Family of Faith Library

The Essentials of American Government

Continuity and Change

2002 EDITION

KAREN O'CONNOR

Professor of Government
American University

LARRY J. SABATO

Robert Kent Gooch Professor
of Government and Foreign Affairs
University of Virginia

Longman

Antcrawl

New York San Francisco Boston
London Toronto Sydney Tokyo Singapore Madrid
Mexico City Munich Paris Cape Town Hong Kong Montreal

Vice President/Publisher: Priscilla McGeehon
Senior Acquisitions Editor: Eric Stano
Development Manager: Lisa Pinto
Senior Development Editor: Dawn Groundwater
Senior Marketing Manager: Megan Galvin-Fak
Supplements Editor: Kelly Villella
Media Supplements Editor: Patrick McCarthy
Senior Production Manager: Eric Jorgensen
Project Coordination, Text Design, Art Studio, and
    Electronic Page Makeup: Electronic Publishing Services Inc., NYC
Cover Designer/Manager: Nancy Danahy
Photo Research: Photosearch, Inc.
Manufacturing Buyer: Al Dorsey
Printer and Binder: RR Donnelley & Sons, Co.
Cover Printer: Phoenix Color Corp.

For permission to use copyrighted material, grateful acknowledgment is made to the copyright holders on the pages where the material appears.

Library of Congress Cataloging-in-Publication Data

O'Connor, Karen,
    The essentials of American government: continuity and change / Karen O'Connor,
Larry J. Sabato--2002 ed.
            p. cm.
    Includes bibliographical references and index.
    ISBN 0-321-08727-5
        1. United States--Politics and government. I. Title: American government. II. Sabato,
Larry. III. Title.

 JK274 .O263 2000
 320.473—dc21   99-045655

Copyright © 2002 by Addison Wesley Longman, Inc.

All rights reserved. No part of this publication may be reproduced, stored in a retrieval system, or transmitted, in any form or by any means, electronic, mechanical, photocopying, recording, or otherwise, without the prior written permission of the publisher. Printed in the United States.

Please visit our website at http://www.ablongman.com

ISBN 0-321-08727-5

2345678910—DOC—04030201

To Meghan,
who grew up with this book
Karen O'Connor

To my Government 101 students
over the years, who all know that
"politics is a good thing"
Larry Sabato

Property of
FAMILY OF FAITH
LIBRARY

BRIEF CONTENTS

DETAILED CONTENTS

APPENDICES

PREFACE

What a year. When we first started writing this text over a decade ago, we could have never envisioned the 2000 presidential election saga. Over the past decade, we experienced 1992's "Year of the Woman" that produced record numbers of women elected to national office, and 1994's "Year of the Angry Male Voter" that produced a Republican revolution in Congress. Both were momentous events that had major consequences in Congress and public policy. The last two editions of this text were written during various phases of various Clinton scandals, including the second impeachment trial of a U.S. president. Then came the 2000 elections when the outcome of this election did not occur until December and then appeared to many to be decided by a single Justice when the court ruled in George W. Bush's favor. The Electoral College, created by the Framers, was in the news as were arcane facts about chads, voting machines, and local politics. Throughout November and December 2000 the entire nation was engaged in an important civics lesson about the voting process that so many of us take for granted.

It can never be said that American politics is boring. For every edition of this text something unexpected or extraordinary has occurred, giving question to the old adage, "Politics as usual." At least on the national level, there appears to be little that is usual. Politics and policy is a vital, fascinating process that affects all our daily lives and we hope that this text reflects that phenomenon as well as provides you with the tools to understand politics as an evolutionary process where history matters.

Teaching introductory American government presents special challenges and rewards. It is a challenge to introduce a new discipline to students. It is a challenge to jump from topic to topic each week. Above all, it is a challenge to motivate large and disparate groups of students to master new material and, one hopes, to enjoy it in the process. The rewards of success, however, are students who pay more attention to their government, who participate in its workings as more informed citizens, and who better understand the workings of democracy as practiced in the United States.

We have witnessed some of these rewards in the classroom. With this book, we hope to offer our experiences in written form. This brief and inexpensive text should work well in classes that are shorter, where policy is not the focus, where a more inexpensive text is desired, or where instructors want to use a basic text supplemented by diverse readings that amplify specific topics. We believe that students need perspective and motivation; they also need to be exposed to information that will withstand the test of time. Our goal with this text is to transmit just this sort of information while creating and fostering student interest in American politics despite growing national skepticism about government and government officials at all levels. We hope that this brief text will explain and put the national mood about politics in better context for students to allow them to understand their role in a changing America.

APPROACH

We believe that one cannot fully understand the actions, issues, and policy decisions facing the U.S. government, its constituent states, or "the people" unless these issues are examined from the perspective of how they have evolved over time. Consequently, the title of this book is *The Essentials of American Government: Continuity and Change.* In its pages we try to examine how the United States is governed today by looking not just at present behavior but also at the Framers' intentions and how they have been implemented and adapted over the years. For example, we believe that it is critical to an understanding of the role of political parties in the United States to understand the Framers' fears of factionalism, how parties evolved, and when and why realignments in party identification occurred.

In addition to questions raised by the Framers, we explore issues that the Framers could never have envisioned, and how the basic institutions of government have changed in response to these new demands. For instance, two centuries ago no one could have foreseen election campaigns in an age when nearly all American homes contain television sets, and the Internet and fax machines allow instant access to information. Moreover, increasing citizen demands and expectations have routinely forced government reforms, making an understanding of the dynamics of change essential for introductory students.

Our overriding concern is that students understand their government as it exists today. In order to do so, they must understand how it was designed in the Constitution. Each chapter, therefore, approaches its topic from a combination of perspectives that we believe will facilitate this approach. In writing this book, we chose to put the institutions of government (Part Two) before political behavior (Part Three). Both sections, however, were written independently, making them easy to switch for those who prefer to teach about the actors in government and elections before discussing its institutions.

WHAT'S CHANGED IN THIS EDITION?

In this 2002 Edition of *The Essentials of American Government: Continuity and Change,* we have retained our basic approach to the study of politics as a constantly changing and often unpredictable enterprise. But we also discuss and analyze the impact of the 2000 election. While most pundits and polls prepared all of us for a close election, no one predicted the scenario that was to unfold. This historic election has refocused attention on the constitutional nature of presidential elections, revived interest in reforming the electoral college, and most importantly, driven home to all that votes do matter. The 2000 election split the Senate evenly between Republicans and Democrats, bringing in new yet familiar faces such as former First Lady Hillary Rodham Clinton. In terms of our political behavior, the 2000 election also changed the way Americans think about voting. From the mail-in presidential ballots in Oregon to the controversial butterfly ballots in Florida, the public learned first hand about archaic state election laws and local politics. And, James Jeffords' switch from the Republican Party to Independent brought another power shift in the Senate.

In addition, we have increased the policy coverage in the text in two ways: First, by transforming the policy portfolio into a full-fledged chapter (Chapter 13: Public Policy). This chapter includes not only the stages of the policy-making process, but discussions of social welfare and economic policies. Second, we have developed a new feature, *Policy in Action*, to examine policy issues and their implications. This feature appears in each chapter.

Chapter Changes

Other changes are reflected in this 2002 Edition. **Chapter 1** includes new data on the 2000 census. **Chapter 3** includes a revised section on federalism and the Supreme Court. **Chapter 4** has new coverage on the Supreme Court's 2000 rulings on student-initiated prayer, *Miranda*, partial-birth abortion, and the Boy Scouts' exclusion of gay men. **Chapter 6** includes coverage on the 107th Congress and its new members. **Chapter 7** provides new coverage on postmodern presidents and presidential expectations, new material on vice-presidential power sharing, the Bush Cabinet, and a new section on ruling through regulation. **Chapter 9** has new coverage of the Supreme Court's role in the outcome of the 2000 presidential election. **Chapter 10** has new coverage on the Voter News Service's role in the 2000 election, the shortcomings of exit polling, and media conflict of interest. **Chapter 11** includes new material on the move toward centrism and an analysis of Ralph Nader's impact on the 2000 election. **Chapter 12** offers indepth coverage of the 2000 presidential campaign and the Supreme Court's historic ruling. **Chapter 13**, as mentioned earlier, examines social welfare and economic policies, as well as the policy-making process.

We have also made a major effort to make certain that this edition contains the most up-to-date scholarship by political scientists, not only on how government works, but what they have said on contemporary debates.

In addition to chapter-by-chapter changes, we have developed several new features designed to enhance student understanding of the political processes, institutions, and policies of American government.

Point/Counterpoint

To involve students in more decision-making issues, we developed a Point/Counterpoint feature that examines a provocative issue from two opposing points of view. Topics like chapter 2's "Is There a Constitutional Right to Privacy?" or chapter 7's "Does the President Need a Mandate to Govern?" are designed to prompt students to take sides in the debate. At the end of each Point/Counterpoint, students are encouraged to take part in an online student chat to post their views.

Analyzing the Data

A feature designed to encourage visual literacy, Analyzing the Data helps students make sense of quantitative information and enables them to get the most out of graphic representations. Topics range from chapter 1's "Changing Age Composition of the United States" to chapter 8's "Presidential Approval Ratings Since 1938." Using annotated leaders and pointers to explain data in bar graphs, line graphs, maps, and charts, these visual learning features appear once in every chapter.

Policy in Action

To strengthen the policy coverage in the book, this edition includes new Policy in Action features that examine policy issues and policy makers. Chapter 2, for example, examines the Supreme Court as a national policy maker, while chapter 4 considers the impending impact of the new "abortion pill" on reproductive rights.

FEATURES

The 2002 Edition has retained the best features and pedagogy from the previous edition and added exciting new ones.

Historical Perspective

Every chapter uses history to serve three purposes: first, to show how institutions and processes have evolved to their present states; second, to provide some of the color that makes information memorable; and third, to provide students with a more thorough appreciation of the fact that government was born amid burning issues of representation and power, issues that continue to smolder today. A richer historical texture helps to explain the present.

Comparative Perspective

Changes in Eastern Europe, the former Soviet Union, North America, and Asia all remind us of the preeminence of democracy, in theory if not always in fact. As new democratic experiments spring up around the globe, it becomes increasingly important for students to understand the rudiments of presidential versus parliamentary government, of multiparty versus two-party systems, and so on. Global Politics boxes compare U.S. politics and institutions with other industrialized democracies and non-western countries such as Russia, China, and Indonesia.

Enhanced Pedagogy

This "essentials" version of our longer text contains many pedagogical features to help students become stronger political thinkers as they explore politics through our theme of evolving change.

Preview and Review   To pique student interest and draw them into each chapter, we begin each one with a contemporary vignette. These vignettes, including how eighteen-year-olds acquired the vote, how special interests are lobbying Congress for laws to allow them to go after student debtors, and congressional efforts to deal with violence in public schools in the aftermath of the Columbine shooting, frequently deal with issues of high interest to students, which we hope will whet their appetites to read the rest of the chapter. Each vignette is followed by a bridge paragraph linking the vignette with the chapter's topics and a roadmap previewing the chapter's major headings. Chapter Summaries restate the major points made under each of these same major headings.

Key Terms   Key terms are boldfaced, listed once more at the end of each chapter, and then defined in the Glossary at the end of the book.

Special Features

- *Global Politics*   To put American government in perspective, these boxes compare American politics with that of other nations. Many of these boxes now include comparisons to non-Western countries such as China, Russia, and Indonesia; some now focus on specific topics. Chapter 11, for example, contains a box on political parties in parliamentary democracies.
- *Politics Now*   These boxes act as a counterpoint to the text's traditional focus on history. Based on current clippings, editorials, and moments in time, these boxes are designed to encourage students to think about current issues in the context of the continuing evolution of the American political system. Chapter 4, for example, examines DNA and changing views about the death penalty.
- *Highlight*   These boxes focus on high student-interest material outside the stream of the text discussion. Chapter 5, for example, looks at professional sports team names coming under attack by ethnic groups. Another describes how one college student's term paper led to the ratification of a constitutional amendment.
- *Continuity & Change*   These sections conclude each chapter. They encourage students to think critically and tie in with the book's theme of change in America. Many of these sections in the 2002 Edition have been revised in order to focus on the evolution of a specific issue. Chapter 3, for example, examines the evolution of marriage in the federal system. We have retained the popular "Cast Your Vote" student polling questions found at the end of each Continuity and Change section.

Using the Web

Web Explorations   Each chapter contains several links to the World Wide Web that prompt students to explore a particular process, topic, or issue in politics on our book-specific website. Identified in the margins with a ⬢ icon, Web Explorations encourage the reader to learn more and think critically about a specific issue or concept (e.g., "For more about local gun initiatives, go to *www.ablongman.com/oconnor").*

LongmanParticipate.com   Each chapter also contains links to interactive activities found on Longman's distinctive Web site for American Government, *LongmanParticipate.com* (www. longmanparticipate.com). Identified in the margins with an icon ⬤, exercises on LongmanParticipate.com help students understand important concepts—and make learning them fun—by getting students involved in several types of activities (e.g., simulations in which the student takes to role of the President, a member of Congress, and more.)

THE ANCILLARY PACKAGE

The ancillary package for *The Essentials of American Government: Continuity and Change, 2002 Edition,* reflects the pedagogical goal of the text: to provide information in a useful context and with colorful examples. We have tried especially hard to provide materials that are useful for instructors and helpful to students.

Instructor Supplements

■ *Instructor's Manual:* Includes chapter overviews, chapter outlines, learning objectives, key terms, and valuable teaching suggestions. Written by Sue Davis of the American Political Science Association.

■ *Test Bank:* Contains hundreds of challenging and thoroughly revised multiple choice, true-false, and essay questions along with an answer key. Written by Sue Davis of the American Political Science Association.

■ *TestGen EQ CD-ROM:* The printed Test Bank is also available through our computerized testing system, TestGen EQ. This fully-networkable, user-friendly program enables instructors to view and edit questions, add their own questions, and print tests in a variety of formats.

■ *Faculty Guide to accompany* LongmanParticipate.com *Web site:* Contains chapter-by-chapter detailed summaries for each of the site's interactive activities, as well as a list of concepts covered, recommendations about how to integrate the site into coursework, and discussion questions and paper topics for every exercise. Instructors may use the table of contents in the front of the guide to locate information on a given activity icon that appears in the margin of this textbook. This guide also provides instructors with detailed instructions and screen shots showing how to register on the site and how to set up and use the administration center. The introductory chapter describes the numerous additional resources included on the Web site. Written by Scott Furlong at the University of Wisconsin.

- *American Government Presentation Library CD-ROM:* This complete multimedia presentation tool provides: a built-in presentation-maker, 200 photographs, 200 figures and graphs from Longman texts, 20 minutes of audio clips, 20 video clips, and links to over 200 websites. Media items can be imported into PowerPoint® and Persuasion® presentation programs.
- *PowerPoint® CD-ROM:* A lecture outline PowerPoint® presentation of the new edition along with graphics from the book. Written by Robert Sterlan of the University of Texas at Tyler.
- *Transparencies:* Color acetates of the figures from the book.
- *Interactive American Government Video:* Contains 27 video segments on topics ranging from the term limit debate to Internet pornography to women in the Citadel. Critical thinking questions accompany each clip, encouraging students to 'interact' with the videos by analyzing their content and the concepts they address.
- *Politics in Action Video:* Eleven "lecture-launchers" covering subjects from conducting a campaign to the passage of a bill. Includes narrated videos, interviews, edited documentaries, original footage, and political ads.
- *American Government Video Program:* Qualified adopters can peruse our list of videos for the American government classroom.
- *Active Learning Guide for American Government:* This unique guide offers an abundance of innovative suggestions for classroom projects and teaching strategies—including scenarios, role plays and debates—that will get students actively involved in course material. Written by Richard H. Foster, Mark K. McBeth, Joseph Morris, Sean K. Anderson and Mark Mussman.
- *Online Course Management:* Longman offers comprehensive online course management systems such as CourseCompass, WebCT, and Blackboard in conjunction with this text. These systems provide complete content, class roster, online quizzing and testing, grade administration, and more, over the Internet. **CourseCompass** combines the strength of Longman content with state-of-the-art eLearning tools! **CourseCompass** is a nationally-hosted, dynamic, interactive online course management system powered by BlackBoard, leaders in the development of Internet-based learning tools. This easy-to-use and customizable program enables professors to tailor content and functionality to meet individual course needs! Every **CourseCompass** course includes a range of pre-loaded content such as testing and assessment question pools. Instructors can redeem pin codes and set up access at *www.coursecompass.com*. Please contact your local Allyn & Bacon/Longman representative for more information.

Student Supplements

- *LongmanParticipate.com (www.longmanparticipate.com):* FREE 6-month student subscription in every new copy of the text. More interactive, more comprehensive and more in-depth than any American government website currently available, *LongmanParticipate.com* offers instructors and students an exciting new resource for teaching and learning about our political system that's easy to integrate into any course. The core of *LongmanParticipate.com* is a set of 5 unique, in-depth learning activities for each of 19 key topics in American government (95 activities in all!):

  - *Simulations* put students in the role of a political actor.

  - *Visual Literacy* exercises get students interpreting, manipulating, and applying data.

  - *Interactive Timelines* through which students experience the evolution of an aspect of government.

  - *Participation* activities personalize politics by either getting students involved or exploring their own thoughts and opinions about our system.

  - *Comparison* exercises in which students compare aspects of our system to those of other countries.

  Students receive feedback at every step and instructors can track student work through the "Instructor Administration Center." The various activities and features were written by:

  Paul Benson, Tarrant County Community College
  James Brent, San Jose State University
  Quentin Kidd, Christopher Newport University
  Laura Roselle, Elon College
  Denise Scheberle, University of Wisconsin
  B. Thomas Schuman, University of New Hampshire
  Sharon Spray, Elon College
  Cara Strebe, San Francisco State University
  Ruth Ann Strickland, Appalachian State University
  Kaare Strøm, University of California, San Diego
  David Tabb, San Francisco State University

- *Interactive Edition CD-ROM:* Offering students a complete multimedia learning experience, this CD-ROM contains the full text of the comprehensive book on CD with hyperlinks to various media - video clips, web links, practices tests, photos and graphics, primary sources, and much more! FREE when ordered packaged with the text.

- *Companion Web site (www.ablongman.com/oconnor):*

  - Web Explorations - critical thinking web exercises (referenced in the text through icons in the margins).

  - Practice Tests - multiple choice, true/false, fill-in-the-blank and essay questions.

- Summaries
- Online Research and Citation Guide
- Chatroom and Message Board

■ *Study Guide:* The printed study guide features chapter outlines, key terms, a variety of practice tests and critical thinking questions to help students learn. Written by Sue Davis of the American Political Science Association.

■ *StudyWizard CD-ROM:* This interactive study guide helps students master concepts in the text through practice tests, chapter and topic summaries, and a comprehensive interactive glossary. Students receive immediate feedback on practice tests in the form of answer explanations and page references in the text to go to for extra help. FREE when ordered packaged with the text. Written by David Dupree at Victor Valley College.

■ *Getting Involved: A Student Guide to Citizenship*: A unique and practical handbook that guides students through political participation with concrete advice and extensive sample material—letters, telephone scripts, student interviews, and real-life anecdotes-for getting involved and making a difference in their lives and communities. FREE when ordered packaged with the text.

■ *Ten Things Every American Government Student Should Read* by Karen O'Connor: We asked American Government instructors across the country to vote for the ten things beyond the text that they believed every student should read. The top vote-getter in each category was put into this unique reader. FREE when ordered packaged with the text.

■ *Discount Subscription to* Newsweek *magazine:* Students receive 12 issues of *Newsweek* at more than 80% off the regular price. An excellent way to keep students up on current events.

■ *CHOICES: An American Government Reader:* This customizable reader allows instructors to choose from a database of over 300 readings to create a reader that exactly matches their course needs. Database includes documents from the 2000 Election!

■ *Penguin-Putnam Paperback Titles at a Deep Discount:* Longman offers 25 Penguin-Putnam titles at more than a 60% discount when packaged with O'Connor & Sabato's text. Titles include De Tocqueville's *Democracy in America* and Lewis' *The Jungle*. Go to *www.ablongman.com/penguin* for a complete list.

■ *Guide to the Internet for American Government:* This easy-to-use guide presents a series of American government exercises using the Internet. It also includes a thorough discussion on evaluating sites for academic usefulness. FREE when ordered packaged.

■ *Writing in Political Science 2/e by* Diane Schmidt: Taking students step-by-step through all aspects of writing in political science, this guide features samples from actual students and expanded information about using the Internet. Available at a significant discount when ordered packaged.

■ *Texas Politics Supplement:* 90-page primer on state and local government and issues in Texas. FREE when packaged. Written by Debra St. John.

■ *California Politics Supplement:* 70-page primer on state and local government and issues in California. FREE when packaged. Written by Barbara Stone.

ACKNOWLEDGMENTS

Karen O'Connor thanks the thousand-plus students in her American Government courses at Emory and American University who, over the years, have pushed her to learn more about American government and to have fun in the process. Long-time friend and co-author Nancy E. McGlen has offered support for more than two decades. Her former students, too, have contributed in various ways to this project, especially John R. Hermann (Trinity University), Laura Van Assendelft (Mary Baldwin College), Bernadette Nye (Union College), and Sue Davis at the American Political Science Association (APSA). For the previous edition of this book, Sarah Brewer, a graduate student at American, took on a growing role in the development and research done to update chapters and write new boxes and vignettes of interest to students. Michael Morey at American provided invaluable assistance for this edition.

Larry Sabato wishes to thank his University of Virginia colleagues and staff, including Joshua Scott, Matthew Wikswo, Lawrence Schack, and technical assistant Nancy Rae.

Particular thanks from both of us go to David Potter of the University of Northern Kentucky, who prepared the Global Politics features, and Sue Davis at APSA for her help with the Point/Counterpoint features. We would also like to thank our editor Eric Stano, our development editor Dawn Groundwater, our marketing manager Megan Galvin-Fak, and Lake Lloyd, our production editor at Electronic Publishing Services, Inc. In the end, we hope that all of these talented people see how much their work and support have helped us to write a better book.

Many of our peers reviewed past editions of the book and earned our gratitude in the process:

Danny Adkinson
Oklahoma State University
Weston H. Agor
University of Texas at El Paso
James Anderson
Texas A&M University
Judith Baer
Texas A&M University

Ruth Bamberger
Drury College
Christine Barbour
Indiana University
Jon Bond
Texas A&M University
Stephen A. Borrelli
University of Alabama

Ann Bowman
*University of
    South Carolina*
Gary Brown
Montgomery College
John Francis Burke
University of Houston–Downtown

Greg Caldeira
Ohio State University
David E. Camacho
Northern Arizona University
David Cingranelli
SUNY, Binghamton
Steve Chan
University of Colorado
Richard Christofferson Sr.
*University of Wisconsin–Stevens
    Point*
Clarke E. Cochran
Texas Tech University
Anne N. Costain
University of Colorado
Cary Covington
University of Iowa
Lane Crothers
Illinois State University
Abraham L. Davis
Morehouse College
Robert DiClerico
West Virginia University
John Domino
Sam Houston State University
Craig F. Emmert
Texas Tech University
Alan S. Engel
Miami University
Frank B. Feigert
University of North Texas
Evelyn C. Fink
*University of Nebraska–
    Lincoln*
Scott R. Furlong
*University of Wisconsin–
    Green Bay*
James D. Gleason
Victoria College
Sheldon Goldman
*University of Massachusetts,
    Amherst*
Roger W. Green
University of North Dakota
Doris Graber
*University of Illinois
    at Chicago*

Charles Hadley
University of New Orleans
William K. Hall
Bradley University
Robert L. Hardgrave Jr.
University of Texas at Austin
Stacie L. Haynie
Louisiana State University
John R. Hermann
Trinity University
Marjorie Hershey
Indiana University
Cornell Hooton
Emory University
Jon Hurwitz
University of Pittsburgh
Chip Hauss
*George Mason University/
    University of Reading*
Joseph Ignagni
University of Texas–Arlington
Dennis Judd
University of Missouri–St. Louis
Carol J. Kamper
Rochester Community College
Kenneth Kennedy
College of San Mateo
Donald F. Kettl
University of Wisconsin
John Kincaid
University of North Texas
Jonathan E. Kranz
*John Jay College of Criminal
    Justice*
Mark Landis
Hofstra University
Sue Lee
North Lake College
Brad Lockerbie
University of Georgia
Larry Martinez
*California State University–Long
    Beach*
Lyn Mather
Dartmouth College
Steve J. Mazurana
University of Northern Colorado

Clifton McCleskey
University of Virginia
Joseph Nogee
University of Houston
Mary Alice Nye
University of North Texas
John O'Callaghan
Suffolk University
Bruce Oppenheimer
Vanderbilt University
Richard Pacelle
University of Missouri–St. Louis
Marian Lief Palley
University of Delaware
Richard M. Pious
Barnard College
David H. Provost
*California State
    University–Fresno*
Lawrence J. Redlinger
The University of Texas at Dallas
Leroy N. Rieselbach
Indiana University
David Robertson
*Public Policy Research Centers, Uni-
    versity of Missouri–St. Louis*
David Robinson
*University of Houston–
    Downtown*
David W. Rohde
Michigan State University
Frank Rourke
Johns Hopkins University
Ronald Rubin
*City University of New York
    Borough of Manhattan Commu-
    nity College*
Daniel M. Shea
University of Akron
Mark Silverstein
Boston University
James R. Simmons
University of Wisconsin–Oshkosh
Elliot E. Slotnick
Ohio State University
Frank J. Sorauf
University of Minnesota

Gerald Stanglin
Cedar Valley College
Richard J. Timpone
SUNY–Stony Brook

Shirlery Anne Warshaw
Gettysburg College
Martin Wiseman
Mississippi State University

Vincent A. Auger
Western Illinois University
Holly Dershem-Bruce
Dawson Community College

Finally, we'd also like to thank our peers who reviewed and aided in the development of the current edition:

Khalil Dokhanchi
University of Wisconsin–Superior
Christopher P. Gilbert
Gustavus Adolphus College
Johanna Hume
Alvin Community College
William P. McLauchlan
Purdue University

William C. Overton
Boise State University
Donald Roy
Ferris State University
Bonita A. Sessing-Matcha
Hudson Valley Community College
Jocelyn D. Shadforth
North Central College

Daniel A. Smith
University of Denver
James A. White
Concord College

(Photo courtesy: William S. Helsel/Stone Images)

The Political Landscape

1

We the People of the United States, in Order to form a more perfect Union, establish Justice, insure domestic Tranquility, provide for the common defense, promote the general Welfare, and secure the Blessings of Liberty to ourselves and our Posterity, do ordain and establish the Constitution for the United States of America.

So begins the Preamble to the United States Constitution. Written in 1787, this document has guided our nation, its government, its politics, its institutions, and its inhabitants for over 200 years.

Back when the Constitution was written, the phrases "We the People" and "ourselves" meant something very different than they do today. Although the Framers—the men who wrote the Constitution—probably intended to include nearly all white men and women, they still envisioned an electorate that was made up of less than half of those who lived in the thirteen original states. After all, voting was largely limited to property-owning white males. Indians, slaves, and women could not vote. Today, through the expansion of the right to vote, the phrase "the People" encompasses men and women of all races, ethnic origins, and social and economic status—a variety of peoples and interests the Framers could not have imagined.

In the goals it outlines, the Preamble describes what the people of the United States can expect from their government. But questions about how much government and at what level services should be performed swirl in every election. Few Americans classify the Union as "perfect;" some feel alienated or excluded from "Justice" and the "Blessings of Liberty." Others are simply disenchanted with government.

Chapter Outline

- The Roots of American Government: Where Did the Ideas Come From?

- Characteristics of American Democracy

- The Changing Political Culture and Characteristics of the American People

- Political Culture and Views of Government

The Framers intended the Constitution to last more than a few years or decades, as we can see from the phrase "our Posterity." Despite a number of turbulent and disruptive episodes in our nation's history, our government has survived: by evolving, changing, accommodating, and compromising. In this text we present you with the tools you need to understand how our political system has evolved, and to prepare you to understand the changes that are yet to come. If you approach the study of American government and politics with an open mind, it should help you become a better citizen. We hope that you learn to ask questions, to understand how various issues have come to be important, and to see why a particular law was enacted and how it was implemented. With such understanding, we further hope you will learn not to accept at face value everything you see on the television news, hear on the radio, or read in the newspaper. Work to understand your government, and use your vote and other forms of participation to help ensure that your government works for you.

We recognize that the discourse of politics has changed dramatically in just the last few years, and more and more Americans—especially

A stunning fireworks display in the nation's Capital was just one of many elaborate world wide celebrations that occured to mark the end of the 1900s.
(Photo courtesy: Robert Trippett/Sipa Press)

the young—are turned off to politics, especially at the national level. Just as Watergate and President Richard Nixon's resignation from office and President Gerald R. Ford's subsequent pardon of him changed Americans' perspectives on the presidency, so did the activities that led to the impeachment and Senate trial of President Bill Clinton. The fallout from these scandals and voting problems in the 2000 election had enormous short- and long-term consequences on how most Americans view politics, politicians, the presidency, and future elections. The recently concluded 2000 election, its failure to produce a clear presidential winner or even determine who would control the Senate, and the role of the media and the importance of your vote, refocused national attention on political participation.

We believe that a thorough understanding of the workings of government will allow you to question and think about the system—the good parts and the bad—and decide for yourself the advantages and disadvantages of possible changes and reforms. Equipped with such an understanding, we hope you will become better informed and more active participants in the political process.

In this chapter, we examine the roots of the American political system. We then look at the characteristics of American democracy as well as those of the American people. The reasons more and more Americans are turned off by politics and frustrated with politicians and their government—at all levels—are also discussed.

PARTICIPATION
You Are Part of the
Political Process

WEB EXPLORATION
For more information
on politics in general, see
www.ablongman.com/oconnor

THE ROOTS OF AMERICAN GOVERNMENT: WHERE DID THE IDEAS COME FROM?

The current American political system did not spring into being overnight. It is the result of philosophy, trial and error, and yes, even luck. To begin our examination of why we came to have the type of government we have today, we look at the theories of government that influenced the Framers: those men who gathered in Philadelphia and drafted a new Constitution, thereby creating the United States of America.

From Aristotle to the Enlightenment

Aristotle (384–322 B.C.) and the Greeks were the first to articulate the notion of **natural law**, the doctrine that human affairs should be governed by certain ethical principles. In the thirteenth century, the Italian priest and philosopher Thomas Aquinas (1225–1274) gave the idea of natural law a new, Christian framework. He argued that natural law and Christianity were compatible because God created the natural law that established individual rights to life and liberty. In contradiction to this view, kings throughout Europe continued to rule as absolute mon-

natural law
A doctrine that society should be governed by certain ethical principles that are part of nature and, as such, can be understood by reason.

archs, claiming this divine right came directly from God. Thus, citizens were bound by the government under which they found themselves, regardless of whether they had a say in its workings: If government reflected God's will, who could argue with it?

In the early sixteenth century, a religious movement to reform the doctrine and institutions of Roman Catholicism began to sweep through Europe. Often, these efforts at reform resulted in the founding of Protestant churches separate from their Catholic source. This Reformation and the resultant growth in the Protestant faith, which promoted the belief that people could talk directly to God without the intervention of a priest, altered the nature of government as people began to believe they could also have a say in their own governance.

During the seventeenth- and eighteenth-century period called the Enlightenment, the ideas of philosophers and scientists such as Galileo Galilei and Isaac Newton worked further to affect peoples' views of government. Newton and others argued that the world could be improved through the use of human reason, science, and religious toleration. He and other theorists directly challenged earlier notions that fate alone controlled an individual's destiny and that kings ruled by divine right. Together the intellectual and religious developments of the Reformation and Enlightenment periods encouraged people to seek alternatives to absolute monarchy and to ponder new methods of governing.

A Growing Idea: Popular Consent

In the late sixteenth century in England, "separatists" split from the Anglican Church. They believed that their ability to speak directly to God gave them the power to participate directly in the governing of their own local congregations. They established self-governing congregations and were responsible for the first widespread appearance of self-government in the form of social compacts. When some separatists settled in America during the 1600s, they brought along their beliefs about self-governance. The Mayflower Compact, deemed sufficiently important to be written while that ship was still at sea, reflects this tradition. Although it addressed itself to secular government, the Pilgrims called it a "covenant" and its form was akin to other common religious "covenants" adopted by Congregationalists, Presbyterians, and Baptists.[1]

Two English theorists of that period, Thomas Hobbes (1588–1679) and John Locke (1632–1704), built on conventional notions about the role of government and the relationship of the government to the people in proposing a **social contract theory** of government. They argued that, even before the creation of God-ordained governments theorized by Aquinas, all individuals were free and equal by natural right. This freedom, in turn, required that all men give their consent to be governed.[2]

Hobbes and Locke.   In his now-classic political treatise *Leviathan* (1651), Hobbes argued pessimistically that man's natural state was war.

WEB EXPLORATION
For more on Aristotle and natural law, see www.ablongman.com/oconnor

social contract theory

The belief that people are free and equal by God-given right and that this in turn requires that all people give their consent to be governed; espoused by John Locke and influential in the writing of the Declaration of Independence.

Government, Hobbes theorized, particularly a monarchy, was necessary to restrain man's bestial tendencies because life without government was a "state of nature." Without written, enforceable rules, people would live like animals—foraging for food, stealing, and killing when necessary. To escape the horrors of the natural state and to protect their lives, Hobbes argued, men must give up to government certain rights. Without government, Hobbes warned, life would basically be "solitary, poor, nasty, brutish, and short"—a constant struggle to survive against the evil of others. For this reason, governments had to intrude on people's rights and liberties to control society and provide the necessary safeguards for property.

In contrast, John Locke—like many other political philosophers of the era—took the basic survival of humanity for granted. He argued that government's major responsibility was the preservation of private property, an idea that ultimately found its way into the Constitution of the United States. Locke also not only denied the divine right of kings to govern, but argued that men were born equal, and with equal rights in nature that no king had the power to void. Under Locke's social contract theory, the consent of the people is the only true basis of any sovereign's right to rule. According to Locke, men form governments largely to preserve life, liberty, and property, and to assure justice. If governments act improperly, they break their "contract" with the people and therefore no longer enjoy the consent of the governed. Because he believed that true justice comes from laws, Locke argued that the branch of government that makes laws—as opposed to the one that enforces or interprets laws—should be the most powerful.

The Theory of Democratic Government

As evidenced by the creation in 1619 of the Virginia House of Burgesses as the first representative assembly in North America, the colonists were quick to create participatory forms of government. The New England town meeting, where all citizens gather to discuss and decide issues facing the town, today stands as a surviving example of a **direct democracy,** such as was used in ancient Greece when all free, male citizens came together periodically to pass laws and "elect" leaders by lot (see Politics Now: The Internet and Our Changing Society).

Direct democracies, in which the people rather than their elected representatives make political decisions, soon proved unworkable in the colonies. As more and more settlers came to the New World, many town meetings were replaced by a system called an **indirect democracy** (this is also called *representative democracy*). This system of government, in which representatives of the people are chosen by ballot, was considered undemocratic by ancient Greeks, who believed that all citizens must have a direct say in their governance.[3]

Initially, many citizens were uncomfortable with the term "democracy" and used the term republic to avoid any confusion between the system

WEB EXPLORATION
For more on Thomas Hobbes and John Locke, see www.ablongman.com/oconnor

WEB EXPLORATION
To connect with others who are interested in politics, see www.ablongman.com/oconnor

direct democracy
A system of government in which members of the polity meet to discuss all policy decisions and then agree to abide by majority rule.

indirect (representative) democracy
A system of government that gives citizens the opportunity to vote for representatives who will work on their behalf.

POLITICS NOW

THE INTERNET AND OUR CHANGING SOCIETY

It is hard to believe that the Internet as we know it was not around when the first edition of this text was published in 1993. What began in 1969 as ARPANET, a communications network developed by the U.S. Department of Defense for its employees to maintain contact with defense contractors and universities in the case of a nuclear attack, has revolutionized how students write papers, people seek information, and even how some individuals date. The Internet is now a vast resource for those interested in politics and may have enormous consequences in the near future as it becomes as critical a part of our daily lives as televisions and telephones.

For the first decade of its existence, the Internet was largely used for e-mail and access to distant data bases, and to facilitate communication among governmental agencies, corporations, and universities.[a] During the early 1980s, all of the interrelated research networks converted to a new protocol that allowed for easy back-and-forth transfer of information; ARPANET became the backbone of the new system, facilitating by 1983 the birth of the Internet we know today.

Only a decade ago, HTML, a hypertext Internet protocol that allowed graphic information to be transmitted over the Internet, was devised. This allowed for the creation of graphic pages—called Web sites—which then became "part of a huge, virtual hypertext network called the World Wide Web."[b] This new, improved Internet was then christened the Web.

By 2000, over 64 percent of all adult Americans reported that they had used the Internet themselves. The vast majority of those aged 18 to 25, however, had used the Web. Almost all schools have Internet access and by 2001, over 50 million households were online. In 2000, female Internet usage surpassed male usage for the first time. Usage by teenage girls soared 126 percent in just four years.[c] Thus, given estimates that computer ownership and Web access are increasing at remarkable rates, the Web's impact on democracy must be considered.

Near-universal usage of home telephones, for example, changed the way that public opinion was measured, and television eventually changed the way that candidates and their supporters reached potential voters. What kinds of political changes can we foresee given the rise of the Web?

- Increased reliance on candidate and party web sites to raise money and supporters
- A more informed electorate given easier access to information about candidates and issues
- A more effective grassroots mechanism for citizens to contact officials, policy makers, large corporations, and so on
- The eventual use of the Internet to conduct polling research
- The use of the Internet to enhance voter turnout
- Online voting.

[a]"Internet History," http://www.tdi.uregina.ca/~ursc/internet/history.html
[b]"Internet History."
[c]Leslie Walker, "Teen Girls Help Create Female Majority Online," *The Washington Post* (August 20, 2000): E3.

adopted throughout the colonies and direct democracies. Historically, the term **republic** implied a system of government in which the interests of the people were represented by more educated or wealthier citizens who were responsible to those who elected them. Today, representative democracies are more commonly called "republics," and the words democracy and republic often are used interchangeably.

republic
A government rooted in the consent of the governed; a representative or indirect democracy.

Why a Capitalist System?

In addition to fashioning a democratic form of government, the colonists also were confronted with the dilemma of what kind of role the government should play in the economy. Concerns with liberty, both personal and economic, were always at the forefront of their actions and decisions in creating a new government. They were well aware of the need for a well-functioning economy and saw that government had a key role in maintaining one. What a malfunction in the economy is, however, and what steps the government should take to remedy it were questions that dogged the Framers and continue to puzzle politicians and theorists today.

PARTICIPATION
Democracy
and the Internet

The American economy is characterized by the private ownership of property and a **free market economy**—two key tenets of **capitalism**, a form of economic system that favors private control of business and minimal governmental regulation of private industry. (For a description of other types of economic systems, see Table 1.1.) In capitalist systems, the laws of supply and demand, interacting freely in the marketplace, set prices of goods and drive production. Under capitalism, sales occur for the profit of the individual. Capitalists believe that both national and individual production is greatest when individuals are free to do with their property or goods as they wish. The government, however, plays an indispensable role in creating and enforcing the rules of the game.

free market economy
The economic system in which the "invisible hand" of the market regulates prices, wages, product mix, and so on.

capitalism
The economic system that favors private control of business and minimal governmental regulation of private industry.

In 1776, at the same time as the signing of the Declaration of Independence, economist Adam Smith (1723–1790) argued that free trade would result in full production and economic health. These ideas were greeted with great enthusiasm in the colonies as independence was proclaimed. Colonists no longer wanted to participate in the mercantile system of Great Britain and other Western European nations. Mercantile systems bound trade and its administration to national governments. Smith and his supporters saw free trade as "the invisible hand" that produced the wealth of nations. This wealth, in turn, became the inspiration and justification for capitalism.

From the mid to late eighteenth century, and through the mid-1930s in the United States and in much of the Western world, the idea of *laissez-faire* economics (from the French, "to leave alone") enjoyed considerable popularity. While most states regulated and intervened heavily in their economies well into the nineteenth century, the U.S. national government routinely followed a "hands-off" economic policy. By the late 1800s, however, the national government felt increasing pressure to regulate some aspects of the economy (often in part because of the

TABLE 1.1   Other Economic Systems

Capitalism is just one type of economic system. Others include socialism, communism, and totalitarianism.

Socialism	Socialism is a philosophy that advocates collective ownership and control of the means of economic production. Socialists call for governmental—rather than private—ownership of all land, property, and industry and, in turn, an equitable distribution of the income from those holdings. In addition, socialism seeks to replace the profit motive and competition with cooperation and social responsibility.
Communism	German philosopher Karl Marx argued that government was simply a manifestation of underlying economic forces and could be understood according to types of economic production.
	Marx believed that it was inevitable for each society to pass through the stages of history: feudalism, capitalism, socialism, and then communism. When society reached communism, Marx theorized, all class differences would be abolished and government would become unnecessary. A system of common ownership of the means of sustenance and production would lead to greater social justice.
	Marx saw the change coming first in highly industrialized countries such as Britain and Germany, where a fully mature capitalism would pave the way for a socialist revolution. But Lenin and the Bolshevik Party wanted to have such a revolution in underdeveloped Russia. Instead of relying on the historical inevitability of the communist future (as Marx envisioned), they advocated forcing that change. Lenin argued that by establishing an elite vanguard party of permanent revolutionaries and a dictatorship of the proletariat (working class), they could achieve socialism and communism without waiting for the historical forces to work. In the 1940s, China followed the Leninist path led by Mao Zedong (formerly transliterated as Mao Tse Tung).
Totalitarianism	A totalitarian system is basically a modern form of extreme authoritarian rule. In contrast to governments based on democratic beliefs, totalitarian governments have total authority over their people and their economic system. The tools of totalitarianism are secret police, terror, propaganda, and an almost total prohibition on civil rights and liberties. These systems also tend to be ruled in the name of an ideology or a personality cult organized around a supreme leader.

difficulties states faced in regulating large, multistate industries such as the railroads, and from industry's desire to override the patchwork regulatory scheme produced by the states). Thereafter, the Great Depression of the 1930s forced the national government to take a much larger role in the economy. Afterward, any pretense that the United States was a purely capitalist system was abandoned. The worldwide extent of this trend, however, varied by country and over time. In post–World War II Britain, for example, the extent of government economic regulation of industry and social welfare was much greater than that attempted by American policy makers in the same period.

CHARACTERISTICS OF AMERICAN DEMOCRACY

The United States, as created by the Framers, is an indirect democracy with several underlying concepts and distinguishing characteristics. Many of these characteristics are often in conflict, a factor that has led to some of the political discontent present in the population and, more specifically, the electorate. The political system, for example, is based on an underlying notion of the importance of balance among the legislative, executive, and judicial branches, between the state and federal governments, between the wants of the majority and the minority, and between the rights of the individual and the best interests of the nation as a whole. The idea of balance permeates many of the concepts and characteristics of American democracy presented below.

Popular Consent

Popular consent, the idea that governments must draw their powers from the consent of the governed, is one distinguishing characteristic of American democracy. Derived from Locke's social contract theory, the notion of popular consent was central to the Declaration of Independence. A citizen's willingness to vote represents his or her consent to be governed and is thus an essential premise of democracy.

Popular Sovereignty

The notion of popular sovereignty, the right of the majority to govern itself, has its basis in natural law: Ultimately, political authority rests with the people, who can create, abolish, or alter their governments. The idea that all governments derive their power from the people is found in the Declaration of Independence and the U.S. Constitution, but the term itself did not come into wide usage until pre-Civil War debates over slavery. (See Highlight: Who Makes Decisions in America? for some theories about who makes decisions about governing.)

Majority Rule

Majority rule, another basic democratic principle, means that only policies that collectively garner the support of a majority of voters will be made into law (50 percent of the total votes cast plus 1). This principle holds for both voters and their elected representatives. Yet the American system also stresses the need to preserve minority rights as evidenced by the myriad protections of individual rights and liberties found in the Bill of Rights.

Individualism

Tremendous value is placed on the individual in American democracy and culture. All individuals are deemed rational and fair, and endowed,

H I G H L I G H T

WHO MAKES DECISIONS IN AMERICA?

How conflicts are resolved is often determined by how the government is operated and by whom. All of these theories provide interesting ways to think about how policy decisions are made, whether we are looking at local, state, or national policies.

Elite Theory

Elite theory posits that all important decisions in society are made by the few, called the elite, so that government is increasingly alienated from the people and rarely responsive to their wishes. In *The Power Elite* (1956), American sociologist C. Wright Mills argued that important policies were set by a loose coalition of three groups with some overlap among each.[a] According to his elite theory, these three major influencers of policy—corporate leaders, military leaders, and a small group of key governmental leaders—are the true "power elite" in America. Other elite theorists have argued that the news media should be included as a fourth source of political power in the United States.

Another proponent of elite theory, political scientist Thomas R. Dye, contends that all societies are divided into elites and masses. The elite are the few who have power, and the masses are the many who don't.[b] This distribution of functions and powers in society is inevitable. Elites, however, are not immune from public opinion, nor do they by definition oppress the masses. Dye argues that in a complex society, such as ours, only a "tiny minority" actually make policy.

Bureaucratic Theory

Max Weber (1864–1920), the founder of modern sociology, argued that all institutions, governmental and nongovernmental, have fallen under the control of a large and ever-growing bureaucracy that carry out policy on a day-to-day basis using standardized procedures. Because all institutions have grown more complex, Weber

as Thomas Jefferson proclaimed in the Declaration of Independence, "with certain unalienable rights." Individualism, which holds that the primary function of government is to enable the individual to achieve his or her highest level of development, makes the interests of the individual more important than those of the state and at the heart of our capitalistic system. It is also a concept whose meaning has changed over time. The rugged individualism of the western frontier, for example, was altered as more citizens moved westward, cities developed, and demands for government services increased. This does not mean, however, that Americans aren't concerned with others as is revealed in Policy in Action: Community Service and the Young.

Equality

Another key characteristic of our democracy is the American emphasis on political equality, the definition of which has varied considerably over time. The importance of political equality is another reflection of American stress on the importance of the individual. Although some

concluded that the expertise and competence of bureaucrats allows them to wrest power from others, especially elected officials

Interest Group Theory

David Truman argues that interest groups—not elites, sets of elites, or bureaucrats—control the governmental process.[c] He believes there are so many potential pressure points in the three branches of the federal government—as well as at the state level—that groups can step in on any number of competing sides. The government then becomes the equilibrium point in the system as it mediates between competing interests.

Pluralist Theory

According to some political scientists, the structure of our democratic government allows only for a pluralistic model of democracy.[d] Borrowing from Truman's work, Robert Dahl argues that resources are scattered so widely in our diverse democracy that no single elite group can ever have a monopoly over any substantial area of policy.

Adding to this debate, Theodore J. Lowi has described how political decision making takes place today in an era of what he terms "interest group liberalism." According to Lowi, participants in every political controversy get something; thus, each has some impact on how political decisions are made. Lowi also states that governments rarely say no to any well-organized interests. Thus, all interests ultimately receive some benefits or rewards. Lowi bemoans the fact that the public interest—that is, what is good for the public at large—often tends to lose in this system.[e]

---

[a]C. Wright Mills, *The Power Elite* (New York: Oxford University Press, 1956).

[b]Thomas R. Dye, *Who's Running America?* (New York: Prentice Hall, 1976).

[c]David B. Truman, *The Governmental Process* (New York: Knopf, 1951).

[d]Robert A. Dahl, *Preface to Democratic Theory* (Chicago: University of Chicago Press, 1956).

[e]Theodore J. Lowi, *The End of Liberalism* (New York: Norton, 1979).

individuals clearly wield more political clout than others, the adage "One man, one vote" implies a sense of political equality for all.

Personal Liberty

Personal liberty is perhaps the single most important characteristic of American democracy. The Constitution itself was written to assure "life" and "liberty." Over the years, however, our concepts of liberty have changed and evolved from "freedom *from*" to "freedom *to*." The Framers intended Americans to be free from governmental infringements on freedom of religion and speech, from unreasonable search and seizure, and so on. The addition of the Fourteenth Amendment to the Constitution and its emphasis on equal protection of the laws and subsequent passage of laws guaranteeing civil rights, however, expanded Americans' concept of liberty to include demands for "freedom to" be free from discrimination. Debates over how much the government should do to guarantee these rights or liberties illustrate the conflicts that continue to occur in our democratic system.

POLICY IN ACTION

COMMUNITY SERVICE AND THE YOUNG

Political scientists such as Robert Putnam have bemoaned the fact that Americans are no longer as civic minded or as engaged in politics as they once were. Pollsters and pundits have predicted further decline based on low voting rates among those under age twenty-five and the dislike of politics reported within that group.

But what many of those commentators fail to note is the extraordinary involvement of those under age twenty-five in community service activities. Beginning in the 1980s, many public and private high schools launched mandatory public service requirements for graduation. Depending on the school or school district, these programs required students to "volunteer" at a wide array of charities or public works projects. The purpose of these programs was to instill in students an awareness of the less fortunate and to stress the importance of continued community and civic involvement. Through these mandated programs, a clear policy designed to encourage lifelong volunteerism emerged. Interestingly, the constitutionality of at least one of these programs was challenged in the federal courts. While studying the Constitution in a social studies class, some students came to believe that these mandatory programs were an unconstitutional form of enforced labor prohibited by the Thirteenth Amendment's ban on slavery and other forms of peonage.

"People should volunteer because they want to, not because of a government threat," said Lynn Steirer, one of the 175 seniors whose graduation was threatened because they failed to perform the sixty hours of public service required by their high school for graduation. They were helped in their challenge by attorneys from the Washington, D.C.-based libertarian Institute for Justice. The federal district court ruled against them, as did the court of appeals. In 1993 the U.S. Supreme Court refused to hear their appeal, thus letting the decision of the lower courts stand.*

This meant that school districts were free to continue their compulsory policies. Their goal seems to be working. More and more college-level students—many schooled on these compulsory programs that whetted their appetite to do for others—are continuing to work on behalf of the less fortunate. Whether it is tutoring inner-city school children, building homes with Habitat for Humanity, or working in soup kitchens or homeless shelters, those under age twenty-five are putting in record numbers of hours on behalf of the less fortunate. They might not be pursuing the kinds of civic engagement studied by political scientists and policy analysts in the past, but they are engaged.

---

*987 F.2d (3rd Cir.) 1993, cert. denied, 510 U.S. 824 (1995).

THE CHANGING POLITICAL CULTURE AND CHARACTERISTICS OF THE AMERICAN PEOPLE

political culture
Attitudes toward the political system and its various parts, and attitudes toward the role of the self in the system.

The concept **political culture** has been defined as the "attitudes toward the political system and its various parts, and attitudes toward the role of the self in the system." It is a set of orientations toward a special set of social objects and processes.[4] Where you live, how you were raised, and even your age or age cohort can affect how you view the government or a governmental program.

Still, at the heart of the American political system is change, be it in population, demographics, or interest in politics. But while America and its population are undergoing rapid change, this is not necessarily a new phenomenon. It is simply new to most of us. In the pages that follow, we take a look at some of the characteristics of the American population. Because the people of the United States are the basis of political power and authority, these characteristics have important implications for how America is governed and how and what policies are made.

Changing Size and Population

One year after the Constitution was ratified, less than 4 million Americans lived in the thirteen states. They were united by a single language and opposition to the king of England. Most shared a similar Protestant-Christian heritage, and those who voted were white, male property owners. The Constitution mandated that each of the fifty-six members of the original House of Representatives should represent 40,000 citizens. However, due to rapid growth, the number of people represented often was much higher. Anti-Federalists, who opposed a strong national government during the founding period, at least took solace in the fact that members of the House of Representatives, who generally represented far fewer people than senators did, would be more in touch with "the people."

As the nation grew westward, the absolute population of the country also grew (see Figure 1.1). Although the physical size of the United States has remained stable since the addition of Alaska and Hawaii in 1959, there are now more than 281.4 million Americans. In 2000, a single member of the House of Representatives from Montana, for example, represented 882,000 people.

As a result of this growth, most citizens today feel far removed from the national government and their elected representatives. Members of Congress, too, feel this change. Often they represent diverse constituencies with a variety of needs, concerns, and expectations, and they can meet only a relative few of these people in face-to-face electioneering.

WEB EXPLORATION
To get a minute-by-minute update on U.S. population, see
www.ablongman.com/oconnor

Changing Demographics of the U.S. Population

As the physical size and population of the United States has changed, so have many of the bases and assumptions on which it was founded. Some of the dynamism of the American system actually stems from the racial and ethnic changes that have taken place throughout our history, a notion that often gets lost in debates about immigration policy. Moreover, for the first time, the U.S. population is getting much older. This "graying" of America also will assuredly lead to changes

FIGURE 1.1   U.S. Population, 1790–2050

Since around 1890, when more and more immigrants came to America, the population of the United States, although largely fueled by new births and increased longevity, has continued to rise.

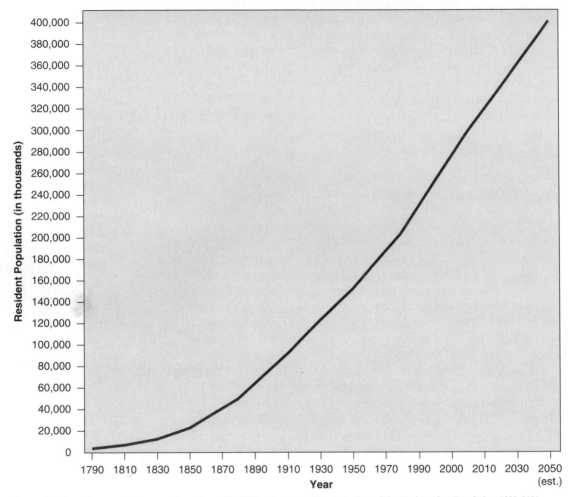

Source: U.S. Census Bureau, U.S. Census of Population: 1920–1990, vol. 1; Population Projections of the Total Resident Population, 1999–2101.

in our expectations of government and in our public policy demands. Below we look at some demographic facts (that is, information on characteristics of America's population) and then discuss some implications of these changes for how our nation is governed and what policy issues might arise.

Changes in Racial and Ethnic Distributions.   From the start, the population of America has been constantly changed by the arrival of various kinds of immigrants to its shores. Immigration to the United States peaked in the first decade of the 1900s, when nearly 9 million people, many of them from Eastern Europe, entered the country. The United

States did not see another major wave of immigration until the late 1980s, when nearly 2 million immigrants were admitted in one year. Unlike the arrivals in other periods of high immigration, however, these "new" Americans were often "nonwhite;" many were Southeast Asians or Latin Americans.

While immigration has been a continual source of changing demographics in America, race, too, has played a major role in the development and course of politics in the United States. As revealed in Figure 1.2, the racial balance in America is changing dramatically. In 2000, for example, whites made up 75.1 percent of the U.S. population, African Americans 12.3 percent, and Hispanics 25 percent, surpassing the number of African Americans in the United States for the first time. Originally demographers did not anticipate Hispanics surpassing African Americans to occur until 2050. In some states, Hispanic population is rivaling white, non-Hispanic populations.

Changes in Age Cohort Composition. Just as the racial and ethnic composition of the American population is changing, so too is the average age of the population. "For decades, the U.S. was described as a nation of the young because the number of persons under the age of twenty greatly outnumber(ed) those sixty-five and older,"[5] but this is no longer the case. While in 1900 only 4 percent of the population was over sixty-five years old and 40 percent was under seventeen, by 2030 more Americans will be over sixty-five than under seventeen.[6] Thus, patterns of fertility, life expectancy, and immigration have changed the nation's age profile drastically. The era in which people are born and the kinds of events they experience can have important consequences on how they view other political, economic, and social events.

Elian Gonzalez holds American and Cuban flags as a crowd of supporters grows outside his uncle's home. The large Cuban community is a powerful force in Miami politics and objected strenuously to Elian's return. (Photo courtesy: AFP/Corbis)

Implications of These Changes

The varied races, ethnic origins, and sizes of the various age cohorts of the American people have important implications for government and politics. Today, in spite of the fact that almost all Americans have ancestors who immigrated to the United States, most Americans oppose unrestricted access to the United States and react negatively to reports that the foreign-born population is increasing. But by 2000, when the U.S unemployment rate was near record lows, this issue largely faded, although Reform Party candidate Patrick Buchanan tried to make what he termed "out of control" immigration an issue. As more and more women graduated from college and entered the workforce, some men criticized efforts to widen opportunities for women,

VISUAL LITERACY
Understanding the Distribution of Wealth in America

WEB EXPLORATION
For more detail on population projections, see www.ablongman.com/oconnor

FIGURE 1.2   Race and Ethnicity in America: 2000 and Beyond

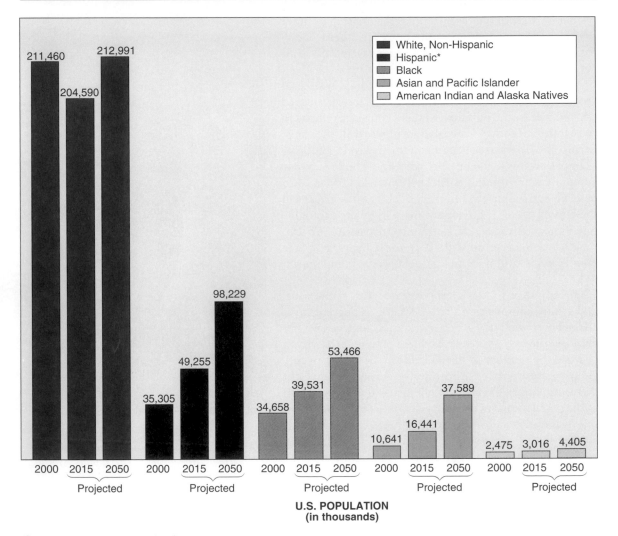

| White, Non-Hispanic |
| Hispanic* |
| Black |
| Asian and Pacific Islander |
| American Indian and Alaska Natives |

White, Non-Hispanic: 211,460 (2000), 204,590 (2015 Projected), 212,991 (2050 Projected)

Hispanic*: 35,305 (2000), 49,255 (2015 Projected), 98,229 (2050 Projected)

Black: 34,658 (2000), 39,531 (2015 Projected), 53,466 (2050 Projected)

Asian and Pacific Islander: 10,641 (2000), 16,441 (2015 Projected), 37,589 (2050 Projected)

American Indian and Alaska Natives: 2,475 (2000), 3,016 (2015 Projected), 4,405 (2050 Projected)

U.S. POPULATION
(in thousands)

*Persons of Hispanic origin can be of any race.

Source: U.S. Census Bureau, www.census.gov/population/projections

while many women complained that a "glass ceiling" prevented them from reaching their highest levels in most occupations.

Hostility to immigrants manifests itself in a variety of ways. Some bemoan the fact that the nation is becoming less white, or criticize those who refuse to adopt "American" ways as they cling to the customs, language, and traditions of their old country. Immigrants often are blamed by the citizenry or elected officials for lost jobs or depressed wages (because they are often willing to take low-wage jobs).

Changing racial, ethnic, and age demographics also seem to intensify—at least for some—an "us" *versus* "them" attitude. Government affirmative action programs, which were created in the 1960s to redress decades of

A N A L Y Z I N G   T H E   D A T A

CHANGING AGE COMPOSITION OF THE UNITED STATES

The elderly are the fastest-growing group in the United States, due to increased life expectancy, immigration, and advanced medical technology. The percentage of elderly individuals is projected to exceed the percentage of young people under seventeen years old by 2030. This is a dramatic increase from 1900, where the elderly comprise only 4 percent of the population. How does this impact government? In one respect, as elderly people steadily retire from the labor force, the proportion of non-working adults will generate ever-greater demands for social programs like Social Security and health care.

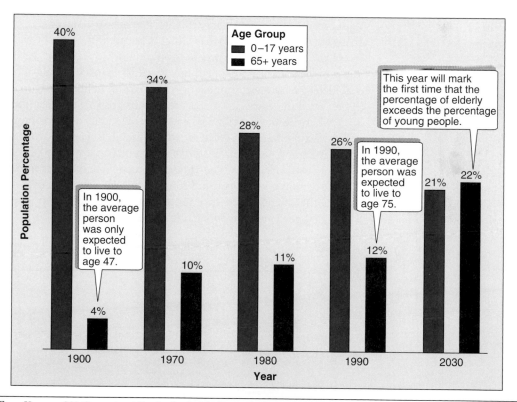

Source: From *Young* v. *Old: Generational Combat in the 21st Century* by Susan A. McManus. Copyright ©1995 by Westview Press, Inc. Reprinted by permission of Westview Press, a member of Perseus Books, L.L.C.

overt racial discrimination, are now under attack as unfair because some people believe that they give minorities and women advantages in the job market. These different worldviews—worker *versus* CEO, educated *versus* uneducated, young *versus* old, white *versus* black, male *versus* female, native-born *versus* immigrant—create deep cleavages in society.

These cleavages and the emphasis many politicians put on our demographic differences play out in many ways in American politics. Baby Boomers and the elderly object to any changes in Social Security or

TIMELINE
Major Events
that Changed
the Political Landscape

Medicare, while those in Generation X vote for politicians who support change, if they vote at all. Many policies are targeted at one group or the other, further exacerbating differences—real or imagined—and lawmakers often find themselves the target of factions. All of this makes it difficult to devise coherent policies to "promote the general welfare," as promised in the Constitution.

The Ideology of the American Public

political ideology
An individual's coherent set of values and beliefs about the purpose and scope of government.

Political ideology is a term used by political scientists to refer to the more or less consistent set of values that historically have been reflected in the political system, economic order, social goals, and moral values of any given society. "It is the means by which the basic values held by a party, class, group, or individual are articulated."[7] A small percentage of Americans are libertarians. They have long believed in the evils of big government and stress that government should not involve itself in the plight of the people or attempt to remedy any social ills. Most who talk about political ideology, however, frame it on a continuum of liberal to conservative. As revealed in Figure 1.3, most Americans are able to place themselves somewhere on this continuum, with more Americans identifying themselves as conservative or moderate than liberal. In general, your ideology often is a good predictor of where you stand on a variety of issues (see Table 1.2) as well as how you view the proper role of government.

The definitions of liberal and conservative have changed over the years. During the nineteenth century, for example, conservatives supported governmental power and favored a role for religion in public life; in contrast,

FIGURE 1.3   Self-Identification as Liberal, Moderate, or Conservative, 1974–2000

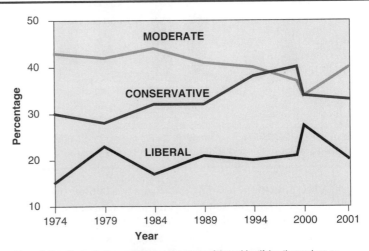

Note: "Liberal" equals the combined percentages of those identifying themselves as extremely liberal, liberal, or slightly liberal; "conservative" equals the combined percentages of those identifying themselves as extremely conservative, conservative, or slightly conservative.

Source: Roper Center at the University of Connecticut, *Public Opinion Online.*

TABLE 1.2   Liberal? Conservative? Libertarian?

	Abortion rights	Environmental regulation	Organized school prayer	Gun control laws	Anti-discrimination laws	Government Support of	
						Poor	School vouchers
Conservatives	Oppose	Oppose	Favor	Oppose	Oppose	Oppose	Favor
Liberals	Favor	Favor	Oppose	Favor	Favor	Favor	Oppose
Libertarians	Favor	Oppose	Oppose	Oppose	Oppose	Oppose	Oppose

liberals supported freedom from undue governmental control. Today, these terms have very different meanings to the general public.

Conservatives.   According to William Safire's *New Political Dictionary,* a **conservative** "is a defender of the status quo who, when change becomes necessary in tested institutions or practices, prefers that it come slowly, and in moderation."[8] Conservatives are thought to believe that a government is best that governs least, and that big government can only infringe on individual, personal, and economic rights. They want less government, especially in terms of regulation of the economy. Conservatives favor local and state action over federal action, and emphasize fiscal responsibility, most notably in the form of balanced budgets.

Liberals.   Safire defines a **liberal** as "currently one who believes in more government action to meet individual needs, originally one who resisted government encroachments on individual liberties."[9] Liberals now are considered to favor big governments that play active roles in the economy. They also stress the need for the government to provide for the poor and homeless, to provide a wide array of other social services, and to take an activist role in protecting the rights of women, the elderly, minorities, and the environment. (See Table 1.2).

Libertarians.   Basically, **libertarians,** although a very diverse lot, favor a free market economy and an end to governmental intrusion in the area of personal liberties. Libertarians have long believed in the evils of big government and stress that government should not involve itself in the plight of the people or attempt to remedy any social ills. Younger voters are more libertarian in political philosophy than older voters and are credited with the election of Governor Jesse Ventura of Minnesota, who while claiming to be a libertarian, ran as a Reform Party candidate.

Problems with Political Labels

Studies reveal that many people who call themselves conservative actually take fairly liberal positions on many policy issues. In fact, anywhere from 20 percent to 68 percent will take a traditionally "conservative" position on one issue and a traditionally "liberal" position on another.[10] People who take conservative stances against "big government," for example, often support increases in spending for the elderly, education,

conservative
One thought to believe that a government is best that governs least and that big government can only infringe on individual, personal, and economic rights.

liberal
One considered to favor extensive governmental involvement in the economy and the provision of social services and to take an activist role in protecting the rights of women, the elderly, minorities, and the environment.

libertarian
One who favors a free market economy and no governmental interference in personal liberties.

 WEB EXPLORATION   For more information about conservatives, liberals, and libertarians, see www.ablongman.com/oconnor

GLOBAL POLITICS

THE UNITED STATES IN COMPARATIVE CONTEXT

Two scholars of American politics recently published books examining their field of study in comparative context. The title of one, *America the Unusual*, speaks volumes about how Americans perceive their national politics. The other, *Only in America?*, wonders whether the political differences make that much difference.* Do political institutions and practices in the United States truly differ from politics elsewhere?

To give you a sense of how different, and in many cases how similar, politics in this country is to politics in other countries, each chapter of this book will include a Global Politics box that compares some aspect of American politics with that in other countries. One line of comparison will be with Canada, France, Germany, Italy, Japan, the United Kingdom, and the United States (known as G-7), which represent a variety of experiences within a common framework. They are all industrial democracies, holding among the highest GNPs in the world and enjoying a comparatively high standard of living. Since the mid-1990s the group has become know as the G-8 by the addition of the Russian president to the annual summit. In this book we continue the G-7 shorthand to stand for a set of advanced capitalist industrial democracies. Even though Russia is now officially a member of this "leadership club," its situation as a country making the transition to capitalism and parliamentary democracy from a socialist economy and political system make its recent political experience qualitatively different from the original G-7 members. There is, however, variation between them on specific indicators. Note, for example, the variations in country size. The United States is far larger than any of its counterparts except Canada. It has more than twice the population of Japan, the next most populous country in the group. More women are in the U.S. workforce, even as a proportion of total adult female population. The United States also has a low unemployment rate, especially compared to the European countries. Thus, the industrial democracies provide a pool of good cases for comparison of politics.

Industrial democracies, however, do not represent the majority of political systems in the world. Of the other 190 or so nation-states in existence today, we will consider China, Indonesia, Mexico, and Russia as representative exam-

WEB EXPLORATION
To determine your ideology, go to www.ablongman.com/oconnor

or health care. It is also not unusual to encounter a person who could be considered liberal on social issues such as abortion and civil rights but conservative on economic or "pocketbook" issues.

Today it seems that there are more extremists than ever. But this perception may be due to the fact that those on the far right or left are often more vocal and vehement about their views than are moderates. Thus, because of television (which is always in search of a quick "sound bite" for the 6 o'clock news) and talk radio shows (which survive on controversy), these views may be the ones voiced and heard most often.

The perception that there are more extremists than ever may not be correct. Since the 1970s, when ideological tracking began to be measured regularly, there actually has been little change in how the American public views itself. General Colin Powell, retired, called this frustrated, moderate electorate "the sensible center."[11] His "sensible center" has remained

ples. The first three are typically classified as developing countries; the indicators above show lower levels of economic development. Mexico is often characterized as a semidemocracy; Indonesia and Russia have only begun the transition to democracy recently. All in one way or another demonstrate the problems many countries face in achieving democracy. China is a socialist country, and as such differs from the G-7 even as to

basic definitions of democracy. Russia is classified as a transitional democracy, attempting to move from the socialist political and economic pattern of the former Soviet Union to parliamentary democracy and a capitalist economy.

---

*John W. Kingdon, *America the Unusual* (New York: Worth Publishers, 1999). Graham K. Wilson, *Only In America?* (Chatham, N.J.: Chatham House, 1998).

Vital Statistics Profiles of G-7 Countries

Country	Area (1000 km²)	Population (million, 2000)	GDP per Capita ($,1995)	Life Expectancy at Birth	Televisions/ 1000 People (1996)	Women in the Labor Force (% of Total Women)
Canada	9,971	31.01	19,439	78.5	714	58.0
China	9,597	1284.9	777[a]	68.6	319	73.0
France	552	59.00	24,739	77.9	591	48.0
Germany	357	82.00	26,183	76.5	564	48.0
Indonesia	1,905	212.1	478	62.7	67	50.0
Italy	301	57.20	20,659	78.1	524	35.0
Japan	378	126.70	29,956	80.5	684	50.0
Mexico	1,958	98.80	4,324	71.5	270	39.0
Russia	17,075	146.9	1,936	64.9	405	50.0
UK	243	58.09	23,934	76.8	516	54.0
USA	9,364	274.1	31,059	76.1	805	60.0

[a]excludes Hong Kong

Sources: Handbook of International Economic Statistics, 1996: OECD Country Trends. http://wn.bilkent.edu.tr/prv/ftp/w . . . ov/cia/ publications/hies96/d/d.html. *Japan, 1997: An International Comparison.* Japan Institute for Social and Economic Affairs, 1997.

---

firm at about 35 percent to 40 percent of the adult population, while those on either end of the spectrum have remained around 12 percent to 15 percent for liberals and 12 percent to 19 percent for conservatives.

POLITICAL CULTURE AND VIEWS OF GOVERNMENT

COMPARATIVE
Comparing Politcal Landscapes

Americans' views about and expectations of government affect the political system at all levels. It has now become part of our political culture to expect negative campaigns, dishonest politicians, and political pundits who make their living bashing politicians and the political process.

Doris "Granny D" Haddock looks out from the U.S. Capitol steps as she completes a 14-month, 3,200-mile trek across America to agitate for campaign finance reform. (Photo courtesy: Reuters/Jamal Wilson/Archive Photos)

High Expectations

In roughly the first 150 years of our nation's history, the federal government had few responsibilities, and its citizens had few expectations of it beyond national defense, printing money, collecting tariffs and taxes, and so on. The state governments were generally far more powerful than the federal government in matters affecting the everyday lives of Americans.

As the nation and its economy grew in size and complexity, the federal government took on more responsibilities such as regulating some businesses, providing poverty relief, and inspecting food. Then, in the 1930s, in response to the Great Depression, President Franklin D. Roosevelt's New Deal government programs proliferated in almost every area of American life (job creation, income security, aid to the poor). Since then, Americans have looked to the government for solutions to all kinds of problems.

Politicians, too, have often contributed to rising public expectations by promising far more than they or the government could deliver. Although President Clinton's vow to end "welfare as we know it" was realized by the end of his first term, his ambitious promises to overhaul the health care system went nowhere. Similarly, several key provisions of the Republicans' highly ambitious Contract with America failed to see the legislative light of day. Term limits, for example, a battle cry of Republicans running for the 104th Congress in 1994, were not really so attractive to them once they took over control of Congress. These rising expectations about government's ability to reform itself, as well as to cure all social and economic ills, have led to cynicism about government and apathy, as evidenced in low voter turnout. It may be that Americans have come to expect too much from the national government and must simply readjust their expectations. Nevertheless, as revealed in Table 1.3, confidence in all institutions is up, although few have much confidence in Congress and the press.

A Missing Appreciation of the Good

During the Revolutionary period, average citizens were passionate about politics because the stakes—the very survival of the new nation—were so high. Today the stakes aren't readily apparent to many, and the government is a target for their blame and frustrations. If you don't have faith in America, its institutions, or symbols (and Table 1.3 shows that

TABLE 1.3   Faith in Institutions

	Percentage of Americans Declaring They had a "Great Deal" of Confidence in the Institution				
	1966	1975	1986	1996	2000
Congress	42%	13%	16%	8%	7%
Executive branch	41	13	21	10	15
The press	29	26	18	11	12
Business & industry	55	19	24	23	9
Colleges/universities	61	36	28	23	37
Medicine	73	51	46	45	39

Sources: Newsweek (January 8, 1996): 32; and *The Public Perspective* 8 (February/March 1994): 4. Data for 2000: Gallup Poll, *Confidence in Institutions,* June 22–25, 2000.

TABLE 1.4 How Americans Are Really Doing

	1945	1970	2000
Population	132 million	203 million	275 million
Life expectancy	65.9	70.8	77
Per capita income (1987 constant dollars)	$6,367	$9,875	$19,241[d]
Adults who are high school grads	25%[a]	55%	83%[e]
Adults who are college grads	5%[a]	11%	27%[e]
Households with phones	46%	87%	94%[b]
Households with televisions	0%	95%	98%[c]
Households with cable TV	0%	4%	65.3%[c]
Households with computers	n/a	n/a	42%
Women in labor force	29%	38%	67%[e]
Own their own home	46%	63%	65%[e]
Annual airline passengers	7 million	170 million	635.4 million[‡e]
Poverty rate	39.7%[†]	12.6%	13.3%[c]
Divorce rate (per 1,000 people)	3.5	3.5	9.9[a]
Children born out of wedlock	3.9%	16.7%	32%[d]

[a]1940 figure [†]1949 figure [b]1996 figure [‡]Estimate [c]1996 figure [d]1997 figure [e]1998 figure [f]1999 figure

Sources: U.S. Census Bureau, Dept. of Economic Analysis, National Center for Health Statistics, Dept. of Education, Statistical Abstract, Bureau of Labor Statistics, the Air Transport Association.

many of us don't), it becomes even easier to blame the government for all kinds of woes—personal as well as societal—in spite of the fact that on many objective measures of progress, Americans are doing better than ever before (as revealed in Table 1.4). Furthermore, while people complain about government, many of us take what government does for us for granted and don't realize all the things governments do well.

In the aftermath of the Great Depression in the United States, for example, the government created the Social Security program, which dramatically decreased poverty among the elderly. Our contract laws and judicial system provide an efficient framework for business, assuring people that they have a recourse in the courts should someone fail to deliver as promised. Government-guaranteed student loan programs make it possible for many students to attend college. Even something as seemingly mundane as our uniform bankruptcy laws help protect both a business enterprise and its creditors when the enterprise collapses.

Mistrust of Politicians

It's not difficult to see why Americans might be distrustful of politicians. In August 1998 after President Clinton announced to the American public that he had misled them concerning his relationship with Monica Lewinsky, 45 percent said they were disgusted, 33 percent were angry, but only 18 percent were surprised, according to a poll conducted by *The Washington Post*. Only 19 percent responded that the president had "high personal, moral and ethical standards," down from 45 percent two years earlier.[12]

The president isn't the only politician to incur the public's distrust. One 1998 poll conducted by the Pew Charitable Trust found that 40 percent of those polled thought that most politicians were "crooks."[13] The

POINT / COUNTERPOINT

IS GOVERNMENT A POSITIVE FORCE OR A NEGATIVE NECESSITY?

Political polls continue to show that most Americans believe government does not do very much for them. Some people feel government ought to be more active in providing services and promoting quality of life. Others believe that government shouldn't be involved in so many facets of daily life. Should there be more or less government? Let's examine these two points of view.

Many people, such as Democrats and Populists, believe that government regulation is good, especially when dealing with protections for the poor, groups that are difficult to mobilize (such as consumers), and public safety. From the cradle to the grave, the government works to provide safety and security, from child safety standards on cribs, car seats, and pajamas, to minimum standards of care for nursing homes to protect the elderly and infirm. Other examples of the positive role government plays in our lives include: Social Security, a program created in the 1930s to assist those too old to work; the Family Leave and Medical Emergency Act that was passed in 1993 to assure maternity leave and leave to care for elderly ill relatives; helmet and seat-belt laws, which have been passed in most states; and many more. These services help provide the life, liberty, and happiness promised in the founding documents of our country.

The government also provides for national defense, regulates the skies and public airwaves, and funds educational programs such as *Sesame Street* and National Public Radio. It also works to guarantee the safety of food and drugs and even requires standardized food labeling so we can compare the nutritional value of our foods. Local and state governments provide sewer systems, garbage collection, recycling programs, roads, and free public education at the elementary and secondary levels, plus low-cost junior colleges and state universities.

Both federal and local governments regulate businesses and even the conduct of private individuals through an extensive code of criminal and civil laws. Without government and its research and development funding, we might not have cellular phones, satellite communications, the Internet, silicon chips (and thus the computer), cable and dish TV, fax machines, Velcro, freeze-dried foods, or four-wheel-drive vehicles.

However, many people, such as Republicans and Libertarians, believe that government regulation is bad. It inhibits freedom and liberty, warps the market forces of the economy, and interferes in areas the government should have nothing to do with. These people believe that

low levels of public confidence in Congress, the executive branch, and even the news media revealed in Table 1.3 underscore this view. Character counts, and the electorate has concluded—rightly or wrongly—that on this measure many elected officials can be found wanting.

Voter Apathy

"Campaigns are the conversation of democracy," an observer once said.[14] But a Gallup poll conducted after the 1988 presidential contest between George Bush and Michael Dukakis found that 30 percent of those who voted would have preferred to check off a "no confidence in either" box had they been given the choice.

government is not a positive force for good but an evil necessity to perform only those functions that individuals cannot do alone. For example, government ought to provide for the national defense, border and immigration controls, and the collection of some minimum level of taxation to pay for the above duties but not for things like the war on drugs and gun control.

Advocates for less government believe that government should not interfere in the lives of individuals and that, by and large, the market and individuals ought to take care of social and economic problems. For example, if the elderly need help, their family or church ought to step in. The government shouldn't provide for services such as day care because the market will provide for day care if there is a need for it. People ought to be responsible for their own safety. If they choose not to wear a helmet or a seat belt, then that is their choice and their responsibility. In addition, they believe that businesses ought to be able to pursue their line of work without undue government interference. In specific policy terms, this viewpoint argues that the problems with Social Security can be fixed by privatizing the program, and that schools can be improved by the introduction of competition through vouchers.

Less government allows for more individual freedom and liberty. No government should be able to tell you that you can't own a gun, smoke a cigarette in a public building, or eat popcorn at the movies. You should be free to read the books you choose to read, watch the movies you choose to watch, and get together with people whom you enjoy, all without government interference.

Smaller, more limited governments would be less likely to be corrupt and could be held accountable more easily than large government. The activities of government would be more transparent because there would be fewer of them, so people would always know what the government was doing.

Government is considered less efficient than the private sector. Proponents of less government argue that if a government agency takes on a task, it will spend more money, hire more people, and produce less than if a private firm or individual were to do the same task. In order to be efficient, supply and demand as well as cost must be an integral part of decision making, and government tends to ignore those principles. The private sector innovates and responds more quickly to changing needs as well.

What do you think? Is government a positive force or a negative necessity? Should we prefer less government or more government?
Go to www.ablongman.com/oconnor

Americans, unlike voters in most other societies, get an opportunity to vote on a host of candidates and issues, but some say those choices may just be too numbing. Responsible voters may simply opt not to go to the polls, fearing that they lack sufficient information of the vast array of candidates and issues facing them.

A Census Bureau report examining the reasons over 5 million eligible voters stayed home from the polls on election day in 1996 showed that time constraints were "the single biggest reason" Americans gave for not voting.[15] The head of the Committee for the Study of the American Electorate thinks that time is an excuse.[16] Instead, he faults the lack of real choices facing voters. Why vote if your vote won't make much

SIMULATION
How to Satisfy
Aunt Martha

difference? In fact, unsuccessful Green Party presidential candidate Ralph Nader tried to run as a alternative to the two major parties, arguing that there was little difference between Republicans and Democrats.

Some commentators have noted that nonvoting may not even be a sign of apathy. If things are good, or you perceive that there is no need for change, why vote? Whatever the reason, declining voter participation is cause for concern. If information is truly a problem, the Internet, access to information and new ways to vote may have major consequences on the course of elections in the future and produce a more informed, and therefore motivated, electorate.

There can be no doubt, however, that many citizens are disengaged from the political process. One 1999 poll found that 59 percent of those queried thought "public officials don't care much what people like me think." Only 28 percent believed that "having elections makes the government pay attention to what the people think."[17]

Redefining Our Expectations

Just as it is important to recognize that governments serve many important purposes, it is also important to recognize that government and politics—the process by which policy decisions are made—are not static. Politics, moreover, involves conflicts over different and sometimes opposing ideologies, and these ideologies are very much influenced by one's racial, economic, sexual, or historical experiences. These divisions are real and affect the political process at all levels.

The current frustration and dissatisfaction about politics and government may be just another phase, as the changing American body politic seeks to redefine its ideas about government. This process is one that is likely to define politics into the millennium, but the individualistic nature of the American system will have long-lasting consequences on how it can be accomplished. Americans want less government but as they get older, they don't want less Social Security. They want lower taxes and better roads, but they don't want to pay for toll roads. They want better education for their children but lower expenditures on schools. Some clearly want less for others but not themselves, which puts politicians in the position of nearly always disappointing voters. This inability to please voters and find a middle ground undoubtedly led to unprecedented recent retirements in the House and Senate in the 1990s.

Politicians, as well as their constituents, are looking for ways to redefine the role of government, much in the same way that the Framers did when they met in Philadelphia to forge a solution between Americans' quest for liberty and freedom tempered by order and governmental authority. While citizens charge that it is still government as usual, a change is taking place in Washington, D.C. The federal government, like most American organizations, is downsizing. Sacrosanct programs such as Social Security and welfare continually are being reexamined, and power and responsibility are slowly being returned to the states. Thus, the times may be different, but the questions about government and its role in our lives remain the same.

Continuity & Change

The Face of America

When early colonists came to what is now the United States, they did so for a variety of reasons. Still, they recognized the critical role that government could play for them in the New World. Even though the colonists in Massachusetts considered themselves British subjects, for example, they knew the importance of fashioning some form of governance, as illustrated by the signatures of agreement on the Mayflower Compact. Those who signed that historic document were largely British, male, and white. They expected the government to be best that governed least, but they also recognized the importance of order and protection of property and were therefore willing to give up some rights in return for government preservation of those ideals.

Over time, in a variety of large and not so large wars, many Americans fought for what they believed was the American ideal. Many saw combat on battlefields far from home, or they worked in hospitals or factories to help the war effort, generally forgoing their personal goals. Immigrants and native-born citizens alike all shared the American dream.

Today, the American dream is more difficult to see. A new wave of immigrants in the 1980s has changed the composition of many U.S. cities and states, often straining scarce resources such as quality public education, which has always been at the forefront of the American political socialization process. Several states, especially California, have attempted to restrict the rights and privileges of noncitizens in unprecedented ways. In a system of majority rule, the rights of those newest to our borders often lose out.

As illustrated by Figure 1.2, however, the "look" of America is changing and it is changing in some places such as California and Florida more quickly than in other areas of the nation.

1. What challenges do you believe national and state governments will face as the racial and ethnic composition of their citizenry changes dramatically?
2. In the wake of the 2000 Census that found Hispanics now to be the largest U.S. minority group, do you foresee any changes in how minorities, especially Hispanics, will be treated?

Cast Your Vote. What other challenges do you think national and state governments will face in the twenty-first century? To cast your vote, go to **www.ablongman.com/oconnor**

SUMMARY

The American political system was based on several notions that have their roots in classical Greek ideas, including natural law, the doctrine that human affairs should be governed by certain ethical principles that can be understood by reason. The ideas of social contract theorists John Locke and Thomas Hobbes, who held the belief that people are free and equal by God-given right, have continuing implications for our ideas of the proper role of government in our indirect democracy.

Key characteristics of this democracy established by the Framers are popular consent, popular sovereignty, majority rule and the preservation of minority rights, equality, individualism, and personal liberty, as is the Framers' option for a capitalistic system.

Several characteristics of the American electorate can help us understand how the system continues to evolve and change. Chief among these are changes in size and demographics of the population, and ideological beliefs.

Americans' views of government are often based on their high expectations. Confounding these high expectations are a missing appreciation of what is good about government, their mistrust of politicians, and the resultant voter apathy. Expectations about government and its role in our lives need to be redefined.

KEY TERMS

capitalism, p. 7
conservative, p. 19
direct democracy, p. 5
free market economy, p. 7

indirect (representative)
   democracy, p. 5
liberal, p. 19
libertarian, p. 19
natural law, p. 3

political ideology, p. 18
political culture, p. 12
republic, p. 7
social contract theory, p. 4

SELECTED READINGS

Almond, Gabriel, and Sidney Verba. *The Civic Culture.* Princeton, N.J.: Princeton University Press, 1963.

Dahl, Robert A. *Polyarchy: Participation and Opposition.* New Haven, Conn.: Yale University Press, 1971.

Elshtain, Jean Bethke. *Democracy on Trial.* New York: Basic Books, 1995.

Glendon, Mary Ann. *Rights Talk: The Impoverishment of Political Discourse.* New York: Free Press, 1991.

Grossman, Lawrence K. *The Electronic Republic: Reshaping Democracy in the Information Age.* New York: Viking, 1995.

Hobbes, Thomas. *Leviathan.* ed. Richard Tuck. New York: Cambridge University Press, 1996.

Hunter, James Davison. *Culture Wars: The Struggle to Define America.* New York: Basic Books, 1991.

Jamieson, Kathleen Hall. *Dirty Politics: Deception, Distraction, and Democracy.* New York: Oxford University Press, 1992.

Locke, John. *Two Treatises of Government,* ed. Peter Lasleti. New York: Cambridge University Press, 1988.

Lowi, Theodore J. *The End of Liberalism.* New York: Norton, 1979.

Putnam, Robert D. *Bowling Alone: The Collapse and Revival of the American Community.* New York: Simon and Schuster, 2000.

Samuelson, Robert J. *The Good Life and Its Discontents: The American Dream in the Age of Entitlement 1945–1995.* New York: Times Books, 1995.

Skocpol, Theda amd Morris Fiorinan, eds. *Civic Engagement in American Democracy.* Washington, D.C.: Brookings Institution Press, 1999.

Tolchin, Susan J. *The Angry American: How Voter Rage Is Changing the Nation.* Boulder, Colo.: Westview Press, 1996.

Truman, David B. *The Governmental Process.* New York: Knopf, 1951.

Verba, Sidney, Kay Schlozman, and Henry Brady. *Voice and Equality: Civic Volunteerism in American Politics.* Cambridge, Mass.: Harvard University Press, 1995.

The Constitution

(Photo courtesy: Pete Souza/Folio, Inc.)

At age eighteen, all American citizens today are eligible to vote in state and national elections. This has not always been the case. It took an amendment to the U.S. Constitution—one of only seventeen amendments that have been added since the Bill of Rights in 1791—to guarantee the franchise to those under twenty-one years of age.

In 1942, during World War II, Representative Jennings Randolph (D–W.Va.), proposed that the voting age be lowered to eighteen, believing that since young men were old enough to be drafted to fight and die for their country, they also should be allowed to vote. He continued to reintroduce his proposal during every session of Congress, and in 1954 President Eisenhower endorsed the idea in his State of the Union message. Presidents Johnson and Nixon—who called upon the nation's young men to fight on foreign shores—also echoed his appeal.[1]

By the 1960s, the campaign to lower the voting age took on a new sense of urgency as hundreds of thousands of young men were drafted to fight in Vietnam and thousands were killed in action. "Old Enough to Fight, Old Enough to Vote" was one popular slogan of the day. By 1970 four states—who under the U.S. Constitution are allowed to set the eligibility requirements for their voters—had lowered their voting ages to eighteen. Under considerable pressure from baby boomers, Congress passed legislation lowering the voting age in national, state, and local elections to eighteen.

The state of Oregon, however, challenged the constitutionality of the law in court, arguing that Congress had not been given the authority to establish a uniform voting age in state and local government under the

Chapter Outline

Constitution. The U.S. Supreme Court agreed.[2] The decision from the badly divided Court meant that those eighteen or older could vote in national elections but that the states were free to prohibit those under twenty-one from voting in state and local elections. The decision presented the states with the logistical nightmare of keeping two sets of registration books—one for those over twenty-one and one for those who were not.

In 1971, Jennings Randolph, now a senator from West Virginia, reintroduced his proposed amendment.[3] Within three months of the Supreme Court's decision, Congress sent the proposed Twenty-Sixth Amendment to the states for their ratification. The required three-fourths of the states ratified the amendment within three months, making its adoption on June 30, 1971, the quickest in the history of the constitutional amending process.

In spite of winning the right to vote through a change in the U.S. Constitution, young people never have voted in large numbers. In spite of issues of concern to those under the age of twenty-five, including Internet privacy, the fate of online music-swapping, reproductive rights, and the continuance of student loan programs, this group has very low voter turnout rates. The 2000 elections showed little change in this phenomenon.

The Constitution was intentionally written to forestall the need for amendment, and the process by which it could be changed or amended was made intentionally time consuming and difficult. Over the years, thousands of amendments—including those to prohibit child labor, provide equal rights for women, grant statehood to the District of Columbia, and balance the budget—have been debated or sent to the states for their approval, only to die slow deaths. Only twenty-seven amendments have made their way into the Constitution. What the Framers came up with in Philadelphia has continued to work, in spite of continually increasing demands and dissatisfaction with our national government. Perhaps Americans are happier with the system of government created by the Framers than they realize. The ideas that went into the making of the Constitution and how the Constitution has evolved to address the problems of a growing and ever-changing nation are at the core of our discussion in this chapter.

THE ORIGINS OF A NEW NATION

Starting in the early seventeenth century, colonists came to the New World for a variety of reasons. Often it was to escape religious persecution. Others came seeking a new start on a continent where land was plentiful. The independence and diversity of the settlers in the New World made the question of how best to rule the new colonies a tricky one. More than merely an ocean separated England from the colonies; the colonists were independent people, and it soon became clear that the Crown could not govern the colonies with the same close rein used at home. King James I thus allowed some local participation in decision making through arrangements such as the first elected colonial assembly, the Virginia House of Burgesses, and the elected General Court that governed the Massachusetts Bay colony after 1629. Almost all the colonists agreed that the king ruled by divine right, but English monarchs allowed the colonists significant liberties in terms of self-government, religious practices, and economic organization. For 140 years, this system worked fairly well.[4]

By the early 1760s, a century and a half of physical separation, colonial development, and the relative self-governance of the colonies led to weakening ties with—and loyalties to—the Crown. By this time, each of the thirteen colonies had drafted its own written constitution, which provided the fundamental rules or laws to govern each colony. Still, the colonists tacitly relinquished to the Crown the authority to regulate trade and conduct international affairs, but they retained the right to levy their own taxes. This fragile agreement, however, was soon put to the test.

The French and Indian War was part of a global war initiated by the British. The American phase of the Seven Years' War was fought between England and France with its Indian allies from 1756 to 1763 on the "western frontier" of the colonies and in Canada. In North America its immediate cause was the rival claims of those two European nations for the lands between the Allegheny Mountains and the Mississippi River. The Treaty of Paris (signed in 1763) signaled the end of the war. The colonists expected that with the "Indian problem" on the western frontier now "under control," westward migration and settlement could begin in earnest. They were shocked when the Crown decreed in 1763 that there was to be no further westward movement by British subjects. Parliament believed that expansion into Indian territory would lead to new expenditures for the defense of the settlers, draining the British treasury, which had yet to recover from the high cost of waging the war.

To raise money to pay for the war, as well as the expenses of administering the colonies, Parliament levied a series of taxes on the colonists. Men throughout the colonies organized the Sons of Liberty, under the leadership of Samuel Adams and Patrick Henry, to protest the taxes. The Stamp Act of 1765, for example, was a direct tax on many items not traditionally under the control of the king, and protests against it were violent and loud. Riots were especially violent in Boston, where the colonial governor's home was burned by an angry mob.

Sam Adams (1722–1803) is best remembered today for the beer that bears his name. Although he did bankrupt his family's brewery, the second cousin of President John Adams was a key player in the development of an independent nation. He signed the Declaration of Independence, attended the Massachusetts convention that ratified the U.S. Constitution, and served as the governor of Massachusetts from 1794 to 1797. (Painting by John Singleton Copely. Courtesy, Museum of Fine Arts, Boston. Reproduced with permission. © 2001 Museum of Fine Arts, Boston. All Rights Reserved.)

First Steps Toward Independence

Stamp Act Congress
First official meeting of the colonies; first step toward unified nation.

In 1765, the colonists called for the **Stamp Act Congress,** the first official meeting of the colonies and the first step toward a unified nation. Nine of the thirteen colonies sent representatives to a meeting in New York City, where a detailed list of Crown violations of their fundamental rights was drawn up.

The Stamp Act Congress and its petitions to the Crown did little to stop the onslaught of taxing measures. In 1767, Parliament imposed duties on all kinds of colonial imports, including tea. Response from the Sons of Liberty was immediate. A boycott was announced, and almost all colonists gave up their favorite drink in a united show of resistance to the tax and British authority.[5] Tensions continued to run high, especially after the British sent 4,000 troops to Boston. On March 5, 1770, English troops opened fire on a mob that included disgruntled dock workers, whose jobs had been taken by British soldiers, and members of the Sons of Liberty who were taunting the soldiers in front of the Boston Customs House. Five colonists were killed in what became known as the "Boston Massacre." Following this confrontation, all duties except those on tea were lifted. The tea tax, however, continued to be a symbolic irritant. In 1772, at the suggestion of Samuel Adams, Boston and other towns around Massachusetts set up **Committees of Correspondence** to articulate ideas and keep communications open around the colony. By 1774, twelve colonies had formed committees to maintain a flow of information among like-minded colonists.

Committees of Correspondence
Groups formed in the colonies to exchange ideas and information about resisting British rule.

Meanwhile, despite dissent in England over the treatment of the colonies, Parliament passed the Tea Act, the effect of which was to force colonial merchants to pay higher prices for tea bought from sources other than Britain. When the next shipment of tea arrived in Boston from Great Britain, the colonists responded by throwing the Boston Tea Party. When the news reached King George, he flew into a rage against the actions of his disloyal subjects. "The die is now cast," the king told his prime minister. "The colonies must either submit or triumph."

His first act was to persuade Parliament to pass the Coercive Acts in 1774. Known in the colonies as the Intolerable Acts, they contained a key provision calling for a total blockade of Boston Harbor until restitution was made for the tea. Another provision reinforced the Quartering Act, giving royal governors the authority to quarter in the homes of private citizens, the additional 4,000 British soldiers sent to patrol Boston.

The Continental Congress

WEB EXPLORATION
For more information on the work of the Continental Congress, see www.ablongman.com/oconnor

The British could never have guessed how the cumulative impact of these actions would unite the colonists. Taxes were no longer the key issue; now the extent of British authority over the colonies was the far more important question. At the request of the colonial assemblies of Massachusetts and Virginia, all but one of the thirteen colonial assemblies agreed to select a group of delegates to attend a continental congress authorized to communicate with the king on behalf of the now united colonies.

The **First Continental Congress** met in Philadelphia from September 5 to October 26, 1774. It was made up of fifty-six delegates from every colony except Georgia. They agreed on a series of resolutions to oppose the Coercive Acts, established a formal organization to boycott British goods, and drafted a Declaration of Rights and Resolves, which called for colonial rights of petition and assembly, trial by peers, freedom from a standing army, and the selection of representative councils to levy taxes.

King George refused to yield, tensions continued to rise, and a **Second Continental Congress** was called. Before it could meet, fighting broke out early in the morning of April 19, 1775, at Lexington and Concord, Massachusetts, with what Ralph Waldo Emerson called "the shot heard round the world." Eight colonial soldiers, called Minutemen, were killed, and 16,000 British troops besieged Boston.

When the Second Continental Congress convened in Philadelphia on May 10, 1775, delegates were united by their increased hostility to Great Britain. The bloodshed at Lexington left no other course but war.

First Continental Congress
Meetings held in Philadelphia from September 5 to October 26, 1774, in which fifty-six delegates (from every colony except Georgia) adopted a resolution that opposed the Coercive Acts.

Second Continental Congress
Meeting convened in Philadelphia on May 10, 1775, at which it was decided an army should be raised and George Washington of Virginia was named commander-in-chief.

THE DECLARATION OF INDEPENDENCE

In January 1776, Thomas Paine, with the support and encouragement of Benjamin Franklin, issued (at first anonymously) *Common Sense,* a pamphlet forcefully arguing for independence from Great Britain. *Common Sense* galvanized the American public against reconciliation with England. As the mood in the colonies changed, so did that of the Second Continental Congress. On June 7, 1776, Richard Henry Lee of Virginia rose to move "that these United Colonies are, and of right ought to be, free and independent States, and that all connection between them and the State of Great Britain is, and ought to be, dissolved." His three-part resolution—which called for independence, the formation of foreign alliances, and preparation of a plan of **confederation**—triggered hot debate among the delegates. A proclamation of independence from Great Britain was treason, a crime punishable by death. Although six of the thirteen colonies had already instructed their delegates to vote for independence, the Second Continental Congress was suspended to allow its delegates to return home to their respective colonial legislatures for final instructions. Independence was not a move to be taken lightly. A committee of five, however, was selected to begin work on a **Declaration of Independence.** Owing to his "peculiar felicity of expression," Thomas Jefferson was selected as chair.

On July 2, twelve of the thirteen colonies (with New York abstaining) voted for independence. Two days later the Second Continental Congress voted to adopt the Declaration of Independence penned by Thomas Jefferson. On July 9, the Declaration, now with the approval of New York, was read aloud in Philadelphia.[6]

confederation
Type of government in which the national government derives its powers from the states; a league of independent states.

Declaration of Independence
Document drafted by Thomas Jefferson in 1776 that proclaimed the right of the American colonies to separate from Great Britain.

A Theoretical Basis for a New Government

In simple but eloquent language, Jefferson set out the reasons for the colonies' separation from Great Britain. Most of his stirring rhetoric drew heavily on the works of sixteenth- and seventeenth-century political philosophers, particularly the English philosopher John Locke, who argued that individuals who give their consent to be governed have the right to rebel against a government that violates the rights of its citizens.

It is easy to see the colonists' debt to Locke. In ringing language, the Declaration of Independence proclaims:

> We hold these truths to be self-evident, that all men are created equal, that they are endowed by their Creator with certain unalienable Rights, that among these are Life, Liberty and the pursuit of Happiness.

The Declaration also justified the colonists' break with the Crown, clarified their ideas about the proper form of government, and enumerated the wrongs that the colonists had suffered under British rule.

The Declaration was signed and transmitted to the king. As the Revolutionary War raged on, the Continental Congress attempted to fashion a new united government to represent the thirteen colonies.

THE FIRST ATTEMPT AT GOVERNMENT: THE ARTICLES OF CONFEDERATION

The British had no written constitution. Representatives to the Second Continental Congress had to codify arrangements never before put into legal terminology. To make things more complicated, the delegates had to arrive at these decisions in a wartime atmosphere. Nevertheless, in late 1777, the **Articles of Confederation,** creating a loose "league of friendship" between the independent states, were passed by the Congress and presented to the states for their ratification.

The Articles created a type of government called a confederation or confederacy. The national government in a confederation derives all of its powers *directly from the states.* The national government in a confederacy is weaker than the sum of its parts, and the states often consider themselves independent states linked together only for limited purposes such as national defense. Key provisions in the Articles creating the confederacy included:

- A national government with a Congress empowered to make peace, coin money, appoint officers for an army, control the post office, and negotiate with Indian tribes.
- Each state's retention of its independence and ultimate authority to govern within its territories.
- One vote in the Continental Congress for each state, regardless of size.

Articles of Confederation

The compact among the thirteen original states that was the basis of their government. Written in 1776, the Articles were not ratified by all the states until 1781.

- The vote of nine states was required to pass any measure (a unanimous vote was necessary for any amendment).
- The selection and payment of delegates to the Congress by their respective state legislatures.

The Articles were finally ratified by all thirteen states in March 1781.

WEB EXPLORATION
For the full text
of the Articles of
Confederation, see
www.ablongman.com/oconnor

Problems Under the Articles of Confederation

No longer united by the war effort, the government quickly fell into chaos. By 1784, just one year after the Revolutionary army was disbanded, governing the new nation under the Articles of Confederation proved unworkable.[7] Congress could rarely assemble the required quorum of nine states to conduct business. Even when it could, there was little agreement among the states. To raise revenue to pay off war debts and run the government, various land, poll, and liquor taxes were proposed. But since Congress had no specific power to tax, all these proposals were rejected. At one point Congress was even driven out of Philadelphia (then the capital) by its own unpaid army.

Problems experienced under the Articles included the following:

- Although the national government could coin money, it had no resources to back up the value of its currency. Continental dollars were worth little, and trade between states became chaotic as some states began to coin their own money.
- Congress had no power to regulate commerce among the states and with foreign nations. As a result individual states attempted to enter into agreements with other countries, and foreign nations were suspicious of trade agreements made with the United States.
- The Articles made no provision for an executive branch of government to execute, or implement, laws passed by the legislative branch. Instead, the "president" was merely the presiding officer at meetings.
- No provision was made for a judicial system to handle the growing number of economic conflicts and boundary disputes among the individual states. Several states claimed the same lands to the west; Pennsylvania and Virginia went to war with each other; Vermont threatened to annex itself to Canada.
- The Articles created only a weak central government. States were unwilling to give up rights, such as the power to tax. The government, moreover, was unable to force the states to abide by the provisions of the Treaty of Paris, signed in 1783, which had officially ended the war.

Daniel Shays leads a group of Revolutionary War veterans at the courthouse in Springfield, Massachusetts, to stop the court from foreclosing on the mortgages on their farms. To quell this uprising, Congress called for a new national militia, but only Virginia agreed to send money. The governor of Massachusetts then tried to raise a state militia, but there were no extra funds in the state treasury. Finally, private funds were rounded up to fund a militia to stop what was called Shays's Rebellion. (Photo courtesy: Bettmann/Corbis)

THE MIRACLE AT PHILADELPHIA: WRITING A CONSTITUTION

On February 21, 1787—in the throes of economic turmoil and with domestic tranquility gone haywire—the Congress called for a Constitutional Convention for "the sole and express purpose of revising the Articles of Confederation." Eventually, all states but Rhode Island sent delegates.

When twenty-nine individuals met in Philadelphia on May 14, they immediately agreed that a new form of government would be necessary. All present recognized that what they were doing could be considered treasonous. Revising the Articles of Confederation was one thing; to call for an entirely new government, as suggested by the Virginia delegation, was another.

The Framers

Fifty-five out of the seventy-four delegates ultimately chosen by their state legislatures to attend the Constitutional Convention labored long and hard that hot summer behind closed doors in Philadelphia. All of them were men; hence they are often referred to as the "Founding Fathers." Most of them, however, were quite young; many were in their twenties and thirties, and only one—Benjamin Franklin, at eighty-one—was very old. (See Analyzing the Data: Facts on the Framers.) Here we generally refer to those delegates as Framers because their work provided the framework for our new government. The Framers brought with them a vast amount of political, educational, legal, and business experience.

Motives of the Framers

Debate about the Framers' motives filled the air during the ratification struggle and has provided grist for the mill of historians and political scientists over the years. Anti-Federalists, who opposed the new Constitution, charged that Federalist supporters of the Constitution were a self-serving, landed, and propertied elite with a vested interest in the capitalistic system that had evolved in the colonies. Federalists countered that they were simply trying to preserve the nation.

In his *Economic Interpretation of the Constitution of the United States* (1913), the highly respected political scientist and historian Charles A. Beard argued that the 1780s were a "critical period" (as the time under governance by the Articles of Confederation had come to be known) not for the nation as a whole, but rather for businessmen.[8] These men feared that a weak, decentralized government could harm their economic interests. Beard argued that the merchants wanted a strong national government to promote industry and trade, protect private property, and most importantly, ensure payment of the public debt—much of which was owed to them.

Therefore, according to Beard, the Constitution represents "an economic document drawn with superb skill by men whose property interests were immediately at stake."[9]

By the 1950s, this view had fallen into disfavor when other historians were unable to find direct links between wealth and the Framers' motives for establishing the Constitution.[10] Robert Brown, for example, faulted Beard's economic approach and his failure to consider the impact of religion and individual views about government.[11] In the 1960s, however, another group of historians began to argue that social and economic factors were, in fact, important motives for supporting the Constitution. In *The Anti-Federalists* (1961), Jackson Turner Main posited that while the Constitution's supporters might not have been the united group of creditors suggested by Beard, they were wealthier, came from high social strata, and had greater concern for maintaining the prevailing social order than the general public.[12]

In 1969, Gordon S. Wood's *The Creation of the American Republic* resurrected this debate. Wood deemphasized economics to argue that major social divisions explained different groups' support for (or opposition to) the new Constitution. He concluded that the Framers were representatives of a class that favored order and stability over some of the more radical ideas that had inspired the Revolution.[13]

The Virginia and New Jersey Plans

The less populous states were concerned with being lost in any new system of government where states were not treated as equals regardless of population. It is not surprising that a large state and then a small one, Virginia and New Jersey, respectively weighed in with ideas about how the new government should operate.

The **Virginia Plan** called for a national system based heavily on the European nation-state model, wherein the national government derives its powers from the people and not from the member states.

Its key features included:

- Creation of a powerful central government with three branches—the legislative, executive, and judicial.
- A two-house legislature with one house elected directly by the people, the other chosen from among persons nominated by the state legislatures.

In general, smaller states felt comfortable with the arrangements under the Articles of Confederation. These states offered another model of government, the **New Jersey Plan**. Its key features included:

- Strengthening the Articles, *not* replacing them.
- Creation of a one-house legislature with one vote for each state and representatives chosen by state legislatures.
- Giving the Congress the power to raise revenue from duties and a post office.

Virginia Plan
The first general plan for the Constitution, proposed by James Madison. Its key points were a bicameral legislature, an executive chosen by the legislature, and a judiciary also named by the legislature.

New Jersey Plan
A framework for the Constitution proposed by a group of small states; its key points were a one-house legislature with one vote for each state, a multiperson "executive," the establishment of the acts of Congress as the "supreme law" of the land, and a supreme judiciary with limited power.

A N A L Y Z I N G   T H E   D A T A

WHO WERE THE FRAMERS?

Who were the Framers? Of the 55 delegates who attended some portion of the Philadelphia meeting, 17 were slaveholders who owned approximately 1,400 slaves (Washington, Mason, and Rutledge were the three largest slaveholders at the time of the Philadelphia Convention). In terms of education, 31 went to college, 24 did not. Those who did not were mostly business, legal, or printing apprentices.

Seven delegates signed both the U.S. Constitution and the Declaration of Independence.

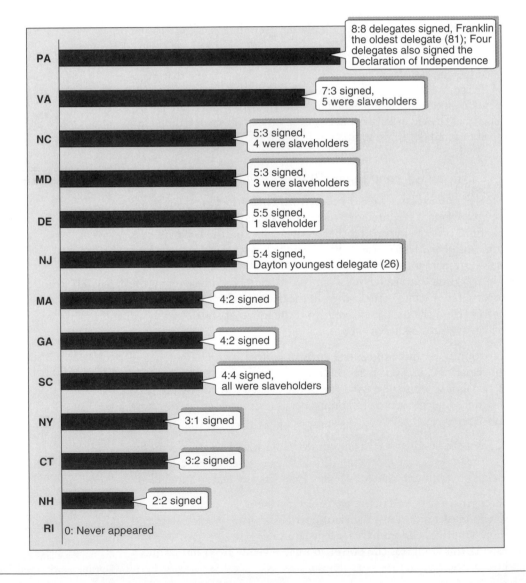

PA — 8:8 delegates signed, Franklin the oldest delegate (81); Four delegates also signed the Declaration of Independence

VA — 7:3 signed, 5 were slaveholders

NC — 5:3 signed, 4 were slaveholders

MD — 5:3 signed, 3 were slaveholders

DE — 5:5 signed, 1 slaveholder

NJ — 5:4 signed, Dayton youngest delegate (26)

MA — 4:2 signed

GA — 4:2 signed

SC — 4:4 signed, all were slaveholders

NY — 3:1 signed

CT — 3:2 signed

NH — 2:2 signed

RI — 0: Never appeared

The most serious disagreement between the Virginia and New Jersey plans concerned representation in Congress. When a deadlock on this point loomed, Connecticut offered its own compromise. Each state would have an equal vote in the Senate. Again, there was a stalemate.

A committee was appointed to work out an agreement. Its solution, known as the **Great Compromise,** took ideas from both the Virginia and New Jersey plans. In recommending a two-house legislature, it suggested that one house be elected directly by the people.

In this one house of the legislature, later called the House of Representatives, there should be fifty-six representatives—one representative for every 40,000 inhabitants. This house was given the power to originate all bills for raising and spending money. In the second house of the legislature, later called the Senate, representatives would be selected by the state legislatures and each state would have an equal vote.[14]

Still, a sticking point remained about how to determine state population. Slaves could not vote, but the Southern states wanted them included for purposes of determining population. After considerable dissension, it was decided that population would be calculated by adding the "whole Number of Free Persons" to "three fifths of all other Persons." "All other Persons" was the delegates' "tactful" way of referring to slaves. Known as the **Three-Fifths Compromise,** this highly political deal assured that the South would hold 47 percent of the House—enough to prevent attacks on slavery but not so much as to foster the spread of slavery northward.[15]

The Great Compromise ultimately met with the approval of all states in attendance. The smaller states were pleased because they got equal representation in the Senate; the larger states were satisfied with the proportional representation in the House of Representatives. The small states then would dominate the Senate while the large states, such as Virginia and New York, would control the House. But because both houses had to pass any legislation, neither body could dominate the other.

Unfinished Business

The Framers next turned to fashioning an executive branch. While they agreed on the idea of a one-person executive, they could not settle on the length of the term of office, nor on how the chief executive should be selected. With Shays's Rebellion still fresh in their minds, the delegates feared putting too much power, including selection of a president, into the hands of the lower classes. At the same time, representatives from the smaller states feared that the selection of the chief executive by the legislature would put additional power into the hands of the large states.

Amid these fears, the Committee on Unfinished Portions, whose sole responsibility was to iron out problems and disagreements concerning the office of chief executive, conducted its work. The committee recommended that the presidential term of office be fixed at four

Great Compromise
A decision made during the Constitutional Convention to give each state the same number of representatives in the Senate regardless of size; representation in the House was determined by population.

Three-Fifths Compromise
Agreement reached at the Constitutional Convention stipulating that each slave was to be counted as three-fifths of a person for purposes of determining population for representation in the U.S. House of Representatives.

years instead of seven, as had earlier been proposed. By choosing not to mention a period of time within which the chief executive would be eligible for reelection, they made it possible for a president to serve more than one term.

The Framers also created the electoral college and drafted rules concerning removal of a sitting president. The electoral college system gave individual states a key role, because each state would select electors equal to the number of representatives it had in the House and Senate. It was a vague compromise that removed election of the president and vice president from both the Congress and the people and put it in the hands of electors whose method of selection would be left to the states. As Alexander Hamilton noted in *Federalist No. 68*, the electoral college was fashioned to avoid "tumult and disorder" that the Framers feared could result if the "masses" were allowed to vote directly for president. Instead, the selection of the president was left to a small number of men (the electoral college) who "possess[ed] the information and discernment requisite" to decide, in Hamilton's words, the "complicated" business of selecting the president. For more on the electoral college see Politics Now: The 2000 Election and Calls to Amend the Constitution and page 45.

In drafting the new Constitution, the Framers also were careful to include a provision for removal of the chief executive. The House of Representatives was given the sole responsibility of investigating and charging a president or vice president with "Treason, Bribery, or other high Crimes and Misdemeanors." A majority vote would then result in issuing Articles of Impeachment against the president. In turn, the Senate was given sole responsibility to try the chief executive on the charges issued by the House. A two-thirds vote of the Senate was required to convict and remove the president from office. The chief justice of the United States was to preside over the Senate proceedings in place of the vice president (that body's usual leader) in order to prevent any appearance of impropriety on the vice president's part.

WEB EXPLORATION
For demographic background on the Framers, see
www.ablongman.com/oconnor

THE U.S. CONSTITUTION

The Preamble to the Constitution, the last section to be drafted, contains exceptionally powerful language that forms the bedrock of American political tradition. Its opening line, "We the People of the United States," boldly proclaimed that a loose confederation of independent states no longer existed.

The simple phrase "We the people" ended, at least for the time being, the question of whence the government derived its power: It came directly from the people, not from the states. The next phrase of the Constitution explained the need for the new outline of government.

WEB EXPLORATION
For the full text of other nations' constitutions, see
www.ablongman.com/oconnor

POLITICS NOW

THE 2000 ELECTION AND CALLS TO AMEND THE CONSTITUTION

After controversial Supreme Court decisions, it is not unusual to hear calls to amend the Constitution. The Court's decision ruling that laws forbidding flag burning are unconstitutional, for example, have elicited proposals to amend the Constitution to forbid the practice in every session of Congress since the Court's decision in 1985. The closeness of the 2000 presidential election, however, began to generate calls to abolish or modify the electoral college created by the Framers in Article II, almost immediately after the November 8 election and before the U.S. Supreme Court got involved in the fray. Other suggestions to amend the Constitution soon also were forthcoming. These include:

1. Abolish the electoral college and allow the candidate with the highest number of popular votes to win, thereby creating the direct popular election of the president. A CNN/Gallup/*USA Today* poll found that 61 percent of the public agree with this just one week after the 2000 election—one month before the process ended.[a]

2. Alter the electoral college to encourage the states to distribute their electors in proportion to the state vote for each candidate. Maine and Nebraska already do this.

3. Establish a nationwide standard for types of voting mechanisms, including voting machines and absentee ballots.

4. Changing the Constitution's grant of life terms to Supreme Court justices to 18 year terms.

What are the merits or drawbacks of each of these proposals? Do you believe that any have a chance of becoming amendments?

***

[a]William Wichterman, "No small matter," *Sunday Gazette Mail*, December 10, 2000, 1C.

"[I]n Order to form a more perfect Union" indirectly acknowledged the weaknesses of the Articles of Confederation in governing a growing nation. Next, the optimistic goals of the Framers for the new nation were set out: to "establish Justice, insure domestic Tranquility, provide for the common defense, promote the general Welfare, and secure the Blessings of Liberty to ourselves and our Posterity"; followed by the formal creation of a new government: "do ordain and establish this Constitution for the United States of America." The Constitution was approved by the delegates from all twelve states in attendance on September 17, 1787.

The Basic Principles of the Constitution

The proposed structure of the new national government owed much to the writings of the French political philosopher Montesquieu, who advocated distinct functions for each branch of government, a concept

separation of powers

A way of dividing power among three branches of government in which members of the House of Representatives, members of the Senate, the president, and the federal courts are selected by and responsible to different constituencies.

checks and balances

A governmental structure that gives each of the three branches of government some degree of oversight and control over the actions of the others.

federal system

Plan of government created in the U.S. Constitution in which power is divided between the national government and the state governments and in which independent states are bound together under one national government.

called **separation of powers,** with a system of **checks and balances** between each branch. The Constitution's concern with the distribution of power between states and the national government also reveals the heavy influence of political philosophers, as well as the colonists' experience under the Articles of Confederation.

Federalism.   Today, in spite of current calls for the national government to return power to the states, the question before and during the Convention was how much power states would give up to the national government. The Framers believed that a strong national government was necessary for the new nation's survival. They fashioned a system now known as the **federal system,** which divides the power of government between a strong national government and the individual states. This system, as the Supreme Court reaffirmed in 1995 in considering term limits, was based on the principle that the federal, or national, government derived its power from the citizens, not the states, as the national government had done under the Articles of Confederation.

Separation of Powers.   Madison and many of the Framers clearly feared putting too much power into the hands of any one individual or branch of government. Separation of powers is simply a way of parceling out power among the three branches of government. It has three key features:

1. Three distinct branches of government: the legislative, the executive, and the judicial.
2. Three separately staffed branches of government to exercise these functions.
3. Constitutional equality and independence of each branch.

As illustrated in Figure 2.1, the Framers were careful to create a system in which lawmaking, law-enforcing, and law-interpreting functions were assigned to independent branches of government. On the national level (and in most states), only the legislature has the authority to make laws; the chief executive enforces laws, and the judiciary interprets them. Moreover, members of the House of Representatives, members of the Senate, the president, and members of the federal courts are selected by, and are therefore responsible to, different constituencies. Madison believed that the scheme devised by the Framers would divide the offices of the new government and their methods of selection among many individuals, providing each office holder with the "necessary means and personal motives to resist encroachment" on his or her power.

Checks and Balances.   The separation of powers among the three branches of the national government is not complete. According to Montesquieu and the Framers, the powers of each branch (as well as the two houses of the national legislature and between the states and

VISUAL LITERACY
The American System
of Checks and Balances

FIGURE 2.1   Separation of Powers and Checks and Balances Illustrated

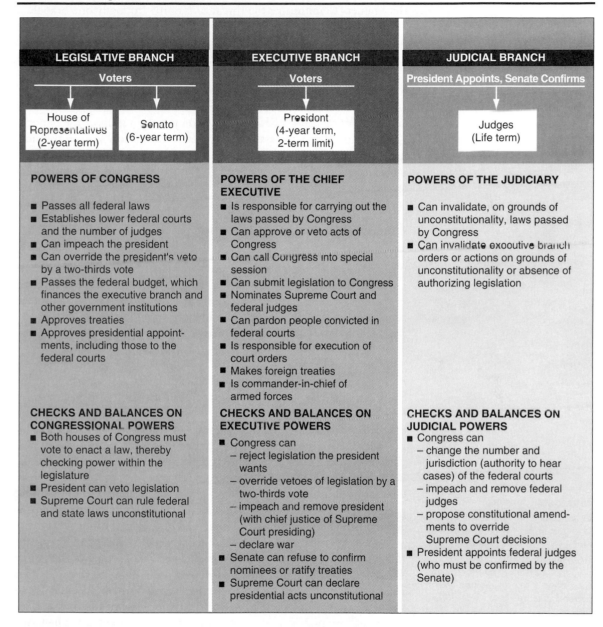

LEGISLATIVE BRANCH	EXECUTIVE BRANCH	JUDICIAL BRANCH
Voters	Voters	President Appoints, Senate Confirms
House of Representatives (2-year term) / Senate (6-year term)	President (4-year term, 2-term limit)	Judges (Life term)

POWERS OF CONGRESS

- Passes all federal laws
- Establishes lower federal courts and the number of judges
- Can impeach the president
- Can override the president's veto by a two-thirds vote
- Passes the federal budget, which finances the executive branch and other government institutions
- Approves treaties
- Approves presidential appointments, including those to the federal courts

POWERS OF THE CHIEF EXECUTIVE

- Is responsible for carrying out the laws passed by Congress
- Can approve or veto acts of Congress
- Can call Congress into special session
- Can submit legislation to Congress
- Nominates Supreme Court and federal judges
- Can pardon people convicted in federal courts
- Is responsible for execution of court orders
- Makes foreign treaties
- Is commander-in-chief of armed forces

POWERS OF THE JUDICIARY

- Can invalidate, on grounds of unconstitutionality, laws passed by Congress
- Can invalidate executive branch orders or actions on grounds of unconstitutionality or absence of authorizing legislation

CHECKS AND BALANCES ON CONGRESSIONAL POWERS

- Both houses of Congress must vote to enact a law, thereby checking power within the legislature
- President can veto legislation
- Supreme Court can rule federal and state laws unconstitutional

CHECKS AND BALANCES ON EXECUTIVE POWERS

- Congress can
  - reject legislation the president wants
  - override vetoes of legislation by a two-thirds vote
  - impeach and remove president (with chief justice of Supreme Court presiding)
  - declare war
- Senate can refuse to confirm nominees or ratify treaties
- Supreme Court can declare presidential acts unconstitutional

CHECKS AND BALANCES ON JUDICIAL POWERS

- Congress can
  - change the number and jurisdiction (authority to hear cases) of the federal courts
  - impeach and remove federal judges
  - propose constitutional amendments to override Supreme Court decisions
- President appoints federal judges (who must be confirmed by the Senate)

the national government) could be used to check the powers of the other two branches of government. This principle, called checks and balances,[16] is illustrated in Figure 2.1. The power of each branch of government is checked, or limited, and balanced because the legislative, executive, and judicial branches share some authority and no branch has exclusive domain over any activity. The creation of this system allowed the Framers to minimize the threat of tyranny from any one branch.

The Supremacy Clause.   Another key constitutional principle that some argue is the linchpin of the entire federal system is the notion of national supremacy. The **supremacy clause** contained in Article VI of the Constitution provides that the "Constitution, and the laws of the United States" as well as all treaties are to be the supreme law of the land. All national and state officers and officials are bound by oath to support the national Constitution above any state law or state constitution. As a result, any legitimate exercise of national power supersedes or preempts any conflicting state action. It is up to the federal courts to determine if such conflict exists. Where it does, national law is always to take precedence.

The Articles of the Constitution

The document finally signed by the Framers condensed numerous resolutions into a Preamble and seven separate articles. The first three articles establish the three branches of government, define their internal operations, and clarify their relationships with one another. The four remaining articles define the relationships among the states, declare national law supreme, and set out ways to amend the Constitution.

Article I: The Legislative Branch.   Article I vests all legislative powers in the Congress and establishes a bicameral legislature, consisting of the Senate and the House of Representatives. It also sets out the qualifications for holding office in each house, the terms of office, methods of selection of representatives and senators, and the system of apportionment among the states to determine membership in the House of Representatives. Article I, section 2, specifies that an "enumeration" of the citizenry must take place every ten years in a manner to be directed by the U.S. Congress. Continuity and Change: Counting Americans reveals how complex and partisan that task has become. Operating procedures and the officers for each house are also outlined and described in Article I.

One of the most important sections of Article I is section 8. It carefully lists the powers the Framers wished the new Congress to possess. These specified or **enumerated powers** contain many key powers that had been denied to the Continental Congress under the Articles of Confederation. For example, one of the major weaknesses of the Articles was Congress's lack of authority to deal with trade wars. The Constitution remedied this problem by authorizing Congress to "regulate Commerce with foreign Nations, and among the several States."

After careful enumeration of seventeen powers of Congress in Article 1, section 8, a final, general clause authorizing Congress to "make all Laws which shall be necessary and proper for carrying into Execution the foregoing Powers" was added to Article I. Often referred to as the **elastic clause**, the necessary and proper clause has been a source of

supremacy clause
The law of the national government stands above any state law or state constitution.

enumerated powers
Seventeen specific powers granted to Congress under Article I, section 8, of the U.S. Constitution; these powers include taxation, coinage of money, regulation of commerce, and the authority to provide for a national defense.

elastic clause
A name given to the "necessary and proper clause" found in the final paragraph of Article I, section 8, of the U.S. Constitution. It gives Congress the authority to pass all laws "necessary and proper" to carry out the enumerated powers specified in the Constitution.

tremendous congressional activity never anticipated by the Framers. The Supreme Court has stretched definitions of "necessary" and "proper" to accommodate changing needs and times. This clause is the source of Congress's **implied powers**—the powers that the Court infers accrue to Congress from its enumerated powers. The Supreme Court, for example, has coupled Congress's authority to regulate commerce with the necessary and proper clause to allow Congress to ban prostitution (where travel across state lines is involved), regulate trains and planes, establish uniform federal minimum-wage and maximum-hour laws, and mandate drug testing for certain workers.

implied power
A power derived from an enumerated power and the necessary and proper clause. These powers are not stated specifically but are considered to be reasonably implied through the exercise of delegated powers.

Article II: The Executive Branch.   Article II vests the executive power, that is, the authority to execute the laws of the nation, in a president of the United States. Section 1 sets the president's term of office at four years and explains the electoral college. It also states qualifications for office and describes a mechanism to replace the president in case of death, disability, or removal.

The powers and duties of the president are set out in section 3. Among the most important of these are the president's role as commander-in-chief of the armed forces, the authority to make treaties with the consent of the Senate, and the authority to "appoint Ambassadors, other public Ministers and Consuls, the Judges of the supreme Court, and all other Officers of the United States." Other sections of Article II instruct the president to report directly to Congress "from time to time," in what has come to be known as the "State of the Union Address," and to "take Care that the Laws be faithfully executed." Section 4 provides the mechanism for removal of the president, vice president, and other officers of the United States for "Treason, Bribery, or other high Crimes and Misdemeanors."

Article III: The Judicial Branch.   Article III establishes a Supreme Court and defines its jurisdiction. During the Philadelphia meeting, the small and large states differed significantly as to the desirability of an independent judiciary and on the role of state courts in the national court system. The smaller states feared that a strong unelected judiciary would trample on their liberties. In compromise, Congress was permitted, but not required, to establish lower national courts. Thus state courts and the national court system would exist side by side with distinct areas of authority. Federal courts were given authority to decide cases arising under federal law. The Supreme Court was also given the power to settle disputes between states, or between a state and the national government. Ultimately, it was up to the Supreme Court to determine what any provisions of the Constitution actually meant.

Judges were given appointments for life, presuming "good behavior." Moreover, their salaries cannot be lowered while they hold office. This provision was adopted to ensure that the legislature did not attempt to punish the Supreme Court or any other judges for unpopular decisions.

POLICY IN ACTION

THE SUPREME COURT AS A NATIONAL POLICY MAKER

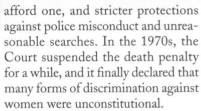

The U.S. Constitution does not mention much about the Supreme Court or its powers. But over time, the justices of the Court have played a major role in carving out the contours of what the Framers meant. In so doing, the Court has become a major player in the policy process, although not necessarily recognized as such by the public.

Historically, the Court has played a key role in issues concerning African Americans and other minorities, the poor, aliens, women, gays and lesbians, and the disabled, among others. In the 1950s, the Court forged the way to end racial segregation in the nation's schools with its decision in *Brown* v. *Board of Education* (1954), in which it declared that school districts violated the Fourteenth Amendment when they sent black and white children to different schools.[a] In the 1960s, the Court forced states to afford criminal defendants a host of rights they had been denied, including the right to a lawyer if they could not afford one, and stricter protections against police misconduct and unreasonable searches. In the 1970s, the Court suspended the death penalty for a while, and it finally declared that many forms of discrimination against women were unconstitutional.

As the new century begins, the Court has continued its critical role in the policy process, although now often finding that congressional laws have gone too far, thereby violating the separation of powers principles agreed to by the Framers and the states that ratified the Constitution. The Court has ruled, for example, that Congress lacked the authority to ban weapons around schools. But perhaps the most noteworthy decision of the Court will prove to be its decision in *Bush* v. *Gore*. There, in a 5–4 opinion, the majority, for the first time in history, in effect, selected the nation's new president.[b]

---

[a]347 U.S. 483 (1954).
[b]531 U.S. (2000)

Articles IV Through VII.   Article IV begins with what is called the full faith and credit clause, which mandates that states honor the laws and judicial proceedings of the other states. Recently, for example, when it appeared that Hawaii might legalize same-sex marriages, the U.S. Congress passed the Defense of Marriage Act to allow states to disregard gay marriages even if they are legal in other states. Since no state has yet to legalize same-sex marriages, although Vermont recognized same-sex partnerships in 2000, this act has not been challenged in the federal courts. But since the full faith and credit clause mandates that states recognize the laws of other states, some question about the legality of the federal law remains. Article IV also includes the mechanisms for admitting new states to the Union. Article V specifies how amendments can be added to the Constitution. Article VI contains the supremacy clause (discussed on page 44). Mindful of the potential problems that could occur if church and state were too enmeshed, Article VI also specifies that no religious test shall be required for holding any office. The seventh and final article of the Constitution concerns the procedures for ratification of the new Constitution: Nine of the thirteen states would have to agree to, or ratify, its new provisions before it would become the supreme law of the land.

THE DRIVE FOR RATIFICATION

While delegates to the Constitutional Convention labored in Philadelphia, the Second Continental Congress continued to govern the former colonies under the Articles of Confederation. The day after the Constitution was signed, the secretary of the Constitutional Convention left for New York City, then the nation's capital, to deliver the official copy of the document to the Congress. He also took with him a resolution of the delegates calling upon each of the states to vote on the new Constitution. Anticipating resistance from the representatives in the state legislatures, however, the Framers required the states to call special ratifying conventions to consider the proposed Constitution.

The Second Continental Congress immediately accepted the work of the convention and forwarded the proposed Constitution to the states for their vote. It was by no means certain, however, that the new Constitution would be adopted. From the fall of 1787 to the summer of 1788, the proposed Constitution was debated hotly around the nation.

Federalists Versus Anti-Federalists

Almost as soon as the ink was dry on the last signature to the Constitution, those who favored the new strong national government chose to call themselves **Federalists.** They were well aware that many still generally opposed the notion of a strong national government. Thus they did not want to risk being labeled "nationalists," so they tried to get the upper hand in the debate by nicknaming their opponents **Anti-Federalists.** Those put in the latter category insisted that they were instead "Federal Republicans" who believed in a federal system. As noted in Table 2.1, Anti-Federalists argued that they simply wanted to protect state governments from the tyranny of a too-powerful national government.[17]

Federalists and Anti-Federalists participated in the mass meetings that were held in state legislatures to discuss the pros and cons of the new plan. Fervent debates were published in newspapers. Articles on both sides of the adoption issue began to appear around the nation, often written under pseudonyms such as "Caesar" or "Constant Reader," as was the custom of the day.

One name stood out from all the rest: "Publius" (Latin for "the people"). Between October 1787 and May 1788, eighty-five articles written under that pen name routinely appeared in newspapers in New York, a state where ratification was in doubt. These eighty-five essays,

Federalists
Those who favored a stronger national government and supported the proposed U.S. Constitution; later became the first U.S. political party.

Anti-Federalists
Those who favored strong state governments and a weak national government; opposed the ratification of the U.S. Constitution.

TABLE 2.1   Federalists and Anti-Federalists Compared

	Federalists	*Anti-Federalists*
Who were they?	Property owners, landed rich, merchants of Northeast and Middle Atlantic states	Small farmers, shopkeepers, laborers
Political philosophy	Elitist: saw themselves and those of their class as most fit to govern (others were to be governed)	Believed in the decency of the common man and in participatory democracy; viewed elites as corrupt; sought greater protection of individual rights
Type of government favored	Powerful central government; two-house legislature; upper house (six-year term) further removed from the people, whom they distrusted	Wanted stronger state governments (closer to the people) at the expense of the powers of the national government. Sought smaller electoral districts, frequent elections, referendum and recall, and a large unicameral legislature to provide for greater class and occupational representation
Alliances	Pro-British Anti-French	Anti-British Pro-French

The Federalist Papers
A series of eighty-five political papers written by John Jay, Alexander Hamilton, and James Madison in support of ratification of the U.S. Constitution.

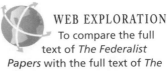

WEB EXPLORATION
To compare the full text of *The Federalist Papers* with the full text of *The Anti-Federalist Papers*, go to www.ablongman.com/oconnor

masterful explanations of the Framers' intentions as they drafted the new Constitution, became known as *The Federalist Papers.*[18]

Forced on the defensive, Anti-Federalists responded with their own series of "letters." Written by men adopting the pen names of "Brutus" and "Cato," two ancient Romans famous for their intolerance of tyranny, these "letters" (actually essays) undertook a line-by-line critique of the Constitution and were designed to counteract *The Federalist Papers.*

Anti-Federalists believed that a strong central government would render the states powerless.[19] They argued that a powerful national government would tax heavily, that the Supreme Court would overwhelm the states by invalidating state laws, and that the president, as commander-in-chief of a large and powerful army, eventually would have too much power.

In particular, the Anti-Federalists feared the power of the national government to run roughshod over the liberties of the people. Their most effective argument concerned the absence of a bill of rights in the Constitution. James Madison answered these criticisms in *Federalist Nos. 10* and *51.* (The texts of these two essays are printed in the Appendix.) In *Federalist No. 10* he pointed out that the voters would not always succeed in electing "enlightened statesmen" as their representatives. The greatest threat to individual liberties would therefore come from factions within the government who might place narrow interests above broader national interests and the rights of citizens. Madison argued that the organization of the new government would minimize the effects of political factions. The great advantage of a federal system,

James Madison (left), Alexander Hamilton (center), and John Jay (right) were important early Federalist leaders. Jay wrote five of *The Federalist Papers* and Madison and Hamilton wrote the rest. Madison served in the House of Representatives (1789–1797) and as secretary of state in the Jefferson administration (1801–1808). In 1808 he was elected fourth president of the United States and served two terms (1809–1817). Hamilton became the first secretary of the treasury (1789–1795). He was killed in 1804 in a duel with Vice President Aaron Burr, who was angered by Hamilton's negative comments about his character. Jay became the first chief justice of the United States (1789–1795) and negotiated the Jay Treaty with Great Britain in 1794. He then served as governor of New York from 1795 to 1801. (Photos courtesy: left, Colonial Williamsburg Foundation; center, The Metropolitan Museum of Art, gift of Henry G. Marquand, 1881 (81.11) copyright © 1987 The Metropolitan Museum of Art; right, Bettmann/Corbis)

Madison maintained, was that it created the "happy combination" of a national government too large to be controlled by any single faction, and several state governments that would be smaller and more responsive to local needs. Moreover, he argued in *Federalist No. 51* that the proposed federal government's separation of powers would prohibit any one branch from either dominating the national government or violating the rights of citizens.

Debate continued in the thirteen states as votes were taken from December 1787 to June 1788, in accordance with the ratifying process laid out in Article VII of the proposed Constitution. Pennsylvania, where Federalists were well organized, was one of the first three states to ratify. New Hampshire became the crucial ninth state to ratify on June 21, 1788. This action completed the ratification process outlined in Article VII of the Constitution and marked the beginning of a new nation. But because New York and Virginia (which between them accounted for more than 40 percent of the new nation's population) had not yet ratified the Constitution, the practical future of the new nation remained in doubt.

SIMULATION
You Are James Madison

Hamilton in New York and Madison in Virginia worked feverishly to convince delegates to their state conventions to vote for the new government. When news of Virginia's acceptance of the Constitution reached the New York convention, Hamilton was finally able to convince a majority of those present to follow suit by a narrow margin of three votes. Both states also recommended the addition of a series of structural amendments, and a bill of rights.

FORMAL METHODS OF AMENDING THE CONSTITUTION

Once the Constitution was ratified, elections were held. When Congress convened, it immediately sent a set of amendments to the states for their ratification. An amendment authorizing the enlargement of the House of Representatives and another to prevent members of the House from raising their own salaries failed to garner favorable votes in the necessary three-fourths of the states (this Twenty-Seventh [Madison] Amendment was ultimately ratified more than 200 years after it was sent to the states, see Highlight Box). The remaining ten amendments, known as the **Bill of Rights** (see Table 2.2), were ratified by 1791 in accordance with the procedures set out in the Constitution. Sought by Anti-Federalists as a protection for individual liberties, they offered

Bill of Rights
The first ten amendments to the U.S. Constitution.

TABLE 2.2   The Bill of Rights

First Amendment	Freedom of religion, speech, press, and assembly
Second Amendment	The right to bear arms
Third Amendment	Prohibition against quartering of troops in private homes
Fourth Amendment	Prohibition against unreasonable searches and seizures
Fifth Amendment	Rights guaranteed to the accused: requirement for grand jury indictment; protections against double jeopardy, self-incrimination; due process guaranteed
Sixth Amendment	Right to a speedy and public trial before an impartial jury, to cross-examine witnesses, and to have counsel
Seventh Amendment	Right to a trial by jury in civil suits
Eighth Amendment	Prohibition against bail fines, and cruel and unusual punishment
Ninth Amendment	Rights not listed in the Constitution retained by the people
Tenth Amendment	States or people reserve those powers not denied to them by the Constitution or delegated to the national government

Note: For the full text of the Bill of Rights, see the Appendix.

H I G H L I G H T

A STUDENT'S REVENGE: THE TWENTY-SEVENTH (MADISON) AMENDMENT

On June 8, 1789, in a speech before the House of Representatives, James Madison stated,

"[T]here is seeming impropriety in leaving any set of men without control [sic] to put their hand into the public coffers, to take out money to put into their pockets. . . . I have gone therefore so far as to fix it, that no law, varying the compensation, shall operate until there is a change in the legislation."

When Madison spoke these words about his proposal, now known as the Twenty-Seventh Amendment, he had no way of knowing that more than two centuries would pass before it would become an official part of the Constitution.

By 1791, when the Bill of Rights was added to the Constitution, only six states had ratified Madison's amendment, and it seemed destined to fade into obscurity. In 1982, however, Gregory Watson, a sophomore majoring in economics at the University of Texas-Austin, discovered the unratified compensation amendment while looking for a paper topic for an American government class. Intrigued, Watson wrote a paper arguing that the proposed amendment was still viable because it had no internal time limit and, therefore, should still be ratified. Watson received a "C" on the paper.

Despite his grade, Watson began a ten-year, $6,000 self-financed crusade to renew interest in

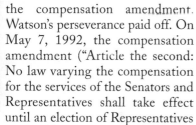

the compensation amendment. Watson's perseverance paid off. On May 7, 1992, the compensation amendment ("Article the second: No law varying the compensation for the services of the Senators and Representatives shall take effect until an election of Representatives shall have intervened"), was finally ratified as the Twenty-Seventh Amendment.

Source: *Fordham Law Review* (December 1992): 497-539, and Anne Marie Kilday, "Amendment Expert Agrees with Congressional Pay Ruling," *Dallas Morning News*, (February 14, 1993): 113A.

Gregory Watson with a document that contains the first ten amendments to the constitution as well as the compensation amendment. (Photo courtesy: Ziggy Kaluzny/*People Weekly* © 1993)

numerous specific limitations on the national government's ability to interfere with a wide variety of personal liberties, some of which were already guaranteed by many state constitutions.

The Amendment Process

Article V of the Constitution creates a two-stage amendment process: proposal and ratification.[20] The Constitution specifies two ways to accomplish each stage. As illustrated in Figure 2.2, amendments to the Constitution can be proposed by:

1. A vote of two-thirds of the members in both houses of Congress; or
2. A vote of two-thirds of the state legislatures specifically requesting Congress to call a national convention to propose amendments.

The second method has never been used. Historically, it has served as a fairly effective threat, forcing Congress to consider amendments that might otherwise never have been debated.

The ratification process is fairly straightforward. When Congress votes to propose an amendment, the Constitution specifies that the ratification process must occur in one of two ways:

1. A favorable vote in three-fourths of the state legislatures; or
2. A favorable vote in specially called ratifying conventions in three-fourths of the states.

 **WEB EXPLORATION** For the text of amendments that failed, see www.ablongman.com/oconnor

The Constitution itself, however, was to be ratified by specifically called ratifying conventions. The Framers feared that the power of special interests in state legislatures would prevent a positive vote on the new Constitution. Since ratification of the Constitution, however, only one ratifying convention has been called. The Eighteenth Amendment, which caused the Prohibition Era by outlawing the sale of alcoholic beverages, was ratified by the first method—a vote in state legislatures. Millions broke the law, others died from drinking homemade liquor, and still others made their fortunes selling bootleg or illegal liquor. After a decade of these problems, Congress decided to act. An additional amendment—the Twenty-First—was proposed to repeal the Eighteenth Amendment. It was sent to the states for ratification, but with a call for ratifying conventions, not a vote in the state legislatures.[21] Members of Congress correctly predicted that the move to repeal the

FIGURE 2.2   Methods of Amending the Constitution Illustrated

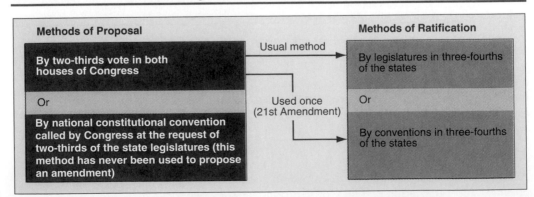

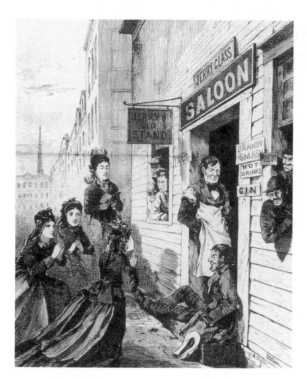

For all its moral foundation in groups like the Women's Christian Temperance Union (WCTU), whose members invaded bars in support of it (left), the Eighteenth Amendment (prohibition) was a disaster. Among its side effects were the rise of powerful crime organizations responsible for (among other things) the cache of over 3,000 bags of bottled beverages uncovered by federal agents (right). Once proposed, it took only ten months to ratify the Twenty-First Amendment, which repealed the Prohibition amendment. (Photos courtesy: left, Hulton Getty/Liaison Agency; right, AP/World Wide Photos)

Eighteenth Amendment would encounter opposition in the state-houses, which were largely controlled by conservative rural interests. Thus Congress's decision to use the convention method led to quick approval of the Twenty-First Amendment.

The intensity of efforts to amend the Constitution has varied considerably, depending on the nature of the change proposed. Whereas the Twenty-First Amendment took only ten months to ratify, an equal rights amendment (ERA) was introduced in every session of Congress from 1923 until 1972, when Congress finally voted favorably on it. Even then, years of lobbying by women's groups were insufficient to garner necessary state support. By 1982, the congressionally mandated date for ratification, only thirty-five states—three short of the number required—had voted favorably on the amendment.[22] Thus the amendment went unratified, although some women's groups continue to press Congress to try the process again.

TIMELINE
The History of Constitutional Amendments

INFORMAL METHODS OF AMENDING THE CONSTITUTION

The Framers did not want to fashion a government that could respond to the whims of the people. The separation of powers and the checks and balances systems are just two indications of the Framers' recognition of the importance of deliberation and thought as a check against government tyranny and the rash judgments of intemperate majorities. James Madison, in particular, wanted to draft a system of government that would pit faction against faction, and ambition against ambition, to design a system of representation and policy making that would strengthen minority factions against possible encroachments by majority factions. Although it took a long time, the Constitution was eventually amended to protect the rights of African Americans through the addition of the Thirteenth, Fourteenth, and Fifteenth Amendments.

The Framers also made the formal amendment process a slow one to ensure that amendments were not added lightly to the Constitution. But the formal amendment process is not the only way that the Constitution has been changed over time. Judicial interpretation and cultural and social change also have had a major impact on the way the Constitution has evolved.

Judicial Interpretation

As early as 1803, under the leadership of Chief Justice John Marshall, the Supreme Court declared that the federal courts had the power to nullify acts of the nation's government when they were found to be in conflict with the Constitution. Over the years this check on the other branches of government and on the states has increased the authority of the Court and has significantly altered the meaning of various provisions of the Constitution, a fact that prompted Woodrow Wilson to call the Supreme Court "a constitutional convention in continuous session." (More detail on the Supreme Court's role in interpreting the Constitution is found in chapters 5, 6, and 10 especially.)

Today some argue that the original intent of the Framers, as evidenced in *The Federalist Papers* as well as in private notes taken by James Madison at the Constitutional Convention, should govern judicial interpretation of the Constitution.[23] Others argue that the Framers knew that a changing society needed an elastic, flexible document that could conform to the ages.[24] In all likelihood, the vagueness of the document was purposeful. Those in attendance in Philadelphia recognized that they could not agree on everything and that it was wiser to leave interpretation to those who would follow them.

Recently, law professor Mark V. Tushnet offered a particularly stinging criticism of any kind of judicial review and exclusive reliance on the courts to say what the Constitution means.[25] He believes that we must

DOONESBURY   Garry Trudeau

(Photo courtesy: DOONESBURY ©G. B. Trudeau. Reprinted with permission of UNIVERSAL PRESS SYNDICATE. All rights reserved.)

create a "populist" constitutional law that allows people to believe that they have the right to enforce the Constitution and not leave it up to the courts. To give this power to the courts, says Tushnet, necessarily means that "We, the people," envisioned by the Framers, lose sight of the true meaning of the Constitution.

Social, Cultural, and Legal Change

Even the most farsighted of those in attendance at the Constitutional Convention could not have anticipated the vast changes that have occurred in the United States. For example, although many were uncomfortable with the Three-Fifths Compromise and others hoped for the abolition of slavery, none could have imagined the status of African Americans today, or that Colin Powell could serve as the U.S. secretary of state and have been frequently mentioned as a viable candidate for president or vice president. Likewise, few of the Framers could have anticipated the diverse roles that women would come to play in American society. The Constitution has often been bent to accommodate such social and cultural changes. Thus, although there is no specific amendment guaranteeing women equal protection of the law, the federal courts have interpreted the Constitution to prohibit many forms of gender discrimination, thereby recognizing cultural and societal change.

Social change has also caused changes in the way institutions of government act. Thus, as problems such as the Great Depression appeared national in scope, Congress took on more and more power at the expense of the states to solve the economic and social crisis. In fact, Yale

POINT / COUNTERPOINT

IS THERE A CONSTITUTIONAL RIGHT TO PRIVACY?

Since 1966, there has been substantial debate about whether there is a constitutional right to privacy in the United States. Privacy is defined simply as areas in which government should not and cannot legislate or otherwise make rules that infringe upon private dealings. In 1965, the Supreme Court, in the case *Griswold* v. *Connecticut*, ruled that the Constitution implied a right to privacy. The Court argued that although the word "privacy" was not specifically mentioned in the Constitution, the concept was so fundamental to our way of thinking and our political system that it is constitutionally protected. Since that time, there have been numerous arguments about whether the Supreme Court went too far in declaring an implied right to privacy that is constitutionally protected or whether the Constitution does protect that right. Is there a constitutional right to privacy? Let's examine these two viewpoints.

The case of *Griswold* v. *Connecticut* concerned a Connecticut law that prohibited the sale and distribution of birth control and information about contraception to married persons in the state. In its ruling, the Court said that the right of a married couple to plan a family is a fundamental constitutional right protected by the right to privacy implied from several amendments: The First Amendment's right to freedom of speech implies a freedom of association and therefore privacy; the Fourth Amendment's protection against unreasonable search and seizure implies a right to privacy in one's home and person; the Fifth Amendment's right to avoid self-incrimination implies a zone of privacy in one's person; the Ninth Amendment guarantees that a person's rights are not limited solely to those written into the Constitution and so allows the Court to use implied rights and not simply enumerate or list rights.

The case in favor of a right to privacy starts with the ruling in *Griswold* that there is a fundamental right for an individual to be free from unwarranted governmental intrusion in matters so fundamentally affecting a person as the decision whether to have a child. This privacy doctrine was also used in *Roe* v. *Wade* (1973), in which a majority of the Court ruled that a woman has a constitutional right to privacy in determining whether or not to end a pregnancy in consultation with her doctor in the first six months of pregnancy.

Those in favor of a constitutional right to privacy, such as so-called judicial activists, the Libertarian Party, and the National Abortion and Reproductive Rights Action League (NARAL), argue that the Framers understood that society would change over time and therefore gave the

law professor Bruce Ackerman argues that on certain occasions, such as the New Deal, extraordinary times call for extraordinary measures, that, in effect, amend the Constitution. Thus, Congress's passage (and the Supreme Court's eventual acceptance) of sweeping New Deal legislation that altered the balance of power between the national government and the states, while possibly bordering on illegality, truly changed the Con-

justices broad authority to interpret the Constitution to reflect the changing times and mores of society. The Framers never intended the Constitution's protections to be limited to the enumerated rights found in the document. Instead, they gave the country a flexible, living document that could cover myriad contingencies in a changing world.

The idea of a right to privacy has been most contentious because it is often thought of in terms of the abortion debate and contraceptive issues. However, proponents of a right to privacy contend that the right to privacy debate includes many other issues, such as Internet privacy (can you be traced online and how can this information be used), online credit card purchases, Social Security and health care information available online or for sale, your credit history, the sale of personal profiles, and even the encoding of information on the back of your driver's license. The right to privacy inherently limits the amount of governmental intrusion into your life and protects you and your right to own information about yourself and your personal habits and movements.

Critics of the idea, sometimes called the Originalists, oppose implied rights in the Constitution, refer to the right to privacy as judicially created or judicial policy making and argue that the Court does not have the power to infer or imply rights. The Constitution does not mention privacy and therefore there is no constitu-

tionally protected right to privacy. Thus, while some actions may be private and beyond the scope of governmental reach or regulation, opponents of a constitutional right to privacy argue that these rights need to be protected by laws, not by the Constitution.

The U.S. Constitution, in this view, does not provide the Court with the authority to invalidate the thoughtful laws of the states regulating public health and welfare because these powers are specifically reserved to the states by the Tenth Amendment. The correct bodies for making laws are the Congress and state legislatures; the courts can only rule on what is specifically written in the Constitution or in laws and statutes. Judicial bodies cannot make laws.

Originalists also care deeply about issues of privacy but do not claim there is a constitutional right that justifies it. Concerns for privacy and issues such as the Internet and whether you can be tracked by your subway ticket or by your cellphone emissions are important but should be dealt with through laws by state legislatures or Congress, not by the courts.

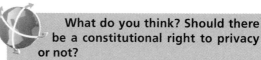

What do you think? Should there be a constitutional right to privacy or not?
Go to www.ablongman.com/oconnor

stitution without benefit of amendment.[26] Today, however, Congress is moving to return much of that power to the states. The actions of the 104th and 105th Congresses to return powers and responsibilities to the states, for example, may be viewed as an *informal* attempt not necessarily to amend the Constitution but to return the balance of power between the national and state government to that which the Framers intended. Again,

GLOBAL POLITICS

COMPARING CONSTITUTIONS

Americans are used to the idea of a durable written constitution. The U.S. Constitution stands out not only for being the first written constitution in the modern world (Poland followed soon after, in 1790), but because it remains the Constitution of the United States today. In fact, the American case is rather anomalous, both in the number of constitutions it has had (two, if we count the Articles of Confederation) and in the continuity of the basic political rules it outlined. Among the cases surveyed here, only Canada and the United Kingdom have had similar experience with a single constitution. Yet Canada's constitutional history is nearly a century shorter than that of the United States. Britain's single constitution is unwritten and has evolved over centuries (parts of it date to the Middle Ages), rendering it difficult to compare with a written constitution. More typically, the European countries and Japan have had multiple constitutions. France is the extreme example, with fifteen constitutional regimes since 1789 (five in the first decade after the French Revolution). External events such as World War II, independence in Asia and Africa, and the collapse of the Soviet Union have had significant impacts on constitution building around the world.

Interestingly, these constitutions have established a wide range of political systems. Since 1789, France has had monarchies, republics, a commune, and a dictatorship in collaboration with a foreign occupier. The first constitutions in Germany, Italy, and Japan were within anti-democratic monarchies. Italy and Germany had fascist constitutional systems in the 1930s and early 1940s. Germany, moreover, had two competing constitutional systems during the Cold War, with a parliamentary democracy in West Germany and a Soviet-style socialist political system in East Germany. In Germany and Japan, postwar occupations by outside powers led to new constitutions. Constitutional amendment practices vary as well. Unlike the Framers' desire to make constitutional change difficult, the European parliamentary systems have rather simple amendment procedures: passage by both houses of the legislature is typically sufficient to effect amendment. The Russian and French presidents have the option to submit an amendment to referendum by the public (both countries' current constitutions were ratified in this manner); French President Chirac exercised the option in 2000. Informal extraconstitutional methods have tended to prevail in nondemocratic settings. Indonesia's 1945 constitution was restored in 1959 amidst civil disorder, and the reality of political power over the next forty years was increasingly remote from constitutional intent. China's three constitutions since 1949 have been largely modifications of their predecessors.

In sum, the United States' constitutional history is rather remarkable for its continuity under a single written document.

Constitutions in 11 Countries

Country	Number of Constitutions	Year Current Constitution Was Established
Canada	1	1867
China	4	1982
France	15	1958
Germany	5	1949
Indonesia	2	1945
Italy	3	1945
Japan	2	1947
Mexico	5	1917
Russia	5	1993
United Kingdom	NA	NA
United States	**2**	**1789**

within the parameters of its constitutional powers, the Congress acted as the Framers intended without changing the document itself.

Advances in technology have also brought about constitutional change. Wiretapping and other forms of electronic surveillance, for example, are now regulated by the First and Fourth Amendments. Similarly, HIV testing must be balanced against constitutional protections. Moreover, all kinds of new constitutional questions are posed in the wake of congressional efforts to regulate what kinds of information can be disseminated on the Internet. Still, in spite of these massive changes, the Constitution still survives, changed and ever changing after more than 200 years.

COMPARATIVE
Comparing
Constitutions

Continuity & Change

Counting Americans

The U.S. Constitution specifically requires that "representatives and direct Taxes shall be apportioned among the several States . . . according to their respective numbers. . . . The actual Enumeration shall be made within three Years after the first Meeting of the Congress of the United States, and within every subsequent Term of then Years in such a Manner as they shall by Law direct." In response to this, the first national census was taken in 1790. But the process itself was very crude. U.S. Marshals and their assistants, providing their own paper, took eighteen months to collect all of the data. Unlike today, when all personal census survey data is confidential, law required that all local reports be posted in at least two public places.

For years, census data were tabulated by hand. In 1890 a punch-card tabulating system was created, revolutionizing the process and allowing for quicker tabulation of data. Over time, compiling the U.S. Census has become more and more complex in response to changing governmental needs as well as changing technology. As the national government has grown, so have the kinds of data collected by the Census Bureau.

By 1990 the nation had grown so large that the Census Bureau admitted its report was inaccurate. Millions of people, especially the poor,

homeless, and minorities, were undercounted. Since the allocation of federal dollars, as well as congressional representation, is based on the results of the decennial census, urban centers and the Democratic Party cried foul, believing they were the most hurt by the undercounting of as many as 5.3 million people. Lawsuits challenging its methods were filed even before the 1990 Census was conducted, and in 1991 Congress passed legislation to compel the Census Bureau to contract with the nonpartisan National Academy of Sciences to study more accurate means for the 2000 Census.

One of the means suggested was statistical sampling—using selected samples to determine the larger group. Actually, the Census Bureau began to use a kind of sampling in 1940, asking only every fourth household more detailed questions. But this is not the kind of sampling suggested by the Clinton administration and subsequently rejected by the Supreme Court in 1999. The Clinton administration wanted to be able to adjust the count to include people that the current system was likely to miss. The Court ruled, however, that sampling could not be used to count citizens for the purposes of reallocating congressional seats among the states, although it didn't prohibit the use of sampling-

(continued)

adjusted numbers when states draw their own congressional and legislative district lines.

The 2000 Census was one of the most unique on record. To get Americans enthused about filling out their forms, a lavish campaign and outreach to minorities and immigrants were augmented with a variety of clever television advertisements throughout the nation, publicizing the importance of an accurate count to the distribution of federal dollars to state and local governments. This enormously expensive campaign worked: Early reports reveal that more Americans filled out their forms than in 1980 or 1990. Sixty-seven percent of all households filled out and returned their questionnaires. Response in the Hispanic community was, to some, surprisingly strong as Hispanics became the largest minority in the U.S.

In spite of these higher returns, the Clinton administration, to the outrage of Republicans in the Congress, also used sampling to revise the census count to add millions more people, particularly minorities. The Court's 1999 decision made it clear that sampling could not be used to apportion congressional seats but it did leave the door open to the use of sampling to redraw legislative boundaries within a state as well as to distribute federal dollars.*

The Census has far more political overtones than the Framers envisioned. Sampling is a well-recognized statistical technique, yet its use to remedy undercounting is highly contentious. In the future, the Census Bureau will continue to be challenged to come up with more accurate measures to count the population. With increasing use of multiple databases, one might envision some sort of super database that could combine and refigure data to enhance the chances that everyone gets counted.

1. What kind of process might be developed to make sure that undercounting, particularly of certain populations with discrete interests, does not occur in the future?
2. How critical do you believe a totally accurate census is to the national government's ability to maintain a representative democracy?

---

*Department of Commerce v. U.S. House of Representatives, No. 98–404 (1999).

Cast Your Vote. Which method of census-taking do you prefer? To cast your vote, go to **www.ablongman.com/oconnor**

SUMMARY

The U.S. Constitution has proven to be a remarkably enduring document. While settlers came to the New World for a variety of reasons, most remained loyal to Great Britain and considered themselves subjects of the king. Over the years, as new generations of Americans were born on colonial soil, those ties weakened. A series of taxes levied by the Crown ultimately led the colonists to convene a Continental Congress and to declare their independence.

The Declaration of Independence (1776), which drew heavily on the writings of John Locke, carefully enumerated the wrongs of the Crown

and galvanized public resentment and willingness to take up arms against Great Britain in the Revolutionary War (1775–1783). To guide the new nation, the Articles of Confederation (1781) created a loose league of friendship between the new national government and the states. Numerous weaknesses in the new government became apparent by 1784. Among the major flaws were Congress's inability to tax or regulate commerce, the absence of an executive to administer the government, and a weak central government.

When the weaknesses under the Articles of Confederation became apparent, the states called for a meeting to reform them. The Constitutional Convention (1787) quickly threw out the Articles of Confederation and fashioned a new, more workable form of government. The Constitution was the result of a series of compromises, including those over representation, questions involving large and small states, and how to determine population. Compromises were also made about how members of each branch of government were to be selected. The electoral college was created to give states a key role in the selection of the president.

The proposed U.S. Constitution created a federal system that drew heavily on Montesquieu's ideas about separation of powers. These ideas concerned a way of parcelling out power among the three branches of government, and checks and balances to prevent any one branch from having too much power.

The drive for ratification became a fierce fight between Federalists and Anti-Federalists. Federalists lobbied for the strong national government created by the Constitution; Anti-Federalists favored greater state power.

The Framers created a formal two-stage amendment process to include the Congress and the states. Amendments could be proposed by a two-thirds vote in Congress or of state legislatures requesting that Congress call a national convention to propose amendments. Amendments could be ratified by a positive vote of three-fourths of the state legislatures or by specially called state ratifying conventions.

The formal amendment process is not the only way that the Constitution can be changed. Judicial interpretation and cultural and technological changes have also caused constitutional change.

KEY TERMS

Anti-Federalists, p. 47
Articles of Confederation, p. 34
Bill of Rights, p. 50
checks and balances, p. 42
Committees of Correspondence, p. 32
confederation, p. 33
Declaration of Independence, p. 33

elastic clause, p. 44
enumerated powers, p. 44
federal system, p. 42
The Federalist Papers, p. 48
Federalists, p. 47
First Continental Congress, p. 33
Great Compromise, p. 39
implied power, p. 45

New Jersey Plan, p. 37
Second Continental Congress, p. 33
separation of powers, p. 42
Stamp Act Congress, p. 32
supremacy clause, p. 44
Three-Fifths Compromise, p. 39
Virginia Plan, p. 37

SELECTED READINGS

Ackerman, Bruce. *We the People*. Cambridge, Mass.: Belknap Press, 1991.

Bailyn, Bernard. *The Ideological Origins of the American Revolution*. Cambridge, Mass.: Belknap Press, 1967.

Beard, Charles. *An Economic Interpretation of the Constitution of the United States*. Reissue edition. New York: Free Press, 1996.

Bernstein, Richard B., and Jerome Agel. *Amending America*. New York: Random House, 1992.

Bowen, Catherine Drinker. *Miracle at Philadelphia*. Boston: Little, Brown, 1986.

Brinkley, Alan, Nelson W. Polsby, and Kathleen M. Sullivan, *New Federalist Papers: Essays in Defense of the Constitution*. New York: Norton, 1997.

Hamilton, Alexander, James Madison, and John Jay. *The Federalist Papers*. New York: Bantam Books, 1989 (1788).

Ketchman, Ralph, ed. *The Anti-Federalist Papers and the Constitutional Convention Debated.* New York: Mentor Books, 1996.

Kuig, Davis E. *Explicit and Authentic Acts: Amending the U.S. Constitution, 1776–1995.* Lawrence: University of Kansas Press, 1996.

Levy, Leonard W., ed. *Essays on the Making of the Constitution,* 2nd ed. New York: Oxford University Press, 1987.

Main, Jackson Turner. *The Social Structure of Revolutionary America.* Princeton, N.J.: Princeton University Press, 1965.

Rossiter, Clinton. *1787: Grand Convention.* Reissue edition. New York: Norton, 1987.

Stoner, James R. Jr. *Common Law and Liberal Theory.* Lawrence, Kans.: University Press of Kansas, 1992.

Vile, John R. *Encyclopedia of Constitutional Amendments, and Amending Issues, 1789-1995.* Santa Barbara, Calif.: ABC-CLIO, 1996.

Wood, Gordon S. *The Creation of the American Republic, 1776-1787.* Reissue edition. New York: Norton, 1993.

(Photo courtesy: Ed Bailey/AP/Wide World Photos)

Federalism 3

A 1998 ruling by the U.S. Supreme Court brought an end to a long controversy between New York and New Jersey over title to Ellis Island, part of the Statue of Liberty national monument, where a museum dedicated to chronicling the history of U.S. immigration is housed.[1] An 1834 compact between the two states set the boundary lines between them as the middle of the Hudson River and gave New York authority over the island even though Ellis Island was on the New Jersey side of the Hudson. New Jersey, however, retained rights to submerged lands on its side. In 1993, New Jersey finally filed suit to gain a final resolution of the land dispute.

Between 1892 and 1954, approximately 12 million steerage and third class passengers who entered the United States through the Port of New York were processed through Ellis Island, where they were examined by physicians and their legal status was reviewed. During that time, when the U.S. government decided to make Ellis Island the gateway to process the flood of immigrants coming to its shores, it also began to fill in around the island's natural shoreline. Eventually 24.5 acres were added to the original island, increasing its size considerably.

While the outcome of the lawsuit filed by New Jersey would have little practical impact, prestige was on the line. Both states wanted bragging rights to this major tourist attraction.[2]

Because two states were involved, the U.S. Supreme Court had what is called original jurisdiction over the case, a term discussed in greater detail in chapter 9. A Special Master was appointed by the Court to investigate the dispute and to report back his findings to the justices. In 1998, the Court ultimately ruled that although New York claimed the land, New Jersey actually had all the rights to the "new lands" added by the federal government to the island.[3]

The states didn't go to war over this boundary dispute; they went to court. When the Framers created the federal system, they were mindful that disputes might arise between the states. Thus, they empowered the Supreme Court to serve as a trial court in these circumstances to provide each state with as fair a hearing as possible.

The nature of the federal relationship between the national government and the states, including their respective duties, obligations, and powers, is outlined in the U.S. Constitution, although the word "federal" does not appear in that document. Throughout history, however, this system and the rules that guide it have been continually stretched, reshaped, and reinterpreted by crises, historical evolution, public expectations, and judicial interpretation. All these forces have had tremendous influence on who makes policy decisions and how these decisions get made.

federalism
The philosophy that describes the governmental system created by the Framers; see also federal system.

Issues involving the distribution of power between the national government and the states affect you on a daily basis. You do not, for example, need a passport to go from Texas to Oklahoma. There is one national currency and a national minimum wage. But many differences exist among the laws of the various states: The age at which you may marry is a state issue, as are laws governing divorce, child custody, and the purchase of guns. Although some policies or programs are under the authority of the state or local government, others, such as air traffic regulation, are solely within the province of the national government. In many areas, however, the national and state governments work together cooperatively in a system of shared powers. The national government, for example, provides significant assistance to states to improve local schools in a variety of ways, from subsidized breakfasts and lunches for students to support for special education teachers. But states and local government retain control over curricula.

In this chapter, we examine the historical development of the allocation of power in the federal system. We also look at how the power of the national government has grown—often at the expense of the states—and current efforts to redress the delicate balance of authority between the national and state governments.

Among issues behind the move to return power to the states are government regulations affecting the environment. Swimming and fishing restrictions such as this one protect people from hazardous lake conditions. (Photo courtesy: Alan Reininger/Contact Press Images)

THE ROOTS OF THE FEDERAL SYSTEM

The relationship between the national and state governments, and their intertwined powers, are the heart of **federalism** (from the Latin *foedus*, or "covenant"), the philosophy that defines

FIGURE 3.1 The Federal, Confederation, and Unitary Systems of Government

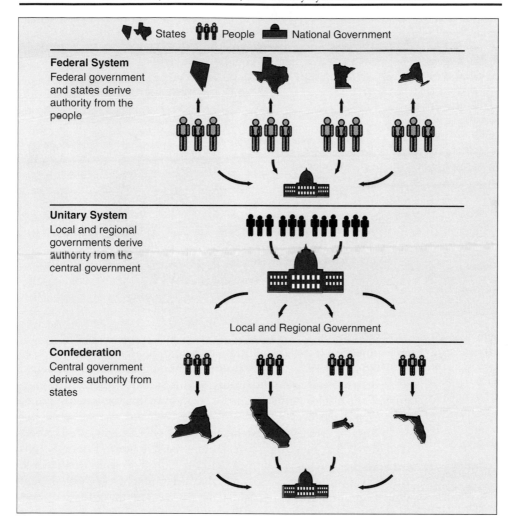

the allocation of power between the national government and the states (see Figure 3.1). Federalist supporters of the new Constitution articulated three major arguments for federalism: (1) the prevention of tyranny; (2) the provision for increased participation in politics; and (3) the use of the states as testing grounds or "laboratories" for new policies and programs.

The national government created by the Framers draws its powers directly from the people, so that both national and state governments are ultimately directly accountable to the public. While each government has certain powers in common with the other (such as the ability to tax) and has its own set of public officials, the Framers also

WEB EXPLORATION
For a directory of federalism, see
www.ablongman.com/oconnor

WEB EXPLORATION
For scholarly works on federalism, see
www.ablongman.com/oconnor

FIGURE 3.2   The Distribution of Governmental Power in the Federal System Illustrated

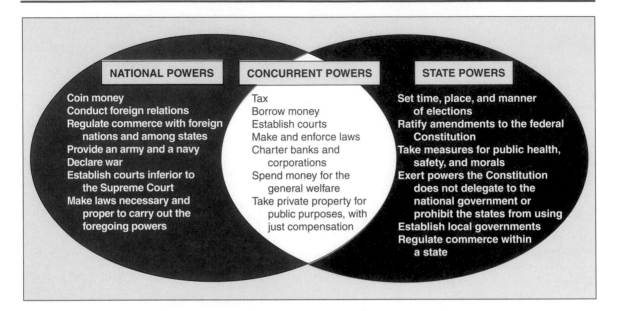

envisioned each government to be supreme in some spheres, as depicted in Figure 3.2. In *Federalist No. 51*, James Madison explained what he perceived to be the beauty of this system: The shifting support of the electorate between the two governments would serve to keep each in balance.

In fashioning the new federal system of government, the Framers recognized that they could not define precisely how all the relations between the national government and the individual states would work. But the Constitution makes it clear that separate spheres of government were to be at the very core of the federal system, with some allowances made for concurrent powers. The addition of Article IV, section 2 of the Constitution underscored the notion that the national government was always to be supreme in situations of conflict between state and national law. What is called the **supremacy clause** declares that the U.S. Constitution, the laws of the United States, and its treaties are to be "the supreme Law of the Land; and the Judges in every State shall be bound thereby."

The federal government's right to tax was also clearly set out in the new Constitution. The Framers wanted to avoid the financial problems that the national government had experienced under the Articles of Confederation. To survive as a strong national government, the power of the national government to raise revenue had to be unquestionable.

The new Constitution left the qualifications of suffrage to the individual states. Thus, over time, the right to vote even in national elections has varied.

supremacy clause

Portion of Article IV of the U.S. Constitution that mandates that national law is supreme to (that is, supersedes) all other laws passed by the states or by any other subdivision of government.

THE POWERS OF GOVERNMENT IN THE FEDERAL SYSTEM

The distribution of powers in the federal system is often described as two overlapping systems, as illustrated in Figure 3.2. On the left are powers specifically granted to Congress in Article I. Chief among the exclusive powers delegated to the national government are the authorities to coin money, conduct foreign relations, provide for an army and navy, declare war, and establish a national court system. All of these powers set out in Article I, section 8 of the Constitution, are called **enumerated powers**. These specified or enumerated powers contain many key provisions that had been denied to the Continental Congress under the Articles of Confederation. For example, one of the major weaknesses of the Articles was Congress's lack of authority to deal with trade wars. The Constitution remedied this problem by authorizing Congress to "regulate Commerce with foreign Nations, and among the several States."

Today, Congress often enacts legislation that no specific clause of Article 1, section 8, appears to authorize. Laws dealing with the environment, welfare, education, and communications, among others, are often justified by reference to a particular power plus the necessary and proper clause. After careful enumeration of seventeen powers of Congress in Article 1, section 8, a final, general clause authorizing Congress to "make all Laws which shall be necessary and proper for carrying into Execution the foregoing Powers" was added to Article I. Often referred to as the elastic clause, the **necessary and proper clause** has been a source of tremendous congressional activity never anticipated by the Framers, as definitions of "necessary" and "proper" have been stretched to accommodate changing needs and times. The clause is the basis for Congress's **implied powers** that it uses to execute its other powers. The Supreme Court, for example, has coupled Congress's authority to regulate commerce with the necessary and proper clause to allow Congress to ban prostitution (where travel across state lines is involved), regulate trains and planes, establish uniform federal minimum-wage and maximum-hour laws, and mandate drug testing for certain workers.

The Constitution does not specifically delegate or enumerate many specific powers to the states. Because states had all the power at the time the Constitution was written, the Framers felt no need, as they did for the new national government, to list and restate the powers of the states. Article I, however, allows states to set the "Times, Places and Manner, for holding elections for senators and representatives," and Article II requires that each state appoint electors to vote for president. States were also given the power to ratify amendments to the U.S. Constitution. Nevertheless, the enumeration of so many specific powers to the national government and so few to the states is a clear indication of the Federalist leanings of the Framers. It was not until the addition of the Bill of Rights and the Tenth Amendment that the states' powers were

enumerated powers

A name given to the clause found in the final paragraph of Article I, section 8, of the U.S. Constitution giving Congress the authority to pass all laws "necessary and proper" to carry out the enumerated powers specified in the Constitution; the "elastic" clause.

necessary and proper clause

A name given to the clause found in the final paragraph of Article I, section 8, of the U.S. Constitution giving Congress the authority to pass all laws "necessary and proper" to carry out the enumerated powers specified in the Constitution; the "elastic" clause.

implied powers

Power given to the national government through inference from the enumerated powers.

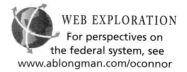

WEB EXPLORATION
For perspectives on the federal system, see
www.ablongman.com/oconnor

reserve (or police) powers

Powers reserved to the states by the Tenth Amendment that lie at the foundation of a state's right to legislate for the public health and welfare of its citizens.

concurrent powers

Powers shared by the national and state governments.

better described: "The powers not delegated to the United States by the Constitution, nor prohibited by it to the States, are reserved to the States respectively, or to the people." These powers, often called the states' **reserve** or **police powers,** include the ability to legislate for the public health, safety, and morals of their citizens. The states' rights to legislate under their police powers today are used as the rationale for many states' restrictions on abortion, including twenty-four-hour waiting requirements and provisions requiring minors to obtain parental consent. Police powers are also the basis for state criminal laws. That is why some states have the death penalty and others do not.

As revealed in Figure 3.2, national and state powers also overlap. The area where the systems overlap represents **concurrent powers**—powers shared by the national and state governments. States already had the power to tax; the Constitution extended this power to the national government as well. Other important concurrent powers include the right to borrow money, establish courts, and make and enforce laws necessary to carry out these powers.

Denied Powers

Article I also denies certain powers to the national and state governments. In keeping with the Framers' desire to forge a national economy, states are prohibited from entering treaties, coining money, or impairing obligation of contracts. States are also prohibited from entering into "compacts" with other states without express congressional approval. In a similar vein, Congress is barred from favoring one state over another in regulating commerce, and it cannot lay duties on items exported from any state.

Both the national and state governments are denied the authority to take arbitrary actions affecting constitutional rights and liberties. Neither national nor state governments may pass a **bill of attainder,** a law declaring an act illegal without a judicial trial. The Constitution also bars either government from passing *ex post facto* **laws,** laws that make an act punishable as a crime even if the action was legal at the time it was committed.

bill of attainder

A law declaring an act illegal without a judicial trial.

ex post facto **law**

Law passed after the fact, thereby making previously legal activity illegal and subject to current penalty; prohibited by the U.S. Constitution.

Guarantees to the States

In return for giving up some of their powers, the states received several guarantees in the Constitution. Among them:

- Article I guarantees each state two members in the U.S. Senate and guarantees that Congress would not limit slavery before 1808.
- Article IV guarantees the citizens of each state the privileges and immunities of citizens of all other states (as discussed in Policy in Action: The States, Poverty, and the Fourteenth Amendment); guarantees each state a "Republican Form of Government," meaning one that represents the citizens of the state; and guarantees that the national government will protect the states against foreign attacks and domestic rebellion.

POLICY IN ACTION

THE STATES, POVERTY, AND THE FOURTEENTH AMENDMENT

On May 18, 1999, the U.S. Supreme Court dusted off the privileges and immunities clause of the Fourteenth Amendment, which had not been used by the Court to anchor a decision in 126 years. The Court's dramatic 7–2 decision came in a case involving a challenge to a California law that allowed it to pay lower welfare benefits to new state residents. Women who fled from abusive relationships in other states were ineligible for higher California state benefits although they still faced higher California cost of living expenses. Under the challenged provision, California paid new residents only the amounts that they were eligible for in the states that they left. So if a person traveled from Oklahoma, they would get but $341 their first year in California. Former Alabamians were eligible for only $120, while long-time Californians could receive $631. "The states' legitimate interest in saving money provides no justification for its decision to dis-criminate among equally eligible citizens," aid Justice John Paul Stevens writing for the Court.[a] The Court said that this two-level benefits system violated citizens' constitutional right to travel and was the justices' first decision dealing with any of the new welfare reform efforts, which critics charge violate the constitutional rights of many of America's poor. The ruling is also important because of the Court's "revival of a constitutional doctrine making citizens of all states equal."[b] Scores of constitutional scholars immediately weighed in, speculating that the Court's use of the privileges and immunities clause could mean far greater protection for what the Court views as fundamental rights and have continued policy ramifications.

---

[a]*Saenz* v. *Roe*, 1999 LEXIS 3174.
[b]Joan Biskupic, "New Resident Limits on Welfare Rejected," *The Washington Post* (May 18, 1999): A1.

Relations Among the States

The Constitution was designed to improve relations among the squabbling states. To that end, it provides that disputes between states are to be settled directly by the U.S. Supreme Court under its original jurisdiction to avoid any sense of favoritism. Moreover, Article IV requires that each state give "Full Faith and Credit . . . to the public Acts, Records and judicial Proceedings of every other State." This clause ensures that judicial decrees and contracts made in one state will be binding and enforceable in another, thereby facilitating trade and other commercial relationships. Article IV also requires states to extradite, or return, criminals to states where they have been convicted or are to stand trial. For example, Timothy Reed, an Indian-rights activist, spent five years in New Mexico fighting extradition to Ohio.[4] In 1998, the New Mexico Supreme Court ordered him released from custody in spite of an order from the New Mexico governor ordering his extradition to Ohio. Reed feared that his parole in Ohio would be revoked without due process, he would be returned to prison, and subject to bodily harm. The U.S. Supreme Court found that the Supreme Court of New Mexico went beyond its authority.[5]

States don't always get along, however. As our opening vignette about Ellis Island illustrates, the U.S. Constitution gives the Supreme Court the final authority to decide controversies between the states. These kinds of land disputes always are decided by the Supreme Court under its original jurisdiction as mandated by Article III of the Constitution.

THE EVOLUTION OF FEDERALISM

The victory of the Federalists—those who supported a strong national government—had long-lasting consequences on the future of the nation. Over the course of our nation's history, the nature of federalism and its allocation of power between the national government and the states have changed dramatically. The debate continues today, too, as many Americans, frustrated with the national government's performance on a number of issues, look for a return of more power to the states. Because the distribution of power between the national and state governments is not clearly delineated in the Constitution, over the years the U.S. Supreme Court has played a major role in defining the nature of the federal system.

McCulloch v. *Maryland* (1819)
The Supreme Court upheld the power of the national government and denied the right of a state to tax the bank. The Court's broad interpretation of the necessary and proper clause paved the way for later rulings upholding expansive federal powers.

McCulloch v. *Maryland* (1819).   *McCulloch* was the first major decision of the Marshall Court to define the relationship between the national and state governments. In 1816, Congress chartered the Second Bank of the United States. (The charter of the First Bank had been allowed to expire.) In 1818, the Democratic-Republican-controlled Maryland state legislature levied a tax requiring all banks not chartered by Maryland (that is, the Second Bank of the United States) to (1) buy stamped paper from the state on which the Second Bank's notes were to be issued; (2) pay the state $15,000 a year; or (3) go out of business. James McCulloch, the head cashier of the Baltimore branch of the Bank of the United States, refused to pay the tax, and Maryland brought suit against him. After losing in a Maryland court, McCulloch appealed his conviction to the U.S. Supreme Court by order of the U.S. secretary of the treasury. In a unanimous opinion, the Court answered the two central questions that had been put to it: First, did Congress have the authority to charter a bank? And, second, if it did, could a state tax it?

Chief Justice Marshall's answer to the first question—whether Congress had the right to establish a bank or another type of corporation, given that the Constitution does not explicitly mention such a power—continues to stand as the classic exposition of the doctrine of implied powers, and as a reaffirmation of the propriety of a strong national government. Although the word "bank" cannot be found in

WEB EXPLORATION
For full text of *McCulloch* v. *Maryland*, see
www.ablongman.com/oconnor

The *Gibbons* v. *Ogden* decision opened the waters to free competition; this is the New York waterfront in 1839. (Photo courtesy: I.N. Phelps Stokes Collection, Miriam and Ira D. Wallach Division of Art, Prints, and Photographs, The New York Public Library Astor, Lenox and Tilden Foundations)

the Constitution, the Constitution enumerates powers that give Congress the authority to levy and collect taxes, issue a currency, and borrow funds. From these enumerated powers, Marshall found, it was reasonable to imply that Congress had the power to charter a bank, which could be considered "necessary and proper" to the exercise of its enumerated powers.

Marshall next addressed the question of whether a federal bank could be taxed by any state government. To Marshall, this was not a difficult question. The national government was dependent on the people, not the states, for its powers. In addition, Marshall noted, the Constitution specifically calls for the national law to be supreme. "The power to tax involves the power to destroy," wrote Marshall. Thus, the state tax violated the supremacy clause, because individual states cannot interfere with the operations of the national government, whose laws are supreme.

Gibbons v. *Ogden* (1824).   Shortly after *McCulloch,* the Marshall Court had another opportunity to rule in favor of a broad interpretation of the scope of national power. *Gibbons* involved a dispute that arose after the New York State legislature granted to Robert Fulton the exclusive right to operate steamboats on the Hudson River. Simultaneously, Congress licensed a ship to sail on the same waters. By the time the case reached the Supreme Court, it was complicated both factually and procedurally. Suffice it to say that both New York and New Jersey wanted to control shipping on the lower Hudson River. But *Gibbons* actually addressed one simple, very important question: What was the scope of Congress's authority under the commerce clause? The states argued that "commerce," as mentioned in Article I, should be interpreted narrowly to include only direct dealings in products. In *Gibbons,* however, the Supreme Court ruled that Congress's power to regulate interstate commerce included the power to regulate commercial activity

Gibbons v. Ogden (1824)
The Court upheld broad congressional power over interstate commerce.

WEB EXPLORATION
For full text of *Gibbons* v. *Ogden,* see
www.ablongman.com/oconnor

as well, and that the commerce power had no limits except those specifically found in the Constitution. Thus, New York had no constitutional authority to grant a monopoly to a single steamboat operator, thereby interfering with interstate commerce.[6]

Dual Federalism

In spite of the nationalist Marshall Court decisions, strong debate continued in the United States over national versus state power. It was under the leadership of Chief Justice Marshall's successor, Roger B. Taney (1835–1863), that the Supreme Court articulated the notions of concurrent power, the belief that separate and equally powerful levels of government is the best arrangement; and **dual federalism,** the belief that the national government should not exceed its enumerated powers expressly set out in the Constitution.

Federalism and Slavery.   During the Taney era, the comfortable role of the Court as the arbiter of competing national and state interests became troublesome when the Court found itself called upon to deal with the highly political issue of slavery. In cases such as *Dred Scott* v. *Sandford* (1857) and others, the Court tried to manage the slavery issue by resolving questions of ownership, the status of fugitive slaves, and slavery in the new territories. These cases generally were settled in favor of slavery and states' rights within the framework of dual federalism. At the urging of President James Buchanan, Chief Justice Roger B. Taney tried to fashion a broad ruling to settle the slavery question. In *Dred Scott* v. *Sandford* (1857) he concluded that the Congress of the United States lacked the constitutional authority to bar slavery in the territories. The decision narrowed the scope of national power while it enhanced that of the states. Moreover, for the first time since *Marbury* v. *Madison* (1803), the Court found an act of Congress—the Missouri Compromise—unconstitutional. By limiting what the national government could do concerning slavery, the Dred Scott decision in all likelihood quickened the march toward the Civil War since its decision seemed to rule out any political (legislative) solution to slavery by the national government.

dual federalism
The belief that the national government should not exceed its enumerated powers expressly set out in the constitution.

"I GUESS I JUST HADN'T NOTICED IT BEFORE"

(Photo courtesy: Copyright 2000 by Herblock in The Washington Post)

The Civil War and Beyond

The Civil War (1861–1865) forever changed the nature of federalism, but the Supreme Court continued to adhere to its belief in the concept of dual federalism. The importance and powers of the states were not diminished in spite of the addition of the Thirteenth, Fourteenth, and Fifteenth Amendments to the Constitution, or by Abraham Lincoln's appointment of the first Republican chief justice, Salmon Chase (1864–1873).

Between 1865 (the end of the Civil War) and 1933 (when the next major change in the federal system occurred), the Court generally continued to support dual federalism along several lines. State courts, for example, were considered to have the final say on the construction of laws affecting local affairs.[7] Generally, the Court upheld any laws passed under the states' police powers, which allow states to pass laws to protect the general welfare of their citizens. These laws included those affecting commerce, labor relations, and manufacturing. After the Court's decision in *Plessy* v. *Ferguson* (1896),[8] in which the Court ruled that state maintenance of "separate but equal" facilities for blacks and whites was constitutional, most civil rights and voting cases also became state matters, in spite of the Civil War amendments.

The Court also developed legal doctrine in a series of cases that reinforced the national government's ability to regulate commerce. By the 1930s these two somewhat contradictory approaches led to confusion: States, for example, could not tax gasoline used by federal vehicles,[9] and the national government could not tax the sale of motorcycles to the city police department.[10] In this period, the Court did recognize the need for national control over new technological developments, such as the telegraph.[11] Beginning in the 1880s, the Court allowed Congress to regulate many aspects of economic relationships such as outlawing monopolies, a type of regulation or power formerly thought to be in the exclusive realm of the states. Passage of laws such as the Interstate Commerce Act in 1887 and the Sherman Anti-Trust Act in 1890 allowed Congress to establish itself as an important player in the growing national economy.

Despite finding that most of these federal laws were constitutional, the Supreme Court did not consistently enlarge the scope of national power. In 1895, for example, the United States filed suit against four sugar refiners, alleging that their sale would give their buyer control of 98 percent of the U.S. sugar-refining business. The Supreme Court ruled that congressional efforts to control monopolies (through passage of the Sherman Anti-Trust Act) did not give Congress the authority to prevent the sale of these sugar-refining businesses, because manufacturing was not commerce. Therefore the companies and their actions were beyond the scope of Congress's authority to regulate.[12]

Friends of Dredd Scott's helped finance a test case seeking Scott's freedom: They believed that his residence in Illinois and later in the Wisconsin Territory, both of which prohibited slavery, in essence made him a free man. After many delays, the U.S. Supreme Court ruled 7–2 that Scott was not a citizen. "Slaves," said the Court, "were never thought of or spoken of except as property." (Photo courtesy: Missouri Historical Society)

The New Deal

The era of dual federalism came to an abrupt end in the 1930s. Its demise began in a series of economic events that ended in the cataclysm of the Great Depression:

- In 1921 the nation experienced a severe slump in agricultural prices.
- In 1926 the construction industry went into decline.
- In the summer of 1929, inventories of consumer goods and automobiles were at an all-time high.

WEB EXPLORATION
For more on the causes of the Great Depression, see www.ablongman.com/oconnor

- Throughout the 1920s bank failures had become common.
- On October 29, 1929, stock prices, which had risen steadily since 1926, crashed, taking with them the entire national economy.

Rampant unemployment (historians estimate it was as high as 40–50 percent) was the hallmark of the Great Depression. To combat this unemployment and a host of other problems facing the nation, in 1933 the newly elected president, Franklin D. Roosevelt, (FDR), proposed a variety of innovative programs under the rubric "the New Deal" and ushered in a new era in American politics, characterized by intense government activity on the national level.

In the first few weeks of the legislative session after FDR's inauguration, Congress and the president acted quickly to bolster confidence in the national government. Soon after, Congress passed a series of acts creating programs proposed by the president. These programs tremendously enlarged the scope of the national government. Those who feared this unprecedented use of national power quickly challenged the constitutionality of New Deal programs in court. At least initially, the Supreme Court often agreed with them.

Through the mid-1930s, the Supreme Court continued to rule that certain aspects of the New Deal went beyond the authority of Congress to regulate commerce. In fact, many believe that the Court considered the Depression to be no more than the sum of the economic woes of the individual states and that it was a problem most appropriately handled by the states. The Court's *laissez-faire*, or "hands-off," attitude toward the economy was reflected in a series of decisions ruling various aspects of New Deal programs unconstitutional.

FDR and the Congress were outraged. FDR's frustration with the attitude of the Court prompted him to suggest what was ultimately nicknamed his "Court-packing plan." Knowing that he could do little to change the minds of those already on the Court, FDR suggested enlarging its size from nine to thirteen justices. This would have given him the opportunity to "pack" the Court with a majority of justices predisposed to the constitutional validity of the New Deal.

Even though Roosevelt was popular, the Court-packing plan was not. Congress and the public were outraged that he even suggested tampering with an institution of government. Nevertheless, the Court appeared to respond to this threat. In 1937 it reversed its series of anti–New Deal decisions and gave Congress (and therefore the national government) broad authority to legislate in areas affecting commerce, including maximum hour and minimum wage laws, and regulation of child labor. Moreover, the Court also upheld the constitutionality of the bulk of the massive New Deal relief programs, such as the National Labor Relations Act of 1935, which authorized collective bargaining between unions and employees;[13] the Fair Labor Standards Act of 1938, which prohibited the interstate shipment of goods made by employees earning less than the federally mandated minimum wage;[14] and the Agriculture Adjustment Act of 1938, which provided crop subsidies to farmers.[15]

The New Deal programs forced all levels of government to work cooperatively with one another. Indeed, local governments—mainly in big cities—became a third partner in the federal system as FDR relied on big-city Democratic political machines to turn out voters to support his programs. In essence, for the first time in U.S. history, cities were embraced as equal partners in an intergovernmental system and became players in the national political arena because many in the national legislature wanted to bypass state legislatures, where urban interests were usually significantly underrepresented.

MODERN FEDERALISM

Before the Depression and the New Deal, most political scientists likened the federal system to a layer cake: Each level or layer of government—national, state, and local—had clearly defined powers and responsibilities. After the New Deal, however, the nature of the federal system changed. Government now looked something like a marble cake:

> Wherever you slice through it you reveal an inseparable mixture of differently colored ingredients. . . . Vertical and diagonal lines almost obliterate the horizontal ones, and in some places there are unexpected whirls and an imperceptible merging of colors, so that it is difficult to tell where one ends and the other begins.[16]

This kind of "marble cake" federalism is often called **cooperative federalism,** a term that describes the relationship between the national, state, and local governments that began with the New Deal as a stronger, more influential national government was created in response to economic and social crises. States began to take a secondary, albeit important, "cooperative" role in the scheme of governance, as did many cities. Nowhere is this shift in power from the states *to* the national government more clear than in the growth of federal grant programs that began in earnest during the New Deal.

cooperative federalism
A term used to characterize the relationship between the national, state, and local governments that began with the New Deal.

Federal Grants

One of the first major redistributions of federal funds to the states for a specific purpose was the Morrill Land Grant Act of 1862. It gave each state 30,000 acres of public land for each representative in Congress. Income from the sale of these lands was to be earmarked for the establishment and support of agricultural and mechanical arts colleges. Sixty-nine land-grant colleges—including Texas A&M University, the University of Georgia, and Michigan State University—were founded, making this grant program the single most important piece of education legislation passed in the United States up to that time.

Franklin D. Roosevelt's New Deal program increased the flow of federal dollars to the states with the infusion of massive federal dollars for a variety of public works programs, including building and road construction. These grants made the imposition of national goals on the states easier. No state wanted to decline funds, so states often secured funds for any programs for which money was available—whether they needed it for that specific purpose or not.

In the boom times of World War II, even more new federal programs were introduced; by the 1950s and 1960s, federal grant-in-aid programs were well entrenched. They often defined federal/state relationships and made the national government a major player in domestic policy. Until the 1960s, however, most federal grants programs were constructed in cooperation with the states and were designed to assist the states in furthering their traditional responsibilities to protect the health, welfare, and safety of their citizens. Most of these programs were categorical grants, ones for which Congress appropriates funds for specific purposes. Funds are allocated by a precise formula and are subject to detailed conditions imposed by the national government, often on a matching basis; that is, states must contribute money to match federal funds, although the national government may pay as much as 90 percent of the total. (For a discussion of the carrot and stick nature of federal grants, see Politics Now: Unspent Dollars: What Happened to the Carrot and the Stick?)

Creative Federalism

By the early 1960s, as concern about the poor and minorities rose, and as states (especially in the South) were blamed for perpetuating discrimination,[17] those in power in the national government saw grants as a way to force states to behave in ways desired by the national government. If the states would not cooperate with the national government to further its goals, it would withhold funds.

In 1964, the Democratic administration of President Lyndon B. Johnson (LBJ) (1963–1969) launched its renowned "Great Society" program, which included what LBJ called a "War on Poverty." The Great Society program was a broad attempt to combat poverty and discrimination. In a frenzy of activity in Washington not seen since the New Deal, federal funds were channeled to states, to local governments, and even directly to citizen action groups in an effort to alleviate social ills that the states had been unable or unwilling to remedy. There was money for urban renewal, education, and poverty programs, including Head Start and job training. The move to fund local groups directly was made by the most liberal members of Congress in order to bypass not only conservative state legislatures, but also conservative mayors and councils in cities like Chicago, who were not frequently moved to help their poor, often African American, constituencies. Thus, these programs often pitted governors and mayors against community activists, who became key players in the distribution of federal dollars.

These new grants altered the fragile federal/state balance of power that had been at the core of most older federal grant programs. During the

Johnson administration, the national government began to use federal grants as a way to further what federal (and not state) officials perceived to be national needs. Thus grants based on what states wanted or believed they needed began to decline, while grants based on what the national government wanted states to do in order to foster national goals increased dramatically. Soon states routinely asked Washington for help: "Pollution, transportation, recreation, economic development, law enforcement and even rat control evoked the same response from politicians: create a federal grant."[18] As shown in Table 3.1, by 1970 federal aid accounted for

TABLE 3.1   Federal Grants-in-Aid Outlays, 1940–2004

		FEDERAL GRANTS AS A PERCENTAGE OF FEDERAL OUTLAYS[a]			
Year	Total Grants-in-Aid (billions)	Total	Domestic Programs[b]	State and Local Expenditures[c]	Gross Domestic Product
1940	$0.9	9.2	—	—	0.9
1945	0.9	0.9	—	—	0.4
1950	2.3	5.3	—	—	0.8
1955	3.2	4.7	—	—	0.8
1960	7.0	7.6	18.0	19.0	1.4
1965	10.9	9.2	18.0	20.0	1.6
1970	24.1	12.3	23.0	24.0	2.4
1975	49.8	15.0	22.0	27.0	3.2
1980	91.4	15.5	22.0	31.0	3.4
1985	105.9	11.2	18.0	25.0	2.6
1986	112.3	11.3	—	—	2.6
1987	108.4	10.8	—	—	2.4
1988	115.3	10.8	—	—	2.3
1989	121.9	10.7	—	—	2.3
1990	135.3	10.8	17.0	21.0	2.4
1991	154.5	11.7	—	—	2.6
1992	178.1	12.9	—	—	2.9
1993	193.6	13.7	—	—	3.0
1994	210.6	14.4	—	—	3.1
1995	225.0	14.8	22.0	25.0	3.1
1996	227.8	14.6	21.0	24.0	3.0
1997	234.2	14.6	21.0	—	2.9
1998	246.1	14.9	21.0	—	2.9
1999(est)	262.2	15.2	21.0	—	3.0
2000(est)	283.5	16.1	22.0	—	3.1
2001(est)	300.7	16.7	22.0	—	3.2
2002(est)	310.3	17.0	23.0	—	3.1
2003(est)	323.6	17.1	23.0	—	3.1
2004(est)	338.8	17.3	23.0	—	3.1

Note: "—" indicates not available. Amounts in current dollars.
[a]Includes off-budget outlays; all grants are on-budget.
[b]Excludes outlays for national defense, international affairs, and net interest.
[c]As defined in the national income and product accounts.
Source: Harold W. Stanely and Richard G. Niemi, *Vital Statistics on American Politics,* 7th ed. (Washington, D.C.: CQ Press, 2000), p. 319. Reprinted by permission of Congressional Quarterly Inc.

20 percent of all state and local government spending; this amount of money made the states ever more dependent on the national government.

As Congress increased the number of grant programs for which cities were eligible, many critics argued that the federal grants system was out of hand. In 1964, the chair of President Johnson's Council of Economic Advisers proposed a new program, called **revenue sharing,** to channel federal dollars back to the states without the strings that went with categorical grants. Johnson, a federalist at heart, rejected the proposal and favored continued national control of grant programs. But President Richard M. Nixon, who ran in 1968 on a Republican Party platform pledging to return power to the states, found the idea attractive. He believed that states and local governments needed federal assistance but should have greater freedom to spend it. Under his revenue-sharing program, money was given to state and local governments to spend where they believed the money was most needed, with no strings attached.

The revenue-sharing idea was popular with the states, which in 1972 were in fiscal crisis. But during the second Reagan administration, when the budget deficit soared, there were few funds to share. Congress terminated the program, over which it had little control, and by 1987 it had been phased out completely.

Between 1965 and 1980, federal aid to cities and states tripled. One political scientist ventured that—in the world of bake-shop metaphors—a "new special" was in the offing: "fruitcake federalism." Not only was it formless, but it also offered (political) plums to all.[19] Negative reaction to this far-reaching federalism was not long in coming. States simply wanted more control.

New Federalism and the Reagan Revolution

In 1976, Jimmy Carter, a former governor of Georgia, successfully ran for president as an "outsider" opposed to big government and federal grants that mandated state spending for a variety of programs, including education and pollution-reduction programs. The unfunded mandates discussed later in the chapter were programs passed by Congress requiring state compliance but that came with no funds for the states to meet federal standards. Although Carter was the first president to reduce intergovernmental grant expenditures, the reforms in federal grant programs Carter introduced were insufficient to override the rest of his political woes, and in 1980 Ronald Reagan former governor of California, was elected president. Reagan pledged to advance what he called a "New Federalism" and a return of power to the states.

President Reagan's New Federalism had many facets. The Republican "Reagan Revolution" as begun by President Reagan and continued by President George Bush had at its heart strong views about the role of states in the federal system. While many argued that grants-in-aid were an effective way to raise the level of services provided to the poor, others, including Reagan, attacked them as imposing national priorities on

revenue sharing
Method of redistributing federal monies back to the states with "no strings attached"; favored by President Richard M. Nixon.

the states. Policy decisions were made at the national level, and the states, always in search of funds, were forced to follow the priorities of the national government. States found it very hard to resist the lure of grants, even though many were contingent on some sort of state investment of matching or proportional funds. Shortly after taking office, Reagan proposed massive cuts in federal domestic programs (which had not become federal functions until the New Deal) and drastic income tax cuts.

The Reagan administration's budget and its policies dramatically altered the relationships among federal, state, and local governments. For the first time in thirty years, federal aid to state and local governments declined.[20] Reagan persuaded Congress to consolidate many categorical grants (for specific programs that often require matching funds) into far fewer, less restrictive **block grants**—broad grants to states for specified activities such as secondary education or health services, with few strings attached.

Reagan's New Federalism initially changed the nature of state politics. Many state governments—as well as cities within a single state—found themselves competing for funds. States were faced with revenue shortfalls caused by the recession of the early 1990s, legal requirements mandating balanced budgets, and growing demands for new social services and the replacement of some formerly provided by the federal government. Many governors around the nation found themselves in political trouble as they had to slash services and ask for tax increases. "A governor with over a 50 percent approval is more the exception than the rule now, and that just wasn't true three or four years ago," noted one pollster in 1991.[21]

Intense competition for federal funds as well as increasing federal regulations, mandates, and conditions of aid all contributed to the need for state and local governments to hire lobbyists to advance their interests in Washington. As revealed in Figure 3.3, there are over 87,000 different governments in the United States. Representatives of these school

block grant
Broad grant with few strings attached given to states by the federal government for specified activities, such as secondary education or health services.

FIGURE 3.3   Number of Governments in the U.S.

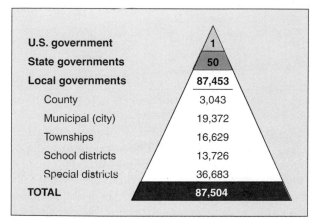

U.S. government	1
State governments	50
Local governments	87,453
County	3,043
Municipal (city)	19,372
Townships	16,629
School districts	13,726
Special districts	36,683
TOTAL	87,504

Source: U.S. Bureau of the Census, http://www.census.gov/govs/www/gid.html.

POLITICS NOW

UNSPENT DOLLARS: WHAT HAPPENED TO THE CARROT AND THE STICK?

On October 1, 2000, a majority of the states lost significant sums that were coming to them from the federal government to repair potholes and bridges or widen roads because they failed to comply with a 1998 federal law that required states to enact legislation to ban motorists from having open containers of alcohol in their cars and to levy harsher penalties on drivers convicted of multiple drunk driving violations. As revealed in the table, this failure has been a costly one for some states. Texas alone lost nearly $50 million.

The case of federal incentives not working is even more striking in the area of health care for poor

States to Lose Money

State	Open Container Loss	Repeat Offender Loss	Child Health Care Insurance Loss
Alaska	$2,953,663	$2,953,663	—
Arkansas	$4,071,994	na	na
California		$25,627,487	590
Colorado	$3,985,768		19.1
Connecticut	$3,216,879	$3,216,879	9.5
Dist. of Columbia		$1,174,747	na
Delaware	$1,376,226	$1,376,268	na
Florida	—	—	69
Georgia	$10,834,373	$10,834,373	na
Illinois		$9,588,695	67.5
Indiana	$7,663,799	—	—
Kansas		$3,723218	na
Kentucky	—	—	—
Louisiana	$4,345,756	$4,345,756	63.7
Maine	—	—	—
Massachusetts	$4,568,670	$4,568,670	—
Maryland	$4,428,357	$4,428,357	—
Minnesota		$4,940, 108	28
Mississippi	$3,813,218	—	na
Missouri	$7,002,701	$7,002,701	—
Montana	$3,232,412	$3,232,412	na
North Dakota		$2,360,860	na

intergovernmental lobby

The pressure group or groups that are created when state and local governments hire lobbyists to lobby the national government.

districts, cities, and states, as well as many more groups, form part of what is called the **intergovernmental lobby.** Some have individual offices in Washington to lobby for funds. Others hire full-time or part-time lobbyists to work solely on their behalf to keep abreast of funding opportunities or to lobby for programs that could be useful back home. Others lobby as well as litigate to make sure that their interests are represented before the courts.[22]

children. Forty-rive percent of the money allocated by Congress to help states pay for health insurance for children in low-income families was not spent during the three-year initial phase of the program. California and Texas, where 29 percent of all of the nation's 11 million children without health insurance live, lost $590 and $446 million respectively.* States had mixed messages about why they failed to spend this money. Some resented that they would have had to pay out some funds to get the federal dollars; others simply were unable to contact children or believed the paperwork to be too onerous.

*Robert Pear, "40 States Forfeit Health Care Funds for Poor Children," *The New York Times* (September 24, 2000), A1.

States to Lose Money (continued)

State	Open Container Loss	Repeat Offender Loss	Child Health Care Insurance Loss
New Hampshire	—	—	7.5
New Jersey		$5,873,430	10
New Mexico	$3,358,574	$3,358,564	57.8
New York		$10,224,067	—
North Carolina	—	—	—
Ohio		$10,036,332	na
Oregon	$3,614,310	$3,614,310	na
Pennsylvania	—	—	—
Rhode Island		$1,490,5544	na
South Carolina		$5,211,242	—
South Dakota		$2,376,404	na
Tennessee	$6,496,493	$6,496,493	—
Texas	$24,091,656	$24,091,656	446
Virginia	$7,543,062		na
Vermont	$1,338,999	$1,338,999	—
Washington			44
Wisconsin		$6,259,241	
West Virginia	$2,211,655	$2,181,655	11.6
Wyoming	$2,515,799	$2,515,799	na

Source: USA Today, September 7, 2000, p. A7. Copyright 2000, USA TODAY. Reprinted with permission.

Not only do individual governments lobby the national government, but myriad types of governments with shared or similar interests also have banded together to advance their collective interests. What scholars term the "Big Seven," which includes the National Governors' Association (NGA) and the National League of Cities, among others are widely recognized as the premier intergovernmental lobbies (see Table 3.2). These groups, primarily founded from the turn of the century to the New Deal,

TABLE 3.2   The "Big Seven" Intergovernmental Associations

Association (Current Title)	Date Founded	Membership
National Governors' Association (NGA)	1908	Incumbent governors
Council of State Governments (CSG)	1933	Direct membership by states and territories; serves all branches of government; has dozens of affiliate organizations of specialists
National Conference of State Legislatures (NCSL)	1948	State legislators and staff
National League of Cities (NLC)	1924	Direct, by cities and state leagues of cities
National Association of Counties (NAC)	1935	Direct by counties; loosely linked state associations; affiliate membership for county professional specialists
United States Conference of Mayors (USCM)	1933	Direct membership by cities with population over 30,000
International City/County Management Association (ICMA)	1914	Direct membership by appointed city and county managers, and other professionals

Source: Allan J. Cigler and Burdett A. Loomis, *Interest Group Politics*, 4th ed. (Washington, D.C.: CQ Press, 1995), p. 135. Reprinted by permission of Congressional Quarterly, Inc.

are well organized and well established. Several of the Big Seven focus on state issues. The NGA is composed of incumbent governors from each state. The governors meet twice a year but have a staff and standing committees that meet more regularly. Adoption of policy positions requires a quorum and vote of three-quarters of the governors. Small states tend to be more active within the group than larger states. The Council of State Governments, located in Washington, D.C., is an umbrella organization designed to gather information and provide assistance to the states. The National Conference of State Legislatures, headquartered in Denver, publishes a monthly magazine, *State Legislatures,* and uses its Washington office to monitor and publish information about the federal government that is useful to the states. It provides a variety of legislative services to all fifty state legislatures plus Puerto Rico.

Three other groups often are called the "urban lobby." The National League of Cities represents medium and small cities, the U.S. Conference of Mayors represents large cities, and the National Association of Counties represents rural, suburban, and urban counties. The remaining member of the Big Seven is the International City/County Management Association, which represents the country's appointed local chief executives.

The Devolution Revolution

In *Federalist No. 17,* Alexander Hamilton noted that "it will always be far more easy for the State government to encroach upon the national authorities than for the national government to encroach upon the State authorities." He was wrong. Today, some argue, the federal/state relationship has moved from "cooperation to coercion,"[23] a situation that in 1994 led many state governors and the Republican Party (remember, both increases in federal power—the New Deal and Great Society Program—were launched during Democratic administrations) to rebel openly against this growth of national power.

Preemption.   One method the federal government has used to cut into the authority of the states to set their own policy preferences derives from the Constitution's supremacy clause. This practice, known as **preemption,** allows the national government to override, or preempt, state or local actions in certain areas.[24] The Tenth Amendment expressly reserves to the states and the people all powers not delegated to the national government. The phenomenal growth of preemption statutes, laws that Congress has passed to allow the federal government to assume partial or full responsibility for traditional state and local governmental functions, began in 1965 during the Johnson administration. Since then, Congress routinely used its authority under the commerce clause to preempt state laws. These statutes not only took authority away from states, they often imposed significant costs on them in the form of unfunded mandates. In fact, the cost to the states—along with the perceived federal interference with local matters—is one reason that the electorate so willingly embraced the campaign message of the Republican Party in 1994.

As governor of Texas, George W. Bush, shown here with his brother Jeb, the governor of Florida, was a member of the National Governors' Association, one of the "Big Seven." (Photo courtesy: Reuters/Jeff Mitchell/Archive Photos)

The **Contract with America,** proposed by then House Minority Whip Newt Gingrich, was a campaign document signed by nearly all Republican candidates (and incumbents) for the House of Representatives in 1994. In it, Republican candidates pledged themselves to force a national debate on the role of the national government in regard to the states. A top priority was scaling back the federal government. Said House Budget Committee Chair John R. Kasich (R–Ohio), Congress wanted to "return money, power, and responsibility to the states," which some called the "devolution revolution."[25]

Republicans lambasted the growth of federal power over the states and were particularly critical of several features of the federal-state relationship that they believed robbed the states of their power to set policy for the health and welfare of their citizens. A key component of the contract was a commitment to end unfunded mandates.

preemption
A concept derived from the Constitution's supremacy clause that allows the national government to override or preempt state or local actions in certain areas.

Contract with America
Campaign pledge signed by most Republican candidates in 1994 to guide their legislative agenda.

WEB EXPLORATION
For more on the Devolution Revolution, see
www.ablongman.com/oconnor

Unfunded Mandates.   From the beginning, most categorical grants were matching grants that came with a variety of strings attached. As

POINT / COUNTERPOINT

WHO SHOULD CONTROL EDUCATION ?

Traditionally, control over public schools has rested with local school districts. But beginning with federal enforcement of civil rights laws and the Great Society programs in the 1950s and 1960s, the national government has been more and more involved in education issues. In 1979, President Jimmy Carter created the U.S. Department of Education, separating it from the Department of Health, Education and Welfare, and in 1994 President Bill Clinton signed into law Goals 2000 or the Educate America Act, which set out eight national education goals and provided money to help states meet them. Among those goals are that children in grades 4, 8, and 12 need to demonstrate competency in English, mathematics, science, foreign languages, civics and government, economics, arts, history, and geography. This particular clause has led to a discussion of nationally mandated standards and to large numbers of standardized tests. The tests are lauded as "outcomes-based assessment" by their supporters and are criticized as interference with the prerogatives of parents and teachers by opponents. But standardized tests is only one aspect of the larger issue of federal involvement in public schools. Vouchers, or school choice, are another proposal designed to address failing schools. Introducing market-based forces into the public schools by allowing parents and students to leave failing schools and take money with them to a better functioning school is designed to increase competition and the quality of education. Opponents argue that vouchers merely undercut the public school system. Let's examine these points of view.

Advocates of strong federal involvement with public education, including many Democrats, argue that schools need national education standards guarantee that all American children get a quality education, regardless of whether they are lucky enough to live in rich school districts or certain states. Advocates for federal involvement also argue that national education standards provide a benchmark with which to measure school reforms and quality. Further, only the federal government seems to be able to guarantee equal treatment for minorities and women.

In addition, the testing and assessment of students in critical grades (4, 8, and 12) is deemed essential to measuring quality and determining

---

mandates

National laws that direct states or local governments to comply with federal rules or regulations (such as clean air or water standards) under threat of civil or criminal penalties or as a condition of receipt of any federal grants.

VISUAL LITERACY
Federalism and Regulations

categorical grants declined, the national government continued to exercise a significant role in state policy priorities through **mandates**—laws that direct states or local governments to comply with federal rules or regulations (such as clean air or water standards) under threat of civil or criminal penalties or as a condition of receipt of any federal grants (a city might not get federal transportation funds, for example, unless the disabled have access to particular means of transportation).

Prior to 1995, the federal government required the states to shoulder the financial programs it did not fund. Unfunded mandates often made up as much as 30 percent of a local government's annual operating budget. Between 1983 and 1990, it is estimated that the cumulative cost of unfunded mandates to state and local governments was between 8.9 and 12.7 billion dollars.[26]

whether school reform is working and how well schools are teaching their students. Testing allows teachers and students to have an objective measure of how well they perform compared with local, state, and national averages.

Advocates of federal involvement are often adamantly opposed to vouchers. If parents opt to send their children to private or parochial schools and are allowed to bring state and federal monies with them, the national education system will be threatened. The worst case scenario is that only the poor and the disadvantaged will be left in public schools. The voucher arguments may also be based on a false assumption: that our public schools are failing. While the problem exist, in many respects public education seems to be improving and is generally high quality. The United States has more of its children going on to college than any country in the world.

Critics of federal involvement, including many Republicans and teachers' unions, argue that state and local authorities, coupled with parents, know and understand what is best for their children and for public education. They fiercely oppose national standards as an effort to impose a national curriculum. They also argue that the education bureaucracy is already expensive and bloated, so why add another layer by increasing the size of the federal education bureaucracy.

The critics also argue that testing is actually having a negative effect on learning. Multiple-choice tests, as most of them are, test only passive recognition, not cognitive ability. Many minority students, women, and students from poor families tend to perform less well on standardized tests. Instead of exploring ways of getting students excited about learning, teachers who teach to the test reduce the quality of education instead of enhancing it.

Many critics of federal involvement also favor vouchers. They see serious flaws in the educational system that, they feel, can be addressed by introducing competition and market forces into the system. If parents start removing their children, and government funding goes with them, poor schools will be forced to change and in the end all children will benefit from higher educational standards.

 What do you think? Who Should control education? *Go to* www.ablongman.com/oconnor

As shown in Figure 3.4, the enactment of federal regulations requiring state and local spending increased tremendously through 1990. During the 1980s, Congress added twenty-seven new programs requiring state spending, and many expensive unfunded provisions were attached to existing grant-in-aid programs. Columbus, Ohio, for example, with 633,000 residents, faced a $1 billion bill to comply with the federal Clean Water Act and the Safe Drinking Water Act at an estimated cost of $685 a year per household.

Unlike the national government, most states are required to have balanced budgets. Mandates increasingly meant more taxes and more trouble for state and local legislators. It is not surprising, then, to understand why Republicans were able to enact the unfunded mandates bill to bar Congress from passing laws that required the states to fund federal

FIGURE 3.4   The Growth of Regulatory Federalism: New Programs Costing States Money, 1931–1990

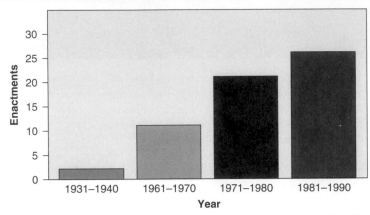

Source: ACIR, *Regulatory Federalism,* Appendix Table 1. Reprinted in Timothy J. Conlan and David R.
Beam, "Federal Mandates: The Record of Reform and Future Products," *Intergovernmental Perspective*
(Fall 1992): 9.

WEB EXPLORATION
For more information
on state and local
governments, see
www.ablongman.com/oconnor

PARTICIPATION
Federal Regulations
and Mandates

WEB EXPLORATION
To analyze where
your state stands
relative to other states, see
www.ablongman.com/oconnor

programs. Moreover, Speaker of the House Newt Gingrich tried to set
aside a day each month called "Corrections Day" to "correct" existing
laws and regulations to ease the financial burdens on states.

By 1999, the cumulative impact of the federal government's moving
some powers back to the states, an improved economy, and decreasing
federal mandates produced record federal and state budget surpluses.
The fifty states are now in the best fiscal shape they have been in since
the 1970s, before federal mandates hurt their ability to prioritize spending. According to the National Conference of State Legislatures, total
state budget surpluses in 1998 exceeded $30 billion. These kinds of sur-
pluses are now allowing states to return money to taxpayers in the form
of tax-cutting measures. But the biggest chunk of these surpluses is
going to educational reforms to help school districts keep up with
enrollment growth caused by the "baby boomlet" generation.[27]

The federal government is also enjoying record surpluses. Federal
surpluses will provide more opportunities for new federal programs.
The new programs, however, are likely to reflect a greater sensitivity to
the needs and desires of the fifty states.

FEDERALISM AND THE SUPREME COURT

Historically, the role of the Supreme Court in determining the parameters of federalism cannot be underestimated. As we have seen in
chapter 2, although Congress passed sweeping New Deal legislation
that some have argued amended the Constitution, it was not until the

H I G H L I G H T

DO YOU HAVE ID? SETTING A NATIONAL ALCOHOL POLICY

The number of fatal crashes involving drivers aged eighteen to twenty-one fell by 14.3 percent from 1983 to 1994. Why? In 1984, after years of often highly emotional lobbying by Mothers Against Drunk Drivers (MADD) and other concerned citizens groups, Congress passed an amendment to the Surface Transportation Act of 1982 designed to withhold 5 percent of federal highway funds from states that did not prohibit those under the age of twenty-one from drinking alcoholic beverages. Prior to that time, MADD had lobbied most state legislators to raise their state drinking ages, with mixed success. Then, its leaders turned their eyes on Congress. In 1984 only sixteen U.S. senators voted against the amendment to the Surface Transportation Act of 1982.

Because the national government did not have the power to regulate the drinking age, it resorted to the carrot-and-stick nature of federalism, whereby the national government dangles money in front of the states but places conditions on its use. To force states to raise their drinking age to twenty-one by 1988, Congress initially decided to withhold 5 percent of all federal highway grants to the recalcitrant states. (This was later raised to 10 percent.) In other words, no raised drinking age, no federal dollars. Even most conservative Republican senators—those most attached to the notion of states' rights—supported the

provision, in spite of the fact that it imposed a national ideal on the states. After congressional action, the bill was signed into law by President Ronald Reagan, another conservative long concerned with how the national government had trampled on state power.

States still retain the power to decide who is legally drunk, however. In 1998, Mothers Against Drunk Driving pressured members of Congress to adopt a national blood alcohol level of 0.08 to indicate drunkenness, but that effort failed. Thus, the blood alcohol content required for determining legal intoxication varied dramatically, from a low of 0.05 in Colorado to a high of 0.1 in several states.

In 1999, however, President Clinton signed legislation that contains incentives for states to lower their blood alcohol levels defining drunk driving to 0.08. By late 2000, eighteen states and the District of Columbia adopted that standard. On the twentieth anniversary of its founding, MADD members rallied to convince Congress to set the 0.08 limit as a mandatory national standard, an action supported by a majority of Americans according to a recent Gallup poll.

Source: Ruth Gastel, "Drunk Driving and Liquor Liability," *Insurance Issues Updates*, April 1999, and Arthur Santana, "On 20th Anniversary, MADD Urges National 0.08% Standard," *The Washington Post* (September 7, 2000) : A6.

Supreme Court finally reversed itself and found those programs to be constitutional that any real change occurred in the federal-state relationship. From the New Deal until the 1980s, the Supreme Court's impact on the nature of the federal system could be found in several areas, but especially in education, the electoral process, and the commerce clause and the functioning of the states.

TIMELINE
Federalism Over Time

GLOBAL POLITICS

FEDERALISM IN COMPARATIVE PERSPECTIVE

All governments face the issue of how to divide political authority geographically. Of the variations presented in the table, federal and unitary systems are the most prevalent throughout the world. The Commonwealth of Independent States (made up of most of the former republics of the Soviet Union) is the rare example of a confederation. The countries presented here are split almost evenly between federal and unitary systems, with the latter slightly more common. While these federal systems divide political authority between national and local government, the near balance suggests that there is nothing inherently better, or even more democratic, in a federal system.

Whether a country adopts one or the other tends to be the result of its political history. The United States and Germany were created out of existing confederacies, so the new governments accommodated theoretically strong state governments as the price of union. Canada was formed in 1867 out of three British provinces that voluntarily sought union. In France, Italy, and Japan, the creation of modern nation-states was driven by central authorities that imposed geographic political arrangements on their provinces. In all three cases, subnational territories were cre-

ated by national governments intent on obliterating then-existing regional identities. China and Russia have always had traditions of strong central government, which makes recent Russian federalism a puzzle.

The ability of the national government to alter local government at will remains a key feature of unitary systems. No better current example can be found than in the British Parliament's decision in 1998 to provide home parliaments for Scotland, Wales, and Northern Ireland. But what Parliament created can be abolished by that body at any time: In 2000, dissatisfied with the lack of progress in peace negotiations in Northern Ireland, the Blair government suspended that region's home parliament and reintroduced direct rule by the Parliament in London.

Power is divided differently even among the federal systems. Canada has had a strong federal government with correspondingly weak provinces, although the latter have asserted their power in recent decades. Quebec is the clearest case, with its threat to separate from the rest of the country forcing the federal government to make concessions on issues like the national language and education. Unlike American states, German state governments cannot raise their

COMPARATIVE
Comparing Federal and Unitary Systems

Through grants-in-aid programs like the Morrill Land Grant Act of 1862, and into the 1950s, Congress long has tried to encourage the states to develop their university and educational systems. Still, education was usually considered a function of the states under their police powers, which allow the states to provide for public health and welfare. That tradition was shattered when the Supreme Court ruled in *Brown v. Board of Education* (1954) that state-mandated segregation has no place in the public schools (see chapter 6). *Brown* forced states to dismantle their segregated school systems and ultimately led the federal courts to play an important role in monitoring the efforts of state and local governments to tear down the vestiges of segregation.

own taxes, but they retain sole control over state police forces, the highest level of regular law enforcement. The Mexican and post-communist Russian federal systems have also been highly centralized. In the original spirit of the U.S. Constitution, Canadian, German, and Russian regional governments are represented in the upper houses of their respective federal parliaments. This gives state governments a direct say in national lawmaking.

Geographic Distribution of Authority

Country	System	Major Subnational Divisions
Canada	federal	10 provinces, 3 territories
China	unitary	23 provinces, 9 other units
France	unitary	96 departments
Germany	federal	16 states
Indonesia	unitary	23 provinces, 3 other units
Italy	unitary	20 regions
Japan	unitary	47 prefectures
Mexico	federal	31 states, 1 federal district
Russia	federal	49 oblasts, 21 republics, 13 other units
United Kingdom	unitary	53 counties
United States	**federal**	**50 states, 1 federal district**

Source: CIA World Factbook 2000 online. http://www.odci.gov/cia.publications/factbook/geos/. Searched September 20, 2000.

A decade after *Brown* v. *Board of Education* (1954), the Supreme Court again involved itself in one of the most sacred areas of state regulation in the federal system—the conduct of elections. As a trade-off for giving the national government more powers, the Constitutional Convention allowed the states control over voter qualifications in national elections, as well as over how elections were to be conducted. But in 1964, the Court began to limit the states' ability to control the process of congressional redistricting. In 1966, for example, the Supreme Court invalidated the poll tax, a state-imposed tax ranging from one to five dollars levied on those who wished to vote. The poll tax was widely used in the Southern states to curtail voting by the poor, who often were black.[28] Most Southern legislators assailed the Court's decision, viewing it as illegal interference with their powers to regulate elections under the Constitution, and as a violation of state sovereignty.

Since the New Deal, and until recently, the commerce clause has been the rationale for virtually any federal intervention in state and local governmental affairs. In *Garcia* v. *San Antonio Metropolitan Transit Authority* (1985), for example, which involved the constitutionality of applying federally imposed minimum wage and maximum hour provisions to state governments, the Court ruled that Congress has broad power to impose its will on state and local governments, even in areas that traditionally have been left to their discretion. The Court ruled that the "political process ensures that laws that unduly burden the states will not be promulgated" and that it should not be up to an "unelected" judiciary to preserve state powers.[29] Furthermore, the majority of the Court concluded that the Tenth Amendment, which ensures that any powers not given to the national government be reserved for the states, was—at least for the time being—essentially meaningless!

The Devolution Revolution and the Court

Growth in federal grants-in-aid programs and unfunded mandates to the states, as well as the Court's apparent bestowal of free rein on the authority of Congress to regulate under the commerce clause, left many states to rethink their position in the federal system. Most were unhappy with it. Some argued that one of the original reasons for federal grants—perceived overrepresentation of rural interests in state legislatures—has been removed, as the Supreme Court has ordered redistricting to ensure better representation of urban and suburban interests. Moreover, state legislatures have become more professional, state and local bureaucracies more responsive, and the delivery of services better. In fact, the greatest growth in government hiring continues to be in the state and local sectors.

Beginning in the late 1980s, however, in what many term a devolution revolution, the Court began to change its willingness to allow Congress to regulate in a variety of areas. Once Ronald Reagan was elected president, he attempted to fashion a Supreme Court in his own image—one of the new justices committed to notions of state rights and rolling back federal intervention in matters that he and many Republicans believed properly resided within the province of the states and not Congress or the federal courts.

SIMULATION
You Are a
Federal Judge

Illustrative of this trend are the Supreme Court's decisions in *Webster v. Reproductive Health Services* (1989)[30] and *Casey v. Planned Parenthood of Southeastern Pennsylvania* (1992).[31] In *Webster,* the Court first gave new latitude—and even encouragement—to the states to fashion more restrictive abortion laws. Since *Webster,* the Court has consistently upheld the authority of the individual states to limit a minor's access to abortion through imposition of parental consent or notification laws. And it has consistently declined to review other restrictions, including twenty-four-hour waiting period requirements. In 2000, however, by a 5–4 vote, the Court struck

ANALYZING THE DATA

STATE-BY-STATE REPORT CARD ON ACCESS TO ABORTIONS

The National Abortion Rights Action League (NARAL) rated each state and the District of Columbia in fourteen categories, including bans on abortion procedures and counseling, clinic violence, the length of waiting periods, access for minors, and public funding. Several states have banned so-called "partial-birth abortions," but in many of these states' courts or attorneys general have blocked enforcement.

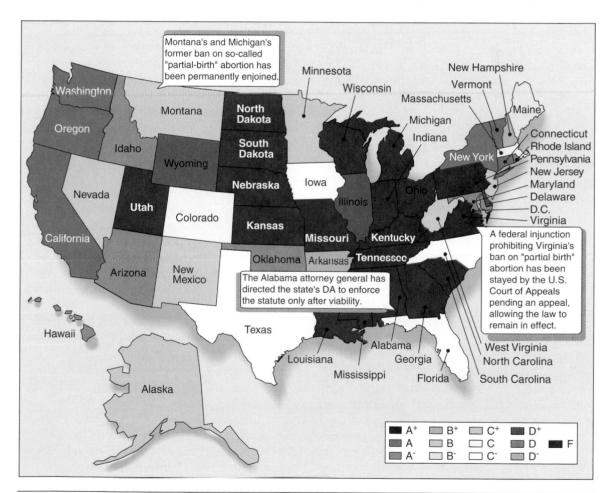

Montana's and Michigan's former ban on so-called "partial-birth" abortion has been permanently enjoined.

A federal injunction prohibiting Virginia's ban on "partial birth" abortion has been stayed by the U.S. Court of Appeals pending an appeal, allowing the law to remain in effect.

The Alabama attorney general has directed the state's DA to enforce the statute only after viability.

Legend: A⁺ B⁺ C⁺ D⁺ A B C D A⁻ B⁻ C⁻ D⁻ F

Source: From NARAL Resource, "State-by-State Report Card on Access to Abortion." Reprinted by permission from The NARAL Foundation.

down a Nebraska ban on so-called "partial birth" abortions (as discussed in chapter 5—see Analyzing the Data: State-by-State Report Card on Access to Abortion).

Continuity &Change

Marriage in the Federal System

When the Framers drafted the Constitution, most of them had clear ideas about what marriage was and the authority of the state (as well as the church) to sanction it. Marriage and the laws surrounding it (as well as its dissolution) were solely within the purview of state authority. Under English common law, when a woman married, she ceased to exist in the eyes of the law; in other words, she was civilly dead and could not make contracts or enter into any other kinds of legal arrangements. Beginning in the 1830s, however, most states began to change their laws to give women more rights in marriage. States regularly determine age at marriage (until the 1970s, it was frequently different for males and females), degree of relationship allowed (can cousins marry?), how married individuals can dispose of property (inheritance laws), pay their taxes, or even whether they can testify against each other in court. Marriage is not only a legal contract recognized by the state, but it carries certain rights and responsibilities with it. Only when some type of law or practice was viewed as discriminatory under the U.S. Constitution has the force of the federal government come into play. Thus, the Supreme Court has struck down as unconstitutional state laws that prohibit interracial marriages,[a] set differential ages for the age of legal capacity for men and women,[b] or allow only women to receive alimony upon dissolution of a marriage.[c] As public perceptions of what was appropriate changed, these changes were marked by changes in state law, and when that didn't happen, sometimes by the federal courts.

Until the 1980s, most people in America thought of marriage as a legal relationship between a male and a female. In the 1980s, however, some cities began recognizing what are termed domestic partnerships. Depending on the locale, these domestic partnership ordinances allowed same-sex couples to register with government officials to ensure that their union could be recognized in some way. In some cases, this provided the force of the state in matters of death and inheritances as well as other issues, including a person's ability to make decisions for an incapacitated partner over the wishes of other family members. Many employers followed suit and began to offer health and insurance benefits to same-sex couples in committed relationships.

In 1993, a decision of the Hawaiian Supreme Court called that state's ban on homosexual marriages into constitutional question. While Hawaii was grappling with this issue, several state legislatures and the U.S. Congress were whipped into a frenzy about the specter of gay and lesbian marriages. In 1996 and 1997 alone, half of the states passed provisions to bar legal recognition of same-sex marriages. The U.S. Congress also got into the act and passed the Defense of Marriage Act, which allows states to disregard gay marriages even if they are legal in other states. (The questionable constitutionality of this provision under the full faith and credit clause is discussed on pp. 46–47.)

In spite of these moves by so many of the states and the federal government, in 2000, Vermont became the first state in the union to sanction civil unions between same-sex couples. These are not marriages; instead, the Vermont law calls them "civil unions." Couples need only pay $20 to receive a license from a town clerk (there are no residency or blood test requirements) and have a ceremony performed by a

(continued)

judge or clergy member. Once so united, the couple is entitled to all of the benefits, protections, and responsibilities that are granted to married couples under Vermont law.

The idea of gay marriage is still upsetting to some, much as interracial marriage was in many sections of the South. Still, there can be no doubt that our notions of what a family is, as well as what (or who) makes up a married couple, are changing, and changing quite rapidly.

1. Are civil union states a good political compromise to diffuse this issue?

2. Should states be pressed to recognize Vermont civil unions under the full faith and credit clause of the U.S. Constitution?

[a]*Loving v. Virginia*, 388 U.S. (1967).
[b]*Stanton v. Stanton*, 421 U.S. 7 (1975).
[c]*Orr v. Orr*, 440 U.S. 268 (1979).

Cast Your Vote. Should other states adopt a civil union law similar to that in Vermont? To cast your vote, go to **www.ablongman.com/oconnor**

SUMMARY

The inadequacies of the confederate form of government created by the Articles of Confederation led the Framers to create an entirely new, federal system of government. From the summer of 1776 until today, the tension between the national and state governments has been at the core of our federal system.

The national government created by the Framers has both enumerated and implied powers, and also exercises concurrent powers with the states. Certain powers are denied to both the state and national governments. Certain guarantees concerning representation in Congress and protection against foreign attacks and domestic rebellion were made to the states in return for giving up some of their powers in the new federal system. Despite limitations, the national government is ultimately supreme.

Over the years, the powers of the national government have increased tremendously at the expense of the states. The Supreme Court, in particular, has played a key role in defining the relationship and powers of the national government through its broad interpretations of the supremacy and commerce clauses. For many years, however, it adhered to the notion of dual federalism, which tended to limit the national government's authority in areas such as slavery and, after the Civil War, civil rights. This notion of a limited role for the

national government in some spheres ultimately fell by the wayside after the Great Depression.

The rapid creation of New Deal programs to alleviate many problems caused by the Depression led to a tremendous expansion of the federal government through the growth of federal services and grant-in-aid programs. This growth escalated during the Johnson administration and in the mid to late 1970s. After his election in 1980, Ronald Reagan, upset by the growth of federal services, tried to reverse the tide through what he termed New Federalism. He built on earlier efforts by Richard M. Nixon to consolidate categorical grants into fewer block grant programs, and to give state and local governments greater control over programs. Since 1993, the national government and the states have been in a constant dialogue to reframe the structure of the federal-state relationship.

Over the years, the Supreme Court has been a major player in recent trends in the federal-state relationship. Its decisions in the areas of education, civil rights, voting rights, and the performance of state functions generally have given the federal government a wider role in the day-to-day functioning of the states, limiting the scope of the states' police powers. Recent decisions, however, indicate the Court's willingness to reassess the federal role in many areas.

KEY TERMS

bill of attainder, p. 68
block grant, p. 79
concurrent powers, p. 68
Contract with America, p. 83
cooperative federalism, p. 75
dual federalism, p. 72
enumerated powers, p. 67

ex post facto law, p. 68
federalism, p. 64
Gibbons v. *Ogden*, p. 71
implied powers, p. 67
intergovernmental lobby,
    p. 80
mandates, p. 84

McCulloch v. *Maryland*, p. 70
necessary and proper clause,
    p. 67
preemption, p. 83
reserve (or police) powers, p. 68
revenue sharing, p. 78
supremacy clause, p. 66

SELECTED READINGS

Bowman, Ann O'M., and Richard C. Kearney. *State and Local Government*, 2nd ed. Boston: Houghton Mifflin, 1993.

Conlan, Timothy J. *From New Federalism to Devolution: Twenty-Five Years of Intergovernmental Reform*. Washington, D.C.: Brookings, 1998.

Derthick, Martha. *The Influence of Federal Grants*. Cambridge, Mass.: Harvard University Press, 1970.

Elazar, Daniel J., and John Kincaid, eds. *The Covenant Connection: From Federal Theology to Modern Federalism*. Lexington, Mass.: Lexington Books, 2000.

Feingold, Kenneth, and Theda Skocpol. *State and Party in America's New Deal*. Madison: University of Wisconsin Press, 1995.

Gillespie, Ed, and Bob Schellhas, eds. *Contract with America*. New York: Times Books, 1994.

Grodzins, Morton. *The American System*. Chicago: Rand McNally, 1966.

Kenyon, Daphne A., and John Kincaid, eds. *Competition Among States and Local Governments*. Washington, D.C.: Urban Institute Press, 1991.

Ostrom, Vincent. *The Meaning of Federalism*. New York: Institute for Contemporary Studies, 1999.

Philips, Kevin. *The Politics of Rich and Poor: Wealth and the American Electorate in the Reagan Aftermath*. New York: Harper Collins, 1990.

Riker, William H. *Federalism: Origin, Operation, Significance*. Boston: Little, Brown, 1964.

Rivlin, Alice M. *Reviving the American Dream: The Economy, the States, and the Federal Government*. Washington, D.C.: Brookings Institution, 1993.

Walker, David B. *The Rebirth of Federalism*. Chatham, N.J.

(Photo courtesy: Alan Diaz/AP/Wide World Photos)

Civil Liberties 4

In spring 2000, the principal of predominantly African American Highland Springs High School in Virginia entered Liz Armstrong's tenth-grade biology class to announce a "random search."[1] In spite of the cry that went up from the class, the principal and other administrators forced students to empty their pockets, pocketbooks, and backpacks. No weapons or drugs were found.

Armstrong, a nine-year veteran of the classroom, was outraged and promised her students that she would find out more about the school district's search policy as well as contact the American Civil Liberties Union (ACLU) on the students' behalf. The next day she received a letter from the president of the Virginia ACLU informing her that the search was "clearly illegal" because it violated not only the students' Fourth Amendment right to be free from unlawful and unwarranted searches and seizures, but also the guidelines of the Virginia Board of Education regarding student searches. Upon receipt of the letter, Armstrong sent a letter to her principal informing him of the unlawfulness of the search and suggesting how a legal policy could be implemented.

Armstrong was suspended a few days later. She wasn't charged with speaking up for her students; instead, she was charged with violating "effective use of instructional time." How did Armstrong do that? By talking to her students about the search. In May, she was dismissed from her position.

In the wake of the 1999 shootings at Columbine High School in Colorado, many school boards and districts instituted zero-tolerance policies for students and teachers. In spite of federal rulings to the contrary, students often fall prey to overzealous administrators who are attempting to keep order in their schools. This balancing of rights—in this case the right of students to be free from unreasonable searches and seizures, as well as

Chapter Outline

- The First Constitutional Amendments: The Bill of Rights
- First Amendment Guarantees: Freedom of Religion
- First Amendment Guarantees: Freedom of Speech and Press
- The Right to Keep and Bear Arms
- The Rights of Criminal Defendants and the Criminal Justice System
- The Right to Privacy

to some expectation of privacy on their persons and their belongings, versus a community's and other students' right to be free from violence and
harm in the classroom—points out how relevant the writings of John Locke
and Thomas Hobbes are today. While these students were victims of an
unlawful search, unless they wish to sue, they have little other recourse.

When the Bill of Rights, which contains many of the most important protections on individual rights, was written, its drafters were not thinking about issues such as abortion, gay rights, or many of the personal liberties discussed in this chapter. Civil liberties issues often present complex problems. The balancing of civil liberties, especially when competing interests are at stake, is made even more difficult by the non-absolute nature of most civil liberties. Frequently, courts or policy makers are called on to balance competing interests and rights. As a society, for example, how much infringement on our personal liberties do we want to give the police? Do we want to have different rules for our homes, classrooms, lockers, dorm rooms, or cars? Similarly, as we discuss later in this chapter, policymakers continue to grapple with the scope of free speech rights on the Internet. Should citizens have unfettered discretion to write and print what they want, or should government impose limits? In many of the cases discussed in the chapter, there is a conflict between an individual or group of individuals seeking to exercise what they believe to be a right, and the government—local, state, or national—seeking to control the exercise of that right in an attempt to keep order and preserve the rights of others: In others, two liberties are in conflict, such as a physician's and her patient's rights to easy access to a clinic versus a pro-lifer's liberty to picket that clinic. It generally falls to the judiciary to balance those interests. Depending on the composition of the Supreme Court and the times, the balance may lean toward civil liberties or toward the right of the government to limit those rights.

civil liberties
The personal rights and freedoms that the federal government cannot abridge by law, constitution, or judicial interpretation.

In this chapter we explore the various dimensions of civil liberties guarantees contained in the U.S. Constitution and the Bill of Rights. **Civil liberties** are the personal rights and freedoms that the federal government cannot abridge, either by law, constitution, or judicial interpretation. Civil liberties guarantees place limitations on the power of the government to restrain or dictate how individuals act. Thus, when we discuss civil liberties such as those found in the Bill of Rights, we are concerned with limits on what governments can and cannot do.

THE FIRST CONSTITUTIONAL AMENDMENTS: THE BILL OF RIGHTS

In 1787, most state constitutions explicitly protected a variety of personal liberties: speech, religion, freedom from unreasonable searches and seizures, trial by jury, and more. It was clear that the new Constitution would redistribute power in the new federal system between the national government and the states. Without an explicit guarantee of specific civil liberties, could the national government be trusted to uphold the freedoms already granted to citizens by their states?

Recognition of the increased power that would be held by the new national government led Anti-Federalists to stress the need for a bill of rights. Anti-Federalists and many others were confident that they could control the actions of their own state legislators, but they didn't trust the national government to be so protective of their civil liberties.

The notion of adding a bill of rights to the Constitution was not a popular one at the Constitutional Convention. Federalists believed it was foolhardy to list things that the national government had no power to do since the proposed Constitution didn't give the national government the power to regulate speech, religion, and the like.

The insistence of Anti-Federalists on a bill of rights, the fact that some states conditioned their ratification of the Constitution on the addition of these guarantees, and the disagreement among Federalists about writing specific liberty guarantees into the Constitution led to prompt congressional action in the First Congress to put an end to further controversy. This was a time when national stability and support for the new government were particularly needed. Thus, in 1789, the proposed Bill of Rights was sent to the states by Congress for ratification, which was finally achieved in 1791.

The Bill of Rights, the first ten amendments to the Constitution, contains numerous specific guarantees, including those of free speech, press, and religion (see Appendix II for the full text). The Ninth and Tenth Amendments, in particular, highlight Anti-Federalist fears of a too-powerful national government. The Ninth Amendment, strongly favored by Madison, makes it clear that this special listing of rights does not mean that others don't exist; and the Tenth Amendment simply reiterates that powers not delegated to the national government are reserved to the states or the people.

WEB EXPLORATION
To view an original copy of the Bill of Rights, see www.ablongman.com/oconnor

The Incorporation Doctrine: The Bill of Rights Made Applicable to the States

The Bill of Rights was intended to limit the powers of the *national* government to infringe on the rights and liberties of the citizenry. In 1833, the Supreme Court ruled that the federal Bill of Rights limited only the U.S. government and not the states.[2] In 1868, however, the Fourteenth Amendment was added to the U.S. Constitution. Section 1 of the Fourteenth Amendment reads: "No State shall . . . deprive any person of life, liberty, or property, without due process of law." This language suggested the possibility that some or even all of the protections guaranteed in the Bill of Rights might be interpreted to prevent state infringement of those rights.

due process clause

Clause contained in the Fifth and Fourteenth Amendments. Over the years, it has been construed to guarantee to individuals a variety of rights ranging from economic liberty to criminal procedural rights to protection from arbitrary governmental action.

incorporation doctrine

Principle in which the Supreme Court has held that most, but not all, of the specific guarantees in the Bill of Rights limit state and local governments by making those guarantees applicable to the states through the due process clause of the Fourteenth Amendment.

Until nearly the turn of the century, the Supreme Court steadfastly rejected numerous arguments urging it to interpret the **due process clause** in the Fourteenth Amendment as making various provisions contained in the Bill of Rights applicable to the states. In 1897, however, the Court began to increase its jurisdiction over the states.[3] It began to hold states to a substantive due process standard whereby state laws had to be shown to be a valid exercise of the state's power to regulate the health, welfare, or public morals of its citizens. Interferences with state power, however, were rare. Thus, many states felt free to pass sedition laws (laws that made it illegal to speak or write any political criticism that threatened to diminish respect for the government, its laws, or public officials), expecting that the Supreme Court would uphold their constitutional validity. All of this changed dramatically in 1925. In *Gitlow* v. *New York* the Supreme Court ruled that the states were not completely free to limit forms of political expression. Instead, the First Amendment's freedom of speech and press guarantees were "among the *fundamental personal rights and 'liberties'* protected by the due process clause of the Fourteenth Amendment from impairment by the states" [emphasis added].[4]

Gitlow was the first step in the slow development of what is now known as the **incorporation doctrine.** After *Gitlow,* it took the Court six more years to "incorporate" another First Amendment freedom—that of the press.

Not all the specific guarantees in the Bill of Rights have been made applicable to the states through the due process clause of the Fourteenth Amendment. Instead, the Court has selectively chosen to limit the rights of states by protecting the personal rights and liberties it considers most fundamental, and thus subject to the Court's most rigorous strict scrutiny review. This process is referred to as selective incorporation.

Selective incorporation requires the states to respect freedoms of press, speech, and assembly among other rights. In 1937 the Court set forth principles that were to guide its interpretation of the incorporation doctrine for the next several decades. Some protections found in the Bill of Rights were absorbed into the concept of due process only because they are so fundamental to our notions of liberty and justice that they cannot be denied by the states unless the state can show what is called a compelling reason for the liberties' curtailment. This is a very high burden of proof for the state. Thus, abridgement of a fundamental right is not often sustained by the Court. Those rights deemed fundamental are not only those selectively drawn from the Bill of Rights and incorporated into the due process clause of the Fourteenth Amendment to apply to the states, but include other unenumerated rights, such as the right to privacy. Other guarantees contained in the Second, Third, and Seventh Amendments, such as the right to bear arms, have not been incorporated because the Court has yet to consider them sufficiently fundamental to national notions of liberty and justice.

FIRST AMENDMENT GUARANTEES: FREEDOM OF RELIGION

Today, many lawmakers bemoan the absence of religion in the public schools and voice their concerns that America is becoming a godless nation. In spite of the fact that 70 percent of all Americans belong to a church or synagogue, many of the Framers were religious men, but they knew what evils could arise if the new nation was not founded with religious freedom as one of its core ideals. Despite the fact that many colonists had fled Europe primarily to escape religious persecution, most colonies actively persecuted those who did not belong to their predominant religious groups.

Nevertheless, the colonists were uniformly outraged in 1774 when the British Parliament passed a law establishing Anglicanism and Roman Catholicism as official religions in the colonies. The First Continental Congress immediately sent a letter of protest announcing its "astonishment that a British Parliament should ever consent to establish . . . a religion [Catholicism] that has deluged [England] in blood and dispersed bigotry, persecution, murder and rebellion through every part of the world."[5]

This distaste for a national church or religion was reflected in the Constitution. Article VI, for example, provides that "no religious Test shall ever be required as a Qualification to any Office or Public Trust under the United States." This simple statement, however, did not reassure those who feared the new Constitution would curtail individual liberty. Thus, the First Amendment to the Constitution was ultimately ratified to lay those fears to rest.

The First Amendment to the Constitution begins, "Congress shall make no law respecting an establishment of religion, or prohibiting the free exercise thereof." This statement sets the boundaries of governmental action. This **establishment clause** ("Congress shall make no law respecting an establishment of religion") directs the national government not to involve itself in religion. It creates, in Thomas Jefferson's words, a "wall of separation" between church and state. The **free exercise clause** ("or prohibiting the free exercise thereof") guarantees citizens that the national government will not interfere with their practice of religion. These guarantees, however, are not absolute. In the mid-1800s, Mormons traditionally practiced and preached polygamy, the taking of multiple wives. In 1879, when it was first called on to interpret the free exercise clause, the Supreme Court upheld the conviction of a Mormon under a federal law barring polygamy. The Court reasoned that to do otherwise would provide constitutional protections to a full range of religious beliefs, including those as extreme as human sacrifice. Later, in 1940, the Supreme Court observed that the First Amendment "embraces two concepts—freedom to believe and freedom

WEB EXPLORATION
For groups with opposing views on how the First Amendment should be interpreted, see www.ablongman.com/oconnor

establishment clause
The first clause in the First Amendment. It prohibits the national government from establishing a national religion.

free exercise clause
The second clause of the First Amendment. It prohibits the U.S. government from interfering with a citizen's right to practice his or her religion.

Meeting with religious leaders at the White House, President Clinton took part in prayer breakfasts. (Photo Courtesy: Stephen Jaffee/AFP Photo)

to act. The first is absolute, but in the nature of things, the second cannot be. Conduct remains subject to regulation of society."[6]

The Establishment Clause

Over the years, the Court has been divided over how to interpret the establishment clause. Does this clause erect a total wall between church and state, or is some governmental accommodation of religion allowed? While the Supreme Court has upheld the constitutionality of many kinds of church/state entanglements such as public funding to provide sign language interpreters for deaf students in religious schools,[7] the Court has held fast to the rule of strict separation between church and state when issues of prayer in school are involved. In 1962, the Court first ruled that the recitation in public school classrooms of a twenty-two-word nondenominational prayer was unconstitutional.[8] In 1992, the Court continued its unwillingness to allow prayer in public schools by finding the saying of prayer at a middle school graduation unconstitutional.[9] In 2000, the Court ruled that student-led, student-initiated prayer at high school football games violated the establishment clause.[10]

The Court has gone back and forth in its effort to come up with a workable way to deal with church/state questions. Since 1980, however, the Supreme Court has appeared more willing to lower the wall between church and state as long as school prayer is not involved. In 1981, for example, the Court ruled that a Missouri law prohibiting the use of state university buildings and grounds for "purposes of religious worship," which had the effect of barring religious groups from using school facilities, was unconstitutional.[11] In 1993 the Court ruled that religious groups must be allowed to use public schools after hours if that access is also given to other community groups.[12]

In 1995 the Court signaled that it was willing to lower the wall between church and state even further. Ironically, it did so in a case involving Thomas Jefferson's own University of Virginia. In a 5–4 decision, the majority held that the university violated the First Amendment's establishment of religion clause by failing to fund a religious student magazine written by a fundamentalist Christian student group even though the university funded similar magazines published by 118 other student groups, some of which were religiously based. In dissent, the importance of this decision was highlighted by Justice David Souter, who noted: "The Court today, for the first time, approves direct funding of core religious activities by an arm of the state."[13] In 1997, the Court decided that it was constitutional for federally funded public school remedial teachers to provide services to students in parochial schools. The lending of computers and library materials to parochial schools was upheld in 2000.[14]

The Free Exercise Clause

The free exercise clause of the First Amendment proclaims that "Congress shall make no law . . . prohibiting the free exercise [of religion]." Although the free exercise clause of the First Amendment guarantees individuals the right to be free from governmental interference in the exercise of their religion, this guarantee, like other First Amendment freedoms, is not absolute. When secular law comes into conflict with religious law, the right to exercise one's religious beliefs is often denied—especially if the religious beliefs in question are held by a minority or by an unpopular or "suspicious" religious group. State statutes barring the use of certain illegal drugs, snake handling, and polygamy—all practices of particular religious sects—have been upheld as constitutional when states have shown compelling reasons to regulate these practices. Nonetheless, the Court has made it clear that the free exercise clause requires that a state or the national government remain neutral toward religion.

Many critics of rigid enforcement of such neutrality argue that the government should do what it can to accommodate the religious diversity in our nation. In the early 1960s, for example, a South Carolina textile mill shifted to a six-day work week, requiring that all employees work on Saturday. When one employee—a Seventh-Day Adventist whose Sabbath was Saturday—said she could not work on Saturdays, she was fired. She sought to receive unemployment compensation and her claim was denied. She then sued to obtain her benefits.

The Supreme Court ordered South Carolina to extend benefits to the woman in spite of its law that required an employee to be available for work on all days but Sundays. The Court ruled that the state law was an unconstitutional violation of the free exercise clause because it failed to accommodate the worker's religious beliefs.[15]

Nevertheless, the Court has interpreted the Constitution to mean that governmental interests can outweigh free exercise rights. In 1990,

GLOBAL POLITICS

RELIGIOUS FREEDOM

As we saw in earlier chapters, the First Amendment to the U.S. Constitution was based in an understanding of comparative politics. The Framers had seen what religious intolerance meant in Europe, and furthermore understood the establishment of official religions as a basic violation of civil liberties.

In terms of constitutional guarantees of religious freedom, the United States today resembles many countries. As the table shows, most countries do not establish a state religion. Until recently, Britain's Anglicanism guaranteed the right of Anglican bishops to sit in the House of Lords. Atheism is arguably the state religion of the People's Republic of China.

The Canadian, French, Japanese, and German constitutions all guarantee religious freedom. Reflecting the heavy American involvement in drafting Japan's current constitution, the guarantee of religious freedom in that document closely paraphrases Article I of the American Bill of Rights. Germany's Basic Law goes further than its American counterpart, guaranteeing the right of conscientious objection as part of religious freedom.

How states interact with religious organizations varies across countries. Many do not share the Jeffersonian insistence on a wall of separation between church and state. Many European countries, including Germany, have Christian democratic parties in their parliaments, most of which emerged out of Catholic parties. The German Basic Law, for example, lacks an establishment clause per se. The government subsidizes both the Catholic church and the Lutheran synods within its borders, and citizens may designate a portion of their income taxes for that purpose. While Indonesia's 1945 constitution does not acknowledge a state religion, the national ideology of Pancasila identifies monotheism as a component of national identity, and therefore of national policy. In practice, the state has supported Islamic organizations financially.

New or minority religions often find themselves at the forefront of civil liberties conflicts. The

for example, the Supreme Court ruled that the free exercise clause did not extend to the protection of sacramental peyote (an illegal hallucinogenic drug) used in some American Indian tribes' traditional religious services.[16] This decision prompted congressional passage of the Religious Freedom Restoration Act to require the courts to give greater protection to religious freedoms and to encourage governments to accommodate religious practices.

FIRST AMENDMENT GUARANTEES: FREEDOM OF SPEECH AND PRESS

A democracy depends on a free exchange of ideas, and the First Amendment shows that the Framers were well aware of this fact. Historically, one of the most volatile areas of constitutional interpre-

Church of Scientology has repeatedly complained that the German government discriminates against it by denying it official religious status. In France, the state has found itself in conflict with Muslims over a number of issues that touch on the heart of French understandings of national identity. In one case, a problem arose from the practice by some Muslim women of covering their heads when away from home. Muslim girls attending school were faced with expulsion because their head coverings were not part of the prescribed school uniform. What one side viewed as an issue of religious freedom, the other saw simply as a matter of enforcing national education policy.

The Establishment Clause in Comparative Perspective

Country	State Religion	Main Religion
Canada	None	Christianity
China	Atheism	Confucianism
France	None	Christianity (Catholicism)
Germany	None	Christianity
Indonesia	None	Islam
Italy	None	Christianity (Catholicism)
Japan	None	Buddhism, Shinto
Mexico	None	Christianity (Catholicism)
Russia	None	Orthodox Christianity
UK	Christianity (Church of England)	Christianity (Church of England)
USA	**None**	**Christianity**

Source: *L'Atlas Geopolitique et Cultural du Petit Robert des Noms Propres* (Paris: Diccionaires le Robert, 1999), 51.

tation has been in the interpretation of the First Amendment's mandate that "Congress shall make no law . . . abridging the freedom of speech, or of the press." Like the establishment and free exercise clauses of the First Amendment, the speech and press clauses have not been interpreted as absolute bans against government regulation. In fact, over the years the Court has used a hierarchical approach, with some items getting greater protection than others. Generally, thoughts have received the greatest protection, and actions or deeds the least. Words have come somewhere in the middle, depending on their content and purpose. (See also Highlight: Political Speech and Student Fees.)

When the First Amendment was ratified in 1791, it was considered to protect only against **prior restraint** of speech or expression, that is, to guard against the prohibition of speech or publication before the fact. The First Amendment was not considered to provide absolute immunity from governmental sanction for what speakers or publishers might

COMPARATIVE

Comparing Civil Liberties

prior restraint
Judicial doctrine stating that the government cannot prohibit speech or publication before the fact.

HIGHLIGHT

POLITICAL SPEECH AND STUDENT FEES

In March 2000, the United States Supreme Court ruled unanimously in *Board of Regents* v. *Southworth* that public universities could charge students a mandatory activity fee that could be used to facilitate extracurricular student political speech so long as the programs are neutral in its application.[a]

Scott Southworth, while a law student at the University of Wisconsin, believed that the university's mandatory fee was a violation of his First Amendment right to free speech. He, along with several other law students, objected that their fees went to fund liberal groups. They particularly objected to the support of eighteen of the 125 various groups on campus that benefited from the mandatory activity, including the Lesbian, Gay, Bisexual, and Transgender Center, the International Socialist Organization, and the campus women's center.[b]

In ruling against Southworth and for the university, the Court underscored the importance of universities being a forum for the free exchange of political and ideological ideas and perspectives. The Southworth case performed that function on the Wisconsin campus even before it was argued before the Supreme Court. A student-led effort called the Southworth Project, for which over a dozen law and journalism students each earned two credits, was begun to make sure that the case was reported on campus in an accurate and sophisticated way. The Southworth Project, said a political science professor, gave "a tremendous boost to the visibility and the thinking process about the case."[c] In essence, the case made the Constitution and what it means come alive on the Wisconsin campus as students pondered the effects of First Amendment protections on their ability to learn in a university atmosphere.

---

[a]*Board of Regents* v. *Southworth*, 529 U.S. 217 (2000).
[b]"U.S. Court Upholds Student Fees Going to Controversial Groups," *Toronto Star* (March 23, 2000), NEXIS.
[c]Mary Beth Marklein, "Fee Fight Proves a Learning Experience," *USA Today* (November 30, 1999): NEXIS.

---

say or print. Thus, over the years, the meaning of this amendment's mandate has been subject to thousands of cases seeking judicial interpretation of its meaning.

Attempts to Limit Speech

Although the Supreme Court has allowed few governmental bans on most types of speech, some forms of expression are not protected. In 1942, the Supreme Court set out the rationale by which it would distinguish between protected and unprotected speech. According to the Court, obscenity, lewdness, libel, and fighting words are not protected by the First Amendment because "such expressions are no essential part of any exposition of ideas, and are of such slight social value as a step to truth that any benefit that may be derived from them is clearly outweighed by the social interest in order and morality."[17]

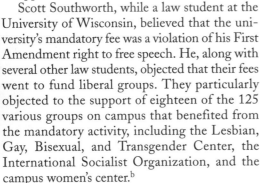

The Alien and Sedition Acts.   In 1798, soon after passage of the Bill of Rights, a constitutional crisis arose when the Federalist Congress enacted the Alien and Sedition Acts. Designed to ban any political criticism by the growing numbers of Jeffersonian Democratic-Republicans, these acts made publication of "any false, scandalous writing against the government of the United States" a criminal offense. Overtly partisan Federalist judges imposed fines and even jail terms on at least ten Democratic-Republican newspaper editors for allegedly violating the acts. The acts became a major issue in the 1800 presidential election campaign, which led to the election of Thomas Jefferson, a vocal opponent of the acts. He quickly pardoned all who had been convicted under their provisions, and the new Democratic-Republican Congress allowed the acts to expire before the Supreme Court had an opportunity to rule on the constitutionality of these serious infringements of the First Amendment.

Anti-Governmental Speech.   There were no more major national efforts to restrict freedom of speech and the press until congressional passage of the Espionage Act of 1917. Nearly 2,000 Americans were convicted of violating its various provisions, especially those that made it illegal to urge resistance to the draft and prohibiting the distribution of antiwar leaflets. In 1919, the Supreme Court interpreted the First Amendment to allow Congress to restrict speech that was "of such a nature as to create a clear and present danger that will bring about the substantive evils that Congress has a right to prevent."[18] Under the **clear and present danger test,** which allowed Congress to ban speech that could cause a clear and present danger to society, the circumstances surrounding the incident count, according to the Court. Antiwar leaflets, for example, may be permissible in peacetime, but they pose too much of a danger in wartime to be allowed.

For decades, the Supreme Court wrestled with what constituted a "danger." Finally, in 1969, the Court fashioned a new test for deciding whether certain kinds of speech could be regulated by the government: the **direct incitement test.** Now the government could punish the advocacy of illegal action only if "such advocacy is directed to inciting or producing imminent lawless action and is likely to incite or produce such action."[19] The requirement of "imminent harm" makes it more difficult for the government to punish speech and is consistent with the Framers' notion of the special role played by speech in a democratic society.

Obscenity and Pornography.   Technically, **obscenity** refers to those things considered "disgusting, foul or morally unhealthy." **Pornography,** in contrast, is often broader in meaning and generally refers to "depictions of sexual lewdness or erotic behavior." While distasteful to many, pornography is not necessarily obscene.[20] Throughout the 1950s and 1960s, the U.S. Supreme Court struggled to find a standard by which to judge whether actions or words were obscene and therefore could be suppressed by law. Some even argued that the Court's public

clear and present danger test
Test used by the Supreme Court to draw the line between protected and unprotected speech; the Court looks to see if there is an imminent danger that illegal action would occur in response to the contested speech.

direct incitement test
The advocacy of illegal action is protected by the First Amendment unless imminent action is intended and likely to occur.

obscenity
Those things considered disgusting or morally unhealthy.

pornography
Depictions of sexual lewdness or erotic behavior.

dilemma fostered the increase in the number of sexually oriented publications designed to appeal to those living amidst what many called the "sexual revolution."

Richard M. Nixon made the growth in pornography a major issue when he ran for president in 1968, and he pledged to appoint to federal judgeships only those who would uphold "law and order" and stop coddling criminals and purveyors of porn. Once elected president, Nixon made four appointments to the Court, including Chief Justice Warren Burger. Not surprisingly, then, in *Miller* v. *California* (1973), the Supreme Court began to formulate rules designed to make it easier for states to regulate obscene materials and to return to communities a greater role in determining what is obscene.[21]

In *Miller,* the Court set out a test that redefined obscenity. To determine whether or not material in question was obscene, the justices concluded that a lower court must ask "whether the work depicts or describes, in a patently offensive way, sexual conduct specifically defined by state law." Moreover, courts were to determine "whether the work, taken as a whole, lacks serious literary, artistic, political or scientific value." The decision also defined community standards to mean local, and not national, standards under the rationale that what is acceptable in New York City might not be tolerated in Peoria, Illinois.

Local community standards still may not be the sole criterion of obscenity. In 1974 the Court overturned a decision of a Georgia state court that found *Carnal Knowledge* (a movie starring Jack Nicholson that included scenes of a partially nude woman) obscene. The Court concluded that the scenes were neither "patently offensive" nor designed to appeal to what the Court termed "prurient interest."[22] As Justice Potter Stewart had once announced, he couldn't define obscenity, but "I know it when I see it."[23] He did not see it in *Carnal Knowledge.*

Time and contexts clearly have altered the Court's and, indeed, much of America's perceptions of what is obscene. *Carnal Knowledge* is now often shown on television on Saturday afternoons with only minor editing. But through the early 1990s, the Court allowed communities greater leeway in drafting statutes to deal with obscenity and, even more important, forms of non-obscene expression. In 1991, for example, the Supreme Court voted 5–4 to allow Indiana to ban totally nude erotic dancing, concluding that its statute did not violate the First Amendment's guarantee of freedom of expression and that it furthered an important or substantial governmental interest.[24]

While lawmakers have been fairly effective in restricting the sale and distribution of obscene materials, Congress has been particularly concerned with two obscenity and pornography issues: (1) federal funding for the arts and (2) the distributions of obscenity and pornography on the Internet that has "embroiled it in constitutional struggles over the proper balance between free expression and the interests of the majority."[25]

In 1990, concern over the use of federal dollars by the National Endowment for the Arts (NEA) for works with controversial religious or sexual themes led to passage of legislation requiring the NEA to "tak(e) into consideration general standards of decency and respect for the diverse beliefs and values of the American public" when it makes its annual awards. In a challenge brought by several performance artists, the Supreme Court ruled that decency standards could be considered by the arts funder as instructed by Congress.[26] (See Figure 4.1 for the chronology of this challenge.)

Congress recently turned to a more difficult task: monitoring the Internet, which some charge has become a vehicle for easy distribution of obscenity and pornography as well as a means for young children to be exposed to these kinds of materials. In 1996, Congress

FIGURE 4.1   Free Speech Challenge

1989

National Endowment for the Arts funding for exhibits that included Robert Mapplethorpe's homoerotic photographs and Andres C. Serrano's "Piss Christ" incite controversy in Congress over federal arts funding and freedom of expression.

1990

Congress adopts a bill instructing the NEA to take "into consideration general standards of decency and respect for the diverse beliefs and values of the American public" when awarding grants.

1991

Four performance artists, including Karen Finley, known for smearing chocolate on her nude body, challenge the new provision in a lawsuit, claiming it violates constitutional free speech and due process protections.

1992

A federal judge in Los Angeles strikes down the decency provision as unconstitutionally vague because it does not clearly define the type of art that would be prohibited.

1993

Part of the lawsuit is settled after the NEA agrees to give $252,000 to the artists who claimed their applications for grants were rejected.

1996

The U.S. Court of Appeals for the 9th Circuit agrees that the "general standards of decency" clause is unconstitutionally vague and adds that it impermissibly restricts artistic content and viewpoint.

1998

The U.S. Supreme Court reverses the 9th Circuit and rules that the government can consider whether a project meets general standards of decency.

Source: Adapted from "'Decency' Can Be Weighed in Arts Agency's Funding," by Joan Biskupic, *The Washington Post,* June 26, 1998, A18.

overwhelmingly passed the Telecommunications Reform Act of 1996. The Act maintained the same ban on obscene material that already applied to the media and criminalized the transmission of "indecent" speech or images to people younger than eighteen years of age. Indecency was defined as any communication that depicts or describes in patently offensive terms any sexual or excretory activities or organs as measured by contemporary community standards. This definition makes no exceptions for materials that have serious literary, artistic, scientific, or other redeeming social value as spelled out in *Miller* v. *California* (1973).

Supporters of the act believed that barring the distribution of certain materials to those under eighteen years of age would protect the act from constitutional challenge. Nevertheless, the act was immediately challenged by the American Civil Liberties Union (ACLU). The Supreme Court agreed with the ACLU in finding that Congress violated freedom of speech rights when it tried to limit pornography on the Internet.[27] To get around this Supreme Court ruling, Congress enacted the Child Online Protection Act in late 1998. It forced commercial Web site operators to collect a credit card number as proof of age before allowing access to any site that could be considered "harmful to minors" if the site lacked a screening device that could enable the material to be available only to adults. It also called for fines of up to $150,000 a day per offense as well as jail time. In June 2000, a federal appeals court ruled that the act, which had never been enforced, was unconstitutional. Pending appeals of this decision, many members of Congress are trying to find alternative solutions to this perceived problem, including proposals to cut off money to public libraries and schools that do not block children's access to Internet pornography.

Libel and Slander.   Today national tabloid newspapers such as the *National Enquirer* and the *Star* boast headlines that cause many just to shake their heads in disbelief. How can they get away with it, some may wonder. The Framers were very concerned that the press not be suppressed. The First Amendment works to allow all forms of speech, no matter how libelous. False or libelous statements are not restrained by the courts, yet the Supreme Court has consistently ruled that individuals or the press can be sued *after the fact* for untrue or libelous statements. **Libel** is a written statement that defames the character of a person. If the statement is spoken, it is **slander.** In many nations—such as Great Britain, for example—it is relatively easy to sue someone for libel. In the United States, however, the standards of proof are much more difficult. A person who believes that he or she has been a victim of libel, for example, must show that the statements made were untrue. Truth is an absolute defense against the charge of libel, no matter how painful or embarrassing the revelations.

libel
False statements or statements tending to call someone's reputation into disrepute.

slander
Untrue spoken statements that defame the character of a person.

It is often more difficult for individuals the Supreme Court considers to be "public persons or public officials" to sue for libel or slander. *New York Times Co. v. Sullivan* (1964) was the first major libel case considered by the Supreme Court.[28] An Alabama state court had found the *Times* guilty of libel for printing a full-page advertisement accusing Alabama officials of physically abusing African Americans during various civil rights protests (the ad was paid for by civil rights activists, including former First Lady Eleanor Roosevelt). The Supreme Court overturned the conviction, ruling that a finding of libel against a public official could stand only if there were a showing of "actual malice." Proof that the statements were false or negligent are not sufficient to prove "actual malice." In 1991, the Court directed lower courts to use the phrases "knowledge of falsity" and "reckless disregard of the truth" when giving instructions to juries in libel cases. This is often difficult to prove, which is why so few public officials or public persons have been able to win libel cases.

What Types of Speech Are Protected?

Not only will the Supreme Court not tolerate prior restraint of speech, but certain types of speech are protected, including symbolic speech.

Prior Restraint. With only a few exceptions, the Court has made it clear that it will not tolerate prior restraint of speech. In 1971, for example, in *New York Times Co. v. United States* (1971)[29] (also called the "Pentagon Papers" case), the Supreme Court ruled that the U.S. government could not block the publication of secret Defense Department documents illegally furnished to the *Times* by antiwar activists. In 1976, the Supreme Court went even further, noting that any attempt by the government to prevent expression carried "a 'heavy presumption' against its constitutionality."[30] In a Nebraska case, a trial court issued a "gag order" barring the press from reporting the lurid details of a crime. In balancing the defendant's constitutional right to a fair trial against the press's right to cover a story, the trial judge concluded that the defendant's right carried greater weight. The Supreme Court disagreed, holding the press's right to cover the trial paramount. Still, judges are often allowed to issue gag orders affecting parties to a lawsuit or to limit press coverage of a case.

Symbolic Speech. In addition to the general protection accorded pure speech, the Supreme Court has extended the reach of the First Amendment to other

New York Times Co. v. Sullivan **(1964)**
The Supreme Court ruled that "actual malice" must be proved to support a finding of libel against a public figure.

(Photo courtesy: Dana Summers/ © Tribune Media Services, Inc. All rights reserved. Reprinted with permission.)

symbolic speech
Symbols, signs, and other methods of expression generally also considered to be protected by the First Amendment.

means of expression often called **symbolic speech**—symbols, signs, and the like—as well as to activities like picketing, sit-ins, and demonstrations. The Supreme Court first acknowledged that symbolic speech was entitled to First Amendment protection in 1931.[31] More recently, the right of high school students to wear black armbands to protest the Vietnam War was upheld in 1969.[32]

Burning the American flag has also been held to be a form of protected symbolic speech. In 1989, a sharply divided Supreme Court (5–4) reversed the conviction of Gregory Johnson, who had been found guilty of setting fire to an American flag during the 1984 Republican national convention in *Texas* v. *Johnson*.[33] There was a major public outcry and a few years later President George Bush and numerous members of Congress called for a constitutional amendment to ban flag burning to overturn the decision.

Instead of a constitutional amendment, Congress passed the Federal Flag Protection Act of 1989. It authorized federal prosecution of anyone who intentionally desecrated a national flag. Those who originally had been arrested burned another flag and were convicted. Their conviction was again overturned by the Supreme Court. The justices again divided 5–4 in holding that the new federal law "suffered from the same fundamental flaw" as had the earlier state law that was declared in violation of the First Amendment.[34] Since that decision, Congress has tried several times to pass a constitutional amendment to allow it to ban flag burning. Those efforts, however, have yet to be successful.

VISUAL LITERACY
What Speech Is
Protected by
the Constitution?

THE RIGHT TO KEEP AND BEAR ARMS

During colonial times, the English tradition of distrust of standing armies was evident: Most colonies required all white men to keep and bear arms, and all white men in whole sections of the colonies were deputized to defend their settlements against Indians and other European powers. These local militias were viewed as the best way to keep order and liberty.

The Second Amendment was added to the Constitution to ensure that Congress could not pass laws to disarm state militias. This amendment appeased Anti-Federalists, who feared that the new Constitution would cause them to lose the right to "keep and bear arms" as well as an unstated right—the right to revolt against governmental tyranny.

WEB EXPLORATION
To learn more about
the gun control issue, see
www.ablongman.com/oconnor

Through the early 1920s, few state statutes were passed to regulate firearms (and generally these laws dealt with the possession of firearms by slaves). The Supreme Court's decision in *Barron* v. *Baltimore* (1833), which limited the application of the Bill of Rights to the actions of Congress alone, prevented federal review of those state laws.[35] Moreover, in *Dred Scott* v. *Sandford* (1857) (see chapter 3), Chief Justice Taney listed the right to own and carry arms as a basic right of citizenship.[36]

In 1934, Congress passed the National Firearms Act in response to the increase in organized crime that occurred in the 1920s and 1930s as a result of Prohibition. The Act imposed taxes on automatic weapons (such as machine guns) and sawed-off shotguns. In *United States* v. *Miller* (1939), a unanimous Court upheld the constitutionality of the Act by stating that the Second Amendment was intended to protect a citizen's right to own ordinary militia weapons and *not* unregistered sawed-off shotguns, which were at issue in the *Miller* case.[37] *Miller* was the last time the Supreme Court directly addressed the Second Amendment. In *Quilici* v. *Village of Morton Grove* (1983), the Supreme Court refused to review a lower court's ruling upholding the constitutionality of a local ordinance banning handguns against a Second Amendment challenge.[38]

In the aftermath of the assassination attempt on President Ronald Reagan in 1981, many lawmakers called for passage of gun control legislation. At the forefront of that effort was Sarah Brady, the wife of James Brady, the presidential press secretary who was badly wounded and left partially disabled by John Hinkley Jr., President Reagan's assailant. In 1993, her efforts helped to win passage of the so-called Brady Bill, which imposed a federal mandatory five-day waiting period on the purchase of handguns.

In 1994, in spite of extensive lobbying by the powerful National Rifle Association (NRA), Congress passed and President Clinton signed the $30.2-billion Violent Crime Control and Law Enforcement Act. In addition to providing money to states for new prisons and law enforcement officers, the act banned the manufacture, sale, transport, or possession of nineteen different kinds of semi-automatic assault weapons.

In 1997, a sharply divided 5–4 U.S. Supreme Court ruled that the section of the Brady Act requiring state officials to conduct background checks of prospective handgun owners violated principles of state sovereignty.[39] The background check provision, while important, is not critical to the overall goals of the Brady Act because a federal record-checking system went into effect in late 1998. School shootings in Littleton, Colorado, and Conyers, Georgia, heightened interest in gun control legislation.

The May 2000, Million Mom March was an attempt to highlight support for additional gun control measures. Celebrities including Rosie O'Donnell led the publicity campaign for the march, but by the November 2000 elections, gun control no longer appeared to be a key issue for many.

Rosie O'Donnell on stage at the "Million Mom March" May 14, 2000 in Washington, D.C. Tens of thousands of mothers, many accompanied by children and husbands, rallied in sight of the Capitol to demand strict control of handguns while memorializing loved ones and strangers killed by bullets. (Photo courtesy: Michael Smith/Liason/Newsmakers/OnlineUSA).

POINT/COUNTERPOINT

ZERO TOLERANCE VS. DUE PROCESS: IS ZERO TOLERANCE TOLERABLE?

Zero tolerance is a policy established under the Reagan administration that originally dealt with adults and drugs and expanded during the late 1980s to include children and drugs, as well as weapons violations and disciplinary infractions in schools. Proponents of the policy, such as police officers and the Drug Enforcement Agency, argue that the courts and prosecutors need additional power and prerogatives when dealing with the threat of drug usage and drug trafficking. Since drugs are often the cause of violence both at the societal and domestic level, powerful laws with no loopholes are needed to assure that drug kingpins and criminals are taken off the streets. Opponents of zero tolerance, such as the American Liberties Union (ACLU) and many Parent Teacher Associations (PTAs), argue that zero tolerance has taken away common sense and the discretion of judges and school administrators to look at extenuating circumstances and has led to some gross injustices and violations of civil liberties. Let's examine these points of view.

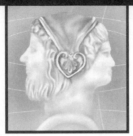

Because drugs are so often cited as the number one problem facing America, proponents of zero tolerance believe that drug use and trafficking are strongly related to violence and child abuse and constitute an enormous cost for society. The White House Office of Drug Policy promotes zero tolerance policies regarding the use of illegal drugs, alcohol, and tobacco within the family, school, workplace, and community. According to President Bill Clinton in his 1999 National Drug Control Strategy message to Congress, the threat of drugs costs our nation more than 14,000 lives and billions of dollars each year. In addition, since drug dealing is so lucrative, drug kingpins can afford the best lawyers. Zero tolerance laws make it easier to convict drug lords because there are no loopholes or room for negotiation—there is literally zero tolerance. Further, proponents argue this policy helps avoid litigation because it is evenhanded and cannot be manipulated by lawyers or judges. In essence, the problem of drugs is considered so severe that it merits special treatment.

In response to shootings in public schools, a 1994 federal law expanded zero tolerance to include guns in schools, while some districts adopted zero tolerance policies for sexual harassment as well. Proponents of zero tolerance argue

THE RIGHTS OF CRIMINAL DEFENDANTS AND THE CRIMINAL JUSTICE SYSTEM

due process rights
Procedural guarantees provided by the Fourth, Fifth, Sixth, and Eighth Amendments for those accused of crimes.

The Fourth, Fifth, Sixth, and Eighth Amendments provide a variety of procedural guarantees (often called **due process rights**) for those accused of crimes. Particular amendments, as well as other portions of the Constitution, specifically provide procedural guarantees to protect individuals accused of crimes at all stages of the criminal justice process. As is the case with the First Amendment, many of these rights have been interpreted by the Supreme Court to apply to the states. In interpreting the amendments dealing with what are fre-

that the safety of students in the public schools is paramount and the only way to get a handle on escalating school violence is through a virtually automatic policy: You get caught and the punishment is severe. Therefore, zero tolerance has a strong deterrent effect. The goal is to provide a safe learning environment for children in schools.

Opponents of zero tolerance argue that the policy allows no extenuating circumstances or common sense in drug and other cases. This policy allows the government to take away your property, search your car, and ignore your civil liberties, including the right to know the charges against you and the right to a hearing if drugs are suspected. There are countless stories about students being suspended or expelled from school for bringing a butter knife to school to cut brownies, having Midol in their backpack, and using water pistols. In one case, officials sought to suspend a six-year-old for kissing another child. Outside the classroom, there are numerous cases of the government confiscating large quantities of cash and luxury items such as yachts for the possession of an ounce of marijuana or for suspicion of a drug-related crime.

Those opposed to zero tolerance argue that our basic civil liberties, such as due process of law established in the Fourth, Fifth, and Fourteenth Amendments, are so fundamental that the threat of drugs and weapons should not cause these rights to be trampled. Zero tolerance also ignores the ideas of innocent until proven guilty and having the punishment fit the crime, while denying discretion and abdicating the responsibility of judges, school administrators, congressional representatives, and others. Opponents argue that lumping all possible cases together under a single rubric is mindless, thoughtless, unjust, and inflexible. It takes time to deal with problems on a case-by-case basis, but our personal liberties are so important that we must make time because if one innocent person is destroyed through a zero tolerance policy, all of our liberties are at stake. As Thomas Jefferson once said, "A society that will trade a little liberty for a little order will lose both, and deserve neither."

What do you think? Should we enforce zero tolerance or not?
Go to www.ablongman.com/oconnor

quently termed "criminal rights," the courts have to grapple not only with the meaning of the amendments, but also with how their protections are to be implemented.

The Fourth Amendment and Searches and Seizures

The Fourth Amendment to the Constitution declares:

> The right of the people to be secure in their persons, houses, papers, and effects, against unreasonable searches and seizures, shall not be violated, and no Warrants shall issue, but upon probable cause, supported by Oath or affirmation, and particularly describing the place to be searched, and the persons or things to be seized.

This amendment's purpose was to deny the national government the authority to make general searches. Over the years, in a number of decisions, the Supreme Court has interpreted the Fourth Amendment to allow the police to search:

1. The person arrested;
2. Things in plain view of the accused person; and
3. Places or things that the arrested person could touch or reach or are otherwise in the arrestee's "immediate control."

In 1995, the Court resolved a decades-old constitutional dispute by ruling unanimously that police must knock and announce their presence before entering a house or apartment to execute a search. But, said the Court, there may be "reasonable" exceptions to the rule to account for the likelihood of violence or the imminent destruction of evidence.[40]

Warrantless searches often occur if police suspect that someone is committing or is about to commit a crime. In these situations, police may "stop and frisk" the individual under suspicion. In 1989 the Court ruled that there need be only a "reasonable suspicion" for stopping a suspect—a much lower standard than "probable cause."[41] Thus, a suspected drug courier may be stopped for brief questioning, but only a frisk search (for weapons) is permitted. The answers to these questions may shift "reasonable suspicion" to "probable cause," thus permitting the officer to search. But except at international borders (or international airports), a *search* requires probable cause.

Searches can also be made without a warrant if consent is obtained, and the Court has ruled that consent can be given by a variety of persons. It has ruled, for example, that police can search a bedroom occupied by two persons as long as they have the consent of one of them.[42]

In situations where no arrest occurs, police must obtain search warrants from a "neutral and detached magistrate" prior to conducting more extensive searches of houses, cars, offices, or any other place where an individual would reasonably have some expectation of privacy.[43] Police can't get search warrants, for example, to require you to undergo surgery to remove a bullet that might be used to incriminate you, since your expectation of bodily privacy outweighs the need for evidence.[44] But courts don't require search warrants in possible drunk driving situations. Thus, the police can require you to take a Breathalyzer test to determine whether you have been drinking in excess of legal limits.[45]

Homes, too, are presumed to be private. Firefighters can enter your home to fight a fire without a warrant. But if they decide to investigate the cause of the fire, they must obtain a warrant before their reentry.[46] In contrast, under the "open fields doctrine" first articulated by the Supreme Court in 1924, if you own a field, and even if you post "No Trespassing" signs, the police can search your field without a warrant to see if you are illegally growing marijuana because you cannot reasonably expect privacy in an open field.[47]

Cars have proven problematic for police and the courts because of their mobile nature. As noted by Chief Justice William Howard Taft as early as 1925, "the vehicle can quickly be moved out of the locality or jurisdiction in which the warrant must be sought."[48] Over the years, the Court has become increasingly lenient about the scope of automobile searches. Today, even the belongings of automobile passengers can be searched without probable cause.

Testing for drugs has become an especially thorny search-and-seizure issue. If the government can require you to take a Breathalyzer test, can it require you to be tested for drugs? In the wake of growing public concern over drug use, in 1986 President Ronald Reagan signed an executive order requiring many federal employees to undergo drug tests. In 1997, Congress passed a similar law authorizing random drug searches of all congressional employees, but the U.S. Supreme Court refused to allow Georgia to require all candidates for state office to pass a urinalysis drug test thirty days before qualifying for nomination or election, concluding that its law violated the search and seizure clause.[49]

While many private employers and professional athletic organizations routinely require drug tests upon application or as a condition of employment, governmental requirements present constitutional questions about the scope of permissible searches and seizures. In 1989, the Supreme Court ruled that mandatory drug and alcohol testing of employees involved in accidents was constitutional.[50] In 1995, the Court upheld the constitutionality of random drug testing of public high school athletes.[51]

In general, all employers can require pre-employment drug screening. Since the Supreme Court has ruled that drug tests are "searches" for the purposes of the Fourth Amendment, public employees enjoy more protection in this area than do employees of private enterprises.[52]

The Fifth Amendment and Self-Incrimination

The Fifth Amendment provides that "No person shall be . . . compelled in any criminal case to be a witness against himself." "Taking the Fifth" is shorthand for exercising one's constitutional right not to self-incriminate. The Supreme Court has interpreted this guarantee to be "as broad as the mischief against which it seeks to guard,"[53] finding that criminal defendants do not have to take the stand at trial to answer questions, nor can a judge make mention of their failure to do so as evidence of guilt. Moreover, lawyers cannot imply that a defendant who refuses to take the stand must be guilty or have something to hide.

Use of "Voluntary" Confessions. The right not to incriminate oneself also means that prosecutors cannot use as evidence in a trial any of a

Even though Ernesto Miranda's confession was not admitted as evidence at his retrial, his ex-girlfriend's testimony and that of the victim were enough to convince the jury of his guilt. He served nine years in prison before he was released on parole. After his release, he routinely sold autographed cards inscribed with the Miranda rights now read to all suspects. In 1976, four years after his release, Miranda was stabbed to death in Phoenix in a bar fight during a card game. Two Miranda cards were found on his body, and the person who killed him was read his Miranda rights upon his arrest. (Photo courtesy: Paul S. Howell/Liaison Agency/Getty Source)

***Miranda* v. *Arizona* (1966)**
The Fifth Amendment requires that individuals arrested for a crime must be advised of their right to remain silent and to have counsel present.

defendant's statements or confessions that were not "voluntary." Police often would beat defendants to obtain their confessions. In 1936, however, the Supreme Court ruled convictions for murder based solely on confessions given after physical beatings were unconstitutional.[54] Police then began to resort to other measures to force confessions. Defendants, for example, were questioned for hours on end with no sleep or food, or threatened with physical violence until they were mentally "beaten" into a confession.

Miranda v. *Arizona* (1966) was the Supreme Court's response to these creative efforts to obtain confessions that were not truly voluntary. On March 3, 1963, an eighteen-year-old girl was kidnapped and raped on the outskirts of Phoenix, Arizona. Ten days later police arrested Ernesto Miranda, a poor, mentally disturbed man with a ninth-grade education. In a police station lineup, the victim identified Miranda as her attacker. Police then took Miranda to a separate room and questioned him for two hours. At first he denied guilt. Eventually, however, he confessed to the crime and wrote and signed a brief statement describing the crime and admitting his guilt. At no time was he told that he did not have to answer any questions or that he could be represented by an attorney.

After Miranda's conviction, his case was appealed on the ground that his Fifth Amendment right not to incriminate himself had been violated because his confession had been coerced. Writing for the Court, Chief Justice Earl Warren, himself a former district attorney and California state attorney general, noted that because police have a tremendous advantage in any interrogation situation, criminal suspects must be given greater protection. A confession obtained in the manner of Miranda's was not truly voluntary; thus it was inadmissible at trial. Later, Miranda was given a new trial and convicted again.

To provide guidelines for police to implement *Miranda*, the Court mandated that:

> Prior to any questioning, the person must be warned that he has a right to remain silent, that any statements he does make may be used as evidence against him, and that he has a right to the presence of an attorney, either retained or appointed.[55]

In response to this mandate from the Court, police routinely began to read suspects their Miranda rights, a practice you undoubtedly have seen repeated over and over in movies and TV police dramas.

The Rehnquist Court has been more tolerant of the use of coerced confessions and has employed a much more flexible standard to allow their admissibility. In 1991, for example, it ruled that the use of a coerced confession in a criminal trial does not automatically invalidate a conviction if its admission is deemed a "harmless error"; that is, if the other evidence is sufficient to convict.[56] But in 2000, in an opinion written by Chief Justice Rehnquist, the Court reaffirmed the central holding of *Miranda,* ruling that defendants must be read *Miranda* warnings. The Court went on to say, that despite an act of Congress that stipulated that voluntary statements made during custodial interrogations were admissible at trial, without *Miranda* warnings, no admissions could be trusted to be truly voluntary.[57]

The Exclusionary Rule.   The **exclusionary rule,** enunciated by the Supreme Court in 1914, bars the use of illegally seized evidence at trial. Thus, although the Fourth and Fifth Amendments do not prohibit the use of evidence obtained in violation of their provisions, the exclusionary rule is a judicially created remedy to deter constitutional violations.[58]

exclusionary rule
Judicially created rule that prohibits police from using illegally seized evidence at trial.

The Burger and Rehnquist Courts and more recently Congress, however, have chipped away at the exclusionary rule. Since 1976, the Court has carved out a variety of limited "good faith exceptions" to the exclusionary rule. The Court has allowed the use of "tainted" evidence in a variety of situations, especially when police have a search warrant and conduct the search "in good faith" on the assumption that the warrant is valid—even if it is subsequently found invalid. Since the purpose of the exclusionary rule is to deter police misconduct, and in this situation there is no police misconduct, the courts have permitted the introduction of the seized evidence at trial.

SIMULATION
You Are the
Police Officer

The Sixth Amendment and the Right to Counsel

The Sixth Amendment guarantees to an accused person "the Assistance of Counsel in his defense." In the past this provision meant only that an individual could hire an attorney to represent him or her in court. Since most criminal defendants are poor, this provision was of little assistance to many who found themselves on trial. Recognizing this, Congress required federal courts to provide attorneys for defendants too poor to afford one. This was first required in capital cases (where the death penalty is a possibility); eventually, attorneys were provided to the poor in all federal criminal cases.[59]

The Supreme Court also began to expand the right to counsel to state offenses, but did so in a piecemeal fashion that gave the states little direction. Given the high cost of providing legal counsel, this ambiguity often made it cost-effective for the states not to provide counsel at all.

These ambiguities came to an end with the Court's decision in *Gideon* v. *Wainwright* (1963).[60] Writing for a unanimous Court, Justice Hugo Black explained that "lawyers in criminal courts are necessities, not luxuries." Therefore, the Court concluded, the state must provide an attorney to poor defendants in felony cases. Underscoring the Court's point, Gideon was acquitted when he was retried with a lawyer to argue his case.

The Sixth Amendment and Jury Trials

The Sixth Amendment (and, to a lesser extent, Article III of the Constitution) provides that a person accused of a crime shall enjoy the right to a speedy and public trial by an impartial jury—that is, a trial in which a group of the accused's peers act as a fact-finding, deliberative body to determine guilt or innocence. It also provides defendants the right to confront witnesses against them. The Supreme Court has held that jury trials must be available if a prison sentence of six or more months is possible.

"Impartiality" is a requirement of jury trials that has undergone significant change, with the method of selecting jurors being the most frequently challenged part of the process. For example, whereas potential individual jurors who have prejudged a case are not eligible to serve, no groups can be systematically excluded from serving. In 1880, for example, the Supreme Court ruled that African Americans could not be excluded from state jury pools (lists of those eligible to serve).[61] And in 1975, the Court ruled that to bar women from jury service violated the mandate that juries be a "fair cross section" of the community.[62]

In the 1980s, the Court expanded the requirement that juries reflect the community by invalidating various indirect means of excluding African Americans. While noting that although lawyers historically had used peremptory challenges to select juries they believed most favorable to the outcome they desired, the use of peremptory challenges specifically to exclude African American jurors violated the equal protection clause of the Fourteenth Amendment.[63] In 1994, the Supreme Court answered the major remaining unanswered question about jury selection: Can lawyers exclude women from juries through their use of peremptory challenges? This question came up frequently because in rape trials and sex discrimination cases, one side or another often finds it advantageous to select jurors on the basis of their sex. The Supreme Court ruled that the equal protection clause prohibits discrimination in jury selection on the basis of gender. Thus, lawyers cannot strike all potential male jurors based on the belief that males might be more sympathetic to the arguments of a man charged in a paternity suit, a rape trial, or a domestic violence suit, for example.

The right to confront witnesses at trial is also protected by the Sixth Amendment. In 1990, however, the Supreme Court ruled that this right was not absolute. In *Maryland* v. *Craig* (1990), the Court ruled that the testimony of a six-year-old alleged child abuse victim via one-way closed circuit television was constitutionally permissible. The clause's central purpose, said the Court, was to ensure the reliability of testimony by subjecting it to rigorous examination in an adversary proceeding.[64] In this case, the child was questioned out of the presence of the defendant, who was in communication with his attorney. The defendant, along with the judge and jury, watched the testimony.

The Eighth Amendment and Cruel and Unusual Punishment

The Eighth Amendment prohibits "cruel and unusual punishments," a concept rooted in the English common-law tradition. In the 1500s, religious heretics and those critical of the Crown were subjected to torture to extract confessions, and then were condemned to an equally hideous death by the rack, disembowelment, or other barbarous means. The English Bill of Rights and its safeguard against "cruel and unusual punishments" was a result of public outrage against those practices. The same language found its way into the U.S. Bill of Rights. Prior to the 1960s, however, little judicial attention was paid to the meaning of that phrase, especially in the context of the death penalty.

In the 1960s, the National Association for the Advancement of Colored People (NAACP) Legal Defense Fund, believing that the death penalty was applied more frequently to African Americans than to members of other groups, orchestrated a carefully designed legal attack on its constitutionality.[65] In *Furman* v. *Georgia* (1972), the Supreme Court effectively put an end to capital punishment, at least in the short run.[66] The Court ruled that because the death penalty was often imposed in an arbitrary manner, it constituted cruel and unusual punishment in violation of the Eighth and Fourteenth Amendments.

Following *Furman,* several state legislatures enacted new laws designed to meet the Court's objections to the arbitrary nature of the sentence. In 1976 in *Gregg* v. *Georgia,* Georgia's rewritten death penalty statute was ruled constitutional by the Supreme Court in a 7–2 decision.[67] Unless the perpetrator of a crime was fifteen years old or younger at the time of the crime, the Supreme Court is currently unwilling to intervene to overrule a state court's imposition of the death penalty even when it appears to discriminate against African Americans.[68] By 2000, executions were commonplace in the United States, as underscored in Politics Now: DNA and the Death Penalty.

ANALYZING THE DATA

CAPITAL PUNISHMENT IN THE UNITED STATES

Since capital punishment was reinstated in 1976, over 650 people have been executed, mostly by lethal injection or electrocution. More than half of the accused (55 percent) were white, over a third (36 percent) were black, and almost a tenth were Latino, Native American, or Asian American. Today, over 3,600 inmates are sitting on death row. Of those inmates, 46.2 percent are white, 42.7 percent black, 8.9 percent Latino, 1.2 percent Native American, and 0.8 percent Asian American. The death-row population is overwhelmingly male, with females only accounting for 1.4 percent of inmates awaiting execution. It is also disproportionately African American. Seven states (New Mexico, Kansas, South Dakota, New York, New Hampshire, New Jersey, and Connecticut) have the death penalty but have had no executions.

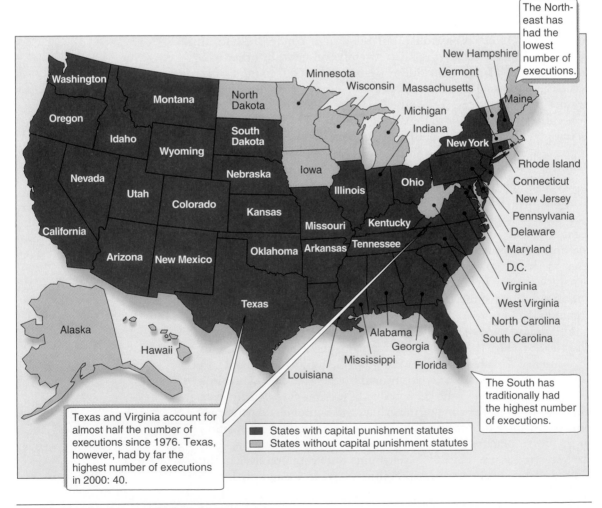

The Northeast has had the lowest number of executions.

Texas and Virginia account for almost half the number of executions since 1976. Texas, however, had by far the highest number of executions in 2000: 40.

The South has traditionally had the highest number of executions.

■ States with capital punishment statutes
□ States without capital punishment statutes

Source: Based on data from www.deathpenalty.org.

POLITICS NOW

DNA AND THE DEATH PENALTY

On June 15, 2000, Paul Nuncio became the 134th prisoner put to death in Texas since Governor George W. Bush took office in 1995. Texas leads the nation in executions, as highlighted in Analyzing the Data: Capital Punishment in the United States, and Bush was questioned about this fact frequently during his presidential campaign. All during the 2000 campaign, study after study was released calling into question the appropriateness of the death penalty as administered. One study from Columbia University revealed that over two-thirds of all death sentences were overturned on appeal—most because of serious errors on the part of police officers, prosecutors, or low paid, often court-appointed defense attorneys.[a] The national average for overturned cases was 68 percent, and Kentucky led the nation with a 100 percent reversal rate.[b]

In March 2000, the Republican governor of Illinois, George Ryan, ordered a moratorium on all executions. Ryan, a death penalty proponent, was disturbed by new evidence collected by students at Northwestern University as part of a class project that led to the release of thirteen men in his state already on death row. The specter of presiding over an irreversible unjust punishment was just too much for Ryan. In May 2000, the New Hampshire state legislature voted to abolish the death penalty, but that action was vetoed by the state's Democratic governor, Jeanne Shaheen.

Public support for the death penalty—now at 66 percent—is down from its high of 80 percent in 1994, and is actually at its lowest point since 1978, when it was 62 percent.[c] Because DNA evidence now can be used as a double check on guilty verdicts, many are clamoring to allow all of those on death row the opportunity to prove their guilt or innocence once and for all, although some public officials are against this. As people are less worried about crime, and at the same time have greater doubts about the fairness of the criminal justice system in light of several well-publicized cases of inmates proved innocent by DNA evidence, even Republicans in Congress are concerned. Senator Orrin Hatch, for example, introduced legislation in 2000 that would expand an inmate's right to seek DNA testing even if the time for his or her appeals had already expired. Under the Hatch bill, convicts would need to prove that identification was a critical issue at their trial and that DNA results could prove their innocence.

[a]This feature draws heavily from Judy Keen, "Death Penalty Issue Looms over Bush Campaign," *USA Today* (June 16, 2000): 17A.
[b]"Error in Courts," *The New York Times* (June 12, 2000): A1.
[c]Fox Butterfield, "Death Sentences Being Overturned in 2 of 3 Appeals," *The New York Times* (June 12, 2000): A1.

THE RIGHT TO PRIVACY

To this point, the rights and freedoms we have discussed have been derived fairly directly from specific guarantees contained in the Bill of Rights. In contrast, the Supreme Court has also given protection to the rights not specifically enumerated in the Constitution or Bill of Rights.

privacy
The right to be left alone; a judicially created doctrine encompassing an individual's decision to use birth control or secure an abortion.

WEB EXPLORATION
For more on other privacy issues, see www.ablongman.com/oconnor

TIMELINE
The History of the Right to Privacy

The ACLU often has been at the forefront of efforts to expand constitutional protections of enumerated and nonenumerated rights.

There is no mention of a right to **privacy** in either the main body of the Constitution or the Bill of Rights. Nevertheless, as Justice William O. Douglas noted in 1965, the notion of privacy is "older than the Bill of Rights." It is questionable, however, whether the Framers would ever have considered birth control, surrogate motherhood, in vitro fertilization, or euthanasia, all defended under "right to privacy" claims, proper subjects of constitutional protection.

Although the Constitution is silent about the right to privacy, the Bill of Rights contains many indications that the Framers expected that some areas of life were "off limits" to governmental regulation. The right to freedom of religion guaranteed in the First Amendment implies the right to exercise private, personal beliefs. The guarantee against unreasonable searches and seizures contained in the Fourth Amendment similarly implies that persons are to be secure in their homes and should not fear that police will show up at their doorsteps without cause. As early as 1928, Justice Louis Brandeis hailed privacy as "the right to be left alone—the most comprehensive of rights and the right most valued by civilized men."[69] It was not until 1965, however, that the Court attempted to explain the origins of this right.

Birth Control

Today most Americans take access to many forms of birth control as a matter of course. This was not always the case. *Griswold* v. *Connecticut* (1965) involved a challenge to the constitutionality of an 1879 Connecticut law prohibiting the dissemination of information about or the sale of contraceptives.[70] In *Griswold,* seven justices decided that various portions of the Bill of Rights, including the First, Third, Fourth, Fifth, and Fourteenth Amendments, cast "penumbras" (unstated liberties on the fringes or in the shadow of more explicitly stated rights), thereby creating zones of privacy, including a married couple's right to plan a family. Thus, the Connecticut statute was ruled unconstitutional as a violation of marital privacy, a right the Court concluded could be read into the U.S. Constitution.

Later, the Court expanded the right of privacy to include the right of unmarried individuals to have access to contraceptives. "If the right of privacy means anything," wrote Justice William J. Brennan, "it is the right of the individual, married or single, to be free from unwarranted governmental intrusion into matters so fundamentally affecting a person as the decision to bear or beget a child."[71]

Abortion

In 1973, the Supreme Court handed down one of its most controversial decisions, *Roe* v. *Wade.*[72] Norma McCorvey was a pregnant, itiner-

Roe v. *Wade* **(1970)**
The Supreme Court found that a woman's right to an abortion was protected by the right to privacy that could be implied from specific guarantees found in the Bill of Rights and the Fourteenth Amendment.

ant circus worker. Unable to secure a legal abortion and frightened by the conditions she found when she sought an illegal, back-alley abortion, McCorvey turned to two young Texas lawyers who were looking for a plaintiff to bring a lawsuit to challenge Texas's restrictive statute, which allowed abortions only when they were necessary to save the life of the mother. McCorvey, who was unable to obtain a legal abortion, later gave birth and put the baby up for adoption. Nevertheless, she allowed her lawyers to proceed with the case using her as their plaintiff, under the pseudonym Jane Roe.

When the case finally came before the Supreme Court, Justice Harry A. Blackmun relied heavily on medical evidence to rule that the Texas law violated a woman's constitutionally guaranteed right to privacy, which he argued included her decision to terminate a pregnancy. Writing for the majority in *Roe* v. *Wade*, Blackmun divided pregnancy into three stages. In the first trimester, a woman's right to privacy gave her an absolute right (in consultation with her physician), free from state interference, to terminate her pregnancy. In the second trimester, the state's interest in the health of the mother gave it the right to regulate abortions—but only to protect the woman's health. Only in the third trimester—when the fetus becomes potentially viable—did the Court find that the state's interest in potential life outweighed the woman's privacy interests. Even in the third trimester, however, abortions to save the life or health of the mother were to be legal.

Roe v. *Wade* unleashed a torrent of political controversy. From the 1970s through the present, the right to an abortion and its constitutional underpinnings in the right to privacy have been under attack by well-organized anti-abortion groups. The Reagan and Bush administrations were strong advocates of the anti-abortion position, regularly urging the Court to overrule *Roe*. They came close to victory in *Webster* v. *Reproductive Health Services* (1989).[73] In *Webster*, the Court upheld state-required fetal viability tests in the second trimester, even though these tests would increase the cost of an abortion considerably. The Court also upheld Missouri's refusal to allow abortions to be performed in state-supported hospitals or by state-funded doctors or nurses. Perhaps most noteworthy, however, is the fact that four justices seemed willing to overrule *Roe* v. *Wade*.

After *Webster*, states began to enact more restrictive legislation. In the most important abortion case since *Roe*, *Planned Parenthood of Southeastern Pennsylvania* v. *Casey* (1992), Justices O'Connor, Anthony Kennedy, and David Souter, in a jointly authored opinion, wrote that Pennsylvania could limit abortions as long as its regulations did not pose "an undue burden" on pregnant women.[74]

While President Clinton attempted to shore up abortion rights through the appointment of pro-choice justices to the Supreme Court, the Republican Congress attempted to restrict abortion rights. There were nearly forty votes on reproductive choice taken in 1995, nearly double the next-highest year of anti-abortion legislative activity in

The anti-abortion group Operation Rescue has staged large-scale protests in front of abortion clinics across the nation. It now has a surprising new member—Norma McCorvey, the "Jane Roe" of *Roe* v. *Wade*, who announced in a 1995 press conference that she had become pro-life.
(Photo courtesy: Tim Sharp/AP/Wide World Photos)

WEB EXPLORATION
To compare different sides of the abortion debate, see www.ablongman.com/oconnor

POLICY IN ACTION

THE POLITICS OF RU-486

Many women wishing to have an abortion must travel very long distances—as much as 300 to 500 miles—to the closest provider. Once there, they often face a barrage of angry protestors and mandatory twenty-four-hour waiting periods before a physician can perform the procedure. Now, all of that may change. When the federal Food and Drug Administration (FDA) approved the abortion pill mifepristone, commonly called RU-486, a wide range of physicians became able to prescribe this new pill so long as the physician had some kind of surgical backup should the two-pill regime prove not effective. This policy decision could have far ranging effects on women's reproductive choices now guaranteed by the Constitution, particularly at a time when the number of hospitals, clinics, and physicians who perform abortions is on the decline (see Figure 4.2).

RU-486 has a long policy history. It was first used in Europe in 1982. It was approved for use in France in 1986 but soon thereafter was taken off the market by its manufacturer after protests from right-to-life activists. The French government, under pressure from women's rights groups, then ordered the manufacturer to bring it back on the market. In June 1989, the Bush administration issued a ban on the importing of RU-486 into the United States. Then, on his first day in office, Bill Clinton lifted the ban. In 1994, the French maker of the drug, at the urging of the Clinton administration, donated the patent for RU-486 to the Population Council. After several successful clinical trials, the Population Council filed a new drug application with the FDA and shortly thereafter licensed the distribution and manufacture to Danco Laboratories. Then, a manufacturer backed out of its agreement to make the drug. In 1996, a FDA committee recommended that RU-486 be approved, which the FDA finally did four years later. But, the Bush administration may attempt to reverse this policy and some members of Congress want to review the FDA's action.

Congress, 1977.[75] In fact, in 1996 and again in 1997, Congress passed and sent to President Clinton bills that for the first time would ban a specific procedure used in late-term abortions.[76] On both occasions the president vetoed the Partial Birth Abortion Act over strong pressure from right-to-life groups. (To learn more about the abortion controversy, see Policy in Action: The Politics of RU-486.) In 2000, the Supreme Court, however, ruled 5–4 that a Nebraska "partial birth" abortion statute was unconstitutionally vague and therefore unenforceable, calling into question the laws of twenty-nine other states with their own bans on late-term procedures.[77] At the same time, it ruled that a Colorado law that prohibited protestors from coming within eight feet of women entering clinics was unconstitutional.[78] This "bubble law" was designed to create an eight-foot buffer zone around women as they walked through protesters into a clinic to receive an abortion.

FIGURE 4.2 Abortion Providers

Clinic violence and a reenergized right to life movement have made it difficult for clinics to attract physicians to perform abortions.

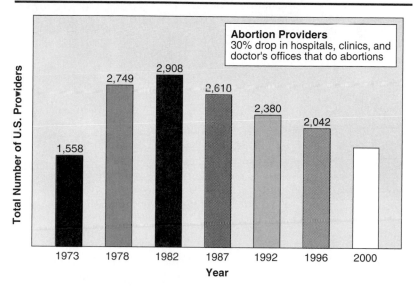

Abortion Providers
30% drop in hospitals, clinics, and doctor's offices that do abortions

Homosexuality

Although the Supreme Court has ruled that the right to privacy includes the right to decide whether "to bear or beget a child," it has declined to interpret the right of privacy to include the right to engage in homosexual acts. In 1985, the Court, in a 4–4 decision (Justice Powell was ill), upheld a lower-court decision that found unconstitutional an Oklahoma law allowing the dismissal of teachers who advocate homosexual relations.[79] The next year, when another case involving homosexual rights, *Bowers* v. *Hardwick* (1986), was argued before the Court, the lawyer representing Michael Hardwick pitched his arguments toward Justice Powell, who he believed would be the crucial swing vote in this controversial area.[80] Hardwick's lawyer argued against the constitutionality of a Georgia law prohibiting consensual heterosexual and homosexual oral or anal sex.

In a 5–4 decision, the Supreme Court upheld the law. At conference, Justice Powell reportedly seemed torn by the case. He believed that the twenty-year sentence that came with conviction was excessive, but he was troubled by the fact that Hardwick hadn't actually been (and never was) tried and convicted. Although he originally voted with the majority to overturn the law, Powell was bothered by the broadness of Justice Blackmun's original draft of the majority opinion. Thus he changed his mind and voted with the minority view to uphold the law, making it the new majority.[81] After his retirement, Justice Powell confessed that he was wrong in *Bowers* and should have voted to overturn the Georgia law.

While the Court has refused to expand the right to privacy to invalidate state laws that criminalize some aspects of homosexual behavior,

James Dale, a one-time Boy Scout leader who sued the organization after he was dismissed for being gay, talks to reporters following the Supreme Court's ruling allowing the Boy Scouts of America to deny entry of gays. A closely divided Court ruled that such a private group has the right to set its own moral code. (Photo courtesy: Archive Photos)

 WEB EXPLORATION
For more on gay rights, see www.ablongman.com/oconnor

in 1996 it ruled that a state could not deny rights to homosexuals simply because they are homosexuals. In *Romer* v. *Evans*, the Court ruled that the equal protection clause bars unreasonable state discrimination against homosexuals.[82] Privacy rights and First Amendment associational rights came into conflict in *Boy Scouts of America* v. *Dale*.[83] The Court ruled that the Boy Scouts could exclude gay men from serving as scoutmasters, a move that disheartened gay rights activists and caused many public groups to withdraw their support from the Boy Scouts.

The Right to Die

While the current Supreme Court is unlikely to expand the scope of the privacy doctrine to include greater protections for homosexuals in the near future, it is likely to continue to get more cases involving claims for personal autonomy. In 1990 the Supreme Court sided with the state against the privacy claims of the parents of Nancy Cruzan. She was a brain-injured woman living in a comatose state. Her parents sued to remove her feeding tube, and the Bush administration and numerous anti-abortion groups filed briefs supporting the state against the Cruzans.

Writing for a five-person majority, Chief Justice Rehnquist rejected any attempts to expand the right of privacy into this thorny area of social policy. The Court did, however, note that individuals could terminate medical treatment if they were able to express, or had done so in writing via a living will, their desire to have medical treatment terminated in the event they became incompetent.[84]

States, too, have entered into this arena. Even before the *Cruzan* case, the New Jersey Supreme Court allowed the parents of a comatose woman to withdraw her feeding tube.[85] More recently, in a different

FIGURE 4.3   Assisted Suicide Laws in the United States

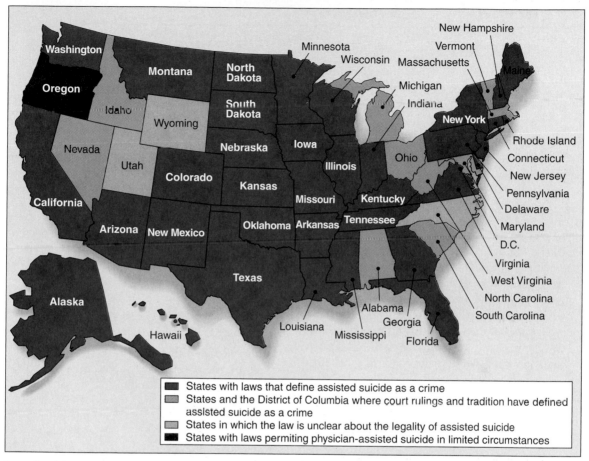

States with laws that define assisted suicide as a crime

States and the District of Columbia where court rulings and tradition have defined assisted suicide as a crime

States in which the law is unclear about the legality of assisted suicide

States with laws permiting physician-assisted suicide in limited circumstances

Source: Copyright 1997, *USA Today.* Reprinted with permission.

but related vein, states have legislated to prevent what is often called "assisted suicide." Jurors, however, often appear unwilling to find loved ones or even Dr. Kervorkian guilty of helping the terminally ill carry out the decision to take their own lives. In 1999, however, after being acquitted in four other trials, Dr. Jack Kervorkian represented himself and was found guilty by a Michigan jury of administering a lethal injection of chemicals to a fifty-two-year-old man. In 1997, the U.S. Supreme Court ruled unanimously that terminally ill persons do not have a constitutional right to physician-assisted suicide. The Court's action upheld the laws of New York and Washington State that make it a crime for doctors to give life-ending drugs to mentally competent but terminally ill patients who wish to die.[86] As revealed in Figure 4.3, state laws and practices concerning assisted suicide vary considerably.

WEB EXPLORATION
For more on the right to die movement, see www.ablongman.com/oconnor

Continuity & Change

Conceptions of Civil Liberties

When the new Constitution was adopted by the citizens in the states, it lacked a Bill of Rights. This absence was a glaring one in the eyes of many Americans. Their state constitutions often protected their civil liberties, and they feared that they already were giving up too many rights to an untested national government. So when the first Congress met in 1789, one of the first items on its agenda was the passage of a Bill of Rights to prevent the national government from infringing the liberties of the citizenry.

In the late 1700s, issues of political speech, freedom of the press, and the right to gather and petition the government were among the rights most cherished. After all, without these rights, the colonists never would have been able to organize and mobilize effectively enough to make the successful break with Great Britain.

Today, our conceptions of civil liberties, as well as their need for protection, are quite different. Poll after poll shows that if Americans were to vote on the Bill of Rights already contained in the Constitution, it would not garner enough votes in the states to be adopted. Over the years the role of the courts—especially the federal courts—in expanding the application of most of the Bill of Rights to the states, as well as in interpreting those provisions, has produced a panoply of rights never envisioned by the Framers. Moreover, the provisions of the Constitution and the Bill of Rights have been interpreted to protect a variety of rights, and liberties that are not explicitly stated, such as protections for criminal defendants, the right to privacy, and reproductive rights.

Just think about how Americans' conceptions of rights have evolved in 200 years. New technologies from cars (police searches) to telephones (wiretaps) to e-mail have created new laws dealing with issues of civil liberties. The development of the Internet will undoubtedly produce even more civil liberties issues than those already addressed by Congress dealing with pornography.

1. As it becomes easier and easier to get more and more information about all of us, what kind of civil liberties protections do you think the government should institute?
2. Conversely, in a Hobbesian sense, what kinds of practices and policies that curtail some rights, such as DNA testing, but may contribute to the betterment of life for the majority, should be permitted?

Cast Your Vote. Which civil liberties deserve protection? To cast your vote, go to **www.ablongman.com/oconnor**

SUMMARY

Most of the Framers originally opposed the Bill of Rights. Anti-Federalists, however, continued to stress the need for a Bill of Rights during the drive for ratification of the Constitution, and some states tried to make their ratification contingent on the addition of a Bill of Rights. During its first session, Congress sent the first ten amendments to the Constitution, the Bill of Rights, to the states for their ratification. Later, the addition of the Fourteenth Amendment allowed the Supreme Court to apply some of the amendments to the states through a process called selective incorporation.

The First Amendment guarantees freedom of religion. The establishment clause, which prohibits the national government from establishing a religion, does not, according to Supreme Court interpretation, create an absolute wall between church and state. While the national and state governments may generally not give direct aid to religious groups, many forms of aid, especially many that benefit children, have been held to be constitutionally permissible. In contrast, the Court has generally barred prayer in public schools. The Court generally has adopted an accommodationist approach when interpreting the free exercise clause by allowing some governmental regulation of religious practices.

The First Amendment also guarantees freedom of speech and of the press. By the twentieth century, several states, and later the national government, passed laws restricting freedoms of speech and of the press. These curtailments were upheld by the Court. Later, the Court used the more liberal direct incitement test, which required a stronger showing of imminent danger before speech could be restricted. The First Amendment also has been interpreted *not* to protect obscenity and some forms of pornography, as well as libel and slander.

Symbolic speech has been afforded the same protection as other forms of speech. Historically, the Supreme Court has disfavored any attempts at prior restraint of speech or press.

The Fourth, Fifth, Sixth, and Eighth Amendments provide a variety of procedural guarantees to individuals accused of crimes. In particular, the Fourth Amendment prohibits unreasonable searches and seizures, and the Court has generally refused to allow evidence seized in violation of this safeguard to be used at trial.

Among other rights, the Fifth Amendment guarantees that "no person shall be compelled to be a witness against himself." The Supreme Court has interpreted this provision to require that the government inform the accused of his or her right to remain silent. This provision has also been interpreted to require that illegally obtained confessions must be excluded at trial.

The Sixth Amendment's guarantee of "assistance of counsel" has been interpreted by the Supreme Court to require that the government provide counsel to defendants unable to pay for it in cases where prison sentences may be imposed. The Sixth Amendment also requires an impartial jury, although the meaning of impartial continues to evolve through judicial interpretation.

The Eighth Amendment's ban against "cruel and unusual punishments" has been held not to bar imposition of the death penalty.

The right to privacy is a judicially created right carved from the implications of several amendments, including the First, Third, Fourth, Fifth, and Fourteenth Amendments. Statutes limiting access to birth control and abortion rights have been ruled unconstitutional violations of the right to privacy. In contrast, the Supreme Court has not expanded the right to privacy to invalidate state statutes criminalizing homosexual acts. The right to privacy does not include the right to physician-assisted suicide, either. Nevertheless, few efforts have been made to alter the basic guarantees contained in the Bill of Rights.

KEY TERMS

civil liberties, p. 96
clear and present danger test, p. 105
direct incitement test, p. 105
due process clause, p. 98
due process rights, 112
establishment clause, p. 99

exclusionary rule, p. 117
free exercise clause, p. 99
incorporation doctrine, p. 98
libel, p. 108
Miranda v. *Arizona*, p. 116
New York Times Co. v. *Sullivan*, p. 109

obscenity, p. 105
pornography, p. 105
prior restraint, p. 103
privacy, p. 122
Roe v. *Wade*, p. 122
slander, p. 108
symbolic speech, p. 110

SELECTED READINGS

Abraham, Henry J., and Barbara A. Perry. *Freedom and the Court: Civil Rights and Civil Liberties in the United States.* 7th ed. New York: Oxford University Press, 1998.

Fiss, Owen M. *The Irony of Free Speech.* Cambridge, Mass.: Harvard University Press, 1996.

Friendly, Fred W. *Minnesota Rag: The Dramatic Story of the Landmark Case That Gave New Meaning to Freedom of the Press.* New York: Random House, 1981.

Gates, Henry Louis Jr., ed. *Speaking of Race, Speaking of Sex: Hate Speech, Civil Rights, and Civil Liberties.* New York: New York University Press, 1995.

Greenawalt, Kent. *Fighting Words: Individuals, Communities, and Liberties of Speech.* Princeton, N.J.: Princeton University Press, 1995.

Lewis, Anthony. *Gideon's Trumpet* (reissue edition). New York: Vintage Books, 1989.

———. *Make No Law: The Sullivan Case and the First Amendment.* New York: Random House, 1991.

Manwaring, David R. *Render Unto Caesar: The Flag Salute Controversy.* Chicago: University of Chicago Press, 1962.

O'Brien, David M. *Constitutional Law and Politics, Vol. 2: Civil Rights and Civil Liberties.* 3rd ed. New York: Norton, 1997.

O'Connor, Karen. *No Neutral Ground: Abortion Politics in an Age of Absolutes.* Boulder, Colo.: Westview Press, 1996.

Perry, Barbara A. *In the Name of Hate: Understanding Hate Crimes.* New York: Routledge, 2001.

Regan, Priscilla M. *Legislating Privacy: Technology, Social Values, and Public Policy.* Chapel Hill: University of North Carolina Press, 1995.

Weddington, Sarah. *A Question of Choice.* New York: Grosset/Putnam, 1993.

(Photo courtesy: Ron Thomas/AP/Wide World Photos)

Civil Rights

5

On February 4, 1999, just as Amadou Diallo, a twenty-two-year-old unarmed African immigrant, stood in the vestibule of his apartment building in the Bronx, four white plainclothes police officers opened fire on him, eventually firing forty-one shots. He died at the scene.[1] There were no witnesses. The four officers, who were eventually charged with second degree murder, were members of New York City's Street Crimes Unit, which was created by the mayor in the early 1990s to help lower the city's crime rate. Known to have targeted black citizens, the unit admits to stopping and searching as many as 225,000 citizens since its creation.[2]

New York City's frightened minority community, African Americans and new immigrants alike, along with liberal activists and everyday citizens turned their anger on city police and Mayor Rudolph Giuliani, who they believe have used overly aggressive, and often racially biased, techniques to reduce crime. In the months after the shooting, citizens from all walks of life—from actress Susan Sarandon to street cleaners—protested at City Hall, and even marched from the federal courthouse over the Brooklyn Bridge into Manhattan, an action reminiscent of many 1960s civil rights marches. Over 1,500 protesters were arrested at one demonstration, the largest New York City had seen in twenty-five years.[3] Eventually all four officers charged in this incident were acquitted at trial.

In the 1980s, crime in the United States, and in particular New York City, was out of control, and Americans demanded that their governments do something about it. Governments at all levels responded with more police and more prisons. Now that crime is on the wane, however, and no longer even on Americans' list of top ten concerns, ordinary citizens are asking the question that troubled John Locke and Thomas Hobbes over three centuries ago: How much liberty should you give up to the government in

Chapter Outline

- Slavery, Abolition, and Winning the Right to Vote, 1800–1885
- The Push for Equality, 1889–1954
- The Civil Rights Movement
- Other Groups Mobilize for Rights

return for safety? In the Diallo case, and many others, it is clear that black Americans, whether native or foreign born, are being targeted for civil rights deprivations at far higher rates than other identifiable groups. In 1999, for example, it was discovered that 40 percent of those strip searched at the Chicago airport by U.S. Customs officials were African American women.[4] In New Jersey and other states, alleged use by state troopers of what is called racial profiling to stop black drivers is under legal challenge.[5] Black college students recently filed suit when they were forced to pay higher room rates than white students in Daytona Beach during spring break.[6]

The Declaration of Independence, written in 1776, boldly proclaims: "We hold these truths to be self-evident, that all men are created equal, that they are endowed by their Creator with certain inalienable rights." The Constitution, written eleven years later, is silent on the concept of equality. Only through constitutional amendment and Supreme Court definition and redefinition of the rights contained in that document have Americans come close to attaining equal rights. Still, as our opening vignette highlights, some citizens have yet to experience full equality and the full enjoyment of civil rights many Americans take for granted.

civil rights

Refers to the positive acts governments take to protect individuals against arbitrary or discriminatory treatment by governments or individuals based on categories such as race, sex, national origin, age, or sexual orientation.

The term **civil rights** refers to the positive acts governments take to protect individuals against arbitrary or discriminatory treatment by governments or individuals. The Framers considered some civil rights issues. But, as James Madison reflected in *Federalist No. 42*, one entire class of citizens—slaves—were treated in the new Constitution more like property than like people. Delegates to the Constitutional Convention put political expediency before the immorality of slavery and basic civil rights. Moreover, the Constitution considered white women full citizens for purposes of determining state population, but voting qualifications were left to the states. Only New Jersey allowed women to vote at the time the Constitution was ratified.

Since the Constitution was written, concepts of civil rights have changed dramatically. The addition of the Fourteenth Amendment, one of three amendments ratified after the Civil War, introduced the notion of equality into the Constitution by specifying that states could not deny "any person within its jurisdiction equal protection of the laws." The Fourteenth Amendment has generated more litigation to determine and specify its meaning than any other provision of the Constitution. Within a few years of its ratification, women—and later, African Americans and other minorities and disadvantaged groups—took to the courts to seek expanded civil rights in all walks of life. But the struggle to augment rights was not limited to the courts. Public protest, civil disobedience, legislative lobbying, and appeals to public opinion have all been part of the arsenal of those seeking equality. The Diallo case incorporates all of those actions. Ordinary citizens and celebrities took to the

WEB EXPLORATION
For more on civil rights generally, see www.ablongman.com/oconnor

streets, legislators held hearings, police officers were put on trial, and the media reported it all.

Since passage of the Civil War amendments (1865–1870), there has been a fairly consistent pattern of the expansion of civil rights to more and more groups. In this chapter we explore how notions of equality and civil rights have changed in this country. To do so we discuss slavery, its abolition, and the achievement of voting rights for African Americans and women. We examine the evolution of African American rights and women's rights in tandem to appreciate how each group has drawn ideas, support, and success from the other. Throughout this chapter we discuss their parallel developments as well as those of other historically disadvantaged political groups.

SLAVERY, ABOLITION, AND WINNING THE RIGHT TO VOTE, 1800–1885

Ever since the first Africans were brought to the New World in 1619, slavery was a divisive issue. Congress banned the slave trade in 1808, after the expiration of the twenty-year period specified by the Constitution. But after the invention of the cotton gin, which separated seeds from cotton very quickly, the South became even more dependent on agriculture and cheap slave labor as its economic base. At the same time, technological advances were turning the Northern states into an increasingly industrialized region, which intensified the cultural and political differences and animosity between North and South.

As the nation grew westward, conflicts between Northern and Southern states intensified over the admission of new states to the Union with "free" or "slave" status. The first major crisis occurred in 1820, when the territory of Missouri applied for admission to the Union as a "slave state"—that is, one in which slavery would be legal. Missouri's admission would have weighted the Senate in favor of slavery and was therefore opposed by Northern senators. The resultant Missouri Compromise of 1820 allowed the admission of Missouri as a slave state, along with the admission of Maine (formed out of the territory of Massachusetts with the permission of Congress and Massachusetts) as a free state. Other compromises concerning slavery were eventually necessitated as the nation continued to grow and new states were added to the Union.

The Abolitionist Movement: The First Civil Rights Movement

The compromise of 1820 solidified the South in its determination to keep slavery legal, but it also fueled the fervor of those who opposed slavery. The abolitionist movement, however, might have fizzled had it not been for William Lloyd Garrison, a white New England newspaper

WEB EXPLORATION
For more information on abolition, the American Anti-Slavery Society, and its leaders, see www.ablongman.com/oconnor

editor, who founded the American Anti-Slavery Society in 1833; by 1838 it had more than 250,000 members.

The Women's Rights Tie-in.   Slavery was not the only practice that people began to question in the decades following adoption of the Constitution. In 1840, for example, Elizabeth Cady Stanton and Lucretia Mott, who were to found the women's movement, attended the meeting of the World's Anti-Slavery Society in London with their husbands. Not allowed to participate because they were women, they sat in the balcony apart from the male delegates and compared their status to the slaves they sought to free. Believing that women were not much better off than slaves, they resolved to call the first women's rights convention.

They finally held such a convention in Seneca Falls, New York, in 1848. The 300 people who attended passed resolutions calling for the abolition of legal, economic, and social discrimination against women. All of the resolutions reflected the attendees' dissatisfaction with contemporary moral codes, divorce and criminal laws, and the limited opportunities for women in education, the church, and in medicine, law, and politics. Only the call to extend the franchise—the legal right to vote—to women failed to win unanimous approval. Most who attended the Seneca Falls meeting continued to press for women's rights along with the abolition of slavery.

The 1850s: The Calm Before the Storm.   By 1850 much was changing in America—the Gold Rush had spurred westward migration, cities grew as people were lured from their farms, railroads and the telegraph increased mobility and communication, and immigrants flooded into the United States. Reformers called for change, the women's movement gained momentum, and slavery continued to tear the nation apart. Harriet Beecher Stowe's *Uncle Tom's Cabin*, a novel that showed the evils of slavery by depicting a slave family torn apart, further inflamed the country. *Uncle Tom's Cabin* sold more than 300,000 copies in a single year, 1852.

The tremendous national reaction to Stowe's work, which later prompted Abraham Lincoln to call Stowe "the little woman who started the big war," had not yet faded when a new controversy over the 1820 Missouri Compromise became the lightning rod for the first major civil rights case to be addressed by the U.S. Supreme Court. In *Dred Scott* v. *Sandford* (1857), the Supreme Court bluntly ruled the 1820 Missouri Compromise unconstitutional, further finding that slaves were not U.S. citizens and therefore could not bring suits in federal court.

The Civil War and Its Aftermath: Civil Rights Laws and Constitutional Amendments

The Civil War had many causes, but slavery was clearly the key issue. During the war (1861–1865), abolitionists kept up their antislavery pressure. They were rewarded when President Abraham Lincoln issued the Emancipation Proclamation, which provided that all slaves in states still in active rebellion against the United States would automatically be freed on January 1, 1863. Designed as a measure to gain favor for the war in the North, the Emancipation Proclamation did not free all slaves—it freed only those who lived in the Confederacy. Complete abolition of slavery did not occur until congressional passage and ultimate ratification of the Thirteenth Amendment in 1865.

The Civil War Amendments.   The **Thirteenth Amendment** was the first of the three so-called Civil War amendments. It banned all forms of "slavery [and] involuntary servitude." Although Southern states were required to ratify the Thirteenth Amendment as a condition of their readmission to the Union after the war, most of the former Confederate states quickly passed laws that were designed to restrict opportunities for newly freed slaves. These Black Codes prohibited African Americans from voting, sitting on juries, or even appearing in public places. Although Black Codes differed from state to state, all empowered local law-enforcement officials to arrest unemployed blacks, fine them for vagrancy, and hire them out to employers to satisfy their fines. Some state codes went so far as to require African Americans to work on plantations or to be domestics.

The outraged Reconstructionist Congress enacted the Civil Rights Act of 1866 to invalidate some state Black Codes. President Andrew Johnson vetoed the legislation, but—for the first time in history—Congress overrode a presidential veto. The Civil Rights Act formally made African Americans citizens of the United States and gave the Congress and the federal courts the power to intervene when states attempted to restrict male African American citizenship rights in matters such as voting. Congress reasoned that African Americans were unlikely to fare well if they had to file discrimination complaints in state courts, where judges were elected. Passage of a federal law allowed African Americans to challenge discriminatory state practices in the federal courts, where judges were appointed by the president.

Because controversy remained over the constitutionality of the act (since the Constitution gives states the right to determine qualifications of voters), the **Fourteenth Amendment** was proposed simultaneously with the Civil Rights Act to guarantee, among other things, citizenship to all freed slaves. Other key provisions of the Fourteenth Amendment barred states from abridging "the privileges or immunities of citizenship" or depriving "any person of life, liberty, or property without due process of law."

Unlike the Thirteenth Amendment, which had near-unanimous support in the North, the Fourteenth Amendment (which specifically added the word "male" to the Constitution for the first time) was opposed by many women who argued against passage of any new amendment that would extend suffrage to black males and not to women.

In spite of sentiments like these, the **Fifteenth Amendment** was also passed by Congress in February 1869. It guaranteed the "right of

Thirteenth Amendment
One of the three Civil War amendments; specifically bans slavery in the United States.

Fourteenth Amendment
One of the three Civil War amendments; guarantees equal protection and due process of the law to all U.S. citizens.

Fifteenth Amendment
One of the three Civil War amendments; specifically enfranchised black males.

citizens" to vote regardless of their "race, color or previous condition of servitude." Again, sex was not mentioned.

Women's rights activists were shocked. Abolitionists' continued support of the Fifteenth Amendment, which was ratified by the states in 1870, prompted many women's rights supporters to leave the abolition movement to work solely for the cause of women's rights. Twice burned, women's rights leaders including Susan B. Anthony and Elizabeth Cady Stanton decided to form their own organization, the National Woman Suffrage Association (NWSA), to achieve that goal. In spite of NWSA's opposition, however, the Fifteenth Amendment was ratified by the states in 1870.

Civil Rights and the Supreme Court

Congress was clear in its wishes that the rights of African Americans be expanded and that the Black Codes be rendered illegal. The Supreme Court, however, was not nearly so protective of those rights under the Civil War amendments. In the first two tests of the scope of the Fourteenth Amendment, the Supreme Court ruled that the citizenship rights guaranteed by the amendment applied only to rights of national citizenship and not to state citizenship.[7]

Claims for expanded rights and requests for a clear definition of U.S. citizenship rights continued to fall on deaf ears in the halls of the Supreme Court. In 1875, for example, the Court ruled that a state's refusal to let a woman vote did not violate the privileges and immunities clause of the Fourteenth Amendment. The justices ruled unanimously that voting was not a privilege of citizenship.[8]

In the same year, continued Southern resistance to African American equality led Congress to pass the Civil Rights Act of 1875, designed to grant equal access to public accommodations such as theaters, restaurants, and transportation. The act also prohibited the exclusion of African Americans from jury service. In 1883, however, a series of cases decided by the Supreme Court severely damaged the vitality of the 1875 act.

The *Civil Rights Cases* (1883) were five separate cases involving the convictions of private individuals found to have violated the Civil Rights Act by refusing to extend accommodations to African Americans in theaters, a hotel, and a railroad.[9] The Supreme Court ruled that Congress could prohibit only *state* or governmental action and not private acts of discrimination. The Court thus seriously limited the scope of the Fourteenth Amendment by concluding that Congress had no authority to prohibit private discrimination in public accommodations.

The Court's opinion in the *Civil Rights Cases* provided a moral reinforcement for segregation. Southern states viewed the Court's ruling as an invitation to gut the Thirteenth, Fourteenth, and Fifteenth Amendments.

In devising ways to make certain that African Americans did not vote, Southerners had to avoid the *intent* of the Fifteenth Amendment. This amendment did not guarantee suffrage; it simply said that states could not deny anyone the right to vote on account of race or color. So to exclude African Americans in a seemingly racially neutral way, Southern states used two devices before the 1890s: (1) poll taxes (small taxes on the right to vote that often came due when poor African American sharecroppers had the least amount of money on hand) or some form of property-owning qualifications; and (2) "literacy" or "understanding" tests, which allowed local registrars to administer difficult reading-comprehension tests to potential voters whom they did not know.

To make certain that these laws didn't further reduce the numbers of poor or uneducated white voters, many Southern states added a **grandfather clause** to their voting qualification provisions, granting

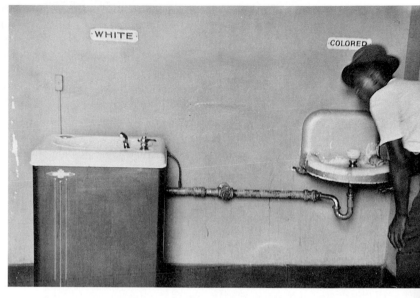

Throughout the South, examples of black codes, or what were more commonly called "Jim Crow laws," abounded. One such law required separate public drinking fountains, shown here. Notice the obvious difference in quality. (Photo courtesy: Bettman/Corbis)

voting privileges to those who failed to pass a wealth or literacy test only if their grandfathers had voted before Reconstruction. Grandfather clauses effectively denied the descendants of slaves the right to vote.

While African Americans continued to face wide-ranging racism on all fronts, women also confronted discrimination. During this period married women, by law, could not be recognized as legal entities. Women often were treated in the same category as juveniles and "imbeciles" and in many states were not entitled to wages, inheritances, or custody of their children.

grandfather clause
Statute that allowed only those whose grandfathers had voted before Reconstruction to vote unless they passed a wealth or literacy test.

THE PUSH FOR EQUALITY, 1889–1954

The Progressive Era (1889–1920) was characterized by a concerted effort to reform political, economic, and social affairs. Prejudice against African Americans was just one target of progressive reform efforts. Distress over the legal inferiority of African Americans was aggravated by the U.S. Supreme Court's decision in *Plessy v. Ferguson* (1896), a case that some commentators point to as the Court's darkest hour. In *Plessy,* the Court upheld the constitutionality of a Louisiana law mandating racial segregation on all public trains. The majority based their decision on their belief that separate facilities for blacks and whites provided equal protection of the laws. After all, they reasoned, African

Plessy v. *Ferguson* **(1896)**
Plessy challenged a Louisiana statute requiring that railroads provide separate accommodations for blacks and whites. The Court found that separate but equal accommodations did not violate the equal protection clause of the Fourteenth Amendment.

Americans were not prevented from riding the train; the Louisiana statute required only that the races travel separately.[10] Justice John Marshall Harlan (1877–1911) was the lone dissenter. He argued that "the Constitution is colorblind" and that it was senseless to hold constitutional a law "which, practically, puts the badge of servitude and degradation upon a large class of our fellow citizens."

The separate-but-equal doctrine enunciated in *Plessy* soon came to mean only "separate," as new legal avenues to discriminate against African Americans were enacted into law throughout the South. While discrimination was widely practiced in many parts of the North, Southern states passed *laws* legally imposing segregation in education, housing, public accommodations, employment, and most other spheres of life. Miscegenation laws, for example, prohibited blacks and whites from marrying.

By the early 1900s a small group of African Americans (largely from the North) had been able to attain some formal education and were ready to push for additional rights. They found some progressive white citizens and politicians amenable to their cause.

The Founding of Key Groups

By 1909, major race riots had occurred in several American cities, and progressive reformers were concerned about these outbreaks of violence and the possibility of others. Oswald Garrison Villard, an influential publisher and grandson of William Lloyd Garrison, called a conference to discuss the problem of "the negro." This group soon evolved into the National Association for the Advancement of Colored People (NAACP).

The NAACP was not the only group getting off the ground. The struggle for women's rights was revitalized in 1890 by the formation of the National American Woman Suffrage Association (NAWSA), devoted largely to securing women's suffrage. Its task was greatly facilitated by the proliferation of women's groups that emerged during the Progressive Era. In addition to the rapidly growing temperance movement—the move to ban the sale of alcohol, which many women blamed for a variety of social ills—women's groups were created to seek protective legislation in the form of maximum hour or minimum wage laws for women and to work for improved sanitation, public morals, education, and the like.

suffrage movement
The drive for women's right to vote that took place in the United States from 1890 to 1920.

NAWSA based its claim to the right to vote largely on the fact that women, as mothers, should be enfranchised. Furthermore, although many members of the **suffrage movement** were NAACP members, the new women's movement—called the suffrage movement because of its focus on the vote alone and not on broader issues of women's rights—took on racist overtones as women argued that if undereducated African Americans could vote, why couldn't women? Some NAWSA members even argued that "the enfranchisement of women would ensure immediate and durable white supremacy."

The growing suffrage movement's roots in the Progressive movement gave it an exceptionally broad base that transformed NAWSA from a small organization of just over 10,000 members in the early 1890s to a true social movement of more than 2 million members in 1917. By 1920, a coalition of women's groups led by NAWSA was able to secure ratification of the Nineteenth Amendment to the Constitution. It guaranteed *all* women the right to vote—fifty-five years after African American males were enfranchised by the Fifteenth Amendment.

After passage of the suffrage amendment in 1920, the fragile alliance of diverse women's groups that had come together to fight for the vote quickly disinte-

Suffragettes demonstrating for the franchise. Parades like this one took place in cities all over the United States. (Photo courtesy: Library of Congress)

grated. Widespread, organized activity on behalf of women's rights did not reemerge until the 1960s. In the meantime, however, the NAACP continued to fight racism and racial segregation. In fact, its activities and those of others in the civil rights movement would later give impetus to a new women's movement.

Litigating for Equality

During the 1930s, leaders of the NAACP began to sense that the time was right to launch a full-scale challenge in the federal courts to the constitutionality of *Plessy*'s separate-but-equal doctrine. The NAACP mapped out a long-range strategy that would first target segregation in professional and graduate education. Clearly, the separate-but-equal doctrine was a bar to any hope of full equality for African Americans. Traditional legislative channels were unlikely to work, given blacks' limited or nonexistent political power. Thus the federal courts and a long-range litigation strategy were the NAACP's only hope.

WEB EXPLORATION
To learn more about the NAACP, see
www.ablongman.com/oconnor

Test Cases. The NAACP opted first to challenge the constitutionality of all-white law schools. In 1935, all Southern states maintained fully segregated elementary and secondary schools. Colleges and universities were also segregated, but most states did not provide for post-graduate education for African Americans. NAACP lawyers chose to target law schools because they were institutions that judges could well understand, and integration there could prove less threatening to most whites.

Lloyd Gaines, a graduate of Missouri's all-black Lincoln University, sought admission to the all-white University of Missouri Law School in 1936. He was immediately rejected, but the state offered to build a law school at Lincoln (although no funds were allocated for the project) or, if he didn't want to wait, to pay his tuition at an out-of-state law school. Gaines lost his appeal of this rejection in the lower court, and the case was appealed to the U.S. Supreme Court.[11]

Gaines's case was filed at an auspicious time. As you may recall from chapter 3, a "constitutional revolution" occurred in Supreme Court decision making in 1937. Prior to 1937, the Court was most receptive to and interested in the protection of economic liberties. In 1937, however, the Court reversed itself in a series of cases and began to place individual freedoms and personal liberties on a more protected footing. Thus, in 1938, it was to a far more sympathetic Supreme Court that Gaines's lawyers finally pleaded his appeal. NAACP attorneys argued that the creation of a separate law school of any less caliber than that of the University of Missouri would not and could not afford Gaines an *equal* education. The justices agreed with the NAACP's contention and ruled that Missouri had failed to meet the separate-but-equal requirements of *Plessy*, and the Court ordered Missouri to admit Gaines to the school.

Recognizing the importance of the Court's ruling, in 1939 the NAACP created a separate, tax-exempt, legal defense fund to devise a strategy to build on the Missouri case to bring about equal educational opportunities for all African American children. The first head of the NAACP Legal Defense and Educational Fund (LDF), as it was called, was Thurgood Marshall, who later became the first African American to serve on the U.S. Supreme Court (1967–1991). Sensing that the Court would be more amenable to the NAACP's broader goals if it was first forced to address a variety of less threatening claims to educational opportunity, Marshall and the LDF brought a series of carefully crafted test cases to the Court.

The first case involved a forty-six-year-old African American mail carrier. In 1946, Herman Sweatt applied for admission to the all-white University of Texas Law School. He was rejected because he was not white, so he sued with the help of the NAACP. The presiding judge gave the state six months to establish a law school or to admit him to the University of Texas. The university then rented a few rooms in downtown Houston and hired two local African American attorneys to be part-time faculty members. The state legislature also authorized $100,000 to create a new negro law school in Austin. This new school was located across the street from the state capitol. It consisted of three small basement rooms, a library of more than 10,000 books and access to the state law library, and three part-time first-year instructors as the "faculty." Sweatt declined the opportunity to obtain an education there and instead chose to continue his legal challenge.

WEB EXPLORATION
To learn more about the NAACP Legal Defense and Education Fund, see www.ablongman.com/oconnor

Eventually, the Supreme Court handled this case together with another NAACP case involving graduate education.[12] The eleven Southern states filed an *amicus curiae* (friend of the court) brief, in which they argued that *Plessy* should govern both cases. In a dramatic departure from the past, however, the Truman administration filed a friend of the court brief urging the Court to overrule *Plessy*. The Court traditionally gives great weight to briefs from the U.S. government.

The Court, however, did not overrule *Plessy*. Instead, the justices found that the measures taken by the states in each case failed to live up to the strictures of the separate-but-equal doctrine. The Court unanimously ruled that the "remedies" to each situation were inadequate to afford a sound education and did not provide an opportunity for a black student to get an "equal" education.

The NAACP LDF concluded that the time now had come to launch a full-scale attack on the separate-but-equal doctrine. The decisions of the Court were encouraging, and the position of the U.S. government and the population in general appeared to be more receptive to an outright overruling of *Plessy*.

That came in the form of **Brown v. Board of Education** (1954). *Brown* was actually four cases brought from different areas of the South and the border states, involving public elementary or high school systems that mandated separate schools for blacks and whites. In *Brown*, NAACP lawyers, again headed by Thurgood Marshall, argued that *Plessy*'s separate-but-equal doctrine was unconstitutional under the **equal protection clause** of the Fourteenth Amendment. The only way to equalize the schools, argued Marshall, was to integrate them.

A major component of the NAACP's strategy was to prove that the intellectual, psychological, and financial damage that befell African Americans as a result of segregation precluded any court from finding that equality was served by the separate-but-equal policy.

On May 17, 1954, Chief Justice Earl Warren delivered the fourth opinion of the day, *Brown v. Board of Education of Topeka, Kansas*. Writing for the Court, Warren stated:

> To separate [some school children] from others . . . solely because of their race generates a feeling of inferiority as to their status in the community that may affect their hearts and minds in a way very unlikely ever to be undone. We conclude, unanimously, that in the field of public education the doctrine of "separate but equal" has no place.[13]

Brown was the most important civil rights case decided in the twentieth century.[14] It immediately evoked an uproar that shook the nation. The governor of South Carolina decried the decision, saying, "Ending

Seven-year-old Linda Brown lived close to a good public school, but her race precluded her attendance there. When the NAACP sought plaintiffs to challenge this discrimination, her father, a local minister, offered Linda to be one of several students named in the NAACP's case. Her name came first alphabetically, hence the case name. (Photo courtesy: Carl Iwasaki/ Life Magazine/ TimePix)

Brown v. Board of Education (1954)
U.S. Supreme Court decision holding that school segregation is inherently unconstitutional because it violates the Fourteenth Amendment's guarantee of equal protection; marked the end of legal segregation in the United States.

equal protection clause
Section of the Fourteenth Amendment that guarantees that all citizens receive "equal protection of the laws"; has been used to bar discrimination against blacks and women.

WEB EXPLORATION
To read the full text
of *Brown*, see
www.ablongman.com/oconnor

segregation would mark the beginning of the end of civilization in the South as we know it."[15] The NAACP LDF lawyers who had argued these cases and those cases leading to *Brown*, however, were jubilant.

THE CIVIL RIGHTS MOVEMENT

Our notion of civil rights has changed profoundly since 1954. First African Americans and then women have built upon existing organizations to forge successful movements for increased rights. *Brown* served as a catalyst for change, sparking the development of the modern civil rights movement. Women's work in that movement and the student protest movement that arose in reaction to the U.S. government's involvement in Vietnam gave women the experience needed to form their own organizations to press for full equality. As African Americans and women became more and more successful, they served as models for others who sought equality—Native Americans, Hispanic Americans, homosexuals, the disabled, and others.

School Desegregation After *Brown*

One year after *Brown*, in a case referred to as *Brown II*, the Court ruled that racially segregated systems must be dismantled "with all deliberate speed."[16] Many in the South, however, entered into a near conspiracy to avoid the mandates of *Brown II*. In Arkansas, the day before school was to begin, Governor Orval Faubus announced that he would surround Little Rock's Central High School with National Guard troops to prevent African American students from entering. While the federal courts in Arkansas continued to order the admission of African American children, the governor remained adamant. Finally, President Dwight D. Eisenhower sent federal troops to Little Rock to protect the rights of the nine students who had attempted to attend Central High.

In *Cooper* v. *Aaron* (1958), the Little Rock School Board asked the federal district court for a two-and-one-half-year delay in implementation of its desegregation plans. In reaction to the state's request and the governor's outrageous conduct, the Court broke with tradition and issued a unanimous decision in which each justice signed the opinion individually, underscoring his individual support for the notion that "no state legislator or executive or judicial officer can war against the Constitution without violating his undertaking to support it."[17] The state's actions were thus ruled unconstitutional and its "evasive schemes" illegal.

A New Move for African American Rights

In December 1955, soon after *Brown II*, the civil rights movement took another step forward—this time in Montgomery, Alabama. Rosa Parks made history when she refused to leave her seat on a bus to move to the

POLICY IN ACTION

ENDING RACIAL PROFILING

In 2001, President George W. Bush announced his commitment to end the practice known as racial profiling. Racial profiling is the practice by which police officers stop motorists of certain racial minorities or ethnic groups because the officers believe that those groups are more likely to commit crimes. Despite the civil rights victories of the 1960s, for many people in America, your skin color can still make you a suspect in America. It can make you more likely to be stopped by police, searched, arrested, and imprisoned. In 2000, the ACLU released its own report, "Driving While Black: Racial Profiling on Our Nation's Highways," that documented the treatment of thousands of innocent motorists on U.S. highways. This report led the ACLU to file a suit against the state of Maryland for engaging in this discriminatory practice. The same year, the U.S. Civil Rights Commission released its recommendation that Congress should make it easier for affected individuals to sue abusive police officers and pass legislation outlawing racial profiling, making any police officer convicted of racial profiling subject to immediate dismissal. Throughout 2000 and 2001, many states debated and or passed legislation to outlaw racial profiling. Governor Jesse Ventura of Minnesota, however, has opposed state-wide legislation believing racial profiling to be a problem of local law enforcement. Some see a need for federal law.

How widespread is racial profiling? To some extent, it depends on where you live and what your race is. A 1999 Gallup Poll, for example, found that while 59 percent of the public believed that racial profiling was widespread, only 6 percent of whites polled believed that they had been victims of racial profiling. In contrast, 42 percent of blacks believed that they had been subject to this type of discrimination. In fact, 75 percent of young black men reported that they had been stopped by police because of their race.[*]

---

[*]The Gallup Organization, "Racial Profiling is Seen as Widespread, Particularly Among Black Men," Poll Releases, December 9, 1999.

---

back to make room for a white male passenger. She was arrested for violating an Alabama law banning integration of public facilities, including buses. After she was freed on bond, the NAACP urged African Americans to boycott the Montgomery bus system.

As the boycott, led by a twenty-six-year-old minister, Dr. Martin Luther King Jr., dragged on, Montgomery officials and local business owners began to harass the city's African American citizens. But King urged Montgomery's African Americans to continue their protest. In 1956 a federal court ruled that the segregated bus system violated the equal protection clause of the Fourteenth Amendment. After a year of walking, African Americans ended their protest as the buses were ordered to integrate. The first effort at nonviolent protest had been successful. Organized boycotts and other forms of nonviolent protest, including sit-ins at segregated restaurants and bus stations, were to follow.

WEB EXPLORATION
For more information about the Montgomery bus boycott and Dr. Martin Luther King Jr., see
www.ablongman.com/oconnor

Formation of New Groups

The recognition and respect that King earned within the African American community helped him to launch the Southern Christian Leadership Conference (SCLC) in 1957, soon after the end of the Montgomery bus boycott. Unlike the NAACP, which had Northern origins and had come to rely largely on litigation as a means of achieving expanded equality, the SCLC had a Southern base and was rooted more closely in black religious culture. The SCLC's philosophy reflected King's growing belief in the importance of nonviolent protest.

Eventually, the SCLC and the Student Nonviolent Coordinating Committee (SNCC), largely made up of activist college students, came to dominate the new civil rights movement. While the SCLC generally worked with church leaders in a community, SNCC was much more of a grassroots organization. Always perceived as more radical than the SCLC, SNCC tended to focus its organizing activities on the young, both black and white.

In addition to holding sit-ins at segregated facilities, SNCC also came to lead what were called "freedom rides," designed to focus attention on segregated public accommodations. Bands of college students and other civil rights activists traveled by bus throughout the South in an effort to force bus stations to desegregate.

While SNCC continued to sponsor sit-ins and freedom rides, in 1963, the Reverend Martin Luther King Jr. launched a series of massive nonviolent demonstrations in Birmingham, Alabama, long considered a major stronghold of segregation. Thousands of blacks and whites marched to Birmingham in a show of solidarity. Peaceful marchers were met there by the Birmingham police commissioner, who ordered his officers to use dogs, clubs, and fire hoses on the marchers. Americans across the nation watched in horror as they witnessed the brutality and abuse heaped on the protesters. As the marchers hoped, these shocking scenes helped convince President John F. Kennedy to propose important civil rights legislation.

The Civil Rights Act of 1964

The older faction of the civil rights movement as represented by the SCLC, and the younger branch, represented by SNCC, both sought a similar goal: full implementation of Supreme Court decisions and an end to racial segregation and discrimination. The cumulative effect of collective actions including sit-ins, boycotts, marches, and freedom rides—as well as the tragic bombings and deaths inflicted in retaliation—led Congress to pass the first major piece of civil rights legislation since the post–Civil War era.

In 1963, President Kennedy requested that Congress pass a law banning discrimination in public accommodations. Seizing the moment and recognizing the potency of a show of massive support, Martin Luther

King Jr. called for the March on Washington for Jobs and Freedom, held in August 1963. More than 250,000 people heard King deliver his famous "I Have a Dream" speech from the Lincoln Memorial. Before Congress had the opportunity to vote on any legislation, however, John F. Kennedy was assassinated on November 22, 1963, in Dallas, Texas.

When Vice President Lyndon B. Johnson, a Southern-born former Senate majority leader, succeeded Kennedy as president, he put civil rights reform at the top of his legislative priority list, and civil rights activists gained a critical ally. In spite of strong presidential support and the sway of public opinion, the Civil Rights Act of 1964 did not sail through Congress. Southern senators conducted the longest filibuster in the history of the Senate. For eight weeks they held up voting on the civil rights bill until cloture, a procedure requiring the votes of sixty senators to end debate, was invoked and their filibuster ended. Once passed, the **Civil Rights Act of 1964:**

VISUAL LITERACY
Race and the Death Penalty

1. Outlawed arbitrary discrimination in voter registration and expedited voting rights lawsuits.
2. Barred discrimination in public accommodations engaged in interstate commerce.
3. Authorized the U.S. Justice Department to initiate lawsuits to desegregate public facilities and schools.
4. Provided for the withholding of federal funds from discriminatory state and local programs.
5. Prohibited discrimination in employment on grounds of race, color, religion, national origin, or sex.
6. Created the Equal Employment Opportunity Commission (EEOC) to monitor and enforce the bans on employment discrimination.

Civil Rights Act of 1964
Legislation passed by Congress to outlaw segregation in public facilities and racial discrimination in employment, education, and voting; created the Equal Employment Opportunity Commission.

The Women's Rights Movement

Just as in the abolition movement in the 1800s, women from all walks of life participated in the civil rights movement. Women were important members of the SNCC and more traditional groups like the NAACP and the SCLC, yet they often found themselves treated as second-class citizens. At one point Stokely Carmichael, chair of the SNCC, openly proclaimed: "The only position for women in SNCC is prone."[18] Statements and attitudes like these led some women to found early women's liberation groups that were generally quite radical, small in membership, and not intended to use more conventional political tactics.

Paternalistic attitudes toward women, and perhaps society as well, continued well into the 1970s. Said one U.S. Supreme Court justice in 1961:

WEB EXPLORATION
To learn more about the women's movement, see www.ablongman.com/oconnor

> Despite the enlightened emancipation of women from the restrictions and protections of bygone years, and their entry into many parts of community life formerly considered to be reserved to men, a woman is still regarded as the center of home and family life.[19]

These attitudes and decisions were insufficient to forge a new movement for women's rights. Soon, however, three events occurred to move women to action. In 1961, soon after his election, President John F. Kennedy created the President's Commission on the Status of Women. The commission's report, *American Women,* released in 1963, documented pervasive discrimination against women in all walks of life. In addition, the civil rights movement and publication of Betty Friedan's *The Feminine Mystique* (1963), which led some women to question their lives and status in society, added to their dawning recognition that something was wrong.[20] Soon after, passage of the Civil Rights Act of 1964 made discrimination based on sex, as well as race, illegal.

In 1966, after the Equal Employment Opportunity Commission failed to enforce the Civil Rights Act of 1964 as it applied to sex discrimination, women activists formed the National Organization for Women (NOW). From its inception, NOW was closely modeled on the NAACP. Women in NOW were quite similar to the founders of the NAACP; they wanted to work within the system to prevent discrimination. Initially, most of this activity was geared toward two goals: achievement of equality through passage of an equal rights amendment to the Constitution, or by judicial decision. But because to that time the Supreme Court had failed to extend constitutional protections to women, the only recourse that remained was an amendment.

WEB EXPLORATION
To learn more
about NOW, see
www.ablongman.com/oconnor

The Equal Rights Amendment (ERA).   Not all women agreed with the notion of full equality for women. Nevertheless, from 1923 to 1972, a proposal for an equal rights amendment was made in every session of every Congress. Every president since Harry S Truman backed it, and by 1972 public opinion favored its ratification.

In response to pressure from NOW, the National Women's Political Caucus, and a wide variety of other feminist groups, Congress in 1972, passed the Equal Rights Amendment (ERA) by overwhelming majorities (84–8 in the Senate; 354–24 in the House). The amendment provided that:

WEB EXPLORATION
To learn more
about the ERA, see
www.ablongman.com/oconnor

- Equality of rights under the law shall not be denied or abridged by the United States or by any state on account of sex.
- The Congress shall have the power to enforce, by appropriate legislation, the provisions of this article.

Within a year, twenty-two states ratified the amendment, most by overwhelming margins. But the tide soon turned. In 1974 and 1975, the amendment only squeaked through the Montana and North Dakota legislatures, and two states—Nebraska and Tennessee—voted to rescind their earlier ratifications.

By 1978, one year before the deadline for ratification was to expire, thirty-five states had voted for the amendment—three short of the three-fourths necessary for ratification. Efforts in key states such as Illinois and Florida failed as opposition to the ERA intensified. Faced with

ANALYZING THE DATA

EEOC SEXUAL HARASSMENT FILINGS

Sexual harassment filings have leveled off since 1995. Interestingly, however, the percentage of charges filed by males has increased steadily since the Supreme Court nomination hearings of Clarence Thomas to the Supreme Court concerning whether he had harassed Anita Hill: from 9.1% of the 10,500 total filings in 1992 to the 13.6% of 15,800 total filings in 2000.

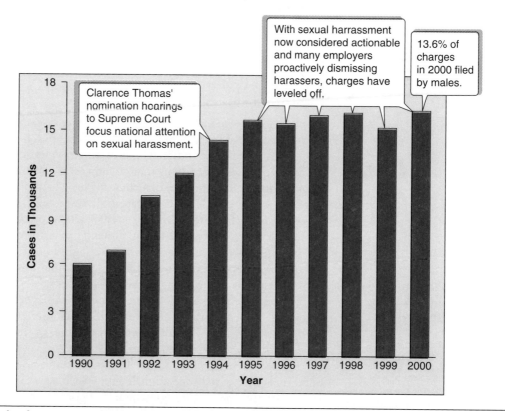

Source: Based on data from www.eeoc.gov/stats/harass. Accessed March 9, 2001.

the prospect of defeat, ERA supporters heavily lobbied Congress to extend the deadline. Congress extended the time period for ratification by three years, but to no avail. No additional states ratified the amendment, and three more rescinded their votes.

What began as a simple correction to the Constitution turned into a highly controversial proposed change. In spite of the fact that large numbers of the public favored the ERA, opponents needed to stall ratification in only thirteen states while supporters had to convince legislators in thirty-eight. The success that women's rights activists were having in the courts was hurting the effort. When women first sought the ERA in the late 1960s, the Supreme Court had yet to rule that women were protected by the Fourteenth Amendment's equal protection clause from any kind of discrimination, thus clearly showing the need for an amendment. But as the Court widened its interpretation of the Constitution to protect women from some sorts of discrimination, in the eyes of many the need for a new amendment became less urgent.

Litigation for Equal Rights.   While several women's groups worked toward passage of the ERA, NOW and several other groups, including the American Civil Liberties Union (ACLU), formed litigating arms to pressure the courts. But women faced an immediate roadblock in the Supreme Court's interpretation of the equal protection clause of the Fourteenth Amendment.

The Equal Protection Clause and Constitutional Standards of Review

The Fourteenth Amendment protects all U.S. citizens from state action that violates equal protection of the laws. Most laws, however, are subject to what is called the rational basis or minimum rationality test. This lowest level of scrutiny means that governments must allege a rational foundation for any distinctions they make. Early on, however, the Supreme Court decided that certain rights were entitled to a heightened standard of review. As early as 1937, the Supreme Court recognized that some rights were so fundamental that a very heavy burden would be placed on any government that sought to restrict those rights. When fundamental rights such as First Amendment freedoms or what the Court terms **suspect classifications** such as race are involved, the Court uses a heightened standard of review called **strict scrutiny** to determine the constitutional validity of the challenged practices (as highlighted in Table 5.1). In legal terms this means that if a statute or governmental practice makes a classification based on race, the statute is presumed to be unconstitutional unless the state can prove the law in question is necessary to accomplish a permissible goal and that it is the least restrictive means through which that goal can be accomplished.

During the 1960s and into the 1970s, the Court routinely struck down as unconstitutional practices and statutes that discriminated on the basis of race. "Whites-only" public parks and recreational facilities, tax-exempt status for private schools that discriminated, and statutes prohibiting racial intermarriage were declared unconstitutional. In contrast, the Court refused even to consider the fact that the equal protection clause might apply to discrimination against women. Finally, in a case brought in 1971 by Ruth Bader Ginsburg as director of the Women's Rights Project of the ACLU, the Supreme Court ruled that an Idaho law granting male parents automatic preference over female parents as the administrator of their deceased children's estates violated the equal protection clause of the Fourteenth Amendment.[21]

suspect classification
Category or class, such as race, which triggers the highest standard of scrutiny from the Supreme Court.

strict scrutiny
A heightened standard of review used by the Supreme Court to determine the constitutional validity of a challenged practice.

WEB EXPLORATION
For more on the ACLU Women's Rights Project, see www.ablongman.com/oconnor

TABLE 5.1   The Equal Protection Clause and Standards of Review Used by the Supreme Court to Determine Whether It Has Been Violated

TYPES OF CLASSIFICATION (What kind of statutory classification is an issue?)	STANDARD OF REVIEW (What standard of review will be used?)	TEST (What does the court ask?)	EXAMPLE (How does the court apply the test?)
Fundamental freedoms: religion, assembly, press, privacy, suspect classifications (including race)	Strict scrutiny or heightened standard	Is classification necessary to the accomplishment of a permissible state goal? Is it the least restrictive way to reach that goal?	*Brown* v. *Board of Education* (1954): Racial segregation not necessary to accomplish the state goal of educating its students
Gender	Intermediate standard	Does the classification serve an important governmental objective, and is it substantially related to those ends?	*Craig* v. *Boren* (1976): Keeping drunk drivers off the roads may be an important governmental objective, but allowing eighteen- to twenty-one-year-old women to drink alcoholic beverages while prohibiting men of the same age from drinking is not substantially related to that goal.
Others (including age, wealth, and sexual preference)	Minimum rationality standard	Is there any rational foundation for the discrimination?	*Romer* v. *Evans* (1996): Colorado constitutional amendment precluding any legislative, executive, or judicial action at any state or local level designed to bar discrimination based on sexual preference is not rational or reasonable.

While the Court did not rule that sex was a suspect classification, it concluded that the equal protection clause of the Fourteenth Amendment prohibited unreasonable classifications based on sex. In 1976 the Court carved out a new "test" to be used in examining claims of sex discrimination, "[T]o withstand constitutional challenge, . . . classifications by gender must serve important governmental objectives and must be substantially related to achievement of those objectives." The Court thus created an intermediate standard of review within what previously was a two-tier distinction—strict scrutiny/rational basis.

Since 1976, the Court has applied the intermediate standard of constitutional review to most claims that it has heard involving gender. Thus the following kinds of practices have been found to violate the Fourteenth Amendment:

■ Single-sex public nursing schools.
■ Laws that consider males adults at twenty-one years but females at eighteen years.
■ Laws that allow women but not men to receive alimony.

- State prosecutors' use of preemptory challenges to reject men or women to create more sympathetic juries.
- Virginia's maintenance of an all-male military college, the Virginia Military Institute.

In contrast, the Court has upheld the following governmental practices and laws:

- Draft registration provisions for males only.
- State statutory rape laws that apply only to female victims.

The level of review used by the Court is crucial. Clearly, a statute excluding African Americans from draft registration would be unconstitutional. But because gender is not subject to the same higher standard of review that is used in racial discrimination cases, the exclusion of women from the requirements of the Military Selective Service Act was ruled permissible because the government policy was considered to serve "important governmental objectives."[22]

This history has perhaps clarified why women's rights activists continue to argue that until the passage of an equal rights amendment, women will never enjoy the same rights as men. An amendment would automatically raise the level of scrutiny that the Court applies to gender-based claims.

Statutory Remedies for Sex Discrimination.   In part because of the limits of the intermediate standard of review and the fact that the equal protection clause applies only to *governmental* discrimination, women's rights activists began to bombard the courts with sex-discrimination cases. These cases have been filed under Title VII of the Civil Rights Act, which prohibits discrimination by private and, after 1972, public employers, or Title IX of the Education Amendments of 1972, which bars educational institutions receiving federal funds from discriminating against female students. Key victories include:

- Consideration of sexual harassment as sex discrimination.
- A broad definition of what can be considered sexual harassment, which includes same-sex harassment.
- Inclusion of law firms, which many argued were *private* partnerships, in the coverage of the act.
- Allowance of voluntary affirmative action programs to redress historical discrimination against women.

Women also have won some important suits for back pay under the Equal Pay Act. Still, a large wage gap between men and women continues to exist (see Politics Now: Equal Pay for Women Workers).

Title IX, which parallels Title VII, has also greatly expanded the opportunities for women in elementary, secondary, and postsecondary institutions. Since women's groups, like the NAACP before them, saw eradication of educational discrimination as key to improving other facets of women's lives, they lobbied for it heavily. Most of today's college students did not go through school being excluded from home eco-

P O L I T I C S   N O W

EQUAL PAY FOR WOMEN WORKERS

Each year the National Committee on Pay Equity, a consortium of 180 organizations including women's groups and labor organizations, mobilizes events around the nation to call attention to the disturbing fact that, in spite of the passage of the Equal Pay Act in 1963, women still earn far less than their male counterparts. In 2000, women leaders gathered at the White House to hear President Clinton urge Congress to pass the Paycheck Fairness Act to fight discrimination in women's wages. Sponsored by Senator Tom Daschle (D–N.Dak.) and Rep. Rosa DeLaura (D–Conn.), its goal is to put teeth into the Equal Pay Act by prohibiting employers from firing employees who inquire about the salaries of their co-workers. At that same meeting, President Clinton announced his administration's Equal Pay initiative, which included the creation of an Equal Pay Task Force within the Equal Employment Opportunity Commission (the federal agency charged with enforcing the provisions of the Equal Pay Act, as well as several other antidiscrimination provisions), and an investment of $20 million to remove barriers to the career advancement of women scientists and engineers. Other events held on Equal Pay Day 2000 were:

- The Maine Women's Lobby handed out oversized dollar bills with large sections missing to visually illustrate the missing portion of women's pay.
- In Green Bay, Wisconsin, women picketed a busy street with placards reading "Where is my 27 cents?" referring to the gap between men's and women's wages.*

But in spite of the wage gap, the Republicans in Congress do not want to bring the Paycheck Fairness Act out of committee.

---

*National Committee on Pay Equity, "Questions and Answers about Equal Pay Day Tuesday, April 3, 2001," http://www.feminist.com/fairpay/epd.htm.

nomics or shop classes because of their sex. Nor, probably, did many attend schools that had no team sports for females. Yet this was commonly the case in the United States prior to passage of Title IX.[23] The performance of women athletes at recent Olympic Games showed the impact of the law on women's participation in sport. There, record numbers of women competed and won.

OTHER GROUPS MOBILIZE FOR RIGHTS

Native Americans

Native Americans are the first "true" Americans, and their status under U.S. law is unique. Under the U.S. Constitution, "Indian tribes" are considered distinct governments, a situation that has affected Native

PARTICIPATION
Statehood for Puerto Rico and the District of Columbia?

WEB EXPLORATION
For more about the Native American Rights Fund, see www.ablongman.com/oconnor

Americans' treatment by the Supreme Court in contrast to other groups of ethnic minorities. And "minority" is a term that accurately describes American Indians. It is estimated that there were as many as 10 million Indians in the New World at the time it was discovered by Europeans in the 1400s, with 3 to 4 million living in what is today the United States. By 1900 the number of Indians in the continental United States had plummeted to less than 2 million.

It was not until the 1960s, at the same time that women were beginning to mobilize for greater civil rights, that Indians too began to mobilize to act. Like the civil rights and women's rights movements, the movement for Native American rights had a radical as well as a more traditional branch. In 1973, for example, national attention was drawn to the plight of Indians when members of the radical American Indian Movement took over Wounded Knee, South Dakota, the site of the massacre of 150 Indians by the U.S. Army in 1890. Other Indians began to file hundreds of test cases in the federal courts involving tribal fishing rights, tribal land claims, and the taxation of tribal profits. The Native American Rights Fund (NARF) was founded in 1970 and soon became the NAACP LDF of the Indian rights movement when the "courts became the forum of choice for Indian tribes and their members."[24]

Native Americans have won some very important victories concerning hunting, fishing, and land rights. They continue to litigate to gain access to their sacred places and have filed lawsuits to stop the building of roads and new construction on ancient burial grounds or other sacred spots. But Native Americans have not fared nearly so well in areas such as religious freedom, especially where tribal practices come into conflict with state law. Native Americans continue to fight the negative stereotypes that plague their progress. Indians contend that even the popular names of thousand of high school, college, and professional teams are degrading (as discussed in Highlight: What's in a Name: Team Names Under Attack).

Latino Americans

Like women's efforts to garner expanded political rights, Latino Americans, too, can date their first real push for equal rights to 1965–1975. Like blacks, women, and Native Americans, Latino Americans have some radical militant groups but have been dominated by more conventional organizations. The more conventional groups have built up ties with existing, powerful mainstream associations, including labor unions and the Roman Catholic church. They have also relied heavily on litigation to secure greater rights. Key groups are the Mexican American Legal Defense and Educational Fund (MALDEF) and the Puerto Rican Legal Defense and Educational Fund.

MALDEF was founded in 1968 after members of the League of United Latin American Citizens (LULAC), the nation's largest and oldest Latino organization, met with NAACP LDF leaders and, with

HIGHLIGHT

WHAT'S IN A NAME: TEAM NAMES UNDER ATTACK

In 1993, Ben Nighthorse Campbell (R–Colo.), the only Native American in Congress, introduced legislation to block approval of a $200 million stadium for the Washington Redskins unless the team changed its name. Campbell, who told a House panel that the word "redskin" was an offensive racial slur, failed to convince his colleagues. Still, Indian activists picketed football games, the World Series, and other sporting events to draw attention to racially insensitive team names such as the Atlanta Braves and the Cleveland Indians. Since the early 1990s, however, over 600 high schools and several universities have abandoned their Indian-themed names.

Around the same time, Suzan Shown Hartjo, a Cheyenne, also tried to drum up support to change the name of the Redskins. Her work brought her to the attention of a trademark lawyer who asked her if she had considered challenging the team name under the provisions of the 1946 Lanham Act, which bars the federal government from registering trademarks that are "disparaging, scandalous, or contemptuous." After seven years of legal pleadings, in 1999 a three-judge trademark panel ordered the cancelation of seven trademarks registered to the Redskins team, a decision that was upheld in 2000. Challenges to the Atlanta Braves and Cleveland Indians trademarks are pending.

The U.S. Justice Department is also investigating names. Recently, one North Carolina high school agreed to drop the term "squaws" in referring to its girls' sports teams. "At some point, there aren't going to be any Indian team names anymore. That's social change," said the dean of Northwestern University's Law School.

Source: Brooke Masters, "Team Name Goes to Court," *The Washington Post* (April 7, 1999): B1, B8.

---

their assistance, secured a $2.2 million start-up grant from the Ford Foundation. It was created to bring test cases to force school districts to allocate more funds to schools with predominantly low-income minority populations, to implement bilingual education programs, to force employers to hire Chicanos, and to challenge election rules and apportionment plans that undercount or dilute Latino voting power.

MALDEF has been quite successful in its efforts to expand voting rights and opportunities to Latino Americans. In 1973, for example, it won a major victory when the Supreme Court ruled that multimember electoral districts (in which more than one person represents a single district) in Texas discriminated against African Americans and Latino Americans.[25] In multimember systems, legislatures generally add members to larger districts instead of drawing smaller districts in which a minority candidate could get a majority of the votes necessary to win.

While enjoying greater access to elective office, their numbers fall far short of African Americans in spite of being the nation's largest minority group. Moreover, Latinos still suffer discrimination. Language

WEB EXPLORATION
For more about Mexican American Legal Defense and Education Fund, see www.ablongman.com/oconnor

POINT / COUNTERPOINT

IS A CRIME JUST A CRIME, OR DO MOTIVES AND INTENTIONS MATTER?

A hate crime is an act of violence against a person or property based on the victim's race, color, gender, national origin, religion, sexual orientation, or disability. Every year, thousands of Americans are documented victims of hate crimes and it is suspected that many more go unreported. Many localities, states, and even the federal government are passing or considering special legislation to make hate crimes a separate type of crime that merits special punishment. But do crimes based on hatred deserve to be in a special category for punishment? Do motivations and intentions matter, or is a crime just a crime? Let's examine these two point of views.

Those who favor hate crimes legislation, including the Democratic Party and the NAACP, believe that hate crimes have a special emotional and psychological impact on the victim and the victim's community that causes the victim to withdraw from broader society. This kind of alienation can damage the very fabric of society by making people and groups feel isolated and untrusting of their fellow citizens. Proponents of hate crimes legislation argue that hate crimes are an assault not only to the victim but on the entire group to which that victim belongs and therefore merit additional attention and punishment because the state has a compelling interest in protecting its citizens against bias. The death of James Byrd Jr. in Texas is an example of a hate crime. Byrd was dragged several miles tied to the back of a pickup truck solely because he was an African American. This act of violence killed Byrd and injured his family and friends. However, many African Americans in and outside of Texas cite this crime as an act that makes them feel less secure and less trusting in society as a whole. In Wyoming, two men cited Matthew Shepard's homosexuality as the reason they brutally beat him and left him tied to a fence. Shepard's murder is another example of a crime that had an impact beyond the immediate victims. These two examples, and many others, have left many people wondering what kind of society we live in and believing that the motivations behind these crimes are so heinous that they deserve extra punishment.

Other groups, such as the Libertarian Party, the Christian coalition, Republicans, and the ACLU express opposition or reservations about hate crimes legislation. The basic arguments against hate crimes legislation are that legislating about motivations and intentions is a dramatic extension of government power. If the government can tell us we can't hate a certain group, can it also tell us we can't use certain words, watch certain movies, or associate with certain people? If a crime is committed, opponents say, there are already laws on the books to punish the guilty. A crime is a crime and should be treated as such. Why is murder worse if it is a hate crime? The victim is dead regardless of the motivations of the killer, so why add more laws? Why not prosecute using existing laws and use the punishments already prescribed, ranging from imprisonment to execution? Is the murder of James Byrd Jr. or Matthew Shepard worse than other murders because it is motivated by hate? Opponents of hate crimes legislation argue that it is not worse.

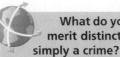

What do you think? Do hate crimes merit distinct treatment or is a crime simply a crime?
Go to www.ablongman.com/oconnor

GLOBAL POLITICS

IMMIGRATION AND CIVIL RIGHTS

Americans are used to being a nation of immigrants, even as new immigration sparks public debate about how much is enough. Immigration into Western Europe and Japan has been an even more problematic issue. In the last decade or so, right-wing political parties in Western Europe have made immigration a national issue.

Immigration is a political issue in these countries for three reasons. First, European and Japanese nationalism since the nineteenth century is based on the notion of the nation as a common ethnic people. Second, most of the postwar immigration into Western Europe and Japan has been from developing countries in Asia, Africa, and the Middle East (many of them former colonies). Third, that immigration, which was assumed after World War II by many governments to be temporary, has been in many cases permanent. Large populations of Turkish "guest workers" in Germany, followed in the 1990s by refugees from Eastern Europe, North Africans in France; and Chinese and Koreans in Japan present problems of how to assimilate people from different backgrounds without radically altering national identity. In a number of ways, then, immigration issues in Europe and Japan resemble ethnic and racial issues in the United States.

More or less permanent outsider status invites civil rights abuses. Right-wing groups across Western Europe have made rhetorical as well as physical attacks on foreign residents. While the constitutions of these countries typically prohibit discrimination, immigrants who are not citizens often do not enjoy the full protection of the law.

Acquiring citizenship as a way to assimilate is not always easy. Japan and Germany provide a striking contrast to the United States on this point. The United States government subscribes to the doctrine of *jus soli*: People born on American soil automatically acquire citizenship even if their parents are not United States citizens. Moreover, American requirements for citizenship for permanent residents are comparatively lenient. The Japanese and German governments, in contrast, subscribe to the doctrine of *jus sanguinis*: Only the children of citizens (and therefore properly German or Japanese) automatically qualify for citizenship. In 2000, the German government eased this restriction to allow for dual citizenship for second-generation aliens, but preference in immigration and naturalization continues to go to ethnic German immigrants. Naturalization by second- and third-generation immigrants in Germany and Japan remains quite low.

---

barriers and substandard educational opportunities continue to plague their progress. In 1973 the U.S. Supreme Court refused to find that a Texas law under which the state appropriated a set dollar amount to each school district per pupil, while allowing wealthier districts to enrich educational programs from other funds, violated the equal protection clause of the Fourteenth Amendment.[26]

Throughout the 1970s and 1980s, inter-school-district inequalities continued, and frequently had their greatest impact on poor Latino children, who often had inferior educational opportunities. Recognizing that

TIMELINE
The Fourteenth
Amendment

SIMULATION
You Are the Mayor

the increasingly conservative federal courts offered no recourse, in 1984 MALDEF filed suit in state court alleging that the Texas school finance policy violated the Texas constitution. In 1989 it won a case in which a state district judge elected by the voters of only a single county declared the state's entire method of financing public schools to be unconstitutional under the state constitution. High on its agenda today is affirmative action, the admission of Latino students to state colleges and universities, health care for undocumented immigrants, and challenging unfair redistricting practices that make it more difficult to elect Latino legislators. Its Census 2000 educational outreach campaign, moreover, sought to ensure all Latinos were counted in 2000.

Gays and Lesbians

COMPARATIVE
Comparing
Civil Rights

Gays and lesbians have had an even harder time than African Americans, women, Native Americans, or Latinos in achieving fuller rights. Gays do, however, have on average far higher household incomes and educational levels than do these other groups, and they are beginning to convert these advantages into political clout at the ballot box. The cause of gay and lesbian rights, like that of African Americans and women early in their quest for greater civil rights, did not fare well in the Supreme Court initially. In *Bowers* v. *Hardwick* (1986), for example, the Supreme Court ruled that a Georgia law that made private acts of consensual sodomy illegal (whether practiced by homosexuals or by heterosexual married adults) was constitutional. Gay and lesbian rights groups had argued that a constitutional right to privacy included the right to engage in consensual sex within one's home, but the Court disagreed. Although privacy rights may attach to relations of "family, marriage, or procreation," those rights did not extend to homosexuals, wrote Justice Byron White for the Court. In a concurring opinion—his last written on the Court—Chief Justice Warren Burger called sodomy "the infamous crime against nature."[27]

WEB EXPLORATION
For more on gay
rights groups, see
www.ablongman.com/oconnor

The Supreme Court's unwillingness to expand privacy rights or special constitutional protections to homosexuals, and Congress's failure to end discrimination in the military, has led many gay and lesbian rights groups to other, potentially more responsive, political forums: state and local governments. (See Chapter 3 for a discussion of moves to recognize gay marriage and domestic partnerships.) Around the nation, such groups have lobbied for antidiscrimination legislation with mixed success. In 1992, for example, Colorado voters passed a state constitutional amendment that rescinded several local gay and lesbian rights ordinances and also prevented the adoption of any such measures. In *Romer* v. *Evans* (1996), however, the U.S. Supreme Court ruled that the amendment was unconstitutional. Although the Court used the rational basis test to invalidate the amendment, it was the first time ever that a majority of the justices applied the equal protection clause of the Fourteenth Amendment to prevent discrimination against homosexuals.[28]

As discussed in chapter 5, however the Court decision allowing the Boy Scouts of America to ban homosexuals from becoming scout masters had a chilling effects on the gay rights activists' optimism about the Court as a source of continued rights expansion.

Disabled Americans

Disabled Americans also have lobbied hard for antidiscrimination legislation. In the aftermath of World War II, many veterans returned to a nation unequipped to handle their disabilities. The Korean and Vietnam wars made the problems of disabled veterans all the more clear. These disabled veterans saw the successes of African Americans, women, and other minorities, and they too began to lobby for greater protection against discrimination.

In 1990, in coalition with other disabled people, veterans were finally able to convince Congress to pass the Americans with Disabilities Act. The statute defines a disabled person as someone with a physical or mental impairment that limits one or more "life activities," or who has a record of such impairment (see Figure 5.1). It thus extends the protections of the Civil Rights Act of 1964 to all of those with physical or mental disabilities, including people with AIDS. It guarantees access to public facilities, employment, and communication services. It also requires employers to acquire or modify work equipment, adjust work schedules, and make existing facilities accessible. This means, for example, that buildings must be accessible to those in wheelchairs, and telecommunications devices be provided for deaf employees.

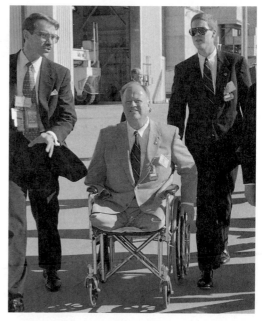

Senator Max Cleland (D–Ga.), shown here in a wheelchair, is a vocal proponent of the rights of those with disabilities. He knows firsthand the problems of noncompliance with the ADA; when he was first elected to the U.S. Senate, it took him several months to find housing to accommodate his wheelchair. (Photo courtesy: Mary Ann Chestain/AP/Wide World Photos)

WEB EXPLORATION
For more about disability advocacy groups, see www.ablongman.com/oconnor

FIGURE 5.1   Defining Disabilities
From 1992 to 1998, there were 108,939 complaints filed with the Equal Employment Opportunity Commission under the Americans with Disabilities Act.

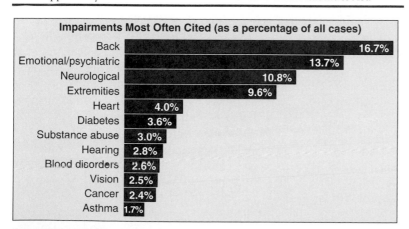

Impairments Most Often Cited (as a percentage of all cases)

Impairment	Percentage
Back	16.7%
Emotional/psychiatric	13.7%
Neurological	10.8%
Extremities	9.6%
Heart	4.0%
Diabetes	3.6%
Substance abuse	3.0%
Hearing	2.8%
Blood disorders	2.6%
Vision	2.5%
Cancer	2.4%
Asthma	1.7%

Source: Based on data from The Washington Post, 1998.

Continuity & Change

Race in America: Affirmative Action

When the Framers met in Philadelphia, they all recognized that the issue of slavery and how it was treated in the new Constitution could make or break their efforts to fashion a new nation and win acceptance in the Southern states. The Three-Fifths Compromise was their politically expedient solution. It got the Southern states on board, but only for a while. In 1861, the Civil War was fought largely over the issue of slavery. After slavery was abolished, the Southern states quickly acted to pass legislation to limit opportunities for newly freed slaves that persisted for nearly the next century.

Nearly one hundred years after the first shots rang out in the Civil War, African Americans and other civil rights supporters gained support for their efforts to attain fuller civil rights, including the right to vote, attend desegregated schools, and be treated fairly in the workplace. *Brown v. Board of Education* (1954) and passage of the Civil Rights Act of 1964, went a long way toward remedying many onerous forms of discrimination. Since the mid-1960s, racial tolerance has increased, although discrimination still exists. In 1997, 77 percent of those surveyed by the Gallup organization said they approved of interracial marriage and 93 percent said that they would vote for a black president.[a] Nevertheless, while most Americans agree that discrimination is wrong, most whites—57 percent—today believe that **affirmative action programs** (policies designed to give special attention or compensatory treatment to members of a previously disadvantaged group) are no longer needed, although 86 percent thought that those programs were needed thirty years ago. As early as 1871, Frederick Douglass ridiculed the idea of racial quotas, arguing that they would promote "an image of blacks as privileged wards of the state." They were "absurd as a matter of practice" because some could use them to argue that blacks "should constitute one-eighth of the poets, statesmen, scholars, authors and philosophers."[b]

The debate over affirmative action and equality of opportunity became particularly intense during the Reagan years. In 1978 the Supreme Court addressed the issue of affirmative action in the case of Alan Bakke, a thirty-one-year-old paramedic, who was wait-listed for admission by the medical school at the University of California at Davis. The medical school maintained two separate admissions committees—one for white students and another for minority students. Bakke was not admitted, although his grades and standardized test scores were higher than those of all of the African American students admitted to the school. In *Regents of the University of California v. Bakke* (1978), a sharply divided Court concluded that Bakke's rejection had been illegal because the use of strict quotas was inappropriate.[c] The medical school, however, was free to "take race into account."

In 1979, the Court ruled that a factory and a union could voluntarily adopt a quota system in selecting black workers over more senior white workers for a training program. These kinds of programs outraged blue-collar Americans who had traditionally voted for the Democratic Party. In 1980, they abandoned the party in droves and supported Ronald Reagan, an ardent foe of affirmative action.

In subsequent affirmative action cases, the newly elected Reagan administration strongly urged the Court to invalidate the plans in question, but to no avail. With changes on the Court, however, including the 1986 elevation to chief

(continued)

"...BACK TO SQUARE ONE."

(Photo courtesy: Mike Peters/©Tribune Media Services, Inc. All rights reserved. Reprinted with permission)

justice of William Rehnquist, a strong opponent of affirmative action, the continued efforts of the Reagan administration finally began to pay off as the Court heard a new series of cases signaling an end to the advances in civil rights law. In a three-month period in 1989, the Supreme Court handed down five civil rights decisions limiting affirmative action programs and making it harder to prove employment discrimination. In 1995, the U.S. Supreme Court ruled that all federal affirmative action programs based on racial classifications are "inherently suspect," virtually ending affirmative action programs.[c]

The next year, the Court refused to review a challenge to a lower court ruling that upheld the constitutionality of a University of Texas practice that prohibited giving a "plus" to minorities applying to its state law school.[d] In the same year, California voters passed Proposition 209, which bans racial preferences throughout the state, including in college admissions. The University of California at Berkeley has seen its African American and Latino minority student populations plummet as a result.

1. With affirmative action now largely a thing of the past, do you see a need for new civil rights legislation to protect the growing minority population in the United States?
2. Do you see the Supreme Court as a vehicle to seek expanded rights or one likely to be curtailing civil rights in the future?

[a]"Poll: Whites, Blacks Differ on Quality of Race Relations," June 17, 1997. CNN Interactive (http://cnn.com/US/9706/10/gallup.poll/index.html)
[b]Frederick Douglass, *Frederick Douglass: Autobiography* (New York: Library of America, 1994), 28.
[c]*Adarand Constructors Inc. v. Pena,* 515 U.S. 2001 (1995).
[d]Cert. denied, *Texas* v. *Hopwood,* 116 S. Ct. 2581 (1996). See also Terrance Stutz, "UT Minority Enrollment Tested by Suit: Fate of Affirmative Action in Education Is at Issue," *Dallas Morning News* (October 14, 1995): 1A.

Cast Your Vote. What groups do you think need protection? To cast your vote, go to **www.ablongman.com/oconnor**

SUMMARY

When the Framers tried to "compromise" on the issue of slavery, they only postponed dealing with a volatile question that was later to rip the nation apart. Ultimately, the Civil War was fought to end slavery. Among its results were the triumph of the abolitionist position and adoption of the Thirteenth, Fourteenth, and Fifteenth Amendments. During this period women also sought expanded rights, especially the right to vote, but to no avail.

Although the Civil War amendments were added to the Constitution, the Supreme Court limited their application. As laws mandating racial segregation were passed throughout the South, the NAACP was founded in the early 1900s to press for equal rights for African Americans. Women's groups were also active during this period, successfully lobbying for passage of the Nineteenth Amendment, which assured them the right to vote.

In 1954, the U.S. Supreme Court ruled in *Brown* v. *Board of Education* that state-segregated school systems were unconstitutional. This victory empowered African Americans as they sought an end to other forms of pervasive discrimination. Bus boycotts and sit-ins were common tactics. As new groups were formed, freedom rides, pressure for voting rights, and massive nonviolent demonstrations became common lobbying tactics. This activity culminated in the passage of the Civil Rights Act of 1964. Now, African American and women's rights groups could attack private discrimination under the Civil Rights Act, or state-sanctioned discrimination under the equal protection clause of the Fourteenth Amendment.

Over the years the Supreme Court developed different tests to determine the constitutionality of various forms of discrimination. In general, strict scrutiny, the most stringent standard, was applied to race-based claims. An intermediate standard of review was developed to assess the constitutionality of sex discrimination claims.

Building on the successes of African Americans and women, other groups, including Native Americans, Latino Americans, gays and lesbians, and the disabled, organized to litigate for expanded civil rights as well as to lobby for antidiscrimination laws. The inadequacies of the confederate form of government created by the Articles of Confederation led the Framers to create an entirely new, federal system of government. From the summer of 1776 until today, the tension between the national and state governments has been at the core of our federal system.

The national government created by the Framers has both enumerated and implied powers, and also exercises concurrent powers with the states. Certain powers are denied to both the state and national governments. Certain guarantees concerning representation in Congress and protection against foreign attacks and domestic rebellion were made to the states in return for giving up some of their powers in the new federal system. Despite limitations, the national government is ultimately supreme.

Over the years, the powers of the national government have increased tremendously at the expense of the states. The Supreme Court, in particular, has played a key role in defining the relationship and powers of the national government through its broad interpretations of the supremacy and commerce clauses. For many years, however, it adhered to the notion of dual federalism, which tended to limit the national government's authority in areas such as slavery and, after the Civil War, civil rights. This notion of a limited role for the national government in some spheres ultimately fell by the wayside after the Great Depression.

The rapid creation of New Deal programs to alleviate many problems caused by the Depression led to a tremendous expansion of the federal government through the growth of federal services and grant-in-aid programs. This growth escalated during the Johnson administration and in the mid- to late 1970s. After his election in 1980, Ronald Reagan, upset by the growth of federal services, tried to reverse the tide through what he termed New Federalism. He built on earlier efforts by Richard M. Nixon to consolidate categorical grants into fewer block grant programs, and to give state and local governments greater control over programs. Since 1993, the national government and the states have been in a constant dialogue to reframe the structure of the federal-state relationship.

Over the years, the Supreme Court has been a major player in recent trends in the federal-state relationship. Its decisions in the areas of education, civil rights, voting rights, and the performance of state functions generally have given the federal government a wider role in the day-to-day functioning of the states, limiting the scope of the states' police powers. Recent decisions, however, indicate the Court's willingness to reassess the federal role in many areas.

KEY TERMS

affirmative action programs, p. 158

Brown v. *Board of Education,* p. 141

civil rights, p. 132

Civil Rights Act of 1964, p. 145

equal protection clause, p. 141

Fifteenth Amendment, p. 135

Fourteenth Amendment, p. 135

grandfather clause, p. 137

Plessy v. *Ferguson,* p. 137

strict scrutiny, p. 148

suffrage movement, p. 138

suspect classification, p. 148

Thirteenth Amendment, p. 135

SELECTED READINGS

Bacchi, Carol Lee. *The Politics of Affirmative Action: 'Women,' Equality and Category Politics.* Thousand Oaks, Calif.: Sage, 1996.

Bergmann, Barbara R. *In Defense of Affirmative Action.* New York: Basic Books, 1996.

Bowen, William G., and Derek C. Bok, *The Shape of the River.* Princeton, N.J. : Princeton University Press, 1998.

Bullock, Charles III, and Charles Lamb, eds. *Implementation of Civil Rights Policy.* Pacific Grove, Calif.: Brooks/Cole, 1984.

Eastland, Terry. *Ending Affirmative Action: The Case for Colorblind Justice.* New York: Basic Books, 1997.

Edley, Christopher, Jr. *Not All Black and White: Affirmative Action, Race, and American Values.* New York: Hill and Wang, 1996.

Freeman, Jo. *The Politics of Women's Liberation.* New York: Longman, 1975.

Kluger, Richard. *Simple Justice.* New York: Vintage, 1975.

Knobel, Dale T. *"America for the Americans": The Nativist Movement in the United States.* Old Tappen, N.J.: Twayne, 1996.

Mansbridge, Jane J. *Why We Lost the ERA.* Chicago: University of Chicago Press, 1986.

McClain, Paula D., and Joseph Stewart Jr. *"Can We All Get Along?" Racial and Ethnic Minorities in American Politics,* 2nd ed. Boulder, Colo.: Westview Press, 1998.

McGlen, Nancy E., and Karen O'Connor. *Women, Politics and American Society,* 2nd ed. Upper Saddle River, N.J.: Prentice Hall, 1998.

Reed, Adolp, Jr., *Without Justice for All: The New Liberalism and Our Retreat from Racial Equity.* Boulder, Colo.: Westview Press, 1999.

Rosales, Francisco A., and Arturo Rosales, eds. *Chicano! The History of the Mexican American Civil Rights Movement.* Houston, Tex.: Arte Publico Press, 1996.

Verba, Sidney, and Gary R. Orren. *Equality in America: The View from the Top.* Cambridge, Mass.: Harvard University Press, 1985.

Williams, Juan. *Eyes on the Prize: America's Civil Rights Years, 1954–1965.* New York: Penguin, 1987.

6 Congress

(Photo courtesy: Reuters New Media Inc./Corbis)

Partisanship is alive and well in the U.S. Congress. Witness the political maneuverings that surrounded the ultimately unsuccessful attempts to enact gun control by Democrats in the 106th Congress and their abandonment of the issue by 2001. On April 21, 1999, two students dressed in long baggy black coats walked into Columbine High School in Littleton, Colorado, unleashing a bombing and shooting spree that left fourteen students and one teacher dead and shocked the nation. It was the fifth episode since 1997 in which one or more students opened fire on other students in a public school.[1]

In the days after the Columbine massacre, Senate Majority Leader Trent Lott (R–Miss.) promised quick Senate action on a gun control measure. The minority leader, Thomas Daschle (D–S.Dak.), initially said more gun control is not the solution. Disagreeing with his party leader, Representative Edward J. Markey (D–Mass.) "predicted the public, angered over 'the toxic cocktail of media violence and easy availability of guns,'" would be quick to demand that their elected representatives take some action on gun control. Still, many wondered if Congress would bow to pressure from the powerful National Rifle Association (NRA), a 2.8-million-member group that spent over $3.4 million backing its preferred candidates in the 1998 congressional elections. The new House Speaker, J. Dennis Hastert (R–Ill.), as he expressed his condolences to the families of the dead and injured Columbine victims, called only for a National Conference on Youth and Culture, never mentioning possible legislation.[2]

Less than a month later, the Republican-controlled Senate turned down a Democratic-sponsored bill to require background checks on all firearms

would be up for reelection every two years. Senators were to be tied to their state legislatures closely and were expected to represent those interests in the Senate. State legislators lost this influence with ratification of the Seventeenth Amendment in 1913, which provides for the direct election of senators by the voters.

In contrast to senators' six-year terms, members of the House of Representatives were to be elected to two-year terms by a vote of the eligible voters in each congressional district. It was expected that the House would be the more "democratic" branch of government because its members would be more responsible to the people (because they were directly elected by them) and more responsive to them (because they were up for reelection every two years).

Apportionment and Redistricting

The U.S. Constitution requires that a census, which entails the counting of all Americans, be conducted every ten years. Because the Constitution requires that representation in the House be based on state population, after each census congressional districts are redrawn by state legislatures to reflect population shifts, so that each member in Congress will represent approximately the same number of residents. This process of redrawing congressional districts to reflect increases or decreases in seats allotted to the states, as well as population shifts within a state, is called **redistricting.** When shifts occur in the national population, as revealed after the Census Bureau makes its report, states gain or lose congressional seats.

redistricting

The redrawing of congressional districts to reflect increases or decreases in seats allotted to the states, as well as population shifts within a state.

Through redistricting, the political party in each statehouse with the greatest number of members tries to assure that the maximum number of its party members can be elected to Congress. This redistricting process, which has gone on since the first census in 1790, often involves what is called **gerrymandering** (see Figure 6.1) as state legislators try to maximize their majority party's chances to win new seats.

Creative redistricting and the actions of state legislators have often created problems that have ended up in litigation. Over the years, the Supreme Court has ruled that

gerrymandering

The legislative process through which the majority party in each statehouse tries to assure that the maximum number of representatives from its political party can be elected to Congress and the statehouse through the redrawing of legislative districts.

- Congressional as well as state legislative districts must have "substantially equal" populations.[8]
- Purposeful gerrymandering of a congressional district to dilute minority strength is illegal under the Voting Rights Act of 1965.[9]
- Redrawing of districts for obvious racial purposes to enhance minority representation is unconstitutional. North Carolina's 12th Congressional district, as originally drawn (see Figure 6.1) was ruled unconstitutional in a 5–4 vote because it denies the constitutional rights of white citizens.[10] In 2001, however, the Supreme Court ruled that the redrawn 12th district, now shorter and fatter with fewer African Americans, was simply old-fashioned gerrymandering and therefore constitutional.

FIGURE 6.1   Gerrymandering

Two drawings—one a mocking cartoon—the other all too real—showing the bizarre geographical contortions involved in gerrymandering. The North Carolina district was found unconstitutional by the Supreme Court.

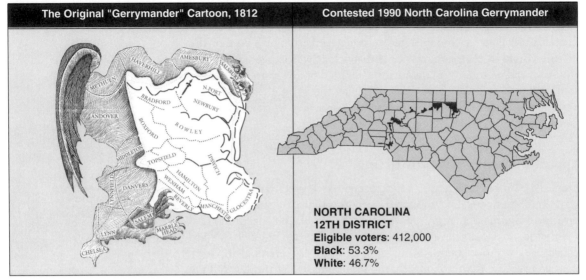

Source: From "Snakes or Ladders?" by David Van Biema, *Time*, July 12, 1993. Copyright ©1993 Time Inc. Reprinted with permission.

Constitutional Powers of Congress

The Constitution specifically gives to Congress its most important power—the authority to make laws. This law-making power is shared by both houses. No bill (proposed law) can become law, for example, without the consent of both houses. Examples of other constitutionally shared powers include the power to declare war, raise an army and navy, coin money, regulate commerce, establish the federal courts and their jurisdiction, establish rules of immigration and naturalization, and "make all Laws which shall be necessary and proper for carrying into Execution the foregoing Powers." As interpreted by the Supreme Court, the *necessary and proper clause,* when coupled with one or more of the specific powers enumerated in Article I, section 8, has allowed Congress to increase the scope of its authority, often at the expense of the states and into areas not necessarily envisioned by the Framers.

Article I also gives special, exclusive powers to each house in addition to their shared role in lawmaking. For example, as noted in Table 6.1, the Constitution specifies that all revenue bills must originate in the House of Representatives. The House also has the power of **impeachment,** the authority to charge the president, vice president, or other "civil officers," including federal judges, with *"Treason, Bribery, or other high Crimes and Misdemeanors."* Only the Senate is authorized to conduct trials of impeachment, with a two-thirds vote being necessary before a federal official can be removed from office.

impeachment

The power delegated to the House of Representatives in the Constitution to charge the president, vice president, or other "civil officers," including federal judges, with "Treason, Bribery, or other high Crimes and Misdemeanors." This is the first step in the constitutional process of removing such officials from office.

TABLE 6.1   Key Differences Between the House and Senate

CONSTITUTIONAL DIFFERENCES

House	*Senate*
Initiates all revenue bills	Offers "advice and consent" on many major
Initiates impeachment procedures and passes	presidential appointments
articles of impeachment	Tries impeached officials
Two-year terms	Six-year terms (one-third up for reelection every
435 members (apportioned by population)	two years)
	100 members (two from each state)
	Approves treaties

DIFFERENCES IN OPERATION

House	*Senate*
More centralized, more formal; stronger leadership	Less centralized, less formal; weaker leadership
Rules Committee fairly powerful in controlling time	No Rules Committee; limits on debate come through
and rules of debate (in conjunction with the Speaker)	unanimous consent or cloture of filibuster
More impersonal	More personal
Power less evenly distributed	Power more evenly distributed
Members are highly specialized	Members are generalists
Emphasizes tax and revenue policy	Emphasizes foreign policy

CHANGES IN THE INSTITUTION

House	*Senate*
Power centralized in the Speaker's inner circle	Senate workload increasing and informality
of advisors	breaking down; filibusters more frequent
House procedures are becoming more efficient	Becoming more difficult to pass legislation
Turnover is relatively high	Turnover is moderate

The House and Senate share in the impeachment process, but the Senate has the sole authority to approve major presidential appointments, including federal judges, ambassadors, and Cabinet- and sub-Cabinet-level positions. The Senate, too, must approve by a two-thirds vote all treaties entered into by the president.

THE MEMBERS OF CONGRESS

Being a member of Congress isn't easy. There are indications that the high cost of living in Washington, maintaining two homes, political scandals, intense media scrutiny, the need to tackle hard issues, and a growth of partisan dissension is taking a toll on many members. And, of course, they are constantly seeking campaign contributions if they plan to seek reelection. Members, moreover, must attempt to appease two constituencies—party leaders, colleagues, and lobbyists in Washington, D.C., and their constituents at home. As revealed in Table 6.2, members spend full days at home as well as in D.C. Most members of Congress try almost frantically to keep in touch with their constituents. Even if they

TABLE 6.2   A Day in the Life of a Member of Congress

Typical Member's At-Home Schedule		*Typical Member's Washington Schedule*	
Monday, March 20		**Wednesday, April 10**	
7:30 A.M.	Business group breakfast, 20 members of the business community leaders (1 hour)	8:00 A.M.	Budget Study Group—Chairman Leon Panetta, Budget Committee, room 340 Cannon Building
8:45	Hoover Elementary School, 6th grade class assembly (45 min)	8:45	Mainstream Forum Meeting, room 2344 Rayburn Building
9:45	National Agriculture Day, speech, Holiday Inn South (45 min)	9:15	Meeting with Consulting Engineers Council of N.C. from Raleigh about various issues of concern
10:45	Supplemental Food Shelf, pass foodstuffs to needy families (1 hour)	9:45	Meet with N.C. Soybean Assn. representatives re: agriculture appropriations projects
12:00	Community College, student/faculty lunch, speech and Q & A (45 min)	10:15	WCHL radio interview (by phone)
1:00 P.M.	Sunset Terrace Elementary School, assembly 4, 5, 6 graders, remarks/Q & A (45 min)	10:30	Tape weekly radio show—budget
(Travel Time: 1:45 P.M.–2:45 P.M.)		11:00	Meet with former student, now an author, about intellectual property issue
2:45	Plainview Day Care Facility, owner wishes to discuss changes in federal law (1 hour)	1:00 P.M.	Agriculture Subcommittee Hearing—Budget Overview and General Agriculture Outlook, room 2362 Rayburn Building
4:00	Town Hall Meeting, American Legion (1 hour)	2:30	Meeting with Chairman Bill Ford and southern Democrats re: HR-5., Striker Replacement Bill, possible amendments
(Travel Time: 5:00 P.M.–5:45 P.M.)		3:15	Meet with Close-Up students from district on steps of Capitol for photo and discussions
5:45	PTA meeting, speech, education issues before Congress (also citizen involvement with national associations) (45 min)	3:45	Meet with Duke professor re: energy research programs
6:30	Annual Dinner, St. John's Lutheran Church Developmental Activity Center (30 min)	4:30	Meet with constituent of Kurdish background re: situation in Iraq
7:15	Association for Children for Enforcement of Support meeting to discuss problems of enforcing child support payments (45 min)	5:30–7:00	Reception—Sponsored by National Assn. of Home Builders, honoring new president Mark Tipton from Raleigh, H-328 Capitol
(Travel Time: 8:00 p.m.–8:30 p.m.)		6:00–8:00	Reception—Honoring retiring Rep. Bill Gray, Washington Court Hotel
8:30	Students Against Drunk Driving (SADD) meeting, speech, address; drinking age, drunk driving, uniform federal penalties (45 min)	6:00–8:00	Reception—Sponsored by Firefighters Assn., room B-339 Rayburn Building
9:30	State University class, discuss business issues before Congress (1 hour)	6:00–8:00	Reception—American Financial Services Assn., Gold Room

Sources: Craig Shultz, ed., *Setting Course. A Congressional Management Guide* (Washington, D.C.: American University, 1994), 335; David E. Price. *The Congressional Experience: A View from the Hill* (Boulder, Colo.: Westview Press, 1992), 38.

come under charges of losing touch, members can try to step up their at-home activities. They send newsletters, hold town meetings throughout their districts, and get important help from their staffs, who help constituents frustrated by the faceless, form-filled federal bureaucracy.

Increasingly, senators and representatives place most of their case-workers back in their home district offices, where they are more accessible to constituents, who can drop by and talk to a friendly face about their problems. In larger districts caseworkers may "ride the circuit," taking the helping hand of the congressional office to county seats, crossroads, post offices, and mobile offices.

The average House member has seventeen full-time staff members; the average size of a senator's office staff is forty-four, although this number varies with state population.[11]

Running for Office and Staying in Office

Despite the long hours and hard work senators and representatives put in, thousands aspire to these jobs every year. Yet only 535 men and women actually serve in the U.S. Congress. Membership in one of the two major political parties is almost always a prerequisite for election because election laws in various states often discriminate against independents (those without party affiliation) and minor-party candidates.

Incumbency is an informal factor that helps members to stay in office once they are elected. Simply put, being in office helps you stay in office. It's often very difficult for outsiders to win because they don't have the advantages enjoyed by incumbents, including name recognition, access to media, and fund raising. Moreover, most Americans approve of their *own* members of Congress. It is not surprising, then, that from 1980 to 1990, an average of 95 percent of the incumbents who sought reelection actually won their primary and general election races. More recent elections saw even higher proportions of incumbents returning to office.

Voluntary retirements, regular district changes, and occasional defeats continue to make turnover in Congress substantial in spite of the benefits reaped by incumbents. The presence of so many new members has made the idea of term limits less pressing to many who viewed the incumbency advantage enjoyed by members of Congress as a roadblock to significant change in the institution and the way it did business.

Representative Bernie Sanders (I–Vt.) one of three non–Republicans or Democrats, is actually a socialist. One of two independents in the House, Sanders said of his election: "What Vermonters wanted is somebody to go down there and stand up and fight for ordinary people, rather than as the vast majority of members of Congress do—protect the interests of the wealthy and the powerful." In 2001, his fellow Vermonter James Jeffords also became an Independent. Jeffords's actions, however, had far greater consequences, as his defection and decision to ally himself with Democrats meant the Democrats took over control of the Senate. (Photo courtesy: Glen Russell/ SIPA Press)

Term Limits.   A **term-limits** movement began sweeping the nation in the late 1980s because of voter frustration with gridlock and ethics problems in Congress and in state legislatures.

In 1994, many Republicans running for Congress signed the Republicans' 1994 Contract with America which called for congressional passage of federal term limits, in 1995 the U.S. Supreme Court ruled that state-imposed limitations on the terms of members of Congress was unconstitutional.[12] Thus, any efforts to enact congressional term limits would necessitate a constitutional amendment—not an easy

incumbency
The status derived by one who holds an office or elected position. This usually provides a substantial advantage in seeking selection.

term limits
Legislation designating that state or federal elected legislators can serve only a specified number of years.

(Photo courtesy: Oliphant, © Universal Press Syndicate. Reprinted with permission. All rights reserved.)

STILL THE BEST CONGRESSIONAL TERM-LIMITING DEVICE.

VISUAL LITERACY
Why Is It So Hard to Defeat an Incumbent?

WEB EXPLORATION
To evaluate your own representative, see
www.ablongman.com/oconnor

feat. In the 104th Congress, a term-limits amendment was brought to the floor for a vote. The proposal fell sixty votes short of the two-thirds vote needed to propose a constitutional amendment. The measure also failed in the Senate, where Republicans failed to muster enough votes to cut off a Democratic filibuster.

What Does Congress Look Like?

Congress is better educated, more white, more male, and richer than the rest of the United States. The Senate, in fact, is often called the "Millionaires' Club," and its members sport names like Rockefeller and DuPont. The average age of House members in the 107th Congress is fifty-four; the average age of Senators is fifty-nine and no Senator is younger than forty.

As revealed in Figure 6.2, the 1992 elections, the first national elections after states redistricted congressional districts in response to the 1990 Census, saw a record number of women, African Americans, and other minorities elected to Congress. In 1992, for the first time ever, both senators elected from a single state—California—were women, Democrats Dianne Feinstein and Barbara Boxer. By the 107th Congress, the total number of women in Congress increased to seventy-five; sixty-two in the House and thirteen in the Senate. This includes two women who serve as the elected (but nonvoting) delegates in the House. The 2000 election also saw the election of First Lady Hillary Rodham Clinton (D–N.Y.) to the Senate and the appointment of Jean Carnahan (D–Mo.) to fill her deceased husband's seat.

The number of African Americans in the House increased by two to thirty-nine. There are twenty-one Hispanics in the 107th —all in the House (sixteen Democrats and one Republican). The number of Asians remained steady at six—two in the Senate and four in the House. There is but a lone Native American in each chamber of Congress.

Jean Carnahan (D–Mo.) was appointed to the Senate seat won by her husband, Mel Carnahan, who died in a plane crash in 2000. (Photo courtesy: Orlin Wagner/AP/Wide World Photos)

FIGURE 6.2   Numbers of Women and Minorities in Congress

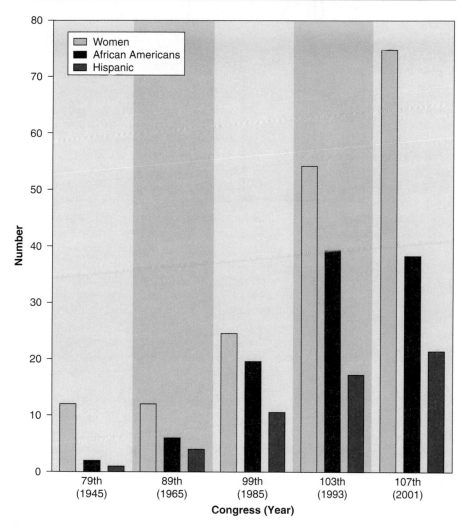

Source: Harold W. Stanley and Richard G. Niemi, eds., *Vital Statistics on American Politics,* 1997–1998 (Washington D.C.: CQ Press, 1998), 197. Data updated by authors.

The Representational Role of Members of Congress

Questions of who should be represented and how that should happen are critical in a republic. British political philosopher Edmund Burke (1729–1787), who also served in the British Parliament, believed that although he was elected from Bristol, it was his duty to represent the interests of the *entire* nation. According to Burke, representatives should be **trustees** who listen to the opinions of their constituents and then can be trusted to use their own best judgment to make final decisions.

trustee

Role played by elected representatives who listen to constituents' opinions and then use their best judgment to make final decisions.

POINT/COUNTERPOINT

IS PORK BARRELING WASTEFUL SPENDING OR LEGITIMATE EXPENDITURE?

The term "pork barrel" dates back to the early 1800s when pork was salted (as a preservative) and kept in a barrel. In the late 1800s, it became used as political slang to mean goodies for the local district paid for by the taxpayers at large. Today, Citizens Against Government Waste (CAGW), a nonpartisan, independent watchdog group, defines pork barreling as any government expenditure that meets at least one of these seven criteria:

- Requested by only one member of Congress;
- Not specifically authorized;
- Not competitively awarded;
- Not requested by the president;
- Greatly exceeds the president's budget request from the previous year;
- Not the subject of congressional hearings; or
- Serves only a local or special interest.

This group argues that any spending that fits this definition is wasteful and should not be allowed. In fiscal year 2000, Citizens Against Government Waste (CAGW) estimated that the budget contained in excess of $14.6 billion in earmarks or pork barrel spending. Measured in the hundreds of millions or billions of dollars, pork barrel spending is not a huge part of the whole trillion dollar federal budget, however. To many members of Congress, one person's pork is another person's legitimate budgetary expenditure. Almost all members of Congress do it and a large number of them argue that what CAGW others call pork is not extravagant and wasteful spending but good constituent service. Let's examine these two points of view.

Opponents of pork barreling, such as CAGW and Common Cause, oppose pork barrel spending as illegitimate and against the national interest and the interests of the general taxpayers. The Libertarian Party even goes as far as defining most government spending as pork barrel and unnecessary. Opponents often cite examples of multi-million or billion dollar spending that is obviously wasteful or downright silly: the multi-million dollar study of cow flatulence, a one million dollar appropriation to determine why Americans don't ride their bikes to work, and, in 2000, the one million dollars given to Texas Tech University for an experiment on growing vegetables in outer space.

delegate

Role played by elected representatives who vote the way their constituents would want them to, regardless of their own opinions.

politico

Role played by elected representatives who act as trustees or as delegates, depending on the issue.

A second theory of representation holds that representatives are **delegates.** True delegates are representatives who vote the way their constituents would want them to, whether or not those opinions are the representative's.

Not surprisingly members of Congress and other legislative bodies generally don't fall neatly into either category. It is often unclear how constituents feel about a particular issue, or there may be conflicting opinions within a single constituency. With these difficulties in mind, a third theory of representation holds that **politicos** alternately don the hats of trustee or delegate, depending on the issue. On an issue of great concern to their constituents, representatives will most likely vote as

Opponents of pork barrel spending argue that government monies ought to be spent on projects that benefit a large number of people and that all spending should go through a deliberative process, not simply be added as a rider to a popular bill (which is how much pork gets signed into law). CAGW and others believe that irresponsible and reckless spending should be curbed through the implementation of the Grace Commission plan. The Grace Commission was impaneled by President Reagan in 1982 and after two years of analyzing government expenditures produced a 47-volume 21,000-page report on wasteful government spending and suggested numerous ways to reduce fraud, errors, and waste through better management, oversight, and enhanced accountability. The Grace Commission proposed cuts of over $141 million per year for three years without cutting any essential services.

Members of Congress, and the people who benefit from these projects, support these spending earmarks as legitimate expenditures as well as positive benefits. Members of Congress have staffs who do constituent service in order to help them get reelected as well as to help them represent the needs and views of their dis-

tricts. These same members see what some have called "pork barrel" spending as another way of representing their constituents and benefiting their districts: Grand Rapids, Michigan, needed that highway to relieve local congestion; Savannah, Georgia, needed the harbor dredged so it could compete with other ports and maintain the local economy; California, hard hit by military base closures in the 1980s, was in desperate need of a refurbished naval base in San Diego; West Virginia is one of the poorest states in the union and needed the jobs provided by the FBI fingerprinting facility and the intelligence branch listening posts. These are instances of effective constituent service. Many members of Congress also argue that if they don't jockey for money for their own district, it will go to other districts instead.

What do you think? Is so-called pork barrel wasteful spending or legitimate expenditure?
Go to www.ablongman.com/oconnor

delegates; on other issues, perhaps those that are less visible, representatives will act as trustees and use their own best judgment.

How a representative views his or her role—as a trustee, delegate, or politico—may still not answer the question of whether or not it makes a difference if a representative or senator is male or female, African American or Hispanic or Caucasian, young or old, gay or straight. Burke's ideas don't even begin to address more practical issues of representation. Can a man, for example, represent the interests of women as well as a woman? Can a rich woman represent the interests of the poor? The combinations are endless. See Politics Now: Seventy-Five and Counting for more discussion of women members.

GLOBAL POLITICS

REPRESENTATION IN THE INDONESIAN LEGISLATURE

As mentioned earlier, the representative function of legislatures is critical to a republic. In most of the industrialized democracies, the legislature is the only directly elected part of the national government. In the United States, members of Congress are first and foremost representatives of electoral districts, which is why district constituents play such a large role in what legislators do. The constitutional requirement that members of Congress reside in their districts reinforces that tendency. Other industrialized democracies such as Japan, Germany, and Italy mix single member districts with proportional representation, where candidates represent a political party, not a district.

Indonesia provides another form of representation. In the 1999 election for the Indonesian house of representatives, thirty-eight seats were reserved for the military. Under the New Order government that had been in power from 1966–1998, the number had been higher. Reserving seats had ensured that the Suharto dictatorship maintained control over the legislature, and the truncated version that followed in 1999 demonstrates the difficulties democratizing governments often face in eliminating the vestiges of powerful nondemocratic interests.

Electoral Rules and Representation in 11 Legislatures

Country	Lower House of Legislature	Seats	Electoral Rules
Canada	House of Commons	301	Single member districts
China	National People's Congress	2,979	Indirectly elected
France	National Assembly	577	Single member districts
Germany	Bundestag	669	Single member districts, proportional representation
Indonesia	House of Representatives	500	Multimember districts, reserved seats
Italy	Chamber of Deputies	630	Single member districts, proportional representation
Japan	House of Representatives	500	Single member districts, proportional representation
Mexico	Chamber of Deputies	500	Single member districts, proportional representation
Russia	State Duma	500	Single member districts, proportional representation
United Kingdom	House of Commons	652	Single member districts
United States	House of Representatives	435	Single member districts

Source: CIA World Factbook 2000 online, http://www.odci.gov/cia/publications/factbook/geos.

Members of Congressional Black Caucus trying to (symbolically) stop Electoral College voting in joint session in January 2001. (Photo courtesy: Marshall/Liaison Agency/Getty Source)

HOW CONGRESS IS ORGANIZED

Every two years, a new Congress is seated. After ascertaining the formal qualifications of new members, the Congress organizes itself as it prepares for the business of the coming session. Among the first items on its agenda are the election of new leaders and the adoption of rules for conducting its business. As illustrated in Figure 6.3, each house has a hierarchical leadership structure.

The House of Representatives

Even in the first Congress in 1789, the House of Representatives was almost three times larger than the Senate. It is not surprising, then, that from the beginning the House has been more tightly organized, more elaborately structured, and governed by stricter rules (see Table 6.1). Traditionally, loyalty to the party leadership and voting along party lines have been more common in the House than in the Senate. House leaders also play a key role in moving the business of the House along. Historically, the Speaker of the House, the majority and minority leaders, and the majority and minority house whips have made up the party leadership that runs Congress. This has now been expanded to include deputy minority whips of both parties.

The Speaker of the House. The **Speaker of the House** is the only officer of the House of Representatives specifically mentioned in the Constitution. The Speaker is formally elected at the beginning of each new Congress by the entire House. Traditionally, the Speaker is a member of the **majority party,** the party in each house with the greatest number of members, as are all committee chairs. The **minority party** is the

COMPARATIVE
Comparing Legislatures

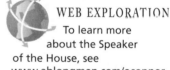

WEB EXPLORATION
To learn more about the Speaker of the House, see www.ablongman.com/oconnor

Speaker of the House
The only officer of the House of Representatives specifically mentioned in the Constitution; elected at the beginning of each new congress by the entire House; traditionally a member of the majority party.

majority party
The political party in each house of Congress with the most members.

minority party
Party with the second most members in either house of Congress.

FIGURE 6.3   Organizational Structure of the House of Representatives and the Senate early in the 107th Congress

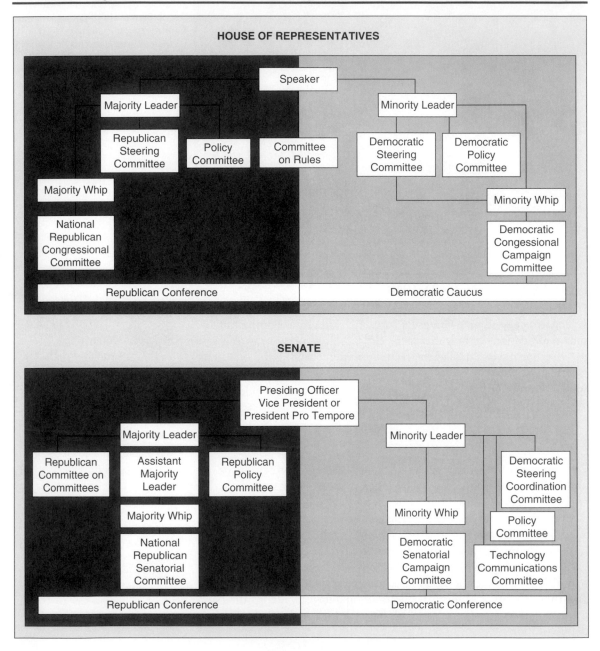

major party with the second most members in either house. While typically not the member with the longest service, the Speaker generally has served in the House for a long time and in other House leadership positions as sort of an apprenticeship.

POLITICS NOW

SEVENTY-FIVE AND COUNTING: WOMEN IN THE U.S. CONGRESS

In 2000, the nine women in the United States Senate—three Republicans and six Democrats—came together to pen a book about their experiences in Congress and their efforts to work together to make a difference in the Senate.[a] By 2001, their numbers had grown to thirteen with the election of four additional women, all Democrats. Gains in the House were far more modest, but together women's representation in the 107th Congress is at an all-time high.

Study after study continues to find that women make a difference in all legislative bodies, especially when it comes to sponsoring legislation involving women's issues from health care to parental leave.[b] Still, their relatively low numbers continue to mean that women's interests are not always addressed. For example, in late 1999, Senate Foreign Relations Chairman Jesse Helms (R–N.C.) actually called Capitol police to remove nine female House members from a committee hearing after they tried

to present him with a letter calling him as committee chair to hold hearings on Senate ratification of the 1979 United Nations Convention to Eliminate All Forms of Discrimination Against Women. Helms had refused to hold hearings on the treaty, which has been ratified by 160 nations. He also would not meet with House members who want the United States to ratify the treaty. After three months of Helms's dodging their request for a meeting, the women opted to confront him. "Now, please be a lady," Helms admonished Rep. Lynn C. Woolsey (D–Calif.), the leader of the House women who stood at the back of the room with blow-ups of the letter with one hundred House signatures. "If they want to be treated like members of Congress," said one Helms aide in defending his boss, "they ought to behave like members of Congress."[c]

While these women of the House were not able to prod Helms, the thirteen female Senators are in an unusually advantageous position in the Senate. With the Senate so closely divided (50–49–1), these thirteen women can provide a potential bloc of moderate votes to urge the passage of policies of particular interest to women from education to health care to Social Security reform.

Rep. Lynn Woolsey (D–Calif.) is one of seventy-five female members of Congress. (Photo courtesy: Dudley M. Brooks, ©1998 *The Washington Post*. Reprinted with permission.)

[a]*Nine and Counting: The Women of the Senate*. Barbara Mikulski...[et al.] written with Catherine Whitney 1st Editor New York: William Morrow ©2000.
[b]Sue Thomas, *How Women Legislate* (New York: Oxford University Press, 1994).
[c]Helen Dewar, "Ladies of the House Rebuffed," *The Washington Post* (October 28, 1999): A31.

The Speaker presides over the House, oversees House business, is the official spokesperson for the House of Representatives, and is second in the line of presidential succession. Moreover, he is the House liaison with the president and generally has great political influence within the chamber. Through his parliamentary and political skills, he is expected to smooth the passage of party-backed legislation through the House.

Newt Gingrich, the first Republican Speaker in forty years, convinced fellow Republicans to return important formal powers to the Speaker. In return for a rule preventing Speakers from serving for more than four consecutive congresses, the Speaker was given unprecedented authority, including the power to refer bills to committee, ending the practice of joint referral of bills to more than one committee, where they might fare better. These formal changes, along with his personal leadership skills, allowed Gingrich to exercise greater control over the House and its agenda than any other Speaker in decades.

TIMELINE
The Speaker
of the House

In time, Gingrich's highly visible role as a revolutionary transformed him into a negative symbol outside the Beltway as his public popularity plunged. Exit polls conducted on election day 1996 revealed that 60 percent had an unfavorable opinion of the Speaker, although that dislike did not appear to translate into votes against incumbent House Republicans. But in 1998, Republicans were stung when they failed to win more seats in the House and Senate—seats they needed if they were to impeach Bill Clinton. Gingrich's general unpopularity with large segments of the public reinforced Republicans' discontent with Gingrich. The 105th Republican Congress had few legislative successes; members were forced to accept a budget advanced by the White House, and Republicans running for office in 1998 lacked the coherent theme that had been so successful for them in 1994. These were but two of many reasons that prompted several members to announce that they would run against the Speaker. Gingrich, who could read the writing on the wall, opted to resign rather than face the prospect that he might not be re-elected to the position that he had coveted so long.

Representative Bob Livingston quickly emerged as Gingrich's successor. Amid the Clinton impeachment fervor, however, news of a longtime Livingston extramarital affair broke, and Livingston stunningly announced that he would give up his expected speakership and resign from the House altogether. Scandal-weary Republicans then turned to someone largely unknown to the public, a well-liked and respected one-time high school coach, J. Dennis Hastert. Since coming into his "accidental speakership," Hastert has shown himself to be a "pragmatic and cautious politician" as he tries to deal with his "whisker thin (ten vote) majority."[13] Through the 106th Congress, Hastert boasted a remarkable record of mobilizing his majority. In fact, "he never lost a vote on a rule to govern floor debate, a feat not seen in at least a decade."[14] Still, he and the House minority leader, Richard Gephart (D–Mo.), enjoy a strained relationship and the Speaker even campaigned for Gephart's opponent, "a blatant departure from traditional leadership decorum."[15]

majority leader
The elected leader of the party controlling the most seats in the U.S. House of Representatives or the Senate; second in authority to the Speaker of the House, and in the Senate is regarded as its most powerful member.

minority leader
The elected leader of the party with the second highest number of elected representatives in either the House or the Senate.

Other House Leaders.   After the Speaker, the next most powerful people in the House are the majority and minority leaders, who are elected in their individual party caucuses. The **majority leader** is the second most important person in the House; his counterpart is the **minority leader.**

Shortly after the 2000 election, Senator Barbara A. Mikulski (D–Md.), second from the right, met with her Republican and Democratic women colleagues to welcome the newly elected Senate members to Capitol Hill. From left, Senator Blanche Lincoln (D–Alaska), Senator-elect Jean Carnahan (D–Mo.), Senator Susan Collins (R–Maine), Senator Patty Murray (D–Wash.), Senator-elect Hillary Rodham Clinton (D–N.Y.), Senator Kay Bailey Hutchison (R–Tex.), Mikulski, and Senator Dianne Feinstein (D–Calif.). (Photo courtesy: Alex Wong/Liaison/Newsmakers/Online USA)

Both work closely with the Speaker, and the majority leader helps the Speaker schedule proposed legislation for debate on the House floor.

The Speaker and majority and minority leaders are assisted in their leadership efforts by the majority and minority **whips,** who are elected by party members in caucuses. The concept of whips originated in the British House of Commons, where they were named after the "whipper in," the rider who keeps the hounds together in a fox hunt. Party whips—who were first designated in the House in 1899 and in the Senate in 1913—do, as their name suggests, try to "whip" fellow Democrats or Republicans into line on partisan issues.

whip
One of several representatives who keep close contact with all members and take "nose counts" on key votes, prepare summaries of bills, and in general act as communications links within the party.

The Senate

The Constitution specifies that the presiding officer of the Senate is the vice president of the United States. He is not a member of the Senate, and he votes only in the case of a tie. Vice President Dick Cheney is the first vice president since 1881 to preside over an evenly divided Senate.

The official chair of the Senate is the president pro tempore, who is selected by the majority party. He presides over the Senate in the absence of the vice president. The position is largely honorific and generally goes to the most senior senator of the majority party. Since presiding over the Senate can be a rather perfunctory duty, the duty actually rotates among junior members.

The true leader of the Senate is the majority leader, elected to the position by the majority party. Because the Senate is a smaller and more collegial body, operating without many of the more formal House rules concerning debate, the majority leader is not nearly as powerful as the Speaker of the House, who presides over a more overtly partisan body that requires more control.

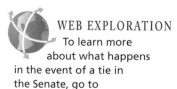

WEB EXPLORATION To learn more about what happens in the event of a tie in the Senate, go to www.ablongman.com/oconnor

WEB EXPLORATION
To get up-to-date data
on House leaders, see
www.ablongman.com/oconnor

The majority and minority whips round out the leadership positions in the Senate and perform functions similar to those of their House counterparts. But leading and whipping in the Senate can be quite a challenge. Senate rules have always given tremendous power to individual senators; in most cases senators can offer any kind of amendments to legislation on the floor, and an individual senator can bring all work on the floor to a halt indefinitely through a filibuster unless sixty senators vote to cut him or her off.[16] Control is likely to be difficult for Tom Daschle, who became the majority leader in the 107th Congress in June 2001 when James Jeffords abandoned the Republican Party to become an Independent, giving the Democrats control.

The Role of Political Parties

The organization of both houses of Congress is closely tied to political parties and their strength in each House. For the party breakdowns in both houses, see Figure 6.4. Parties play a key role in the committee system, an organizational feature of Congress that facilitates its law-making and oversight functions. The committees, controlled by the majority party in each chamber, often set the congressional agendas.[17] At the beginning of each new Congress—the 106th Congress, for example, sat in two sessions, one in 1999 and one in 2000—the members of each party gather in a party caucus or conference. The party caucuses—called "caucus" by House Democrats and "conference" by House and Senate Republicans and Senate Democrats—have several roles, including nominating or electing party officers, reviewing committee assignments, discussing party policy, imposing party discipline, setting party themes, and coordinating media, including talk radio. Conference chairs are recognized party leaders who work with others who are part of the House or Senate leadership.[18]

FIGURE 6.4   Party Strength in the 107th Congress

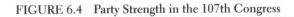

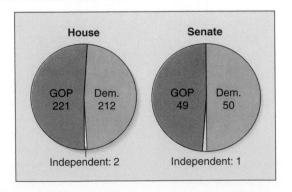

The Committee System

The saying "Congress in session is Congress on exhibition, whilst Congress in its committee rooms is Congress at work" may not be as true today as it was when Woodrow Wilson wrote it in 1883.[19] Still, "the work that takes place in the committee and subcommittee rooms of Capitol Hill is critical to the productivity and effectiveness of Congress."[20] **Standing committees** are the first and last places that most bills go. When different versions of a bill are passed in the House and Senate, a **conference committee** with members of both houses meets to iron out the differences. Usually committee members who play key roles in floor debate in the full House or Senate about the merits of the proposed bill. Committees are especially important in the House of Representatives because its size makes organization and specialization key.

Types of Committees.   There are four types of congressional committees:

1. *Standing committees,* so called because they continue from one Congress to the next, are the committees to which proposed bills are referred for consideration.
2. *Ad hoc, special,* or *select committees* are temporary committees appointed for specific purposes, generally to conduct special investigations or studies and to report back to the chamber that established them.
3. *Joint committees* include members from both houses of Congress who conduct investigations or special studies.
4. *Conference committees* are a special kind of joint committee that reconciles differences in bills passed by the House and Senate.

The House and Senate standing committees listed in Table 6.3 are created by rule. In the 107th Congress, the House had nineteen standing committees, each with an average of thirty-one members. Together, they had a total of eighty-six subcommittees that collectively acted as the eyes, ears, and hands of the House. They considered issues roughly parallel to those of the departments represented in the president's Cabinet. For example, there were committees on agriculture, national security, the judiciary, veterans' affairs, transportation, and commerce.

Although most committees in one house parallel those in the other, the House Rules Committee, for which there is no counterpart in the Senate, plays a key role in the law-making process. Indicative of the importance of Rules, majority party members are appointed directly by the Speaker. This committee reviews most bills after they come from a committee and before they go to the full chamber for consideration. Performing a "traffic cop" function, the House Rules Committee gives each bill what is called a *rule,* which contains the date the bill will come up for debate and the time that will be allotted for discussion, and often specifies what kinds of amendments can be offered. Bills considered under a closed rule cannot be amended.

Standing committees have considerable power. They can kill bills, amend them radically, or hurry them through the process. A committee

standing committee
Committee to which proposed bills are referred.

conference committee
Joint committee created to iron out differences between Senate and House versions of a specific piece of legislation.

WEB EXPLORATION
To learn more about specific committees, see
www.ablongman.com/oconnor

TABLE 6.3   Committees of the 107th Congress (with a Subcommittee Example)

STANDING COMMITTEES

House	Senate
Agriculture	Agriculture, Nutrition, and Forestry
Appropriations	Appropriations
Armed Services	Armed Services
Banking and Financial Services	Banking, Housing, and Urban Affairs
Budget	Budget
Commerce	Commerce, Science, and Transportation
Education and the Workforce	Energy and Natural Resources
Government Reform	Environment and Public Works
House Administration	Finance
International Relations	Foreign Relations
Judiciary	Governmental Affairs
Resources	Health, Education, Labor, and Pensions
Rules	Judiciary—Judiciary Subcommittees:
Science	Administrative Oversight and the Courts
Small Business	Antitrust, Business Rights, and Competition
Standards of Official Conduct (Ethics)	Constitution, Federalism, and Property Rights
Transportation and Infrastructure	Immigration
Veterans' Affairs	Technology, Terrorism, and Government Information
Ways and Means	Youth Violence
	Rules and Administration
	Small Business
	Veterans' Affairs

SELECT, SPECIAL, AND OTHER COMMITTEES

House	Senate
Select Intelligence	Special Aging
	Select Ethics
	Select Intelligence
	Indian Affairs

JOINT COMMITTEES

Economics
Inaugural Ceremonies
Library
Printing
Taxation

discharge petition

Petition that gives a majority of the House of Representatives the authority to bring an issue to the floor in the event of committee inaction.

WEB EXPLORATION
To learn more about the members of the 107th Congress, go to www.ablongman.com/oconnor

reports out to the full House or Senate only a small fraction of the bills assigned to it. Bills can be "forced" out of a House committee by a **discharge petition** signed by a majority (218) of the House membership, but legislators are reluctant to take this drastic measure.

In the 107th Congress, the Senate had sixteen standing committees that ranged in size from twelve to twenty-eight members. It also had sixty-eight subcommittees, which allowed all majority party senators to chair one. For example, the Senate Judiciary Committee had six subcommittees, as illustrated in Table 6.3.

In contrast to the House, whose members hold few committee assignments (an average of 1.8 standing and three subcommittees), Senators are spread more thinly, with each serving on an average of three to four committees and seven subcommittees. Whereas the committee system allows House members to become policy or issue specialists, Senate members are often generalists.

Senate committees enjoy the same power over framing legislation as do House committees, but the Senate, being an institution more open to individual input than the House, gives less deference to the work done in committees. In the Senate, legislation is more likely to be rewritten on the floor, where all senators can participate and add amendments at any time.

Committee Membership.   Many newly elected members of Congress come into the body with their sights set on certain committee assignments. One political scientist notes that committee assignments are to members what stocks are to investors—they seek to acquire those that will add to the value of their portfolios.[21] Representatives often seek committee assignments that have access to what is known as the **pork barrel.** Pork barrel legislation allows representatives to "bring home the bacon" to their districts in the form of public works programs, military bases, or other programs designed to benefit districts directly.

Pork isn't the only motivator for those seeking committee assignments. Some committees, such as Commerce, facilitate reelection by giving members influence over decisions that affect large campaign contributors. A third motivator for certain committee assignments is the desire to have power and influence within the chamber. The Appropriations and Budget Committees provide that kind of reward for some members.

In both the House and the Senate, committee membership generally reflects the party distribution within that chamber. For example, at the outset of the 107th Congress, Republicans held a narrow majority of House seats (221) and thus claimed about a 52 percent share of the seats on several committees, including International Relations, Commerce, and Education and the Workforce. On committees more critical to the operation of the House or to setting national policy, the majority often takes a disproportionate share of the slots. Since the Rules Committee regulates access to the floor for legislation approved by other standing committees, control by the majority party is essential for it to manage the flow of legislation. For this reason, no matter how narrow the majority party's margin in the chamber, it makes up at least two-thirds of Rules's membership. In the Senate, during its brief 50–50 split, the leaders agreed to equal representation on committees, along with equal staffing, office space, and budgets.

Committee Chairs.   Before recent changes giving the House Speaker more power, committee chairs long enjoyed tremendous power and prestige. Even today's House chairs may choose not to schedule hearings on a bill to kill it. (Senate power sharing rules allow either party to bring legislation to the floor, thereby diminishing its chairs' powers.) Chairs also carry with them the power to draft legislation, manage a staff budget of over a million dollars, and "hear pleas from lobbyists, Cabinet secretaries, and even presidents who need something only a committee can provide."[22] Chairs may convene meetings when opponents are absent, or they may adjourn meetings when things are going badly. Personal skill, influence, and expertise are a chair's best allies.

pork barrel
Legislation that allows representatives to "bring home the bacon" to their districts in the form of public works programs, military bases, or other programs designed to benefit their districts directly.

Historically, committee chairs have generally been the majority party member with the longest continuous service on the committee. Reforms made by Republicans in 1995 dramatically limited the long-term power of committee chairs. New rules prevent chairs from serving more than six years—three consecutive Congresses—or heading their own subcommittees. In return, committee chairs were, however, given some important powers. They are authorized to select all subcommittee chairs, call meetings, strategize, and recommend majority members to sit on conference committees. Committee chairs in the House no longer are selected by seniority, as is the case in the Senate. Thus, thirteen House committee chairs are new in the 107th Congress.[23]

THE LAWMAKING FUNCTION OF CONGRESS

The organization of Congress allows it to fulfill its constitutional responsibilities, chief among which is its lawmaking function. Only members of the House or Senate can formally submit a bill for congressional consideration. Once a bill is proposed, it usually reaches a dead end. Of the approximately 9,000 bills introduced during each session of Congress, fewer than 5 percent to 10 percent are enacted, or made into law.

It is probably useful to think of Congress as a system of multiple vetoes, which was what the Framers desired. As a bill goes through Congress, a dispersion of power occurs as roadblocks to passage must be surmounted at numerous steps in the process. In addition to realistic roadblocks, caution signs and other opportunities for delay abound. A member who sponsors a bill must get through *every* obstacle; in contrast, successful opposition means winning at only one of many stages, including: (1) the subcommittee, (2) the House full committee, (3) the House Rules Committee, (4) the House, (5) the Senate subcommittee, (6) the full Senate committee, (7) the Senate, (8) floor leaders in both Houses, (9) the House-Senate conference committee, and (10) the president.

How a Bill Becomes a Law

A bill must survive three stages before it becomes a law. It must be approved by one or more standing committees and both chambers, and, if House and Senate versions differ, a conference report resolving those differences must be accepted by each house. A bill may be killed during any of these stages, so it is much easier to defeat a bill than it is to get one passed. The success or failure of a bill may be affected by unforeseen events, as is underscored in Analyzing the Data: Gun Control Legislation Following Publicized Shootings.

The House and Senate have parallel processes, and often the same bill is introduced in each chamber at the same time. A bill must be

A N A L Y Z I N G   T H E   D A T A

GUN CONTROL LEGISLATION FOLLOWING PUBLICIZED SHOOTINGS

Machine-gun violence during Prohibition and the attempted assassination of President Franklin D. Roosevelt in 1933 was followed by the National Firearms Act of 1934, which required registration of automatic weapons. Other gun control legislation has followed highly publicized shootings. As the gun control legislation saga described in our opening vignette underscores, the path a particular piece of legislation takes is often as varied as the content of the legislation itself. In the wake of so many school shooting tragedies, many Americans regard some form of gun control legislation as a must. Legislators, with their election campaigns always in sight, are mindful of this fact. With 64 percent of the American public responding that they would consider a candidate's position on gun control important when voting in the next election, it is reasonable to expect Congress to act. Congress frequently reacts to external stimuli that produce citizen demands for action. Still, gun control legislation was defeated in spite of public opinion, perhaps underscoring the potency of the gun lobby.

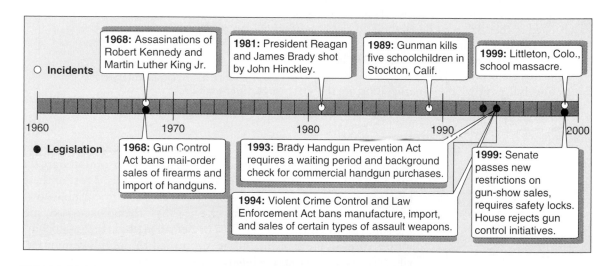

○ **Incidents**

1968: Assassinations of Robert Kennedy and Martin Luther King Jr.

1981: President Reagan and James Brady shot by John Hinckley.

1989: Gunman kills five schoolchildren in Stockton, Calif.

1999: Littleton, Colo., school massacre.

1960   1970   1980   1990   2000

● **Legislation**

1968: Gun Control Act bans mail-order sales of firearms and import of handguns.

1993: Brady Handgun Prevention Act requires a waiting period and background check for commercial handgun purchases.

1994: Violent Crime Control and Law Enforcement Act bans manufacture, import, and sales of certain types of assault weapons.

1999: Senate passes new restrictions on gun-show sales, requires safety locks. House rejects gun control initiatives.

Source: USA Today (May 26, 1999): p. 2A. Reprinted by permission. Updated by author.

introduced by a member of Congress, but it is often sponsored by a whole list of other members in an early effort to show support for it. Once introduced, the bill is sent to the clerk of the chamber, who gives it a number (for example, HR 1 or S 1—indicating House or Senate bill number one for the session). The bill is then printed, distributed, and sent to the appropriate committee or committees for consideration. It is at this stage that a bill is named.

The first action takes place within the committee, after it is referred there by the Speaker. The committee usually refers the bill to one of its

H I G H L I G H T

W H A T ' S   I N   A   N A M E ?

Naming a bill has become a not-so-subtle art of late. In times past, Franklin D. Roosevelt could propose a Social Security Act without calling it the "Dignity in Old Age Act" or the "Keep Grandma Out of the Poorhouse Act." Since Republicans took over control of Congress in 1995, bills have been named much more creatively and usually have value-laden names. A tax-cutting bill, for example, was named the "American Dream Restoration Act," and the Omnibus Budget Reconciliation bill's name was changed to the "Balanced Budget" bill to garner more favorable attention.

Representative Barney Frank (D–Mass.) wondered aloud on the House floor if the immigration bill entitled the "Immigration in the National Interest Act" should be renamed the "Statue of Liberty Was Wrong Act." One Republican representative, in an attempt to promote a bill requiring football, baseball, basketball, and hockey to use instant replays, named his proposal the "What Really Happened Bill" after rejecting his first choice, "It Wasn't a Touchdown, Stupid, Bill."

The names of bills such as the "Partial Birth Abortion Bill" can be particularly value laden and put opponents on the defensive. Can you think of other examples?

Source: This draws heavily from Adam Clymer, "When 'Ketchup' Is 'Tomato Achievement,'" *The New York Times* (March 24, 1996): section 4.2.

subcommittees, which researches the bill and decides whether to hold hearings on it. The subcommittee hearings provide the opportunity for those on both sides of the issue to voice their opinions. Most of these hearings are now open to the public because of 1970s sunshine laws, which require open sessions. After the hearings, the bill is revised, and the subcommittee votes to approve or defeat the bill. If the subcommittee votes in favor of the bill, it is returned to the full committee, which then either rejects the bill or sends it to the House or Senate floor with a favorable recommendation (see Figure 6.5).

The second stage of action takes place on the House or Senate floor. In the House, before a bill may be debated on the floor, it must be approved by the Rules Committee and given a rule and a place on the calendar, or schedule. (House budget bills don't go to the Rules Committee.) In the House, the rule given to a bill determines the limits on the floor debate and specifies what types of amendments, if any, may be attached to the bill. Once the Rules Committee considers the bill, it is put on the calendar.

When the day arrives for floor debate, the House may choose to form a Committee of the Whole. This allows the House to deliberate with only 100 members present to expedite consideration of the bill. On the

FIGURE 6.5   How a Bill Becomes a Law

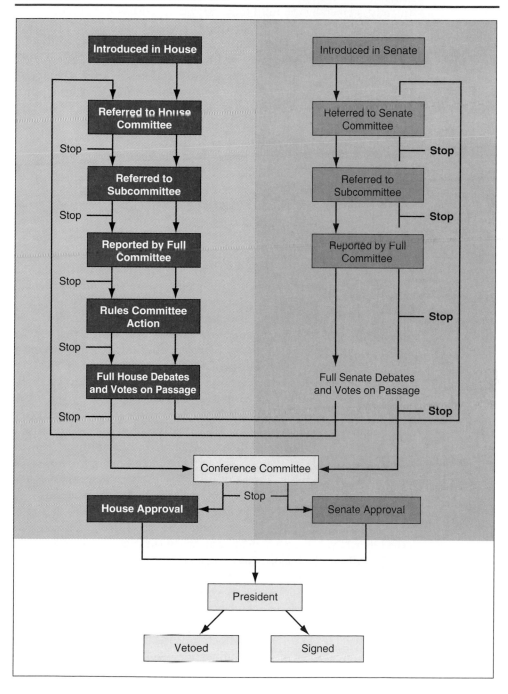

House floor, the bill is debated, amendments are offered, and a vote ultimately is taken by the full House. If the bill survives, it is sent to the Senate for consideration if it was not considered there simultaneously.

Unlike the House, where debate is necessarily limited given the size of the body, bills may be held up by a hold or a filibuster in the Senate. A **hold** is a tactic by which a senator asks to be informed before a particular bill is brought to the floor. This request signals the Senate leadership and the sponsors of the bill that a colleague may have objections to the bill and should be consulted before further action is taken. Because any single member can filibuster a bill or other action to death, the Senate leadership is very reluctant to bring actions with a hold on them to the floor.

Filibusters, which allow for unlimited debate on a bill, grew out of the absence of rules to limit speech in the Senate and are often used to "talk a bill to death." In contrast to a hold, a filibuster is a more formal and public way of halting action on a bill by means of long speeches or unlimited debate in the Senate. To end a filibuster, **cloture** must be invoked. To cut off debate, sixteen senators must first sign a motion for cloture, then sixty senators must vote to end debate. If cloture is invoked, no more than thirty additional hours can be devoted to debate before the legislation at issue is brought to a vote.

The third stage of action takes place when the two chambers of Congress approve different versions of the same bill. When this happens, a conference committee is established to iron out the differences between the two versions of a bill. The president is not given a multiple choice and allowed to select which version he prefers. The conference committee, whose members are from the original House and Senate committees, hammers out a compromise, which is returned to each chamber for a final vote. Sometimes, as was the case with gun control legislation discussed in our opening vignette, the conference committee fails to agree and the bill dies there. No changes or amendments are allowed at this stage. If the bill is passed, it is sent to the president, who either signs it or vetoes it. If the bill is not passed in both houses, it dies.

The president has ten days to consider a bill. He has five options: (1) He can sign the bill, at which point it becomes law. (2) He can veto the bill, which is more likely to occur when the president is of a different party from the majority in Congress. In the 103rd Congress, when Democrats controlled both houses of Congress, President Clinton became the first president in 140 years not to veto a single bill during a two-year Congress. Congress may override the president's veto with a two-thirds vote in each chamber, a very difficult task. (3) He can wait the full ten days, at the end of which time the bill becomes law without his signature if Congress is still in session. (4) If the Congress adjourns before the ten days are up, the president can choose not to sign the bill, and it is considered "pocket vetoed." A **pocket veto** figuratively allows bills stashed in the president's pocket to die. The only way for a bill then to become law is for it to be reintroduced in the next session and go through the process all over again. Because Congress sets its own date

hold
A tactic by which a Senator asks to be informed before a particular bill is brought to the floor.

filibuster
A formal way of halting action on a bill by means of long speeches or unlimited debate in the Senate.

cloture
Motion requiring sixty Senators to cut off debate.

pocket veto
If Congress adjourns during the ten days the president has to consider a bill passed by both houses of Congress, without the president's signature, the bill is considered vetoed.

of adjournment, technically the session could be continued the few extra days necessary to prevent a pocket veto. Extensions are unlikely, however, as sessions are scheduled to adjourn close to the November elections or the December holidays.

The president can no longer exercise a **line-item veto**, a power that was an item in the Contract with America that was passed, and signed into law in 1996. Presidents since Ulysses S. Grant urged Congress to give them a line-item veto as a way to curb wasteful spending, particularly in pork barrel projects added to bills to assure member support. Line-item vetos allow executives to strike or reduce any discretionary budget authority or eliminate any targeted tax provision (the line item) in any bill. As passed by Congress, the line-item veto required the president to prepare a separate rescissions package for each piece of legislation he wished to veto and then submit his proposal to Congress within twenty working days. The president's proposed rescissions were to take effect if Congress did nothing, unless both houses of Congress passed a disapproval bill by a two-thirds vote within twenty days of receiving the rescissions.[24]

In 1998, however, the U.S. Supreme Court struck down the line-item veto as unconstitutional. In a 6–3 decision, a majority of the Court concluded that the provision violated a constitutional provision that mandates that legislation be passed by both houses of Congress and then be sent to the president—in its entirety—for his signature or veto.[25] Allowing the president to pick and choose among budget authorizations submitted by Congress gives the presidents the power "to enact, to amend or to repeal statutes," said the Court, a constitutional power the Framers never intended presidents to have. President Clinton, who had used the power eighty-two times, bemoaned the Court's decision.

line-item veto

The power to veto specific provisions of a bill without vetoing the bill in its entirety.

HOW MEMBERS MAKE DECISIONS

As a bill makes its way through the labyrinth of the lawmaking process described above, members are confronted with the question: How should I vote? Members often listen to their own personal beliefs on many matters, but those views can often be moderated by other considerations. To avoid making any voting mistakes, members look to a variety of sources for cues.

Constituents

If an issue affects their constituency, a representative often will try to determine how the people back home feel. Only if legislators have strong personal preferences will they vote against a clearly expressed desire of their constituents. Studies by political scientists show that members vote in conformity with prevailing opinion in their districts

PARTICIPATION
Write to Your
Member of Congress

about two-thirds of the time.[26] Members also are influenced by events and their constituents' perceptions of them, as illustrated in Analyzing the Data: Gun Control Legislation Following Publicized Shootings.

Colleagues

The range and complexity of issues confronting Congress means that no one can be up to speed on more than a few topics. When members must vote on bills about which they know very little, they often turn for advice to colleagues who have served on the committee that handled the legislation. On issues that are of little interest to a legislator, *logrolling*, or vote trading, often occurs. Logrolling often takes place on specialized bills targeting money or projects to selected congressional districts. A yea vote by an unaffected member often is given to a member in exchange for the promise of a future yea vote on a similar piece of specialized legislation.

Party

Political parties are another important source of influence. Members often look to party leaders for indicators of how to vote. Indeed, it is the whips' job in each chamber to reinforce the need for party cohesion, particularly on issues of concern to party. From 1970 to the mid-1990s, the incidence of party votes in which majorities of the two parties took opposing sides roughly doubled to more than 60 percent of all roll-call votes. When the Republicans took control of Congress with the Contract with America as its agenda, the parties divided over three-quarters of the time in both the House and the Senate, making 1995 the most partisan year in generations.

Today, many members of Congress elected on a partisan ticket feel a degree of obligation to their party and to the president if he is of the same party. The national political parties have little say in who gets a party's nomination for the U.S. Senate or the House. But once a candidate has emerged successfully from a primary contest, both houses have committees that provide campaign assistance. It is to each party's advantage to win as many seats as possible in each house. If a member is elected with the financial support or campaign visits from popular members and party leaders, the member is much more inclined to toe the party line.

Caucuses

Special interest caucuses were created to facilitate member communication—often across party lines—over issues of common concern. By 1994 there were at least 140 special interest caucuses, including many formed to promote certain industries, such as textiles, tourism, wine, coal, steel, mushrooms, and cranberries, or to advance particular views or interests.

Before 1995 twenty-seven caucuses enjoyed special status as legislative service organizations (LSOs) and congress provided staff, office space and budgets for them. Included among these were the liberal Black Caucus, the Congressional Caucus for Women's Issues, and the Democratic Study Group. In 1995 the Republican majority voted to abolish LSOs.[27] Without institutional support, most of the caucuses died while others have lost influence and members.

Interest Groups and Political Action Committees

The primary function of most interest group lobbyists is to provide information to supportive or potentially supportive legislators, committees, and their staffs. Interest groups can win over undecided legislators or confirm the support of their friends by providing information that legislators use to justify the positions they have embraced. Pressure groups also use grassroots appeals to pressure legislators by urging their members in a particular state or district to call, write, fax, or e-mail their congressional representatives. Lobbyists can't vote, but voters back home can and do.

While a link to a legislator's constituency may be the most effective way to influence behavior, that is not the only path of interest group influence on member decision-making. The high cost of campaigning has made members of Congress—especially those without huge personal fortunes—attentive to those who help pay the tab for tens of thousands of dollars worth of television commercials that have become staples in contested elections. The 4,000 or so political action committees (PACs) organized by interest groups are a major source of most members' campaign funding. When an issue comes up on which a legislator has no strong opinion and which is of little consequence to his or her constituents, there is, not surprisingly, a tendency to support the stand taken by those nice folks who helped pay for the last campaign. After all, who wants to bite the hand that feeds him or her?

Staff and Support Agencies

Members of Congress rely heavily on members of their staffs for information on pending legislation. Staff members prepare summaries of bills and brief the legislator based on their research. If the bill is nonideological or one on which the legislator has no real position, staff members can be very influential. Staff members also do research on and even draft bills that a legislator wishes to introduce.

Even with the reductions in congressional committee staff enacted by Republicans in 1995, the ranks of those working on the Hill still total more than 15,000. In addition, members of Congress rely on several agencies for information about complex issues, as described in Table 6.4.

SIMULATION
You Are a Member of Congress

CONGRESS AND THE PRESIDENT

The Constitution envisioned that the Congress and the president would have discrete powers and that one branch would be able to hold the

divided government
The situation that arises when the congressional majority and the president are from different political parties.

other in check. When these two branches are controlled by different political parties we call it **divided government.** As revealed in Figure 6.6, Republicans controlled the Congress and presidency briefly in 2001, for the first time since 1954. Divided government often makes it more difficult for Congress and the president to agree on major legislation, as was the case in the 106th Congress.

Over the years, and especially since the 1930s, the president has often held the upper hand. In times of crisis or simply when it was unable to meet public demands for solutions, Congress has willingly handed over its authority to the chief executive. Even though the chief executive has been granted greater latitude, legislators do, of course, retain ultimate legislative authority to question executive actions, and to halt administration activities by cutting off funds. Congress also wields the ultimate oversight power—the power to impeach and even remove the president from office.

Congressional Oversight of the Executive Branch

Since 1961 there has been a substantial increase in congressional oversight of the executive branch. Oversight generally involves a committee or subcommittee reviewing activities of an agency, department, or office to see if it has carried out its responsibilities the way Congress intended. It also includes checking on possible abuses of power by governmental officials, including the president.

Key to Congress's performance of its oversight function is its ability to question members of the administration and the bureaucracy to see if they are enforcing and interpreting the laws passed by Congress as the members intended. These committee hearings, now routinely televised, are among Congress's most visible and dramatic actions. Recent

TABLE 6.4   Congressional Support Agencies

Congressional Research Service (CRS)	*General Accounting Office (GAO)*	*Congressional Budget Office (CBO)*
Created in 1914 as the Legislative Research Service (LRS), the CRS is administered by the Library of Congress and responds to more than a quarter of a million congressional requests for information each year. The service provides nonpartisan studies of public issues, compiling facts on both sides of issues, and it conducts major research projects for committees at the request of members. The CRS also prepares summaries of all bills introduced and tracks the progress of major bills.	The GAO was established in 1921 as an independent regulatory agency for the purpose of auditing the financial expenditures of the executive branch and federal agencies. Today, the GAO performs four additional functions: It sets government standards for accounting, it provides a variety of legal opinions, it settles claims against the government, and it conducts studies upon congressional request.	The CBO was created in 1974 to evaluate the economic effect of different spending programs and to provide information on the cost of proposed policies. It is responsible for analyzing the president's budget and economic projections. The CBO provides Congress and individual members with a valuable second opinion to use in budget debates.

research reveals that the more the legislative body sees the oversight committee as not representative of the House or Senate as a whole, the more likely it will allow the executive branch leeway in adopting regulations to implement congressional policy.[28]

Hearings are also used to improve the administration of programs. Hearings that focus on particular executive branch actions often signal that Congress believes changes in policy need to be made before that agency's next budgetary requests are reviewed. Since most members of House and Senate committees and subcommittees are interested in the issues under their jurisdiction, they often *want* to help bureaucrats and not hinder them.

Legislators also augment their formal oversight of the executive branch by allowing citizens to appeal adverse bureaucratic decisions to agencies, Congress, and even the courts. **Congressional review,** a procedure adopted by the 104th Congress, is another method of exercising congressional oversight.[29] Legislation authorizing Congressional review provides Congress with sixty days to disapprove newly drafted executive agency regulations, which often are passed to implement some sort of congressional action. A regulation is disapproved if the resolution is passed by both chambers and signed by the president, or when Congress overrides a presidential veto of a disapproving resolution.

Congressional review differs from another form of legislative oversight called the **legislative veto,** a procedure by which one or both houses of Congress can disallow an act of an executive agency by a simple majority vote. Provisions for so-called legislative vetoes were first added to statutes in 1932 but were not used frequently until the

congressional review

The process by which Congress can nullify an executive branch regulation by a resolution passed in both houses within sixty days of announcement of the regulation.

legislative veto

A procedure by which one or both houses of Congress can disallow an act of the president or executive agency by a simple majority vote; ruled unconstitutional by the Supreme Court.

FIGURE 6.6   Divided Government
In 2001 Republicans briefly had control of the White House and Congress for the first time since 1954.

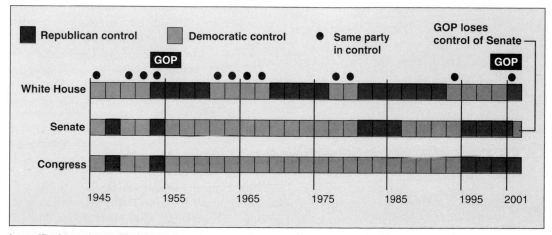

Source: "Total Control," *The Washington Post*, January 20, 2001. Copyright ©2001, The Washington Post. Reprinted with permission.

1970s. They were usually included in laws that delegated congressional powers to the executive branch while retaining the power of Congress to restrict their use. By 1981 more than 200 statutes contained legislative veto provisions.

In 1983, however, the U.S. Supreme Court ruled that the legislative veto as it was used in many circumstances was unconstitutional because it violated separation of powers principles.[30] The Court concluded that although the Constitution gave Congress the power to make laws, the Framers were clear in their intent that Congress should separate itself from executing or enforcing the laws. It is the president's responsibility to sign or veto legislation, not the Congress's. This case offered a classic example of the separations of powers doctrine underlying the Constitution. The legislative veto, however, continues to play an important role in executive-legislative relations. In signing the Omnibus Consolidation Rescission and Appropriation Act in April 1996, for example, President Clinton noted that Congress had included a legislative veto that the Supreme Court would in all likelihood find unconstitutional. Nevertheless, he signed the bill. The continued use by Congress, and acceptance by the president, of the legislative veto underscores the limits of judicial intervention without the cooperation of the other branches of government.

Until the Bush administration, congressional review had never been exercised. But, as noted in Policy in Action: Scrapping Ergonomics Regulations, Congress exercised congressional review to reject Clinton administration ergonomics regulations. It is likely that Congress will opt to use this procedure and abandon its use of legislative vetoes, which have been ruled unconstitutional because they cut the president out of the lawmaking process.

Foreign Affairs Oversight.   The Constitution divides foreign policy powers between the executive and the legislative branches. The president has the power to wage war and negotiate treaties, whereas the Congress has the power to declare war and the Senate alone has the power to ratify treaties. Throughout the twentieth century, the executive branch has become preeminent in foreign affairs despite the constitutional division of powers. This is partly due to the series of crises and the development of nuclear weapons in this century; both have necessitated quick decision-making and secrecy, which is far easier to manage in the executive branch.

Confirmation of Presidential Appointments.   The Senate plays a special oversight function through its ability to confirm key members of the executive branch, as well as presidential appointments to the federal courts. As discussed in chapters 9 and 10, although the Senate generally confirms most presidential nominees, it does not always do so. A wise president considers senatorial reaction before nominating poten-

POLICY IN ACTION

SCRAPPING ERGONOMICS REGULATIONS

Since 1990 when Elizabeth Dole was the secretary of labor, there has been concern about repetitive stress injuries in the workplace. After a decade of study and debate, in the waning days of the Clinton administration thousands of new rules and regulations were issued throughout January 2001. Among them were 608 pages of new ergonomics rules announced by the Occupational Safety and Health Administration (OSHA) to cover 102 million workers that would have required employers to adjust key board heights, revamp assembly lines, and take a host of other costly actions to prevent on the job injuries to workers who do repetitive tasks. The new regulations were to go into effect in October 2001.

Generally, new administrations and Congress are stuck with rules promulgated by an old administration. But, soon after the Republicans first took control of the Congress in 1995, the Congressional Review Act was passed in 1996. It empowered Congress to examine executive branch rules and regulations to determine if they were within the purview of the intent of Congress in enacting the legislation delegating authority to a particular agency or bureau. The Congressional Review Act also strictly limits debates and bars amendments on legislation aimed at reviewing executive branch rules. Prior to 2001, it had never been used.

As Bill Clinton left office he did so with his administration issuing a flurry of new regulations. Among them were the OSHA regulation that had been lobbied for heavily by labor unions. But, George W. Bush was elected president with the support of big business, not labor, and unions no longer have a friend in the White House. And, although the Senate is split evenly among Republicans and Democrats, several Democratic senators come from states carried by George W. Bush. And, President Bush was sympathetic to the claims of lobbyists for big business, who charged that the new rules would cost employers billions of dollars.

At the urging of these lobbyists, and supported by the Bush administration, a resolution of disapproval of the OSHA rules was brought to the floor for a vote in both houses in March 2001, under the Congressional Review Act, which was used for the first time. Voting in both houses was largely on party lines (although all six of the Democratic senators who voted to repeal the rules were from states carried by President Bush). The policy outcome? No rules to prevent workers from repetitive motion injuries and the likelihood that the Republican Congress, which no longer must fear a presidential veto, will continue to pass more probusiness legislation.

---

tially controversial individuals to his administration or to the federal courts. In the case of federal district court appointments, senators often have a considerable say in the nomination of judges from their states through what is called **senatorial courtesy**, a process by which presidents generally defer selection of district court judges to the choice of senators of their own party who represent the state in which a vacancy occurs (see chapter 9).

senatorial courtesy
A process by which presidents, when selecting district court judges, defer to the senator in whose state the vacancy occurs.

Presidential appointees during the Clinton administration faced a particularly hostile Congress. "Appointments have always been the battleground for policy disputes," says political scientist G. Calvin MacKenzie, but now, "what's new is the rawness of it—all of the veneer is off."[31] Thus, while Congress's power seems to have waned over the years, its oversight function gives it a potent weapon to presidential efforts to appoint extreme or controversial individuals to executive or judicial positions.

The Impeachment Process.   The impeachment process is Congress's ultimate oversight of the U.S. president (as well as federal court judges). The U.S. Constitution is quite vague about the impeachment process and much of the debate about it of late concerns what is an impeachable offense. The Constitution specifies that a president can be impeached for treason, bribery, or other "high crimes and misdemeanors." Most commentators agree that this phrase was meant to mean significant abuses of power. The question for the U.S. House then in considering whether President Clinton should be removed from office was, were President Clinton's statements to the Grand Jury lies, and if so, did lying to a grand jury constitute a "high crime and misdemeanor" deserving of possible removal from office? In *The Federalist Papers* Alexander Hamilton noted his belief that impeachable offenses "are of a nature which may with peculiar propriety be denominated POLITICAL, as they relate chiefly to injuries done immediately to society itself."

House and Senate rules control how the impeachment process operates. Yet, because the process is used so rarely, and under such disparate circumstances, there are few hard and fast rules. Until 1998, the U.S. House of Representatives had voted to impeach only sixteen federal officials—and only one of those was a president, Andrew Johnson. (Of those, seven were convicted and removed from office and three resigned before the process described below was completed.)

Until late 1998, only three resolutions against presidents had resulted in further action: (1) John Tyler, charged with corruption and misconduct in 1843; (2) Andrew Johnson, charged with serious misconduct in 1868; and (3) Richard M. Nixon, charged with obstruction and the abuse of power in 1974. The House rejected the charges against Tyler; Johnson was acquitted by the Senate by a one-vote margin; and Nixon resigned before the full House voted on the articles of impeachment. Four articles of impeachment were voted on in the House against President Clinton; two of those failed. The Senate acted on the remaining two and found the president not guilty on both articles.

The impeachment process itself has eight distinct stages as illustrated in Table 6.5.

TABLE 6.5   The Eight Stages of the Impeachment Process

The Resolution A resolution, called an inquiry of impeachment, is sent to the House Judiciary Committee. Members may also introduce bills of impeachment, which will be referred to the Judiciary Committee.

The Committee Vote After the consideration of voluminous evidence, the Judiciary Committee votes on the resolution or bill of impeachment. A positive vote from the committee indicates its belief that there is sufficiently strong evidence for impeachment in the House.

The House Vote If the articles of impeachment are reccommended by the House Judiciary Committee, the full House votes to approve (or disapprove) a Judiciary Committee decision to conduct full-blown impeachment hearings.

The Hearings Extensive evidentiary hearings are held by the House Judiciary Committee concerning the allegations of wrongdoing. Witnesses may be called and the scope of the inquiry may be widened at this time. The committee heard only from the independent counsel in the Clinton case.

The Report The committee votes on one or more articles of impeachment. Reports supporting this finding (as well as dissenting views) are forwarded to the House and become the basis for its consideration of specific articles of impeachment.

The House Vote The full House votes on each article of impeachment. A simple majority vote on any article is sufficient to send that article to the Senate for its consideration.

The Trial in the Senate A trial is conducted on the floor of the Senate with the House Judiciary Committee bringing the case against the president, who is represented by his own private attorneys. The Senate, in essence, acts as the jury, with the chief justice of the United States presiding over the trial.

The Senate Vote The full Senate votes on each article of impeachment. If there is a two-thirds vote on any article, the president is automatically removed from office and the vice president assumes the duties of the president. Both articles issued against President Clinton, charging him with lying to the grand jury and encouraging a grand jury witness to lie or mislead, were defeated in the Senate.

Continuity & Change

Representatives—In or Out of Touch?

When the Framers met in Philadelphia, they were concerned that their representatives not get too far away from the American people. Thus the House of Representatives was created with members to stand for election every two years. The House was truly to be "the people's house." The Framers envisioned those elected to this body would well represent the interests of their constituents, go back home frequently, and not view the House as their ultimate career.

Over time, not only did members come to represent more people, but the kinds of people who could vote for members changed. Thus, as those who didn't own property, blacks, and women were added to the rolls of voters, the kinds of interests that members were expected to represent should have changed, but did not necessarily.

Today, although women make up more than half of the population, they make up only about

(continued)

13 percent of our national lawmakers. African Americans constitute more than 12.1 percent of the population but have no representation in the United States Senate. When members of the Congressional Black Caucus wanted to challenge the Joint Sessions' counting of the electoral college votes, they could not do so when they failed to get the signature of a single senator. Even more distressing to some is the fact that although Hispanics make up more than 12.5 percent of the population, they hold a small share of the seats in Congress and, like African Americans, none in the Senate.

As the nation becomes more diverse ethnically and racially and minorities as well as women hold so few seats in Congress, can that body still be seen as a representative body? Representative of whom, some might ask. Particu-larly when one sees the power of corporate interests, or in Senator John McCain's pleas for campaign finance reform, one begins to wonder how much drastic change might take place before the interests of the citizens, as envisioned by the Framers, are truly being represented.

1. Do you see the present racial, economic, and male/female composition of the Congress as a problem in truly representing the interests of "the people"?
2. What steps might be taken to make Congress more representative?

Cast Your Vote. Is Congress representative of the American people? To cast your vote, go to **www.ablongman.com/oconnor**

SUMMARY

Congress was molded after the bicameral British Parliament, but with an important difference. The U.S. Senate is probably the most powerful upper house in any national legislature. The Senate has unique powers to ratify treaties and to approve presidential nominees.

Article I of the Constitution sets forth qualifications for office, specifies age minimums, and specifies how legislators are to be distributed among the states. The Constitution also requires seats in the House of Representatives to be apportioned by population. Thus, after every census, district lines must be redrawn to reflect population shifts. The Constitution also provides a vast array of enumerated and implied powers to Congress. Some, such as lawmaking and oversight, are shared by each house of Congress; others are not.

Members of Congress live in two worlds—in their home districts and in the District of Columbia. Casework is one way to keep in touch with the district, since members, especially those in the House, never stop running for office. Incumbency is an important factor in winning reelection. Thus many have called for limits on congressional terms of office. Several theories exist concerning how members represent their constituents.

Political parties play a major role in the way Congress is organized. The Speaker of the House is always a member of the majority party, and members of the majority party chair all committees. Congress has a labyrinth of committees and subcommittees that cover the entire range of government policies, often with a confusing tangle of shared responsibilities. Each legislator serves on one or more committees and multiple subcommittees. It is in these environments that many policies are shaped and that members make their primary contributions to solving public problems.

The road to enacting a bill into law is long and strewn with obstacles, and only a small share of the proposals introduced become law. A multitude of factors impinge on legislators as they decide policy issues. The most important of the many considerations are constituents' preferred options and the advice given by better informed colleagues. When clear and consistent cues are given by voters back home, legislators usually heed their demands. In the absence of strong constituency preferences, legislators may turn for advice to colleagues who are experts on the topic or to interest group lobbyists, especially those who have donated to their campaign.

The president can successfully twist arms or appeal to party loyalty when dealing with legislators who belong to his party. A president's influence with fellow partisans and opponents is related to the chief executive's popularity with the public.

While the president is often a legislative leader, Congress ulimately has legislative power as well as its oversight and impeachment powers at its disposal to reassert itself in the political system.

KEY TERMS

bicameral legislature, p. 164
cloture, p. 188
conference committee,
   p. 181
congressional review, p. 193
delegate, p. 172
discharge petition, p. 182
divided government, p. 193
filibuster, p. 188
gerrymandering, p. 165

hold, p. 188
impeachment, p. 166
incumbency, p. 169
legislative veto, p. 193
line-item veto, p. 189
majority leader, p. 178
majority party, p. 175
minority leader, p. 178
minority party, p. 175
pocket veto, p. 188

politico, p. 172
pork barrel, p. 183
redistricting, p. 165
senatorial courtesy, p. 195
Speaker of the House,
   p. 175
standing committee, p. 181
term limits, p. 169
trustee, p. 171
whip, p. 178

SELECTED READINGS

Aberbach, Joel D. *Keeping a Watchful Eye*. Washington, D.C.: Brookings Institution, 1990.

Bianco, William T., ed. *Congress on Display, Congress at Work*. Ann Arbor: University of Michigan Press, 2000.

Davidson, Roger H., and Walter J. Oleszek. *Congress and Its Members*, 7th ed. Washington, D.C.: Congressional Quarterly Press, 1999.

Deering, Christopher J., and Steven S. Smith, *Committees in Congress*, 3d ed. Washington, D.C.: Congressional Quarterly Press, 1997.

Dodd, Lawrence C., and Bruce Ian Oppenheimer, eds. *Congress Reconsidered*, 7th ed. Washington, D.C.: CQ Press, 2000.

Fenno, Richard F., Jr. *Home Style: House Members in Their Districts*. Boston: Little, Brown, 1978.

Fox, Richard Logan. *Gender Dynamics in Congressional Elections*: Beverly Hills, Calif.: Sage, 1996.

Gill, Laverne McCain. *African American Women in Congress: Forming and Transforming History*. New Brunswick, N.J.: Rutgers University Press, 1997.

Hammond, Susan Webb. *Congressional Caucuses in National Policy Making*. Baltimore, Md.: John Hopkins University Press, 1998.

Hibbing, John R., and Elizabeth Theiss-Morse. *Congress as Public Enemy: Public Attitudes Toward American Political Institutions*. New York: Cambridge University Press, 1996.

Kaptur, Marcy. *Women of Congress*. Washington, D.C.: CQ Press, 1996.

Mayhew, David R. *Congress: The Electoral Connection*. New Haven, Conn.: Yale University Press, 1986.

Oleszek, Walter J. *Congressional Procedures and the Policy Process*, 5th ed. Washington, D.C.: Congressional Quarterly Press, 2000.

Price, David E. *The Congressional Experience: A View from the Hill*, 2nd ed. Boulder, Colo.: Westview Press, 2000.

Thurber, James A., and Roger Davidson, eds. *Remaking Congress: Change and Stability in the 1990s*. Washington, D.C.: Congressional Quarterly Press, 1995.

7 The Presidency

(Photo courtesy: Robert Trippett/SIPA Press)

The shootings at Littleton, Colorado, and other schools around the nation. The bombing in Oklahoma City. The burning of churches throughout the South. The series of national floods, hurricanes, tornadoes, and other national disasters. The explosion of the space shuttle *Challenger.* The killing of 241 Marines in Beirut, Lebanon.

What do all of these horrific disasters have in common? All allowed a sitting president to show his ability to heal and lead the nation. President Bill Clinton, like President Ronald Reagan before him, showed himself to be a master in bringing the nation together in times of personal crisis. Clinton was always quick to hop on a plane to console the affected families in private and then to lead the nation in prayer. The ability to act as a national unifier often transcends partisan politics, usually to the dismay of the party that does not control the White House.

Not all presidents have this kind of ability to mold national tragedies into celebrations of heroes and American spirit. Without the personal charisma exercised by Presidents Clinton and Reagan, the bombings in Oklahoma City and in Beirut, Lebanon, could have turned into indictments of executive branch misfeasance.

Similarly, the *Challenger* explosion could have been the fault of the Reagan administration's cost-cutting efforts, which led to faulty inspection procedures. That did not happen. But when Americans were held hostage in Iran, President Jimmy Carter took personal blame.

The ability to heal the nation is a natural talent that likely cannot be taught. The ability to use the symbols of office, and how a president uses the power, scope, and gravity of his office, often defines his administration. This critical dynamic also underscores the importance of understanding sources of a president's unwritten powers as well as his specific constitutional grants of authority.

The constitutional authority, statutory powers, and burdens of the presidency make it a powerful position and an awesome responsibility. Most of the men who have been president in the past two decades have done their best; yet, in the heightened expectations of the American electorate, most have come up short. Not only did the Framers not envision such a powerful role for the president, they could not have foreseen the skepticism with which many presidential actions are now greeted in the press, on talk radio, and on the Internet. These expectations have also led presidents into policy areas never dreamed of by the Framers.

The modern media, often used by modern presidents to help advocate their agendas, have brought us "closer" to our presidents, making them seem more human, a mixed blessing for those trying to lead. Only two photographs exist of Franklin D. Roosevelt in a wheelchair—his paralysis was a closely guarded secret. Five decades later, Bill Clinton was asked on national TV what kind of underwear he preferred (briefs). Later revelations about his conduct with Monica Lewinsky made this exchange seem tame. This "demythifying" of the president, along with simultaneous increases in our general mistrust of government, have made governing a difficult job.

A president does not rely only on the formal powers of office to lead the nation: Public opinion and public confidence are key components of a president's ability to get programs adopted and to implement his or her vision of the nation. As political scientist Richard E. Neustadt has noted, the president's power often rests on the power to persuade.[1] To persuade, a president must not only be able to forge links with members of Congress, but must also have the support of the American people and the respect of foreign leaders.

The ability to persuade and to marshal the unenumerated powers of the presidency have become more important over time. In fact, the presidency of George W. Bush and the times that surround it are dramatically different from the presidency of his father and the years 1989–1993. America is changing dramatically and so are the responsibilities of the president and people's expectations of the person who holds that office. Presidents in this century battled the Great Depression, fascism, communism, and several wars involving American soldiers. With the Cold War over, there is less to expect from presidents, and fewer episodic instances to demonstrate their clear leadership in the face of adversity. Moreover, it is hard to lead on the domestic front when divided government has become the norm. Still, there are myriad opportunities to lead for most presidents, as we will discuss throughout this chapter.[2]

The tension between public expectations and the formal powers of the president permeates our discussion of how the presidency has evolved from its humble origins in Article II of the Constitution to its current stature. In this chapter, we explore the constitutional powers of the president, the evolution of presidential power, the role of the president in the American political system, and the impact of public opinion on the president.

THE ROOTS OF THE OFFICE OF PRESIDENT OF THE UNITED STATES

Like most of America's political institutions, the roots of the presidency date back to the Constitutional Convention.

The Constitutional Convention

The delegates to the Constitutional Convention in Philadelphia quickly decided to dispense with the Articles of Confederation and fashion a new government composed of three branches—the legislative (to make the laws), the executive (to execute, or implement, the laws), and the judicial (to interpret the laws). The Framers had little difficulty in agreeing that executive authority should be vested in one person, although some delegates suggested multiple executives to diffuse the power of the executive branch. The Articles of Confederation had no executive branch of government. The eighteen different men who served as the president of the Continental Congress of the United States of America were president in name only—they had no actual authority or power in the new nation. Yet, because the Framers were so sure that George Washington—whom they had trusted with their lives during the Revolutionary War—would become the first president of the new nation, many of their deepest fears were calmed. They agreed on the necessity of having one individual speak on behalf of the new nation, and they all agreed that one individual should be George Washington.

The manner of the president's election haunted the Framers for a while, and their solution to the dilemma—the electoral college—is described in detail in chapter 12. For now, we turn to details of the issues the Framers resolved quickly.

Qualifications for Office.   The Constitution requires that the president (and the vice president, whose major function was to succeed the president in the event of his death or disability) be a natural-born citi-

WEB EXPLORATION
To learn more about specific presidents, see www.ablongman.com/oconnor

zen of the United States, at least thirty-five years old, and a resident of the United States for at least fourteen years.

Term of Office.   At one time, the length of a president's term was controversial. Four-, seven-, and eleven-year terms with no eligibility for reelection were suggested by various delegates to the Constitutional Convention. The Framers of the Constitution reached agreement on a four-year term with eligibility for reelection. In the 1930s and 1940s, Franklin D. Roosevelt ran successfully in four elections as Americans fought first the Great Depression and then World War II. Despite Roosevelt's popularity, negative reaction to his long tenure in office ultimately led to passage (and ratification in 1951) of the Twenty-Second Amendment, which limits presidents to two four-year terms or a total of ten years in office, should a vice president assume a portion of a president's remaining term.

Removal.   During the Constitutional Convention, Benjamin Franklin was a staunch supporter of *impeachment,* a process for removing an official from office. He noted that "historically, the lack of power to impeach had necessitated recourse to assassination."[3] Not surprisingly, then, he urged the rest of the delegates to formulate a legal mechanism to remove the president and vice president.

Just as the president's veto power was a check on Congress, the impeachment provision included in Article II was adopted as a check on the power of the president. It gives each house of Congress a role to play in the impeachment process to assure that the chief executive can be removed only for "Treason, Bribery, or other high Crimes and Misdemeanors."

The Constitution gives the House of Representatives the power to conduct a thorough investigation to determine whether or not the president has engaged in any of those offenses. If the finding is positive, the House can vote to impeach the president by a simple majority vote. The Senate may then act as a court of law and try the president for the charged offenses. (The chief justice of the United States presides over the Senate hearing and the vote.) A two-thirds majority vote in the Senate on any count contained in the articles of impeachment is necessary to remove the president from office. Only two presidents, Andrew Johnson and William Jefferson Clinton, were impeached by the House of Representatives. Neither Clinton nor Johnson, however, was removed from office by the Senate.

Succession.   Through 2001, eight presidents died in office from illness or assassination. The Framers created the office of the vice president to ensure an orderly transfer of power. Moreover, the Constitution directs Congress to select a successor if the office of vice president is vacant. To clarify this provision, Congress passed the Presidential

WEB EXPLORATION
For a chronology of the Clinton impeachment, see www.ablongman.com/oconnor

Succession Act of 1947, which lists—in order—those in line (after the vice president) to succeed the president:

1. Speaker of the House of Representatives
2. President *pro tempore* of the Senate
3. Secretaries of state, treasury, and defense, and other Cabinet heads in order of the creation of their department

The Succession Act has never been used because there has always been a vice president to take over when a president died in office. The Twenty-Fifth Amendment, in fact, was added to the Constitution in 1967 to assure that this will continue to be the case. Should a vacancy occur in the office of the vice president, the Twenty-Fifth Amendment directs the president to appoint a new vice president, subject to the approval (by a simple majority) of both houses of Congress.

The Vice President

The Framers paid little attention to the office of vice president beyond the need to have an immediate official "stand-in" for the president. Initially, for example, the vice president's one and only function was to assume the office of president in the case of the death of the president or some other emergency. After further debate the delegates made the vice president the presiding officer of the Senate (except in cases of presidential impeachment). They feared that if the Senate's presiding officer was chosen from the Senate itself, one state would be short a representative. The vice president was given the authority to vote only in the event of a tie, however.

Power and fame generally come only to those vice presidents who become president. Just "one heartbeat away" from the presidency, the vice president serves as a constant reminder of the president's mortality. In part, this situation has given rise to a trend of uneasy relationships between presidents and vice presidents that began as early as Adams and Thomas Jefferson. As historian Arthur M. Schlesinger Jr. once noted, "The Vice President has only one serious thing to do: that is, to wait around for the President to die. This is hardly the basis for a cordial and enduring friendship."[4]

In the past, presidents chose their vice presidents largely to balance the presidential ticket—politically, geographically, or otherwise—with little thought given to the possibility of the vice president becoming president. Since Jimmy Carter's presidency (1977–1981), however, presidents not only have selected running mates they viewed as capable of succeeding them, but they also have given their vice presidents more and more responsibility.

President George W. Bush's sharing of power with his vice president, Dick Cheney, a former secretary of defense in his father's administration, has been almost unprecedented. Cheney was at Bush's side when every major appointment to his new administration was

WEB EXPLORATION
For more on the
vice president, see
www.ablongman.com/oconnor

announced. His greater interest and experience in foreign affairs have led to considerable speculation that Bush has delegated considerable authority to Cheney in the area of foreign affairs. No matter how much authority President Bush has opted to share with Vice President Cheney, it is clear that the days of inactive, out-of-the-loop vice presidents in America are over.

The question still exists, however, as to whether or not the vice presidency is a stepping stone to the presidency. As the 2000 campaign underscored, the vice president of a very popular president at a time of unprecedented economic prosperity was unable to translate that good will into election for himself. Since the presidency of Franklin D. Roosevelt, several vice presidents have become president, as revealed in Table 7.1. In fact, five of the twelve men who served as vice president from 1945 until 2000 became president. Three of those five, however—Presidents Truman, Johnson, and Ford—came to the office through the death or resignation of the president. (Truman and Johnson were then later elected in their own right.) Only two, Republican Presidents Nixon and Bush, were elected after serving as vice president. Richard M. Nixon actually was defeated by John F. Kennedy when he ran for president in 1960 while vice president; it wasn't until 1968, when he ran as a private citizen, that he was elected. Two vice presidents, Hubert H. Humphrey and Al Gore, ran for president and lost. Vice President J. Danforth Quayle sought the Republican Party nomination for the pres-

TABLE 7.1 The Vice Presidency: A Modern Stepping Stone to the Presidency?

President	Vice President	President Through Death or Resignation	Ran for Office	Won
Franklin Roosevelt	Harry S Truman	Death		
Harry S Truman	(vacant 1945–49) Alben Barkley		1948	Won
Dwight Eisenhower	Richard M. Nixon		1960 1968	Lost Won
John F. Kennedy	Lyndon B. Johnson	Death	1964	Won
Lyndon B. Johnson	Hubert H. Humphrey		1968	Lost
Richard M. Nixon	Spiro Agnew (resigned 1973) Gerald Ford	Resignation		
Gerald R. Ford	Nelson Rockefeller Ford ran as president		1976	Lost
Jimmy Carter	Walter Mondale		1984	Lost
Ronald Reagan	George Bush		1988	Won
George Bush	J. Danforth Quayle		Sought party nomination	Lost
Bill Clinton	Al Gore		2000	Lost

idency but lost at that stage. Thus, since 1945 at least, the vice presidency can no longer be viewed as an especially advantageous place from which to make a run for the presidency.

THE CONSTITUTIONAL POWERS OF THE PRESIDENT

The Framers were quite divided about the proper role and authority of the president. In contrast to Article I's laundry list of provisions for authority of the legislative branch, Article II details few presidential powers beyond noting that "the executive Power shall be vested in a President of the United States of America." Distrust of a powerful chief executive led to the Constitution's intentionally vague prescriptions for the presidency. Nevertheless, it is these constitutional powers, when coupled with a president's own personal style and abilities, that allow him or her to lead the nation.

The Appointment Power

To help the president enforce the laws passed by Congress, the Constitution authorizes him to appoint, with the advice and consent of the Senate, "Ambassadors, other public Ministers and Consuls, judges of the supreme Court, and all other Officers of the United States, whose Appointments are not herein otherwise provided for, and which shall be established by Law." Although this section of the Constitution deals only with appointments, behind that language is a powerful policy-making tool. Not only does the president have the authority to make more than 3,000 appointments (including over 1,000 senior-level appointments) to his or her administration (see Table 7.2), many of those appointees are in positions to wield substantial authority over the course and direction of public policy. Although Congress has the authority "to make all

WEB EXPLORATION
To learn more about the number of confirmed presidential appointees in the Bush administration, go to www.ablongman.com/oconnor

TABLE 7.2   Presidential Teams (Senior Administrative Positions Requiring Senate Confirmation)

	Total Appointments	Total Women	Percentage Women
Jimmy Carter	1,087	191	17.6%
Ronald Reagan	2,349	277	11.8%
George Bush	1,079	215	19.9%
Bill Clinton	1,257	528	42.0%

Sources: "Insiders Say White House Has Its Own Glass Ceiling," *Atlanta Journal Constitution* (April 10, 1995): A-4; and Judi Hasson, "Senate GOP Leader Lott Says He'll Work With Clinton," *USA Today* (December 4, 1996): 8A

laws," through the president's enforcement power—and chosen assistants—the chief executive often can set the policy agenda for the nation. Especially in the context of appointments to the federal courts, a president's influence can be felt far past the term of office.

It is not surprising, then, that selecting the "right" people is often one of a president's most important tasks. Presidents look for a blend of loyalty, competence, and integrity. Identifying these qualities in people is a major challenge that every new president faces. Recent presidents, especially Bill Clinton and George W. Bush, also have tried to appoint more women and minorities to top positions.

Many presidential appointments are subject to Senate approval—a potentially strong check on the power of the president. Nevertheless, especially when the president and Senate are from the same political party, the Senate traditionally gives a president's preferences great respect—especially those for the **Cabinet**. In fact, the vast majority (97 percent) of all presidential nominations were confirmed.[5] But even a few rejections can have a major impact on the course of an administration. Rejections leave a president without first choices, have a chilling effect on other potential nominees, affect a president's relationship with the Senate, and affect how the president is perceived by the public.

Cabinet
The formal body of presidential advisers who head the fourteen departments. Presidents often appoint others to this body of formal advisers.

The Power to Convene Congress

The Constitution requires the president to inform the Congress periodically of "the State of the Union," and authorizes the president to convene either or both houses of Congress on "extraordinary Occasions." The power to convene Congress was important when Congress did not sit in nearly year-round sessions. Today this power has little more than symbolic significance.

The Power to Make Treaties

The president's power to make treaties with foreign nations is checked by the Constitution's stipulation that all treaties must be approved by at least two-thirds of the members of the Senate. Only sixteen treaties that have been put to a vote in the Senate have been rejected, often under highly partisan circumstances. The chief executive also can "receive ambassadors," wording that has been interpreted to allow the president to recognize the very existence of other nations.

The Senate may require substantial amendment of a treaty prior to its consent. When President Carter proposed the controversial Panama Canal Treaties in 1977, for example, the Senate required several conditions to be ironed out between the Carter and Torrijos administrations before its approval was forthcoming.

Presidents often try to get around the "advise and consent" requirement for ratification of treaties and the congressional approval required for trade agreements by entering into an **executive agreement,** which

executive agreement
Secret and highly sensitive arrangements with foreign nations entered into by the president that do not require the "advise and consent" of the Senate.

allows the president to enter into secret and highly sensitive arrangements with foreign nations without Senate approval. Presidents have used these agreements since the days of George Washington, and their use has been upheld by the courts. Although executive agreements are not binding on subsequent administrations, since 1900 they have been used far more frequently than treaties, further cementing the role of the president in foreign affairs.

Veto Power

veto power
The formal, constitutional authority of the president to reject bills passed by both houses of Congress, thus preventing their becoming law without further congressional action.

In keeping with the system of checks and balances, the Constitution gives the president the authority to reject, or veto, any act of Congress (with the exception of joint resolutions that propose constitutional amendments), but gives Congress the authority to override an executive veto by a two-thirds vote in each house. This **veto power** is a powerful policy tool because Congress cannot usually muster enough votes to override a veto. Thus, in over 200 years, there have been approximately 2,500 presidential vetoes and only 100 or so have been overridden.

The Line-Item Veto.   As early as 1873 in his State of the Union message, President Ulysses S. Grant proposed a constitutional amendment to give the president a *line-item veto,* the power enjoyed by many governors to disapprove of individual items within a spending bill and not just the bill in its entirety. Since then, over 150 resolutions calling for a line-item veto were introduced in Congress. Finally, in 1996, Congress enacted legislation giving the president the authority to veto specific spending provisions of a bill without vetoing the bill in its entirety. It was expected that the line-item veto would allow the president to project his policy priorities into the budget by vetoing any programs inconsistent with his policy goals. It also allowed the president to do away with more outrageous examples of "pork" (legislators' pet projects, which often find their way into a budget) and to eliminate needless fat in the budget. In 1998, however, the state of New York challenged the line-item veto law when President Clinton used the line-item veto to stop payment of some congressionally authorized funds to the state. The Supreme Court then ruled that the line-item veto was unconstitutional because it gave powers to the president denied him by the U.S. Constitution. Those kinds of alterations of power, said the Court, require constitutional amendments.[6]

WEB EXPLORATION
To see the number of presidential vetoes from Washington to Clinton, go to www.ablongman.com/oconnor

The Power of the President to Preside over the Military as Commander-in-Chief

One of the most important constitutional executive powers is the president's authority over the military. Article II states that the president is "Commander-in-Chief of the Army and Navy of the United States." While the Constitution specifically grants Congress the authority to

Chief law enforcer: National Guard troops sent by President Eisenhower enforce federal court decisions ordering the integration of public schools in Little Rock, Arkansas. (Photo courtesy: Bettman/Corbis)

Leader of the party: George W. Bush accepts his party's nomination for president at the 2000 Republican National Convention. (Photo courtesy: Mark Wilson/Newsmakers/Liaison Agency)

Commander-in-chief: President Bush and Barbara Bush, with troops in the Persian Gulf. (Photo courtesy: Wally McNamee/Folio, Inc.)

The President's Many Hats

Shaper of domestic policy: President Johnson confers with the Reverend Martin Luther King, Jr. and Ralph Abernathy about Johnson's War on Poverty. (Photo courtesy: Bettmann/Corbis)

Key player in the legislative process: President Clinton proposes legislation to Congress and the nation. (Photo courtesy: Dirck Halstead/Liaison Agency/Getty source)

Chief of state: President Kennedy and Jacqueline Kennedy are greeted by the president of France and his wife during the Kennedys' widely publicized 1961 trip to that nation. (Photo courtesy: Bettmann/Corbis)

declare war, presidents since Abraham Lincoln have used the commander-in-chief clause in conjunction with the chief executive's duty to "take Care that the Laws be faithfully executed" to wage war (and to broaden various powers).

Modern presidents continually clash with Congress over the ability to commence hostilities. In 1973 Congress passed the **War Powers Act** to limit the president's authority to introduce American troops into hostile foreign lands without congressional approval. President Nixon's veto of the act was overridden by a two-thirds majority in both houses of Congress.

Presidents since Nixon have continued to insist that the War Powers Act is an unconstitutional infringement of their executive power. Thus, over and over again, presidents—Democratic and Republican—have ignored one or more provisions of the act. For example, in 1993 President Clinton sent U.S. troops to Haiti to restore its president to power. Some members of Congress criticized Clinton, as they did other presidents who ordered troops abroad without congressional authorization. Yet the president's actions in each case have been judged in terms of the success of the operation and not on the possible abuse of power.

In 1999 Congress attempted to reassert itself in the foreign affairs process but managed to give the president mixed signals. The House of Representatives divided down the middle on a resolution showing simple support for the air war in Yugoslavia. Then, six weeks after the bombings began, the House took another vote. This time, it barred the president from sending ground troops to Yugoslavia without prior approval.[7]

The Pardoning Power

Presidents can exercise a check on judicial power through their constitutional authority to grant reprieves or pardons. A **pardon** is an executive grant releasing an individual from the punishment or legal consequences of a crime before or after conviction, and restores all rights and privileges of citizenship. Presidents exercise complete pardoning power for federal offenses except in cases of impeachment, which cannot be pardoned. President Gerald R. Ford granted the most famous presidential pardon when he pardoned former President Richard M. Nixon—who had not been formally charged with any crime—"for any offenses against the United States, which he, Richard Nixon, has committed or may have committed while in office." This unilateral, absolute pardon, which prevented the former president from ever being tried for any crimes he may have committed, unleashed a torrent of public criticism against Ford and questions about whether or not Nixon had discussed the pardon with Ford before Nixon's resignation. Many attribute Ford's ultimate defeat in his 1976 bid for the presidency to that pardon.

War Powers Act
Law requiring presidents to obtain congressional approval before introducing U.S. troops into a combat situation; passed in 1973 over President Nixon's veto.

pardon
An executive grant providing restoration of all rights and privileges of citizenship to a specific individual charged or convicted of a crime.

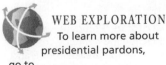

WEB EXPLORATION
To learn more about presidential pardons, go to
www.ablongman.com/oconnor

THE DEVELOPMENT OF PRESIDENTIAL POWER

Each person who has served as president of the United States has had some expectation about the use of presidential authority and some vision (often outlined in campaign promises) of how the country could be improved through his guidance and leadership. Yet most presidents have found accomplishing their goals much more difficult than they envisioned, even if they were elected with a sizable majority. As he was leaving office, Harry S Truman mused about what surprises awaited his successor, Dwight Eisenhower, a former general: "He'll sit and he'll say, "Do this! Do that! *And nothing will happen.* Poor Ike—it won't be a bit like the army. He'll find it very frustrating."[8]

A president's personal expectation of authority (and the public's expectations of him) is limited by the formal powers bestowed on the president by the Constitution and by the Supreme Court's interpretation of those constitutional provisions. These formal checks on presidential power are also affected by the times in which the president serves, the selection of confidantes and advisers, and by the president's personality and leadership abilities. (See Highlight: George Washington's Impact on the Presidency.) The postwar era of good feelings and economic prosperity presided over in the 1950s by the grandfatherly former war hero Dwight D. Eisenhower, for instance, called for a very different kind of leader from that needed by the Civil War–torn nation governed by Abraham Lincoln.

During that war, Lincoln argued that he needed to act quickly for the very survival of the Union. He suspended the writ of *habeas corpus,* which allows those in prison to petition to be released, citing the need to jail persons even suspected of disloyal practices. He ordered a blockade of Southern ports, in effect initiating a war without the approval of Congress. He also closed the U.S. mails to treasonable correspondence. Lincoln argued that the **inherent powers** of his office allowed him to do these things in a time of war or national crisis.

inherent powers
Powers of the president that can be derived or inferred from specific powers in the Constitution.

Presidents who take strong actions argue that their power derives not only from specific grants of authority in Article II, but also from inferences that can be drawn from the Constitution. Since the Constitution conferred on the president the duty to make sure that the laws of the United States are faithfully executed, reasoned Lincoln, the acts enumerated above were constitutional. He simply refused to allow the nation to crumble because of what he viewed as technical requirements of the Constitution. Noting the secession of the Southern states and their threat to the sanctity of the Union, Lincoln queried, "Are all of the laws *but one* to go unexecuted, and the Government itself go to pieces lest that one be violated?"[9] Once the Congress and Supreme Court ultimately approved of Lincoln's actions

H I G H L I G H T

GEORGE WASHINGTON'S IMPACT ON THE PRESIDENCY

In furtherance of his belief in the importance of the executive office to the development of the new nation, George Washington set several important precedents for future presidents:

- He took every opportunity to establish the primacy of the national government. In 1794, for example, Washington used the militia of four states to put down the Whiskey Rebellion, an uprising of 3,000 western Pennsylvania farmers opposed to the payment of federal excise tax on liquor. Leading those 1,500 troops was Secretary of the Treasury Alexander Hamilton, whose duty it was to collect federal taxes. Washington's action helped establish the idea of federal supremacy and the authority of the executive branch to collect the taxes levied by Congress.

- Washington began the practice of regular meetings with his advisers (called the Cabinet), thus establishing the Cabinet system.

- He asserted the prominence of the role of the chief executive in the conduct of foreign affairs. He sent envoys to negotiate the Jay Treaty with Great Britain. Then, over senatorial objection, he continued to assert his authority to negotiate treaties first and then simply submit them to the Senate for its approval. Washington made it clear that the Senate's function was limited to approval of treaties and did *not* include negotiation with foreign powers.

- He claimed the inherent power of the presidency as the basis for proclaiming a policy of strict neutrality when the British and French were at war. Although the Constitution is silent about a president's authority to declare neutrality, Washington's supporters argued that the Constitution granted the president inherent powers, that is, powers that can be derived or inferred from what is formally described in the Constitution. They argued that the president's power to conduct diplomatic relations could be inferred from the Constitution. Since neither Congress nor the Supreme Court later disagreed, this power was presumed added to the list of specific, enumerated presidential powers found in Article II.

taken during the Civil War, the theory of inherent powers gained legitimacy, transformed the presidency, and led to the broad powers that the president enjoys today.

Not only do different times call for different kinds of leaders, but they also often provide limits, or conversely, wide opportunities, for whomever serves as president at the time. As was the case with Lincoln and the Civil War, crises often trigger expansions of presidential power. The danger to the Union posed by the Civil War in the 1860s required a strong leader to take up the reins of government. Because of his leadership during this crisis, Lincoln is generally ranked as the "best" president (see Table 7.3).

TABLE 7.3   The Best and the Worst Presidents

Who was the best president and who was the worst? Many surveys of scholars have been taken over the years to answer this question, and virtually all have ranked Abraham Lincoln the best. A 2000 C-Span survey of fifty-eight historians, for example, came up with these results:

Ten Best Presidents	Ten Worst Presidents
1. Lincoln (best)	1. Buchanan (worst)
2. F. Roosevelt	2. A. Johnson
3. Washington	3. Pierce
4. T. Roosevelt	4. Harding
5. Truman	5. W. Harrison
6. Wilson	6. Tyler
7. Jefferson	7. Fillmore
8. Kennedy	8. Hoover
9. Eisenhower	9. Grant
10. L. Johnson (10th best)	10. Arthur (10th worst)

Source: Steve Neal, "Putting Presidents in Their Place: Longtime Favorites Top the List," *Chicago Sun-Times* (November 19,1995); and Susan Page, "Putting Presidents in Their Place," *The Washington Post* February 21, 2000.

The Modern Presidency

Before the days of instantaneous communication, the nation could afford to allow Congress, with its relatively slow deliberative processes, to make most decisions. Furthermore, decision making might have been left to Congress because its members, and not the president, were closest to the people. As times and technology have changed, however, so has the public's expectations about the role of the president. For example, the breakneck speed with which the electronic media such as the Cable News Network (CNN) report national and international events has intensified the public's expectation that the president will be the individual to act quickly and decisively on behalf of the entire nation in a crisis. Congress is often just too slow to respond to fast-changing events—especially in foreign affairs.

In the twentieth and twenty-first centuries, the general trend has been for presidential—as opposed to congressional—decision making to be more and more important. The start of this trend can be traced to the four-term presidency of Franklin D. Roosevelt (FDR), who led the nation through several crises, including the Great Depression and World War II. This growth of presidential power and the growth of the federal government and its programs in general are now criticized by many.

FDR took office in 1933 in the midst of the Great Depression during which as many as 25 percent of the U.S. workforce was unemployed. To jump-start the American economy, FDR asked Congress for and was given "broad executive powers to wage a war against the emergency, as great as the power that would be given to me if we were in fact invaded by a foreign foe."[10]

Just as Abraham Lincoln took bold steps to deal with the South's split from the Union, Roosevelt also acted quickly. He immediately

PARTICIPATION
Rate the Presidents

New Deal
The name given to the program of "Relief, Recovery, Reform" begun by President Franklin D. Roosevelt in 1933 designed to bring the United States out of the Great Depression.

fashioned a plan for national recovery called the **New Deal**, a package of bold and controversial programs designed to invigorate the failing American economy. As part of that plan, Roosevelt:

- Declared a bank holiday to end public runs on the depleted resources of many banks
- Persuaded Congress to pass legislation to provide for emergency relief, public works jobs, regulation of farm production, and improved terms and conditions of work for thousands of workers in a variety of industries
- Made standard the executive branch practice of sending legislative programs to Congress for its approval; before, the executive branch had generally just reacted to congressional proposals
- Increased the size of the federal bureaucracy from fewer than 600,000 to more than 1 million workers

Throughout Roosevelt's unprecedented twelve years in office (he was elected to four terms but died shortly after beginning the last one), which saw the nation go from the economic "war" of the Great Depression to the real international conflict of World War II, the institution of the presidency changed profoundly and permanently. All kinds of new federal agencies were created to implement New Deal programs, and the executive branch became more and more involved in implementing the wide variety of programs overseen by these agencies.

Not only did FDR create a new bureaucracy to implement his pet programs, but he also personalized the presidency by establishing a new relationship between the presidency and the people. In his radio addresses—or "fireside chats," as he liked to call them—he spoke directly to the public in a relaxed and informal manner about serious issues. He opened his radio addresses with the words, "My friends . . . ," which made it seem as though he were speaking directly to each listener. In response to these chats, Roosevelt began to receive about 4,000 letters per day, in contrast to the forty letters per day received by his predecessor, Herbert Hoover.

To his successors FDR left the "modern presidency," including a large federal bureaucracy, an active and usually leading role for the president in both domestic and foreign policy and legislation, and a nationalized executive office that used technology—first radio and then television—to bring the president closer to the public than ever before.

TIMELINE
The Executive
Order over Time

THE PRESIDENTIAL ESTABLISHMENT

As the responsibilities and scope of presidential authority have grown over the years, especially since FDR's time, so has the executive branch of government and the number of people working directly for the president in the White House itself. While the U.S. Constitution makes no special mention of a Cabinet, it does imply that a president will be assisted by advisers.

WEB EXPLORATION
For more on the modern White House, see
www.ablongman.com/oconnor

The Cabinet

The Cabinet, which has no basis in the Constitution, is an informal institution based on practice and precedent whose membership is determined by tradition and presidential discretion. By custom, this advisory group selected by the president includes the heads of major departments. Presidents today also include their vice presidents in Cabinet meetings, as well as any other agency heads or officials to whom the president would like to accord Cabinet-level status. As a body, the Cabinet's major function is to help the president execute the laws and assist in making decisions.

As revealed in Table 7.4, over the years the Cabinet has grown as departments have been added to accommodate new pressures on the

TABLE 7.4   The U.S. Cabinet

Department	Date of Creation	Responsibilities
Department of State (DOS)	1789	Responsible for the making of foreign policy, including treaty negotiation
Department of the Treasury	1789	Responsible for government funds and regulation of alcohol, firearms, and tobacco
Department of Defense (DOD)	1789, 1947	Created by consolidating the former Departments of War, the Army, the Navy, and the Air Force; responsible for national defense
Department of Justice (DOJ)	1870	Represents U.S. government in all federal courts, investigates and prosecutes violations of federal law
Department of the Interior (DOI)	1849	Manages the nation's natural resources, including wildlife and public lands
Department of Agriculture (USDA)	Created 1862; elevated to Cabinet status 1889	Assists the nation's farmers, oversees food-quality programs, administers food stamp and school lunch programs
Department of Commerce (DOC)	1903	Aids businesses and conducts the U.S. Census (originally the Department of Commerce and Labor)
Department of Labor (DOL)	1913	Runs labor programs, keeps labor statistics, aids labor through enforcement of laws
Department of Health and Human Services (HHS)	1953	Runs health, welfare, and Social Security programs; created as the Department of Health, Education, and Welfare (lost its education function in 1979)
Department of Housing and Urban Development (HUD)	1965	Responsible for urban and housing programs
Department of Transportation (DOT)	1966	Responsible for mass transportation and highway programs
Department of Energy	1977	Responsible for energy policy and research, including atomic energy
Department of Education	1979	Responsible for the federal government's education programs
Department of Veterans' Affairs	1989	Responsible for programs aiding veterans

president to act in areas that were not initially considered within the scope of concern of the national government. As interest groups, in particular, pressured Congress and the president to recognize their demands for services and governmental action, they often were rewarded by the creation of an executive department. Since each was headed by a secretary who automatically became a member of the president's Cabinet, powerful groups including farmers (Agriculture), business people (Commerce), workers (Labor), and teachers (Education) saw the creation of a department as increasing their access to the president.

The size of the president's Cabinet has increased over the years at the same time that most presidents' reliance on their Cabinet secretaries has decreased, although some individual members of a president's Cabinet may be very influential. Because the Cabinet secretaries and high-ranking members of their departments are routinely subjected to congressional oversight and interest group pressures, they often have divided loyalties. In fact, Congress, through the necessary and proper clause, has the authority to reorganize executive departments, create new ones, or abolish existing ones altogether. For this reason most presidents now rely most heavily on members of their inner circle of advisers (the Executive Office of the President and the White House Office) for advice and information. (Chapter 8 provides a more detailed discussion of the Cabinet's role in executing U.S. policy.)

The Executive Office of the President (EOP)

Executive Office of the President (EOP)
Establishment created in 1939 to help the president oversee the bureaucracy.

The **Executive Office of the President (EOP)** was established by FDR in 1939 to oversee his New Deal programs. It was created to provide the president with a "general staff" to help him direct the diverse activities of the executive branch. In fact, it is a mini-bureaucracy of several advisers and offices located in the ornate Executive Office Building next to the White House on Pennsylvania Avenue, as well as in the White House itself, where his closest advisers often are located.

The EOP has expanded over time to include the Office of the Vice President, as well as several advisory and policy making agencies and task forces. Over time, the units of the EOP have become more responsive to individual presidents rather than to the executive branch as an institution. They are often now the prime policy makers in their fields of expertise as they play key roles in advancing the president's policy preferences. Among its most important members are the National Security Council, the Council of Economic Advisors, the Office of Management and Budget, the Office of the Vice President, and the U.S. Trade Representative.

The National Security Council (NSC) was established in 1947 to advise the president on American military affairs and foreign policy. The NSC is composed of the president, the vice president, and the secretaries of state and defense. The president's national security adviser

POLICY IN ACTION

THE PRESIDENT AND THE PULPIT

All during the 2000 presidential campaign, George W. Bush made it clear that he was a devoutly religious man who believed that his faith had saved him from his wilder ways. Like his father before him, Bush fervently believes in the relevance and importance of religious institutions in improving the social welfare of the nation.

Still, it surprised some observers when he acted to abolish the White House Office on Women's Initiatives and Outreach. Instead, President Bush created an Office of Faith-Based and Community Initiatives to lead the executive branch's efforts to coordinate a wide range of programs to enhance the policy formulation and implementation role of faith-based institutions as Bush sought more partnerships with churches and the federal government.

The mandate of this office is considerable and shows how much a change in presidential administrations can affect the nature of public policy as well as the delivery of programs at the national, state, and local level. President Bush's announcement of the new office made it clear that he and his administration saw an important role for churches in the alleviation of poverty and homelessness, and in the provision of better education for America's youth. Interestingly, at the same time he appeared to lower the profile of offices dealing with AIDS and drugs, he sought religious solutions to some pressing social problems although even some religious leaders, including Pat Robertson, voiced concern about this mingling of church and state.

runs the staff of the NSC, coordinates information and options, and advises the president. Although the president appoints the members of each of these bodies, they must still perform their tasks in accordance with congressional legislation. Thus, like the Cabinet, depending on who serves in key positions, these mini-agencies may not be truly responsible to the president.

Presidents can give clear indications of their policy preferences by the kinds of offices they include in the EOP. President Bush, for example, not only abolished some offices when he became president in 2001, he quickly moved to create a new office, the Office of Faith-Based and Community Initiatives, which critics immediately attacked as an unconstitutional mingling of church and state. See Policy in Action: The President and the Pulpit.

The White House Staff

The personal assistants to the president, including senior aides, their deputies, assistants with professional duties, and clerical and administrative aides make up the White House staff. As personal assistants, these advisers are not subject to Senate confirmation, nor do they have divided loyalties. Their power is derived from their personal relationship to the president and they have no independent legal authority.

Although each president organizes the White House staff in different ways, presidents typically have a chief of staff whose job is to facilitate the smooth running of the staff and the executive branch of government. Successful chiefs of staff have also protected the president from mistakes and helped implement their policies to obtain the maximum political advantage for the president. Other key White House aides include those who help plan domestic policy, maintain relations with Congress and interest groups, deal with the media, provide economic expertise, and execute political strategies.

Senior White House staffers often have worked as campaign aides or are longtime friends or confidants. While White House staffers prefer to be located in the White House, in spite of its small offices, many staffers are relegated to the old Executive Office Building next door because White House office space is limited. In Washington, the size of the office is not the measure of power that it often is in corporations. Instead, power in the White House goes to those who have the president's ear, and influence is often measured by how close an aide's office is to the Oval Office.

THE ROLE OF THE PRESIDENT IN THE LEGISLATIVE PROCESS: THE PRESIDENT AS POLICY MAKER

When FDR sent his first legislative package to Congress, he broke the traditional model of law making. As envisioned by the Framers, Congress was to make the laws. Now FDR claimed a leadership role for the president in the legislative process. Said the president of this new relationship, "It is the duty of the President to propose and it is the privilege of the Congress to dispose."[11] With those words and the actions that followed, FDR shifted the presidency into a law- and policy-maker role. Now not only did the president and the executive branch *execute* the laws, he and his aides generally suggested them, too.

FDR's view of the role of the president in the lawmaking process of government is often called a **presidentialist** view. Thus a president such as FDR could claim that his power to oversee and direct the vast and various executive departments and their policies is based on the simple grant of executive power found in Article II that includes the duty to take care that the laws be faithfully executed. Presidentialists take an expansive view of their powers and believe that presidents should take a key role in policy making. For various reasons, Democratic presidents since FDR have tended to embrace this view of the president's role in law and policy making. In contrast, Republicans in the White House and in Congress have

presidentialist
One who believes that Article II's grant of executive power is a broad grant of authority and power allowing a president wide discretionary powers.

generally subscribed to what is called the **congressionalist** view, which holds that Article II's provision that the president should ensure "faithful execution of the laws" should be read as an injunction against substituting presidential authority for legislative intent.[12] These conflicting views of the proper role of the president in the lawmaking process should help you understand why presidents, especially Democratic presidents who have faced Republican majorities in the Congress or Republican presidents who have faced Democratic majorities, have experienced difficulties in governing in spite of public expectations.

congressionalist
A view of the president's role in the lawmaking process that holds Article II's provision that the president should ensure "faithful execution of the laws" should be read as an injunction against substituting presidential authority for legislative intent.

From FDR's presidency to the Republican-controlled 104th Congress, the public routinely looked to the president to formulate concrete legislative plans to propose to Congress, which then adopted, modified, or rejected his plans for the nation. Then, in 1994, it appeared for a while that the electorate wanted Congress to reassert itself in the legislative process. In fact, the Republicans' Contract with America was a Republican call for Congress to take the reins of the law-making process. But, several Republican Congresses' failure to pass many of the items of the contract, and President Clinton's continued forceful presence in the budgetary process made a resurgent role for Congress largely illusory. Thus, the president continues to play a major role in setting the legislative agenda, especially in the era where the House and the Senate are so narrowly divided on partisan lines. Without working majorities, President Bush recognizes that "merely placing a program before Congress is not enough," as President Lyndon B. Johnson (LBJ) once explained. "Without constant attention from the administration, most legislation moves through the congressional process at the speed of a glacier."[13] The president's most important power (and often the source of greatest frustration), then, in addition to support of the public, is his ability to construct coalitions within Congress that will work for passage of his legislation. FDR and LBJ were among the best presidents at "working" Congress, but they were helped by Democratic majorities in both houses of Congress.[14]

On the whole, presidents have a hard time getting Congress to pass their programs. Passage is especially difficult if the president presides over what is called a "divided government," which occurs when the presidency and Congress are controlled by different political parties. Recent research by political scientists, however, shows that presidents are much more likely to win on bills central to their announced agendas than to secure passage of legislation proposed by others.[15] Presidents generally experience declining support throughout their terms for policies they advocate. That's why it is so important for a president to propose key plans early in an administration during the honeymoon period, a time when the good will toward the president often allows passage of legislation that would not be possible at a later period. Even LBJ, who was able to get about 57 percent of his programs through Congress, noted: "You've got to give it all you can, that first year . . . before they start worrying about themselves. . . . You can't put anything through when half the Congress is thinking how to beat you."[16] For example, during his

POINT/COUNTERPOINT

DOES THE PRESIDENT NEED A MANDATE TO GOVERN?

George W. Bush lost the popular vote in 2000 by about 500,000 votes and only won the electoral college after prolonged battles over the state of Florida's election process. According to conventional wisdom, and many media pundits, Bush will have a difficult time governing the United States because he lacks a mandate—the authority to act on behalf of the people. In the United States, most people consider a mandate to be an overwhelming number, or at least a majority, of popular votes in an election. If a president has a mandate, he can govern authoritatively, using leverage with the Congress to get his policies enacted, holding news conferences to rally public support, and giving speeches to pressure the legislative branch to pass his agenda. In addition, the media tend to give the president more support and attack him less if he is popular with the people. Does a president need a mandate to govern, or can he run the country successfully without the popular vote majority? Let's examine these two points of view.

Democrats argue that Bush is going to have a difficult time getting any of his programs passed because he lacks the authority of a mandate. Because Republicans lost seats in the House and the Senate during the 2000 election as well as the presidential popular vote, Bush does not have a mandate to enact his agenda and so must cooperate and run the government in a bipartisan fashion. Many Democrats promise to block Bush's policies in Congress if they are considered too conservative and will try to force the Republicans to take up the Democratic agenda since Al Gore won the popular vote.

Democrats cite a number of presidents in history who have governed poorly due to their lack of a mandate. In 1824, the House of Representatives selected John Quincy Adams as president after no candidate managed to win a majority in the electoral college. He had nothing but trouble with Congress because many members viewed him as illegitimate. The 1876 election between Rutherford B. Hayes and Samuel Tilden was

first one hundred days, President George W. Bush pushed hard to win congressional support for his tax reduction and education proposals.

Presidential Involvement in the Budgetary Process

Since the 1970s, Congress has spent more time debating the budget than it has legislating.[17] The annual high-stakes showdowns that occur nearly every November are a way for presidents to exert their authority over Congress and to demonstrate leadership at the same time they drive home to the public and the Congress their policy priorities. In addition to proposing new legislation or new programs, a president can also set national policy and priorities through his or her budget proposal and his continued insistence on their intact congressional passage. The budget proposal not only outlines the programs the president proposes but indicates the importance of each program by the amount of

WEB EXPLORATION
To try your hand at balancing the budget, go to www.ablongman.com/oconnor

quite similar to the 2000 election. Tilden had won the popular vote by 250,000 votes but South Carolina, Florida, and Louisiana were strongly divided and sent two sets of electors to the electoral college. A highly controversial commission chose the Republican contender, Hayes. The House rejected the commission's findings while the Senate accepted them. A political compromise was finally reached that allowed Hayes to take office. He is not remembered as a particularly good president, and many members of Congress referred to him as "his Fraudulency." In 1888, Benjamin Harrison won the electoral vote while Grover Cleveland won the popular vote. Harrison had an uneventful presidency and was beaten four years later in a rematch with Cleveland.

George W. Bush and the Republicans argue that winning the White House is its own mandate, regardless of the margin in the election. He is the legitimate president of the United States and will govern effectively. Because the Republican Party controls the House and can often muster 51 votes in the Senate, Bush might be able to push his programs through Congress. Histor-

ically speaking, several presidents have governed well despite their lack of a mandate as traditionally defined. In 1800, Thomas Jefferson became president when the House of Representatives selected him following an inconclusive vote in the electoral college, and most Americans today cite him as one of history's best presidents. In 1960, only 100,000 votes separated John F. Kennedy and Richard M. Nixon. The election hinged on the state of Illinois, where Kennedy won by 8,000 votes. Nixon was fond of saying that if one additional voter in each precinct in Illinois had voted for him, he would have won the presidency. Despite lacking a decisive voter mandate, however, Kennedy is also commonly listed as one of the best presidents in history. To most Republicans, these historical vignettes indicate that a traditional mandate is not necessary for a successful presidency.

 What do you think? Does a president need a mandate to govern?
Go to www.ablongman.com/oconnor

funding requested for each program and its associated agency or department. Because the Framers gave Congress the power of the purse, Congress had primary responsibility for the budget process until 1930. The economic disaster set off by the stock market crash of 1929, however, gave FDR the opportunity to assert himself in the congressional budgetary process, just as he inserted himself into the legislative process. In 1939, the Bureau of the Budget, which had been created in 1921 to help the president tell Congress how much money it would take to run the executive branch of government, was made part of the newly created Executive Office of the President. In 1970, President Nixon changed its name to the Office of Management and Budget (OMB) to clarify its function in the executive branch.

OMB works exclusively for the president and employs hundreds of budget and policy experts. Key OMB responsibilities include preparing the president's annual budget proposal, designing the president's program, and reviewing the progress, budget, and program proposals of the executive department agencies. It also supplies economic forecasts to the president and conducts detailed analyses of proposed bills and agency rules. OMB reports allow the president to attach price tags to legislative proposals and defend the presidential budget. The OMB budget is a huge document, and even those who prepare it have a hard time deciphering all of its provisions. Even so, the expertise of the OMB directors often gives them an advantage over members of Congress.

The importance of the executive branch in the budget process has increased in the wake of the Balanced Budget and Emergency Deficit Reduction Act of 1985 (often called Gramm-Rudman, for two of the three senators who sponsored it). This act outlined debt ceilings and targeted a balanced budget for 1993. To meet that goal, the act required that the president bring the budget in line by reducing or even eliminating cost-of-living and similar automatic spending increases found in programs such as Social Security. It also gave tremendous power to the president's director of the Office of Management and Budget, who was made responsible for keeping all appropriations in line with congressional understanding and presidential goals.

In 1990, Congress, recognizing that its goal of a balanced budget would not be met, gave OMB the authority to access each appropriations bill. Although this action gutted the Gramm-Rudman Balanced Budget Act, it "had the effect of involving [OMB] even more directly than it already is in congressional law-making."[18] Growing public (and even congressional) concern over the deficit contributed to the president's and executive branch's increasing role in the budget process. As a single actor, the president may be able to do more to harness the deficit and impose order on the federal budget and its myriad programs than the 535 members of Congress, who are torn by several different loyalties.

Interestingly, many critics hailed the joint efforts of the president and Congress in coming up with a balanced budget in 1998—a goal that long eluded Bill Clinton's predecessors and earlier Congresses. The feat of avoiding a deficit budget was achieved without benefit of a balanced budget amendment. Although both parties to the budget dance have sought to take credit for their thriftiness, much of the surplus that occurred is a result of savings brought about by the end of the Cold War, which has led to much lower military spending, and a strong economy. Still, the president was happy to take credit for the balanced budget as he became the first president since Richard M. Nixon to sign a budget that had no red ink.

Questions about what to do with the budget surplus came to the fore in every 2000 presidential debate and often seemed to define the Bush and Gore campaigns. Bush cited the projected surplus as exhibit one that the federal government was taking too much of the people's money and therefore should give some back in the form of lower taxes across the board. The tax cuts, as well as many targeted tax cuts including the end of the marriage tax penalty supported by President Bush, may signal the first indications of his ability to wield the budget as a vehicle for policy change.

Ruling Through Regulation

Proposing legislation and using the budget to advance policy priorities are not the only ways that presidents can affect the policy process, especially in times of highly divided government. Executive orders (discussed in detail in chapter 9) offer the president an opportunity to make policy without legislative approval. Major policy changes have been made when a president has issued an **executive order,** a rule or regulation issued by the president that has the effect of law. While many executive orders are issued to help clarify or implement legislation enacted by Congress, other executive orders have the effect of making new policy. President Harry S Truman ordered an end to segregation in the military through an executive order, and affirmative action was institutionalized as national policy through Executive Order 11246, issued by Lyndon B. Johnson in 1966.

A president's policies have been clearly evident in the use of executive orders to limit or advance access to abortion, depending on the views of the occupant of the White House. Ronald Reagan, for example, ordered a stop to federal funding of fetal tissue research and an end to federal monies to any group providing abortion counseling. When Bill Clinton took office in 1993, he immediately rescinded those orders. Over the course of his presidency, Clinton used the force of his office to set aside vast acreage of wilderness lands and go after tobacco companies.

In the waning days of his presidency, Clinton marshaled the full force of the executive branch to issue thousands of regulations and executive orders, recognizing that the incoming Republican administration would have difficulty ferreting out all of the new directives. Among some of the midnight regulations issued by Clinton were regulations to limit emissions from diesel-powered trucks and buses, limits on the release of medical information by physicians and hospitals, and new requirements concerning workplace safety.[19] Several of those regulations were later reversed by the Bush administration or repealed by Congress.

Winning Support for Programs

As we have seen, the job of the president is ever expanding, a trend that makes it more and more difficult for any one individual to govern well enough to meet the rising expectations of the American public. Yet ability to govern often comes down to a president's ability to get his or her programs through Congress.

According to one political scientist, presidents have three ways to improve their role as legislative lobbyist to get favored programs

executive order
A rule or regulation issued by the president that has the effect of law. All executive orders must be published in the *Federal Register*.

During the thousand days the Kennedys lived in the White House, it became a trend-setting center of culture and style, a royal palace, a "Camelot." John F. Kennedy and his family had looks, youth, and wealth, and JFK was a witty and gifted speaker. (Photo courtesy: Bettmann/Corbis)

passed.[20] The first two involve what you may think of as traditional political avenues such as jobs, or other special favors or rewards to win support. Invitations to the White House and campaign visits to districts of members of Congress running for office are two ways to curry favor with legislators. Inattention to key members can prove deadly to a president's legislative program. House Speaker Thomas P. O'Neill reportedly was quite irritated when the Carter team refused O'Neill's request for extra tickets to Carter's inaugural. This did not exactly get the president off to a good start with the powerful Speaker.

A second political way presidents can bolster support for their legislative package is to call on their political party. As the informal leader of the party, the president should be able to take advantage of that position in Congress, where party loyalty is very important. This strategy works best for presidents who have carried members of the party into office on their coattails, as was the case in the Johnson and Reagan landslides of 1964 and 1984, respectively. In fact, many scholars regard LBJ as the most effective legislative leader. Not only had he served in the House and as Senate majority leader, but he also enjoyed a comfortable Democratic Party majority in Congress.[21]

Presidential Style.   The third way a president can influence Congress is a less political and far more personalized strategy. A president's ability to lead and to get programs adopted or implemented depends on many factors, including personality, approach to the office, others' perceptions of his or her ability to lead, and the ability to mobilize public opinion to support his or her actions. Many call this the president's style.

Frequently, the difference between great and mediocre presidents centers on their ability to grasp the importance of leadership style. Truly great presidents, such as Lincoln and Franklin D. Roosevelt, understood that the White House was a seat of power from which decisions could flow to shape the national destiny. They recognized that their day-to-day activities and how they went about them should be designed to bolster support for their policies and to secure congressional and popular backing that could translate their intuitive judgment into meaningful action. Mediocre presidents, on the other hand, have tended to regard the White House as "a stage for the presentation of performances to the public" or a fitting honor to cap a career.[22]

Presidential Leadership.   Leadership is not an easy thing to exercise. It remains an elusive concept for scholars to identify and measure but it is important to all presidents seeking support for their programs and policies. Moreover, ideas about the importance of effective leaders have deep roots in our political culture. The leadership abilities of the "great presidents"—Washington, Jefferson, Lincoln, and FDR—have been extolled over and over again, leading us to fault modern presidents who fail to cloak themselves in the armor of leadership. Americans have

TABLE 7.5 Barber's Presidential Personalities

Does character seriously affect how a president handles his job? Many of the presidents ranked highest by historians had major flaws.

Not all discussions of presidential character center around lying, as was the case with Richard M. Nixon, or womanizing and draft evasion, as was the case with Bill Clinton. In an approach to analyzing and predicting presidential behavior criticized or rejected by many political scientists, political scientist James David Barber has suggested that patterns of behavior, many that may be ingrained during childhood, exist and can help explain presidential behavior. Barber believes that there are four presidential character types, based on (1) energy level (whether the president is active or passive) and (2) the degree of enjoyment a president finds in his job (whether the president has a positive or negative attitude about his job). Barber believes that active and positive presidents are more successful than passive and negative presidents. Active-positive presidents generally enjoyed warm and supportive childhood environments and are basically happy individuals open to new life experiences. They approach the presidency with a characteristic zest for life and have a drive to lead and succeed. In contrast, passive presidents find themselves reacting to circumstances, are likely to take direction from others, and fail to make full use of the enormous resources of the executive office. The table classifies presidents from Taft through George Bush according to Barber's categories. Where would you place Bill Clinton? George W. Bush?

	Active	*Passive*
Positive	F. D. Roosevelt Truman Kennedy Ford Carter[a] Bush	Taft Harding Reagan
Negative	Wilson Hoover L. B. Johnson Nixon	Coolidge Eisenhower

[a]Some scholars think that Carter better fits the active-negative typology.

Source: James David Barber, *The Presidential Character: Predicting Performance in the White House,* 4th ed. (Englewood Cliffs, N.J.: Prentice Hall, 1992).

thus come to believe that "If presidential leadership works some of the time, why not all of the time?"[23] This attitude, in turn, directly influences what we expect presidents to do and how we evaluate them (see Table 7.5). Research by political scientists shows that presidents can exercise leadership by increasing their public attention to particular issues. Analyses of presidential State of the Union Addresses, for example, reveal that mentions of particular policies translate into more Americans mentioning those policies as the most important problems facing the nation.[24]

The Power to Persuade. In trying to lead against long odds, presidents must not only exercise the constitutional powers of the chief executive, but also persuade enough of the country that their actions are the right ones so that they can carry them out without national

POLITICS NOW

WHAT A DIFFERENCE A PRESIDENT MAKES

Although George W. Bush came into office without any kind of clear mandate down nearly a half million popular votes, he did not let that stop him from setting to work immediately to put his stamp on a wide array of bold public policies. One of his first actions found tremendous approval from the conservative wing of his party. On his third day in office he reimposed what is called the "Mexico City Policy" of the previous Reagan and Bush administrations, which bans federal aid to organizations that use their own money to perform or promote abortions, whether through counseling, public information campaigns, or lobbying to legalize abortions.

This change in policy was predicted by prochoice activists in the campaign. Other quick steps by the new Bush administration, however, appeared to make some—even members of his Cabinet—by surprise. During the 2000 presidential campaign, for example, President Bush pledged to seek reductions in carbon dioxide emissions from the nation's power plants. Christine Todd Whitman, the administrator of the Environmental Protection Agency, in fact, told her staff to come up with a plan to brand carbon dioxides as a pollutant, but her actions were suspended when the president announced that he had changed his mind because limits on carbon dioxide would cause energy costs to escalate further. His actions were hailed by industry lobbyists but triggered widespread condemnation from environmentalists.

President Bush's affinity with big business showed through loud and clear again with his sup-

---

strife.[25] A president's personality and ability to persuade others are key to amassing greater power and authority.

Presidential personality and political skills often determine how effectively a president can exercise the broad powers of the modern president. To be a successful president, says political scientist Richard E. Neustadt, a president must not only have a will for power but must use that will to set the agenda for the nation. In setting that agenda, in effect, the president can become a true leader. According to Neustadt, "Presidential power is the *power to persuade,*" which comes largely from an individual's ability to bargain. Neustadt states that persuasion is key because constitutional powers alone don't provide modern presidents with the authority to meet rising public expectations.[26]

VISUAL LITERACY
Presidential Success in Congress

PUBLIC OPINION AND THE PRESIDENT

Presidents have long recognized the power of the bully pulpit and the importance of going public. Since Watergate, however, the American

port of bankruptcy reform legislation, which the Clinton administration opposed. Instead, over the strong objections of consumer groups, President Bush signed legislation to make it harder for individuals to go bankrupt and made it easier for the nation's banks to collect on consumer credit loans.

President Bush also quickly moved to create an Office of Faith-Based Initiatives to allow for an increased participation in the nation's churches in implementing executive policies, a move that would have never happened during the Clinton administration. He also acted forcefully to support congressional efforts to overrule Clinton era ergonomics regulations hotly contested by big business, showing organized labor that they no longer had a friend in the White House.

President Bush also made it quickly evident that the United States was no longer to be a peace negotiator around the world. In meetings with Britain's Tony Blair, he made it clear that he would not take the kind of role that his predecessor did in the North Ireland peace process. Ditto to the administration's resolve to intervene in the Middle East peace process.

President Bush as we went to press was also considering ending the American Bar Association's 50-year role in evaluating nominees to the federal bench, finding that the liberal ABA is often too critical in its evaluation of conservative judges of the kind that Mr. Bush expects to nominate to the federal courts.

Quick out of the starting gate in spite of a protracted election that shortened the time to put his administration in place, President Bush, the first president with an advanced degree in business administration, has shown himself to be an effective manager able to get policies he wants in place quickly.

---

public has been increasingly skeptical of presidential actions, and few presidents have enjoyed extended periods of the kind of popularity needed to help win support for programmatic change.

In 1974, President Richard M. Nixon resigned from office rather than face the certainty of impeachment, trial, and removal from office for his role in covering up details about a break-in at Democratic Party national headquarters in the Watergate office complex.

What came to be known simply as Watergate also produced a major decision from the Supreme Court on the scope of what is termed **executive privilege**. In *United States* v. *Nixon* (**1974**) the Supreme Court ruled unanimously that there was no overriding executive privilege that sanctioned the president's refusal to comply with a court order to produce information to be used in the trial of the Watergate defendants.

Watergate forever changed the nature of the presidency. Because the president long had been held up as a symbol of the nation, the knowledge that corruption could exist at the highest levels of government changed how Americans viewed all institutions of government, and mistrust of government ran rampant. Watergate demythified the office and its occupant. As Nixon toppled, so did the prestige of the office

executive privilege
An assertion of presidential power that reasons that the president can withhold information requested by the courts in matters relating to his office.

United States v. Nixon (1974)
The Supreme Court ruled that there is no constitutional absolute executive privilege that would allow a president to refuse to comply with a court order to produce information needed in a criminal trial.

Watergate
Term used to describe the events and scandal resulting from a break-in at the Democratic National Committee headquarters in 1972 and the subsequent coverup of White House involvement.

GLOBAL POLITICS

THE PRESIDENCY IN COMPARATIVE PERSPECTIVE

Presidents in the industrial democracies, faced with the difficulties of leading governments, often wish they had those powers exercised by the other kind of executive, the prime minister. Is the president of the United States more powerful than the prime ministers of the parliaments of Europe, Canada, and Japan?

In some ways, the president has significant powers that prime ministers do not. First, presidents typically appoint 3,000 positions in the executive branch and judiciary, two to three times the number prime ministers appoint. Second, presidents have larger staffs than prime ministers, a significant information-gathering resource. Third, the separation of powers places the president at the center of the political system, which gives him the ability to focus popular attention on key issues and to appeal to the public.

Presidents are harder to remove from office. Impeachment proceedings require that the president have committed "high crimes or misdemeanors." Prime ministers can be removed by a vote of no confidence, which requires only that a simple majority of the lower house of parliament agrees that it does not support the prime minister's leadership.

Prime ministers, on the other hand, have powers American presidents often wish they had. Prime ministers do not face formal term limits and, with the exception of Germany's chancellor, can call for elections whenever they choose (within limits). Unlike recent American presidents, prime ministers have long prior experience in the legislature (an informal requirement for the position) and cabinet: "Outsiders" do not take over the reins of government. Finally, because the majority party or coalition in the lower house of parliament elects the prime minister, the latter is virtually assured of support from the legislature. Unlike both the American and French presidents in 1999, for example, no prime minister in the G-7 faces a hostile majority in the parliament or Congress. As a result, prime ministers have a much easier time getting their legislative agendas passed into law; the success rate

itself. After Watergate, no longer was the president to be considered above the law or the scrutiny of the public or of the press.

Watergate not only forever changed the public's relationship to the president; it also spurred many reforms in how government and politics were run. Ethics and campaign finance laws were tightened up, and an independent counsel law, which allowed for independent investigation of the executive branch, was enacted. Perhaps even more than these changes, Watergate bruised Americans' optimism about what was good about America. Furthermore, intensive media attention brought the president and the presidency closer to the people (*and* to their intense public criticism) at the same time that the public expectations about the presidency itself increased. People began to look to the president rather than Congress to solve pressing and increasingly complex national

for cabinet-sponsored bills in the parliamentary systems is 80–90 percent, which no American president can match.

When we look farther afield, we run into a problem of comparison. "President" in countries like Mexico, China, and Indonesia means something rather different from what it means in the United States. In many developing countries, for different reasons, presidents typically have powers no American president enjoys. Among many of these presidencies, the chief executives are not faced with courts that can overturn executives' decisions. In China and Indonesia, the president is elected by the legislature, a device intended (until recently in Indonesia's case) to ensure that the incumbent remained in office. The domination of Mexican national politics by the Institutional Revolutionary Party until 1990s had similar consequences; President Fox represents a break from the domination. The existence of a president doesn't guarantee a government based on meaningful checks and balances.

China represents an extreme in this regard. Jiang Zemin is not chief executive because he is president so much as because he occupies a number of positions in the government and the Communist Party that enable him and his supporters to control government. Jiang's predecessor, Deng Xiao-Ping, was commonly referred to as "paramount leader," a term that fully conveys the idea that the executive power in China lies outside the constitutinal provisions of any particular office.

Chief Executives, 2001

Country	Chief Executive	Office
Canada	Jean Chretien	Prime minister
China	Jiang Zemin	President
France	Jacques Chirac	President
Germany	Gerhard Schroder	Chancellor
Indonesia	Abdurrahim Wahid	President
Italy	Silvio Berlusconi	Prime minister
Japan	Junichiro Koizumi	Prime minister
Mexico	Vicente Fox	President
Russia	Vladimir Putin	President
United Kingdom	Tony Blair	Prime minister
United States	George W. Bush	President

problems even as their respect for the office—and often even its occupant—declined.

The complex interactions of public opinion and the president are of considerable interest to scholars as well as members of the media and politicians. Presidents can mold public opinion and use public opinion to garner support for their favored programs. While all presidents try to manipulate public opinion to win support of their programs, they also are very mindful of their own standing in the polls.

Going Public

On average, President Bill Clinton spoke to the public in a variety of venues about 550 times a year. President Reagan, often remembered as

WEB EXPLORATION
For more details on Watergate, see www.ablongman.com/oconnor

COMPARATIVE
Comparing Chief Executives

a master of public relations and the media, averaged 320 appearances a year; the folksy President Truman, only 88 times a year.[27] What's the difference? The postmodern president has to try to govern amidst the din of several competing twenty-four-hour news channels, the Internet, and a news cycle that makes events of an hour ago old news. This rapid change provides presidents with rare opportunities while at the same time representing daunting challenges.

Historically, even before the days of radio and television, presidents tried to reach out to the public to gain support for their programs through what President Theodore Roosevelt (1901–1909) called "the bully pulpit."

In this century, the development of commercial air travel and radio, news reels, television, and communication satellites have made direct communication to larger numbers of voters easier. Presidents no longer stay at home but instead travel all over the world to expand their views and to build personal support as well as support for their programs.

Direct, presidential appeals to the electorate like those that often were made by Bill Clinton are referred to as "going public." Going public means that a president goes over the heads of members of Congress to gain support from the people, who can then place pressure on their elected officials in Washington. George W. Bush appears to prefer a more subtle form. Instead of taking to the national airwaves, he is a frequent visitor to key states.

Presidential Approval Ratings

Historically, presidents have the best chance of convincing Congress to follow their policy lead when public opinion ratings are high. Presidential popularity, however, generally follows a cyclical pattern. These cycles have occurred since 1938, when pollsters first began to track presidential popularity.[28]

Typically, presidents enjoy their highest level of popularity at the beginning of their terms and try to take advantage of this honeymoon period to get their programs passed by Congress as soon as possible. Each action a president takes, however, is divisive—some people will approve, and others will disapprove. Disapproval tends to have a cumulative effect. Inevitably, as a general rule, a president's popularity wanes, although Bill Clinton was a notable exception to this rule.

As revealed in Analyzing the Data, since Lyndon Johnson's presidency, only four presidents finished their terms with approval ratings of more than 50 percent. Many credit this trend to events such as Vietnam, Watergate, the Iran hostage crisis, and the Iran-Contra scandal, which have made the public increasingly skeptical of presidential performance. Presidents George Bush and Bill Clinton, however, experienced increases in their presidential performance scores during the course of their presidencies. Bush's rapid rise in popularity occurred after the major and, perhaps more important, quick victory in the 1991

A N A L Y Z I N G   T H E   D A T A

PRESIDENTIAL APPROVAL SINCE 1938

Presidential approval ratings have generally followed a cyclical pattern. Presidents generally have enjoyed their highest ratings at the beginning of their terms and experienced lower ratings toward the end. Presidents Bush and Clinton, however, have enjoyed popularity surges during the course of their terms. Despite the Monica Lewinsky crisis and the threat of impeachment, Clinton's approval ratings continued to rise in 1998 and 1999. They peaked at 73% at the end of 1998—the highest rating of his administration. Clinton left office with a 66% approval rating.

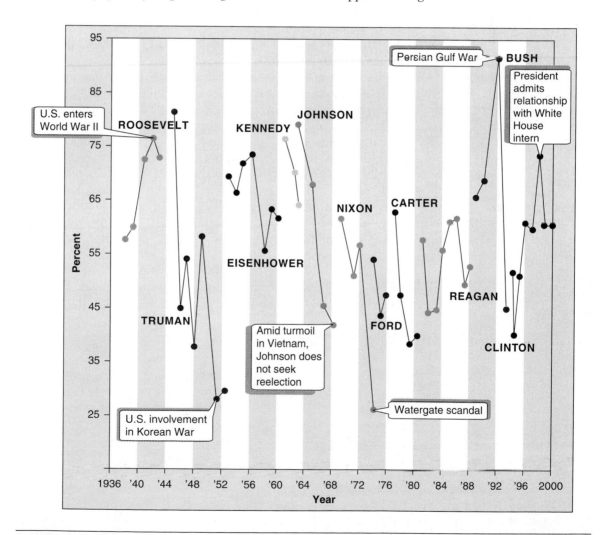

Source: USA Today (August 14, 2000), p. 6A. Copyright 2000, USA TODAY. Reprinted by permission.

Persian Gulf war. His popularity, however, plummeted as the good feelings faded and Americans began to feel the pinch of recession. In contrast, Bill Clinton's approval scores skyrocketed after the 1996 Democratic National Convention. More interestingly, Clinton's high approval ratings continued in the wake of allegations of wrongdoing in the Oval Office, his eventual admission of inappropriate conduct, and through his impeachment proceedings.

When Clinton went to the American public and admitted that he misled them about his relationship with Monica Lewinsky, an ABC poll conducted immediately after his speech showed a 10-point jump in his job approval rating.[29]

Presidential popularity in domestic or foreign affairs is likely to hold some sway on the president's ability to build support for programs, although some political scientists question direct linkages between presidential support and policy influence.[30] Still, it is critical to remember that the president—whether you voted for him, like him, or agree with him on any particular issue or philosophical debate—is the elected leader of the nation and a key player in the policy process. A president is many things to many people: a symbol of the nation, a political organizer, a moral teacher. As we discussed in chapter 1, until the 1960s most Americans looked up to their president. Watergate heightened cynicism about the president and government in general. Nevertheless, until the 1990s it was highly unusual to see a sitting president vilified in the press or on radio or television talk shows. Never before have Americans known so much about the activities of their presidents, their background, who they dated in high school and college, what affairs they've had, and what they eat. Unlike the U.S. Supreme Court, whose members deliberate in secret and wear long, black judicial robes, Bill Clinton's legs, his running shorts (and even his undershorts) were often the frequent objects of public attention and comment. The Lewinsky affair opened a whole new line of what is considered "fair" game. In fact, one of the strengths of George W. Bush's candidacy was that there was no recent hint of scandal in his personal life.

Continuity & Change

A Woman President?

When the Constitution was first adopted, women could not vote, let alone dream of being president. By the mid-1800s, however, some women had begun to mobilize for expanded rights and opportunities, and the right to vote in particular. As early as 1871, Victoria Woodhull, an outspoken proponent of "free love" and editor of a weekly newspaper, tried to convince women suffrage leaders to form their own political party, the Cosmo-

(continued)

Political Party.[a] Woodhull would then run for president in the 1872 elections. Susan B. Anthony soon vetoed the idea because she was distrustful of Woodhull and her motives.[b]

Campaigning for Woodhull in 1872 was Belva Lockwood, who in 1867 founded the first D.C. franchise group, the Universal Suffrage Association. Lockwood was a strong believer in the role of publicity in the cause of women's rights. In 1884, Lockwood met with a handful of other women in California and founded the National Equal Rights Party, which nominated Lockwood for president.[c] Her platform included equal rights for all, liquor restrictions, uniform marriage and divorce laws, and universal peace. Her run for the presidency was opposed by most women suffrage leaders; still, she received 4,149 votes in the six states where she was on the ballot. She ran again in 1888 but received even fewer votes.

In 1964, Senator Margaret Chase Smith (R–Maine), the only woman in the U.S. Senate, announced her candidacy for her party's nomination. Her name was placed in nomination at the convention, but she garnered few votes from the delegates. In 1984, the Democratic Party and its presidential candidate, former Vice President Walter Mondale, thought it could capitalize on its growing support from women voters and reenergize the party by nominating Geraldine Ferraro as his vice presidential running mate.[d] The Mondale/Ferraro ticket, however, was trounced by popular incumbent Ronald Reagan. Still, women's hopes to have a woman president did not die. In fact, in 1998 a nonpartisan group called the White House Project was founded to change the political climate so that the public would be more receptive to the idea of a woman president. In 2000, it cooperated with Mattel to produce "Madame President Barbie" to help socialize young girls to think about being president.

Today, the idea of a woman president is becoming more and more accepted. In 1937, only 33 percent of those polled said they would vote for a woman for president.[e] By 1999, when Elizabeth Dole announced her exploratory committee for president, 92 percent of those polled said that they could vote for a woman, up 10 percent since 1987.[f] But due to the inability to raise funds, Dole dropped out of the race in October 1999 before a single vote was cast. To facilitate the election of a woman to the White House by the year 2004, the nonpartisan White House Project launched a campaign in 1998 with a straw ballot in women's magazines offering twenty women as potential nominees. Over 100,000 people responded. The top five winners were Hillary Rodham Clinton, Elizabeth Dole, Dianne Feinstein, Christine Todd Whitman, and General Claudia Kennedy, the highest ranking woman in the U.S. military.[g]

The election of First Lady Hillary Rodham Clinton to the U.S. Senate and the naming of Christine Todd Whitman to head the Environmental Protection Agency give these women more national exposure. Still, it is interesting to note that several other nations have been headed by women, yet in the United States few see that happening soon.

1. What kind of barriers face women seeking the presidency?
2. Who will emerge as likely candidates in the future?

[a] *Woodhull and Clafin's Weekly*, April 22, 1871.
[b] Carol Hymowitz and Michaele Weissman, *A History of Women in America* (New York: Bantam Books, 1978), 172.
[c] Louis Filler, "Belva Lockwood," in Edward T. James, ed., *Notable American Women*, vol. 2 (Cambridge, Mass.: Harvard University Press, 1971), 413–16.
[d] Nancy E. McGlen and Karen O'Connor, *Women, Politics, and American Society*, 2nd ed. (Upper Saddle River, N.J.: Prentice Hall, 1998), 47–8.
[e] Frank Newport, "Americans Today Much More Accepting of a Woman, Black, Catholic, or Jew as President," *Poll Releases*, Gallup Organization, March 29, 1999.
[f] Newport, "Americans Today Much More Accepting of a Woman."
[g] Gloria Negri, "Liswood's Goal: A Woman in the White House," *Boston Globe, City Weekly* (May 2, 1999): 1.

Cast Your Vote. What female candidate would you elect as president of the United States? To cast your vote, go to **www.ablongman.com/oconnor**

SUMMARY

Because the Framers feared a tyrannical monarch, they gave considerable thought to the office of the chief executive. Since ratification of the Constitution, the office has changed considerably—more through practice and need than from changes in the Constitution.

Distrust of a too-powerful leader led the Framers to create an executive office with limited powers. They mandated that a president be thirty-five years old and opted not to limit the president's term of office. To further guard against tyranny, they also made provisions for the removal of the president and created an office of vice president to provide for an orderly transfer of power.

The Framers gave the president a variety of specific constitutional powers in Article II, including the appointment power, the power to convene Congress, the power to make treaties, and the power to veto. The president also derives considerable power from being commander-in-chief of the military. The Constitution also gives the president the power to grant pardons.

The development of presidential power has depended on the personal force of those who have held the office. The election of FDR ushered in a new era of the modern presidency. A hallmark of the modern presidency is the close relationship between the American people and their chief executive.

As the responsibilities of and expectations about the president have grown, so has the executive branch of government. The cabinet has grown, and FDR established the Executive Office of the President to help him govern. Perhaps the most key policy advisers are those closest to the president—those in the White House office and some members of the Executive Office of the President.

Since FDR, the public has looked to the president to propose legislation to Congress. The modern president also plays a major role in the budgetary process. To gain support for programs or a proposed budget, the president can use patronage, personal rewards, and party connections, and can go directly to the public. How presidents go about winning support is determined by their leadership and personal style, their character and ability to persuade, and, in general, their ability to maintain high ratings in public opinion polls.

Presidents long have recognized the importance of using the bully pulpit to advance their interests. Since Watergate, however, the American public has grown increasingly skeptical of presidential effects to manipulate public opinion.

KEY TERMS

Cabinet, p. 207
congressionalist, p. 219
executive agreement, p. 207
Executive Office of the
    President (EOP), p. 216
executive order, p. 223

executive privilege, p. 227
inherent powers, p. 211
New Deal, p. 214
pardon, p. 210
presidentialist, p. 218

United States v. *Nixon* (1974):
    p. 227
veto power, p. 208
War Powers Act, p. 210
Watergate, p. 227

SELECTED READINGS

Barber, James David. *The Presidential Character: Predicting Presidential Performance in the White House,* 4th ed. Englewood Cliffs, N.J.: Prentice Hall, 1992.

Daynes, Byron W., and Glen Sussman. *The American Presidency and the Social Agenda.* Upper Saddle River, N.J.: Prentice Hall, 2001.

Campbell, Karlyn Kohr, and Kathleen Hall Jamieson. *Deeds Done in Words: Presidential Rhetoric and the Genres of Governance.* Chicago: University of Chicago: Chicago Press, 1990.

Corwin, Edwin S. *The Presidential Office and Powers,* 4th ed. New York: New York University Press, 1957.

Edwards, George C., III., *Presidential Leadership: Politics and Policy Making.* New York: Bedford Books, 2000.

Kellerman, Barbara. *The Political Presidency.* New York: Oxford University Press, 1986.

Kernell, Samuel. *Going Public: New Strategies for Presidential Leadership,* 3rd ed. Washington, D.C.: CQ Press, 1997.

Levy, Leonard W., and Louis Fisher, eds. *Encyclopedia of the American Presidency.* Englewood Cliffs, N.J.: Prentice Hall, 1994.

Nelson, Michael, ed. *The Presidency and the Political System,* 5th ed. Washington, D.C.: CQ Press, 1998.

Neustadt, Richard E. *Presidential Power and the Modern Presidency.* New York: Free Press, 1991.

Pfiffner, James P. *Modern Presidency.* New York: Bedford Press, 2000.

Pious, Richard M. *The Presidency.* Boston: Allyn and Bacon, 1996.

Ragsdale, Lyn. *Vital Statistics on the Presidency: Washington to Clinton.* Washington, D.C.: CQ Press, 1998.

Rossiter, Clinton. *The American Presidency.* Baltimore, Md.: Johns Hopkins University Press, 1987.

Skowronek, Stephen. *The Politics Presidents Make: Leadership from John Adams to Bill Clinton.* Cambridge, Mass.: Harvard University Press, 1997.

Walcott, Charles E., and Karen Hult. *Governing the White House.* Lawrence: University Press of Kansas, 1995.

Warshaw, Shirley Anne. *The Domestic Presidency: Policy Making in the White House.* Boston: Allyn and Bacon, 1996.

—————. *Managing the Presidency. The Keys to Power.* New York: Addison-Wesley, 1999.

8 The Executive Branch and the Federal Bureaucracy

(Photo courtesy: Lisa Quinones/Black Star)

Chapter Outline

From January through April of 2000, there was little that most Americans could do to avoid hearing about Elian Gonzalez. The story of a boy adrift in the ocean after his mother died attempting to flee Cuba pulled at the heartstrings of most Americans, regardless of whether or not they believed that he should be returned to his father or granted asylum in the United States and allowed to live with his relatives in Miami. While much of the action in this case took place in the courts as well as in the media, it was federal employees in the Immigration and Naturalization Services (INS), in consultation with Justice Department officials, who eventually made the decision to return Elian to his father, as well as to how they were reunited.

Federal bureaucrats made many of the important decisions in the Elian Gonzalez case and were charged with implementing directives from Attorney General Janet Reno, who presided over the Justice Department and its many branches, including one in Miami. Although many Americans often are critical of the federal government and those who work for it, even in the wake of the extraordinarily publicized armed raid on the Gonzalez home and Elian's removal by INS officials, Americans overwhelmingly approved of the action. Neither did most Americans want members of Congress, who are charged with oversight of the executive branch, to launch into more hearings on the executive branch's handling of the entire Gonzalez matter. In fact, 68 percent of those polled opposed the proposed hearings.[1] Weary of the many highly partisan hearings over Whitewater, Travelgate, Filegate, Ruby Ridge, and Waco, many of them costing millions of dollars and leading to few concrete findings, the American public seemed sick of hearings and appeared to want Congress to let the executive branch get on with its function: executing the laws of the land and allowing bureaucrats to do their jobs.

D uring the 2000 presidential race, George W. Bush painted Al Gore as a proponent of big federal government and federal programs, while he professed to want to devote more power and money back to the states and the people. The **bureaucracy** is often called the "fourth branch of government" because of the tremendous power that agencies and bureaus can exercise, as was illustrated in the case of Elian Gonzalez. George W. Bush and many other Republicans charge that the bureaucracy, the thousands of federal government agencies and institutions that implement and administer the laws and programs enacted by Congress or the president and the executive branch, is too large, too powerful, and too unaccountable to the people or even to elected officials. Often, many charge that the bureaucracy is too wasteful. Interestingly, few discuss the fact that laws and policies are also implemented by state and local bureaucracies and bureaucrats.

While many Americans are uncomfortable with the large role of the federal government in policy making, current studies show that most users of federal agencies rate the agencies and the services received quite favorably. Although many of those polled by the Pew Research Center as part of its efforts to assess America's often seemingly conflicting views about the federal government and its services were frustrated by complicated rules and the slowness of a particular agency, most gave most agencies overall high marks. Most of those polled drew sharp distinctions between particular agencies and the government as a whole, although the federal government, especially the executive branch, is largely composed of agencies, as we will discuss later in this chapter. For example, 84 percent of physicians and pharmacists rated the Food and Drug Administration favorably, while only one half were positive about the government.[2] Not surprisingly, the Internal Revenue Service got the lowest marks, but it even got a positive rating from 42 percent of the taxpayers surveyed. The survey also found that attitudes toward particular agencies were related to public support for their function. Thus, the public, which views clean air and water as a national priority, was much more likely to rate the Environmental Protection Agency highly. Since missions of the agencies aren't likely to change, most agencies are trying to improve their service to the public, and the public appears to be responding.

Harold D. Lasswell once defined political science as the "study of who gets what, when, and how."[3] It is by studying the bureaucracy that those questions can perhaps best be answered.

In this chapter, we examine the development of the bureaucracy, what bureaucrats do, and the role of bureaucrats and the bureaucracy in the policy-making process.

bureaucracy

A set of complex hierarchical departments, agencies, commissions, and their staffs that exist to help carry out the president's constitutionally mandated charge to enforce the laws of the nation.

THE ROOTS AND DEVELOPMENT OF THE EXECUTIVE BRANCH AND THE FEDERAL BUREAUCRACY

German sociologist Max Weber believed bureaucracies, the set of complex hierarchical departments, agencies, commissions, and their staffs that help carry out the president's constitutionally mandated charge to enforce the laws of the nation, were a rational way for complex societies to organize themselves. Model bureaucracies, said Weber, are characterized by certain features, including:

1. A chain of command in which authority flows from top to bottom.
2. A division of labor whereby work is apportioned among specialized workers to increase productivity.
3. A specification of authority where there are clear lines of authority among workers and their superiors.
4. A goal orientation that determines structure, authority, and rules.
5. Impersonality, whereby all employees are treated fairly based on merit and all clients are served equally, without discrimination, according to established rules.
6. Productivity, whereby all work and actions are evaluated according to established rules.[4]

From George Washington to the Progressive Era

Weber's characterization more or less aptly describes the development of the federal bureaucracy since George Washington's time. George Washington's bureaucracy consisted of only three departments, which had existed under the Articles of Confederation: State (called Foreign Affairs under the Articles of Confederation), War, and Treasury. Soon, the head of each department was called its *secretary*. To help the president with legal advice, Congress created the office of attorney general. The original status of the attorney general, however, was unclear—was he a member of the judicial or executive branch? That confusion was remedied in 1870 with the creation of the Justice Department as part of the executive branch, with the attorney general as its head.

From the beginning, individuals appointed as Cabinet secretaries (as well as the attorney general) were subject to approval by the U.S. Senate, but were "removable by the president" alone. Even the first Congress realized how important it was for a president to be surrounded by those in whom he had complete confidence and trust.

The Civil War and Its Effect on Government Growth.   The Civil War (1861–1865) permanently changed the nature of the federal bureaucracy. As the nation geared up for war, thousands of additional employees were added to existing departments. The Civil War also spawned the need for new government agencies. A series of poor harvests and marketing problems led President Abraham Lincoln (who understood that one needs food in order to conduct a war) to create the Department of Agriculture in 1862, although it was not given full Cabinet-level status until 1889.

After the Civil War, the need for big government continued unabated. The Pension Office was established in 1866 to pay benefits to the thousands of northern veterans who had fought in the war. Justice was made a department in 1870, and other departments were added through 1900.

The Progressive Era and Government Growth.   During the late 1800s, Progressives raised the public cry for governmental regulation of business. In the wake of the tremendous growth of big business (especially railroads), widespread price fixing and other unfair business practices, and lobbying from reformers, Congress created the Interstate Commerce Commission (ICC). It became the first **independent regulatory commission,** an agency outside of the major executive departments. Independent regulatory commissions such as the ICC are created by Congress to be independent of direct presidential authority. Commission members, although appointed by the president, hold their jobs for fixed terms and are not removable by the president unless they fail to uphold their oaths of office. In 1887, the creation of the ICC also marked a shift in the focus of the bureaucracy from service to regulation. Its creation gave the government—in the shape of the bureaucracy—vast powers over individual and property rights.

independent regulatory commission
An agency created by Congress that is generally concerned with a specific aspect of the economy.

The ratification of the Sixteenth Amendment to the Constitution in 1913 also affected the size of government and the possibilities for growth. It gave Congress the authority to implement a federal income tax to supplement the national treasury and provided an infusion of funds to support new federal agencies, services, and governmental programs.

The New Deal and Bigger Government

The stock market crashed in 1929, ushering in the Great Depression, which was characterized by high unemployment and weak financial markets. Franklin D. Roosevelt proposed and the Congress enacted far-ranging legislation to create hundreds of new government agencies to regulate business practices and various aspects of the economy. The desperate mood of the nation supported these moves, as most Americans began to change their ideas about the proper role of government and the provision of governmental services. Formerly, Americans had believed in a hands-off approach; now they considered it the government's job to get the economy going and get Americans back to work.

Within the first hundred days of Roosevelt's administration, Congress approved every new regulatory measure proposed by the president. In a series of key decisions made through 1937, however, the Supreme Court repeatedly invalidated key provisions in congressional legislation designed to regulate various aspects of the economy. The Court and others who subscribed to what are termed *laissez-faire* principles argued that natural economic laws at work in the marketplace control the buying and selling of goods. Advocates of *laissez-faire* believed that the government had no right to regulate business in any way.

In response, FDR, frustrated by the decisions of the Court, proposed his famous Court-packing plan, which would have allowed him to add appointees to the Court. In the wake of that institution-threatening proposal, the Court quickly fell into sync with public opinion. In a series of cases, the Supreme Court reversed a number of its earlier decisions and upheld what some have termed the "alphabetocracy." For example, the Court upheld the constitutionality of the National Labor Relations Act of 1935 (NLRA), which allowed recognition of unions and established formal arbitration procedures for employers and employees.[5] Once new programs were declared constitutional, the proverbial floodgates were open to the creation of more governmental agencies. With the growth in the bureaucracy came more calls for reform of the system.

TIMELINE
Evolution of the Federal Bureaucracy

THE MODERN BUREAUCRACY

spoils system
The firing of public-office holders of a defeated political party and their replacement with loyalists of the newly elected party.

Pendleton Act
Reform measure that created the Civil Service Commission to administer a partial merit system. It classified the federal service by grades to which appointments were made based on the results of a competitive examination. It made it illegal for federal political appointees to be required to contribute to a particular political party.

civil service system
The system created by civil service laws by which many appointments to the federal bureaucracy are made.

merit system
The system by which federal civil service jobs are classified into grades or levels to which appointments are made on the basis of performance on competitive examinations.

In 1831, describing President Andrew Jackson's populating the federal government with his political cronies, Senator William Learned Marcy of New York commented, "To the victor belong the spoils." From his statement derives the phrase **spoils system** to describe the firing of public-office holders of the defeated political party and their replacement with loyalists of the new administration. Many presidents, including Jackson, argued that in order to implement their policies, they had to be able to appoint those who subscribed to their political views as rewards for their support.

Increasing public criticism of the spoils system prompted Congress to pass the Civil Service Reform Act in 1883, more commonly known as the **Pendleton Act,** to reduce patronage. It established the principle of federal employment on the basis of open, competitive exams and created a bipartisan three-member Civil Service Commission, which operated until 1978. Initially, only about 10 percent of the positions in the federal **civil service system** were covered, but later laws and executive orders have extended coverage of the act to over 90 percent of all federal employees. This new system was called the **merit system,** a characteristic of Weberian democracy.

The civil service system as it has evolved today provides a powerful base for federal agencies and bureaucrats. Federal workers have tenure and the leverage of politicians is reduced. The good part is that the spoils system was reduced (but not eliminated). The bad part, however, is that federal agencies can and often do take on a life of their own, making administrative law, passing judgments, and so on. With 90 per-

POLICY IN ACTION

STUDENT LOANS

Without student loans, many of you probably would not be in college. As college costs have soared over the years, fewer and fewer families and individuals can afford to attend college without some kind of outside support. Frequently, that comes in the form of financial aid, which often includes state or federal loans.

Federal student loan programs now provide or guarantee nearly $35 billion a year. In 2000, President Clinton announced two new initiatives to make college loans more affordable and to provide debt relief to loan recipients who agree to work in poor and inner-city schools. Throughout his presidency, Clinton remained committed to putting more teachers into failing public schools. His Department of Education tried several programs, some to good success; others appeared to make little impact.

While some question whether a program that will drop the interest on the loans of those who teach will serve to attract more students to that profession, it will help reduce costs for those who become teachers who incurred debt as they worked toward their degrees.

You might not think that a loan program has much to do with the bureaucracy. Yet it is the federal government that sets the interest rates for the loans that you pay, negotiates with cooperating banks and universities, and is using a new program to influence the career directions of some through a loan program. Again, it's policy in action.

---

cent of the federal workforce secure in their positions, some bureaucrats have been able to thwart reforms passed by legislators and wanted by the people. This often makes the bureaucracy the target of public criticism and citizen frustration.

Critics continually lament that the national government is not run like a business. But the national government differs from private business in ways too numerous to cover here adequately. Governments exist for the public good, not to make money. Businesses are driven by a profit motive; government leaders, but not bureaucrats, are driven by reelection. Businesses get their money from customers; the national government gets its money from taxpayers. Another difference between a bureaucracy and a business is that it is difficult to determine to whom bureaucracies are responsible. Is it the president? Congress? The citizenry? (The range of programs involved is highlighted in Policy in Action: Student Loans.)

These kinds of differences have a tremendous consequence on the way the bureaucracy operates.[6] Because all of the incentive in government "is in the direction of not making mistakes," public employees view risks and rewards very differently than their private sector counterparts.[7] The key to the modern bureaucracy is to understand not only who bureaucrats are, how the bureaucracy is organized, and how it works, but also to see that it cannot be run like a business. An understanding of these facts and factors can help in the search for ways to motivate positive change in the bureaucracy.

The Formal Organization of the Federal Bureaucracy

While even experts can't agree on the exact number of separate governmental agencies, commissions, and departments that make up the federal bureaucracy,[8] there are probably at least 1,149 civilian agencies. A distinctive feature of the executive bureaucracy is its traditional division into areas of specialization. For example, one agency, the Occupational Safety and Health Administration, handles occupational safety, and the Department of Education specializes in education, the State Department in foreign affairs, and the Environmental Protection Agency in the environment. It is not unusual, however, for more than one agency to be involved in a particular issue or for one agency to be involved in myriad issues. In fact, numerous agencies often have authority in the same issue areas, making administration even more difficult. Agencies fall into four general types: (1) departments, (2) independent regulatory commissions, (3) independent executive agencies, and (4) government corporations.

The Cabinet Departments.   The fourteen Cabinet **departments** are major administrative units that have responsibility for conducting a broad area of government operations. Cabinet departments account for about 60 percent of the federal workforce.

As depicted in Figure 8.1, executive branch departments are headed by Cabinet members called secretaries (except the Justice Department, which is headed by the attorney general). The secretaries are responsible for establishing their department's general policy and overseeing its operations. Cabinet secretaries are directly responsible to the president but are often viewed as having two masters—the president and those affected by their department. Cabinet secretaries are also tied to Congress, from which they get their appropriations and the discretion to implement legislation and make rules and policy.

Although departments vary considerably in size, prestige, and power, they share certain features. Each department covers a broad area of responsibility generally reflected by its name. Each secretary is assisted by a deputy or undersecretary to take part of the administrative burden off the secretary's shoulders, as well as by several assistant secretaries, who direct major programs within the department. In addition, each secretary, like the president, has numerous assistants who help with planning, budgeting, personnel, legal services, public relations, and other key staff functions. Most departments are subdivided into bureaus, divisions, sections, or other smaller units, and it is at this level that the real work of each agency is done. Most departments are subdivided along functional lines, but the basis for division may be geography, work processes

WEB EXPLORATION
For more on federal governmental agencies, see www.ablongman.com/oconnor

department
A major administrative unit with responsibility for a broad area of government operations. Departmental status usually indicates a permanent national interest in that particular governmental function, such as defense, health, or agriculture.

WEB EXPLORATION
For more information on Cabinet departments, independent regulatory commissions, and independent executive agencies, see www.ablongman.com/oconnor

FIGURE 8.1   Departments of the Executive Branch

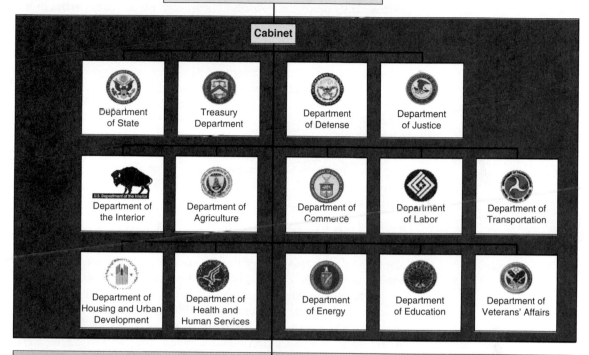

(for example, the Economic Research Service in the Department of Agriculture), or clientele (such as the Bureau of Indian Affairs in the Department of the Interior). In addition to national offices in Washington, D.C., or its immediate suburbs, each executive department has regional offices to serve all parts of the United States.

Departmental status generally signifies a strong permanent national interest to promote a particular function. Moreover, departments often are organized to foster and promote the interests of a given clientele—that is, a specific social or economic group. The Departments of Agriculture, Education, Energy, Labor, and Veterans' Affairs and the Bureau of Indian Affairs in the Department of the Interior are examples of clientele agencies/bureaus.

Because many of these agencies were created at the urging of well-organized interests to advance their particular objectives, it is not surprising that clientele groups are powerful lobbies with their respective agencies in Washington.

Independent Regulatory Commissions.   Independent regulatory commissions are agencies that were created by Congress to exist outside of the major departments to regulate a specific economic activity or interest. Because of the complexity of modern economic issues, Congress sought to create agencies that could develop expertise and provide continuity of policy with respect to economic issues because neither Congress nor the courts have the time or talent to do so. Examples of independent regulatory commissions include the National Labor Relations Board, the Federal Reserve Board, the Federal Communications Commission, and the Securities and Exchange Commission (SEC).

Most of the older independent agencies were specifically created to be relatively free from immediate (partisan) political pressure. Each is headed by a board composed of five to seven members (always an odd number, to avoid ties) who are selected by the president and confirmed by the Senate for fixed, staggered terms to increase the chances of a bipartisan board. Unlike executive department heads, they cannot be easily removed by the president. In 1935, the U.S. Supreme Court ruled that in creating independent commissions, the Congress had intended that they be independent panels of experts as far removed as possible from immediate political pressures.[9]

independent executive agency
Governmental unit that closely resembles a Cabinet department but has a narrower area of responsibility (such as the Central Intelligence Agency) and is not part of any Cabinet department.

Independent Executive Agencies.   **Independent executive agencies** closely resemble Cabinet departments but have narrower areas of responsibility. Generally speaking, independent agencies perform a service or administrative rather than regulatory function. Many of these agencies are tied to the president and Congress as closely as executive departments because the heads of these agencies are appointed by the president and serve, like Cabinet secretaries, at his or her pleasure. The heads of some of these agencies require Senate confirmation.

Independent agencies exist apart from executive departments for practical or symbolic reasons. The National Aeronautics and Space

Administration (NASA), for example, could have been placed within the Department of Defense. That kind of placement, however, could have conjured up thoughts of a space program dedicated solely to military purposes, rather than for civilian satellite communication or scientific exploration. Similarly, the Environmental Protection Agency (EPA) was created in 1970 to administer federal programs aimed at controlling pollution and protecting the nation's environment. It administers all congressional laws concerning the environment and pollution. Along with the Council on Environmental Quality, a staff agency in the Executive Office of the President, the EPA advises the president on environmental concerns. It also administers programs transferred to it along with personnel from the Departments of Agriculture, Energy, Interior, and Health and Human Services, as well as the Nuclear Regulatory Commission, among others. The expanding national focus on the environment, in fact, has brought about numerous calls to elevate the EPA to Cabinet-level status to reinforce a long-term national commitment to improved air and water and other environmental issues.

Government Corporations. **Government corporations** are the most recent addition to the bureaucratic maze. Dating from the early 1930s, they are businesses set up and created by Congress to perform functions that could be provided by private businesses. The corporations are formed when the government chooses to engage in activities that are primarily commercial in nature, produce revenue, and require greater flexibility than Congress generally allows regular departments. Some of the better-known government corporations include the U.S. Postal Service, Amtrak, and the Federal Deposit Insurance Corporation. Unlike other governmental agencies, government corporations charge for their services.

government corporation
Business set up and created by Congress that performs functions that could be provided by private businesses (such as the U.S. Postal Service).

Who Are Bureaucrats?

Federal bureaucrats are career government employees who work in the executive branch, in the fourteen Cabinet-level departments and the more than sixty independent agencies that comprise more than 2,000 bureaus, divisions, branches, offices, services, and other subunits of the federal government. There are approximately 2 million federal workers in the executive branch. Nearly one-third of all civilian employees work in the postal service. The remaining federal civilian workers are spread out among the various executive departments and agencies throughout the United States. Most of these federal employees are paid according to what is called the "General Schedule" (GS). They advance within GS grades and onto higher GS levels and salaries as their careers progress.

As a result of reforms made during the Truman administration that built on the Pendleton Act, most civilian federal governmental employees today are selected by merit standards, which include tests (such as civil service or foreign service exams) and educational criteria. Merit systems protect federal employees from being fired for political reasons.

ANALYZING THE DATA

NUMBER OF FEDERAL EMPLOYEES IN THE EXECUTIVE BRANCH, 1789–2000

The federal government grew slowly until the 1930s, when Franklin D. Roosevelt's New Deal programs were created in response to the high unemployment and weak financial markets of the Great Depression. A more modest spike in the federal workforce occurred in the mid-1960s during Lyndon B. Johnson's "Great Society" program. Since that time, six executive branch departments have been created: Department of Housing and Urban Development (1965), Department of Transportation (1966), Department of Energy (1977),

Department of Education (1979), Department of Heath and Human Services (1979), (which were created out of the old department of Health, Education and Welfare) and the Department of Veterans' Affairs (1989). Of all the federal departments, the Department of Defense is by far the largest, employing nearly 800,000 workers. In comparison, the smallest federal department—the Department of Education, a branch frequently under fire by the Republican Congress—employs approximately 5,000 workers.

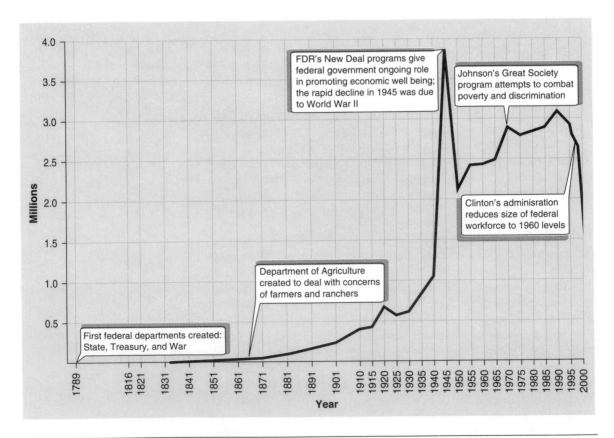

Source: U.S. Department of Commerce, Bureau of the Census, *Historical State of U.S.: Colonial through 1970* (Washington D.C.: U.S. Government Printing Office, 1975): U.S. Bureau of Labor Statistics, *Monthly Labor Review,* November 1988, and U.S. Office of Personnel Management, *The Fact Book,* http://www.opm.gov/feddata/factbook/html/fb-p08.html.

At the lower levels of the U.S. Civil Service, most positions are filled by competitive examinations. These usually involve a written test, although the same position in the private sector would not. Mid-level to upper ranges of federal positions don't normally require tests; instead, in the past, applicants had to fill out lengthy Form 171 job applications. Now, as a result of the Clinton administration's National Performance Review's call for the reduction of paperwork, they can simply submit a resume, or even apply by phone. Personnel departments then evaluate potential candidates and rank candidates according to how well they fit a particular job opening. Only the names of those deemed "qualified" are then forwarded to the official filling the vacancy. This can be a time-consuming process; it is not unusual for it to take six to nine months before a position can be filled in this manner.

Who are the bureaucrats? Mulder and Scully, of Fox TV's *The X-Files,* a series about federal agents who investigate the paranormal, might not be your idea of bureaucrats. But as employees of the Federal Bureau of Investigation, that's exactly what they are supposed to be! (Photo courtesy: 20th Century Fox/Shooting Star)

The remaining 10 percent of the federal bureaucracy is made up of persons not covered by the civil service system. These positions generally fall into three categories:

1. Appointive policy-making positions. About 600 persons are appointed directly by the president. Some of these, including Cabinet secretaries, are subject to Senate confirmation. These appointees, in turn, are responsible for appointing the high-level policy-making assistants who form the top of the bureaucratic hierarchy.
2. Independent regulatory commissioners. Although each president gets to appoint as many as 100 commissioners, they become independent of the president's direct political influence once they take office.
3. Low-level, nonpolicy patronage positions. At one time, the U.S. Post Office was the largest source of these government jobs. In 1971 Congress reorganized the Post Office and removed positions such as local postmaster from the political patronage/rewards pool. Since then, these types of positions generally refer to secretarial assistants to policy makers.

Federal employees are stereotyped as "paper pushers," but more than 15,000 job skills are represented in the federal government, and its workers are perhaps the best trained and most skilled and efficient in the world. Government employees, whose average age is 45.9 years, with an average length of service at 16.9 years, include forest rangers,

FBI agents, foreign service officers, computer programmers, security guards, librarians, administrators, engineers, plumbers, lawyers, doctors, postal carriers, and zoologists, among others. The diversity of government jobs mirrors the diversity of jobs in the private sector. The federal workforce, itself, is also diverse. As revealed in Figure 8.2, the federal workforce largely reflects the racial and ethnic composition of

FIGURE 8.2   Characteristics and Rank Distribution of Federal Civilian Employees, 2000

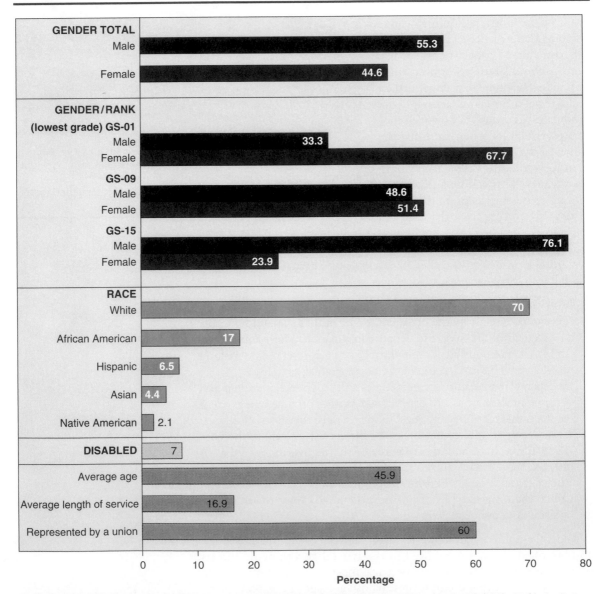

Source: Fact Book: Trend of Employment, http://www.opm.gov/feddata/factbook/html/fb-p10i.html and "Government at Work," *The Washington Post,* September 4, 2000. A23, and Demographic Profile of the Federal Workforce; office of Workforce information, n.d.

the United States as a whole, although the employment of women lags behind that of men. Women also appear to hit the same glass ceiling in the federal workforce that they find in the private sector. Not only do women make up over two-thirds of the lowest GS levels, but less than 25 percent of the positions at the highest levels of the federal General Service are held by women.

Only about 11 percent of all federal bureaucrats work in the nation's Capitol; the rest are located in regional, state, and local offices scattered throughout the country. The decentralization of the bureaucracy facilitates accessibility to the public. The Social Security Administration, for example, has numerous offices so that its clients may have a place nearby to take their paperwork, questions, and problems. Decentralization also helps distribute jobs and incomes across the country.

Many Americans believe that the federal bureaucracy is growing bigger each year, but they are wrong. Efforts to reduce the federal workforce have worked. Although it is true that the number of total government employees has been increasing until lately, most growth has taken place at the state and local levels. As more federal programs are shifted back to the states, the size of state payrolls and state bureaucracies are likely to rise to reflect these new responsibilities.

WEB EXPLORATION
To compare the federal workforce by gender, race, and ethnicity, see www.ablongman.com/oconnor

Politics and Government Workers

As an increasing proportion of the American workforce came to work for the U.S. government as a result of the New Deal recovery programs, many began to fear that the members of the civil service would play major roles not only in implementing public policy but also in electing members of Congress and even the president. Consequently, Congress enacted the Political Activities Act of 1939, commonly known as the **Hatch Act,** which was designed to prohibit federal employees from becoming directly involved in working for political candidates.

Although presidents as far back as Thomas Jefferson had advocated efforts to limit the opportunities for federal civil servants to influence the votes of others, over the years many criticized the Hatch Act as too extreme. Critics argued that it denied millions of federal employees the First Amendment guarantees of freedom of speech and association, and discouraged political participation among a group of people who might otherwise be strong political activists. Critics also argued that civil servants *should* become more involved in campaigns, particularly at the state and local level, in order to understand better the needs of the citizens they serve.

In response to criticisms of the Hatch Act and at the urgings of President Bill Clinton, in 1993, Congress enacted the **Federal Employees Political Activities Act.** This liberalization of the Hatch Act among other things allows employees to run for public office in nonpartisan elections, contribute money to political organizations, and campaign for or against candidates in partisan elections. They still, however, are prohibited from

PARTICIPATION
Who Wants to Be a Bureaucrat?

Hatch Act
Law enacted in 1939 to prohibit civil servants from taking activist roles in partisan campaigns. This act prohibited federal employees from making political contributions, working for a particular party, or campaigning for a particular candidate.

Federal Employees Political Activities Act
1993 liberalization of Hatch Act. Federal employees are now allowed to run for office in nonpartisan elections and to contribute money to campaigns in partisan elections.

engaging in political activity while on duty, soliciting contributions from the general public, or running for office in partisan elections. During the signing ceremony, Clinton said the law will "mean more responsive, more satisfied, happier, and more productive federal employees."[10]

POLICY MAKING

One of the major functions of the bureaucracy is policy making—and bureaucrats can be, and often are, major policy makers. When Congress creates any kind of department, agency, or commission, it is actually delegating some of its powers listed in Article I, section 8, of the U.S. Constitution. Therefore the laws creating departments, agencies, corporations, or commissions carefully describe their purpose and give them the authority to make numerous policy decisions, which have the effect of law. Congress recognizes that it does not have the time, expertise, or ability to involve itself in every detail of every program; therefore it sets general guidelines for agency action and leaves it to the agency to work out the details. How agencies execute congressional wishes is called **implementation,** the process by which a law or policy is put into operation.

Practically, many decisions are left to individual government employees on a day-to-day basis. Justice Department lawyers, for example, make daily decisions about whether or not to prosecute someone. Similarly, street-level Internal Revenue Service agents make many decisions during personal audits.[11] These street-level bureaucrats make policy on two levels. First, they exercise wide discretion in decisions concerning citizens with whom they interact. Second, taken together, their individual actions add up to agency behavior.[12] Thus how bureaucrats interpret or apply (or choose not to apply) various policies are equally important parts of the policy-making process. Administrative discretion allows decision makers (whether they are in a Cabinet-level position or at the lowest GS levels) a tremendous amount of leeway.

Iron Triangles and Issue Networks

At each stage of the policy-making process, the effect of what some call iron triangles or issue networks can be seen. The term **iron triangle** has been coined to describe the relatively stable relationships and patterns of interaction that occur among an agency, interest groups, and congressional committees or subcommittees as policy is made.

Policy-making triangles are "iron" because they are virtually impenetrable to outsiders and are largely autonomous. Even presidents have difficulty piercing the workings of these subgovernments, which have endured over time. Examples of iron triangles abound. The Department of Veterans' Affairs, the House Committee on Veterans Affairs,

implementation
The process by which a law or policy is put into operation by the bureaucracy.

iron triangle
The relatively stable relationship and pattern of interaction that occur among an agency, interest groups, and congressional committees or subcommittees.

and the American Legion and Veterans of Foreign Wars—the two largest organizations representing veterans—usually agree on the need for expanded programs for veterans and work together toward that end.

The policy decisions made within these iron triangles often foster the interests of a clientele group and have little to do with the advancement of national policy goals. In part, subgovernmental decisions often conflict with other governmental policies and tend to tie the hands of larger institutions such as Congress and the president. The White House is often too busy dealing with international affairs or crises to deal with smaller issues like veterans' benefits. Likewise, Congress defers to its committees and subcommittees. Thus these subgovernments decentralize policy making and make policy making difficult to control.[13]

Administrative Discretion

Essentially, bureaucrats make as well as implement policy. They take the laws and policies made by Congress, the president, and the courts, and develop rules and procedures for making sure they are carried out. Most policy implementation involves what is called **administrative discretion,** the ability to make choices concerning the best way to implement congressional intentions. Administrative discretion can also be exercised through two formal administrative procedures: rule making and administrative adjudication. This process is illustrated in Highlight: Enforcing Gender Equity in College Athletics.

Rule Making.   **Rule making** is a quasi-legislative administrative process that results in regulations and has the characteristics of a legislative act. **Regulations** are the rules that govern the operation of all government programs and have the force of law. In essence, then, bureaucratic rule makers often act as lawmakers as well as law enforcers when they make rules or draft regulations to implement various congressional statutes. Thus, rule making is called a quasi-legislative process. Some political scientists say that "[R]ulemaking is the single most important function performed by agencies of government."[14]

Because regulations often involve political conflict, the 1946 Administrative Procedure Act established rule-making procedures to give everyone the chance to participate in the process. The act requires that (1) public notice of the time, place, and nature of the rule-making proceedings be provided in the *Federal Register;* (2) interested parties be given the opportunity to submit written arguments and facts relevant to the rule; and (3) the statutory purpose and basis of the rule be stated. Once rules have been written, thirty days must generally elapse before they take effect.

Sometimes an agency is required by law to conduct a formal hearing before issuing rules. Evidence is gathered, and witnesses testify and are cross-examined by opposing interests. The process can take weeks, months, or even years, at the end of which agency administrators must

administrative discretion
The ability of bureaucrats to make choices concerning the best way to implement congressional intentions.

rule making
A quasi-legislative administrative process that has the characteristics of a legislative act.

regulation
Rule that governs the operation of a particular government program and has the force of law.

WEB EXPLORATION
To see federal agency rules and regulations of the *Federal Register,* go to www.ablongman.com/oconnor

HIGHLIGHT

ENFORCING GENDER EQUITY IN COLLEGE ATHLETICS

In 2000, there were approximately 148,802 female student-athletes,[a] a number up dramatically from 1971 when there were only 31,352 women participating in collegiate athletics.[b] A major source of that difference? The passage in 1972 of legislation popularly known as Title IX, which prohibits discrimination against girls and women in federally funded education, including in athletics programs. This legislation mandates that "No person in the United States shall, on the basis of sex, be excluded from participation in, be denied the benefits of, or be subjected to discrimination under any education program or activity receiving federal financial assistance." It wasn't until December 1978—six years after passage of the Education Amendments—that the Office for Civil Rights in HEW released a "policy interpretation" of the law, dealing largely with the section that concerned intercollegiate athletics.[c] More than thirty pages of text were devoted to dealing with a hundred or so words from the statute. Football was recognized as unique, because of the huge revenues it produces, so it could be inferred that male-dominated football programs could continue to outspend women's athletic programs. The more than sixty women's groups that had lobbied for equality of spending were outraged and turned their efforts toward seeking more favorable rulings on the construction of the statute from the courts.

Increased emphasis on Title IX enforcement has led many women to file lawsuits to force compliance. In 1991, in an effort to trim expenses, Brown University cut two men's and two women's teams from its varsity rosters. Several women on the downgraded gymnastics team filed a Title IX complaint against the school, arguing that it violated the act by not providing women varsity sport opportunities in relation to their population in the university. The women also argued that cutting the two women's program saved $62,000, whereas the men's cuts saved only $16,000. Thus the women's varsity programs took a bigger hit, in violation of federal law.

A U.S. district court refused to allow Brown to cut the women's programs. A U.S. court of appeals upheld that action, concluding that Brown had failed to provide adequate opportunities for its female students to participate in athletics.[d] In 1997, in *Brown University* v. *Cohen*, the U.S. Supreme Court declined to review the appeals court's decision.[e] This put all colleges and universities on notice that discrimination against women would not be tolerated, even when, as in the case of Brown University, the university had, since the passage of Title IX, tremendously expanded sports opportunities for women.

Women have made significant strides on all college campuses, but true equity in athletics is

---

review the entire record and then justify the new rules. Although cumbersome, the process has reduced criticism of some rules and bolstered the deference given by the courts to agency decisions.

administrative adjudication
A quasi-judicial process in which a bureaucratic agency settles disputes between two parties in a manner similar to the way courts resolve disputes.

Administrative Adjudication. **Administrative adjudication** is a quasi-judicial process in which a bureaucratic agency settles disputes between two parties in a manner similar to the way courts resolve disputes.

still a long way away at many colleges and universities. Since 1972, for every new dollar allocated to men's sports, women's teams have received but one dollar. While the number of women participating in college level sports is increasing, the proportion of women coaches is decreasing (at the same time the pool of women who could be coaches is increasing). Most colleges still provide far fewer opportunities to women given their numbers in most universities, and enforcement still lags. This has required groups including the National Women's Law Center to take the lead in the Brown case and to devote millions of dollars in legal fees to fuller enforcement.[f] Title IX is not self-enforcing.

Individual colleges and universities must comply with the law, aggrieved students must complain of inequities, and the Department of Education's Office of Civil Rights must enforce the law.

---

[a]NCAA Homepage: http://www.ncaa.org.
[b]*Intercollegiate Athletics: Status of Efforts to Promote Gender Equity*, U.S. General Accounting Office, October 25, 1996.
[c]See Joyce Gelb and Marian Lief Palley, *Women and Public Policies* (Charlottesville: University of Virginia Press, 1996), ch. 5.
[d]*Cohen v. Brown University*, 101 F.3d 155 (1996).
[e]117 S.Ct. 1469 (1997).
[f]http://www.edc.org/WomensEquity/resource/title9/report/athletic.html.

In 1992 Congress enacted Title IX of the Education Amendments of 1972, which mandated nondiscrimination in women's sports. Congress, however, left it up to an executive department to implement the law. Title IX guidelines, especially those dealing with intercollegiate athletics, have been very controversial and yet to be implemented fully. Still, since its passage, there has been a dramatic increase in the number of high school and college women competing in school sports. According to the Soccer Industry Council of America, the number of girls playing soccer in the United States grew from 85,173 in 1986 to 191,358 in 1995. (Photo courtesy: Karen O'Connor)

Administrative adjudication, like rule making, is referred to as "quasi" (Latin for "seemingly") judicial, because law making by any body other than Congress or adjudication by any body other than the judiciary would be a violation of the constitutional principle of separation of powers.

Agencies regularly find that persons or businesses are not in compliance with the federal laws the agencies are charged with enforcing, or that they are in violation of an agency rule or regulation. To force compliance, some agencies resort to administrative adjudication, which is generally less formal than a trial. Several agencies and boards employ administrative law judges to conduct the hearings. Although these judges are employed by the agency, they are strictly independent and cannot be removed except for gross misconduct. Congress, for example, empowers the Federal Trade Commission (FTC) to determine what constitutes an unfair trade practice.[15] Its actions, however, are reviewable in the federal courts.

SIMULATION
You Are the
Administrator

GOVERNMENT CONTROL: MAKING AGENCIES ACCOUNTABLE

The question of to whom bureaucrats should be responsible is one that continually comes up in any debate about governmental accountability. Should the bureaucracy be answerable to itself? To organized interest groups? To its clientele? To the president? To Congress? Or to some combination of all of these? At times an agency becomes so removed from the public it serves that Congress must step in. (See Politics Now: Can I Help You? It All Depends on Whether Congress Allocates Enough Money.) While many would argue that bureaucrats should be responsive to the public interest, the public interest is difficult to define. As it turns out, several factors work to control the power of the bureaucracy, and, to some degree, the same kinds of checks and balances that operate among the three branches of government serve to check the bureaucracy.

Executive Control

As the size and scope of the American national government have grown, particularly the executive branch and the bureaucracy, presidents have delegated more and more power to bureaucrats. But most presidents have continued to try to exercise some control over the bureaucracy, although they have often found that task more difficult than they first envisioned.

Presidents try to appoint the best possible persons to carry out their wishes and policy preferences. Although presidential appointments make up less than 1 percent of all federal jobs, presidents usually fill most top policy-making positions. Presidents can also, with the approval of Congress, reorganize the bureaucracy. They can make changes in an agency's annual budget requests and ignore legislative initiatives originating within the bureaucracy.

Presidents also issue **executive orders** to provide direction to bureaucrats. Executive orders are presidential directives to an agency that provide the basis for carrying out laws or for establishing new policies. Even before Congress acted to protect women from discrimination by the federal government, for example, the National Organization for Women

executive order
Presidential directive to an agency that provides the basis for carrying out laws or for establishing new policies.

P O L I T I C S   N O W

CAN I HELP YOU? IT DEPENDS ON WHETHER CONGRESS ALLOCATES ENOUGH MONEY

There are few letters that most Americans shudder to open: A letter from the Internal Revenue Service pointing to some problem with a recent tax return is one of them. Until recently, the cause for that nervousness was not necessarily unfounded. Throughout 1997 and 1998, Congress held extensive hearings about abuses at the Internal Revenue Service (IRS), one of the most hated and feared federal agencies in America. Senate hearings in particular exposed abuses of ordinary citizens who found themselves in a nightmare of bureaucratic red tape and agency employee abuse of power. As a result of these hearings, Congress ordered the new IRS commissioner to overhaul the way the IRS deals with the public.[a]

To do this, a computer "whiz kid" was appointed to totally reorganize the agency. "We're going to burn the house down and build it back from the foundation," said a member of the reorganization team that proposed dispatching IRS vans to neighborhoods, using e-mail to communicate with taxpayers, and setting up anonymous Internet chatrooms for taxpayers to engage in a give and take with the IRS on a range of problems that affect their tax status.[b] Other changes include twenty-four-hour customer service help lines, allowing use of credit cards to pay tax bills, and stepped-up electronic filing and assistance.

Under the new reorganization, regional offices were abolished and replaced with four operating divisions to handle specific tax areas.

This move was designed to create a more specialized workforce and allow employees to learn more about a single area, cutting down on the transmission of misinformation. "Early reports are that the agency's workers as well as its leadership are taking seriously Congress's and the public's demand for good manners and pleasant service."[c] One of its changes, however, has proven almost too good to be true. To help taxpayers settle their debts, the IRS created a new plan called the "offer in compromise" process, which allows the IRS to accept compromise offers before costly hearings. So many taxpayers, however, tried to take advantage of this process that the IRS was quickly overwhelmed, creating just the kind of logjam that the congressional investigations tried to get the IRS to fix. Tight budget restrictions won't allow the IRS to hire more staffers to handle the flood of requests, so the agency again is under attack for failing to fulfill its pledges to Congress to handle these complaints within six months.[d]

---

[a]Stephen Barr, "For IRS, a Deadline to Draft a Smile," *The Washington Post* (January 31, 1999): H1.
[b]Barr, "For IRS, a Deadline."
[c]Albert B. Crenshaw, "Another Tax Year, A Whole New Attitude at the IRS; Overhaul Produces Nicer Treatment, Better Service," *The Washington Post* (April 15, 1999): E9.
[d]Liz Pulliam Weston, "IRS Deluged over Tax-Debt Plan: Agency Can't Keep Up with the Applications," *Milwaukee Journal Sentinel* (October 23, 2000): 10D.

---

convinced President Lyndon B. Johnson to sign Executive Order 11375 in 1967. This amended an earlier order prohibiting the federal government from discriminating on the basis of race, color, religion, or national origin in the awarding of federal contracts, by adding to it the category of "gender." Nevertheless, although the president signed the order, the

POINT/COUNTERPOINT

SHOULD THE CIA BE ABOLISHED?

The Central Intelligence Agency (CIA) is an independent government agency created in 1947 as an instrument for waging the Cold War between the United States and the Soviet Union through spying. But when the Cold War ended following the independence of Eastern Europe and the fall of the Soviet Union in the early 1990s, the CIA's role in the post–Cold War world became uncertain. Because many different agencies collect intelligence, such as the Defense Intelligence Agency, the State Department Bureau of Research and Intelligence, the National Security Agency, and others, some believe the CIA—with its expensive intelligence operations—is no longer necessary. So why does the CIA still exist? Some believe that intelligence is even more important today, given the complexities of the world, the rise of terrorism, and the fact that nuclear and biological weapons still exist. Should the CIA be abolished? Let's examine these two points of view.

Opponents of the CIA, including the Libertarian Party and a number of groups on the far left as well as the far right, argue that the intelligence agency enjoys unlimited budgets with no accountability and little public scrutiny. The oversight that exists is minimal and is mostly congressional staff and members of Congress who have vested interests in maintaining huge expenditures for intelligence work. For example, members of Congress from Virginia favor spending on submarine-based intelligence work because it supports the ship-building industry, and the jobs that come with it, in that state. CIA opponents argue that there are plenty of other agencies collecting information and that the CIA is redundant and costly. Intelligence budgets are often top secret, but estimates are that all U.S. intelligence operations combined cost $28 billion per year. Some officials even wonder about the overall effectiveness of the agency in recent years.

Office of Federal Contract Compliance (the executive agency charged with implementing the order) failed to draft appropriate guidelines for implementation of the order until several years later.[16]

The power of the purse is also an important control that presidents exercise over the bureaucracy. They may alter or reduce an agency's annual budget request. They can also initiate or adjust policies that would, if enacted by Congress, change the scope and nature of an agency's activities.

Congressional Control

Congress, too, plays an important role in checking the power of the bureaucracy. Constitutionally, it possesses the authority to create or abolish departments and agencies as well as to transfer agency functions. It can also expand or contract bureaucratic discretion.

The CIA failed to predict the 1979 capture of American hostages in Iran, the fall of the Berlin Wall in 1989, or India's nuclear tests in 1999. The mission of the CIA was espoused during the height of the Cold War, and since the Cold War is over, the mission is also over.

Supporters of the CIA, including the Republican Party, argue that it is even more essential today than ever before to have accurate and timely intelligence about our adversaries and our allies. They see an expanded mission for intelligence agencies, not a need for cutting back. In the information age, the currency of the modern nation state and of security is intelligence. CIA advocates believe that congressional oversight provides adequate accountability while maintaining the need for security. Because the president must approve many of the riskier ventures the intelligence community pursues, the executive branch provides additional oversight. In defending rising intelligence budgets, CIA supporters argue that it is more expensive to keep tabs on the world today—

with more than 200 states—than it was to watch the Soviet Union and its allies during the height of the Cold War. Technology such as satellites, specially outfitted submarines, and Internet surveillance used in collecting intelligence is more expensive and expansive today than ever before. In addition, the time leaders have to respond to crises has dramatically decreased. News sources such as CNN now report twenty-four hours a day, and leaders often have to respond immediately in crisis situations. During the Cuban Missile Crisis of 1961, John F. Kennedy had days and weeks in which to respond, while George W. Bush will have only hours or minutes to respond to a similar crisis. Thus, accurate and immediate intelligence information is even more crucial today.

What do you think? Should the CIA be abolished or retained and strengthened?
Go to www.ablongman.com/oconnor

Congress can also pass legislation to affect an agency's activities or even abolish existing programs. It can investigate bureaucratic actions and force bureaucrats to testify about them before Congress. As illustrated in Politics Now: Can I Help You?, Congress at times even responds to constituent complaints about the bureaucracy. In that case, hearings resulted in total reorganization of the IRS. The Senate's power to approve presidential appointments of agency heads and other top officials is also a form of control over the bureaucracy.

Legislators also augment their formal oversight of the executive branch by allowing citizens to appeal adverse bureaucratic decisions to agencies, Congress, and even the courts. Congressional review, a procedure adopted by the 104th Congress by which agency regulations can be nullified by joint resolutions of legislative disapproval, is another method of exercising congressional oversight. (This form of oversight is discussed in greater detail in chapter 5.)

WEB EXPLORATION
For more about the IRS and its modernization efforts, see www.ablongman.com/oconnor

Judicial Control

Federal judges have the authority to determine whether or not agency rulings or actions are constitutional, a potent form of oversight. While the president's and Congress's control over the actions of the bureaucracy is very direct, the judiciary's oversight function is less so. The federal judiciary, for example, can directly issue injunctions or orders to an executive agency even before a rule is formally promulgated. The courts have also ruled that agencies must give all affected individuals their due process rights guaranteed by the U.S. Constitution. A Social Security recipient's checks cannot be stopped, for example, unless that individual is provided with reasonable notice and an opportunity for a hearing. On a more informal, indirect level, litigation, or even the threat of litigation, often exerts a strong influence on bureaucrats. Injured parties can bring suit against agencies for their failure to enforce the law, and can challenge agency interpretations of the law. In general, however, the courts give great weight to the opinions of bureaucrats and usually defer to their expertise.[17]

Research by political scientists shows that government agencies are strategic. They often implement Supreme Court decisions "based on the costs and benefits of alternative policy choices."[18] Specifically, the degree to which agencies appear to respond to Supreme Court decisions is based on the "specificity of Supreme Court opinions, agency policy preferences, agency age, and amicus curiae support."[19]

The development of specialized courts has altered the relationship of some agencies with the federal courts and apparently resulted in less judicial deference to agency rulings. Research by political scientists reveals that specialized courts such as the Court of International Trade defer less to agency decisions than do more generalized federal courts because of their expertise. Additionally, decisions from executive agencies are more likely to be reversed than those from more specialized independent regulatory commissions.[20]

The kinds of oversight engaged in by the president, Congress, and the courts do not always work to control the bureaucracy, as evidenced by the repeated calls by lawmakers and the public for reform. Calls for bureaucratic reform usually center on one main issue: accountability. Congress essentially created its own bureaucracy to keep an eye on what the executive branch and *its* bureaucracy were doing. Today the General Accounting Office (GAO) not only tracks how money is spent in the bureaucracy but also monitors how policies are

President Clinton and Vice President Gore stand in front of a forklift loaded with tons of government regulations to dramatize their plan to cut and reshape government in an effort to trim over $100 billion from the national budget. (Photo courtesy: J. Scott Applewhite/AP/Wide World Photos)

GLOBAL POLITICS

BUREAUCRACIES IN SELECTED INDUSTRIALIZED COUNTRIES

The bureaucracy plays a significant role in European and Japanese government. Unlike in the United States, employment in the national bureaucracy is considered an elite career that competes for prestige with the best positions in the private sector. In Britain, France, and Japan, top civil servants are recruited from elite institutions of higher education and are recognized as having professional qualifications specifically to manage government and the economy.

The higher civil service in the parliamentary systems is intimately involved in all aspects of policy making. Cabinet ministers drawn from the ranks of the legislature typically do not have expertise in the specific policy areas that their ministries oversee, so they rely on the higher civil service to draft the bills that will be introduced in their names. Top bureaucrats, of course, oversee the implementation of that legislation. In Germany and France, bureaucrats frequently run for election in the parliament without giving up their civil service status; retired Japanese bureaucrats have often done the same. In these coun-

tries, the elite civil service is therefore represented not only in the bureaucracy, but in the legislature and executive as well.

France and Japan demonstrate that the size of the bureaucracy may be less important than the role it plays in society. France has one of the largest public sectors in the industrial democracies, Japan the smallest. Yet both are characterized by public policies that give the national civil service a great deal of power to manage the economy and lower levels of government.

Government Employment as a Proportion of Total Employment, 1995

Country	Percent
France	19.3
Germany	14.9
Japan	5.9
United Kingdom	19.3
United States	14.5

Source: From *European Politics Today,* 3rd ed. by Frank Wilson. Copyright ©1999. Reprinted by permission of Prentice-Hall, Inc., Upper Saddle River, N.J.

implemented. The Congressional Budget Office (CBO) also conducts oversight studies. If it or the GAO uncovers problems with an agency's work, Congress is notified immediately.

Accountability—that is, holding members of the bureaucracy responsible for how they implement laws and presidential directives—is one major issue facing Congress and the president. Because the way bureaucracies are designed affects the way they operate, most presidents have tried with little success to change the structure and design of many agencies to make them function better and to facilitate oversight. This would make bureaucrats more accountable to both the president and Congress for their decisions. Attempts to achieve greater accountability for the bureaucracy have included efforts to curb waste, reduce spending, decrease redundancy, and ultimately reduce the size of the bureaucracy itself.

COMPARATIVE
Comparing
Bureaucracies

VISUAL LITERACY

The Changing Face of the Federal Bureaucracy

All recent presidents have tried to streamline the bureaucracy, a persistent goal of government reform, to make it smaller and thus more accountable. The Clinton administration was especially bullish on reform. In early 1993, Clinton signed executive orders to

- Cut the size of the federal workforce by 252,000 people within five years.
- Cut in half the growing number of federal regulations within three years.
- Set customer service standards to direct agencies to put the people they serve first.

These actions allowed President Clinton and the Congress to make dramatic reforms in the bureaucracy not seen since the New Deal.

Continuity & Change

Technology and the Bureaucracy

We rely on government bureaucrats to make sure that our cars are registered, to get our drivers' licenses, voter registration, and passports, and even to keep track of our contributions to the Social Security system. That is a far cry from what governments did in the late 1700s or what citizens expected of it. When the United States was first founded, there were but three departments in the executive branch, and an attorney general who provided the president with legal advice. The State Department, headed by Thomas Jefferson, a consistent opponent of big government, had but nine employees. The Treasury Department, headed by Federalist Alexander Hamilton, had a much larger staff. The bureaucracy continued to increase in size, albeit slowly. From 1816 to 1861, the size of the bureaucracy grew as demands on the national government increased. The Civil War and its aftermath greatly accelerated the growth of government.

Technology was barely existent. Ledgers and federal records were compiled and maintained with pen and ink. The development of the typewriter, carbon paper, and later, copying machines, while making the maintenance of records easier, also were to contribute tremendously to the red tape and paper woes of the bureaucracy. Computers totally revolutionized the way the federal government did business. Detailed records are now maintained about individuals by several different agencies, and some even fear that the government knows way too much about them. But even computers become obsolete.

Today, local, state, and the national governments are adopting and embracing technology at breathtaking speed. States, in particular, are using the Internet to provide information and services to their citizens, cutting costs, increasing efficiency, and making government more responsive to the people, just as the Framers intended. "Well-run, efficiently organized Websites improve the attitude of citizens toward government," concluded one major study of federal and state websites that ranked them according to twenty-seven factors, including the ability to register a vehicle online and access searchable records.

(continued)

In September 2000, the federal government went online with a new homepage to allow Americans to access all of its services from a single location. Firstgov.gov provides connections to over 27 million federal agency web pages on 20,000 sites.[a] Unlike the federal government, this site is accessible twenty-four hours a day. Better yet, for those who aren't familiar with federal bureaucratic structures, the site contains a search engine to allow the public to connect with the correct agency. This site contains connections to all branches of government and federal agencies, as well as to state and local governments.

It is not just governments that are making more information available to citizens to cut through the bureaucracy and red tape. Several Internet sites have sprung up to bring the government and the bureaucracy closer to the people. Govworks.com, now defunct, claimed that it could help you "take care of virtually all your government needs on line"[b] from locating the right office for reporting a pothole, paying property taxes, or registering to vote.

How technology can be used to make government more efficient and effective—especially as the number of federal employees decreases—may have important implications for how the federal government of the future operates.

1. What uses do you see for technology?
2. How could governmental services and accountability be improved through the use of new technologies?

[a]Bob Dart, "Feds Open 'All-in-One' Web Site for the Public," *Atlanta Journal and Constitution* (September 23, 2000): A1.
[b]Full-page advertisement, *New York Times* (March 18, 2000): A19.

Cast Your Vote. How would you modernize federal agencies? To cast your vote, go to **www.ablongman.com/oconnor**

SUMMARY

The federal bureaucracy plays a major role in America as a shaper of public policy, earning it the nickname the "fourth branch" of government.

According to Max Weber, all bureaucracies have similar characteristics. These characteristics can be seen in the federal bureaucracy as it developed from George Washington's time, when the executive branch had only three departments—State, War, and Treasury—through the Civil War. Significant gains occurred in the size of the federal bureaucracy as the government geared up to conduct a war. Today, the modern bureaucracy is composed of nearly 2 million civilian workers. In general, bureaucratic agencies fall into four general types: departments, government corporations, independent agencies, and independent regulatory commissions. These agencies and those who staff them not only make but implement public policy. Iron triangles or issue networks often can be used to describe how this policy making occurs. Much policy making occurs at the lowest levels of the bureaucracy, where administrative discretion can be exercised on an informal basis. More formal policy is often made through rule making and administrative adjudication.

Agencies enjoy considerable discretion, but they are also subjected to many formal controls. The president, Congress, and the judiciary all exercise various degrees of control over the bureaucracy.

Accountability is a key issue in bureaucratic politics. To improve accountability, to reduce waste and duplication, and to save money, most presidents have suggested bureaucratic reforms but to little avail because systems problems make reform difficult.

KEY TERMS

administrative adjudication, p. 252

administrative discretion, p. 251

bureaucracy, p. 237

civil service system, p. 240

department, p. 242

executive order, p. 254

Federal Employees Political Activities Act, p. 249

government corporation, p. 245

Hatch Act, p. 249

implementation, p. 250

independent executive agency, p. 244

independent regulatory commission, p. 239

iron triangle, p. 250

merit system, p. 240

Pendleton Act, p. 240

regulation, p. 251

rule making, p. 251

spoils system, p. 240

SELECTED READINGS

Bennett, Linda L. M., and Stephen E. Bennett. *Living with Leviathan: Americans Coming to Terms with Big Government.* Lawrence: University of Kansas Press, 1990.

Brehm, John, and Scott Gates. *Working, Shirking, and Sabotage: Bureaucratic Response to a Democratic Public.* Ann Arbor: University of Michigan Press, 1997.

Derthick, Martha, and Paul J. Quirk. *The Politics of Deregulation.* Washington, D.C.: Brookings Institution, 1985.

Goodsell, Charles T. *The Case for Bureaucracy: A Public Administration Polemic.* Chatham, N.J.: Chatham House, 1994.

Gormley, William T., Jr. *Taming the Bureaucracy: Muscles, Prayers and Other Strategies.* Princeton, N.J.: Princeton University Press, 1989.

Handler, Joel F. *Down the Bureaucracy: The Ambiguity of Privatization and Empowerment.* Princeton, N.J.: Princeton University Press, 1996.

Ingraham, Patricia Wallace. *The Foundation of Merit: Public Service in American Democracy.* Baltimore, Md.: Johns Hopkins University Press, 1995.

Kerwin, Cornelius M. *Rulemaking: How Government Agencies Write Law and Make Policy,* 2nd ed. Washington, D.C.: CQ Press, 1999.

Mackenzie, G. Calvin. *The Irony of Reform: Roots of Political Disenchantment.* Boulder, Colo.: Westview Press, 1996.

Osborne, David, and Peter Plastrik. *Banishing Bureaucracy: The Five Strategies for Reinventing Government.* Boston: Addison-Wesley, 1997.

Peters, B. Guy. *The Politics of Bureaucracy.* 4th ed. New York: Longman, 1995.

Richardson, William D. *Democracy, Bureaucracy and Character.* Lawrence: University of Kansas Press, 1997.

Rourke, Francis E. *Bureaucracy, Politics and Public Policy.* Boston: Little, Brown, 1988.

Wilson, James Q. *Bureaucracy: What Government Agencies Do and Why They Do It.* New York: Basic Books, 1991.

(Photo courtesy: Catherine Karnow/Woodfin Camp & Associates)

The Judiciary

9

O n December 1, 2000, hundreds of protesters gathered outside the U.S. Supreme Court. In spite of the bone-chilling temperatures, individuals had started lining up two days before to be one of the 250 lucky individuals who would be given tickets to hear *Bush* v. *Gore.* All of the surrounding roads were closed by Court police to ensure public safety. Hundreds of media crews staked out positions outside the building.

As the new century dawned, Americans were accustomed to seeing Congress deliberate a full range of issues from the most mundane to presidential impeachment on C-SPAN or one or more of the other networks. Political junkies could get their fill of the 2000 presidential election contest as the trial, circuit, and Florida supreme court proceedings were televised in their entirety.

But the U.S. Supreme Court hearings were not televised. In the first challenge to the Florida vote count, after Theodore Olson, a lawyer for the Bush campaign, finished his presentation, Roger Cossack of CNN rushed out of the Court breathlessly to report on what had happened. His colleague, Greta Van Sustern, remained in the courtroom to cover the opposing arguments offered by Harvard University Law Professor Laurence Tribe on behalf of the Gore campaign.

Olson's arguments in the first of the two cases the Court was to hear concerning the election were dramatic as he attempted to fend off attacks from various justices who questioned whether Governor Bush even had a federal case. The mood and nature of the questioning then shifted during Tribe's turn at the lectern. But very few people in America were able to see either presentation, even though the gallery looked like a who's who in American politics—among the onlookers were retired Justice Byron White, several members of Congress, and even Caroline Kennedy Schlossberg.

Members of the news media, as well as the American Political Science Association, have been urging the U.S. Supreme Court to open its arguments to the public for years, to no avail. With the outcome of the presidential contest at stake, the call was raised anew, with C-SPAN and CNN leading the charge for a one-time deal. Still, it was a no go at the Court, where many of the justices have taken an "over my dead body" stand on the issue of cameras in the Court while condoning their use in other courts. The Court's lone concession to the magnitude of the case before it? Recordings of the oral arguments were released in their entirety one hour after conclusion of the attorneys' presentations, instead of being made available two weeks later on the Court's Web site.

Even before the high-stakes presidential cases were accepted by the Court, several members of the Senate were upset with the Court's refusal to make its "public" appearances more public. In fact, Senators Arlen Specter (R–Pa.) and Joseph Biden Jr. (D–Del.) of the Judiciary Committee have sponsored a bill to require television cameras in the Supreme Court. Nevertheless, although many commentators argued that the legitimacy of the Court was on the line *Bush* v. *Gore*, the Justices remained undeterred in their commitment to keep their proceedings as private as possible.

In 1787, when Alexander Hamilton wrote to urge support of the U.S. Constitution, he firmly believed that the judiciary was the weakest of the three departments of government. Today the role of the courts, particularly the U.S. Supreme Court, is significantly different from that envisioned in 1788, the year the national government came into being. What Hamilton envisioned as the "least dangerous branch" is now perceived by many as having too much power. In this chapter we describe the American legal system, the federal court system, and how the Supreme Court has come to play a pivotal role in American life.

A note on terminology: When we refer to the "Supreme Court," the "Court," or the "high Court" here, we always mean the U.S. Supreme Court, which sits at the pinnacle of the federal and state court systems. The Supreme Court is referred to by the name of the chief justice who presided over it during a particular period (for example, the Marshall Court is the Court presided over by John Marshall from 1801 to 1835). When we use the term "courts," we refer to all federal or state courts unless otherwise noted.

The Constitution and the Creation of the National Judiciary

The detailed notes James Madison took at the Philadelphia Convention make it clear that the Framers devoted little time to the writing of or the content of Article III, which created the judicial branch of government. The Framers believed that a federal judiciary posed little of the threat of tyranny that they feared from the other two branches.

Anti-Federalists, however, were quick to object to a judiciary whose members had life tenure and the ability to interpret what was to be "the supreme law of the land," a phrase that Anti-Federalists feared would give the Supreme Court too much power.

The Framers also debated the need for any federal courts below the level of the Supreme Court. A compromise left the final choice to Congress, and Article III, section 1, begins simply by vesting "The judicial Power of the United States ... in one supreme Court, and in such inferior Courts as the Congress may from time to time ordain and establish."

Had the Supreme Court been viewed as the potential policy maker it is today, it is highly unlikely that the Framers would have provided for life tenure with "good behavior" for federal judges in Article III. This feature was agreed on because the Framers did not want the justices (or any federal judges) subject to the whims of politics, the public, or politicians. Moreover, Alexander Hamilton argued in *Federalist No. 78* that the "independence of judges" was needed "to guard the Constitution and the rights of individuals."

Article III, section 1, also gave Congress the authority to establish other courts as it sought fit. Section 2 specifies the "judicial power" of the Supreme Court (see Table 9.1) and discusses the Court's original and appellate jurisdiction. This section also specifies that all federal crimes, except those involving impeachment, shall be tried before a jury in the state

Pro-life protesters march before the Supreme Court. The Court has often been the target of interest group protests on account of its decisions on such controversial issues as abortion, affirmative action, gay rights, and physician-assisted suicide. (Photo courtesy: Larry Downing/Woodfin Camp & Associates)

TABLE 9.1 The Judicial Power of the United States Supreme Court

The following are the types of cases the Supreme Court was given the jurisdiction to hear as initially specified in the Constitution:

All cases arising under the Constitution and laws or treaties of the United States

All cases of admiralty or maritime jurisdiction

Cases in which the United States is a party

Controversies between a state and citizens of another state

Controversies between two or more states

Controversies between citizens of different states

Controversies between citizens of the same states claiming lands under grants in different states

Controversies between a state, or the citizens thereof, and foreign states or citizens thereof

All cases affecting ambassadors or other public ministers

in which the crime was committed. The third section of the Article defines treason and mandates that at least two witnesses appear in such cases.

Although it is the duty of the chief justice of the United States to preside over presidential impeachments, this is not noted in Article III. Instead, Article I, section 3 notes in discussing impeachment, "When the President of the United States is tried, the Chief Justice shall preside."

Some checks on the power of the judiciary were nonetheless included in the Constitution. The Constitution gives Congress the authority to alter the Court's jurisdiction (its ability to hear certain kinds of cases). Congress can also propose constitutional amendments that, if ratified, can effectively reverse judicial decisions, and it can impeach and remove federal judges. In one further check, it is the president who (with the "advice and consent" of the Senate) appoints all federal judges.

THE JUDICIARY ACT OF 1789 AND THE CREATION OF THE FEDERAL JUDICIAL SYSTEM

In spite of the Framers' intentions, the pervasive role of politics in the judicial branch quickly became evident with the passage of the Judiciary Act of 1789. Congress spent nearly the entire second half of its first session deliberating the various provisions of the act to give form and substance to the federal judiciary.

Judiciary Act of 1789
Established the basic three-tiered structure of the federal court system.

The **Judiciary Act of 1789** established the basic three-tiered structure of the federal court system. At the bottom are the federal district courts. Circuit courts were created to handle appeals from district courts. Initially, each court was composed of one district court judge and two itinerant Supreme Court justices who met as a circuit court twice a year.

The Supreme Court of the United States sits atop the federal judicial system. Although the Constitution mentions "the supreme Court," it is silent on its size. The Judiciary Act set the size of the Supreme Court at six—the chief justice plus five associate justices. (Since 1869, the Supreme Court has been composed of nine justices—the chief and eight associates.)

The first session of the Court was presided over by John Jay, who was appointed chief justice of the United States by George Washington. It decided only one really important case. Moreover, in an indication of its lowly status, one associate justice left the Court to become chief justice of the South Carolina Supreme Court. Nevertheless, in its first decade, the Court took several actions to help mold the new nation. For example, by declining to give George Washington advice on

The Supreme Court held its first two sessions in this building, called the Exchange. (Photo courtesy: Bettman/Corbis)

the legality of some of his actions, the justices attempted to establish the Supreme Court as an independent, nonpolitical branch of government. The early Court also tried to advance principles of nationalism and to maintain the national government's supremacy over the states. In a series of decisions, the justices paved the way for announcement of the doctrine of judicial review by the third chief justice, John Marshall. (Oliver Ellsworth served as chief justice from 1796 to 1800.)

The Marshall Court (1801–1835)

John Marshall was appointed chief justice by President John Adams in 1801, three years after he declined to accept a nomination as associate justice. An ardent Federalist, Marshall later came to be considered the most important justice ever to serve on the high Court. Part of his reputation is the result of the duration of his service and the historical significance of this period in our nation's history. Marshall also, however, brought much-needed respect and prestige to the Court through his leadership in a progression of cases and a series of innovations.

Marshall, for example, began the practice of writing opinions on behalf of the Court. For the Court to take its place as an equal branch of government, Marshall strongly believed, the justices needed to speak as a *Court* and not as six individuals. He also claimed for the Court the right of judicial review, from which the Supreme Court derives much of its day-to-day power and impact on the policy process.

Judicial Review

During the Philadelphia Convention, the Framers debated and rejected the idea of judicial veto of legislation or executive acts, and they rejected the Virginia Plan's proposal to give the judiciary explicit authority over Congress. They did, however, approve Article VI, which contains the supremacy clause.

In *Federalist No. 78,* Alexander Hamilton first publicly endorsed the idea of **judicial review**, noting, "Whenever a particular statute contravenes the Constitution, it will be the duty of the judicial tribunals to adhere to the latter and disregard the former." Nonetheless, because the power of judicial review is not mentioned in the U.S. Constitution, the actual authority of the Supreme Court to review the constitutionality of acts of Congress was an unsettled question. During its first decade, the Supreme Court had reviewed acts of Congress, but it had not found any unconstitutional. But in *Marbury v. Madison* (1803), John Marshall claimed this sweeping authority for the Court. *Marbury*'s long-term effect was to establish the rule that "it is emphatically the province and duty of the judicial department to say what the law is."[1] Through

John Marshall was an ardent Federalist and a third cousin of Democratic-Republican President Thomas Jefferson, whose administration he faced head on in *Marbury* v. *Madison*. Marshall came to head the Court with little legal experience and *no* judicial experience, unlike the situation on the current Supreme Court, where all of the justices *except* Chief Justice Rehnquist had prior judicial experience. Still, it is unlikely that any contemporary justice will have anywhere near the impact that Marshall had on the Court and the course of U.S. politics. (Photo courtesy: Boston Athenaeum)

judicial review

Power of the courts to review acts of other branches of government and the states.

Marbury v. Madison **(1803)**

Supreme Court case in which the Court first asserted the power of judicial review in finding that a congressional statute extending the Court's original jurisdiction was unconstitutional.

HIGHLIGHT

MARBURY V. MADISON AND JUDICIAL REVIEW

Perhaps the most important power of the Supreme Court, although it is not mentioned in the Constitution, is that of judicial review, the authority of a court to determine the constitutional validity of acts of the legislature. During the Constitutional Convention, the Framers debated and rejected the idea of a judicial veto of legislation or executive acts, but they did approve Article VI, which contains the supremacy clause.

During its first decade, the Supreme Court reviewed acts of Congress, but it did not find any to be unconstitutional. The actual authority of the Supreme Court to review acts of Congress to determine their constitutionality thus was an unsettled question. But in *Marbury* v. *Madison* (1803), Chief Justice John Marshall claimed this sweeping authority for the Court by asserting the right of judicial review was a power that could be implied from the Constitution's supremacy clause.

Marbury v. *Madison* arose amidst a sea of political controversy. In the final hours of the Adams administration, William Marbury was appointed a justice of the peace for the District of Columbia. But in the confusion winding up matters, Adams's secretary of state failed to deliver Marbury's commission. Marbury then asked James Madison, Thomas Jefferson's secretary of state, for the commission. Under direct orders from Jefferson, who was irate over the Adams administration's last-minute appointment of several federal judges (quickly confirmed by the Federalist Senate),

Madison refused to turn over the commission. Marbury and three other Adams appointees who were in the same situation then filed a writ of *madamus* (a legal motion) asking the Supreme Court to order Madison to deliver their commissions.

Political tensions ran high as the Court met to hear the case. Jefferson threatened to ignore any order of the Court. Marshall realized that he and the prestige of the Court could be devastated by any refusal of the executive branch to comply with the decision. Responding to this challenge, in a brilliant opinion that in many sections reads more like a lecture to Jefferson than a discussion of the merits of Marbury's claim, Marshall concluded that although Marbury and the others were entitled to their commissions, the Court lacked the power to issue the writ sought by Marbury. In *Marbury* v. *Madison,* Marshall further ruled that the parts of the Judiciary Act of 1789 that extended the jurisdiction of the Court to allow it to issue writs were inconsistent with the Constitution and therefore unconstitutional.

Although the immediate effect of the decision was to deny power to the Court, its long-term effect was to establish the principle of judicial review, a power that Marshall concluded could be implied from the Constitution. Since *Marbury,* the Court has routinely exercised the power of judicial review, although periodically various groups and individuals have criticized judicial review as beyond the scope of the court's intended authority.

WEB EXPLORATION
To read the full text on *Marbury* v. *Madison,* go to www.ablongman.com/oconnor

judicial review, the power of the Court to review acts of Congress, the president, or the states to determine their constitutionality, the Supreme Court most dramatically exerts its authority to determine what the Constitution means. Since *Marbury,* the Court has routinely exercised the power of judicial review to determine the constitutionality of acts of Congress, the executive branch, and the states. (See Highlight: *Marbury* v. *Madison* and Judicial Review for more on judicial review.)

THE AMERICAN LEGAL SYSTEM

The judicial system in the United States can best be described as a dual system consisting of the federal court system and the judicial systems of the fifty states. Cases may arise in either system. Both systems are basically three tiered. At the bottom of the system are **trial courts**, where litigation begins. In the middle are appellate courts in the state systems and the courts of appeals in the federal system. At the top of each pyramid sits a high court. (Some states call these Supreme Courts; New York calls it the Court of Appeals; Oklahoma and Texas call the highest state court for criminal cases the Court of Criminal Appeals.) The federal courts of appeals and Supreme Court as well as state courts of appeals and Supreme Courts are **appellate courts** that, with few exceptions, review on appeal only cases that already have been decided in lower courts. These courts generally hear matters of both civil and criminal law.

trial court
Court of original jurisdiction where cases begin.

appellate court
Court that generally reviews only findings of law made by lower courts.

Jurisdiction

Before a state or federal court can hear a case, it must have **jurisdiction**, which means the authority vested in a particular court to hear and decide the issues in any particular case. The jurisdiction of the federal courts is controlled by the U.S. Constitution and by statute. Jurisdiction is conferred based on issues, money involved in a dispute, or the type of offense. Procedurally, we speak of two types of jurisdiction: original and appellate. **Original jurisdiction** refers to a court's authority to hear disputes as a trial court. (O. J. Simpson's criminal and civil cases, for example, were heard in Los Angeles County, California, state trial courts of original jurisdiction. The lawsuit against the Virginia Military Academy over its failure to admit women into the cadet corps was originally heard in federal district court.) More than 90 percent of all cases, whether state or federal, end at this stage. **Appellate jurisdiction** refers to a court's ability to review cases already decided by a trial court. Appellate courts do not ordinarily review the factual record; instead, they review legal procedures to make certain that the law was applied properly to the issues presented in the case. Table 9.2 shows the jurisdiction of the three major federal courts and enumerates the types of cases that the Supreme Court was given the jurisdiction to hear as initially specified in the Constitution. Figure 9.1 illustrates how rarely the Court exercises its original jurisdiction. Instead, most cases are heard by the Court under its appellate jurisdiction.

jurisdiction
Authority vested in a particular court to hear and decide the issues in any particular case.

original jurisdiction
The jurisdiction of courts that hear a case first, usually in a trial. Courts determine the facts of a case under their original jurisdiction.

appellate jurisdiction
The power vested in an appellate court to review and revise the decision of a lower court.

Criminal and Civil Law

Criminal law is the body of law that regulates individual conduct and is enforced by the government.[2] Crimes are graded as felonies, misdemeanors, or offenses, according to their severity. Some acts—for

criminal law
The body of law that regulates individual conduct, is enforced by the state, and provides punishment for violations.

TABLE 9.2   Federal Court Jurisdiction

The Supreme Court rarely exercises its original jurisdiction. Instead, most cases are heard by the Court under its appellate jurisdiction.

	Original Jurisdiction *(Approximately 2-5% of Cases Heard)*	*Appellate Jurisdiction* *(Approximately 95-97% of Cases Heard)*
The Supreme Court	Cases are heard in Supreme Court first when they involve: • Two or more states • The United States and a state • Foreign ambassadors and other diplomats • A state and a citizen of another state (if the action is begun by the state)	The Supreme Court can agree to hear cases first heard or decided on in lower courts or the state courts (generally the highest state court) involving appeals from: • U.S. courts of appeals • State highest courts (only in cases involving federal questions) • Court of Military Appeals
U.S. Courts of Appeals	None	Hears appeals of cases from: • Lower federal courts • U.S. regulatory commissions • Legislative courts, including the U.S. Court of Federal Claims and the U.S. Court of Veterans' Appeals
U.S. District Courts	Cases are heard in U.S. district courts when they involve: • The federal government • Civil suits under federal law • Civil suits between citizens of different states if the amount in issue is more than $50,000 • Admiralty or maritime disputes • Bankruptcy • Other matters assigned to them by Congress	None

example, murder, rape, and robbery—are considered crimes in all states. Although all states outlaw murder, their penal, or criminal, codes treat the crime quite differently; the penalty for murder differs considerably from state to state. Other crimes—such as sodomy and some forms of gambling, such as lotteries or bingo—are illegal only in some states.

Criminal law assumes that society itself is the victim of the illegal act; therefore, the government prosecutes, or brings an action, on behalf of an injured party (acting as a plaintiff) in criminal but not civil cases. The kinds of cases prosecuted on *Law and Order* are criminal cases. Criminal cases are traditionally in the purview of the states. But a burgeoning set of criminal laws is contributing significantly to case delays in the federal courts.

civil law
The body of law that regulates the conditions and relationships between private individuals or companies.

Civil law is the body of law that regulates the conduct and relationships between private individuals or companies. Because the actions at

FIGURE 9.1   The Dual Structure of the American Court System

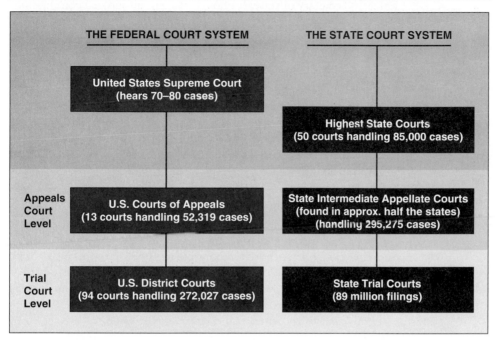

THE FEDERAL COURT SYSTEM

THE STATE COURT SYSTEM

United States Supreme Court
(hears 70–80 cases)

Highest State Courts
(50 courts handling 85,000 cases)

Appeals Court Level

U.S. Courts of Appeals
(13 courts handling 52,319 cases)

State Intermediate Appellate Courts
(found in approx. half the states)
(handling 295,275 cases)

Trial Court Level

U.S. District Courts
(94 courts handling 272,027 cases)

State Trial Courts
(89 million filings)

Note: Numbers are approximate. With the exception of cases actually decided by the U.S. Supreme Court, most other numbers increase each year.

issue in civil law do not constitute a threat to society at large, people who believe they have been injured by another party must take action on their own to seek judicial relief. Civil cases, then, involve lawsuits filed to recover something of value, whether it is the right to vote, fair treatment, or monetary compensation for an item or service that cannot be recovered. The cases seen on *Divorce Court* or *Judge Judy* are civil cases.

Before a criminal or civil case gets to court, much has to happen. In fact, most legal disputes that arise in the United States never get to court. Individuals and companies involved in civil disputes routinely settle their disagreements out of court. Often these settlements are not reached until minutes before the case is to be tried. Many civil cases that go to trial are settled during the course of the trial—before the case can be handed over to the jury or submitted to a judge for a decision or determination of guilt.

Each civil or criminal case has a plaintiff, who brings charges against a defendant. Sometimes the government is the plaintiff. The government may bring criminal or civil charges on behalf of the citizens of the state or the national government against a person or corporation for violating the law, but it is always the government that brings a criminal case. Cases are known by the name of the plaintiff first and the defendant second. So in *Marbury* v. *Madison*, William Marbury was the plaintiff, suing the defendants, the U.S. government and James Madison as its secretary of state, for not delivering his judicial commission.

During trials, judges must often interpret the intent of laws enacted by Congress and state legislatures as they bear on the issues at hand. To do so, they read reports, testimony, and debates on the relevant legislation and study the results of other similar legal cases. They also rely on the presentations made by lawyers in their briefs and at trial. If it is a jury trial, the jury ultimately is the finder of fact, while the judge is the interpreter of the law.

WEB EXPLORATION
For more on how civil and criminal trials progress, see www.ablongman.com/oconnor

THE FEDERAL COURT SYSTEM

The federal district courts, circuit courts of appeals, and the Supreme Court are called **constitutional** (or Article III) **courts** because Article III of the Constitution either established them (as is the case with the Supreme Court) or authorizes Congress to establish them. Judges who preside over these courts are nominated by the president (with the advice and consent of the Senate), and they serve lifetime terms, as long as they engage in "good behavior."

In addition to constitutional courts, **legislative courts** are set up by Congress, under its delegated powers, generally for special purposes. The U.S. Territorial Courts (which hear federal cases in the territories) and the U.S. Court of Veterans' Appeals are examples of legislative courts, or what some call Article I courts. The judges who preside over these federal courts are appointed by the president (subject to Senate confirmation) and serve fixed, limited terms.

constitutional courts
Federal courts specifically created by the U.S. Constitution or by Congress pursuant to its authority in Article III.

legislative courts
Courts established by Congress for specialized purposes, such as the Court of Military Appeals.

District Courts

Today there are ninety-four federal district courts staffed by a total of 653 judges and over 300 retired, or senior, judges who work part-time. (See Figure 9.1.) No district court cuts across state lines. Every state has at least one federal district court, and the largest states—California, Texas, and New York—each have four.

Federal district courts, where the bulk of the judicial work takes place in the federal system, have original jurisdiction over only specific types of cases, as indicated in Table 9.2. (Cases involving other kinds of issues generally must be heard in state courts.) Although the rules governing district court jurisdiction can be complex, cases heard in federal district courts by a single judge (with or without a jury) generally fall into one of three categories:

1. They involve the federal government as a party.
2. They present a question of federal law based on a claim under the U.S. Constitution, a treaty with another nation, or a federal statute.
3. They involve civil suits in which citizens are from different states, and the amount of money at issue is more than $50,000.[3]

WEB EXPLORATION
To view the hierarchy of the U.S. court system, go to www.ablongman.com/oconnor

Each federal judicial district has a U.S. attorney, who is nominated by the president and confirmed by the Senate. The U.S. attorney in each district is that district's chief law enforcement officer. The size of the staff and the number of assistant U.S. attorneys who work in each district depend on the amount of litigation in each district. U.S. attorneys, like district attorneys within the states, have a considerable amount of discretion as to whether they pursue criminal or civil investigations or file charges against individuals or corporations.

The Courts of Appeals

The losing party in a case heard and decided in a federal district court can appeal the decision to the appropriate court of appeals. The United States courts of appeals (known as the circuit courts of appeals prior to 1948) are the intermediate appellate courts in the federal system and were established in 1789 to hear appeals from federal district courts. The present structure of the appeals courts, however, dates from the Judiciary Act of 1891. There are eleven numbered circuit courts. A twelfth, the D.C. Court of Appeals, handles most appeals involving federal regulatory commissions and agencies, including, for example, the National Labor Relations Board and the Securities and Exchange Commission. The thirteenth federal appeals court is the U.S. Court of Appeals for the Federal Circuit, which deals with patents, contract, and financial claims against the federal government.

In 2001 the eleven circuit appeals courts and the D.C. Circuit Courts of Appeals were staffed by 179 active and more than 80 senior judges, who were appointed by the president, subject to Senate confirmation. The number of judges within each circuit varies—depending on the workload and the complexity of the cases—and ranges from six to nearly thirty. In deciding cases, judges are divided into rotating three-judge panels. In rare cases, all the judges in a circuit may choose to sit together (*en banc*) to decide a case by majority vote.

Once a decision is made by a federal court of appeals, a litigant no longer has an automatic right to an appeal. The losing party may submit a petition to the U.S. Supreme Court to hear the case, but the Court grants few of these requests. In its 1999–2000 term, for example, 8,445 petitions for review were filed. The Supreme Court accepted only 84 cases for full review and issued full opinions in only 73 (see Figure 9.2).

In general, courts of appeals try to correct errors of law and procedure that have occurred in lower courts or administrative agencies. Courts of appeals hear no new testimony; instead, lawyers submit written arguments, in what is called a **brief** (also submitted in trial courts), and then appear to orally present and argue the case to the court.

The Supreme Court

The U.S. Supreme Court is often at the center of the storm of highly controversial issues that have yet to be resolved successfully in the

SIMULATION
You Are a
Young Lawyer

brief
A document containing the collected legal written arguments in a case filed with a court by a party prior to a hearing or trial.

FIGURE 9.2　Supreme Court Caseload 1950–2000 Terms
The caseload of the Supreme Court has remained fairly consistent from its 1992–1993 through 1998–1999 term, although the Court accepted far fewer cases for its review than it did in earlier decades. In its 1999–2000 term, although the number of cases filed experienced a significant bump, in deciding only seventy-three cases, the Court hit a low not seen in fifty years.

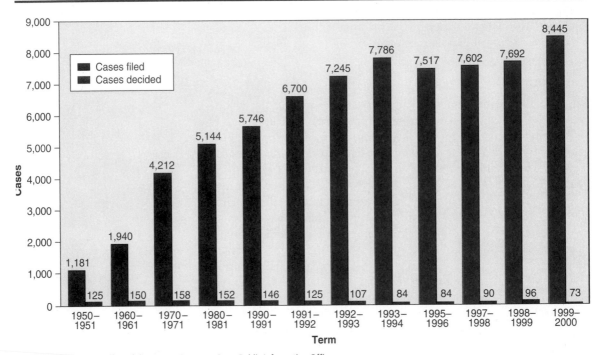

Source: Administrative Office of the Courts; Supreme Court Public Information Office.

political process. As the court of last resort at the top of the judicial pyramid, it reviews cases from the U.S. courts of appeals and state supreme courts and acts as the final interpreter of the U.S. Constitution. It not only decides many major cases with tremendous policy significance each year, but it also ensures uniformity in the interpretation of national laws and the Constitution, resolves conflicts among the states, and maintains the supremacy of national law in the federal system.

Decisions of the U.S. Supreme Court are binding throughout the nation and establish national **precedents**. This reliance on past decisions or precedents to formulate decisions in new cases is called *stare decisis* (a Latin phrase meaning "let the decision stand"). The principle of *stare decisis* allows for continuity and predictability in our judicial system. Although *stare decisis* can be helpful in predicting decisions, at times judges carve out new ground and ignore, decline to follow, or even overrule precedents in order to reach a different conclusion in a case involving similar circumstances. In one sense, that is why there is so much litigation in America today. Parties know that one cannot always predict the outcome of a case; if such prediction were possible, there would be little reason to go to court.

precedent
Prior judicial decision that serves as a rule for settling subsequent cases of a similar nature.

stare decisis
In court rulings, a reliance on past decisions or precedents to formulate decisions in new cases.

The chief justice presides over public sessions of the Court, conducts the Court's conferences, and assigns the writing of opinions (if he is in the majority; otherwise, the most senior justice in the majority makes the assignment). By custom, he administers the oath of office to the president and the vice president on Inauguration Day (any federal judge can administer the oath, as has happened when presidents have died in office).

Compared with the president or even members of Congress, the Supreme Court operates with few support staff. Along with the three or four clerks each justice employs, there are about 400 staff members at the Supreme Court.

WEB EXPLORATION
For more on the Supreme Court, plus the full text of major Supreme Court decisions, go to www.ablongman.com/oconnor

HOW FEDERAL COURT JUDGES ARE SELECTED

Although specific, detailed provisions in Articles I and II specify the qualifications for president, senator, and member of the House of Representatives, the Constitution is curiously silent on the qualifications for federal judges. This may have been because of an assumption that all federal judges would be lawyers, but to make such a requirement explicit might have marked the judicial branch as too elite for the tastes of common men and women. Also, it would have been impractical to require formal legal training, given that there were so few law schools in the nation, and that most lawyers became licensed after clerking or apprenticing with another attorney.[4]

The selection of federal judges is often a very political process with important political ramifications because judges are nominated by the president and must be confirmed by the U.S. Senate. Unlike the other two branches of government, there are no formal requirements for federal judges (except Senate confirmation). During the Reagan–Bush years, for example, 553 basically conservative Republican judges were appointed to the lower federal bench. The Clinton years, in contrast, saw the appointment of more moderate judges—at least partly because the Senate was controlled by Republicans throughout the last five years of his presidency. (See Figure 9.3.)

Typically, federal district court judges have held other political offices, such as those of state court judge or prosecutor. Most have been involved in politics, which is what usually brings them into consideration for a position on the federal bench.

Presidents generally defer selection of district court judges to senators of their own party who represent the state in which a vacancy occurs on the federal bench, a practice called senatorial courtesy. By tradition, the Senate Judiciary Committee will not confirm a presidential nominee who has not been agreed to by the senator of the nominee's home state. This tradition is an important source of political patronage for senators.

FIGURE 9.3   How a President Affects the Federal Judiciary
This depicts the number of judges appointed by each president and how quickly a president can make an impact on the makeup of the Court.

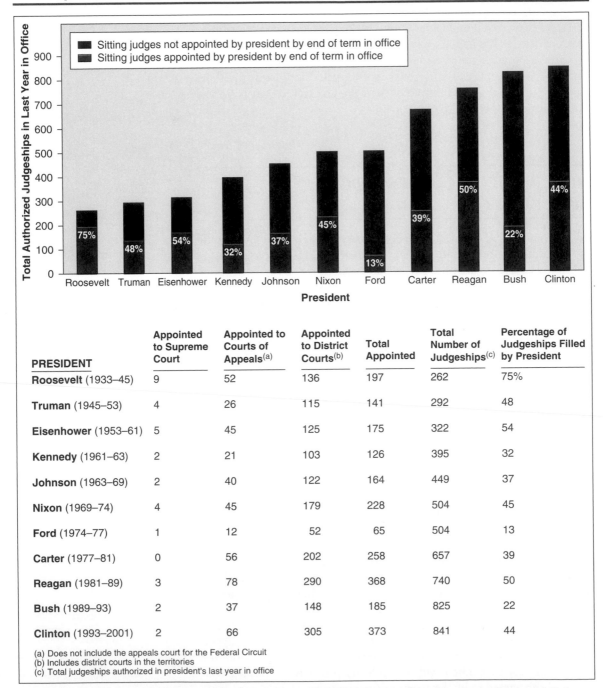

PRESIDENT	Appointed to Supreme Court	Appointed to Courts of Appeals[a]	Appointed to District Courts[b]	Total Appointed	Total Number of Judgeships[c]	Percentage of Judgeships Filled by President
Roosevelt (1933–45)	9	52	136	197	262	75%
Truman (1945–53)	4	26	115	141	292	48
Eisenhower (1953–61)	5	45	125	175	322	54
Kennedy (1961–63)	2	21	103	126	395	32
Johnson (1963–69)	2	40	122	164	449	37
Nixon (1969–74)	4	45	179	228	504	45
Ford (1974–77)	1	12	52	65	504	13
Carter (1977–81)	0	56	202	258	657	39
Reagan (1981–89)	3	78	290	368	740	50
Bush (1989–93)	2	37	148	185	825	22
Clinton (1993–2001)	2	66	305	373	841	44

(a) Does not include the appeals court for the Federal Circuit
(b) Includes district courts in the territories
(c) Total judgeships authorized in president's last year in office

Source: "Imprints on the Bench," *CQ Weekly Report* (January 19, 1991): p. 173. Reprinted by permission of Copyright Clearance Center on behalf of Congressional Quarterly Inc. Data on Bush and Clinton provided by the Senate Judiciary Committee.

Since the 1970s, most presidents have pledged (with varying degrees of success) to do their best to appoint more African Americans, women, and other groups traditionally underrepresented on the federal bench. Each president, moreover, has created a special group to help him identify and nominate candidates for the bench.

Appointments to the U.S. Supreme Court

Like other federal court judges, the justices of the Supreme Court are nominated by the president and must be confirmed by the Senate. Historically, because of the special place the Supreme Court enjoys in our constitutional system, its nominees have encountered more opposition than district or court of appeals judges. As the role of the Court has increased over time, so too has the amount of attention given to nominees. With this increased attention has come greater opposition, especially to nominees with controversial views.

Nomination Criteria

Justice Sandra Day O'Connor once remarked that "You have to be lucky" to be appointed to the Court.[5] Although luck is certainly important, over the years nominations to the bench have been made for a variety of reasons. At least five criteria today are especially important: competence, ideology or policy preferences, pursuit of political support, race, and gender.

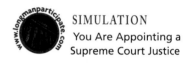

SIMULATION
You Are Appointing a Supreme Court Justice

Competence.   Most prospective nominees are expected to have had at least some judicial or governmental experience. In 2001 all sitting Supreme Court justices except the chief justice had prior judicial experience before they were appointed. The American Bar Association (ABA), the politically powerful organization that represents the interests of the legal profession, rates each nominee based on his or her qualifications, as Well-Qualified, Qualified, or Not Qualified. (The same system is used for lower federal court nominees; over the years, however, the exact labels have varied.) Of the nine sitting justices, only Clarence Thomas received less than at least a unanimous Qualified rating.

WEB EXPLORATION
To learn the extent of the ABA's legislative advocacy, go to www.ablongman.com/oconnor

Ideological or Policy Preferences.   Most presidents seek to appoint to the Court individuals who share their policy preferences, and almost all have political goals in mind when they appoint a justice. Presidents Franklin D. Roosevelt, Richard M. Nixon, and Ronald Reagan were very successful in molding the Court to their own political beliefs. Nixon and Reagan, in fact, publicly proclaimed that they would nominate only conservatives who favored a **strict constructionist** approach to constitutional decision making—that is, an approach emphasizing the original intentions of the Framers.

strict constructionist
An approach to constitutional interpretation that emphasizes the Framers' initial intentions.

POINT/COUNTERPOINT

SHOULD JUDGES BE ELECTED OR APPOINTED?

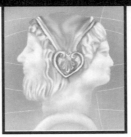

At both the federal and the state levels, judges are selected in a variety of ways. Some are elected in partisan election, some in nonpartisan election, others are appointed and then confirmed by elections, and others simply appointed. Basically, this boils down to two methods: election and appointment. Currently, twenty-nine states plus the District of Columbia use some form of appointment and twenty-one states some form of election. The goal in either method is an independent judiciary that is able to make impartial judgments on the meaning of the law and pass judgment fairly. In addition, judges ought to be accountable to society at large and make rulings according to the laws, not their own wishes. How should we best balance the interests of an independent, and an accountable, judiciary? Let's examine both point viewpoints.

Advocates of judicial election, such as the Federalist Society for Law and Public Policy Studies, argue that it is more democratic to elect judges than to have some elite body choose them for us. Elections provide accountability so that judges cannot run amuck with our inalienable rights. In addition, judicial elections reinforce one of our most cherished ideals: self government. Advocates of judicial election argue that the appointment process is riddled with partisan struggles, litmus tests, and bias so that it does not what advocates claim: assuring meritorious and independent judges. Instead, it gives U.S. judges chosen in smoke-filled rooms by a political elite. Appointments, then, replace open electoral processes with back-room elite manipulation. If a governor or president is the appointing party, that person's political affiliation comes to bear. If the appointing party is a committee, the committee is usually composed of experts who are lawyers. Why is this preferable to the will of voters?

Advocates of appointment, such as the American Judicature Society, argue that the appointment process allows qualified individuals and groups to carefully weigh the credentials of judicial aspirants and make selections based solely on merit to assure that judges are chosen from a pool of highly qualified candidates through the method of providing an appropriate balance between judicial independence and public accountability. Appointment minimizes the political considerations in the selection of judges and gets rid of the issues of campaign finance. How can a judge rule fairly in a case regarding one of his or her campaign contributors? Advocates of judicial appointment argue that the elections are merely popularity contests and reward name recognition, not wisdom and sagacity. In addition, elections tip the balance between judicial accountability so far in the direction of accountability that independence is often forfeit.

What do you think? Should judges be elected or appointed?
Go to www.ablongman.com/oconnor

Pursuit of Political Support.   During Ronald Reagan's successful campaign for the presidency in 1980, some of his advisers feared that the gender gap would hurt him. Polls repeatedly showed that he was far less popular with female voters than with men. To gain support from women, Reagan announced that should he win, he would appoint a woman to fill the first vacancy on the Court. When Justice Potter Stewart, a moderate, announced his early retirement from the bench, President Reagan nominated Sandra Day O'Connor of the Arizona Court of Appeals to fill the vacancy. It probably did not hurt President Clinton politically with women or Jews that his first appointment (Ruth Bader Ginsburg) was a Jewish woman (at a time when no Jews served on the Court).

Race and Gender.   Only two African Americans and two women have served on the Court. Race was undoubtedly a critical issue in the appointment of Clarence Thomas to replace Thurgood Marshall, the first African American justice. But President George Bush refused to acknowledge his wish to retain a "black seat" on the Court. Instead, he announced that he was "picking the best man for the job on the merits," a claim that was met with considerable skepticism by many observers.

In contrast, O'Connor was pointedly picked because of her gender. Ginsburg's appointment was more matter-of-fact, and her selection surprised many because the Clinton administration appeared to be considering seriously several men for the appointment first.

Religion.   Ironically, religion, which historically has been an important issue, was hardly mentioned during the most recent Supreme Court vacancies. Some, however, hailed Clinton's appointment of Ginsburg, noting that the traditionally "Jewish" seat on the Court had been vacant for over two decades. Through 2001, of the 108 justices who have served on the Court, almost all have been members of traditional Protestant faiths.[6] Only nine have been Catholic and only seven have been Jewish.[7] Twice during the Rehnquist Court, more Catholics—Brennan, Scalia, and Kennedy, and then Scalia, Kennedy, and Thomas—served on the Court at one time than at any other period in history. Today, however, it is clear that religion cannot be taken as a sign of a justice's conservative or liberal ideology: When William Brennan was on the Court, he and fellow Catholic Antonin Scalia were at ideological extremes.

The Supreme Court Confirmation Process

The Constitution gives the Senate the authority to approve all nominees to the federal bench. Before 1900 about one-fourth of all presidential nominees to the Supreme Court were rejected by the Senate. Today, rejections are rare.

As a president begins to narrow his list of possible nominees to the Supreme Court, those names are sent to the Federal Bureau of Investigation before a nomination is formally made. Once the formal nomination is made and sent to the Senate, the Senate Judiciary Committee begins its own investigation of the nominee. (The same process is used for nominees to the lower federal courts, although such investigations generally are not nearly as extensive as for Supreme Court nominees.)

ANALYZING THE DATA

CHARACTERISTICS OF DISTRICT COURT APPOINTEES, CARTER TO CLINTON

Traditionally, white males have dominated federal court appointments. Of Reagan's 290 appointees, for example, 92.4 percent were white males. By the end of Clinton administration, however, the percentage of white male federal appointees decreased sig- nificantly, comprising only 52.1 percent of his 305 court appointees. While most presidents in recent years have pledged to appoint more African Americans, women, and Hispanics to the federal bench, Clinton has thus far been the most successful.

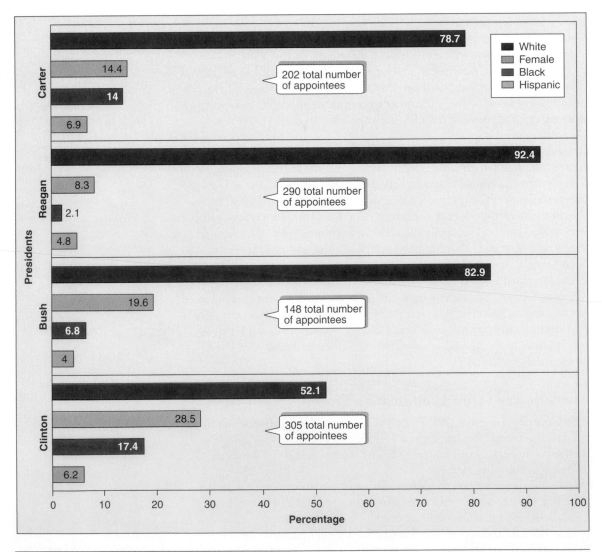

Source: Sheldon Goldman and Elliot E. Slotnick, "Clinton's First Term Judiciary: Many Bridges to Cross," *Judicature* (May–June 1997), p. 261. Reprinted by permission.

Lobbying by Interest Groups.   While the ABA historically was the only organization asked formally to rate nominees, other groups are also keenly interested in the nomination process.

The Bush administration, concerned with the liberalness of the ABA, in fact, has pledged to rely more on the conservative Federalist Society, to screen its nominees. Until recently, interest groups played a minor and backstage role in most appointments to the Supreme Court. Today, it is common for interest groups to lobby *against* prospective nominees. In 1987 the Democratic-controlled Senate Judiciary Committee allowed liberal interest groups enough time to mobilize the most extensive radio, television, and print media campaign ever launched against a nominee to the U.S. Supreme Court. This opposition was in spite of the fact that Robert H. Bork sat with distinction on the D.C. Court of Appeals and was a former U.S. solicitor general, a top-ranked law school graduate, and a Yale Law School pro-

The scrutiny by the public and press of President Reagan's Supreme Court nominee Robert H. Bork set a new standard of inquiry into the values—political and personal—of future nominees. Bork's nomination was rejected by the Senate in 1987. Here NARAL president Kate Michelman speaks out against Bork.
(Photo courtesy: Frank Fournier/Contact Press Images)

fessor. (His actions as solicitor general, especially his firing of the Watergate special prosecutor, made him a special target for traditional liberals.)

The Senate Committee Hearings and Senate Vote.   After its investigation is complete, the Senate Judiciary Committee holds public hearings. As the uneventful 1994 hearings of Stephen Breyer attest (he was confirmed by a Senate vote of 97–3), not all nominees inspire the kind of intense reaction that kept Bork from the Court, and more recently, almost blocked the confirmation of Clarence Thomas. Until recently, however, modern nomination hearings were not particularly thorough. In 1969, for example, Chief Justice Warren E. Burger was confirmed by the Senate on a vote of 94-3, just nineteen days after he was nominated.

Since the 1980s it has become standard for senators to ask the nominees probing questions, but most nominees (with the notable exception of Robert H. Bork) have declined to answer most of them on the grounds that these issues might ultimately come before the Court. After hearings are concluded, the Senate Judiciary Committee usually makes a recommendation to the full Senate. Any rejections of presidential nominees to the Supreme Court generally occur only after the Senate Judiciary Committee has recommended against a nominee's appointment. Few recent confirmations have been close; prior to Clarence Thomas's 52–48 vote in 1991, Rehnquist's nomination in 1971 as associate justice (68–26) and in 1986 as chief justice (69–33) were the tightest in recent history.[8]

THE SUPREME COURT TODAY

Given the judicial system's vast size and substantial, although often indirect, power over so many aspects of our lives, it is surprising that so many Americans know next to nothing about the judicial system in general and the Supreme Court in particular. Even today, at a time when all other institutions of government and government officials receive unprecedented media attention, the work of the Court proceeds in relative anonymity. Few Americans can correctly name the current chief justice, let alone the other eight justices. A poll conducted in 1990 for the Court's 200th anniversary revealed that only 23 percent of Americans queried knew how many justices sit on the Court, and nearly two-thirds could not name a single member of the Court.[9] A 1999 Roper poll of teenagers found that only 7 percent could identify William H. Rehnquist as the chief

TABLE 9.3   The Supreme Court, 2001

Name	Year of Birth	Year of Appointment	Political Party	Law School	Appointing President	Religion	Prior Judicial Experience	Prior Government Experience
William H. Rehnquist	1924	1971/1986*	R	Stanford	Nixon	Lutheran	Associate Justice U.S. Supreme Court	Assistant U.S. Attorney General
John Paul Stevens	1920	1975	R	Chicago	Ford	Nondenom- inational Protestant	U.S. Court of Appeals	
Sandra Day O'Connor	1930	1981	R	Stanford	Reagan	Episcopalian	Arizona Court of Appeals	State Legislator
Antonin Scalia	1936	1986	R	Harvard	Reagan	Catholic	U.S. Court of Appeals	
Anthony Kennedy	1936	1988	R	Harvard	Reagan	Catholic	U.S. Court of Appeals	
David Souter	1939	1990	R	Harvard	Bush	Episcopalian	U.S. Court of Appeals	New Hamp- shire Assistant Attorney General
Clarence Thomas	1948	1991	R	Yale	Bush	Catholic	U.S. Court of Appeals	Chair, Equal Employment Opportunity Commission
Ruth Bader Ginsburg	1933	1993	D	Columbia	Clinton	Jewish	U.S. Court of Appeals	
Stephen Breyer	1938	1994	D	Harvard	Clinton	Jewish	U.S. Court of Appeals	Chief Counsel, Senate Judiciary Committee

*Promoted to chief justice by President Reagan in 1986.

justice. To fill in any gaps in your knowledge of the current Supreme Court, see Table 9.3.

Much of this ignorance can be blamed on the American public's lack of interest. But the Court itself has taken great pains to ensure its privacy and sense of decorum. Its rites and rituals contribute to the Court's mystique and encourage a "cult of the robe."[10] Consider, for example, the way Supreme Court proceedings are conducted. Oral arguments are not televised, and deliberations concerning the outcome of cases are conducted in utmost secrecy. In contrast, C-SPAN brings us daily coverage of various congressional hearings and floor debate on bills and important national issues, and Court TV (and sometimes other networks) provides gavel-to-gavel coverage of many important state court trials. The Supreme Court, however, remains adamant in its refusal to televise its proceedings—including public oral arguments, as discussed in the opening vignette.

Deciding to Hear a Case

Although more than 8,400 cases were filed at the Supreme Court in 1999–2000, this was not always the case. From 1790 to 1801, the Court heard only eighty-seven cases under its appellate jurisdiction.[11] As recently as the 1940s, fewer than 1,000 cases were filed annually. Since that time, filings have increased at a dramatic rate until the 1993–1994 term. Filings then leveled off but skyrocketed during the Court's 1999–2000 term. These high filings, however, do not mean that the Court actually is deciding more cases. In fact, of the 8,445 petitions it received during the 1999–2000 term, it handed down signed opinions in only seventy-four. The process by which cases get to the Supreme Court is outlined in Figure 9.4.

The Supreme Court's Jurisdiction

The Court has two types of jurisdiction, as indicated in Table 9.2. Its original jurisdiction is specifically set out in the Constitution. The Court has original jurisdiction in "all Cases affecting Ambassadors, other public Ministers and Consuls, and those in which a State shall be a party." Most cases arising under the Court's original jurisdiction involve disputes between two states, usually over issues such as ownership of offshore oil deposits, territorial disputes caused by shifting river boundaries, or controversies caused by conflicting claims over water rights, such as when a river flows through two or more states.[12]

A second kind of jurisdiction enjoyed by the Court is appellate jurisdiction (see Table 9.2). The appellate jurisdiction of the Court can be changed by the Congress at any time, a power that has been a potent threat to the authority of the Court. The Judiciary Act of 1925 gave the Court discretion over its own jurisdiction, meaning that it does not have to accept all appeals that come to it. The idea behind the act was that the intermediate courts of appeals should be the final word for almost

FIGURE 9.4   How a Case Goes to the United States Supreme Court

This figure illustrates how cases get on the Court's docket; what happens after a case is accepted for review is detailed in Figure 9.5.

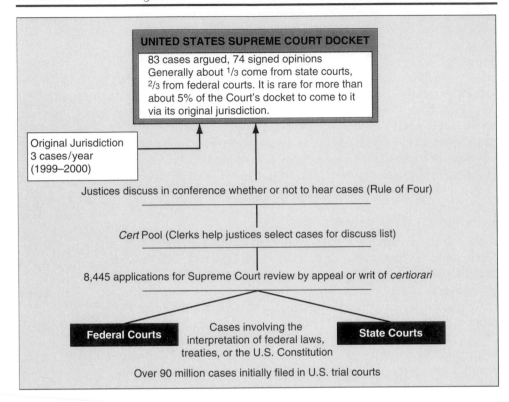

writ of *certiorari*
A formal document issued from the Supreme Court to a lower federal or state court that calls up a case.

in forma pauperis
Literally, "in the form of a pauper"; a way for an indigent or poor person to appeal a case to the U.S. Supreme Court.

all federal litigants, thus freeing the Supreme Court to concentrate on constitutional issues, unless the Court decided that it wanted to address other matters. The Court, then, is not expected to exercise its appellate jurisdiction simply to correct errors of other courts. Instead, appeal to the Supreme Court should be taken only if the case presents important issues of law, or what is termed "a substantial federal question." Since 1988 nearly all appellate cases that had gone to the Supreme Court arrived there on a petition for a **writ of *certiorari*** (from the Latin "to be informed"), which is a request for the Supreme Court—at its discretion—to order up the records of the lower courts for purposes of review.

About one-third of all Supreme Court filings involve criminal law issues.[13] Many of these, in fact more than half of all petitions to the Court, are filed *in forma pauperis* (IFP) (literally from the Latin, "as a pauper"). About 80 percent of these are filed by indigent prison inmates seeking review of their sentences. Permission to proceed *in forma pauperis* allows the petitioner to avoid filing and printing costs. Any criminal defendant who has had a court-appointed lawyer in a lower court proceeding is automatically entitled to proceed in this fashion.

The Supreme Court today. From left to right: Clarence Thomas, Antonin Scalia, Sandra Day O'Connor, Anthony Kennedy, David Souter, Stephen Breyer, John Paul Stevens, William Rehnquist, and Ruth Bader Ginsburg.
(Photo courtesy: Ken Heinen/Pool/AP/Wide World Photos)

The Rule of Four.   Unlike other federal courts, the Supreme Court controls its own caseload through the *certiorari* process, deciding which cases it wants to hear, and rejecting most cases that come to it. All petitions for *certiorari* must meet two criteria:

1. The case must come either from a U.S. court of appeals, a special three-judge district court, or a state court of last resort. Generally, this means that the case has already been decided by the state supreme court.
2. The case must involve a federal question. This means that the case must present questions of interpretation of federal constitutional law or involve a federal statute or treaty. The reasons the Court should accept the case for review and legal argument supporting that position are set out in the petition (also called a brief).

The clerk of the Court's office transmits petitions for writs of *certiorari* first to the chief justice's office, where his clerks review the petitions, and then to the individual justices' offices. Those cases that the justices deem noteworthy are placed on what is called the "discuss list"—a list of cases to be discussed—prepared by the chief justice's clerks and circulated to the chambers of the justices. Only about 30 percent of submitted petitions make it to the discuss list. During one of the justices' weekly conference meetings, the cases on the discuss list are reviewed. The chief justice speaks first, then the rest of the justices,

Rule of Four

At least four justices of the Supreme Court must vote to consider a case before it can be heard.

according to seniority. The decision process ends when the justices vote, and by custom, *certiorari* is granted according to the **Rule of Four**— when at least four justices vote to hear a case.

The Role of Clerks.   As early as 1850, the justices of the Supreme Court had beseeched Congress to approve the hiring of a clerk to assist each justice. Congress denied the request, so when Justice Horace Gray hired the first law clerk in 1882, he paid the clerk himself. Justice Gray's clerk was a top graduate of Harvard Law School whose duties included cutting Justice Gray's hair and running personal errands. Finally, in 1886, Congress authorized each justice to hire a "stenographer clerk" for $1,600 a year.

Supreme Court clerks are typically selected from candidates at the top of the graduating classes of prestigious law schools. They perform a variety of tasks, ranging from searching for arcane facts to playing tennis or taking walks with the justices. Clerks spend most of their time researching material relevant to particular cases, reading and summarizing cases, and helping justices write opinions. The clerks also make the first pass through the petitions that come to the Court, undoubtedly influencing which cases get a second look. Just how much help they provide in the writing of opinions is unknown.[14]

Over time, the number of clerks employed by the justices has increased. Through the 1946 to 1969 terms, most justices employed two clerks. By 1970 most had three, and by 1980 all but three had four. In 2000 there were thirty-four clerks. This growth in clerks has had many interesting ramifications for the Court. "Between 1969 and 1972—the period during which the justices each became entitled to a third law clerk— . . . the number of opinions increased by about 50 percent and the number of words tripled."[15] Until recently, the number of cases decided annually increased as more help was available to the justices.

The relationship between clerks and the justices for whom they work is close and confidential, and many aspects of the relationship are kept secret. Clerks may sometimes talk among themselves about the views and personalities of their justices, but rarely has a clerk leaked such information to the press. In 1998, a former clerk to Justice Harry Blackmun broke the silence. Edward Lazarus published a book that shocked many Court watchers by penning an insider's account of how the Court really works.[16] He also charged that the justices give their young, often ideological clerks far too much power.

How Does a Case Survive the Process?

It can be difficult to determine why the Court decides to hear a particular case. Sometimes it involves a perceived national emergency, as was the case with appeals concerning the outcome of the 2000 presidential election. The Court does not offer reasons, and "the standards by which the justices decide to grant or deny review are highly personalized and necessarily discretionary," noted former Chief Justice Earl Warren. Moreover, he continued, "those standards cannot be captured in rules or guidelines that would be meaningful."[17] Political scientists have nonetheless attempted to determine the characteristics of the cases that the Court accepts; not surprisingly, they are similar to those that help a case get on the discuss list. Among the cues are the following:

- The federal government is the party asking for review.
- The case involves conflict among the circuit courts.
- The case presents a civil rights or civil liberties question.
- The case involves ideological or policy preferences of the justices.
- The case has significant social or political interest, as evidenced by the presence of interest group *amicus curiae* briefs.

Federal Government as a Party. One of the most important cues for predicting whether the Court will hear a case is the position the **solicitor general,** as chief lawyer for the U.S. government, takes on it. The solicitor general, appointed by the president, is the fourth-ranking member of the Justice Department and is responsible for handling all appeals on behalf of the U.S. government to the Supreme Court. The solicitor's staff is like a small, specialized law firm within the Justice Department. But because this office has such a special relationship with the Supreme Court, even having a suite of offices within the Supreme Court building, the solicitor general is often referred to as the Court's "ninth and a half member."[18] Moreover, the solicitor general, on behalf of the U.S. government, appears as a party or as an *amicus curiae* in more than 50 percent of the cases heard by the Court each term.

This special relationship with the Court helps explain the overwhelming success the solicitor general's office enjoys before the Supreme Court. The Court generally accepts 70 to 80 percent of the cases where the U.S. government is the petitioning party, compared to about 5 percent of all others.[19]

Conflict Among the Circuits. Conflict among the lower courts is apparently another reason the justices take cases. When interpretations of constitutional or federal law are involved, the justices seem to want consistency throughout the federal court system.

Interest Group Participation. A quick way for the justices to gauge the ideological ramifications of a particular case is by the amount of interest group participation. Richard C. Cortner has noted that "Cases do not arrive on the doorstep of the Supreme Court like orphans in the night."[20] Instead, most cases heard by the Supreme Court involve either the government or an interest group—either as the sponsoring party or as an *amicus curiae.* Liberal groups such as the ACLU, People for the

solicitor general
The fourth-ranking member of the Justice Department; responsible for handling all appeals on behalf of the U.S. government to the Supreme Court.

amicus curiae
"Friend of the court"; a third party to a lawsuit who files a legal brief for the purpose of raising additional points of view in an attempt to influence a court's decision.

WEB EXPLORATION
To examine the recent filings of the office of the solicitor general, see www.ablongman.com/oconnor

Demonstrators gathered outside the U.S. Supreme Court as the justices began hearing arguments in the case that ultimately decided the 2000 election. (Photo courtesy: Rob Crandall/The Image Works)

American Way, the NAACP Legal Defense Fund, and conservative groups including the Washington Legal Foundation, Concerned Women for America, or Americans United for Life Legal Defense Fund routinely sponsor cases or file *amicus* briefs either urging the Court to hear a case or asking it to deny *certiorari*. Research by political scientists has found that "not only does [an *amicus*] brief in favor of *certiorari* significantly improve the chances of a case being accepted, but two, three and four briefs improve the chances even more.[21]

Clearly, it's the more the merrier, whether or not the briefs are filed for or against granting review.[22] Interest group participation may highlight lower court and ideological conflicts for the justices by alerting them to the amount of public interest in the issues presented in any particular case.

Starting the Case.   Once a case is accepted for review, a flurry of activity begins (see Figure 9.5). If a criminal defendant is proceeding *in forma pauperis,* the Court appoints an expert lawyer to prepare and argue the case. Unlike the situation in many state courts, where appointed lawyers are often novices, it is considered an honor to be asked to represent an indigent before the Supreme Court in spite of the fact that such representation is on a *pro bono,* or no fee, basis.

Whether they are being paid or not, lawyers on both sides of the case begin to prepare their written arguments for submission to the Court. In these briefs lawyers cite prior case law and make arguments as to why the Court should find in favor of their client.

More often than not, these arguments are echoed or expanded in *amicus curiae* briefs filed by interested parties, especially interest groups. In the 1987 term, for example, 80 percent of the cases decided by the Court had at least one *amicus curiae* brief. All sorts of interest groups, then, find that joining ongoing cases through *amicus* briefs is a useful way of advancing their policy preferences. Interest groups also provide the Court with information not necessarily contained in the major-party briefs, help write briefs, and assist in practice moot-court sessions. In these sessions the lawyer who will argue the case before the nine justices goes through a complete rehearsal, with prominent lawyers and law professors playing the roles of the various justices.

FIGURE 9.5   How Supreme Court Decisions Get Made

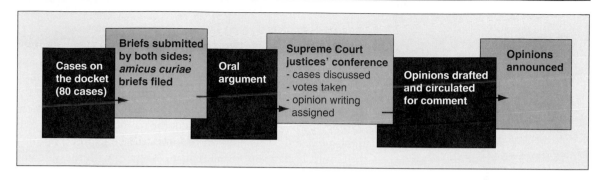

Oral Arguments.   After briefs and *amicus* briefs are submitted on each side, oral argument takes place. Oral argument is generally limited to the immediate parties in the case, although it is not uncommon for the U.S. solicitor general to appear to argue orally as an *amicus curiae*. Oral argument at the Court is fraught with time-honored tradition and ceremony. At precisely 10:00 every morning when the Court is in session, the Court marshal (dressed in a cutaway) emerges to intone "Oyez! Oyez! Oyez!" as the nine justices emerge from behind a reddish-purple velvet curtain to take their places on the raised and slightly angled bench. The chief justice sits in the middle with the other justices to the right and left, alternating in seniority.

Almost all attorneys are allotted one-half hour to present their cases, and this allotment includes the time taken by questions from the bench. Although many Court watchers have tried to figure out how a particular justice will vote based on the questioning at oral argument, most find that the nature and number of questions asked does not help much in predicting the outcome of a case.

The Conference and the Vote.   The justices meet in closed conference once a week when the Court is hearing oral argument. Since 1836 the justices have begun each conference session with a round of hand-shaking. Once the door to the conference room closes, no others are allowed to enter. The justice with the least seniority acts as the door-keeper for the other eight, communicating with those waiting outside to fill requests for documents, water, and so on.

Conferences highlight the importance and power of the chief justice, who presides over them and makes the initial presentation of each case. Each individual justice then discusses the case in order of his or her seniority on the Court, with the most senior justice speaking next. On the Rehnquist Court, the justices generally vote at the same time they discuss the case. Initial conference votes are not final, allowing justices to change their minds before final votes are taken later.

Writing Opinions.   There are basically five kinds of opinions that can be written:

1. A *majority opinion* is written by one member of the Court, and as such reflects the views of at least a majority of the justices. This opinion usually sets out the legal reasoning justifying the decision, and this legal reasoning becomes a precedent for deciding future cases.
2. A *concurring opinion* is one written by a justice who agrees with the outcome of the case but not with the legal rationale for the decision.
3. A *plurality opinion* is one that attracts the support of three or four justices. Generally, this opinion becomes the controlling opinion of the Court. Usually one or more justices agrees with the outcome of the decision in a concurring opinion, but there is no solid majority for the legal reasoning behind the outcome. Plurality decisions do not have the precedential value of majority opinions.
4. A *dissenting opinion* is one that is written by one or more justices who disagree with the opinion of a majority or plurality of the Court.
5. A *per curiam opinion* is an unsigned opinion issued by the Court. Justices may dissent from *per curiam* opinions but do so rarely.

The chief justice, if in the majority, has the job of assigning the writing of the opinion; otherwise, the assignment falls to the most senior justice in the majority. This privilege enables him to wield tremendous power.

HOW THE JUSTICES VOTE

Justices are human beings, and they do not make decisions in a vacuum. Principles of *stare decisis* dictate that the justices follow the law of previous cases in deciding cases at hand. But other factors are usually operating. A variety of legal and extra-legal factors have been found to affect Supreme Court decision making. As Politics Now: Lobbying Jurists suggests, there may be other ways too.

judicial restraint
A philosophy of judicial decision-making that argues courts should allow the decisions of other branches of government to stand, even when they offend a judge's own sense of principles.

judicial activism
A philosophy of judicial decision making that argues judges should use their power broadly to further justice, especially in the areas of equality and personal liberty.

Legal Factors

One of the primary issues concerning judicial decision making focuses on what is called the activism/restraint debate. Advocates of **judicial restraint** argue that courts should allow the decisions of other branches to stand, even when they offend a judge's own sense of principles.[23] Restraintists defend their position by asserting that the federal courts are composed of unelected judges, which makes the judicial branch the least democratic branch of government. Consequently, the courts should defer policy making to other branches of government as much as possible.

Restraintists refer to *Roe* v. *Wade* (1973), the case that liberalized abortion laws, as a classic example of **judicial activism** run amok. They maintain that the Court should have deferred policy making on this

POLITICS NOW

LOBBYING JURISTS

By now you should realize that judges, appointed and confirmed through an often highly political process, may reflect political or ideological biases. How else might we explain the high number of 5–4 decisions of late from the U.S. Supreme Court? Today some judges lobby for spots on the federal bench, and interest groups bring cases to courts they believe are amenable to their causes. Interest groups are also involved in another form of perhaps more insidious lobbying that has received very little attention.

From 1992 to 1998, more than 230 federal judges took all-expenses-paid trips to resort locations (some might call these vacations) to attend legal seminars paid for by corporations and foundations that have interests in cases already in or likely to be soon in federal court. These seminars are always held in warm places and have been occurring since the early 1980s. The most recent seminars have been devoted to issues of environmental litigation, where the message from the seminar sponsors was that regulation should be limited and that "the free market should be relied upon to protect the environment."*

In fact, judges who attended those seminars wrote ten of the most crucial rulings handed down during the 1990s dealing with curbing environmental protection, including decisions invalidating a provision of the Endangered Species Protection Act and another regulation that attempted to abate soot and smog. Although judges are asked each year to report outside income, which itself is also controversial, many judges do not note these seminars on their financial disclosure forms. Whether undue influence is felt at these seminars, there is at least the appearance of a conflict of interest. Do you think that judges who go on these trips should rule on cases involving the parties hosting these events?

*Abner Mikva, "The Wooing of Our Judges." *The New York Times*, August 28, 2000, A17.

sensitive issue to the states or to the other branches of the federal government—the legislative and executive—because their officials are elected and therefore are more receptive to the majority's will.

Advocates of judicial activism contend that judges should use their power broadly to further justice, especially in the areas of equality and personal liberty. Activists argue that it is the Court's appropriate role to correct injustices committed by the other branches of government. Explicit in this argument is the notion that courts need to protect oppressed minorities.[24]

The debate over judicial activism versus judicial restraint often focuses on how the Court should interpret the meaning of the Constitution. Advocates of judicial restraint generally agree that judges should be strict constructionists; that is, they should interpret the Constitution as it was written and intended by the Framers. They argue that in determining the constitutionality of a statute or policy, the Court should rely on the explicit meanings of the clauses in the document, which can be clarified by looking at the intent of the Framers.

Precedent.   Most Supreme Court decisions are laced with numerous references to previous Court decisions. Some justices, however, believe that *stare decisis* and adherence to precedent is no longer as critical as it once was. Chief Justice Rehnquist, for example, has noted that while "*stare decisis* is a cornerstone of our legal system . . . it has less power in constitutional cases."[25] In contrast, Justices O'Connor, Kennedy, and Souter explained their reluctance to overrule *Roe* v. *Wade* (1973) in *Planned Parenthood of Southeastern Pennsylvania* v. *Casey* (1992): "to overrule under fire in the absence of the most compelling reason to reexamine a watershed decision would subject this Court's legitimacy beyond any serious question."[26]

Interestingly, a 1990 study of the American public's knowledge and perceptions of the Court indicated that only 44 percent believed that the Court decides cases primarily on the basis of facts and law. Nearly 50 percent believe that the Court makes decisions based on other factors, including political pressures (28 percent), political/personal beliefs (18 percent), and religious beliefs (1 percent). More recently, a study conducted after *Bush* v. *Gore* found that 29 percent of those polled saw political reasons as motivating that decision. Although *theoretically* the Framers envisioned the Court to be above these pressures, the American public does not appear to be particularly upset about the role of politics and personal beliefs in the decision-making process. In fact, those polled want the Court to take a more active role in the areas of discrimination against women and minorities.

Extra-Legal Factors

Most political scientists who study what is called judicial behavior conclude that a variety of extra-legal forces shape judicial decision making. Of late, many have attempted to explain how judges vote by integrating a variety of models to offer a more complete picture of judicial decision making.[27] Many of those models attempt to take into account justices' behavioral characteristics and attitudes, as well as what are called the fact patterns of the case. Others argue that their clerks play a role.

Behavioral Characteristics.   Some political scientists argue that social background differences, including childhood experiences, religious values, education, earlier political and legal careers, and political party loyalties are likely to influence how a judge evaluates the facts and legal issues presented in any given case. Justice Harry A. Blackmun's service at the Mayo Clinic is often pointed to as a reason his opinion for the Court in *Roe* v. *Wade* was so soundly grounded in medical evidence. Similarly, Justice Potter Stewart, who was generally considered a moderate on most civil liberties issues, usually took a more liberal position on cases dealing with freedom of the press. Why? It may be that Stewart's early job as a newspaper reporter made him more sensitive to these claims.

Ideology. Critics of the social background approach argue that attitudes or ideologies can better explain the justices' voting patterns. Since the 1940s the two most prevailing political ideologies in the United States have been conservative and liberal. On the Supreme Court, justices with "conservative" views generally vote against affirmative action, abortion rights, expanded rights for criminal defendants, and increased power for the national government. In contrast, "liberals" tend to support the parties advancing these positions.

The Attitudinal and Strategic Models. The attitudinal approach hypothesizes that there is a substantial link between judicial attitudes and decision making.[28] Simply stated, the attitudinal model holds that Supreme Court justices decide cases in light of the facts of the cases according to their personal preferences toward issues of public policy. Among some of the factors used to derive attitudes are a justice's party identification,[29] the party of the appointing president,[30] and the liberal/conservative leanings of a justice.

Although by 1995 many judicial scholars were claiming that the attitudinal model could be used to explain all judicial decision making, by 2000 that was no longer the case. Now, several scholars who study the courts are advocating their belief that judges act strategically, meaning that they weigh and assess their actions against those of other justices to optimize the chances that their preferences will be adopted by the whole court.[31] Moreover, this approach seeks to explain not only a justice's vote but also the range of forces such as congressional/judicial relations and judicial/executive relations that also affect the outcome of legal disputes.

Public Opinion. Many political scientists also have examined the role of public opinion in Supreme Court decision making.[32] Not only do the justices read legal briefs and hear oral arguments, they also read newspapers, watch television, and have some knowledge of public opinion—especially on controversial issues. According to Chief Justice Rehnquist,

> Judges, so long as they are relatively normal human beings, can no more escape being influenced by public opinion in the long run than can people working at other jobs. And if a judge on coming to the bench were to decide to hermetically seal himself off from all manifestations of public opinion, he would accomplish very little; he would not be influenced by current public opinion, but instead would be influenced by the state of public opinion at the time he came to the bench.[33]

One political scientist, however, has discovered substantial variation in the degree to which particular justices' decisions are in line with public opinion.[34]

The courts, especially the Supreme Court, also can be the direct target of public opinion. During the spring of 1989, when the case of *Webster* v. *Reproductive Health Services* was about to come before the Supreme Court, the Court was subjected to unprecedented lobbying as groups and individuals on both sides of the abortion issue marched and sent appeals to the Court. Not only did pro-choice activists mount one of the largest demonstrations in the history of the United States when more than 300,000 people marched from the Mall to the Capitol building, just across the street from the Supreme Court, full-page advertisements appeared in prominent newspapers urging supporters of *Roe* v. *Wade* to contact members of the Court to voice their support. Mail at the Court, which usually averages about 1,000 pieces a day, rose to an astronomical 46,000 pieces a day when *Webster* reached the Court, virtually paralyzing normal lines of communication.

It is not surprising, then, that public confidence in the Court, like other institutions of government, has ebbed and flowed. Public support for the Court was highest after the Court issued *U.S.* v. *Nixon* (1974). At a time when Americans lost faith in the presidency, they could at least look to the Supreme Court to do the right thing. Of late, however, the Court and the judicial system as a whole have taken a beating in public confidence. In the aftermath of the O. J. Simpson criminal trial, many white Americans faulted the judicial system. This dissatisfaction was reflected in low levels of confidence in the system, although the Supreme Court itself continues to enjoy considerable popular support. In 2001, 59 percent of those sampled by the Gallup Organization had a favorable opinion of the Supreme Court. Still, race seems to color individual perceptions of the court. Nearly 80 percent of blacks disagreed with the court's decision in *Bush* v. *Gore;* only 18 percent of whites did.

PARTICIPATION
The Court and
School Prayer

JUDICIAL POLICY MAKING AND IMPLEMENTATION

The Supreme Court also appears to affect public opinion. Political scientists have found that the Court affects public opinion when it first rules in controversial cases such as those involving abortion or capital punishment but that subsequent decisions have little effect.[35]

All judges, whether they like it or not, make policy. Judges can interpret a provision of a law to cover matters not previously understood to be covered by the law, or can "discover" new rights, such as that of privacy, from their reading of the Constitution. This power of the courts to make policy presents difficult questions for democratic theory, because democratic theorists believe that the power to make law resides only in the people or their elected representatives. Yet court rulings, especially Supreme Court decisions, routinely affect policy far beyond the interests of the immediate parties.

Policy Making

One measure of the power of the courts is that more than one hundred federal laws have been declared unconstitutional. Although many of these laws have not been particularly significant, others have.

Another measure of the power of the Supreme Court is its ability to overrule itself. Although the Court generally abides by the informal rule of *stare decisis,* by one count it has overruled itself in more than 140 cases since 1810. Moreover, in the past few years, the Court has repeatedly reversed earlier decisions in the areas of criminal defendants' rights, affirmative action, and the establishment of religion, thus revealing its powerful role in determining national policy. At no time was this power clearer than in 2000 when its decision, in effect, decided the outcome of the 2000 election as discussed in Policy in Action: The Supreme Court as a National Policy Maker.

A measure of the growing power of the federal courts is the degree to which they now handle issues that, after *Marbury* v. *Madison* (1803), had been considered to be political questions more appropriately left to the other branches of government to decide.

The 1989 pro-choice rally in Washington, D.C., was part of an intense lobbying effort to influence the Court's decision in the *Webster* case. Justice Sandra Day O'Connor, viewed as a swing vote on the case, was a particular target of the lobbying. (Photo courtesy: Jodi Buren/Woodfin Camp & Associates)

Implementing Court Decisions

President Andrew Jackson, annoyed about a particular decision handed down by the Marshall Court, is alleged to have said, "John Marshall has made his decision; now let him enforce it." Jackson's statement raises a question: How do Supreme Court rulings translate into public policy? In fact, although judicial decisions carry legal and even moral authority, all courts must rely on other units of government to carry out their directives. If the president or Congress, for example, doesn't like a particular Supreme Court ruling, they can underfund programs needed to implement a decision or seek only lax enforcement. **Judicial implementation** refers to how and whether judicial decisions are translated into actual public policies affecting more than the immediate parties to the lawsuit.

How well a decision is implemented often depends on how well crafted or popular it is. Hostile reaction in the South to *Brown* v. *Board of Education* (1954) and the absence of precise guidelines to implement the decision meant that the ruling went largely unenforced for years. The *Brown* experience also highlights how much the Supreme Court needs the support of federal and state courts as well as other governmental agencies to carry out its judgments. For example, you may have graduated from high school since 1992, when the Supreme Court ruled that

TIMELINE
Umpiring the
Government

judicial implementation
Refers to how and whether judicial decisions are translated into actual public policies affecting more than the immediate parties to a lawsuit.

GLOBAL POLITICS

THE POWERS OF THE COURTS

Judicial review is an American innovation that reflects the concern with balancing the branches of government under a system of separation of powers. It does not exist in all political systems, and how it is used in practice varies.

The United Kingdom and China occupy one extreme; these two countries do not afford the courts judicial review. In the British case, judicial review is seen as a violation of the principle of parliamentary sovereignty, that Parliament is the supreme organ of government. Consistent with this principle, the House of Lords, which combines a history of legislative and judicial functions, acts as the highest court. Judicial review is also inconsistent with socialist legality, which places the Communist Party above the law, so Chinese courts do not exercise judicial review.

A number of constitutions afford their courts limited powers of judicial review. In Russia and Mexico, the courts can overturn legislative acts but not executive actions. France stands out in this group because the Constitutional Council is not a court. It is a body of eminent persons appointed respectively by the president and the two houses of Parliament, and it rules only on the constitutionality of legislation current under debate. The deliberations of the council can be seen as part of the legislative process itself.

Japan's experience illustrates another aspect of judicial review. Japan's 1947 constitution was written during the American Occupation at the end of World War II (as was West Germany's), and judicial review was accordingly given to the courts. Yet, the Supreme Court has been reluctant to use that power. In the 1950s, the court made a series of declarations stating that issues involving national defense, operations of the Parliament and imperial household were the responsibility of the Parliament and were therefore not proper concerns of the judiciary. In so doing, the Supreme Court removed itself from the most controversial issues of the time, issues which had engendered numerous lawsuits by citizens.

Malapportionment of electoral seats in the Parliament illustrates the high court's reluctance

public middle school and high school graduations could not include a prayer. Yet your own commencement ceremony may have included one.

For effective implementation of a judicial decision, potential enforcers must understand the original decision. For example, in *Reynolds* v. *Sims* (1964) the Supreme Court ruled that every person should have an equally weighted vote in electing governmental representatives.[36] This "one person, one vote" decision might seem simple enough at first glance, but in practice it can be very difficult to understand. State legislatures and local governments, which determine voting districts for federal, state, and local offices, are largely responsible for implementing this decision. If a state legislature draws districts in such a way that African American voters are spread thinly across a num-

to intervene in parliamentary operations. As the Japanese population shifted from the countryside to the cities in the postwar era, rural electoral districts became overrepresented at the expense of their urban counterparts. In extreme cases voters in some districts had the equivalent of nearly five times as many votes as did citizens in certain other districts, a violation of the constitutional principle of one person, one vote. The Supreme Court first ruled on a suit brought in the wake of elections in 1976, ruling that while overrepresented rural districts violated the constitution, it was up to the Parliament to provide a remedy. Using similar arguments, the courts have continued to issue rulings that refuse to overturn the results of parliamentary elections. In the most recent case involving the 1998 House of Representatives election, plaintiffs sued the government alleging that malapportionment continues, despite electoral reforms enacted in the mid-1990s (which had had the support of the judiciary): the Supreme Court again refused to nullify the results of the election.

Japan's case suggests that judicial activism is not necessarily part and parcel of judicial review. Whether the courts are active in shaping politics has to do with how the courts perceive their role in relation to other parts of government.

Judicial Review in Industrial Judiciaries

Country	Name of Highest Court	Power of the Courts
Canada	Supreme Court	judicial review
France	Constitutional Council	limited judicial review
Germany	Federal Constitutional Court	judicial review
Italy	Constitutional Court	judicial review
Japan	Supreme Court	judicial review
United Kingdom	House of Lords	no judicial review
United States	Supreme Court	judicial review

ber of separate constituencies, the chances are slim that any particular district will elect a representative who is especially sensitive to blacks' concerns. Does that violate "equal representation"? (In practice, through the early 1990s, courts and the Justice Department intervened in many cases to ensure that elected officials would include minority representation only ultimately to be overruled by the Supreme Court.)

The second requirement of effective implementation mandates that "enforcers" must actually follow Court policy. Thus, when the Court ruled that women could not be denied admission to the Virginia Military Institute, the implementing population—in this case, university administrators and the state of Virginia—were ordered to enroll qualified female students.

COMPARATIVE
Comparing
Judiciaries

POLICY IN ACTION

THE SUPREME COURT AS A NATIONAL POLICY MAKER

On December 12, 2000 all eyes in the United States were cast on the Supreme Court as all major networks went live to the steps of the Court where hundreds of people were amassed to report on the Court's much anticipated decision in *Bush* v. *Gore*. In the weeks and months after that decision was rendered, legal scholars continued to debate the appropriateness of the Court's action. In an unassigned opinion which was accompanied by sharp dissents from the Court's four more liberal members—Justices Breyer, Ginsburg (both Democratic appointees), Stevens, and Souter—the Court effectively stopped the recounting of all Florida votes that the Florida Supreme Court had ordered. Since George W. Bush was ahead by a few hundred votes at that stage, George W. Bush became the 43rd president of the United States.

When the Constitution was drafted, Alexander Hamilton was of the opinion that the Supreme Court would be "the least dangerous," or weakest branch. As the Court's decision in this case indicates, however, the Court can be a powerful player in the political and policy process. Although the majority grounded its opinion in legal doctrine, critics charge that the desired outcome was first reached and then an opinion cobbled together. This decision had enormous policy consequences, no matter what the Court's rationale. Among some of the indirect policy outcomes of the case that the Justices had to have been mindful of were:

- The future direction of the Court. By awarding the presidency to George W. Bush, the majority, in effect, had a powerful voice in selecting the kinds of justices (conservative) who would become their colleagues. Thus, 5–4 conservative decisions could become clearer majorities in the future.
- The continued legality of abortion. Most court watchers believe that *Roe* v. *Wade* and the continued legality of abortion hangs on by a narrow margin. Changes in Court personnel, as well as the president, could do much to limit reproductive rights as was evidenced by President Bush's appointment of conservative abortion foe John Ashcroft to attorney general.
- The end of affirmative action.

Can you think of other policies the Supreme Court has weighed in on that were likely to be affected by the election of a conservative president?

WEB EXPLORATION
For an analysis of the Court's 2000 election decision by constitutional scholars, go to www.ablongman.com/oconnor

Judicial decisions are most likely to be implemented smoothly if responsibility for implementation is concentrated in the hands of a few highly visible public officials, such as the president or a governor.

The third requirement for effective implementation is that what political scientists term the consumer population must be aware of the rights that a decision grants or denies them.[37] Teenagers seeking abortions, for example, are consumers of the Supreme Court's decisions on parental consent and notification requirements for abortions. They need to know that most states require them to inform their parents of their intention to have an abortion or to get parental permission to do so.

Continuity &Change

Participation in the Judicial Process

At the time the Constitution was adopted, women and African Americans were largely excluded from the judicial process. Neither could vote, and largely on that basis, both groups were excluded from jury service. Similarly, no women or African Americans were lawyers or judges. A handful of black lawyers practiced in the North in the mid-1880s, and John Swett Rock was admitted to practice before the Supreme Court in 1861. The first women lawyers were admitted to practice in the late 1860s. When Belva Lockwood's petition to be admitted to the Supreme Court bar was denied in 1876, she energetically lobbied Congress, which passed a law requiring the Court to admit qualified women to practice. In 1879 she became the first woman admitted to practice before the Supreme Court.

Women and blacks were often excluded from jury service because many states selected jurors from those registered to vote. Since African Americans were systematically excluded from the voter rolls throughout the South until after passage of the Voting Rights Act of 1965, they have only recently begun to be part of the judicial system. As early as 1888, however, the Supreme Court ruled that African Americans could not be barred from serving as jurors.[a] It was not until 1975 that the Supreme Court was to rule that states could not exclude women from jury service.[b]

As a result of the civil rights and women's rights movements (detailed in chapter 5), the number as well as percentage of all lawyers and judges has grown tremendously. Today, 29 percent of all lawyers are women, and 8 percent are African American, Hispanic, or Native American.

In 2001, women, for the first time in history, made up over half of all first-year law students. Similarly, beginning with President Carter's efforts to appoint more women and minorities to

(continued)

SUMMARY

The judiciary and the legal process—on the national and state levels—are complex and play a far more important role in the setting of policy than the Framers ever envisioned. Many of the Framers viewed the judicial branch of government as little more than a minor check on the other two branches, ignoring Anti-Federalist concerns about an unelected judiciary and its potential for tyranny. The Judiciary Act of 1789 established the basic federal court system we have today. It was the Marshall Court (1801–1835), however, that interpreted the Constitution to include the Court's major power, that of judicial review.

Ours is a dual judicial system consisting of the federal court system and the separate judicial systems of the fifty states. In each system there are two basic types of courts: trial courts and appellate courts. Each type deals with cases involving criminal and civil law. Original jurisdiction refers to a court's ability to hear a case as a trial court; appellate jurisdiction refers to a court's ability to review cases already decided by a trial court.

The federal court system is made up of constitutional and legislative courts. Federal district courts, courts of appeals, and the Supreme Court are constitutional courts. District court and court of appeals judges are nominated by the president and subject to Senate confirmation. Senators often play a key role in recommending district court appointees from their home state. Supreme Court

the federal courts, women and minorities are a rising proportion of the federal judiciary, with African Americans holding 10 percent of all federal judgeships and white women another 15 percent (Hispanics hold 4 percent of the seats, Asian Americans less than 1 percent, and there are but 2 Native American federal judges). While no state can bar African Americans or women from serving on a jury, it was not all that unusual, until recently, for lawyers to use their peremptory challenges (those made without a reason) to systematically dismiss women or African Americans if they believed that they would be more hostile jurors to their side. In two cases, however, the Supreme Court ruled that race or gender could not be used as reasons to exclude potential jurors.[c] Thus, today, juries are much more likely to be truly representative of the community and capable of offering litigants in a civil or criminal matter a jury of their peers.

Many studies of the judicial process have concluded that male and female justices decide cases differently. Women and African American judges tend to be more liberal than their white male counterparts. Thus, the presence of more women and more minority judges could lead to enhanced public support for the judiciary. The O. J. Simpson case brought home to most Americans quite vividly that whites and blacks view the judicial process quite differently, often based on group treatment within that process.

1. As we move into a society with more African American, Hispanic, and female jurists, lawyers, and jurors, what consequences will this have on public perceptions of the American legal system?
2. Will greater participation by women, Hispanic, and African American judges have a difference on how cases are decided and the ways that laws are interpreted?

[a] *Strauder* v. *West Virginia*, 100 U.S. 303 (1888).
[b] *Duren* v. *Missouri*, 439 U.S. 357 (1979).
[c] *Batson* v. *Kentucky*, 476 U.S. 79 (1986) (African Americans) and *J.E.B.* v. *Alabama*, 511 U.S. 127 (1994) (women).

Cast Your Vote. What changes, if any, do you foresee in the judicial process? To cast your vote, go to **www.ablongman.com/oconnor**

justices are nominated by the president but must also win Senate confirmation. Presidents use different criteria for selection, but important factors include competence, ideology, pursuit of political support, race, and gender.

Several factors go into the Court's decision to hear a case. Not only must the Court have jurisdiction, but at least four justices must vote to hear the case, and cases with certain characteristics are most likely to be heard. Once a case is set for review, briefs and *amicus curiae* briefs are filed and oral argument scheduled. The justices meet after oral argument to discuss the case, votes are taken, and opinions are written and circulated.

Several legal and extra-legal factors affect how the Court arrives at its decision. Legal factors include judicial philosophy, the original intent of the Framers, and precedent. Extra-legal factors include public opinion, behavioral characteristics, ideology, and strategic choices of the justices.

The Supreme Court is an important participant in the policy-making process. The process of judicial interpretation gives the Court powers never envisioned by the Framers.

Unlike the other two branches of government, the Supreme Court and the federal judiciary have not been the subjects of many reform efforts, and periodic calls for change have met with little support. Yet the question remains: Should jurists be political?

KEY TERMS

amicus curiae, p. 287
appellate courts, p. 269
appellate jurisdiction p. 269
brief, p. 273
civil law, p. 270
constitutional court p. 272
criminal law, p. 269
in forma pauperis, p. 284

judicial activism, p. 290
judicial implementation, p. 295
judicial restraint, p. 290
judicial review, p. 267
Judiciary Act of 1789, p. 266
jurisdiction, p. 269
legislative court, p. 272
Marbury v. *Madison* p. 267

original jurisdiction, p. 269
precedent, p. 274
Rule of Four, p. 286
solicitor general, p. 287
stare decisis, p. 274
strict constructionist, p. 277
trial court, p. 269
writ of *certiorari*, p. 284

SELECTED READINGS

Abraham, Henry J. *The Judicial Process,* 7th ed. New York: Oxford University Press, 1997.

Barrow, Deborah J., Gary Zuk, and Gerard S. Gryski, *The Federal Judiciary and Institutional Change.* Ann Arbor: University of Michigan Press, 1996.

Baum, Lawrence. *The Supreme Court,* 7th ed. Washington, D.C.: CQ Press, 2000.

———. *The Puzzle of Judicial Behavior.* Ann Arbor: University of Michigan Press, 1997.

Epstein, Lee, et al. *The Supreme Court Compendium: Data, Decisions, and Developments,* 2nd. ed. Washington, D.C.: Congressional Quarterly Inc., 1996.

Goldman, Sheldon. *Picking Federal Judges: Lower Court Selection from Roosevelt Through Reagan.* New Haven, Conn.: Yale University Press, 1997.

Hall, Kermitt L., ed. *The Oxford Companion to the Supreme Court of the United States.* New York: Oxford University Press, 1992.

Irons, Peter, and Stephanie Guitton, eds. *May It Please the Court: 23 Live Recordings of Landmark Cases As Argued Before the Court.* New York: New Press, 1993.

Lazarus, Edward. *Closed Chambers: The First Eyewitness Account of the Epic Struggles Inside the Supreme Court.* New York: Times Books, 1998.

Marshall, Thomas R. *Public Opinion and the Supreme Court.* Boston: Unwin and Hyman, 1989.

Maveety, Nancy. *Justice Sandra Day O'Connor: Strategist on the Supreme Court.* Lanham, Md.: Rowman & Littlefield, 1996.

O'Brien, David M. *Storm Center: The Supreme Court in American Politics,* 4th ed. New York: Norton, 1996.

Perry, H. W. *Deciding to Decide: Agenda Setting in the United States Supreme Court.* Cambridge, Mass.: Harvard University Press, 1994.

Provine, Doris Marie. *Case Selection in the United States Supreme Court.* Chicago: University of Chicago Press, 1980.

Salokar, Rebecca Mae. *The Solicitor General: The Politics of Law.* Philadelphia: Temple University Press, 1992.

Slotnick, Elliot E., and Jennifer A. Segal. *Television News and the Supreme Court: All the News That's Fit to Air.* Boston: Cambridge University Press. 1998.

Woodward, Bob, and Scott Armstrong. *The Brethren: Inside the Supreme Court.* New York: Avon, 1996.

10 Public Opinion and the News Media

(Photo courtesy: Bob Daemmrich)

On 2:18 A.M. November 8, 2000, one of the major television networks made the call that George W. Bush would become the forty-third president of the United States. All the major networks quickly followed suit. But, as we all know now, that was not to be the end of it. As calls for recounts and litigation went on, one of the longest presidential elections in the nation's history became a field day for pollsters and their critics. Interestingly, the original call awarding Florida to Al Gore came early in the evening and was based on projections from the Voter News Service, an exit poll service used by a consortium of news organizations, not on actual vote totals.

Pollsters sprang into action in the wake of Al Gore's decision to retract his concession to Governor Bush. The Gallup Organization polled Americans to determine if they favored or opposed the hand recounts favored by Gore. Nationwide on November 11–12, 55 percent of those polled favored a recount, 85 percent of the Gore voters but only 20 percent of those who voted for Bush. Sixty percent believed that those votes should be included in the final totals.[1] On November 26, 2000, when asked whom they considered the real winner in Florida, 51 percent said Bush but 32 percent were unsure. By then, only 15 percent thought Gore was the "real" winner. But after the U.S. Supreme Court's decision that stopped all further vote counting and, in essence, declared George W. Bush the winner, voters were asked from December 15–17, "Just your best guess, if the Supreme Court had allowed the vote recount to continue in Florida, who do you think would have ended up with the most votes in Florida?" Of the national sample, 46 percent said Gore; 45 percent said Bush. Again, just as in the November 11–12 poll, there was a huge chasm between Bush and Gore voters. Nearly three-quarters (74 percent) of the Gore voters continued to believe that he was the rightful winner; 77 percent of the Bush voters believed that their man was the winner. The same poll found that only 51 percent of those sampled believed that the electoral college outcome was "fair." Again, huge gaps were evident. Eighty-five percent of the Bush voters thought the election outcome was fair; only 23 percent of the Gore voters did. Nationally, 68 percent of black voters believed that their votes were less likely to have been counted fairly in Florida than whites. Still, 61 percent of the public reported their belief that George W. Bush would work hard to "represent the interests of all Americans," but only 22 percent of blacks polled agreed with this statement.

Polling gives us a unique view into the psyche of Americans. Politicians read the polls, as do their advisors. George W. Bush, who prided himself on his good relations with Hispanic and African American communities in Texas, was undoubtedly shocked and troubled by the feelings of Gore supporters and African Americans. Some might even argue that the diversity of his first Cabinet appointments reflected his concern with American sentiment as he sought to lead the nation and establish the legitimacy of his victory in light of continued public skepticism.

The networks and many major newspapers measured and reported on public opinion slavishly during the 2000 campaign and based their election-night calls on the work of pollsters. Today, many Americans don't know what to think about polls or the media. While there was a lot of hyperbole about the effects of polls on the election outcome, most polls came close to predicting the final vote. The detailed reports that many members of the media provided in the wake of the elections show how diverse America is, but yet how much agreement continues about many fundamental issues. Most want less government, particularly at the national level. So did many citizens in 1787. Most want to leave a nation better for their children. So did the Framers. But the Framers did not have sophisticated public opinion polls to tell them this, nor did they have national news media to tell them the results of those polls or put a particular spin on those findings, compounding the problem of measuring **public opinion,** what the public thinks about a particular issue or set of issues at any point in time.

Today many people wonder what shapes public opinion: poll results or people's opinions. Do the polls drive public opinion, or does public opinion drive the polls? In this chapter we examine public opinion and the media and their roles in the making of policy.

public opinion
What the public thinks about a particular issue or set of issues at any point in time.

During World War I, as part of "the world's greatest adventure in advertising," the Committee on Public Information created a vast gallery of posters designed to shore up public support for the war effort. (Photo courtesy: Bettmann/Corbis)

EARLY EFFORTS TO INFLUENCE AND MEASURE PUBLIC OPINION

From the very early days of the republic, political leaders recognized the importance of public opinion and used all the means at their disposal to manipulate it for political purposes. By the early 1800s, the term "public opinion" was frequently being used by the educated middle class. As more Americans became educated, they became more vocal about their opinions and were more likely to vote. A more educated, reading public led to increased demand for newspapers, which in turn provided more information about the process of government. As the United States grew, there were more elections and more opportunities for citizens to express their political opinions through the ballot box. As a result of these trends, political leaders were more frequently forced to try to gauge public opinion in order to remain responsive to the wishes and desires of their constituents.

During World War I, some people argued that public opinion didn't matter at all. But President Woodrow Wilson (1913–1921) argued that public opinion would temper the actions of international leaders. Therefore, only eight days after the start of the war, Wilson created a Committee on Public Information. Run by a prominent journalist, the committee immediately undertook to unite U.S. public opinion behind the war effort. It used all of the tools available—pamphlets, posters, and speakers who exhorted the patrons of local movie houses during every intermission—in an effort to garner support and favorable opinion for the war. In the words of the committee's head, it was "the world's greatest adventure in advertising."[2]

Public opinion polling as we know it today did not begin to develop until the 1930s. Researchers in a variety of disciplines, including political science, tried to use scientific methods to measure political thought through the use of surveys or polls. As methods for gathering and interpreting data improved, survey data began to play an increasingly important role in all walks of life, from politics to retailing.

Early Election Forecasting

As early as 1824, one Pennsylvania newspaper tried to predict the winner of that year's presidential contest. Later, in 1883, the *Boston Globe* sent reporters to selected election precincts to poll voters as they exited voting booths, in an effort to predict the results of key contests. In 1916, *Literary Digest,* a popular magazine, began mailing survey postcards to potential voters in an effort to predict election outcomes. *Literary Digest* drew its survey sample from "every telephone book in the United States, from the rosters of clubs and associations, from city directories, lists of registered voters [and] classified mail order and occupational data."[3] Using the data it received from the millions of postcard ballots sent out throughout the United States, *Literary Digest* correctly predicted every presidential election from 1920 to 1932.

Literary Digest used what were called **straw polls** to predict the popular vote in those four presidential elections. Its polling methods were widely hailed as "amazingly right" and "uncannily accurate."[4] In 1936, however, its luck ran out. *Literary Digest* predicted that Republican Alfred M. Landon would beat incumbent President Franklin D. Roosevelt by a margin of 57 percent to 43 percent of the popular vote. Roosevelt, however, won in a landslide election, receiving 62.5 percent of the popular vote and carrying all but two states.

Through the late 1940s, the number of polling groups and increasingly sophisticated polling techniques grew by leaps and bounds as new businesses and politicians relied on the information they provide to market products and candidates. In 1948, however, the polling industry suffered a severe, although fleeting, setback when Gallup and many other pollsters incorrectly predicted that Thomas E. Dewey would defeat President Harry S Truman.

What Went Wrong

Literary Digest reached out to as many potential respondents as possible, with no regard for modern sampling techniques that require that respondents be selected or sampled according to strict rules of cross-sectional representation. Respondents, in essence, were like "straws in the wind," hence the term "straw polls."

Literary Digest's sample had three fatal errors. First, its sample was drawn from telephone directories and lists of automobile owners. This technique oversampled the upper middle class and the wealthy, groups heavily Republican in political orientation. Moreover, in 1936, voting polarized along class lines. Thus the oversampling of wealthy Republicans was particularly problematic, because it severely underestimated the Democratic vote.

Literary Digest's second problem was timing. Questionnaires were mailed in early September. Thus the changes in public sentiment that occurred as the election drew closer were not measured.

Its third error occurred because of a problem we now call self-selection. Only highly motivated individuals sent back the cards—a mere 22 percent of those surveyed responded. Those who respond to mail surveys are quite different from the general electorate; they often are wealthier and better educated and care more fervently about issues. *Literary Digest*, then, failed to observe one of the now well-known cardinal rules of survey sampling: "One cannot allow the respondents to select themselves into the sample."[5]

At least one pollster, however, correctly predicted the results of the 1936 election: George Gallup. Gallup had written his dissertation on how to measure the readership of newspapers, and then expanded his methods to study public opinion about politics. He was so confident

straw poll
Unscientific survey used to gauge public opinion on a variety of issues and policies.

about his methods that he gave all of his newspaper clients a money-back guarantee: If his poll predictions weren't closer to the actual election outcome than those of the highly acclaimed *Literary Digest*, he would refund them their money. The *Digest* predicted Alf Landon to win; Gallup predicted Roosevelt. Although he underpredicted Roosevelt's victory by nearly 7 percent, the fact that he got the winner right was what everyone remembered, especially given *Literary Digest*'s dramatic miscalculation.

The Gallup Organization, now run by George's Gallup's son, continues to be a successful predictor of the popular vote. But as the 2000 presidential election reminded most Americans, it is the vote in the electoral college, not the popular vote, that ultimately counts. Thus, while George W. Bush's lead in the polls continued to shrink in the final days of polling, he won by a single vote in the electoral college. On November 7, 2000, the Gallup Organization announced, in what turned to be a major understatement, that the election was too close to call. Ultimately, Bush got 48 percent of the popular vote; Gore 49 percent.

TIMELINE
Public Opinion and
Presidential Approval

POLITICAL SOCIALIZATION AND OTHER FACTORS THAT INFLUENCE OPINION FORMATION

political socialization
The process through which an individual acquires particular political orientations; the learning process by which people acquire their political beliefs and values.

Political scientists believe that many of our attitudes about issues are grounded in our political values. We learn these values through a process called **political socialization,** "the process through which an individual acquires his [or her] particular political orientations—his [or her] knowledge, feeling and evaluations regarding his [or her] political world."[6] Family, the mass media, schools, and peers are often important influences or agents of political socialization. For example, try to remember your earliest memory of the president of the United States. It may have been Ronald Reagan or George Bush (older students probably remember earlier presidents). What did you think of him? Of the Republican or Democratic Party?

It's likely that your earliest feelings or attitudes were shaped by what your parents thought about that particular president and his party. Similar processes also apply to your early attitudes about the flag of the United States, or even the police. Other factors, too, often influence how political opinions are formed or reinforced. These include political events; the social groups you belong to, including your church; demographic group, including your race, gender, and age; and even the region of the country in which you live. Many of these factors have cross-cutting effects, too. Thus, while more women than men hold liberal political views, a married, Christian fundamentalist woman living in the rural South is likely to hold more conservative than liberal views.

The Family.   The influence of the family on political attitudes and party affiliation can be traced to two factors: communication and receptivity. Children, especially during their preschool years, spend tremendous amounts of time with their parents; early on they learn their parents' political values, even though these concepts may be vague. By the age of ten or eleven, for example, children become more selective in their perceptions of the president. By this age children raised in Democratic households are much more likely to be critical of a Republican president than are those raised in Republican households. In 1988, for example, 58 percent of children in Republican households identified themselves as Republicans, and many developed strong positive feelings toward Ronald Reagan, the Republican president. Support for and the popularity of Ronald Reagan translated into strong support for the Republican Party through the 1988 presidential election.

Religion.   Today religion plays a very important role in the life of Americans. Although only one in five citizens in 1776 belonged to a church or synagogue, today two-thirds of all Americans attend church.

In 1997, 58 percent of Americans identified themselves as Protestant, 27 percent as Catholic, 36 percent as born-again or evangelical Christians, 2 percent as Jewish, and 5 percent as other.[7] Only 9 percent claimed to have no religious affiliation. Over the years, analysts have found continuing opinion differences among these groups, with Protestants being the most conservative on many issues and Jews the most liberal. Evangelical Christians, in particular, have strong conservative views and have mobilized to have their views and beliefs converted into public policy.

Shared religious attitudes, generally transmitted through family ties, tend to affect voting and stances on particular issues. Catholics tend to vote Democratic more than do Protestants, and they tend to vote for other Catholics. For example, in 1960, Catholics overwhelmingly cast their ballots for John F. Kennedy, who became the first Catholic president. Catholics as a group also favor aid to parochial schools, most Jews support aid to Israel, and many fundamentalist Protestants support organized prayer in public schools. Seventy-eight percent of regular church-attending evangelicals voted Republican in the 1994 elections.[8] Roman Catholics and Jews, in contrast, tend to vote more Democratic. In 2000, for example, the Al Gore and Joe Lieberman ticket attracted 79 percent of the Jewish vote and 50 percent of the Catholic vote.

Gender.   From the time that the earliest public opinion polls were taken, women have been known to hold more negative views about war and military intervention than do men, and more strongly positive attitudes about issues touching on social welfare concerns, such as education, juvenile justice, capital punishment, and the environment. Some suggest that women's more "nurturing" nature and their prominent role as mothers lead women to have more liberal attitudes on issues affecting the family or the safety of their children. Research by Pamela

Johnson Conover and Virginia Sapiro, however, finds no support for a maternal explanation.[9]

Poll after poll continues to reveal that women hold very different opinions from men on a variety of issues, as shown in Table 10.1. These differences on political issues have often translated into substantial gaps in the way women and men vote. Women, for example, are more likely to be Democrats, and they often provide Democratic candidates with their margin of victory.

The charges made by former Clinton/Gore campaign volunteer Kathleen Willey against President Clinton, on one of the all-time highest-rated editions of *60 Minutes*, reveal especially interesting gender differentials. Women polled by *The Washington Post* in January 1998, for example, were less likely than men to believe that the president had an affair with Monica Lewinsky (60 percent vs. 46 percent) or sexually harassed Paula Jones (35 percent vs. 29 percent). But polls showed no **gender gap** when respondents were asked if Bill Clinton should be impeached.[10]

The historic gender gap on military issues appears to be closing. In 1999 public opinion polls on Kosovo showed no more than a ten-point gap. One *NBC News/Wall Street Journal* poll showed only a four-point difference. Experts offer several reasons for this shrinking gap, including the increased participation of women in the workforce and in the military, the "sanitized nature of much of the war footage" shown on TV, and the humanitarian reasons offered for NATO involvement in Yugoslavia.[11]

Race.   Differences in political socialization of African Americans and whites appear at a very early age. Young Black children, for example, show "great affection for the national political community, [but] this attachment becomes seriously undermined with maturation." Black children fail to hold the president in the esteem accorded him by white children; indeed, older African American children in the 1960s viewed the government primarily in terms of the U.S. Supreme Court. These differences continue through adulthood.[12]

During the O. J. Simpson trial, public opinion poll after public opinion poll revealed in stark numbers the immense racial divide that continues to exist in the nation. Blacks distrust governmental institutions far more than do whites, and are much more likely to question police

gender gap
The difference between the voting choices of men and women.

TABLE 10.1   Gender Differences on Political Issues

Favored or Supporting	*Males*	*Females*
Approve of Bill Clinton's handling of the presidency (1998)	60%	66%
Favor affirmative action for women and minorities (1998)	49	63
Favor the death penalty (1998)	71	63
Favor gun control legislation (1999)	53	75
Health care important in 2000 presidential vote	76	89

Source: Data from CNN/USA Today (December 28–30, 1994); *The Public Perspective* (June/July 1995): 38 and (April/May 1996): 39; Roper Center, *Public Opinion Online* (1998) and Gallup polls (2000).

FIGURE 10.1   Racial Attitudes on Selected Issues

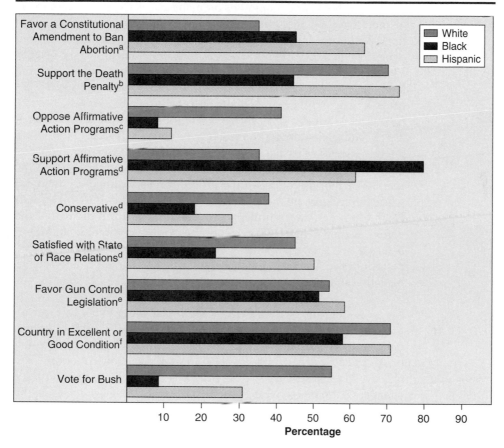

Source: Compiled by authors from 1999 National Election Study. Marjorie Connelly, "Who Voted: A Portrait of American Politics, 1976–2000," *New York Times,* November 12, 2000, C4.Questions from the Roper Center, *Public Opinion Online.*
[a]December 1996   [b]August 1997   [c]March 1998   [d]April 1998   [e]December 1998   [f]January 1999

actions. Not surprisingly, then, while a majority of whites believed that Simpson was guilty, a majority of blacks believed that he was innocent.

Race is an exceptionally important factor in elections and in the study of public opinion. As highlighted by the O. J. Simpson example, the direction and intensity of African American opinion on a variety of hot-button issues is often quite different from that of whites. As revealed in Figure 10.1, whites oppose affirmative action plans at significantly higher levels than do Blacks or Hispanics. Likewise, significant differences in public opinion can be seen in other areas, including public assistance and welfare, food stamps, federal aid for cities, support for the death penalty, and support for President Clinton after release of The Starr Report chronicling his affair with Monica Lewinsky.

Hispanics, Asians/Pacific Islanders, and Native Americans are other identifiable ethnic minorities in the United States that often respond differently to issues than do whites. Generally, Hispanics and Native Americans hold similar opinions on many issues largely because many of them have low incomes and find themselves targets of discrimination. Within the Hispanic community, however, existing divisions often depend on national origin. Generally, Cuban Americans who cluster in Florida (and in the Miami-Dade County area in particular) are more likely to be conservative. They fled from communism and Fidel Castro in Cuba, and they generally vote Republican. In contrast, Latinos (people of Mexican origin) voting in California, New Mexico, Arizona, Texas, and Colorado are more likely to vote Democratic. On issues directly affecting a particular group, sentiments are often markedly different. As our opening vignette illustrated, black voters perceived the fairness of Florida vote counting procedures very differently than did whites. Similarly, public sentiment in the Cuban community about Elian Gonzales, for example, was quite different from the rest of the nation. Although nearly 90 percent of the Cuban community in Miami believed that Elian should be allowed to say in the United States,[13] 56 percent of the American public believed that he should be returned to his father in Cuba.[14]

Age.   As a group, senior citizens are much more likely to favor an increased governmental role in the area of medical insurance and to oppose any cuts in Social Security benefits. In the future the "graying of America" will have major social and political consequences. The elderly over age seventy vote in much larger numbers than do their younger counterparts. Moreover, the fastest-growing age group in the United States is that of citizens over the age of sixty-five. Thus not only are there more people in this category, but they are more likely to be registered to vote, and often vote conservatively.

Age also seems to have a decided effect on one's view of the proper role of government, with older people continuing to be affected by having lived through the Depression and World War II. Political scientist Susan A. MacManus predicts that as Baby Boomers age, the age gap in political beliefs about political issues, especially governmental programs, will increase.[15] Young people, for example, resist higher taxes to fund Medicare, while the elderly resist all efforts to limit medicare or Social Security.

Region.   Regional and sectional differences have been important factors in the development and maintenance of public opinion and political beliefs since colonial times. As the United States grew and developed into a major industrial nation, waves of immigrants with different religious traditions and customs entered the United States and often settled in areas they viewed as hospitable to their way of life. For example, thousands of Scandinavians settled in cold, snowy, rural Minnesota, and many Irish settled in the urban centers of the Northeast, as did many Italians and Jews. All brought with them unique views about many issues, as well as about the role of government. Many of these regional differences continue to affect public opinion today and sometimes result in conflict at the national level.

Recall, for example, that during the Constitutional Convention most southerners staunchly advocated a weak national government. Nearly a hundred years later, the Civil War was fought in part because of basic differences in philosophy toward government (states' rights in the South versus national rights in the North). As we know from the results of modern political polling, the South has continued to lag behind the rest of the nation on support for civil rights, while continuing to favor return of power to the states at the expense of the national government.

The South is also much more religious than the rest of the nation, as well as more Protestant. Sixty-four percent of the South is Protestant (versus 39 percent for the rest of the nation), and 45 percent identify themselves as born-again Christians. Nearly half of all Southerners believe that "the United States is a Christian country, and the government should make laws to keep it that way."[16] It is not surprising, then, that the Christian Coalition has been very successful at mobilizing voters in the South.

Southerners also are much more supportive of a strong national defense. They accounted for 41 percent of the troops in the Persian Gulf in the early days of that war, even though they made up only 28 percent of the general population.

The West, too, now appears "different" from other sections of the nation. Some people have moved there to avoid city life; other residents have an antigovernment bias. Many who have sought refuge there are staunchly against any governmental action, especially on the national level.

The Impact of Events.   You probably have some professors who remember what they were doing on the day that President John F. Kennedy was killed—November 22, 1963. This dramatic event is indelibly etched in the minds of virtually all people who were old enough to be aware of it. Similarly, most college students today remember where they were when the space shuttle *Challenger* exploded, or when they learned about the Oklahoma City bombing.

President Richard M. Nixon's fall from grace and forced resignation in 1974 also had a profound impact on the socialization process of all Americans. It made a particular impression on young people, who were forced to realize that their government was not always right or honest.

In fact, one problem in discussing political socialization is that many of the major studies on this topic were conducted in the aftermath of these and other crucial events, including the civil rights movement and the Vietnam War, all of which produced a marked increase in Americans' distrust of government. Dramatic drop-off of trust in government began in the mid-1960s and continued through the election of Ronald Reagan in 1980. In a study of Boston children conducted in the aftermath of the Watergate scandal, for example, one political scientist found that children's perception of the president went from that of a benevolent to a "malevolent" leader.[17] These findings are indicative of the low confidence most Americans had in government in the aftermath of Watergate and President Nixon's ultimate resignation from office to avoid impeachment.

Interestingly, confidence in government remained high during the Clinton scandal in 1998, although still down from the Watergate years. But the issues surrounding the Clinton impeachment have raised concerns about their impact on young people, especially Generation Y. Some studies show that their views toward the president and political affairs are significantly more negative than ever before—including Watergate.[18] It is still probably too early to determine what, if any, long-term impact the tumultuous 2000 presidential election will have on views toward the presidency and the electoral system more generally.

The Mass Media.   The media today are taking on a growing role as a socialization agent and molder of public opinion. Adult Americans spend nearly thirty hours a week in front of their television sets; children spend even more.[19] Television has a tremendous impact on how people view politics, government, and politicians. TV talk shows and talk radio are an important source of information about politics for many, yet the information that people get from these sources is often skewed. One study, for example, found that 25 percent of all Americans learned about presidential campaigns from David Letterman and Jay Leno.[20] By 2000, another study was estimating that 51 percent of all adults regularly got information about the election or candidates from alternative sources such as comedy shows like *Saturday Night Live* or MTV. For those younger than thirty, that figure soared to 79 percent.[21]

Television can serve to enlighten voters or encourage voter turnout. For example, MTV began coverage of presidential campaigns in 1992 and had reporters traveling with both major candidates to heighten young people's awareness of the stakes in the campaign. Its "Choose or Loose" campaign in the 1992, 1996, and 2000 elections was designed to enhance the abysmal turnout rates of young voters. When an MTV poll found only 33 percent of those age eighteen to twenty-four planned to vote, it stepped up its efforts.[22] Recognizing this, both candidates appeared on *Saturday Night Live* poking fun at themselves. Both also appeared on *Jay Leno, David Letterman, Oprah Winfrey*, and *Live with Regis*. George W. Bush even donned a Regis-like monochromatic shirt and tie for the event. After his appearances with Oprah and Regis, Bush's poll numbers rose.[23]

All of the major candidates in the 2000 election also attempted to use another form of "media" to sway and inform the voters: the Internet, a form of campaigning that was, believe it or not, still considered new in 1996. By 2000, although some still doubt its effectiveness, not only had each presidential and most other major and minor campaigns launched their own Internet sites, but all of the major networks and newspapers had their own Internet sites reporting on the election. There was an Internet Alley at the Republican and Democratic National Conventions, and on election night, millions of hits were counted on election-related news sites as voters logged on to get the most up to date coverage. In fact, the outcome of the presidential election was first called online, prompting other forms of media to follow quickly.

One poll conducted after the 2000 election found that one in three voters followed the campaign online—three times the number who did in 1996. Nationwide, 11 percent of voters listed the Internet as their major source of information about campaign news; an additional 19 percent reported that they got some of their information about the election online.[24] Forty-two percent of voters under age thirty reported that the net was their major source of information about the campaign.

Political Ideology and Public Opinion About Government.   As discussed in chapter 1, an individual's coherent set of values and beliefs about the purpose and scope of government is called his or her **political ideology.** Americans' attachment to strong ideological positions has varied over time. In sharp contrast to spur-of-the-moment responses, these sets of values, which are often greatly affected by political socialization, can prompt citizens to favor a certain set of policy programs and adopt views about the proper role of government in the policy process.

Conservatives are generally likely to support smaller, less activist governments, limited social welfare programs, and limited government regulation of business. In contrast, liberals generally believe that the national government has an important role to play in a wide array of areas, including helping the poor and disadvantaged. Unlike most conservatives, they generally favor activist governments.

Political scientists and politicians often talk in terms of conservative and liberal ideologies, and most Americans believe that they hold a political ideology. In a study by the Roper Center, when asked, most Americans (42 percent) responded that their political beliefs are "middle of the road" or moderate, although a substantial number called themselves conservatives (39 percent).

political ideology
An individual's coherent set of values and beliefs about the purpose and scope of government.

VISUAL LITERACY
Who Are Liberals and Conservatives? What's the Difference?

WEB EXPLORATION
For the most recent Roper Center polls, go to www.ablongman.com/oconnor

HOW WE FORM POLITICAL OPINIONS

Many of us hold opinions on a wide range of political issues, and our ideas can be traced to our social group and the different experiences each of us has had. Some individuals (called ideologues) think about politics and vote strictly on the basis of liberal or conservative ideology. Others use the party label. Most people, however, don't do either. Most people—those who are not ideologues—filter their ideas about politics through the factors discussed earlier but are also influenced by

PARTICIPATION
Which Are You: Liberal or Conservative?

(1) personal benefits, (2) political knowledge, and (3) cues from various leaders or opinion makers.

Personal Benefits.   Most polls reveal that Americans are growing more and more "I" centered. This perspective often leads people to choose policies that best benefit them personally. You've probably heard the adage, "People vote with their pocketbooks." Taxpayers generally favor lower taxes; hence, the popularity of candidates pledging "No new taxes." Similarly, the elderly usually support Social Security increases, and Generation X, worried about the continued stability of the Social Security program, is not very supportive of federal retirement programs. Generation Y, or Generation NeXt, appears even less willing to support retirement programs. Similarly, African Americans support strong civil rights laws and affirmative action programs, while most whites do not.

Some government policies, however, don't really affect us individually. Legalized prostitution and the death penalty, for example, are often perceived as moral issues that few citizens experience. Individuals' attitudes on these issues are often based on underlying values they have acquired through the years.

When we are faced with policies that don't affect us personally and don't involve moral issues, we often have difficulty forming an opinion. Foreign policy is an area in which this phenomenon is especially true. Most Americans often know little of the world around them, and public opinion is likely to be volatile in the wake of any new information.

Political Knowledge.   Americans enjoy a relatively high literacy rate, and most Americans (82 percent) graduate from high school. Most Americans, moreover, have access to a range of higher education opportunities. In spite of that access to education, however, Americans' level of actual political knowledge is low. Americans generally don't know much about politics. In a survey one month before the 2000 presidential election, for example, MTV found that one-quarter of those age eighteen to twenty-four could not name both presidential candidates; 70 percent couldn't name the running mates.[25] Knowledge, however, is often related to interest. Given both major candidates' emphasis on issues of concern to the elderly such as Social Security, Medicare, and prescription drugs, it may be that young people, turned off, tuned out.

In 1925 Walter Lippmann critiqued the American democratic experience and highlighted the large but limited role the population plays. Citizens, said Lippmann, cannot know everything about candidates and issues but they can, and often do, know enough to impose their views and values as to the general direction the nation should take.[26] This generalized information often stands in contrast and counterbalance to the views held by more knowledgeable political elites "inside the Beltway."

As early as 1966, V. O. Key argued in his book *The Responsible Electorate* that voters "are not fools." Since then, many political scientists have argued that generalizable knowledge is enough to make democracy work.

WEB EXPLORATION
To test your political knowledge, see
www.ablongman.com/oconnor

Research, for example, shows citizens' perception "of the policy stands of parties and candidates were considerably more clear and accurate when the stands themselves were more distinct: in the highly ideological election of 1964, for example, as opposed to that of 1957, or in the primaries rather than the general election of 1968."[27] In elections with sharper contrasts between candidates, voters also seemed to pay more attention to issues when they cast their ballots, and to have more highly structured liberal-conservative belief systems.[28] In addition, the use of more sophisticated analytical methods involving perceived issue distances between candidates and voters seemed to reveal more issue voting in general than had previously been discovered.[29]

Cues from Leaders   Low levels of knowledge can lead to rapid opinion shifts on issues. The ebb and flow of popular opinion can be affected dramatically (some might say "manipulated") by political leaders. Given the visibility of political leaders and their access to the media, it is easy to see the important role they play in influencing public opinion. Political leaders, members of the news media, and a host of other experts have regular opportunities to influence public opinion because of the lack of deep conviction with which most Americans hold many of their political beliefs.

The president, especially, is often in a position to mold public opinion through effective use of the "bully pulpit." Political scientist John E. Mueller concludes, in fact, that there is a group of citizens—called *followers*—who are inclined to rally to the support of the president no matter what he does.[30]

HOW WE MEASURE PUBLIC OPINION

Public officials at all levels use a variety of measures as indicators of public opinion to guide their policy decisions. These measures include election results; the number of telephone calls, faxes, or e-mail messages received pro and con on any particular issue; letters to the editor in hometown papers; and the size of demonstrations or marches. But the most commonly relied-on measure of public sentiment continues to be the public opinion survey, more popularly called a **public opinion poll.** Polling has several key phases.

Determining the Content and Phrasing the Questions.   Once a candidate, politician, or news organization decides to use a poll to measure the public's attitudes, special care has to be taken in constructing the questions to be asked. For example, if your professor asked you, "Do you think my grading procedures are fair?" you might give a slightly different answer than you would if asked, "In general, how fair do you think the grading is in your American Politics course?" The wording of the first question tends to put you on the spot and personalize the grading

public opinion poll
Interviews or surveys with a sample of citizens that are used to estimate public opinion of the entire population.

style; the second question is more neutral. Even more obvious differences appear in the real world of polling, especially when interested groups want a poll to yield particular results. Responses to highly emotional issues such as abortion, busing, and affirmative action are often skewed, depending on the wording of the question.

Selecting the Sample.　Once the decision is made to take a poll, pollsters must determine the *universe,* or the entire group whose attitudes they wish to measure. This universe could be all Americans, all voters, all city residents, all women, or all Democrats. Although in a perfect world each individual would be asked to give an opinion, this kind of polling is simply not practical. Consequently, pollsters take a sample of the universe in which they are interested. One way to obtain this sample is by **random sampling.** This method of selection gives each potential voter or adult the same chance of being selected. In theory, this sounds good, but it is actually impossible to achieve because no one has lists of every person in any group. This is why the method of poll taking is extremely important in determining the validity and reliability of the results.

Most national surveys and commercial polls use samples from 1,000 to 1,500 individuals and use a variation of the random sampling method called **stratified sampling.** Stratified sampling is based on census data that provides the number of residences in an area and their location. Researchers divide the country into four sampling regions. They then randomly select a set of counties and standard metropolitan statistical areas in proportion to the total national population.

About twenty respondents from each primary sampling unit are selected to be interviewed. Generally four or five city blocks or areas are selected, and then four or five target families from each district are used. Large, sophisticated surveys like the National Election Study and General Social Survey, which produce the data commonly used by political scientists, attempt to sample from lists of persons living in each household. The key to the success of the stratified sampling method is not to let people volunteer to be interviewed—volunteers as a group often have different opinions from those who don't volunteer.

Stratified sampling (the most rigorous sampling technique) is generally not used by those who do surveys reported in the *New York Times* and *USA Today* or on network news programs. Instead, those organizations or pollsters working for them randomly survey every tenth, hundredth, or thousandth person or household. If those individuals are not at home, they go to the home or apartment next door.

Contacting Respondents.　After selecting the methodology to conduct the poll, the next question is how to contact those to be surveyed. Television stations often ask people to call in, and some surveyors hit the streets. Telephone polls, however, are becoming the most frequently used mechanism by which to gauge the temper of the electorate.

The most common form of telephone polls are random-digit dialing surveys, in which a computer randomly selects telephone numbers

random sampling
A method of selection that gives each potential voter or adult the same chance of being selected for a poll.

stratified sampling
A variation of random sampling; census data are used to divide a country into four sampling regions. Sets of counties and standard metropolitan statistical areas are then randomly selected in proportion to the total national population.

to be dialed. Because it is estimated that as many as 95 percent of the American public have telephones in their homes, samples selected in this manner are likely to be fairly representative.

Individual, in-person interviews are conducted by some groups, such as by the University of Michigan for the National Election Studies. Some analysts favor such in-person surveys, but others argue that the unintended influence of the questioner or pollster is an important source of errors. How the pollster dresses, relates to the person being interviewed, and even asks the questions can affect responses. (Some of these factors, such as tone of voice or accent, can also affect the results of telephone surveys.)

Political Polls.   As polling has become more and more sophisticated and networks, newspapers, and magazines compete with each other to report the most up-to-the-minute changes in public opinion on issues or political candidates, new types of polls have been suggested and put into use. Each type of poll has contributed much to our knowledge of public opinion and its role in the political process.

During the 2000 presidential elections, **tracking polls,** which were taken on a daily basis by some news organizations (see Figure 10.2), were introduced to allow candidates to monitor short-term campaign developments and the effects of their campaign strategy.

Tracking polls involve small samples and are conducted every twenty-four hours (usually of registered voters contacted at certain times of day). They are usually combined with some kind of a moving statistical average to boost the sample size and therefore the statistical reliability.[31] Even though such one-day surveys are fraught with reliability problems, many major news organizations continued their use as they reported on the 2000 presidential campaign. As revealed in Figure 10.2, the 2000 tracking polls failed to pick up the upswing in Vice

(Photo courtesy: © Tribune Media Services, Inc. All rights reserved. Reprinted with permission.)

tracking poll
Continuous surveys that enable a campaign to chart its daily rise or fall.

FIGURE 10.2   A Daily Update Tracking Poll of the 2000 Presidential Election

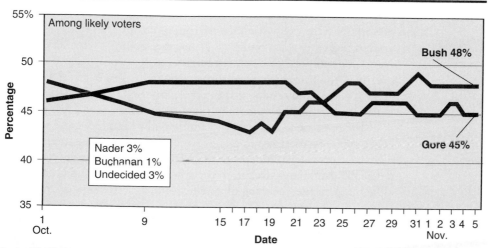

Source: "Washington Post Daily Tracking Poll," *The Washington Post.* November 7, 2000, p. A17. Copyright ©2000, The Washington Post. Reprinted with permisson

POINT / COUNTERPOINT

SHOULD POLITICS BE DRIVEN BY POLLS?

Polling is everywhere. Every newspaper and TV station seems to run polls about everything from your preference on toilet tissue to your attitude toward immigration policies. The Internet is awash with polls, some scientific and some not so scientific. Good polls can help us understand the world around us, and bad polls can confuse us. The use of polling in politics is controversial in part because there are good and bad polls, but also because polls are being used today as a means of governance and not just for information. Since FDR, all American presidents have used polls in some way, but their use has become more controversial in the last ten years. Bill Clinton was an avid and frequent user of polls. George W. Bush says he will not be guided by polls but by principle. Should a president use polls on a frequent basis, or should a president be guided more by principle and ideology? Let's examine these two points of view.

Advocates of poll-driven politics, such as former Presidents Bill Clinton and George Bush, believe that it can help the public good. During his presidency, Clinton relied on techniques designed to constantly gauge public opinion and respond to it in a variety of ways. According to *The Washington Post*, "no previous president read public opinion surveys with the same hypnotic intensity" (December 30, 2000). Clinton's administration took hundreds of polls, from daily polls during the campaign or crises to weekly polls during quieter times. Policy decisions that were heavily poll-driven include devoting the surplus to "save Social Security first," protecting the privacy of medical and financial records, and prohibiting needle exchanges for drug addicts to combat AIDS. Phrases such as "risky tax scheme" were tested and refined through polling. Mark Penn, Clinton's primary pollster, argued that polls are all about democracy, allowing voices to be heard that

President Gore's popular vote, although the differences between the two candidates were well within the margin of error of the poll.

Exit polls are polls conducted at selected polling places on Election Day. Generally, large news organizations send pollsters to selected precincts to sample every tenth voter as he or she emerges from the polling place. The results of these polls are used to help the television networks predict the outcome of key races, often just a few minutes after the polls close in a particular state and generally before voters in other areas—sometimes in a later time zone—have cast their ballots. They also provide an independent assessment of why voters supported particular candidates "free from the spin that managers and candidates alike place on the 'meaning of an election.'"[32]

exit poll
Poll conducted at selected polling places on Election Day.

Shortcomings of Polling.   In 1990, the major television networks consolidated their polling operations under the umbrella of Voter News Ser-

might otherwise be silent. Clinton himself said that polling is a tool that a president ought to use to find out what the people want. According to supporters of this use for polls, polling helps politicians find consensus and is democratic because those polled are the people themselves. They claim that the alternative to polling is relying heavily on special interest groups and people with lots of money, access, and influence.

Opponents of governing through polls, such as George W. Bush and former U.S. Senator Bob Dole, argue that too heavy a reliance on polls drains politics of meaning and encourages cynicism. Many of Clinton's political opponents believe that the manipulation of public opinion by the former president increased public cynicism about government and harmed the public good. They argue that elected officials ought to lead the people, not follow polls that often twitch and change with the political winds; sometimes the right thing to do is the unpopular thing. Leaders should educate the people and inform them about their ideas, not simply ask everyone their opinion. A president should not aim to be popular but should accomplish something and maintain his principles. According to comments made during the 2000 campaign, George W. Bush seems to agree with these sentiments.

In addition, there seems to be skepticism about the accuracy of polls. Many opponents of governing by polls question whether polls measure public opinion or simply give a snapshot of a certain point in time. Accurate polling is very difficult, and political polling can often be deliberately inaccurate. Some doubt whether a sample of 1,500 to 2,000 randomly selected people can represent a population of 280 million.

What do you think? Should politics be driven by polls?
Go to www.ablongman.com/oconnor

vice (VNS), which was a major cost-saving measure for all involved. But the construction of a single questionnaire and one data set meant that problems could arise, as was evident in the 2000 Election Night projections. In 1992 the VNS data significantly overpredicted the support for Republican candidate Patrick Buchanan in the New Hampshire primary, and showed President Bush to be in much more trouble than he was. Armed with these erroneous survey results, commentator after commentator (all relying on the same data) predicted a narrow victory for Bush—who actually went on to win by a healthy sixteen-point margin. Nevertheless, "many Americans went to bed believing that the president had been badly damaged."[33] This kind of reporting based on inaccurate polls can skew the rest of a campaign, particularly in an era when campaigns are viewed as horse races and everyone wants to know who's winning and by how much. Thus polls and the way they are reported can affect election outcomes; they are a powerful tool that gives the media

POLICY IN ACTION

A NEW GENERATION OF POLLING

As more dissatisfaction with traditional polling methods becomes clear, a variety of new forms of measuring public sentiment are now being devised using the Internet as a new medium. One company, DiscoveryWhy.com, used Internet polling to measure the responses of potential voters to Al Gore's speech accepting the presidential nomination at the 2000 Democratic National Convention.[a] Participants rated his performance with mouse clicks as they watched the address on television and the results could be known almost instantaneously. The 300 watchers—a smaller sample than used for phone polls—were drawn from lists created by the company and were by invitation only. Thus, DiscoveryWhy.com attempts to approximate the same kind of reliability as phone surveys, but with potentially quicker gauges of public opinion for politicians, policy makers, and pundits.

Harris Interactive, an Internet-based marketing firm, used the Internet to achieve a 99 percent accuracy rate in seventy-three political contests in November 2000.[b] Harris's margin of error was 1.9 percent; conventional polling was off by 3.9 percent for Gore and 3.9 percent for Bush. Harris even predicted that Gore would win the popular vote but lose the electoral college vote. How did they do it? Over 300,000 members of the voting-age public participated in the poll online from October 30 through November 6, 2000. The company processed over 40,000 online interviews per hour, including 7,800 simultaneous interviews. The final data were then weighted and tabulated. The results could change the face of polling as we know it, especially in light of the errors in traditional methods that occurred in 2000.

---

[a]Steve Marantz, "Dotcom Finds a Future Cyber Polling," *Boston Herald* (September 25, 2000): 21.
[b]"2000 Election Winners: George W. Bush and Online Polling," *Business Wire* (December 14, 2000).

WEB EXPLORATION
For problems with early VNS-based calls in the 2000 election, go to www.ablongman.com/oconnor

additional sway in the democratic process. (For more on VNS see Politics Now: Exit Polling and the 2000 Election.)

The accuracy of any poll depends on the quality of the sample that was drawn. Small samples, if properly drawn, can be very accurate if each unit in the universe has an equal opportunity to be sampled. If a pollster, for example, fails to sample certain populations, his or her results may reflect that shortcoming. Often, the opinions of the poor and homeless are underrepresented because insufficient attention is given to making certain that these groups are representatively sampled. In the case of tracking polls, if you choose to sample only on weekends or from 5 P.M. to 9 P.M., you may get more Republicans, who are less likely to have jobs that require them to work in the evening or on weekends. There comes a point in sampling, however, where increases in the size of the sample have little effect on a reduction of the **sampling error** (also called **margin of error**), the difference between the actual universe and the sample.

sampling error or margin of error
A measure of the accuracy of a public opinion poll.

HIGHLIGHT

IS THERE TOO MUCH POLLING?

You may be one of those people who questions the polls because you have never been sampled. You need only to read a daily paper or watch television to recognize that polls are being conducted all the time. In the wake of this potential for too much information, the Gallup Organization has even polled Americans to see if there has been too much coverage of media events. They didn't ask, however, if there was too much polling about beliefs concerning those events.

What events did Gallup select to ask about? The 2000 post-election controversy, the Columbine High School shootings, the Clinton-Lewinsky scandal, and the death of Britain's Princess Diana. Gallup reports that 51 percent of the public thought that post-election coverage was about right. Similar sentiments were reported about the shootings (50%) and the death of the princess (49%). Only the Clinton-Lewinsky affair was judged by the American public to be overreported by the news media—72 percent believed it was overdone; only 22 percent thought coverage was about right.

Clearly, there is a poll for every issue. What are the merits of these kinds of polls? Who might be swayed by their findings?

Source: All data reported here are from The Gallup Organization, "Poll Releases: Americans Divided Over Whether There Is Too Much Media Coverage of the Election," http://www.gallup.cpm/poll/releases/pr001201.asp.

All polls contain errors. Standard samples of approximately 1,000 to 1,500 individuals provide fairly good estimates of actual behavior (in the case of voting, for example). Typically, the margin of error in a sample of 1,500 will be about 3 percent. If you ask 1,500 people "Do you like ice cream?" and 52 percent say "yes" and 48 percent say "no," the results are too close to tell whether more people like ice cream than not. Why? Because the margin of error implies that somewhere between 55 percent (52 + 3) and 49 percent (52 - 3) of the people like ice cream, while between 51 percent (48 + 3) and 45 percent (48 - 3) do not. The margin of error in a close election makes predictions very difficult.

Polls can be inaccurate when they limit responses. If you are asked, "How do you like this class?" and are given only like or dislike options, your full sentiments may not be tapped if you like the class very much or feel only so-so about it.

SIMULATION
You Are a Polling
Consultant

Public opinion polls may also be off when they attempt to gauge attitudes about issues that some or even many individuals don't care about or about which the public has little information. For example, few Americans probably care about the elimination of the electoral college. If a representative sample were polled, many would answer pro or con without having given much consideration to the question.

POLITICS NOW

EXIT POLLING AND THE
2000 ELECTIONS

When the *Literary Digest* miscalled the 1948 presidential election, its call went into the error hall of fame. The Voter News Service (VNS), however, is likely to take the overall prize for bad judgment although it never actually called the 2000 race for either candidate. Instead, the networks and news services looked at data provided by VNS and made their own calls. None, however, were aware of the problems below.

According to a confidential report of VNS, its polling was plagued with errors all night long in Florida. The polling firm had no reliable way of estimating the number of Florida's absentee ballots, which were nearly double the expected number. It estimated that the absentee ballots would make up 7.2 percent of all of the ballots cast; instead, they were 12 percent. VNS also misprojected how many of those absentee votes would go to Governor Bush, estimating 22.4 percent when it actually was 23.7. "That mistake alone accounted for 1.3 percentage points of the 7.3 percent lead that Gore was projected to hold at 7:50 that night."*

Prior to the election, VNS failed to conduct any telephone polling in Florida as it had done in traditionally absentee-heavy states such as California, Oregon, and Washington, in an effort to estimate the magnitude or direction of absentee voting. Essentially, it overlooked the politics of the state where the Republican Party was headed by the brother of one of the candidates. Phone polling is labor intensive and expensive, and according to VNS, its budget simply didn't allow it to sample every state.

An additional part of Gore's projected lead—2.8 percent—was inflated because of results from forty-five sample polls. This error, while in the range of acceptable error for exit polls, added to the inaccuracy of VNS's actions on Election Night. The rest of its error—3.2 percent—came from the exit poll model that it used. Instead of relying on the vote model of 1996 Republican presidential candidate Bob Dole, VNS used the 1998 Florida gubernatorial vote for Jeb Bush as an indicator of how his older brother would fare in 2000. Critics charge that since more voters turn out in presidential elections, 1996 should have been used as a baseline instead of 1998 when comparisons were being made to project the winner in 2000. Finally, at 7:50 P.M., VNS's Tampa exit poll was off by 16 percentage points, but no actual votes were yet reported there or in Miami. Thus, VNS was unable to modify any of its exit poll errors in Tampa and Miami, where its polls were the most off.

VNS's quality control was also off. It failed to reject, for example, an early report that 95 percent of Duval County's votes were for Gore. Moreover, because it used far smaller samples than the networks had used before creation of VNS, it overestimated the size of the black vote and underestimated the Cuban vote. The likely outcome of this debacle? Increased mistrust of polls, heightened discretion in calling elections, and the creation of a new polling consortium to replace VNS, whose credibility has been irreparably damaged.

What other effects do you think the failures of this polling firm will have?

Do you see problems with all major media outlets relying on a single source for their election-night polling?

---

*This account of errors in the VNS poll draws heavily on "New Group Admits Poll Errors: Probe Also Reveals Use of Risky Techniques," *The Washington Post* (December 24, 2000): A7.

Most academic public opinion research organizations, such as the National Election Study, use some kind of filter question that first asks respondents whether or not they have thought about the question. These screening procedures generally allow surveyors to exclude as many as 20 percent of their respondents, especially on complex issues like the federal budget. Questions on more personal issues such as moral values, drugs, crime, race, and women's role in society get far fewer "no opinion" or "don't know" responses.

Another shortcoming of polls concerns their inability to measure intensity of feeling about particular issues. Whereas a respondent might answer affirmatively to any question, it is likely that his or her feelings about issues such as abortion, the death penalty, or support for U.S. troops in the Gulf are much more intense than are his or her feelings about the electoral college.

David Duke, the controversial Louisiana politician with ties to the Ku Klux Klan, ran in a special election in 1999 for the seat vacated by Rep. Bob Livingston. Duke came in third.(Photo courtesy: J. Pat Carter/AP/Wide World Photos)

THE NEWS MEDIA

The media have the potential to exert enormous influence over Americans. Not only does the press tell us what is important by setting the agenda for what we will watch and read, but it can also influence what we think about issues through the content of the news stories. The simple words of the Constitution's First Amendment, "Congress shall make no law . . . abridging the freedom of the speech, or of the press" have shaped the American republic as much as or more than any others in the Constitution and its amendments. This freedom has been crucial in facilitating the political discourse and education necessary for the maintenance of democracy.

The American Press of Yesteryear

The first newspapers were published in the American colonies in 1690 and quickly had an impact on public opinion. The number of newspapers grew throughout the 1700s, as colonists began to realize the value of a press free from government oversight and censorship. Thus it was not surprising that one of the most important demands made by Anti-Federalists during our country's constitutional debate was that an amendment guaranteeing the freedom of the press be included in the final version of the Constitution.

It is important to remember that the reference to the media as "the fourth branch of government," while a provocative notion, is a complete fiction. In other words, an American media outlet might choose, or have chosen, stridently to support a particular political party, platform, issue, or official, but it would do so as an independent voice of private citizens or a private organization, not as the concealed organ of the government in power (contrast this system with those of totalitarian regimes, in which a state news agency is often the only, and inevitably a highly biased, source of information). This distinction can be difficult to maintain under some circumstances, as this chapter will discuss, but its basic reliability continues to provide the basis for journalistic integrity in America.

Thomas Jefferson was instrumental in establishing an Anti-Federalist newspaper. The *National Gazette* was created to compete with the *Gazette of the United States* founded earlier by Alexander Hamilton and his anti-Jefferson Federalists. The era of party newspapers extended from Washington's tenure through Andrew Jackson's presidency. The editor of Jackson's party paper, *The Globe,* was included in the president's influential "Kitchen Cabinet" (a group of informal advisers), and all of Jackson's appointees with annual salaries greater than $1,000 were required to buy a subscription.

The partisan presses eventually gave way to what was called the penny press. In 1833 Benjamin Day founded the *New York Sun,* which cost a penny at the newsstand. Because it was not tied to one party, it was politically more independent than the party papers. The *Sun* was the forerunner of the modern press built on mass circulation and commercial advertising to produce profit.

The press thus became markedly less partisan but not necessarily more respectable. Mass-circulation dailies sought wide readership, and readers were clearly attracted by the sensational and the scandalous. The sordid side of politics became the entertainment of the times. One of the best-known examples occurred in the presidential campaign of 1884, when the *Buffalo Evening Telegraph* headlined "A Terrible Tale" about Grover Cleveland, the Democratic nominee.[34] In 1871, while sheriff of Buffalo, the bachelor Cleveland had allegedly fathered a child. Even though the woman in question had been seeing other men, Cleveland willingly accepted responsibility since all the other men were married, and he had dutifully paid child support for years. Fortunately for Cleveland, another newspaper, the *Democratic Sentinel,* broke a story that helped to offset this scandal: Republican presidential nominee James G. Blaine and his wife had had their first child just three months after their wedding. There is a lesson for politicians in this double-edged morality tale. Cleveland acknowledged his responsibility forthrightly and took his lumps, whereas Blaine told a fabulously elaborate, completely unbelievable story about having had two marriage ceremonies six months apart. Cleveland won the election (although other factors also played a role in his victory).

In the late 1800s and early 1900s, the era of the intrusive press was in full flower. First yellow journalism and then muckraking were in fashion. Pioneered by prominent publishers such as William Randolph

Hearst and Joseph Pulitzer, **yellow journalism**[35] featured pictures, comics, and color designed to capture a share of the burgeoning immigrant population market. These newspapers also oversimplified and sensationalized many news developments. The front-page editorial crusade became common, the motto for which frequently seemed to be, "Damn the truth, full speed ahead."

After the turn of the century, the muckrakers—so named by President Theodore Roosevelt after a special rake designed to collect manure[36]—took charge of a number of newspapers and nationally circulated magazines. **Muckraking** journalists searched out and exposed real and apparent misconduct by government, business, and politicians in order to stimulate reform.[37] There was no shortage of corruption to reveal, of course, and much good came from these efforts. But an unfortunate side effect of the emphasis on crusades and investigations was the frequent publication of gossip and rumor without sufficient proof.

The modern press corps may also be guilty of this offense, but it has achieved great progress on another front. Throughout the nineteenth century, payoffs to the press were not uncommon. Andrew Jackson, for instance, gave one in ten of his early appointments to loyal reporters,[38] and during the 1872 presidential campaign, the Republicans slipped cash to about 300 newsmen.[39] Wealthy industrialists also sometimes purchased editorial peace or investigative cease-fire for tens of thousands of dollars. Examples of such press corruption are exceedingly rare today, and not even the most extreme of the modern media's critics believe otherwise.

As the news business grew, its focus gradually shifted from passionate opinion to corporate profit. Newspapers, hoping to maximize profit, were more careful to avoid alienating the advertisers and readers who produced their revenues, and the result was less harsh, more objective reporting. Meanwhile, media barons such as Joseph Pulitzer and William Randolph Hearst became pillars of the establishment; for the most part, they were no longer the antiestablishment insurgents of yore.

Technological advances had a major impact on this transformation in journalism. High-speed presses and more cheaply produced paper made mass-circulation dailies possible. The telegraph and then the telephone made news gathering easier and much faster, and nothing could compare to the invention of radio and television. When radio became widely available in the 1920s, millions of Americans could hear national politicians instead of merely reading about them. With television— first introduced in the late 1940s, and nearly a universal fixture in U.S. homes by the mid-1950s—citizens could see and hear candidates and presidents. The removal of newspapers and magazines as the foremost conduits between politicians and voters had profound effects on the electoral process, as we discuss shortly.

yellow journalism

A form of newspaper publishing that featured pictures, comics, color, and sensationalized, oversimplified news coverage.

muckraking

A form of newspaper publishing concerned with reforming-government and business conduct.

WEB EXPLORATION
For examples of nineteenth-century yellow journalism, go to www.ablongman.com/oconnor

TIMELINE
300 Years of
U.S. Media

The Contemporary Media Scene

The editors of the first partisan newspapers could scarcely have imagined what their profession would become more than two centuries later. The number and diversity of media outlets existing today are stunning. The **print press** includes many thousands of daily and weekly newspapers, periodicals, magazines, newsletters, and journals; the **electronic media** include radio and television stations and networks, computerized information services, and the Internet. In some ways the news business is more competitive now than at any time in history; yet paradoxically, the news media have expanded in some ways and contracted in others, dramatically changing the ways in which they cover politics.

Although the number of journalists continues to grow, they are not necessarily attracting a larger audience, at least on the print side. Daily newspaper circulation peaked in 1970 at 62 million; by 1998 it had dropped to less than 57 million papers in circulation per day. Barely half of the adult population reads a newspaper every day. Among young people only one-third are daily readers—a decline of 50 percent in two decades although many claim to get their news online.

Part of the cause of the newspapers' declining audience has been the increased numbers of television sets and cable subscribers and the increased popularity of television as a news source. At the dawn of the 1960s, a substantial majority of Americans reported that they got most of their news from newspapers. A 1997 study commissioned by the major networks found that 69 percent of Americans over eighteen cite television as the source of most of their news. Thirty-seven percent named newspapers while 15 percent get their news online. Radio was the fourth source of news. Fifty-three percent rated TV news as "the most credible"; 23 percent cited newspapers as most credible.[40] There can be little question that television news is increasingly important. Despite its many drawbacks (such as simplicity, brevity, and entertainment orientation), television news is "news that matters."[41] It has the power to greatly effect which issues viewers say are important.[42]

Additionally, at least one study of television and print news finds differences in the level of independence each shows in their reporting. Television news was less questioning of the "government line" during the Gulf War, while newspapers exhibited a greater deal of journalistic autonomy and diversity of opinion about the conduct of the war in their coverage.[43]

print press
The traditional form of mass media, comprising newspapers, magazines, and journals.

electronic media
The newest form of broadcast media, including television, radio, cable, and the Internet.

Politicians today rely on the print and electronic media to communicate their policy views to the American public. (Photo courtesy: Reuters NewMedia Inc./Corbis)

A N A L Y Z I N G   T H E   D A T A

CIRCULATION OF DAILY NEWSPAPERS, 1850–1998

In the second half of the nineteenth century, newspapers were the primary news medium, and circulation expanded dramatically as the penny press reduced the cost of newspapers and universal public education boosted literacy rates. In the second half of the twentieth century—with the advent of new media from television to the Internet—newspaper circulation dropped just as dramatically. This does not mean necessarily that people are less well informed; they may simply be getting their news from other sources.

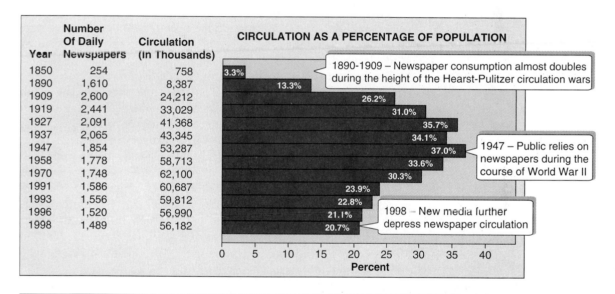

Year	Number Of Daily Newspapers	Circulation (In Thousands)
1850	254	758
1890	1,610	8,387
1909	2,600	24,212
1919	2,441	33,029
1927	2,091	41,368
1937	2,065	43,345
1947	1,854	53,287
1958	1,778	58,713
1970	1,748	62,100
1991	1,586	60,687
1993	1,556	59,812
1996	1,520	56,990
1998	1,489	56,182

CIRCULATION AS A PERCENTAGE OF POPULATION

- 1850 – 3.3%
- 1890 – 13.3%
- 1909 – 26.2%
- 1919 – 31.0%
- 1927 – 35.7%
- 1937 – 34.1%
- 1947 – 37.0%
- 1958 – 33.6%
- 1970 – 30.3%
- 1991 – 23.9%
- 1993 – 22.8%
- 1996 – 21.1%
- 1998 – 20.7%

1890-1909 – Newspaper consumption almost doubles during the height of the Hearst-Pulitzer circulation wars

1947 – Public relies on newspapers during the course of World War II

1998 – New media further depress newspaper circulation

Source: Adapted from Harold W. Stanley and Richard G. Niemi, *Vital Statistics on American Politics, 1997-1998 (6th ed.).* (Washington, D.C.: Congressional Quarterly, Inc. 1998, Table 4-2, pp 163–64. *Editor & Publisher Yearbook 1999.*

The television news industry differs from its print counterpart in a variety of ways. The number of outlets has been increasing, not declining, as with newspapers. The four major networks now receive broadcast competition from Cable News Network (CNN), C-SPAN, Fox News, and MSNBC, as well as PBS's *News Hour/Jim Lehrer.* Although the audiences of all the alternate shows are relatively small compared with those of the network news shows, they are growing while the networks' audience shares of the viewing audience get smaller. The growth of cable television has been tremendous over the last thirty years. Today, over 80 percent of American households possess access to cable or satellite television, as revealed in Figure 10.3. Smaller satellite dishes and lower prices are sure to make satellite television a more attractive media source in the future.

VISUAL LITERACY
What's in an Ad?

Adding to television's diversity, the national television news corps is often outnumbered on the campaign trail by local television reporters. Satellite technology has provided any of the 1,300 local stations willing to invest in the hardware an opportunity to beam back reports from the field. On a daily basis, local news is watched by more people (67 percent of adults) than is network news (49 percent), so increased local attention to politics has some real significance. Unfortunately, however, studies also show that local news, compared to newspapers and network reports, contains the least substantive coverage. Criticism and analysis of policy positions and candidates are much more likely to be found in national news reports than local broadcasts.[44]

Another growing source of political news and commentary is the Internet. All major national and even many local networks have Web pages, and Web-based information has become standard fare for anyone interested in politics. Three Web sites among the hundreds now available are those of the *National Journal*, which includes its famous Hotline report (www.cloakroom.com); *The Washington Post*, whose site is widely considered the best political site on the Web (www.washingtonpost.com); and an all-politics collaboration between CNN, *Time* magazine, and other media sources (www.cnn.com/ALLPOLITICS). Virtually every major newspaper, opinion magazine, and news magazine now has a site, as well as all the television networks, which endlessly offer not only the pieces that appear on the evening news, but additional commentary and information too lengthy to include on the original thirty-minute broadcast. The percentage of Americans getting their information about news and politics online at least once a week tripled from 1997 to 1999—from 11 to 36 million news users. Interestingly, people who go online don't necessarily alter their other news habits.[45]

FIGURE 10.3   The Growth in Television, Cable, and Satellite Use in America, 1950–1998

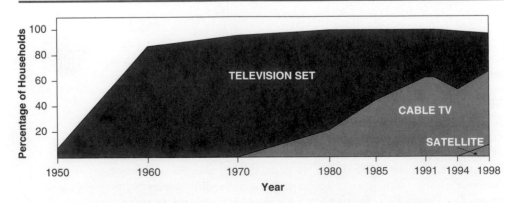

Source: Adapted from Harold W. Stanley and Richard G. Niemi, *Vital Statistics on American Politics, 1997–1998,* 6th ed. (Washington, D.C.: Congressional Quarterly, Inc., 1998), Table 4-1, p. 162. Television Bureau of Advertising.

How the Media Cover Politicians and Government

Much of the media's attention is focused on our politicians and the day-to-day operations of our government. In this section we will discuss how the press covers the three constitutionally created branches of government (Congress, the president, and the courts) and show how the tenor of this coverage has changed since the Watergate scandal of the early 1970s.

At the outset, it is useful to distinguish between several terms associated with the release and discussion of information by elected officials, public figures, and their staffs. A **press release** is a written document offering an official comment or position on an issue or news event; it is usually printed on paper and handed directly to reporters, or, increasingly, released by e-mail or fax. A **press briefing** is a relatively restricted live engagement with the press, in which the range of questions accepted is limited to one or two specific topics and a public figure or elected official is usually represented by his or her press secretary or other aides but does not appear in person. In a full-blown **press conference**, an elected official appears in person to talk with the press at greater length about an unrestricted range of topics. Press conferences are significant media events, providing a field on which reporters struggle to get the answers they need and public figures attempt to retain control of their message and "spin" the news and issues in ways favorable to them.

press release
An official statement on an issue or news event.

press briefing
A restricted engagement with the press usually conducted by aides to a public figure.

press conference
An unrestricted appearance by public figure to talk with the press.

The President.   In the world of media coverage, the president is first among equals. All television cables lead to the White House, and a president can address the nation on all networks almost at will. Since Franklin D. Roosevelt's time, chief executives have used the presidential press conference to shape public opinion and explain their actions. The presence of the press in the White House enables a president to appear even on very short notice and to televise live, interrupting regular programming. The White House's press-briefing room is a familiar sight on the evening news, not just because presidents use it so often, but also because presidential press secretaries have almost daily question-and-answer sessions there.

Although the president receives the lion's share of the press attention, political scientist Thomas Patterson suggests that much of this focus is unfavorable. Since the 1960s, press coverage of the president has become dramatically more negative. In fact, all major presidential contenders in 1992, 1996, and 2000 received more negative than positive coverage. Patterson also found that coverage of President George Bush's handling of important national problems was almost solely negative.[46]

During his 2000 presidential campaign, George W. Bush promised to restore character and honor to the presidency. In recent years, the press has focused more and more on character issues rather than on policy proposals during presidential elections. (Photo courtesy: Jenny Warburg/Impact Visuals)

Congress.   Press coverage of Congress is very different from media coverage of the president. The size of the institution alone (535 members) and its decentralized nature (bicameralism, the committee system, and so on) make it difficult for the media to survey. Nevertheless, the congressional press corps has more than 3,000 members.[47] Most news organizations solve the size and decentralization problems by concentrating coverage on three groups of individuals. First, the leaders of both parties in both houses receive the lion's share of attention because only they can speak for a majority of their party's members. Usually the majority and minority leaders in each house and the Speaker of the House are the preferred spokespersons. Second, key committee chairs command center stage when subjects in their domain are newsworthy. Third, local newspapers and broadcast stations will normally devote some resources to covering their local senators and representatives, even when these legislators are junior and relatively lacking in influence. Most office holders, in turn, are mainly concerned with meeting the needs of their local media contingents, since these reporters are the ones who directly and regularly reach the voters in their home constituencies.

One other kind of congressional news coverage is worth noting: investigative-committee hearings. Occasionally, a sensational scandal leads to televised congressional committee hearings that transfix and electrify the nation. In the early 1950s, Senator Joseph R. McCarthy (R–Wisc.) held a series of hearings to expose and root out what he claimed were Communists in the State Department and other U.S. government agencies, as well as Hollywood's film industry. The senator's style of investigation, which involved many wild charges made without proof and the smearing and labeling of some innocent opponents as Communists, gave rise to the term *McCarthyism*.

Coverage of Congress has been greatly expanded through use of the cable industry channel C-SPAN, the Cable Satellite Public Affairs Network, founded in 1979. C-SPAN1 and C-SPAN2 provide gavel-to-gavel coverage of House and Senate sessions as well as many committee hearings. Americans can watch their representatives in action (or inaction, as the case may be), and do so twenty-four hours a day.

The Judiciary.   The branch of government that is the most different, in press coverage as in many other respects, is the judicial branch. Cloaked in secrecy—because judicial deliberations and decision making are conducted in private—the courts receive scant coverage under most circumstances. However, a volatile or controversial issue, such as abortion, can change the usual type of coverage, especially when the Supreme Court is rendering the decision. Each network and major newspaper has one or more Supreme Court reporters, people who are usually well schooled in the law and whose instant analysis of court opinions interprets the decisions for the millions of people without legal training. Gradually, the admission of cameras into state and local courtrooms across the United States and the popularity of Court TV are offering people a more in-depth look at the operation of the judicial system. Many judges, however, can use their discretion to keep cameras out of their courtrooms, as was the case in the O. J. Simpson civil trial. As yet, though, the Supreme Court does not permit televised proceedings.

Even more than the Court's decisions, presidential appointments to the high Court are the focus of intense media attention. As the judiciary has assumed a more important role in modern times, the men and women considered for the post are being subjected to withering scrutiny of their records and even of their private lives. For example, the media's coverage of the Clarence Thomas Supreme Court nomination hearings in 1991 made Thomas a household word.

Investigative Journalism

Writing in 1999, Bob Woodward notes that the Watergate scandal of the Nixon administration had the most profound impact of any modern event on the manner and substance of the press's conduct.[48] In many respects Watergate began a chain reaction that today allows for intense scrutiny of public officials' private lives. Moreover, coupled with the civil rights movement and the Vietnam War, Watergate shifted the orientation of journalism away from mere description (providing an account of happenings) and toward prescription—helping to set the campaign's (and society's) agenda by focusing attention on the candidates' shortcomings as well as on certain social problems.

A volatile mix of guilt and fear is at work in the post-Watergate press. The guilt stems from regret that experienced Washington reporters failed to detect the telltale signs of the Watergate scandal early on; that even after the story broke, most journalists underplayed the unfolding disaster until forced to take it more seriously by the two young *Post* reporters; that over the years journalism's leading lights had become too close to the politicians they were supposed to check and therefore for too long failed to tell the public about dangerous excesses in the government. The press's ongoing fear is deep-seated and complements the guilt. Every political journalist is apprehensive about missing the next big story, of being left on the platform when the next scandal train leaves Union Station.

Another clear consequence of Watergate has been the increasing emphasis by the press on the character of candidates. The character issue may in part have been an outgrowth of the "new journalism" popularized by author Tom Wolfe in the 1970s.[49] Contending that conventional journalism was sterile and stripped of color, Wolfe and others argued for a reporting style that expanded the definition of news and, novel-like, highlighted all the personal details of the newsmaker. Then, too, reporters had witnessed the success of such books as Theodore H. White's *The Making of the President* series and Joe McGinniss's *The Selling of the President 1968*, which offered revealing, behind-the-scenes vignettes of the previous election's candidates.[50] Why not give readers

WEB EXPLORATION
Should television cameras be allowed in the courtroom, particularly the Supreme Court? To learn more about both sides of the debate, go to www.ablongman.com/oconnor

SIMULATION
You Are the News Editor

and viewers this information before the election, the press reasoned. There was encouragement from academic quarters as well. "Look to character first" when evaluating and choosing among presidential candidates, wrote Duke University political science professor James David Barber in a widely circulated 1972 volume, *The Presidential Character* (see chapter 6).[51]

Loosening the Libel Law.   Another factor permits the modern press to undertake character investigations. In the old days, a reporter would think twice about filing a story critical of a politician's character, and the editors probably would have killed the story had the reporter been foolish enough to do so. The reason? Fear of a libel suit. The first question editors would ask about even an ambiguous or suggestive phrase about a public official was, "If we're sued, can you prove beyond a doubt what you've written?"

Such inhibitions were ostensibly lifted in 1964, when the Supreme Court ruled in *New York Times Co. v. Sullivan* that simply publishing a defamatory falsehood is not enough to justify a libel judgment.[52] Henceforth a public official would have to prove "actual malice," a requirement extended three years later to all public figures, such as Hollywood stars and prominent athletes.[53] The Supreme Court declared that the First Amendment requires elected officials and candidates to prove that the publisher either believed the challenged statement was false or at least entertained serious doubts about its truth and acted recklessly in publishing it in the face of those doubts. The actual malice rule has made it very difficult for public figures to win libel cases.

Despite *Sullivan,* the threat of libel litigation (and its deterrent effect on the press) persists for at least two reasons. First, the *Sullivan* protections do little to reduce the expense of defending defamation claims. The monetary costs have increased enormously, as have the required commitments of reporters' and editors' time and energy. Small news organizations without the financial resources of a national network or *The New York Times* are sometimes reluctant to publish material that might invite a lawsuit because the litigation costs could threaten their existence. The second reason for the continuing libel threat is a cultural phenomenon of heightened sensitivity to the harm that words can do to an individual's emotional tranquility. As a result, politicians are often more inclined to sue their press adversaries, even when success is unlikely.

Bias and the Media.   Whenever the media break an unfavorable story about a politician, the politician usually counters with a cry of "biased reporting"—a claim that the press has told an untruth, has told only part of the truth, or has reported facts out of the complete context of the event. Who is right? Are the news media biased? The answer is simple and unavoidable: Of course they are. Journalists are fallible human beings who inevitably have values, preferences, and attitudes galore— some conscious, others subconscious, but all reflected at one time or

New York Times Co. v. Sullivan **(1964)**
Supreme Court decision ruling that simply publishing a defamatory falsehood is not enough to justify a libel judgment.

Many media outlets prematurely named George W. Bush the winner of the 2000 presidential contest before all the votes in Florida had been counted. The final outcome was not determined until weeks later. (Photo courtesy: Chris Hondros/Liaison Agency/Newsmakers)

another in the subjects selected for coverage or the slant of that coverage. Given that the press is biased, it is important to know in what ways it is biased and when and how the biases are shown.

Truth be told, most journalists lean to the left. First of all, those in the relatively small group of professional journalists (not many more than 100,000, compared with more than 4 million teachers in the United States) are drawn heavily from the ranks of highly educated social and political liberals, as a number of studies, some conducted by the media themselves, have shown.[54] Journalists are substantially Democratic in party affiliation and voting habits, progressive and anti-establishment in political orientation, and well to the left of the general public on most economic, foreign policy, and social issues (such as abortion, affirmative action, gay rights, and gun control). Second, dozens of the most influential reporters and executives entered (or reentered) journalism after stints of partisan involvement in campaigns or government, and a substantial majority worked for Democrats.[55]

Third, this liberal press bias does indeed show up frequently on screen and in print. A study of reporting on the abortion issue, for example, revealed a clear slant to the pro side on network television news, matching in many ways the reporters' own abortion-rights views.[56]

Conservative bias exists in the media as well. One example is the world of AM radio talk shows. Some studies have indicated that liberal programs actually enjoy more air-time than conservative ones, but there is no question that conservatives host by far the most popular shows, as exemplified by Rush Limbaugh. These radio hosts are the political equivalent of "shock jocks." They strive for controversy and attack

WEB EXPLORATION
Compare news coverage on a particular news story for evidence of political bias. Go to www.ablongman.com/oconnor

liberals with ferocious and inflammatory rhetoric. The Limbaugh show, for example, attracts millions of listeners every day and is tremendously profitable and successful in increasing voter preferences for Republican candidates, according to one analysis of panel-study data.[57]

One other source of bias, or at least of non-objectivity, in the press is the increasing celebrity status of many people involved in reporting the news. In an age of media stardom and blurring boundaries between forms of entertainment, journalists in prominent media positions have unprecedented opportunities to attain fame and fortune, of which they often take full advantage. Already commanding multimillion-dollar salaries, journalists can often secure lucrative speaker's fees by addressing corporations, trade societies, private political organizations, universities, and other media gatherings. Especially in the case of journalists with highly ideological perspectives, close involvement with wealthy or powerful special interest groups can blur the line between reporting on policy and issues and influencing them. Some journalists even find work as political consultants or members of government—which seems reasonable, given their prominence, abilities, and expertise, but which can become problematic when they move between spheres not once, but repeatedly. A good example of this troublesome revolving-door phenomenon is the case of Pat Buchanan, who has enjoyed prominent positions in media (as host of CNN's *Crossfire*) and government (as perennial presidential candidate). If American journalism is to retain the watertight integrity for which it is justly renowned, it is essential that key distinctions between private and media enterprise and conscientious public service continue to command our respect.

PARTICIPATION
Where Do You Get Your News, and How Reliable Is It?

During the 2000 campaign, George W. Bush appeared on informal talk shows like *Oprah Winfrey* and *Live with Regis* in an effort to appeal to women voters.
(Photo courtesy: Wilfredo Lee/AP/Wide World Photos)

THE MEDIA'S INFLUENCE ON THE PUBLIC AND PUBLIC OPINION

Some bias in media coverage clearly exists. But how does this bias affect the public that reads or views or listens to biased reporting? In most cases the press has surprisingly little effect. To put it bluntly, people tend to see what they want to see; that is, human beings will focus on parts of a report that reinforce their own attitudes and ignore parts that challenge their core beliefs. Most of us also selectively tune out and ignore reports that contradict our preferences in politics and other fields. In other words, most voters are not empty vessels into which the media can pour their own beliefs. This fact dramatically limits the ability of news organizations to sway public opinion.

Yet this is not the only view. Some political scientists find that the content of network television news accounts for a large portion of the volatility and change in policy preferences of Americans, when measured over relatively short periods of time.[58] These changes are called **media effects.** Let's examine how these media-influenced changes might occur. First, reporting can sway people who are uncommitted and have no strong opinion in the first place. Second, the press has a much greater impact on topics far removed from the lives and experiences of its readers and viewers. News reports can probably shape public opinion about events in foreign countries much more easily than they can about neighborhood crime, or child rearing. Third, news organizations can help tell us what to think about, even if they cannot determine what we think. The press often sets the agenda for government or a campaign by focusing on certain issues or concerns.

media effects
The influence of news sources on public opinion.

The media appear to have a greater influence on political independents than on strong partisans.[59] Indeed, many studies from the 1940s and 1950s, an era when partisanship was very strong, suggested that the media had no influence at all on public opinion. The last forty years, however, have seen the rapid decline in political partisanship,[60] thereby opening the door to greater media influence.

GOVERNMENT REGULATION OF THE ELECTRONIC MEDIA

The U.S. government regulates the electronic component of the media. Unlike radio or television, the print media are exempt from most forms of government regulation, although even print media must not violate community standards for obscenity, for instance. There are two reasons for this unequal treatment. First, the airwaves used by the electronic media are considered public property; they are leased by the federal government to private broadcasters. Second, those airwaves are in limited supply, and without some regulation, the nation's many radio and television stations would interfere with one another's frequency signals. It was not, in fact, the federal government but rather private broadcasters, frustrated by the numerous instances in which signal jamming occurred, that initiated the call for government regulation in the early days of the electronic media. Newspapers, of course, are not subject to these technical considerations.

The first government regulation of the electronic media came in 1927, when Congress enacted the Federal Radio Act, which established the Federal Radio Commission (FRC) and declared the airwaves to be public property. In addition, the act required that all broadcasters be licensed by the FRC. In 1934 the Federal Communications Commission (FCC), an independent regulatory commission, replaced the FRC as the electronic media regulatory body. FCC members are selected by

GLOBAL POLITICS

MEDIA FREEDOM

What role the media plays in politics is partly determined by how free the media are. In 2000, Freedom House, an independent civil liberties organization, rated the degree of media freedom in 186 countries of the world. Using as criteria the degree of government ownership of the media, pressures on media, and actual violations of media freedom, the organization rated countries on a 100-point scale. The lower the score, the freer the media is from government interference. Countries rated between 0 and 30 are considered to have free media, those between 31 and 60 partly free, and those between 61 and 100 not free.

The United States in this respect is in good company. All industrial democracies are considered to have free presses, although they vary in degree. The U.S. and German media are rated freest among the group. State restrictions on the media are highest in Italy and France, which are close to the partly free threshold. The press in Russia, Mexico, and Indonesia are considered

partly free because recent trends toward independent, competitive media institutions still face governments that control significant media resources and which continue to try to control the content of private media.

Restrictions on the media vary. All the industial democracies have public media outlets, most of which are more visible and influential than National Public Radio or the Public Broadcasting Service are in the United States, but the degree of government editorial control varies. In the late 1990s, Japan and the United Kingdom adopted freedom of information acts, but restrictions on the press remain. The British, American, and German governments have passed legislation that makes certain kinds of media communications illegal (i.e., libel in Britain, Internet pornography in the United States, and hate speech and Nazi propaganda in Germany). The Russian government includes a ministry, directly responsible to the president, which supervises the media. China ranks near the bottom of Freedom House's ratings, with near universal control over media

---

the president for five-year terms on an overlapping basis. In addition to regulating public and commercial radio and television, the FCC oversees telephone, telegraph, satellite, and foreign communications in the United States.

COMPARATIVE
Comparing
News Media

In 1996 Congress passed the sweeping Telecommunications Act, deregulating whole segments of the electronic media. The goal of the legislation was to break down the barriers required by federal and state laws and by the legal settlement that broke up the AT&T/Bell monopoly in 1984. This required the separation of local phone service, long-distance service, and cable television service. This deregulation and increased competition is expected to create cheaper and better programming options for consumers and increase the global competitiveness of U.S. telecommunications firms. Consumers can now receive phone service from their cable provider, television programming from their local phone company, or local phone service from their long-distance phone provider. Besides more flexible service options, the legis-

outlets and routine harassment of journalists critical of the government.

Media self-censorship is a problem in many countries. Corporate ownership of media outlets in Italy and the United States is acknowledged as potentially restrictive because corporate-owned media outlets are tempted to try to suppress news that is critical of their owners. Mexico's Institutional Revolutionary Party (PRI) owns the major television station, allowing it to dominate the country's main news outlet. The press club system in Japan is an example of self-censorship in a society generally considered to have a free press. Nearly every government agency has a press club, access to which is limited by the agencies themselves. Press clubs exercise informal restraints on the media because they control the flow of official information and because they can deny membership to

journalists who are too critical of the agency. This can have an impact on the coverage of Japanese government. In contrast to the sensational coverage of Britain's royal family, similar coverage is absent in Japan in no small part because the Imperial Household Agency manages the flow of information about the imperial family and denies tabloid journalists access to its press club.

Freedom House Scores for Media Freedom

Country	Freedom House Score (1–100)	Freedom House Rating
Canada	14	Free
China	80	Not Free
France	24	Free
Germany	13	Free
Indonesia	49	Partly Free
Italy	27	Free
Japan	19	Free
Mexico	50	Partly Free
Russia	60	Partly Free
United Kingdom	20	Free
United States	13	Free

Source: Freedom House, Press Freedom Survey 2000. http://freedomhouse.org/pfs2000/reports.html.

lation spurred the development of new products and services such as unlimited movie selections, interactive television, and advanced computer networking that permits more people to work from their homes.

The legislation provoked criticism by civil libertarian groups who objected to provisions designed to curb "cyberpornography." The act banned the dissemination of "indecent" material on the Internet and online services. The act also requires all large-screen televisions to include built-in "v-chips" that permit parents to block objectionable material they do not wish their family to view. In 1997, the U.S. Supreme Court ruled that the "cyberporn" provisions of the act were unconstitutional, as discussed in chapter 4.

Content Regulation

The government also subjects the electronic media to substantial **content regulation** that, again, does not apply to the print media. Charged

content regulation
Governmental attempts to regulate the electronic media.

equal time rule
The rule that requires broadcast stations to sell campaign air time equally to all candidates if they choose to sell it to any.

with ensuring that the airwaves "serve the public interest, convenience, and necessity," the FCC has attempted to promote equity in broadcasting concerning politics. For example, the **equal time rule** requires that broadcast stations sell campaign air time equally to all candidates if they choose to sell it to any, which they are under no obligation to do. An exception to this rule is a political debate: Stations may exclude from this event less well-known and minor-party candidates.

Until 2000, broadcasters also were required to give candidates the opportunity to respond to personal attacks and political endorsements by the station under FCC rules. In October 2000, however, a federal court of appeals found these rules, long attacked by broadcasters as having a chilling effect on free speech, to be unconstitutional when the FCC was unable to justify these regulations to its satisfaction.

Censorship

The media in the United States, while not free of government regulation, enjoy considerably more liberty than do their counterparts in Great Britain. In the United States, only government officials can be prosecuted for divulging classified information; no such law applies to journalists. Nor can the government, except under extremely rare and confined circumstances, impose prior restraints on the press—that is, the government cannot censor the press. This principle was clearly established in *The New York Times* v. *United States* (1971).[61] In this case the Supreme Court ruled that the government could not prevent publication by the *The New York Times* of the Pentagon Papers, classified government documents about the Vietnam War that had been stolen, photocopied, and sent to the *Times* and *The Washington Post* by Daniel Ellsberg, an antiwar activist. "Only a free and unrestrained press can effectively expose deception in the government," Justice Hugo Black wrote in a concurring opinion for the Court. "To find that the President has 'inherent power' to halt the publication of news by resort to the courts would wipe out the First Amendment."

During the 1991 Persian Gulf War, reporters were upset that the military was not forthcoming about events on and off the battlefield, while some Pentagon officials and many persons in the general public accused the press of telling the enemy too much in their dispatches. The U.S. government had little recourse but to attempt to isolate offending reporters by keeping them away from the battlefield. Even this maneuver was highly controversial and very unpopular with news correspondents because it directly interfered with their job of reporting the news.

Such arguments are an inevitable part of the landscape in a free society. Whatever their specific quarrels with the press, most Americans would probably prefer that the media tell them too much rather than not enough.

Continuity & Change

The News Media and Public Opinion

The Federalist Papers were one of the earliest uses of the mass media to influence public opinion. James Madison, John Jay, and Alexander Hamilton authored eighty-five essays on a variety of issues posed by the proposed Constitution in order to convince the sometimes skeptical citizenry of the need for a new, more powerful national government. These essays were printed in newspapers all over the thirteen states. The Federalists' efforts were countered by Anti-Federalists who tried to respond to each of these essays, but their endeavors were less successful.

Throughout most of our nation's history, the print media played a dominant role in the course of politics and public opinion. Publication of Harriet Beecher Stowe's *Uncle Tom's Cabin*, for example, fueled abolitionist sentiments throughout the North and Abraham Lincoln credited Stowe as the "little woman who started the big war." Later, during the First and Second World Wars, the government used the print media to drum up support for the war effort.

The dawn of the television era brought a new twist to the media's influence on public opinion. The press could no longer be relied on as an instrument of government propaganda. In contrast to the role of the press in earlier wars, television coverage of the Vietnam War significantly transformed the public's perceptions and support of this effort.

The key broadcast in all of television's early years may have occurred in 1968, when television journalist Walter Cronkite traveled to Vietnam after the Tet Offensive, in which North Vietnamese forces surprised Americans at home and abroad with widespread military offensives. Cronkite covered this crucial psychological setback and critically scrutinized President Lyndon Johnson's claim that there was "light at the end of the tunnel" (that is, a clear prospect of military and political success in Vietnam). Cronkite all but concluded that there was little hope for victory, and Lyndon Johnson himself, sitting in the White House and watching Cronkite's report, turned to an aide and said, "We've lost the war, now that we've lost Walter Cronkite."

Today, more and more people rely on the Internet as a source of their news about politics. The Starr Report, which became the basis of the impeachment of President Clinton, was released online, and the public and public opinion largely reacted negatively to Congress's release of the document. In addition to its ability to disseminate large volumes of information at a moment's notice, the Internet is more interactive than the press and television coverage of the news.

1. Is the likely increased interactivity of the media in the future necessarily a positive trend?
2. What are some of the negative consequences of increasing the public voice directly into the political process? Do the potential benefits outweigh the likely costs?

Cast Your Vote. Will the Internet serve as an effective and accurate tool for political polling? To cast your vote, go to **www.ablongman.com/oconnor**

SUMMARY

Public opinion is a subject constantly mentioned in the media, especially in presidential election years or when important policies (such as health care, balancing the budget, race, or crime) are under consideration.

Public opinion is what the public thinks about an issue or a particular set of issues. Public opinion polls are used to estimate public opinion. Almost since the beginning of the United States, various attempts have been made to influence public opinion about particular issues or to sway elections. Modern-day polling did not begin until the 1930s. Over the years, polling to measure public opinion has become more and more sophisticated and more accurate.

The first step in forming opinions occurs through a process called political socialization. The family, religion, gender, race, age, and where you grow up or live all affect how one views political events and issues, as do the major events themselves. Our political ideology—whether we are conservative, liberal, or moderate—also provides a lens through which we filter our political views. So does our level of personal benefit, our political knowledge of issues and events, and cues from leaders.

Measuring public opinion can be difficult. The most frequently used measure is the public opinion poll. Determining the content, phrasing the questions, selecting the sample, and choosing the right kind of poll are critical to obtaining accurate and useable data.

The modern media consist of print press (newspapers, magazines, journals) and electronic media (television, radio, and Internet). In the United States, the media are relatively uncontrolled and free to express many views, although that has not always been the case.

The media have shifted focus in recent years, first toward investigative journalism in the Watergate era, and then toward character issues. Studies have shown that by framing issues for debate and discussion, the media have clear and recognizable effects on voters.

The press is a business—big business, in the case of networks and large newspapers—and it is regulated to some extent by the government. The government has gradually loosened its restrictions on the media. Officially, the Federal Communications Commission licenses and regulates broadcasting stations, although in practice it has been quite willing to grant and renew licenses, and recently it has reduced its regulation of licensees. Additionally, cable transmission was first allowed on a widespread basis in the late 1970s, from whence it has grown to a large supplier of information. Finally, content regulations have loosened, with the courts using a narrow interpretation of libel. All these trends toward deregulation were accelerated by the passage of the massive 1996 telecommunications bill.

KEY TERMS

SELECTED READINGS

Asher, Herbert. *Polling and the Public: What Every Citizen Should Know,* 4th ed. Washington, D.C.: CQ Press, 1998.

Bennet, W. Lance, and David L. Paletz. *Taken by Storm: The Media, Public Opinion, and U.S. Foreign Policy in the Gulf War.* Chicago: University of Chicago Press, 1994.

Carmines, Edward G., and James A. Stimson. *Issue Evolution.* Princeton, N.J.: Princeton University Press, 1990.

Erikson, Robert S., and Kent L. Tedin. *American Public Opinion: Its Contents, Origins and Impact,* 6th ed. New York: Longman, 2000.

Gamson, William A. *Talking Politics.* New York: Cambridge University Press, 1992.

Graber, Doris A. *Mass Media in American Politics,* 5th ed. Washington, D.C.: CQ Press, 1996.

Herbst, Susan. *Numbered Voices: How Opinion Polling Has Shaped American Politics.* Chicago: University of Chicago Press, 1995.

Iyengar, Shanto, and Richard Reeves, eds. *Do the Media Govern?: Politicians, Voters, and Reporters in America.* Beverly Hills, Calif.: Sage, 1997.

Jacobs, Lawrence R. and Robert Y. Shapiro. 2000. *Politicians Don't Pander: Political Manipulation and the Loss of Democratic Responsiveness.* Chicago: Univeristy of Chicago Press.

Jamieson, Kathleen Hall. *Everything You Think You Know About Politics... and Why You Were Wrong.* New York: Basic Books, 2000.

Jennings, M. Kent, and Richard Niemi. *Generations and Politics: A Panel Study of Young Adults and Their Parents.* Princeton, N.J.: Princeton University Press, 1981.

Key, V. O., Jr. *Public Opinion and American Democracy.* New York: Random House, 1961.

Lippmann, Walter. *Public Opinion,* reissue. New York: Free Press, 1997.

Muntz, Diana. *Impersonal Influence: How Perceptions of Mass Collectives Affect Political Attitudes.* Cambridge, Mass.: Cambridge University Press, 1998.

Rubenstein, Sondra Miller. *Surveying Public Opinion.* Belmont, Calif.: Wadsworth Publishing, 1994.

Sabato, Larry J. *Feeding Frenzy: How Attack Journalism Has Transformed American Politics,* updated ed. New York: Macmillan Free Press, 1993.

Stephens, Mitchell. *A History of News: From the Drum to the Satellite.* New York: Viking, 1989.

Stimson, James A. *Public Opinion in America: Moods, Cycles and Swings.* Boulder, Colo.: Westview Press, 1991.

Woodward, Bob. *The Shadow: Five Presidents and the Legacy of Watergate.* New York: Simon and Schuster, 1999.

Zaller, John. *The Nature and Origins of Mass Opinion.* New York: Cambridge University Press, 1992.

11 Political Parties and Interest Groups

(Photo courtesy: Michael Newman/PhotoEdit)

Chapter Outline

- Political Parties
- Interest Groups

At times it is difficult to figure out the difference between political parties and interest groups and the respective roles that each plays in the American political system. It's not surprising. Often, the two work hand in hand, and it's difficult to see which is which. Consider this example: In June 1999, the 223-member House Republican Caucus let a health care lobbyist explain her proposals to them. Some Republicans, however, protested after Deborah Steelman was allowed to speak to the group that has one sacrosanct rule: no lobbyists allowed. Nevertheless, she was allowed to speak without disclosing her clients' financial stake in the proposed Medicare reforms legislation she discussed.

The facts about this lobbyist? Steelman is a top pharmaceutical and hospital lobbyist, a recognized health policy expert, a Republican Party donor, a political party operative, and was a "top domestic policy advisor to then Texas Governor George W. Bush."[1] As the head of her own lobbying and consulting shop, Steelman was the former director of domestic policy for the senior Bush's 1988 presidential campaign. Later, she chaired a 13-member commission that proposed changes to medicare and Social Security. Public Citizen, the Ralph Nader watchdog group, accused Steelman of a "serious conflict of interest," charging that her clients would be affected by Medicare changes. Nevertheless, she earns over $2 million each year from corporations including Bristol-Myers Squibb and Johnson & Johnson. Republican operatives saw her contributions to the party and to the health care debate as key. Her story shows how closely allied parties, interest groups, special interests, and lobbyists are in Washington, D.C.

When James Madison warned of the dangers of faction in *Federalist No. 10*, he never envisioned the development of political parties, or the role that organized interests would eventually play in politics and policy making. It was not long after the ink was dry on the new Constitution that factions arose concerning the desirability to the new system of government that it created. And, soon after, political parties were formed to reflect those political divisions.

At the most basic level, a **political party** is a group of office holders, candidates, activists, and voters who identify with a group label and seek to elect to public office individuals who run under that label. Notice the goal is to *win* office, not just compete for it. This objective is in keeping with the practical nature of Americans and the country's historical aversion to most ideologically driven, "purist" politics. Nevertheless, the group label—also called party identification—can carry with it clear messages about ideology and issue positions. Although this is especially true of minor, less broad-based parties that have little chance of electoral success, it also applies to the national, dominant political parties—the Democrats and the Republicans.

In contrast to political parties, **interest groups,** which go by a variety of names—special interests, pressure groups, organized interests, political groups, lobby groups, and public interest groups—are organizations that "seek or claim to represent people or organizations which share one or more common interests or ideals."[2] Distinguished political scientist V. O. Key Jr. tried to differentiate political parties from interest groups by arguing that "interest groups promote their interests by attempting to influence government rather than by nominating candidates and seeking responsibility for the management of government."[3]

In this chapter we trace the evolution of the role of political parties and interest groups in the American political process. First, we begin by examining political parties. Next, we turn to a discussion of interest groups.

political party

A group of office holders, candidates, activists, and voters who identify with a group label and seek to elect to public office individuals who run under that label.

interest group

An organized group that tries to influence public policy.

POLITICAL PARTIES

Political parties have evolved considerably and changed form from time to time. Nevertheless, they usually have been reliable vehicles for mass participation in a representative democracy.

The Evolution of American Party Democracy

Upset with the political divisions he saw in his administration, George Washington warned the nation against parties in his public farewell. Nevertheless, his departure from office marked the effective end of the brief era of partyless politics in the United States. His vice president, John Adams, was closely allied with Alexander Hamilton, a leading Federalist, who served as secretary of the treasury in the Washington administration. Hamilton was a long-time arch rival of Thomas Jefferson, who also served in Washington's Cabinet. During the heated debates over ratification of the Constitution, Hamilton led Federalist efforts while Jefferson was a leader of the Anti-Federalist faction.

Adams narrowly defeated Jefferson in a bitter election to win the presidency in 1796. Over the course of Adams's single presidential term, two competing congressional party groupings (or caucuses) gradually organized around these men and their clashing principles. Hamilton's Federalists supported a strong central government; the Democratic-Republicans, headed by Thomas Jefferson and James Madison, inherited the mantle of the Anti-Federalists, and preferred a federal system in which the states would be relatively more powerful.

In the presidential election of 1800, the Federalists supported Adams's bid for a second term. But the Democratic-Republicans prevailed. Their nominee, Thomas Jefferson, won and became the first American president elected as the nominee of a political party.

Jefferson was deeply committed to the ideas of his party, but not nearly as devoted to the idea of a party system. He regarded his Democratic-Republican Party as a temporary measure necessary to defeat Adams and Hamilton. Neither Jefferson's Democratic-Republicans nor Hamilton's Federalists enjoyed widespread "party identification" among the citizenry akin to that of today's Democrats and Republicans. Although Southerners were overwhelmingly partial to the Democratic-Republicans and New Englanders to the Federalists, no broad-based party organizations existed on either side to mobilize popular support. Rather, as political scientist John H. Aldrich observes, the congressional factions organized around Hamilton and Jefferson were primarily governmental parties designed to settle the dispute over how strong the new federal government would be.[4]

What is sometimes called the second-party system began around 1824, when Andrew Jackson ran for president (see Figure 11.1). Around that time the base of political parties broadened along with the electorate. Small caucuses of congressional party leaders had previously nominated candidates. But, after much criticism of the system as elitist and undemocratic, it gave way to nominations at large party conventions. The country's first major national presidential nominating convention was held in 1832 by the Democratic Party,[5] the successor to the old Jeffersonian Democratic-Republicans. (The shortened name had gradually come into use in the 1820s.) Formed around the charismatic populist President Andrew Jackson, the Democratic Party attracted most of the newly enfranchised voters, who were drawn to Jackson's style. Jackson's strong personality helped to polarize politics. Opposition to him and Democrats coalesced into the Whig Party, which descended from the Federalists. Its early leaders included Henry Clay, the Speaker of the House from 1811 to 1820. The incumbent Jackson defeated Clay in the 1832 presidential contest and became the first chief executive to win the White House as the nominee of a truly national, popularly based political party.

FIGURE 11.1   American Party History at a Glance

This table shows the transformations and evolution of the various parties that have always made up the basic two-party structure of the American political system.

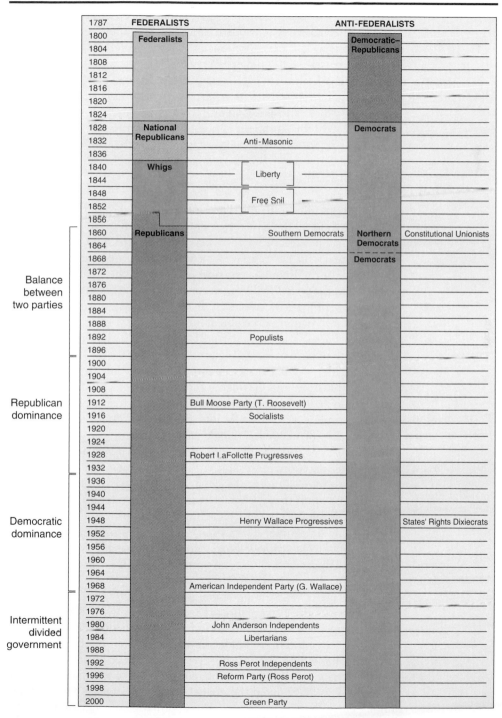

The Whigs and the Democrats continued to strengthen after 1832, establishing state and local organizations almost everywhere. Their competition was usually fierce and closely matched.[6] Unfortunately for the Whigs, the issue of slavery sharpened many already present and divisive internal party tensions that led to its gradual dissolution and replacement by the new Republican Party. Formed in 1854 by anti-slavery activists, the Republican Party set its sights on the abolition (or at least the containment) of slavery. After a losing presidential effort for John C. Frémont in 1856, it was able to assemble enough support from the Whigs, antislavery Northern Democrats, and others to win the presidency for Abraham Lincoln in a fragmented 1860 vote. In that year the South voted solidly Democratic, beginning a habit so strong that not a single Southern state voted Republican for president again until 1920.

Democrats and Republicans: The Golden Age. From that election in 1860 to this day, the same two parties—the Republicans and the Democrats—have dominated American elections, and control of an electoral majority has seesawed back and forth between them. The dominance of the Republicans (now often called the Grand Old Party, or GOP) in the post–Civil War Reconstruction era eventually gave way to a closely competitive system from 1876 to 1896, in part because the Democrats were more successful at integrating new immigrants to port cities like New York, Boston, and Chicago. This is often called the "golden age of parties."

This golden age occurred when emigration from Europe (particularly Ireland, Italy, and Germany) fueled the development of big-city party organizations that ruled their domains with an iron hand. Party and government were virtually interchangeable, and the parties were the providers of needed services, entertainment, and employment. These big city organizations were called **political machines**. A political machine is a party organization that recruits its members with tangible incentives—money, political jobs, an opportunity to get favors from government—and that is characterized by a high degree of leadership control over member activity. Machines were a central element of life for millions of people: They sponsored community events such as parades and picnics, provided social services such as helping new immigrants settle in, and gave food and temporary housing to those in immediate need, all in exchange for votes.

The parties offered immigrants not just services, but also the opportunity for upward social mobility as they rose in the organization. Because they held the hope for social advancement, the parties engendered among their supporters and office holders intense devotion that helped to produce startlingly high voter turnouts—75 percent or better in all presidential elections from 1876 to 1900, compared with less than 50 percent today.[7] They also fostered the greatest party-line voting ever achieved among party contingents in Congress and many state legislatures.[8]

political machine
A party organization that recruits its members with tangible incentives and is characterized by a high degree of control over member activity.

Democrat Franklin D. Roosevelt won the presidency in 1932 with a coalition of Southern voters, racial and ethnic groups, organized labor, farmers, liberals, and big-city "machines." This New Deal coalition basically characterized both the Democratic Party and the prevailing national majority until at least the late 1960s. Since 1970, neither party has been clearly dominant, as more and more voters have seemed to view their partisan attachments as less important. In general, Republicans either have dominated presidential elections while Democrats have controlled the Congress, or the president has been a Democrat and Republicans have controlled Congress. As explained in chapter 6, this is called divided government.

The Modern Era versus the Golden Age.   The modern era seems very distant from the golden age of parties from the 1870s to the 1920s. The heyday of the party—at least this certain kind of party—has passed. In the twentieth century many social, political, technological, and governmental changes have contributed to party decline. Historically, the government's gradual assumption of important functions previously performed by the parties—such as printing ballots, conducting elections, and providing social welfare services—had a major impact. Social services began to be seen as a right of citizenship rather than a privilege extended in exchange for a person's support of a party, and as the flow of immigrants slowed dramatically in the 1920s, party organizations gradually withered in most places.

At the same time, the **direct primary,** whereby party nominees were determined by the ballots of qualified voters rather than at party conventions, was widely adopted by the states in the first two decades of the twentieth century. The primary removed the power of nomination from party leaders and workers, giving it instead to a much broader and more independent electorate and thus loosening the tie between the party nominee and the party organization. Civil service laws also removed much of the patronage used by the parties to reward their followers. **Civil service laws** require appointment on the basis of merit and competitive examinations, whereas **patronage**—also called the spoils system—awards jobs on the basis of party loyalty. These changes were encouraged by the Progressive movement, which flourished in the first two decades of the twentieth century.

In the post–World War II era, extensive social changes fed the movement away from strong parties. Broad-based education gave rise to politics that focuses on specific issues, such as civil rights, tax cutting, environmentalism, and abortion, rather than on party labels. Issue politics tends to cut across party lines and encourages voters to vote for candidates of different parties for various offices in the same election, called **ticket-split** voting. Population shifts also have affected the parties. As millions of people moved out of the more densely populated cities, where they were easy to organize, the sprawling suburbs became a challenge to even the most energetic party organizers.

TIMELINE
Parties that Made
American History

www.longmanparticipate.com

direct primary
The selection of party candidates through the ballots of qualified voters rather than at party nomination conventions.

civil service laws
These acts removed the staffing of the bureaucracy from political parties and created a professional bureaucracy filled through competition.

patronage
Jobs, grants, or other special favors that are given as rewards to friends and political allies for their support.

ticket-split
To vote for candidates of different parties for various offices in the same election.

Politically, many other trends have also contributed to the parties' decline. Television has come to dominate American politics, and the medium naturally emphasizes candidate personality rather than abstract concepts such as party labels. The modern parties have many rivals for the affections of their candidates, including **political consultants,** the hired guns who manage campaigns and design television advertisements. Both television and consultants have replaced the party as intermediaries between the candidate and the voter. It is little wonder that some office holders who have been elected without much help from their parties don't feel tied to their party.

The Basic Structure of American Political Parties

While the distinctions might not be as clear today as they once were, basic structure of the two major parties is not elaborate. Each has national, state, and local branches (see Figure 11.2). At each level, these largely independent entities act fairly autonomously as they represent diverse interests in Washington, D.C., state capitols, and local governments throughout the nation.

The National Party.   The first national party committees were skeletal and formed some years after the creation of the presidential nominating conventions in the 1830s. Every four years, each party holds a **national convention** to nominate its presidential and vice presidential candidates. First the Democrats in 1848 and then the Republicans in 1856 established national governing bodies—the Democratic National Committee (DNC), and the Republican National Committee (RNC)—to make arrangements for the conventions and to coordinate the subsequent presidential campaigns. Although the nomination of the presidential ticket naturally receives the lion's share of attention, the convention also fulfills its role as the ultimate governing body for the party itself. The rules adopted and the platform passed at the quadrennial conclave are durable guideposts that steer the party for years after the final gavel has been brought down.

The key national party official is the chairperson of the DNC or RNC. The chair is formally elected by the national committee, but is usually selected by the sitting president or newly nominated presidential candidate, who is accorded the right to name the individual for at least the duration of the campaign. The chair often becomes the prime spokesperson and arbitrator for the party during the four years between elections, and is called on to damp down factionalism, negotiate candidate disputes, raise money, and prepare the machinery for the next presidential election. Balancing the interests of all potential White House contenders is a particularly difficult job, and strict neutrality is normally expected from the chair.

To serve their interests, the congressional party caucuses in both houses organized their own national committees, loosely allied with the

---

political consultant
Professional who manages campaigns and political advertisements for political candidates.

national convention
A party conclave (meeting) held in the presidential election year to nominate a presidential and vice presidential ticket and adopt a platform.

FIGURE 11.2   Political Party Organization in America: From Base to Pinnacle

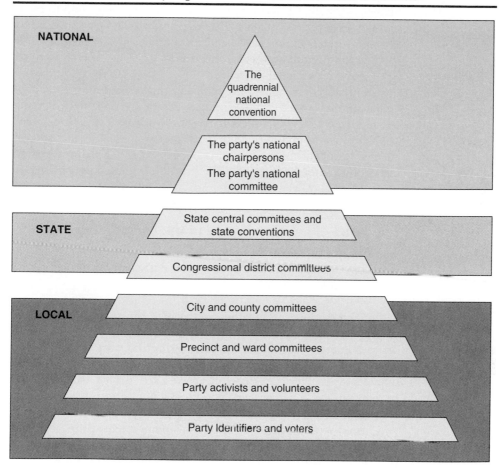

DNC and RNC. This three-part arrangement of national party committee, House party committee, and Senate party committee has persisted in both parties until the present day, and each party's three committees are located together in Washington.

State and Local Parties.   Although national committee activities of all kinds attract most of the media attention, the party is structurally based not in Washington but in the states and localities. Except for the campaign finance arena, virtually all governmental regulation of political parties is left to the states, and most elected officials give their allegiance to the local party divisions they know best. Most important, the vast majority of party leadership positions are filled at subnational levels.

The pyramidal arrangement of political parties provides for a broad base of support. The smallest voting unit, the precinct, usually takes in a few adjacent neighborhoods and is the fundamental building block of the party, and each of the more than 100,000 precincts in the United States potentially has a committeeman or committeewoman to represent it in each party's councils. The precinct committee persons are the key foot soldiers of any party, and their efforts are supplemented by party committees above them in the wards, cities, counties, towns, villages, and congressional districts.

The state governing body supervising this collection of local party organizations is usually called the state central (or executive) committee, and it is made up of representatives from all major geographic units, as determined by and selected under state law. Generally, state parties are free to act within the limits set by their state legislatures without interference from the national party, except in the selection and seating of presidential convention delegates.

The Roles of Political Parties in the United States

The two-party system has helped organize and resolve social and political conflict for 150 years. Political parties perform many other important roles.

Mobilizing Support and Gathering Power.   Elected leaders count on disproportionate support among their partisans. The parties thus aid office holders by giving them maneuvering room and by mobilizing support for their policies. When the president addresses the nation and requests support for his policies, his party's activists are usually the first to respond to the call, perhaps flooding Congress with telegrams urging action on the president's agenda. Moreover, because there are only two major parties, pragmatic citizens who are interested in politics or public policy are mainly attracted to one or the other standard, creating natural majorities or near-majorities for party office holders to command. The party creates a community of interest that bonds disparate groups over time into what is called a coalition—and this eliminates the necessity of creating a new coalition for every campaign or every issue. Imagine the chaos and mad scrambles for public support that would constantly ensue without the continuity provided by the parties.

A Force for Stability.   The parties represent continuity in the wake of changing issues and personalities, anchoring the electorate in the midst of the storm of new political people and policies. Because of its unyielding, pragmatic desire to *win* elections (not just contest them), each party in a sense acts to moderate public opinion. The party tames its own extreme elements by pulling them toward an ideological center in order to attract a majority of votes on Election Day.

Unity, Linkage, Accountability.   Parties provide the glue to hold together the disparate elements of the fragmented American governmental and political apparatus. The Framers designed a system that

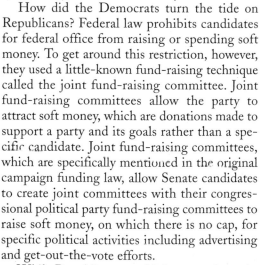

POLICY IN ACTION

THE CHALLENGE OF CAMPAIGN FINANCING

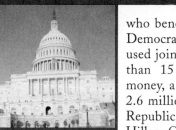

In the 2000 election cycle, Senate Democrats for the first time raised more unlimited, unregulated funds than their Republican counterparts. Their unprecedented success undoubtedly will make it more difficult for many Democratic Senators to support extensive campaign finance reform; clearly it was more attractive when they had more to gain from its passage symbolically as well as financially

How did the Democrats turn the tide on Republicans? Federal law prohibits candidates for federal office from raising or spending soft money. To get around this restriction, however, they used a little-known fund-raising technique called the joint fund-raising committee. Joint fund-raising committees allow the party to attract soft money, which are donations made to support a party and its goals rather than a specific candidate. Joint fund-raising committees, which are specifically mentioned in the original campaign funding law, allow Senate candidates to create joint committees with their congressional political party fund-raising committees to raise soft money, on which there is no cap, for specific political activities including advertising and get-out-the-vote efforts.

While Republicans used joint committees in the 2000 election cycle, it was the Democrats who benefited the most. Fourteen Democratic Senate candidates who used joint committees raised more than 15 million dollars in soft money, a figure far higher than the 2.6 million dollars raised by seven Republican Senatorial candidates.[*] Hillary Clinton was the rock star of soft money campaign financing—she raised over 9.6 million dollars in 2000.

Given the Democrats' successes in 2000, many in the Senate fear that the abolition of soft money will give the Republican Party with its tremendous ties to big business and its deep pockets an advantage that will make it impossible for the Democrats to win the House or the Senate in the 2002 elections.

How does the process work? In the case of Senator Clinton, her joint committee, New York Senate 2000, sent $6 million back to the state Democratic Party for television advertisements and other activities to help elect her senator from New York. Donations to her committee included $100,000 from a prominent union, and $72,000 from Denise Rich, whose ex-husband later received a controversial pardon from President Clinton.

---

[*]Katharine Q. Seelye, "Senate Democrats Surpassed G.O.P. in Soft Financing," *The New York Times* (March 16, 2001): A1.

---

divides and subdivides power, making it possible to preserve individual liberty but difficult to coordinate and produce action in a timely fashion. Parties help to compensate for this drawback by linking all the institutions of power one to another. Although rivalry between the executive and legislative branches of American government is inevitable, the partisan affiliations of the leaders of each branch constitute a common basis for cooperation, as any president and his fellow party members in Congress usually demonstrate daily.

One of the last of the big-city party bosses, Chicago Mayor Richard J. Daley controlled a powerful political machine for more than twenty-five years. (Photo courtesy: Bettmann/Corbis)

hard money
Federal campaign contributions strictly regulated by federal law.

soft money
Under a loophole in federal campaign law, money donated to a political party for noncandidate specific purposes; not covered by federal campaign spending laws.

Moreover, party identification and organization are natural connectors and vehicles for communication between the voter and the candidate as well as between the voter and the office holder. The party connection is one means of increasing accountability in election campaigns and in government. Candidates on the campaign trail and elected party leaders in office are required from time to time to account for their performance at party-sponsored forums, nominating primaries, and conventions.

Political parties, too, can take some credit for unifying the nation by dampening sectionalism. Since parties must form national majorities to win the presidency, any single, isolated region is guaranteed minority status unless it establishes ties with other areas. The party label and philosophy are the bridge that enables regions to join forces; in the process a national interest, rather than a merely sectional one, is created and served.

The Electioneering Function.   The election, proclaimed H. G. Wells, is "democracy's ceremonial, its feast, its great function," and the political parties assist this ceremony in essential ways. First, the parties funnel talented (and some not-so-talented) individuals into politics and government. Thousands of candidates are recruited each year by the two parties, as are many of candidates' staff members—the ones who manage the campaigns and go on to serve in key governmental positions once the election has been won.

The national, state and local parties also help raise money for candidates. The contemporary Republican Party has fund-raising prowess unparalleled in American history and unrivaled by the Democrats. The Republicans have outraised the Democrats by large margins in all recent election cycles, although in 2000, Democratic fund-raising reached record highs, as revealed in Figure 11.3. As is also revealed in Figure 11.3, however, in addition to "hard dollars," or **hard money,** those that are regulated by federal election law and cap how much individuals and political action committees (PACs) may contribute to the parties of candidates, what is called **soft money** now is a significant proportion of all campaign spending. These soft dollars, funds raised outside the limits and prohibitions of the Federal Election Campaign Act, cannot be spent on specific candidates. Soft money, instead, is given to state and national political parties to enhance issue awareness and get out the vote efforts. As revealed in Figure 11.3, soft money contributions doubled in the last election cycle.

Much of this soft money was spent on television issue ads, get out the vote efforts, and other party-building activities. Unlike political action committee contributions, there are no limits on soft money contributions. Thus, most soft money comes from big businesses and labor unions. Among the top contributors to the Democratic Party were the

FIGURE 11.3   Party Funding Escalates

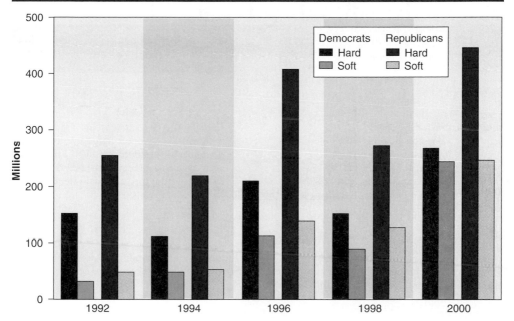

Source: Federal Elections Commission.

American Federation of State, County, and Municipal Employees and the Communications Workers of America. In contrast, leading donors to the Republican Party were the Phillip Morris Co. and AT&T. All four contributed more than $2 million each.

In addition to being able to attract money from wealthy corporate sponsors and groups like the Business Roundtable, a significant amount of Republican money is raised through highly successful mail solicitation, which was begun in the early 1960s and accelerated in the mid-1970s when postage and production costs were relatively low. From a base of just 24,000 names in 1975, for example, the national Republican Party expanded its mailing list of proven donors to several million by the 2000s. Mailings produce about three-quarters of its total revenue, and they do so with an average contribution of under $35. In this fashion the GOP may have broadened its committed base, because contributing money usually strengthens the tie between a voter and any organization. Most of the rest of the GOP's funds come from larger donors.

The money raised by both parties is used to support a dazzling variety of party activities and campaign services, including party staff, voter contact in the form of phone centers and mass mailings, media advertising, and campaign staff and training. The Republican and Democratic National Committees, for example, spend millions of dollars for national, state, and local public opinion surveys. In important contests the party will frequently commission tracking polls—continuous surveys that enable a campaign to chart its daily rise or fall. The information

HIGHLIGHT

SELECTED CONTRASTS IN THE 2000 PARTY PLATFORMS

DEMOCRATS

Taxes

Tax cuts for middle class families; enable families to "live their values by helping them save for college, invest in their job skills and lifelong learning, pay for health insurance, afford child care, eliminate the marriage penalty for working families, care for elderly or disabled loved ones."

REPUBLICANS

Taxes

Replace the five current tax brackets with four lower ones; help families by doubling the child tax credit to $1000; encourage entrepreneurship and growth by capping the top marginal rate, ending the death tax.

Abortion

Support a woman's right to choose to have an abortion in all circumstances currently legal. "Respect the individual conscience of each American on this difficult issue."

Support a human life amendment to outlaw abortions. No specific mention of tolerance for other views on abortion.

Social Security

"Democrats believe in using our prosperity to save Social Security."

"Personal savings accounts must be the cornerstone of restructuring."

Immigration

Permit the children of illegal immigrants to attend public schools; allow legal immigrants to receive welfare and other benefits; make it easier for eligible immigrants to become United States citizens. Support restoration of basic due process protections and essential benefits for legal immigrants.

"Prohibit the children of illegal immigrants from attending public schools; restrict welfare to legal immigrants; support a constitutional amendment denying automatic citizenship to children born in the United States to illegal immigrants and legal immigrants who are in this country for a short time."

provided in such polls is invaluable in the tense concluding days of an election. The national Republican Party, in particular, also operates a sophisticated in-house media division that specializes in the design and production of television advertisements for party nominees at all levels.

Party as a Voting and Issue Cue.   A voter's party identification acts as an invaluable filter for information, a perceptual screen that affects how he or she digests political news. Therefore party provides a useful cue for voters who can use the party as a shortcut or substitute for interpreting issues and events they may not fully comprehend.

Legislative Organization.   In no segment of American government is the party more visible or vital than in the Congress. In this century the political parties have dramatically increased the sophistication and

Education

Support strengthening public schools. "Advocate raises for teachers and accountability for under-performing schools."

Favor using federal money to help parents pay private school tuition. "Support increased local and state control of education."

Homosexual Rights

We support continued efforts … to end workplace discrimination against gay men and lesbians. We support the full inclusion of gay and lesbian families in the life of the nation.

"We do not believe sexual preference should be given special legal protection of standing in the law."

Gun Control

Support mandatory child safety locks, and a photo license I.D., a full background check, and a gun safety test to buy a new handgun in America. Support "more federal gun prosecutors, ATF agents and inspectors, and giving states and communities another 10,000 prosecutors to fight gun crime."

"Defend the constitutional right to keep and bear arms" and favor mandatory penalties for crimes committed with guns.

Environment

Emphasize government regulation to protect the environment.

Emphasize consideration of private property rights and economic development in conjunction with environmental protection.

Star Wars

Oppose revival of the landbased missile defense system, known as Star Wars.

Favor development of the missile defense system.

Source: 2000 Democratic and Republican Party Platforms.

impact of their internal congressional organizations. Prior to the beginning of every session, each party in both houses of Congress gathers (or "caucuses") separately to select party leaders (House Speaker or minority leader, Senate majority and minority leaders, party whips, and so on) and to arrange for the appointment of members of each chamber's committees. In effect, then, the parties organize and operate the Congress.

Policy Formulation and Promotion.   Every four years, the two major national political parties meet to select their nominee for president. At that time they also draft their **national party platforms,** the most visible instrument by which parties formulate, convey, and promote public policy. Each party platform is a lengthy document containing its positions on key issues, and the parties hold very different positions on a variety of issues, as revealed in Highlight: Selected Contrasts in the 2000 Party Platforms.

VISUAL LITERACY
Comparing Party Platforms

national party platform
A statement of the general and specific philosophy and policy goals of a political party, usually promulgated at the national convention.

Historically, the Democratic and Republican Party platforms have been quite different because the political philosophies of each party are also quite different. Historically, the Democratic Party advocates abortion rights, affirmative action, and public funding for the arts—all policies opposed by the Republican Party. Likewise, the Republican Party advocates federal assistance to allow parents to send their children to private schools, development of the missile defense system, and a capital gains cut—all policies opposed by the Democratic Party.

Each U.S. party also has several institutionalized sources of policy ideas. Though unconnected to the parties in any official sense, these so-called *think tanks* (institutional collections of policy-oriented researchers and academics) are quite influential. In the current Bush administration, for instance, the conservative Mountain States Legal Foundation's Gail Norton is the secretary of interior. Conservative think tanks including the Heritage Foundation (where Lynne Cheney, wife of the vice president, works) and the more moderate and bipartisan American Enterprise Institute, supply the Bush team with people and ideas. On the Democratic side, liberal think tanks proliferated during the party's Reagan- and Bush-induced exile. More than a half-dozen policy institutes formed after 1980 in an attempt to nurse the Democrats back to political health. The Center for National Policy and the Progressive Policy Institute, to cite two, sponsored conferences and published papers on Democratic policy alternatives.

To promote their policy positions, the leaders of each party in Congress try to advance legislation to further their interests. Party labels, in fact, have consistently been the most powerful predictor of congressional roll-call voting, a process in which the votes of each member are recorded. In the last few years even more votes have closely followed the partisan divide. A member's party affiliation has proven to be the indicator of his or her votes more than 80 percent of the time in recent years; that is, the average representative or senator sides with his or her party on about 80 percent of the votes that divide a majority of Democrats from a majority of Republicans. In most recent years more than half of the roll-call votes in the House and Senate also found majorities of Democrats and Republicans on opposite sides (see Figure 11.4), and most Democrats and Republicans found themselves voting with members of their party on roll-call votes.

High levels of party cohesion are especially likely to be seen when votes are taken in several areas. The votes that organize the legislative chambers (such as the election of a Speaker), set up the election machinery and campaign laws, and seat-challenged members command nearly unanimous support on behalf of the party's basic interests. Those votes involving key parts of the president's program also frequently divide the parties. Finally, certain policy issues (such as Social Security, welfare programs, and union-management relations) as well as party platform issues that directly and manifestly affect the party's image or its key constituencies produce substantial party voting.

WEB EXPLORATION
To explore the partisan and ideological agendas of unaffiliated think tanks and search for connections to specific parties, go to www.ablongman.com/oconnor

FIGURE 11.4   Congressional Party Unity Scores, 1959–1999
Note how party-based voting has increased conspicuously since the 1970s.

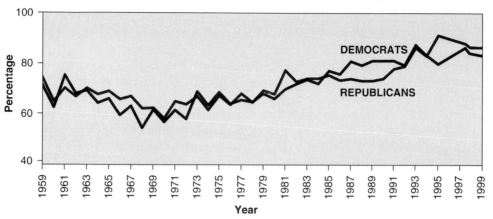

Source: *Congressional Quarterly Almanacs* (Washington, D.C.: Congressional Quarterly, Inc).

The Two-Party System and Third-Partyism

The **two-party system,** for all of its advantages, has not gone unchallenged. At the state level, two-party competition was severely limited or nonexistent in much of the country for most of this century. Even in some two-party states, many cities and counties had a massive majority of voters aligned with one or the other party and thus were effectively one-party in local elections. The spread of two-party competition, while still uneven in some respects, is one of the most significant political trends in recent times and virtually no one-party states are left.

Ironically, the growth of two-party competition has been spurred less by the developing strength of the two parties than by party system as illustrated by the decline in partisan loyalty of the electorate. In other words, citizens are now more inclined to cross party lines to support an appealing candidate, thus making a victory for the minority party possible regardless of whether the victory was earned though the hard work of the party organization.

Third-partyism has proven more durable than one-partyism, though its nature is sporadic and intermittent, and its effects on the political system are on the whole less weighty. Third parties find their roots in sectionalism (as did the South's states' rights Dixiecrats, who broke away from the Democrats in 1948); in economic protest (such as the agrarian revolt that fueled the Populists, an 1892 prairie-states party); in specific issues (such as the Green Party's support of the environment); in ideology (the Socialist, Communist, and Libertarian Parties are examples); and in appealing, charismatic personalities (Theodore Roosevelt's Bill Moose Party is perhaps the best case). Many of the minor parties have drawn strength from a combination

two-party system
The political system in which two major parties dominate the electoral process; rules and customs operate to make it very difficult for third parties to become dominant.

third-partyism
The tendency of third parties to arise with some regularity in a nominally two-party system.

WEB EXPLORATION
Minor parties prolif-
erate, but finding one
that represents your views on
several issues is difficult. To
compare the planks of several
different minor parties, go to
www.ablongman.com/oconnor

In the 2000 presidential campaign, Green Party candidate
Ralph Nader attracted liberals,
environmentalists, and campaign
finance reformers, among others,
to his cause. As a third-party candidate, the former consumer
advocate garnered 3 percent of
the popular vote. (Photo courtesy:
AFB/Corbis)

of these sources. The American Independent Party enjoyed a measure
of success because of a dynamic leader (George Wallace), a firm geographic base (the South), and an emotional issue (civil rights). In 1992
Ross Perot, the billionaire with a folksy Texas manner, was a charismatic leader whose campaign was fueled by the deficit issue (as well as
by his personal fortune).

The 2000 election saw Green Party nominee Ralph Nader, the environmentalist and consumer advocate who ran for president in 1996,
lead a nationwide grassroots, anti-establishment campaign to oppose
the corporate-backed main party candidates, Vice President Al Gore
and Texas Governor George W. Bush. Although Nader collected just
2.86 million votes (or 2.72 percent nationwide, well below the 5 percent required for the Green Party to receive matching federal funding
in 2004), there is little question that Nader cost Democrat Al Gore the
presidency in 2000. In the critical state of Florida—the state that effectively decided the election—Nader received 97,488 votes, while the
official margin between Gore and Bush in that state was 537 votes out
of 5,963,070 votes cast. At least half of all Nader voters indicated in exit
polls that they would have voted for Gore in a two-way race, while most
of the rest said they would not have voted at all, and only a small percentage of Nader voters said that they would have voted for Bush over
Gore. Nader's 22,188 votes in New Hampshire also cost Gore the state
of New Hampshire, which Bush won by a mere 7,211 votes out of
567,795 cast. Gore, however, carried some states where Nader did well:
Wisconsin, Oregon, New Mexico, and Washington. Nader did relatively well in the critical state of California, but Gore won there any-
way, with an 11 percent margin over Bush.

Minor party and independent candidates are not limited to presidential elections; many also run in congressional elections, and the numbers
appear to be growing. In the 2000 congressional elections, for example,
more than 850 minor party and independent candidates ran for seats in
the House and Senate—almost eight times as many as in 1968 and nearly
three times the number who ran in 1980. In 2001, senator James Jeffords
switched from the Republican Party to Independent. A recent study shows
that minor party candidates for the House are most likely to emerge under
three conditions: (1) when a House seat becomes open, (2) when a minor
party candidate has previously competed in the district, and (3) when partisan competition between the two major parties in the district is close.[9]

Third parties make electoral progress in direct proportion to the failure of the two major parties to incorporate new ideas or alienated
groups or to nominate attractive candidates as their standard-bearers.
Usually, though, these third parties are eventually co-opted by one of
the two major parties. Third parties in the United States, however, are
basically akin to shooting stars that appear briefly and brilliantly but do
not long remain visible in the political constellation. In fact, the United
States is the only major Western nation that does not have at least one
significant, enduring national third party.

HIGHLIGHT

ARE YOU A DEMOCRAT? REPUBLICAN? GREEN? REFORM? LIBERTARIAN?

Choosing a political party can be easy or quite difficult. The answer depends on you and your values.

Republicans since the 1980s are generally identified as more conservative than Democrats and tend to be associated with free market economics, lower taxes, family values, hawkish foreign policy, and devolution of power from the federal government to the states.

Democrats of the last two decades, on the other hand, are associated with greater economic intervention, protection of minorities, a social safety net, including Social Security and Medicare, government regulation, protection of the environment, a less aggressive foreign policy, and the cause of poor and working-class people.

Of course, the descriptions of the political parties above are generalizations of their views. Clearly, many people are concerned about a combination of issues that are associated with both of the political parties. In addition, third parties perennially, if often fleetingly, emerge to appeal to highly focused voters, or to average voters when circumstances make urgent issues out of what are usually secondary concerns. For example, the Green Party's primary plank is based predominantly on environmentalism; the Reform Party's, on the need for nonpartisan reform of government corruption and inefficacy; the Libertarian Party's on the philosophical conviction that democracy functions

best with the least intervention from the state. These choices can be tempting for voters with strong opinions but without strong major-party affiliation, or voters who happen to place a great deal of importance on a third party's one key issue. The difficult question is: *How do you decide which party is generally more in line with your values?*

Try this exercise. Think about an issue or set of issues that is important to you. Ask yourself, are the positions taken by well-known politicians from the Republican and Democratic parties different? In what ways? If there are independent or minor-party candidates, do their views differ greatly from those of major-party candidates?

Of course, the choice of a political party is not usually made on the basis of one issue but on the basis of *many* issues taken together. Parties are not made up of one type of person but many diverse groups of people combined. The people who make up the membership of these parties have compromised on some issues and emphasized others in their choice of party. The bottom line is that it is up to you to choose the combination of issues that concern you the most and the party you believe best represents your values.

Do you consider yourself a Democrat or a Republican? Does it matter? Perhaps you are one of the almost one-third of Americans who claim to be independents?

Party Identification

In spite of the critical role that parties play in the political system, few Americans actually *belong* to a political party in any formal sense. Instead, most American voters *identify* with a party. To determine your party identification if you don't already have one, see Highlight: Are you a Democrat? Republican? Green? Reform? Libertarian? There is no universally enrolled party membership; there are no prescribed dues;

GLOBAL POLITICS

POLITICAL PARTIES IN
SELECTED DEMOCRACIES

The United States has a limited range of political parties at the national level. While there are many parties in this country, the Reform Party is currently the most prominent third party. Since the Civil War, the Republican and Democratic Parties have always controlled the federal government. Currently only one member of Congress, Bernie Sanders of Vermont, is a member of a third party.

Election rules offer a partial explanation for this. The "winner-take-all" single-member district system found here tends to produce a two-party system. Yet Canada and the United Kingdom also use the winner-take-all election rule, with two parties dominating their parliaments, but other parties also have at least a few members representing them in the legislature. In Britain's House of Commons, for example, even the Sinn Fein, the political arm of the Irish Republican Army, now has two seats (currently vacant because the party opposes British govern-

ment policy in Northern Ireland). Canada and the United Kingdom are thus better described as two-plus party systems. In the United States and the United Kingdom, the two dominant parties are far larger than any of their rivals, consistent with the understanding of the effects of single-member districts. The near destruction of the once-dominant Progressive Liberal Party in Canada has evened out the distribution of parliamentary seats.

The European countries and Japan have multiparty systems. Typically, there are several parties that can expect to control the executive branch, and a coalition of parties in the cabinet is a frequent feature of these systems. Again, election rules tend to produce such a party configuration. Germany, Italy, and Japan all have two-ballot elections in which voters elect part of the legislature from single-member districts and part by proportional representation based on party lists. Proportional representation tends to benefit

---

party identification

A citizen's personal affinity for a political party, usually expressed by his or her tendency to vote for the candidates of that party.

no formal rules concerning an individual's activities; no enforceable obligations to the party assumed by the voter. The party has no real control over or even an accurate accounting of its adherents, and the party's voters subscribe to few or none of the commonly accepted tenets of organizational membership, such as regular participation and some measure of responsibility for the group's welfare. Still, the party in the electorate—the mass of potential voters who identify with a particular party's label—is the most significant element of the political party. **Party identification** or affiliation is an informal and impressionistic exercise whereby a citizen acquires a party label and accepts its standard as a shorthand summary of his or her political views and preferences.

However, just because the acquisition is informal does not mean that it is unimportant. The party label becomes a voter's central political reference symbol and perceptual screen, a prism or filter through which the world of politics and government flows and is interpreted. For many

smaller parties, because their electoral bases are not confined to districts. Not only do these countries' parliaments have several medium-sized parties (Japan is a bit different because the conservative party is far larger than any of its rivals), but they have parties that span the political spectrum. On the left, social democratic parties are represented in every legislature. France, Germany, and Japan have communist parties (a reformed one in Germany's case). In France, the reactionary National Front has emerged in the last decade as a powerful alternative to the mainstream conservative Union for French Democracy and the Rally for the Republic.

China, Mexico, and Indonesia challenge American assumptions about what the term "political party" means. China is a one-party state in which the Communist Party is guaranteed the leading role in politics by the constitution. The eight other parties represented in the National People's Congress form a token opposition that publicly acknowledges the Communist Party's preeminent position as the price for being allowed to exist. Until the 1999 elections, Indonesian legislative politics was dominated by GOLKAR, an official party created and supported by the military and the civil service. Since 1999, the once dominant GOLKAR finds itself in the uncomfortable position of being the second largest of twenty parties but it still dwarfs the smaller parties in the legislature. The Institutional Revolutionary Party (PRI) in Mexico dominated politics there until recently, although less by statutory provision than by skillful manipulation of patronage.

Number of Political Parties in the Lower House of National Legislatures, 1999

Country	Number of Parties
Canada	5
France	6
Germany	6
Italy	8
Japan	8
United Kingdom	11
United States	**3**

Americans, party identification is a significant aspect of one's political personality and a way of defining and explaining oneself to others. The loyalty generated by the label can be as intense as any enjoyed by sports teams and alma maters; in a few areas of the country, "Democrat" and "Republican" are still fighting words.

On the whole, though, Americans regard their partisan affiliation with lesser degrees of enthusiasm, viewing it as a convenience rather than a necessity. The individual identifications are reinforced by the legal institutionalization of the major parties. Because of restrictive ballot laws, campaign finance rules, the powerful inertia of political tradition, and many other factors, voters for all practical purposes are limited to a choice between a Democrat and a Republican in virtually all elections—a situation that naturally encourages the pragmatic choosing up of sides. The party registration process that exists in about half of the states, requiring a voter to state a party preference (or independent status) when registering

POLITICS NOW

THE MOVE TOWARD THE CENTER

The 2000 election played itself out in a most unconventional manner, but one aspect of the campaign proceeded pretty much by the book: a move toward centrism—a convergence of candidate platforms around the center of the political-ideological spectrum—resulting almost entirely from the open nature of the election (i.e., neither candidate was an incumbent).

Open contests for the presidency are almost always more competitive than elections contested by an incumbent president (there are of course exceptions, such as the elections of 1980 and 1992). Basically, the Democrats and Republicans each control between 33 and 40 percent of the electorate, based on nationwide party identification numbers, while 20 to 33 percent of the electorate considers themselves independents. Independents tend to be more center-oriented or moderate in some views, so if a candidate can secure his or her base, he or she will then articulate a moderate position to capture more of the independent, moderate voters. The first politician to define the "move to the center" in such a way was Richard M. Nixon, who advised Republican presidential candidates to run to the right for the primaries and to the center for the general election. For Democrats, the reverse is true: run to the left for the primaries, then run to the middle for the general election.

In 2000, true to form, centrism offered the key to victory. However widely mocked by skeptical liberals, Bush's centrist platform of "compassionate conservatism" enabled him to make some improvements in his ratings with women and Hispanics. Bush still lost both groups to Gore, but he did considerably better than his predecessor in 1996, Bob Dole, and this slight gain was one of many small things that made the critical difference for Bush.

Al Gore, on the other hand, declined to make similar centrist gestures and paid the penalty. In a close-running and open election, his strong advocacy of gun control, environmentalism, and reproductive freedom likely failed to endear him to moderate voters. The best evidence of this failure was the loss of both his home state, Tennessee, and the usually heavily Democratic West Virginia. Why did Gore lose two states that he almost certainly should have carried? The answer is simple: his liberal position on guns, coal, and abortion.

to vote and restricting participation in primaries to party registrants, also is an incentive for voters to affiliate themselves with a party.[10]

Sources of Party Identification.   As revealed in Table 11.1, Republicans are much more likely to be white, male, and have at least some college education. The sharpest difference between Democrats and Republicans is political ideology, although there is a move to the ideological center in the United States, as is underscored in Politics Now. More than half of the Republicans but only 22 percent of the Democrats surveyed by the Gallup Organization say that they are conservative. Democrats are more likely than Republicans to identify themselves as moderate.

TABLE 11.1   Who Makes Up Republican and Democratic Parties?

	Republicans/ Including Independents Who Lean Republican	Democrats/ Including Independents Who Lean Democratic
Gender		
Male	53%	43%
Female	47%	57%
Age		
18–29	21%	20%
30–49	43%	40%
50–64	19%	21%
65+	15%	18%
Race		
White	93%	75%
Black	3%	19%
Other nonwhite	4%	6%
Education		
Postgraduate degree	12%	13%
Undergraduate degree	14%	11%
Some college	37%	29%
No college	38%	47%
Household Income		
$75,000 and over	22%	15%
$50,000–$74,999	21%	16%
$30,000–$49,999	24%	25%
$20,000–$29,999	12%	14%
Less than $20,000	15%	23%
Region		
East	20%	25%
Midwest	24%	22%
South	33%	31%
West	22%	21%

Source: www.gallup.com/poll/releases/pr000728e.asp.

Whatever the societal and governmental forces undergirding party identification, the explanations of partisan loyalty at the individual's level are understandably more personal. Not surprisingly, parents are the single greatest influence in establishing a person's first party identification. Politically active parents with the same party loyalty raise children who will be strong party identifiers, while parents without party affiliations or with mixed affiliations produce offspring more likely to be independents. Early socialization is hardly the last step in the acquisition and maintenance of a party identity; marriage and other facts of adult life can change one's loyalty. Gender and race, too, are compelling predictors of party identification. Women and African

Americans, for example, are much more likely to identify as Democrats than as Republicans.

Charismatic political personalities, particularly at the national level (such as Franklin D. Roosevelt and Ronald Reagan), cataclysmic events (the Civil War and the Great Depression are the best examples), and maybe intense social issues (for instance, abortion) also lead some individuals to identify with a particular party. Interestingly, social class is not an especially strong indicator of likely partisan choice in the United States, at least in comparison with Western European democracies. Not only are Americans less inclined than Europeans to perceive class distinctions—preferring instead to see themselves and most others as members of an exceedingly broad middle class—but other factors, including sectionalism and candidate-oriented politics, tend to blur class lines in voting.

INTEREST GROUPS

The face of interest group politics in the United States is changing as quickly as laws, political consultants, and technology allow. The activities of big business and trade groups like the Bankruptcy Coalition are increasing at the same time that there is conflict in evidence concerning whether or not ordinary citizens even join political groups. In an influential essay, "Bowling Alone: America's Declining Social Capital," one political scientist argues that fewer Americans are joining groups,[11] while another political scientist concludes that America is in the midst of an "explosion of voluntary groups, activities and charitable donations [that] is transforming our towns and cities."[12] While bowling leagues have withered, other groups including soccer associations, health clubs, and environmental groups are flourishing. Old groups like the Elks Club and the League of Women Voters, whose membership was tracked in the original study, are no longer attracting members. At the same time, people also are reporting more *individual* acts—many of them designed to pressure policy makers at all levels of government.

The major national parties are not always recognized as progressive forces, but in fact many advances in suffrage and voting rights have been spearheaded by the parties as they search for new sources of support. Although still seriously underrepresented, women in recent years have made inroads as delegates, candidates, and office holders. (Photo courtesy: Paul J. Richards/AFP/Corbis)

Today, community soccer associations may be playing the same role that bowling leagues once played in the United States. Political scientists, many trained in the 1960s and 1970s, may have overlooked the kinds of contributions most frequently made by young people today: involvement in voluntary community service work (as opposed to that often required by many school districts). Young people often don't see involvement in groups such as Habitat for Humanity or working in a soup kitchen as political, but it often is.

Interest groups often fill voids left by the traditional political parties and give Americans another opportunity to take their claims directly to the government. Interest groups give the underrepresented and unrepresented an opportunity to have their voices heard, thereby making the government and its policy-making processes more representative of diverse populations and perspectives.

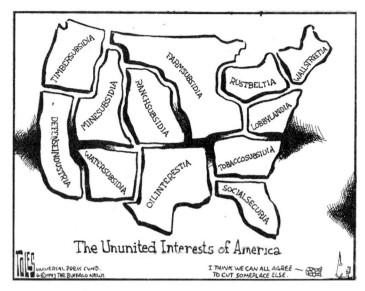

The Ununited Interests of America

I THINK WE CAN ALL AGREE — TO CUT SOMEPLACE ELSE.

(Photo courtesy: Toles ©*The Buffalo News*. Reprinted with permission of Universal Press Syndicate. All rights reserved.)

Why and How Interest Groups Form and Maintain Themselves

As with the many different definitions of interest groups, a variety of sound reasons have been offered to explain why interest groups form. Generally, however, interest groups tend to arise in response to changes. These can be political or economic changes, changes in the population, technological changes, or even changes in society itself. According to one study, nearly 70 percent of today's D.C.–based political organizations established their offices after 1960.[13] Nearly half opened their offices after 1970. Not surprisingly, given the social and economic thrust of President Lyndon B. Johnson's Great Society programs, most of the new groups were formed to take advantage of the money and opportunities those programs offered.

David B. Truman, one of the first political scientists to study interest groups, posed what he termed **disturbance theory** to explain why interest groups form. He hypothesized that groups form in part to counteract the activities of other groups or of organized special interests. According to Truman, the government's role is to provide a forum in which the competing demands of groups and the majority of the U.S. population can be heard and balanced. He argued that the government's role in managing competing groups is to balance their conflicting demands.[14]

Political scientist Robert H. Salisbury expanded upon Truman by arguing that groups are formed when resources—be they clean air,

www.longmanparticipate.com

TIMELINE
Interest Groups
in America

disturbance theory
The theory offered by political scientist David B. Truman that posits that interest groups form in part to counteract the efforts of other groups.

women's rights, or rights of the unborn, for example—are inadequate or scarce.[15] Moreover, unlike Truman, he stresses the role that leaders, or what he terms "entrepreneurs," play in the formation of groups.

Leaders and Patrons.   Interest-group theorists such as Robert Salisbury frequently acknowledge the key role that leaders play in the formation, viability, and success of interest groups. Jack L. Walker contends that without what he terms patrons (those who often finance a group) few organizations could begin.[16] The role of an interest-group leader is similar to that of an entrepreneur in the business world. As in the marketing of a new product, an interest-group leader must have something attractive to offer to persuade members to join. Potential members of the group must be convinced that the benefits of joining outweigh the costs. Union members, for example, must be persuaded that the cost of their union dues will be offset by the union's winning higher wages for them.

WEB EXPLORATION
To join Rock the Vote, see
www.ablongman.com/oconnor

Funding.   Funding is crucial to all interest groups whether a labor union, the National Rifle Association, an environment group, or Rock the Vote. Government, foundations, and wealthy individuals can serve as patrons providing crucial start-up funds for groups, especially public interest groups. Groups also rely heavily on membership contributions, dues, and other fund-raising activities.[17]

Members.   Alexis de Tocqueville, a French aristocrat and philosopher, toured the United States extensively during 1831 and 1832. A keen observer of American politics, he was very much impressed by the tendency of Americans to join groups in order to participate in the policy-making process. "Whenever at the head of some new undertaking you see government in France, or a man of rank in England, in the United States you will be sure to find an association,"[18] wrote de Tocqueville.

Groups vary tremendously in their ability to enroll what are called potential members. Economist Mancur Olson Jr. notes that all groups provide some **collective good**—that is, something of value, such as money, a tax write-off, a good feeling, or a better environment—that can't be withheld from a nonmember of the group.[19] If one union member at a factory gets a raise, for example, all other workers at that factory will, too. Therefore those who don't join or work for the benefit of the group still reap the rewards of the group's activity. This phenomenon is called the **free rider** problem. Consequently, Olson asserts, potential members are unlikely to join a group because they realize that they will receive many of the benefits the group achieves regardless of their participation. Not only is it irrational for free riders to join any group, but the bigger the group, the greater the free rider problem. Thus groups need to provide a variety of other incentives to convince potential members to join. These can be newsletters, discounts, or simply a good feeling. While many interest groups individually are experiencing

collective good
Something of value that cannot be withheld from a nonmember of the group, for example, a tax write-off, a good feeling.

free rider
A problem that occurs when those who don't join or work for the benefit of the group still reap the rewards of the group's activity.

difficulty in recruiting new members, the actual role of interest groups in the political process continues to grow.

The Rise of the Interest Group State

During the 1960s and 1970s, the Progressive spirit found renewed vigor in the rise of all kinds of organized interests including public interest groups, conservative groups, business groups, trade and professional organizations, and labor unions.

Public Interest Groups. **Public interest groups** are organizations "that seek a collective good, the achievement of which will not selectively and materially benefit the membership or activists of the organization."[20] These public interest groups were formed by Americans who were cynical about trusting government to enforce minority rights, protect the environment, or police itself. Common Cause, for example, was founded as a "good government" group. Ralph Nader's Public Citizen was founded to monitor product safety and government regulation. A plethora of groups devoted to representing the interests of African Americans, women, the elderly, the poor, or on behalf of the environment were also established. Many of them had as their patron the liberal Ford Foundation, which helped to bankroll numerous groups including the Mexican American Legal Defense and Education Fund, and the Native American Rights Fund.

public interest group
An organization that seeks a collective good that will not selectively and materially benefit the members of the group.

 WEB EXPLORATION
For more about Common Cause and Public Citizen, see www.ablongman.com/oconnor

Conservative Backlash: Religious and Ideological Groups. The growth and successes that various public interest groups had in the 1960s and 1970s and the civil rights and women's rights movements ultimately led to a conservative backlash. Conservatives became very concerned about the successes of liberal groups in shaping and defining the public agenda, and religious and ideological conservatives became a potent force in U.S. politics. The first major new religious group was the Reverend Jerry Falwell's Moral Majority, founded in 1978. It was widely credited with assisting Ronald Reagan's 1980 presidential victory as well as the defeats of several liberal Democratic senators that same year. Falwell claimed to have sent from 3 million to 4 million newly registered voters to the polls. Falwell, however, disbanded the Moral Majority in 1989.[21]

In 1990 televangelist Pat Robertson, host of the popular *700 Club*, formed a new group, the Christian Coalition, to fill the void left by the demise of the Moral Majority. Since then, it has grown in power and influence by leaps and bounds. Its exit polling showed that religious conservatives accounted for one-third of all votes cast in 1994 and provided the margin of victory for all Republicans who won with 53 percent of the vote or less.[22]

The reorganized coalition continued its efforts to inform voters of issues of concern to it without specifically endorsing candidates. The

WEB EXPLORATION
For more on the
Christian Coalition, see
www.ablongman.com/oconnor

weekend before the November 2000 elections, the Christian Coalition distributed more than 70 miller voter guides in churches throughout the United States. In Florida, it passed out over 3 million voter guides; 1 million were in Spanish.[23]

The Christian Coalition is not the only conservative interest group to play an important role in the policy process as well as in elections at the state and national level. The National Rifle Association (NRA) has been an active opponent of gun control legislation and of late has seen its membership rise as well as its importance in Washington, D.C. (See Analyzing the Data.) Its political action committee raised $11.4 million and spent $1.6 million dollars to help elect President George W. Bush. Before the election, an NRA vice president boasted about Bush: "We'll have a president…where we work out of their office—unbelievably friendly relations."[24] To motivate voters, NRA President Charlton Heston barnstormed through close states, including Tennessee and West Virginia, recognizing that the election of a president sympathetic to its cause would make ultimate passage of NRA-supported legislation more likely.[25]

Business Groups, Trade and Professional Associations.   Businesses and corporations, too, can be powerful individually or collectively as organized interests. Most large corporations, for example, employ D.C.-based lobbyists to keep them apprised of legislation that may affect them or to lobby for the consideration of legislation that could help them as well as to lobby bureaucrats for government contracts. The Business Roundtable, for example, was created in 1972 (largely made up of the chief executive officers of major businesses). The Roundtable, say some, is "a fraternity of powerful and prestigious business leaders that tells 'business's side of the story' to legislators, bureaucrats, White House personnel, and other interested public officials."[26] It urges its members to engage in direct lobbying to influence the course of policy formation.

Organizations like the Chamber of Commerce and the Business Roundtable, as well as trade associations (groups that represent specific industries), enjoy many of the benefits other businesses do as lobbyists: They already have extensive organization, expertise, large numbers, a strong financial base, and a longstanding relationship with key actors in government. Such natural advantages have led to a huge number of business groups. Many of these national groups devote tremendous resources to fighting government regulation.

Large corporations also gave large sums to favored politicians or political candidates. In 1998, for example, when Senate Majority Leader Trent Lott (R–Miss.) sought reelection to his Senate seat, he received $367,498 from the National Association of Realtors, $333,126 from Auto Dealers and Drivers for Free Trade (manufacturers of Japanese cars), $33,000 from Federal Express, and $58,202 from National Security PAC (defense interest advocacy). In the 2000 election, the 1,000 biggest companies gave a record $187 million to candidates for president and other national

WEB EXPLORATION
For more
information on
business, trade, and professional organizations, go to
www.ablongman.com/oconnor

A N A L Y Z I N G   T H E   D A T A

HOW NRA MEMBERSHIP HAS RISEN

The National Rifle Association (NRA), a single-issue interest group, lobbies against any law that it considers a restriction on an individual's right to bear arms. NRA membership has spiked in recent years in reaction to proposed gun control legislation. Interestingly, following the Columbine High School shooting in 1999, in which twelve people were killed, membership has increased dramatically.

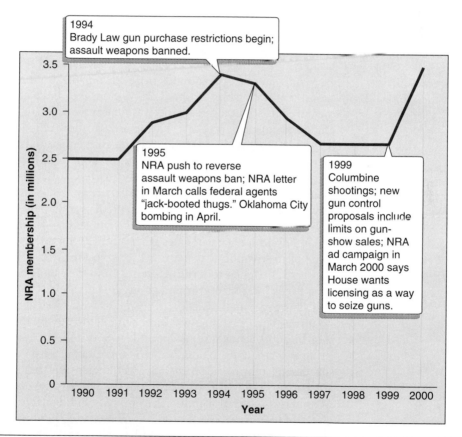

Source: "How the NRA Membership Has Risen" by Genevieve Lynn, *USA Today,* May 18, 2000: p. A1. Copyright 2000, USA TODAY. Reprinted with permission.

offices. Microsoft was number 1. After recognizing the importance of having friends in Washington, it gave a total of $3.7 million (in 1996 Microsoft gave only $237,000 to candidates). AT&T, which wants Congress to instruct the Federal Elections Commission to relax rule that limit ownership in the pay-television market, was a close second.[27]

WEB EXPLORATION
For more information
on labor unions, see
www.ablongman.com/oconnor

Organized Labor   Membership in labor unions held steady throughout the early and mid 1900s and then skyrocketed toward the end of the Depression. By then, organized labor began to be a potent political force as it was able to turn out its members in support of particular political candidates. Labor became a stronger force in U.S. politics when the American Federation of Labor merged with the Congress of Industrial Organizations in 1955. Concentrating its efforts largely on the national level, the new AFL-CIO immediately turned its energies to pressuring the government to protect concessions won from employers at the bargaining table and to other issues of concern to its members, including minimum wage laws, the environment, civil rights, medical insurance, and health care.

But the once-fabled political clout of organized labor has been on the wane at the national level. Union membership has plummeted as the nation has changed from a land of manufacturing workers and farmers to a nation of white-collar professionals and service workers. As a consequence, unions and agricultural organizations no longer have the large memberships or the political clout they once held in governmental circles. By the late 1970s, it was clear that even during a Democratic administration (Carter's), organized labor lacked the impact it had during earlier decades. During the Reagan administration, organized labor's influence fell to an all-time modern-day low. In spite of the tremendous resources behind the AFL-CIO and other unions, membership dropped through 1998 but remained constant in 1999, prompting union leaders to hope. In 1970, over 25 percent of workers were unionized; in 2000, only 13.9 percent were.

Organized labor recognizes its troubles and has tried to recapture some of its lost political clout. Since 1996 the AFL-CIO has ambitiously campaigned to return Congress into the hands of the Democratic Party, long a good friend to organized labor. Targeted TV and radio ads were run in districts of members who voted against the minimum wage increase that was later signed into law by President Clinton. In 2000, labor unions spent over $60 million, with 98 percent going to Democrats. Not only did unions around the nation contribute substantial sums to elect pro-labor candidates, but they also launched a massive get-out-the-vote effort to get fellow workers to the polls. Members made over 8 million phone calls and distributed 12 million pieces of literature. The AFL-CIO alone had 2,000 full-time coordinators working to mobilize union households.[28] While the presidential election was being contested in Florida, unions played an important role in turning out Gore supporters in several count-the-vote rallies.

lobbying
The activities of groups and organizations that seek to influence legislation and persuade political leaders to support a group's position.

What Interest Groups Do

Lobbying.   Most interest groups put lobbying at the top of their agendas. **Lobbying** is the process by which interest groups attempt to assert

TABLE 11.2   Lobbying Techniques of Interest Groups

Technique	STATE-BASED GROUPS		D.C.-BASED GROUPS
	Lobbyists	Organizations	
The Proportion of Each Group Reporting Each Act	(n = 595)	(n = 301)	(n = 175)
Testifying at legislative hearings	98%	99%	99%
Contacting government officials directly to present point of view	98	97	98
Helping to draft legislation	96	88	85
Alerting state legislators to the effects of a bill on their districts	96	94	75
Having influential constituents contact legislator's office	94	92	80
Consulting with government officials to plan legislative strategy	88	84	85
Attempting to shape implementation of policies	88	85	89
Mounting grassroots lobbying efforts	88	86	80
Helping to draft regulations, rules, or guidelines	84	81	78
Shaping government's agenda by raising new issues and calling attention to previously ignored problems	85	83	84
Engaging in informal contacts with officials	83	81	95
Inspiring letter-writing or telegram campaigns	82	83	84
Entering into coalitions with other groups	79	93	90
Talking to media	73	74	86
Serving on advisory commissions and boards	58	76	76
Making monetary contributions to candidates	—	45	58
Attempting to influence appointment to public office	44	42	53
Doing favors for officials who need assistance	41	36	56
Filing suit or otherwise engaging in litigation	36	40	72
Working on election campaign	—	29	24
Endorsing candidates	—	24	22
Running advertisements in media about position	18	21	31
Engaging in protests or demonstrations	13	21	20

Sources: State-based groups: Anthony J. Nownes and Patricia Freeman, "Interest Group Activity in the States," *Journal of Politics* (February 1998): 92. D.C.-based groups: Kay Lehman Schlozman and John Tierney, "More of the Same: Washington Pressure Group Activity in a Decade of Change," *Journal of Politics* 45 (1983): 358.

their influence on the policy process. As Table 11.2 indicates, there are many ways to lobby. Lobbying allows interest groups to try to convince key governmental decision makers and the public of the correctness of their positions. Almost all interest groups lobby by testifying at hearings and contacting legislators. Other groups also provide information that decision makers might not have the time, opportunity, or interest to gather on their own.

Lobbying Congress.   Members of Congress are the targets of a wide variety of lobbying activities: congressional testimony on behalf of a group, individual letters from interested constituents, campaign contributions, trips, speaking fees, or the outright payment of money for votes. Of course, the last item is illegal, but there are numerous documented instances of money changing hands for votes. Many lobbying firms pay millions yearly to former lawmakers to lobby their old

WEB EXPLORATION
For information on groups that monitor lobbying activity, see
www.ablongman.com/oconnor

WEB EXPLORATION
For more on orga-
nized lobbyists, see
www.ablongman.com/oconnor

colleagues. Many former U.S. senators including Robert Dole, as well as former Texas Governor Ann Richards, all earn well over a half million dollars a year as lobbyists for D.C.-based lobbying firms who are hired by interest groups and other special interests to advance their causes.[29]

Because lobbying plays such an important role in Congress, many effective lobbyists often are former members of that body, former staff aides, former White House officials or Cabinet officers, or Washington insiders. This type of lobbyist frequently drops in to visit members of Congress or their staff members and often takes them to lunch, golf, or parties. Although much of that activity may be ethically questionable, most is not illegal.

Attempts to Reform Congressional Lobbying.   In 1946, in an effort to limit the power of lobbyists, Congress passed the Federal Regulation of Lobbying Act, which required anyone hired to lobby any member of Congress to register and file quarterly financial reports. Few lobbyists actually file these reports. For years, numerous good government groups argued that lobbying laws should be strengthened. Civil liberties groups such as the American Civil Liberties Union (ACLU), however, argue that registration provisions violate the First Amendment's freedom of speech and the right of citizens to petition the government.

But public opinion polls continued to reveal that many Americans believed that the votes of numerous members of Congress were often available to the highest bidder. In late 1995, after nearly fifty years of inaction, Congress passed the first effort to regulate lobbying since the 1946 act. The new act, the 1995 Lobbying Disclosure Act, was passed overwhelmingly in both houses of Congress. The new rules employ a strict definition of lobbyist, which should trigger far greater reporting of lobbyist activities. They also require lobbyists to:

1. Register with the clerk of the House and the secretary of the Senate.
2. Report their clients and issues and the agency or house they lobbied.
3. Estimate the amount they are paid by each client.

SIMULATION
You Are a Lobbyist

The reporting of clients and issues should make it easier for those kinds of activities to be monitored by watchdog groups or the media. But the new law hasn't done much to stem the proliferation of lobbyists or money spent on lobbying. In fact, first comprehensive analysis by the Center for Responsible Politics revealed that by June 1999, 20,512 lobbyists were registered—a 35 percent jump from just two years earlier. The number of organizations reporting spending more than one million dollars a year on lobbying also jumped dramatically to 117. In 1998, $2.7 million was spent on lobbying for every member of Congress.[30] See Figure 11.5 for the expenditures of top lobbyists.

FIGURE 11.5   Expenditures of Top Lobbyists

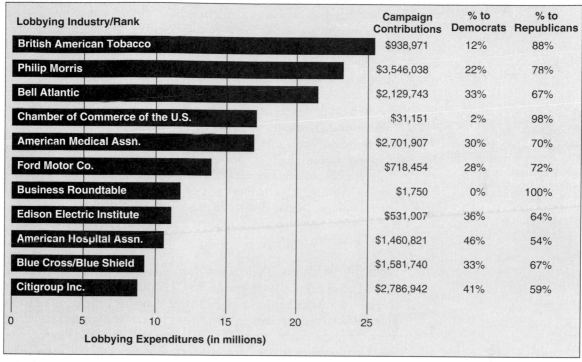

Lobbying Industry/Rank	Campaign Contributions	% to Democrats	% to Republicans
British American Tobacco	$938,971	12%	88%
Philip Morris	$3,546,038	22%	78%
Bell Atlantic	$2,129,743	33%	67%
Chamber of Commerce of the U.S.	$31,151	2%	98%
American Medical Assn.	$2,701,907	30%	70%
Ford Motor Co.	$718,454	28%	72%
Business Roundtable	$1,750	0%	100%
Edison Electric Institute	$531,907	36%	64%
American Hospital Assn.	$1,460,821	46%	54%
Blue Cross/Blue Shield	$1,581,740	33%	67%
Citigroup Inc.	$2,786,942	41%	59%

Lobbying Expenditures (in millions)

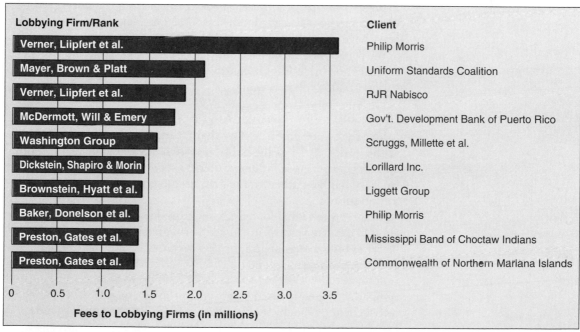

Lobbying Firm/Rank	Client
Verner, Liipfert et al.	Philip Morris
Mayer, Brown & Platt	Uniform Standards Coalition
Verner, Liipfert et al.	RJR Nabisco
McDermott, Will & Emery	Gov't. Development Bank of Puerto Rico
Washington Group	Scruggs, Millette et al.
Dickstein, Shapiro & Morin	Lorillard Inc.
Brownstein, Hyatt et al.	Liggett Group
Baker, Donelson et al.	Philip Morris
Preston, Gates et al.	Mississippi Band of Choctaw Indians
Preston, Gates et al.	Commonwealth of Northern Mariana Islands

Fees to Lobbying Firms (in millions)

Sources: http://www.opensecrets.org/pubs/lobby98/topspend.html; http://www.opensecrets.org/pubs/lobby98/topfees.html.

Lobbying the Executive Branch and Executive Agencies.   Groups often target one or more levels of the executive branch because there are so many potential access points—the president and White House staff, and the numerous levels of the executive branch bureaucracy. Groups try to work closely with the administration in an effort to influence policy decisions at their formulation and implementation stages. Most presidents specifically set up staff positions "explicitly to serve as brokerages or clearinghouses to provide greater access to presidential attention for professional, demographic or specialized organizations."[31]

An especially strong link exists between interest groups and regulatory agencies. While these agencies are ostensibly independent of Congress and the president, interest groups often have clout there. Because of the highly technical aspects of much regulatory work, many groups employ Washington attorneys to deal directly with the agencies. So great is interest group influence in the decision-making process of these agencies that many people charge that the agencies have been captured by the interest groups.

Lobbying the Courts.   The courts, too, have proved a useful target for interest groups.[32] Although you might think that the courts decide cases that affect only the parties involved or that they should be immune from political pressures, interest groups have for years recognized the value of lobbying the courts, especially the Supreme Court, and many political scientists view it as a form of political participation. As shown in Table 11.2, 72 percent of the Washington-based groups surveyed participated in litigation as a lobbying tool. Most major cases noted in this book have either been sponsored by an interest group, or one or both of the parties in the case have been supported by an *amicus curiae* (friend of the court) brief. Highly controversial cases often attract the participation of 100 groups or more.

Grassroots Lobbying.   As the term implies, *grassroots lobbying* is a form of pressure-group activity that attempts to involve those people at the bottom level of the political system. The goal of many organizations is to persuade ordinary voters to serve as their advocates. In the world of lobbying, there are few things more useful than a list of committed supporters.

Some professional lobbyists use grassroots lobbying as a cover for another client. Typically, in these kinds of grassroots campaigns, a "large business hires a Washington firm to organize a coalition of small business, nonprofit groups, and individuals across the nation."[33] This coalition (or better yet, arranged marriage) then draws public attention and sympathy to the proposed policy or legislation sought by the lobbyists' initial client—who, by the time the issue gets on the public agenda, has faded from the public. This kind of grassroots lobbying occurs on most major pieces of legislation.

WEB EXPLORATION
To experience how the lobbying process works, see www.ablongman.com/oconnor

The simple grassroots campaigns of just a few years ago (fill-in-the-blank post cards and forms torn out of the newspaper) have grown much more sophisticated and become much more effective. Some groups buy television ad time, many interest groups and trade groups have installed banks of computerized fax machines to send faxes automatically around the country overnight, instructing each member to ask his or her employees, customers, or other people to write, call, or fax their members of Congress. Other interest groups now run carefully targeted and costly television advertisements pitching one side of an argument. Their opponents must generally respond or lose. Many of these advertisements end with a toll-free phone number that viewers can call if they find the pitch convincing. New telemarketing companies answer these calls and transfer the callers directly to the offices of the appropriate members of Congress.[34]

The Internet is the newest weapon in the arsenal of interest groups and lobbyists. Each major party's political convention had an Internet Alley, with "dot-com delegates" participating in a virtual convention. Many see this as a way of encouraging grassroots political involvement that politicians and political parties will soon need to respond to. E-mail is a way for groups to connect with supporters as well as to urge supporters to connect with policy makers. Digital activism can be especially effective at the local level. "Flash campaigns," as they are called, can be generated with the click of a mouse to contact hundreds or thousands of concerned citizens.[35]

PARTICIPATION
Interest Groups
and Gun Control

Protest Activities.   Most groups have few members so devoted as to put everything on the line for their cause. Some will risk jail or even death, but it is much more usual for a group's members to opt for more conventional forms of lobbying or to influence policy through the electoral process. When these forms of pressure group activities are unsuccessful or appear to be too slow to achieve results, however, some groups (or individuals within groups) resort to more forceful legal and illegal measures to attract attention to their cause.

Groups on both ends of the political spectrum historically have resorted to violence in the furtherance of their objectives. Abolitionists, anti–nuclear power activists, antiwar activists, animal-rights advocates, and other groups on the "left" have broken laws, damaged property, and even injured or killed people, as have groups on the "right" such as the Army of God (an anti-abortion group) and the Ku Klux Klan (KKK). From the early 1900s until the 1960s, African Americans were routinely lynched by KKK members. Today some radical anti-abortion groups regularly block the entrances to abortion clinics; others active in the anti-abortion movement have taken credit for clinic bombings.

Other protest activities are less violent, sometimes tasteless, and often also illegal. After New York City Mayor Rudy Giuliani announced that he had prostrate cancer, People for the Ethical Treatment of Animals (PETA) put up controversial billboards that linked prostrate cancer with drinking milk. PETA activists also have trespassed on private property to "free" animals from testing by humans, and they have thrown red paint on women sporting fur coats.

Election Activities

In addition to trying to achieve their goals or, at least, draw attention to them, through the conventional and unconventional forms of lobbying and protest activity, many interest groups also become involved more directly in the electoral process. The 2000 Republican and Democratic presidential nominating conventions both were the target of significant organized interest group protest concerning each party's stance on a variety of issues, including U.S. involvement in Colombian drug wars, support for Iraqi sanctions, the death penalty, abortion, and third-world sweatshops.

Endorsements.   Many groups claim to be nonpartisan, that is, nonpolitical. Usually they try to have friends in both political parties to whom they can look for assistance and access. Some organizations, however, routinely endorse candidates for public office, pledging money, group support, and often even campaign volunteers. Figure 11.5, shows that spenders tend to give more to Republicans.

EMILY's List, a women's group (EMILY stands for "Early Money Is Like Yeast—it makes the dough rise"), not only endorses candidates but contributes heavily to races of pro-choice women. In 1998, Planned Parenthood broke with tradition and endorsed candidates for the first time. This pro-choice group believed the change of only three senators could allow the Senate to override President Clinton's veto of anti-abortion restrictions. It is not unusual, moreover, for conservation or environmental groups to endorse candidates that they view as friends.

Once groups become overly political, however, their tax-exempt status is jeopardized. Federal law precludes tax-exempt organizations from taking partisan positions (unless it is through a PAC). The Christian Coalition for years claimed to be nonpartisan, although the FEC charged that it used money to promote specific candidates, causing it to redesign its scorecards into voters guides.

Endorsements from some groups may be used by a candidate's opponent to attack a candidate. While labor union endorsements can add money to candidates' campaign coffers, for example, they risk being labeled a "tool of the labor unions" by their opponents.

Rating the Candidates or Office Holders.   Many liberal and conservative ideological groups rate candidates to help their members (and the general public) evaluate the voting records of members of Congress.

The American Conservative Union (conservative) and the Americans for Democratic Action (liberal)—two groups at ideological polar extremes—routinely rate candidates and members of Congress based on their votes on key issues of importance to the group, as illustrated in Table 11.3. These scores help voters to know more about their representatives votes on issues that concern them.

WEB EXPLORATION
For more information on the ACU and on the ADA, go to www.ablongman.com/oconnor

Creating Political Parties. Another interest group strategy is to form a political party to publicize a cause and even possibly win a few public offices. In 1995, many in the Ross Perot–founded United We Stand formed the Reform Party to highlight the group's goals including reform of campaign finance laws. Similarly, consumer advocate Ralph Nader was the nominee of the new Green Party, created to bring attention to environmental issues as well as some people's perceived similarities in the two major parties. Groups often see forming political parties as a way to draw attention to their legislative goals and to drive one of the major political parties to give their demands serious attention.

WEB EXPLORATION
For more on the Reform Party and the Green Party, see www.ablongman.com/oconnor

Interest Groups and Political Action Committees. Throughout most of history, powerful interests and individuals have often used their money to "buy" politicians or their votes. Even if outright bribery was not involved, huge corporate or other interest group donations certainly made some politicians look as if they were in the "pocket" of certain special interests. Congressional passage of the Federal Election Campaign Act began to change most of that. The 1971 act required

TABLE 11.3 Interest Group Ratings of Selected Members of Congress, 2000*

Member	ACU	ACLU	ADA	AFL-CIO	CC	CoC	CFA	LCV
Senate								
Dianne Feinstein (D–Calif.)	28	57	100	78	10	53	86	100
Jesse Helms (R–N.C.)	100	29	0	22	100	82	14	0
Kay Bailey Hutchison (R–Tex.)	96	29	0	0	91	94	29	0
Edward M. Kennedy (D–Mass.)	12	71	95	88	0	47	71	89
House								
Tom DeLay (R–Tex.)	88	14	0	0	100	92	33	6
Sheila Jackson-Lee (D–Tex.)	4	86	100	78	7	29	83	75
C.W. Bill Young (R–Fla.)	72	21	20	38	100	86	50	0

Key
ACU = American Conservative Union
ACLU = American Civil Liberties Union
ADA = Americans for Democratic Action
AFL–CIO = American Federation of Labor–
   Congress of Industrial Organizations

CC = Christian Coalition
CoC = Chamber of Commerce
CFA = Consumer Federation of America
LCV = League of Conservation Voters

*Members are rated on a scale from 1 to 100, with 1 being the lowest and 100 being the highest support of a particular group's policies.

POINT/COUNTERPOINT

DO INTEREST GROUPS HURT OR HELP DEMOCRACY?

Since the 1960s, interest groups have proliferated dramatically, and some people claim that this explosion of interest groups harms democracy. Others claim that the number of interest groups today shows the health of our democracy and enhance the representation of the people. Do interest groups help or hurt democracy? Let's examine these two points of view.

Opponents of interest-group political influence, like the Reform Party and populists, argue that James Madison was right in the *Federalist Paper No. 10* when he warned of the factions. The proliferation of single-issue interest groups has tipped the governmental balance in favor of the minority—be it ideological or other—at the expense of the majority. They believe that minority groups, ranging from ultra-conservative to ultra-liberal, hold the political system hostage. The result is gridlock and an ever expanding role for the government as it gives in to ever more strident demands from all of these groups. Opponents of interest-group influence argue that none of these groups think about the public good, only about their own little issue area. Labor unions demand more money and more benefits without regard for the needs of business owners. At the same time, business owners, represented by chambers of commerce or the National Association of Manufacturers, demand to make maximum profits and pay minimum wages at the expense of workers. Neither extreme position is in the best interest of the nation.

Advocates of the interest group system, including many interest group like AARP, the AFL-CIO, Right to Life groups, chambers of commerce, and the Business Roundtable argue that interest groups have an important and healthy role to play in modern society. They agree that interest groups make many demands, but they argue that that the political system is designed to balance those demands and tends to do a pretty good job of it. For example, in the 1960s, conservative groups sought to maintain a wholly private system of health care and liberal groups lobbied for national health care; the result was Medicaid and Medicare for those most in need—the poor and elderly—and everyone else had private health care.

Interest groups are not evil pressure groups seeking to destroy the national interest but groups with similar interests who get together to make their voices louder (strength in numbers) and advocate their position. This is true democracy. Members of Congress and government officials are lobbied by advocates and opponents of environmental regulations, and so on. Through this clash of interests we arrive at good policy and true public good.

What do you think? Do interest groups hurt or help democracy?
Go to www.ablongman.com/oconnor

candidates to disclose all campaign contributions and limited the amount of money that they could spend on media advertising.

In 1974, amendments to the act made it more far-reaching by sharply limiting the amount of money any interest group could give to

FIGURE 11.6   PACs in Decline

Created in the early 1970s, political action committees (PACs) allowed individuals to collect money and contribute to political campaigns. PACs saw explosive growth in the 1980s, but their numbers have declined in recent years, although their ability to raise money has increased.

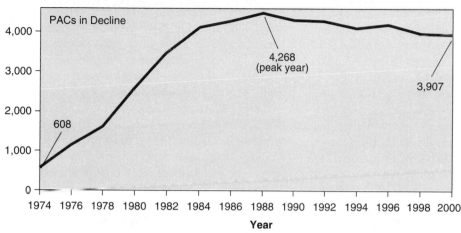

Source: Federal Elections Commission.

a candidate for federal office. However, the act also made it legal for corporations, labor unions, and interest groups to form what were termed **political action committees** (PACs), which could make contributions to candidates for national elections.

Technically, a PAC is a political arm of a business, labor, trade, professional, or other interest group legally authorized to raise funds on a voluntary basis from employees or members in order to contribute to a political candidate or party. These monies have changed the face of U.S. elections. Unlike some contributions to interest groups, however, contributions to PACs are not tax deductible, and PACs generally don't have members who call legislators; instead, PACs have contributors who write checks specifically for the purpose of campaign donations. PAC money plays a significant role in the campaigns of many congressional incumbents, often averaging over half of a House candidate's total campaign spending. PACs generally contribute to those who have helped them before and who serve on committees or subcommittees that routinely consider legislation of concern to that group.

While continuing to be important, PACs are actually on the decline. Although there were 4,268 in 1988, their number is now less than 4,000. (See Figure 11.6) While Republicans complain about labor PACs (there were 317 in 2001), it was the 1,545 corporate and not interest-group PACs that led the way in contributions.

political action committee

A federally registered fund-raising committee that represents an interest group in the political process through campaign donations.

VISUAL LITERACY

PACs and the Money Trail

Continuity &Change

The Evolution of Interest Groups and Parties

Interest groups and political parties long have been a factor in the course of American political history. Members of many discrete religious groups first settled in America seeking religious freedom. Later, after the Revolutionary War was fought and a new nation was created, political factions or groups—Federalists and Anti-Federalists—emerged with strong leaders and even publications clearly setting forth their goals and political philosophies. Both groups later evolved into political parties.

When Alexis de Tocqueville toured the United States in the 1830s, he was struck by the tendency of Americans to join groups of all kinds. Interest groups, particularly labor and big business, also played a critical role in the development of the new nation, especially after the Civil War and into the Progressive Era. They also significantly affected the development of political parties.

The development of what some term the modern interest-group society began in the 1960s with the development of myriad civil rights and public interest groups reminiscent of the kinds of interest-group formation and activity that occurred during the Progressive movement. Environmental groups were a new interest-group phenomenon, whose formation and successes in part spurred the development of new conservative groups and public interest law firms to counter their claims in the legislature, before executive agencies, and in the courts. In many ways, however, the power exerted by big business through trade associations, the hiring of professional lobbyists, and PACs is still quite reminiscent of the power big business enjoyed just before and well into the Progressive movement.

Today, technology-based firms and corporations contributed as much if not more to the economy than major U.S. car manufacturers. This new wealth is creating with it new interests and demands on the political parties. In addition, the Internet is becoming an increasingly effective tool for grassroots mobilization and may be usurping the role of patrons in the formation of new groups whose start-up costs are now much lower. While Robert Putnam may be correct that people are no longer bowling in leagues, they are spending more and more time on the Internet, where organized groups, existing political parties, and new parties all seek new adherents.

1. What kinds of groups do you believe would be particularly amenable to start-up on the Internet?
2. Will the research and conventional wisdom about political parties and their effectiveness have to be rewritten in light of the growth of the Internet?

Cast Your Vote. In what ways will the Internet succeed as an interest-group mobilizing tool? In what ways will it fail? Will it help third-party candidates in disseminating their platforms? To cast your vote, go to **www.ablongman.com/oconnor**

SUMMARY

Political parties and interest groups play very important roles in the American political system. Political parties have been a key method of selecting candidates, organizing Congress, and other elected bodies, and setting policy agendas since the 1800s to lesser or greater degrees. While parties no longer enjoy the public support or clout with the citizenry, they still are powerful predictors of voting—especially in terms of how elected officials vote.

Both major political parties are similarly organized at the local, state, and national levels. Their ability to incorporate ideas of fledgling parties, historically, has made it more difficult for third parties to flourish as they do in other nations.

Just as an individual citizen's likelihood of affiliating with a political party is on the wane, so is individual involvement in interest groups. Interest groups, like political parties, arise for a variety of reasons, but are more focused in their concern over particular issues. Strong leaders and patrons can often make or break the success of an interest group, which often must look to private sources of funds outside of membership dues to keep afloat.

Interest groups today are involved in a variety of activities including lobbying all three branches of government, stirring up grassroots efforts for policy change, and all sorts of legal and illegal protest activities. They also often play key roles in the election process by providing endorsements, volunteers, as well as funds, often in the form of contributions from political action committees.

KEY TERMS

civil service laws, p. 347
collective good, p. 366
direct primary, p. 347
disturbance theory, p. 365
free rider, p. 366
hard money, p. 352
interest group, p. 343
lobbying, p. 370

national convention, p. 348
national party platform, p. 355
party identification, p. 360
patronage, p. 347
political action committee, p. 379
political consultant, p. 348
political machine, p. 346

political party, p. 343
public interest group, p. 367
soft money, p. 352
third-partyism, p. 357
ticket-split, p. 347
two-party system, p. 357

SELECTED READINGS

Beck, Paul Allen, and Marjorie Rardon Hershey. *Party Politics in America,* 9th ed. New York: Longman, 2001.

Berry, Jeffrey M. *The Interest Group Society,* 3rd ed. New York: Longman, 1997.

Cigler, Allan J., and Burdett A. Loomis, eds. *Interest Group Politics,* 5th ed. Washington, D.C.: Congressional Quarterly Press, 1998.

Fiorina, Morris P. *Divided Government.* Boston: Allyn and Bacon, 1996.

Herrnson, Paul S., Ronald G. Shaiko, and Clyde Wilcox. *The Interest Group Connection.* Chatham, N.J.: Chatham House, 1998.

Kollman, Ken. *Outside Lobbying: Public Opinion and Interest Group Strategies.* Princeton, N.J.: Princeton University Press, 1998.

Key, V. O., Jr. *Politics, Parties, and Pressure Groups,* 5th ed. New York: Crowell, 1964.

Maisel, L. Sandy, ed. *The Parties Respond: Changes in American Parties and Campaigns,* 3rd ed. Boulder, Colo.: Westview Press, 1998.

McGlen, Nancy E., and Karen O'Connor. *Women, Politics and American Society,* 2nd ed. Upper Saddle River, N.J.: Prentice-Hall, 1998.

Olson, Mancur, Jr. *The Logic of Collective Action: Public Good and the Theory of Groups.* Cambridge, Mass.: Harvard University Press, 1965.

Price, David E. *Bringing Back the Parties.* Washington, D.C.: CQ Press, 1984.

Riordon, William L., ed. *Plunkitt of Tammany Hall.* New York: Signet, 1995.

Schattschneider, E. *Party Government.* New York: Hoyt, Rinehart and Winston, 1942.

Schlozman, Kay Lehman, and John T. Tierney. *Organized Interests and American Democracy.* New York: Harper & Row, 1986.

Wattenberg, Martin P. *The Decline of American Political Parties, 1952–1992.* Cambridge, Mass.: Harvard University Press, 1994.

Wilson, James Q. *Political Organizations.* Princeton, N.J.: Princeton University Press, 1995.

12 Campaigns, Elections, and Voting

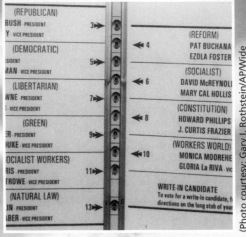

(Photo courtesy: Gary I. Rothstein/AP/Wide World Photos)

For what should have been a relatively tame election, the 2000 presidential contest turned out to be one of the most historic elections in United States history. The race between Democratic Vice President Al Gore and Texas Governor George W. Bush was not a banner contest because of the charisma of the candidates, the strength of their platforms, or a particularly exciting campaign season. The real drama began to unfold *after* Election Day, as a near tie between the candidates developed into a near crisis. With the entire country and the rest of the world watching, the election struggle waged for thirty-six days after November 7 as Americans waited to learn who the new chief executive would be. Those who witnessed the 2000 election will never forget the chaos, intrigue, and indecision wrought by it. Historians and analysts likened the election to the fabled 1876 contest between Republican Rutherford B. Hayes and Democrat Samuel L. Tilden, in which Hayes was delivered a controversial win despite clearly losing the popular vote. In addition, 2000 marked the first election since 1888 in which the man who would eventually become president did not receive the plurality of the national vote. Gore won the popular vote by about 540,000 votes out of 105 million ballots cast. This amount, incidentally, is about the same as the margin by which Richard Nixon defeated Hubert Humphrey in 1972 and nearly five times the margin by which John F. Kennedy bested Nixon in 1968. But as Americans learned anew in 2000, the popular vote matters much less than the vote of the electoral college.

With most election prognosticators targeting Florida and its twenty-five electoral votes as the key to the election, the Sunshine State did not disappoint. Even before all of the polls closed in Florida, the networks declared Gore the winner of the state. Several hours after calling the state for Gore, then recanting and announcing Bush the winner, the major media outlets were forced to once again retract their projection, as the election returns showed a margin of less than 1,000 votes between the two candidates. With no precedent to draw on, the country entered a virtually uncharted moment in history and the outcome came down to the judicial system, bouncing from court to court within Florida and eventually ending up in the Supreme Court. In a 5–4 vote, the justices ruled to shut down manual recount efforts and accept the votes that were certified by Florida Secretary of State Katherine Harris, a Republican who had been appointed by the Republican governor and brother of the victor, Jeb Bush. The Supreme Court's decision effectively elected George W. Bush the forty-third president of the United States. It was an inauspicious start to a presidential term for Bush, but he was grateful for the decision. The ruling and subsequent victory of Bush met with mixed reactions. The country had been eager for an outcome, and most were glad the ordeal was over. There was, however, strong resentment from many Democrats, especially African American voters, who believed that their vote had been invalidated by overt political maneuvering on the part of the Republicans.

While every race is not as close or as controversial as the 2000 presidential election, each is important in the way it dictates the course that the country will take in the coming years. Whether the contest is for commander-in-chief or county clerk, each represents an opportunity for the voice of the American people to be heard.

Every November, a plurality of the voting electorate, simply by casting ballots peacefully across a continent-sized nation, reelect or replace politicians at many levels of government. Every four years they elect a president; every two years the entire House and one-third of the Senate are up for reelection. Many countries do not have the luxury of a peaceful transition of political power. We tend to take this process for granted, but in truth it is a marvel. Fortunately, most Americans, though not enough, understand why and how elections serve their interests. Elections take the pulse of average people and gauge their hopes and fears. The study of campaigns, elections, and voting permits us to trace the course of the American revolution over 200 years of voting.

Today the United States of America is a democrat's paradise in many respects because it probably conducts more elections for more offices more frequently than any nation on earth. Popular election confers on a government the legitimacy that it can achieve no other way. Even many authoritarian and Communist systems around the globe recognize this. From time to time, they hold "referenda" to endorse their regimes or one-party elections, even though these so-called elections offer no real choice that would ratify their rule. The symbolism of elections as mechanisms to legitimize change, then, is important, but so is their practical value. After all, elections are the means to fill public

The home page of Al Gore's presidential campaign Web site. Campaign Web sites were substantially more widespread and sophisticated in the 2000 election than when they first appeared in 1996. (Photo courtesy: Gore 2000 Campaign)

offices and staff the government. The voters' choice of candidates and parties helps to organize government as well. Because candidates advocate certain policies, elections also involve a choice of platforms and point the society in certain directions on a wide range of issues, from abortion to civil rights to national defense to the environment. In recent times, the U.S. electorate (those citizens eligible to vote) has been the most universal in the country's history; no longer can one's race or sex or creed prevent participation at the ballot box. But challenges still remain. After all the blood spilled and energy expended to expand the suffrage (as the right to vote is called), only a little more than half the potentially eligible voters bother to go to the polls.

This chapter focuses on the purposes served by elections, the various kinds of elections held in the United States, and patterns of voting over time. We concentrate in particular on presidential and congressional contests, both of which have rich histories that tell us a great deal about the American people and their changing hopes and needs. We conclude by returning to contemporary presidential elections and addressing some topics of electoral reform.

primary election
Election in which voters decide which of the candidates within a party will represent the party in the general election.

closed primary
A primary election in which only a party's registered voters are eligible to vote.

open primary
A primary in which party members, independents, and sometimes members of the other party are allowed to vote.

crossover voting
Participation in the primary of the party with which the voter is not affiliated.

TYPES OF ELECTIONS

In the U.S. political system, elections come in many varieties. In **primary elections,** voters decide which of the candidates within a party will represent the party's ticket in the general elections. There are also different kinds of primaries. For example, **closed primaries** allow only a party's registered voters to cast a ballot. **Open primaries** allow independents and sometimes members of the other party to participate. Closed primaries are considered healthier for the party system ballot because they prevent members of one party from influencing the primaries of the opposition party. Studies of open primaries indicate that **crossover voting**—participation in the primary of a party with which the voter is not affiliated—occurs frequently.[1] On the other hand, little evidence exists that much **raiding** occurs—an *organized* attempt by voters of one party to influence primary results of the other party.[2] In **blanket primaries,** voters are permitted to vote in either party's primary (but not both) on an office-by-office basis. In all three primary systems, if none of the candidates in the initial primary secures a majority of the votes, there is a **runoff primary,** a contest between the two candidates with the greatest number of votes. Another type of primary, used in Nebraska, Louisiana, and hundreds of cities large and small across America, is the **nonpartisan primary,** which is used to select candidates without regard to party affiliation, whether in the initial slate of contenders or the final choice presented to the voters. For example, a nonpartisan primary would be used to select two final candidates, perhaps both of the same party, from a slate of several candidates, perhaps from many parties, to run for some local elected office.

Once a party's candidates for various offices are chosen, general elections are held. In a **general election,** voters decide which candidates will actually fill the nation's elective public offices. These elections are held at many levels, including municipal, county, state, and national. While primaries are contests between the candidates within each party, general elections are contests between the candidates of opposing parties.

Three other types of elections are the initiative, the referendum and the recall. Used in about twenty states, initiatives and referenda involve voting on issues (as opposed to voting for candidates). An **initiative** is a process that allows citizens to propose legislation and submit it to the state electorate for popular vote, as long as they have a certain number of signatures on petitions supporting the proposal. A **referendum** is a procedure whereby the state legislature submits proposed legislation to the state's voters for approval. The third type of election (or "de-election") found in many states is the **recall,** whereby an incumbent can be removed from office by popular vote. Recall elections are very rare, and sometimes they are thwarted by the official's resignation or impeachment prior to the vote.

PRESIDENTIAL ELECTIONS

Variety aside, no U.S. election can compare to the presidential contest. This spectacle, held every four years, brings together all the elements of politics and attracts the most ambitious and energetic politicians to the national stage. The election itself, though altered by a front-loaded primary season, remains a collection of fifty separate state elections within each party in which delegates to each party's national convention are allotted. The election of delegates is followed in midsummer by the parties' grand national conventions and then by a final set of fifty separate state elections all held on the Tuesday after the first Monday in November. This lengthy process exhausts candidates and voters alike, but it allows the diversity of the United States to be displayed in ways a shorter, more homogeneous presidential election process could not. Every state has its moment in the sun, every local and regional problem has a chance to be aired, and every candidate has an opportunity to break away from the pack.

raiding

An organized attempt by voters of one party to influence primary results of another party.

blanket primary

A primary in which voters may cast ballots in either party's primary (but not both) on an office-by-office basis.

runoff primary

A second primary election between the two candidates receiving the greatest number of votes in the first primary.

nonpartisan primary

A primary used to select candidates without regard to party affiliation.

general election

Election in which voters decide which candidates will actually fill elective public offices.

initiative

A process that allows citizens to propose legislation and submit it to the state electorate for popular vote.

referendum

A procedure whereby the state legislature submits proposed legislation to the state's voters for approval.

recall

Removal of an incumbent from office by popular vote.

In our analysis of presidential elections, we also trace the structure of a campaign, which has five basic parts, no matter what level of office a candidate seeks: (1) nomination campaign, (2) general election campaign, (3) personal campaign, (4) organizational campaign, and (5) media campaign. In the nomination campaign, the target is the party elite, the leaders and activists who choose nominees in primaries or conventions. Party leaders are concerned with electability, while party activists are often ideologically and issue oriented, so a candidate must appeal to both bases.

The Nomination Campaign: Campaigning for Delegates

front-loading

The tendency of states to choose an early date on the primary calendar.

Candidates for a party's presidential nomination try to get as many delegates as they can, as early as they can. The primary schedule, in fact, has been altered by a process called **front-loading**, the tendency of states to choose an early date on the primary calendar. In 2000, the vast majority of delegates to both major party conventions were chosen before the end of March. This trend is hardly surprising, given the added press emphasis on the first contests and the voters' desire to cast their ballots before the competition is decided. Front-loading has had other important effects on the nomination process. First, a front-loaded primary schedule generally benefits the front-runner, since opponents have little time to turn the contest around once they fall behind. Second, front-loading favors the candidate who can raise the bulk of the money *before* the nomination season begins, since there will be little opportunity to raise money once the process is up and running and since candidates will need to finance campaign efforts simultaneously in many states. Finally, front-loading has amplified the importance of the "invisible primary"—the year or so prior to the start of the official nomination season when candidates begin raising money and unofficially campaigning.[3]

State party organizations use a number of methods to elect national convention delegates:

1. *Winner-take-all:* The candidate who wins the most votes in a state secures all of that state's delegates. The Democrats moved away from this mode of delegate selection in 1976. Republicans allow winner-take-all contests, thus enabling a GOP candidate to amass a majority of delegates more quickly.
2. *Proportional representation:* Candidates who secure a threshold percentage of votes (usually around 15 percent) are awarded delegates in proportion to the number of popular votes won. This system is now strongly favored by Democrats.
3. *Proportional representation with bonus delegates; beauty contest with separate delegate selection; delegate selection with no beauty contest:* Used rarely, the first of these awards delegates to candidates in propor-

tion to the popular vote won and then gives one bonus delegate to the winner of each district. The second serves as an indication of popular sentiment for the conventions to consider as they choose the actual delegates. Finally, under the "delegate selection with no beauty contest" system, the primary election chooses delegates to the national conventions who are not linked on the ballot to specific presidential contenders.

4. *The caucus:* The caucus is the oldest, most party-oriented method of choosing delegates to the national conventions. Traditionally, the caucus was a closed meeting of party members in each state that selected the party's choice for presidential candidate. In the late nineteenth and early twentieth centuries, however, these caucuses came to be viewed by many people as elitist and antidemocratic, and reformers succeeded in replacing them with direct primaries in most states. While there are still presidential nominating caucuses today, as in Iowa, they are now more open and attract a wider range of the party's membership.

The Party Conventions.   The seemingly endless nomination battle does have a conclusion: the national party convention held in the summer of presidential election years. The out-of-power party traditionally holds its convention first, in late July, followed by the party holding the White House in mid-August. At one time the conventions were deliberative bodies that made actual decisions, where party leaders held sway and deals were sometimes cut in "smoke-filled rooms" to deliver nominations to little-known contenders called "dark horses." But this era predated the modern emphasis on reform, primaries, and proportional representation, all of which have combined to make conventions mere ratifying agencies for pre-selected nominees.

Today the convention is fundamentally different. First, its importance as a party conclave, at which compromises on party leadership and policies can be worked out, has diminished. Second, although the convention still formally selects the presidential ticket, most nominations are settled well in advance. New preconvention political processes have lessened the role of the convention in three areas:

1. *National Candidates and Issues:* The political perceptions and loyalties of voters are now influenced largely by national candidates and issues, a factor that has undoubtedly served to diminish the power of state and local party leaders at the convention. The national candidates have usurped the autonomy of state party leaders with their preconvention ability to garner delegate support.

2. *The News Media:* The mass media have helped to transform the national conventions into political extravaganzas for the television audience's consumption. They have also helped to preempt the convention, by keeping count of the delegates committed to the candidates; as a result, the delegates and even the candidates now

The 2000 presidential candidates and their running mates. On the left, Joseph Lieberman and Al Gore On the right, George W. Bush and Dick Cheney (Photos courtesy: left, Doug Mills/AP/Wide World Photos; right, M. Spencer Green/AP/Wide World Photos)

have much more information about nomination politics well before the convention. From the strategies of candidates to the commitments of individual delegates, the media covers it all. The business of the convention has been irrevocably shaped to accommodate television: Desirous of presenting a unified image to kick off a strong general election campaign, the parties assign important roles to attractive speakers, and most crucial party affairs are saved for prime-time viewing hours.

3. *Delegate Selection:* The selection of delegates to the conventions is no longer the function of party leaders but of primary elections and grassroots caucuses.

Who Are the Delegates?　In one sense, party conventions are microcosms of the United States: every state, most localities, and all races and creeds find some representation there. (See Table 12.1: Women and Conventions.) Yet delegates are an unusual and unrepresentative collection of people in many other ways. It is not just their exceptionally keen interest in politics that distinguishes delegates. These activists also are ideologically more pure and financially better off than most Americans.

In 2000, for example, both parties drew their delegates from an elite group that had income and educational levels far above the average American's. The distinctiveness of each party was also apparent. Democratic delegates tended to be younger and were more likely to be African American, female, divorced or single, and a member of a labor union. Because of George W. Bush's "compassionate conservatism," the GOP

TABLE 12.1   Women and Conventions

Since 1980, Democratic Party rules have required that women comprise at least 50 percent of the delegates to its national convention. The Republican Party has no similar quotas. Nevertheless, both parties have tried to increase the role of women at the convention. Some "firsts" for women at conventions include:

1876	First woman to address a national convention
1890	First women delegates to conventions of both parties
1940	First woman to nominate a presidential candidate
1951	First woman asked to chair a national party
1972	First woman keynote speaker
1984	First major party woman nominated for vice president (Democrat Geraldine Ferraro)
1996	Wives of both nominees make major addresses
2000	Daughter of a presidential candidate nominates her father

Source: Center for the Study of American Women in Politics.

made a special effort (but with mixed results) to attract minorities who were featured prominently to its convention.

The delegates in each party exemplify the philosophical gulf separating the two parties. Democratic delegates are well to the left of their own party's voters on most issues, and even further away from the opinions held by the nation's electorate as a whole. Republican delegates are a mirror image of their opponents—considerably to the right of GOP voters and even more so of the entire electorate. Although it is sometimes said that the two major parties present U.S. citizens with a "clear choice" of candidates, it is possible to argue the contrary. Our politics are perhaps too polarized, with the great majority of Americans, moderates and pragmatists overwhelmingly, left underrepresented by parties too fond of ideological purity.

The General Election Campaign: Launching the Presidential Campaign

Once the two major-party nominees are selected by delegates at the conventions, both candidates can get to work. Most significant interest groups are courted for money and endorsements, although the results are mainly predictable: liberal, labor, and minority groups usually back Democrats, while conservative and business organizations support Republicans. The most active and intense groups are often coalesced around emotional issues such as abortion and gun control, and these organizations can produce a bumper crop of money and activists for favored candidates. Race and class divisions can often play an important role in general elections, although this tends not to be true in the United States.

Virtually all candidates adopt a brief theme, or slogan, to serve as a rallying cry in their quest for office. The first to do so was William Henry Harrison in 1840, with the slogan "Tippecanoe and Tyler, Too."

Tippecanoe was a nickname given to Harrison, a reference to his participation in the battle of Tippecanoe, and Tyler was Harrison's vice-presidential candidate, John Tyler of Virginia. Candidates try to avoid controversy in their selection of slogans, and some openly eschew ideology. The clever candidate also attempts to find a slogan that cannot be lampooned easily.

The Personal Campaign

In the effort to show voters that they are hard working, thoughtful, and worthy of the office they seek, candidates try to meet personally as many citizens as possible in the course of a campaign. A candidate for high office may deliver up to a dozen speeches a day, and that is only part of the exhausting schedule most contenders maintain. The day may begin at 5 A.M. at the entrance gate to an auto plant with an hour or two of handshaking, followed by similar gladhanding at subway stops until 9 A.M. Strategy sessions with key advisers and preparation for upcoming presentations and forums may fill the rest of the morning. A luncheon talk, afternoon fundraisers, and a series of television and print interviews crowd the afternoon agenda. The light fare of cocktail parties is followed by a dinner speech, and a civic-forum talk or two. More meetings with advisers and planning for the next day's events can easily take a candidate past midnight. Following only a few hours of sleep, the candidate starts all over again. After months of this grueling pace, the candidate may be functioning on automatic pilot and unable to think clearly.

Beyond the strains this fast-lane existence adds to a candidate's family life, the hectic schedule leaves little time for reflection and long-range planning. Is it any wonder that under these conditions many candidates commit gaffes and appear to have foot-in-mouth disease?

The Organizational Campaign

If the candidate is the public face of the campaign, the organization behind the candidate is the private face. Depending on the level of the office sought, the organizational staff can consist of a handful of volunteers or hundreds of paid specialists supplementing and directing the work of thousands of volunteers. The most elaborate structure is found in presidential campaigns. Tens of thousands of volunteers distribute literature and visit neighborhoods. They are directed by paid staff that may number 500 or more, including dozens of lawyers and accountants.

Right-wing 1964 Republican candidate Barry Goldwater's famous slogan, "In your heart, you know he's right," was quickly lampooned by incumbent Democratic opponent President Lyndon B. Johnson's campaign as "In your guts you know he's nuts." (Photo courtesy: Bettmann/Corbis)

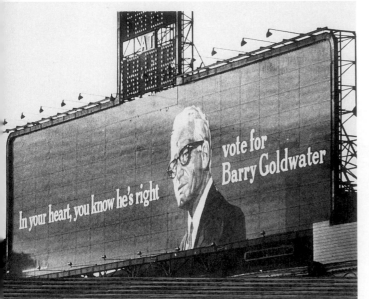

At the top of the organizational chart is the **campaign manager,** who coordinates and directs the various aspects of the campaign. Beside the manager is the **political consultant,** whose position is one of the most important evolutions in campaigning for office in this century. The political consultant is a private-sector individual or team of individuals that sells to a candidate the technologies, services, and strategies required to get that candidate elected to his or her office of choice. The number of consultants has grown exponentially since they first appeared in the 1930s, and their specialties and responsibilities have increased accordingly, to the point that they are now an obligatory part of campaigns at almost any level of government. Candidates hire general consultants to oversee their entire campaign from beginning to end. Their responsibilities range from defining campaign objectives to formulating strategy and developing tactics. Alongside the general consultant are more specialized consultants who focus on the new and complex technologies for only one or two specialties such as fundraising, polling, mass mailings, media relations, advertising, and speech-writing. The best-known consultants for any campaign are usually the **media consultant,** who produces the candidate's television and radio advertisements; the **pollster,** who takes the public opinion surveys that guide the campaign; and the **direct mailer,** who supervises direct-mail fundraising. After the candidate, however, the most important person in the campaign is probably the finance chair, who is responsible for bringing in the large contributions that pay most of the salaries of the consultants and staff.

In addition to raising money, the most vital work of the candidate's organization is to get in touch with voters. Some of this is done in person by volunteers who walk the neighborhoods, going door to door to solicit votes. Some is accomplished by volunteers who use computerized telephone banks to call targeted voters with scripted messages. Both contact methods are termed **voter canvass.** Most canvassing takes place in the month before the election, when voters are paying attention. Close to Election Day, the telephone banks begin the vital **get-out-the-vote (GOTV)** effort, reminding supporters to vote and arranging for their transportation to the polls if necessary.

Many critics claim that consultants strip campaigns of substance and reduce them to a clever bag of tricks for sale, even blaming the degeneration of American politics in the latter half of this century on the rise of the political consultant. Disappointed office-seekers sometimes blame their loss entirely on their consultants, while successful candidates often retain their consultants after the election as political advisers, thereby lending even more credibility to the claim that politics now is all about appearance and not about issues. Candidates, always busy with making appearances and canvassing, often entrust the entire management of campaigns to their consultants without understanding entirely what those consultants do. Sometimes, as in the famous case of Mary Matalin and James Carville, the consultants become media stars in their own right.

campaign manager
A professional who directs the various aspects of a campaign.

political consultant
A private-sector individual or team of individuals that sells to a candidate the technologies, services, and strategies required to get that candidate elected.

media consultant
A professional who produces political candidates' television, radio, and print advertisements.

pollster
A professional who takes public opinion surveys that guide political campaigns.

direct mailer
A professional who supervises a political campaign's direct-mail fundraising strategies.

voter canvass
The process by which a campaign gets in touch with individual voters: either by door-to-door solicitation or by telephone.

get-out-the-vote (GOTV)
A push at the end of a political campaign to encourage supporters to go to the polls.

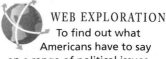

WEB EXPLORATION To find out what Americans have to say on a range of political issues and to experience poll taking firsthand, go to www.ablongman.com/oconnor

Yet there are others who insist that despite the consultants, running for office is still about the bread and butter of campaigns: shaking hands, speaking persuasively, and listening to the voters. Voters, they say, are smart enough to tell the difference between a good candidate and a bad one, regardless of the smoke-and-mirrors tactics of their consultants. Nevertheless, consultants do make a difference. Recent research on political consultants conducted by political scientists indicates that consultants have a significant impact in elections. In campaigns for the U.S. House, for example, the use of professional campaign consultants has been shown to have a positive impact on candidates' fundraising ability[4] and on candidates' final vote shares.[5]

WEB EXPLORATION
To learn more about the functions of the FEC, go to www.ablongman.com/oconnor

To run all aspects of a campaign successfully requires a great deal of money. In 2000, more than $858 million was raised for U.S. House and Senate races, up 39 percent from 1997–1998 levels. As humorist Will Rogers once remarked early in the twentieth century, "Politics has got so expensive that it takes lots of money even to get beat with."

All of the money spent in national elections is regulated by the federal government under the terms of the Federal Election Campaign Act of 1971, first passed in 1971 and substantially strengthened after Watergate in 1974 and again in 1976. (Still more amendments were passed in 1979.) Table 12.2 summarizes the important provisions of the law, which limits what individuals, interest groups, and political parties can give to candidates for president, U.S. senator, and U.S. representative.

TABLE 12.2   Current Contribution Limits for House and Senate Candidates (under the Federal Election Campaign Act)

Contributions From	Given to Candidate (per election)[a]	Given to National Party (per calendar year)	Total Allowable Contributions (per calendar year)
Individual	$1,000	$20,000	Limited to $25,000
Political action committee[b]	$5,000	$15,000	No limit
Any political party committee[c]	$5,000	No limit	No limit
All national and state party committees taken together	To House candidates: $30,000 plus "coordinated expenditures"[d] To Senate candidates: $27,500 plus "coordinated expenditures"[d]		

[a]Each of the following is considered a separate election: primary (or convention), run-off, general election.

[b]Multicandidate PACs only. Multicandidate committees have received contributions from at least fifty persons and have given to at least five federal candidates.

[c]Multicandidate party committees only. Multicandidate committees have received contributions from at least fifty persons and have given to at least five federal candidates.

[d]Coordinated expenditures are party-paid general election campaign expenditures made in consultation and coordination with the candidate under the provisions of section 441(a)(d) of the Federal Code.

The Media Campaign

What voters actually see and hear of the candidate is primarily determined by the **paid media** (such as television advertising) accompanying the campaign and the **free media** (newspaper and television coverage). The two kinds of media are fundamentally different: Paid advertising is under the control of the campaign, whereas the press is independent. Great care is taken in the design of the television advertising, which takes many approaches.

Positive ads stress the candidate's qualifications, family, and issue positions with no direct reference to the opponent. These are usually favored by the incumbent candidate. **Negative ads** attack the opponent's character and platform and may not even mention the candidate who is paying for their airing (except for a brief, legally required identification at the ad's conclusion). In the final weeks of the 2000 presidential campaign, Al Gore used negative ads to attack George W. Bush's record as governor of Texas. Bush, in turn, ran ads accusing Gore and Bill Clinton of making America vulnerable to a nuclear attack from China. **Contrast ads** compare the records and proposals of the candidates, with a bias toward the sponsor. Whether the public likes them or not, all three kinds of ads can inject important (as well as trivial) issues into a campaign. Some of the ads aired in modern campaigns are sponsored *not* by candidates but by interest groups. These ads usually focus on issues and are independent of the actual campaigns, though it may be easy to tell which candidate the interest group favors.

Occasionally, advertisements are relatively long (ranging from four-and-one-half-minute ads up to thirty-minute documentaries). Usually, however, the messages are short **spot ads**, sixty, thirty, or even ten seconds long.

While there is little question that negative advertisements have shown the greatest growth in the past two decades, they have been a part of American campaigns for some time. In 1796, Federalists portrayed Thomas Jefferson, one of the chief authors of the Declaration of Independence, as an atheist and a coward. Clearly, although negative advertisements are more prevalent today, they are not solely the function of the modern media. Furthermore, their effects are well documented. While voters normally need a reason to vote for a candidate, they also frequently vote *against* the other candidate—and negative ads can provide the critical justification for such a vote.

Before the 1980s, well-known incumbents usually ignored negative attacks from their challengers, believing that the proper stance was to be above the fray. But after some well-publicized defeats of incumbents in the early 1980s in which negative television advertising played a prominent role, incumbents began attacking their challengers in earnest. The new rule of politics became "An attack unanswered is an attack agreed to." In a further attempt to stave off brickbats from challengers, incumbents even began anticipating the substance of their opponents' attacks and airing **inoculation advertising** early in the campaign to protect

paid media
Political advertisements purchased for a candidate's campaign.

free media
Coverage of a candidate's campaign by the news media.

positive ad
Advertising on behalf of a candidate that stresses the candidate's qualifications, family, and issue positions, without reference to the opponent.

negative ad
Advertising on behalf of a candidate that attacks the opponent's platform or character.

contrast ad
Ad that compares the records and proposals of the candidates, with a bias toward the sponsor.

spot ad
Television advertising on behalf of a candidate that is broadcast in sixty-, thirty-, or ten-second duration.

inoculation advertising
Advertising that attempts to counteract an anticipated attack from the opposition before the attack is even launched.

POINT/COUNTERPOINT

SHOULD THE PRESIDENTIAL NOMINATION AND CAMPAIGN PROCESS BE SHORTENED?

The presidential nomination process is the first hurdle a politician must clear in order to have a chance at holding the nation's top elected office. Candidates court the party faithful and try to secure enough support within their own respective parties to receive the endorsement at the national convention. Individual states hold Republican and Democratic primaries and caucuses over a four- or five-month span, with New Hampshire and Iowa as the traditional kick-off states, followed by the summer conventions and then the intense general campaign and election in the fall. The real campaigning, however, begins long before the primaries and continues well beyond Election Day. Campaigns for president are practically on a four-year cycle; the newly elected president is hardly sworn in before candidates from his party and opposing parties begin jockeying for position among the party elite in hopes of becoming anointed the next presidential candi-

date. At the same time, the long campaign enables the public to become acquainted with candidates who are vying for the most powerful office in the world. Should the presidential nomination and campaign process be shortened? Let's examine these two points of view.

Many reform-minded citizens and legislators believe that shortening the nomination and campaign process would reduce exorbitant spending (about $360 million in the 2000 presidential election) and benefit the democratic process by encouraging participation. Many European nations have a much more abbreviated political season, and most have higher turnout and lower campaign spending than the United States. Under the British system, for example, campaigns and elections are held in a period of six weeks after the election is called. Shortening the nomination and campaign process in the United States into a series of regional primaries held shortly before the conventions, an idea with a

themselves in advance of the other side's spots. Inoculation advertising attempts to counteract an anticipated attack from the opposition before the attack is even launched. For example, a senator who fears a broadside about her voting record on Social Security issues might air advertisements featuring senior citizens praising her support of Social Security.

The news media present quite a challenge to candidates. Although politicians and their staffs cannot control the press, they nonetheless try to manipulate press coverage. They use three techniques to accomplish this aim. First, the staff often seeks to isolate the candidate from the press, thus reducing the chances that reporters will bait a candidate into saying something that might damage the candidate's cause.

Second, the campaign stages media events—activities designed to include brief, clever quotes called *sound bytes* and staged with appealing

wide range of support from political organizations, could reduce the cost involved in campaigning and might keep people from tuning out during the elections. In addition, many see set regional primaries as fairer than the current front-loaded system. Due to tradition and the constitutional freedom to set their own primary dates, first-in-the-nation New Hampshire (whose population is 98 percent white) and Iowa (97 percent white), though largely unrepresentative of America as a whole, yield incredible power in setting the course of presidential elections.

On the other hand, many political practitioners and elected officials are hesitant to reduce the formal processes of nomination and campaigning. The political parties have a responsibility for the nominating process, although it is often shared with state governments, who actually set the dates of primary elections. Congress has been hesitant to take the authority away from the states and mandate a set primary and caucus schedule. Supporters say that the apparently chaotic nature of the primary system and general

election is by design—candidates are forced to appeal not only to members of their own party, but to a broad base of Americans that does not necessarily reflect all of their views. Candidates try out slogans and develop their message over the course of the primary, and they build on those positions during the general campaign. True, the selection system is not perfect, but attempts to reduce the formal apparatuses of the nomination process would likely have little impact on the tendency for politicians to begin their presidential bids earlier and earlier. In addition, reform opponents suggest that there is not necessarily cause to believe that shortening the campaign process will have any effect on voter education or participation.

> **What do you think? Should the presidential nomination and campaign process be shortened, or is the system effective in its current form?**
> *Go to* www.ablongman.com/oconnor

backdrops so that they are all but irresistible, especially to television news. In this fashion, the candidate's staff can successfully fill the news hole reserved for campaign coverage on the evening news programs and in the morning papers.

Third, the handlers and consultants have perfected the technique termed *spin*—that is, they put the most favorable possible interpretation for their candidate on any circumstance occurring in the campaign, and they work the press to sell their point of view or at least to ensure that it is included in the reporters' stories. Televised candidate debates, especially the televised presidential variety, are also showcases for the consultants' spin patrol, and teams of staffers from each side swarm the press rooms to declare victory even before the candidates finish their closing statements.

SIMULATION
You Are a Presidential
Campaign Consultant

The Electoral College: How Presidents Are Elected

Given the enormous amount of energy, money, and time expended to nominate two major-party presidential contenders, it is difficult to believe that the general election could be more arduous than the nominating contests, but it usually is. The actual campaign for the presidency (and other offices) has many facets but the object is clear: winning a majority of the **electoral college**. A uniquely American institution, the electoral college consists of electors from each state who cast the final ballots that actually elect a president as highlighted in Table 12.3.

The electoral college was the result of a compromise at the Constitutional Convention. The electoral college compromise, while not a perfect solution, had practical benefits. Since there were no mass media in those days, it is unlikely that common citizens, even reasonably informed ones, would know much about candidates from other states. This situation could have left voters with no choice but to vote for someone from their own states, making it improbable that any candidate would secure a national majority. On the other hand, the **electors** (members of the electoral college) were envisioned to be men of good character with a solid knowledge of national politics who would be able to identify, agree on, and select prominent national statesmen above the fray of partisan politics to guide the nation.

There are three essentials to understanding the Framers' design of the electoral college. (1) It was meant to work without political parties. (2) It was designed to cover both the nominating and electing phases of presidential selection. (3) It was constructed to produce a nonpartisan president.

Presidents were not to be popularly elected. Instead, each state was to designate electors (through appointment or popular vote) equal in number to the sum of its representation in the House and Senate. Figure 12.1 shows a map of the United States drawn in proportion to each state's electoral college votes. Each elector had two votes to cast in the electoral college's selection for the president and vice president. The rules of the college stipulated that each elector was allowed to cast only one vote for any single candidate, and by extension obliged each elector to use his second vote for another candidate. There was no way to designate votes for president or vice president; instead, the candidate with the most votes (provided he also received votes from a majority of the electors) won the presidency and the runner-up won the vice presidency. If two candidates received the same number of votes and both had a majority of electors, the election was decided in the House of Representatives, with each state delegation acting as a unit and casting one vote. In the event that no candidate secured a majority, the election would be decided in the House, with each state delegation casting one vote for any of the top five electoral vote-getters. In both these scenarios, a majority of the total number of states was necessary for victory.

This system seems almost insanely unpredictable, complex, and unwieldy until one remembers that the Framers devised it specifically

electoral college

Representatives of each state who cast the final ballots that actually elect a president.

elector

Member of the electoral college chosen by methods determined in each state.

TABLE 12.3   How the Electoral College Works

1. Each state is allotted one elector for each U.S. representative and senator it has. Washington, D.C., receives three electors, the same number of electors as the least populous state. The total number of electoral votes is 538.

2. Mostly, electors are nominated at state party conventions. The electors' names are given to the state's election official.

3. On Election Day, voters in each state cast their ballot for the slate of electors representing their choice of presidential ticket. The electors' names do not usually appear on the ballot.

4. The slate of electors for the presidential ticket that receives the most votes is appointed, and all the electoral votes for that state go to those candidates. (Except for Maine and Nebraska, which each give two at-large delegates to whoever wins the state and the rest to whoever wins in each congressional district.)

5. A candidate needs to win a majority of electoral votes—270—to be elected president. If no candidate wins a majority of electoral votes, the House chooses the president and the Senate chooses the vice president.

6. In December, in a largely ceremonial gesture, the electors cast ballots for president and vice president and are expected to follow the popular vote of their state. On rare occasions, "faithless" electors have voted for another candidate.

7. The votes are counted at a joint session of Congress, and the president officially is elected.

Previous Close Calls

It is possible for the candidate who wins the popular vote to loose the election. This has happened four times, including 1824, when the House decided the election because no candidate won a majority of electoral votes.

Election year/ candidates	Popular vote percentage	Electoral votes received	Electoral votes needed for majority
1824			131
John Quincy Adams	→30.92%	84	
Andrew Jackson	41.34	99	
Henry Clay	12.99	37	
William H. Crawford	11.17	41	
1876			185
Rutherford B. Hayes	→47.95%	185	
Samuel J. Tilden	50.97	184	
1888			201
Benjamin Harrison	→47.82%	233	
Grover Cleveland	48.62	168	
2000			270
George W. Bush	→47.87%	271	
Al Gore	48.38	266	

Sources: "How the Electoral College Works," *The Washington Post,* November 19, 2000, p. A1. ©2000, The Washington Post. Reprinted with permission.

for the type of political system that existed when they framed the Constitution and which they (erroneously) foresaw for America in perpetuity: a nonpartisan (one-party), consensus-based, indirectly representative, multi-candidate system. In such a system, the electoral college would function admirably, as indeed it did for several elections. In

FIGURE 12.1   **The States Drawn in Proportion to their Electoral College Votes**
This table visually represents the electors "weight" of the 50 states.

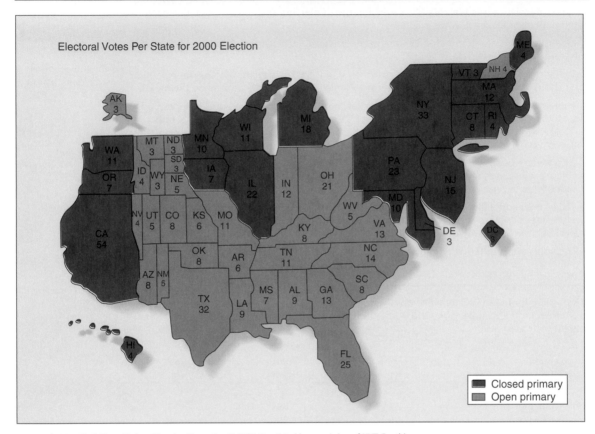

Electoral Votes Per State for 2000 Election

Closed primary
Open primary

Source: The New York Times National Sunday, November 5, 2000. Reprinted by permission of NYT Graphics.

practice, electors with a common basic political understanding would arrive at a consensus preference for president, and most, if not all, would plan to cast one of their votes for that candidate, thereby virtually guaranteeing one clear winner, who would then become president; a tie was an unlikely and unhappy outcome. Each would then plan to cast his remaining vote for another candidate, the one whom the elector implicitly preferred for vice president. Consensus on the vice presidency would presumably be less clear than for the more important position of president, so there might be a closer spread among the runners-up, but in any case, the eventual president and vice president—indeed, all the candidates—would still have been members of the same one party!

Early Problems with the Electoral College.   The republic's fourth presidential election revealed a flaw in the Framers' plan. In 1800, Thomas Jefferson and Aaron Burr were, respectively, the presidential and vice presidential candidates advanced by the Democratic-Republican Party, and supporters of the Democratic-Republican Party controlled a majority of the electoral college. Accordingly, each Democratic-Republican elector in the states cast one of his two votes for Jefferson and the other one for Burr, a situation that resulted in a tie for the presidency between Jefferson and Burr, since there was no way under the constitutional arrangements for electors to earmark their votes separately for president and vice president. Even though most understood Jefferson to be the actual choice for president, the Constitution mandated that a tie be decided by the House of Representatives. So it was, of course, and in Jefferson's favor, but only after much energy was expended to persuade lame-duck Federalists not to give Burr the presidency.

VISUAL LITERACY
American Electoral Rules: How Do They Influence Campaigns?

The Twelfth Amendment was ratified in 1804 to remedy the confusion between the selection of vice presidents and presidents that beset the election of 1800. The amendment provides for separate elections for each office, with each elector having only one vote to cast for each office. Forty-eight of the fifty states have winner-take-all systems and twenty-six states, by law, require electors to cast their vote for the candidate garnering the most votes in their state. Maine and Nebraska each gives two at-large delegates to the candidate who receives the most votes there; the rest go to the candidate who wins in each congressional district. Penalties for 'faithless' electors are practically nonexistent and occasionally electors have opted not to vote for the candidate to whom they were committed. Electors cast their votes in December. If no candidate receives a majority of the total number of electors, the election still goes to the House of Representatives; now, however, each state delegation has one vote to cast.

The Twelfth Amendment hasn't solved all the problems of the electoral college system (see Table 12.3). In the 1824 election between incumbent John Quincy Adams and Andrew Jackson, neither presidential candidate won a majority of electoral votes, again throwing the election into the House. Although Jackson had more electoral and popular votes than Adams, Adams won in the House. On two other occasions in the nineteenth century, the presidential candidate with fewer popular votes than his opponent won the presidency. In the 1876 contest between Republican Rutherford B. Hayes and Democrat Samuel J. Tilden, no candidate received a majority of electoral votes; the House decided in Hayes's favor even though he had only one more (disputed) electoral vote and 250,000 fewer popular votes than Tilden. In the election of 1888, President Grover Cleveland secured about 100,000 more popular votes than did Benjamin Harrison, yet Harrison won a majority of the electoral college vote, and with it the presidency.

The Electoral College in the Twentieth and Twenty-First Centuries.
A number of near crises pertaining to the electoral college have occurred more recently. The election of 1976 was almost a repeat of those nineteenth-century contests in which the candidate with fewer popular votes

won the presidency: Even though Democrat Jimmy Carter received about 1.7 million more popular votes than Republican Gerald Ford, a switch of some 8,000 popular votes in Ohio and Hawaii would have secured for Ford enough votes to win the electoral college, and hence the presidency. Had Ross Perot stayed in the 1992 presidential contest without a hiatus, it is possible that he could have thrown the election into the House of Representatives. His support had registered from 30 percent to 36 percent in the polls in early 1992. When he reentered the race, some of that backing had evaporated, and he finished with 19 percent of the vote and carried no states. However, Perot drained a substantial number of Republican votes from George Bush, thus splitting the GOP base, enabling Clinton to win many normally GOP-leaning states.

Throughout the 2000 campaign for the presidency, many Americans foresaw that the election would likely be the closest election since the 1960 race between John F. Kennedy and Richard M. Nixon. Few realized, however, that the election would be so close that the winner would not be officially declared for over five weeks after Election Day, and that a mere 500 votes in Florida would effectively decide the presidency of the United States. In such a time of uncertainty, reformers have seized the opportunity to bring forward several proposals for improving the American electoral system, as described in Policy in Action: The Politics of Redistricting. While this kind of amendment is uncertain, it would certainly change the way candidates would seek the presidency in the future. The winner-take-all nature of the current, constitutionally mandated electoral college system is a major detriment to the creation and survival of third parties, who must win the plurality of votes in any state to win any electoral votes.

In the wake of the closeness of the 2000 presidential election, in which the candidate who won the popular vote did not win the general election, three major reform ideas have developed:

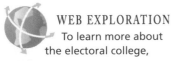

WEB EXPLORATION
To learn more about the electoral college, go to www.ablongman.com/oconnor

1. *Abolition.* This reform proposes to abolish the electoral college entirely and have the president selected by popular vote. This reform is by far the most unlikely to succeed, given that the Constitution of the United States would have to be amended to change the electoral college. Even assuming that the House of Representatives could muster the two-thirds majority necessary to pass an amendment, the proposal would almost certainly never pass the Senate. This is because small states have the same representation in the Senate as populous ones, and the Senate thus serves as a bastion of equal representation for all states, regardless of population—a principle which is generally reinforced by the existing configuration of the electoral college, which ensures a minimum of electoral influence for even the smallest states.

2. *Congressional district plan.* Under this plan, each candidate would receive one electoral vote for each congressional district that he wins in a state, and the winner of the overall popular vote in each state would receive two bonus votes (one for each senator) for that state.

POLICY IN ACTION

THE POLITICS OF REDISTRICTING

The Voting Rights Act of 1965 protects the interests of black voters. This protection is given heightened scrutiny every decade when state legislators begin the onerous and highly contentious task of redrawing congressional district lines. As a result of the 2000 Census, for example, Arizona, Florida, Georgia, and Texas will gain two and several other states will gain one member of Congress, Texas, in fact, has now become the second most populous state in the Union.

Watch closely as this process goes on. During redistricting, the Republican Party will champion enforcement of the act because for every majority black district created, "there is a good chance of creating two or more districts that are overwhelmingly white and Republican."[a] In the South, in particular, this practice has resulted in record numbers of African American (largely Democratic) representatives and an increasing number of white Republican House members. Knowing this, Democratic Southern state legislators will try to fashion districts that that have 25 to 40 percent African American voters, figuring that those voters will vote Democratic along with a sufficient number of white Democrats to send a Democrat to Con-

gress. In contrast, Republicans in the state houses will try to pack large numbers of African Americans into a single district so as not to dilute Republican strengths.

Democrats are seeking ways to try to prevent this practice and both parties have lawyers ready to challenge new districts in federal court. "Our goal is to not allow Republicans to use redistricting to put us in a permanent minority status," said the counsel to the Democratic Party's major redistricting organization.[b] After the last redistricting, the Supreme Court rejected plans drawn with race as the predominant factor, which produced exceptionally oddly drawn, widely spread out districts. In fact, court battles over redistricting were fought in 41 states after the 1990 Census. Still, as the Voting Rights Act was implemented and enforced, over time it has ironically meant that black representation from black districts has produced Republican electoral victories in much of the South, which was not necessarily a goal of the original law.

---

[a]Thomas B. Edsall, "Parties Play Voting Rights Role Reversal," *The Washington Post* (February 25, 2001): A4.
[b]Edsall, "Parties Play."

Take for example Virginia, which has eleven Representatives and two Senators for a total of thirteen electoral votes. If the Democratic candidate wins five congressional districts, and the Republican candidate wins the other six districts and also the statewide majority, the Democrat wins five electoral votes and the Republican wins a total of eight. This reform can be adopted without a constitutional amendment. This electoral system currently exists only in Maine and Nebraska, but any state can adopt this system on its own because the Constitution gives states the right to determine the place and manner by which electors are selected. There are, however, some unintended consequences to this reform. First, the winner of the overall election might change in some circumstances. Richard Nixon would have won the 1960 election instead of John F. Kennedy under a congressional district plan. George W. Bush would have likely won by a wider margin if the entire nation used this system in 2000. Second, this reform would further politicize the redistricting process that takes place every ten years according to census results. Fair and objective redistricting already suffers at the hands of many political interests, and if electoral votes were at stake, it would suffer further as the parities made nationwide efforts to maximize the number of safe electoral districts for their presidential nominee while minimizing the number of competitive districts. The third consequence of state-by-state adoption is that the nation would quickly come to resemble a patchwork of different electoral methods, with some states being awarded by congressional districts and some states awarded solely by popular vote. California, for example, would be unlikely to adopt this system because it would reduce tremendously the power of the state that comes with having fifty-four electoral votes in one package and induces California legislators to keep their electoral votes together. In the end, the United States and its democracy might be better served by preserving the more uniform system that currently prevails, despite its other shortcomings. Finally, candidates would quickly learn to focus their campaigning on competitive districts while ignoring secure districts, since secure districts would contribute electoral votes only through the senatorial/statewide-majority component.

3. *Keep the college, abolish the electors.* This proposal calls for the preservation of the college as a statistical electoral device but would remove all voting power from actual human electors and their legislative appointors. This would eliminate the threat of so-called faithless electors—that is, electors who are appointed by state legislators to vote for the candidate who won that state's vote, but who then choose, for whatever reason, to vote for the other candidate. This reform is widely accepted, although—perhaps even because—the problem of faithless electors is only a secondary and little-realized liability of the electoral college.

While the fate of these major policy reform proposals has yet to be determined, any change in the existing system would inevitably have a profound impact on the way that candidates go about the business of seeking votes for the U.S. presidency.

Patterns of Presidential Elections

Electoral college results reveal more over time than simply who won the presidency. They show which party and which regions are coming to dominance and how voters may be changing party allegiances in response to new issues and generational changes. Political scientists who study elections note several important patterns in presidential elections.

Party Realignments.   Usually such movements are gradual, but occasionally the political equivalent of a major earthquake swiftly and dramatically alters the landscape. During these rare events, called **party realignments,**[6] existing party affiliations are subject to upheaval: Many voters may change parties, and the youngest age group of voters may permanently adopt the label of the newly dominant party. Until recent times, at least, party realignments have been spaced about thirty-six years apart in the U.S. experience.

A major realignment is precipitated by one or more **critical elections,** which may polarize voters around new issues and personalities in reaction to crucial developments, such as a war or an economic depression. With the aid of timely circumstances, realignments are accomplished in two main ways.[7] Some voters are simply converted from one party to the other by the issues and candidates of the time. New voters may also be mobilized into action: Immigrants, young voters, and previous nonvoters may become motivated and then absorbed into a new governing majority. However vibrant and potent party coalitions may be at first, as they age, tensions increase and grievances accumulate. The majority's original reason for existing fades, and new generations neither remember the traumatic events that originally brought about the realignment nor possess the stalwart party identifications of their ancestors. New issues arise, producing conflicts that can be resolved only by a breakup of old alignments and a reshuffling of individual and group party loyalties. Viewed in historical perspective, party realignment has been a mechanism that ensures stability by controlling unavoidable change.

In the entire history of the United States, there have been six party alignments; three tumultuous eras in particular have produced significant critical elections. First, during the period leading up to the Civil War, the Whig Party gradually dissolved and the Republican Party developed and won the presidency. Second, the populist radicalization of the Democratic Party in the 1890s enabled the Republicans to strengthen their majority status and make lasting gains in voter attachments. Third, the Great Depression of the 1930s propelled the Democrats to power, causing large numbers of voters to repudiate the GOP and embrace the Democratic Party. In each of these cases, fundamental and enduring alterations in the party equation resulted.

The last confirmed major realignment happened in the 1928–1936 period, as Republican Herbert Hoover's presidency was held to one term because of voter anger about the Depression. In 1932 Democrat Franklin D. Roosevelt swept to power as the electorate decisively rejected Hoover and the Republicans. This dramatic vote of "no confidence" was followed by substantial changes in policy by the new president, who demonstrated in fact or at least in appearance that his policies were effective. The people responded to his success, accepted his vision of society, and ratified their choice of the new president's party in subsequent presidential and congressional elections.

party realignment
A shifting of party coalition groupings in the electorate that remains in place for several elections.

critical election
An election that signals a party realignment through voter polarization around new issues.

Simultaneously, the former majority party (Republican) reluctantly but inevitably adjusted to its new minority role. So strong was the new partisan attachment for most voters that even when short-term issues and personalities that favored the Republican Party dislodged the Democrats from power, the basic distribution of party loyalties did not shift significantly. In 1952, 1956, 1968, and 1972, Republicans won the presidency, but the New Deal Democratic coalition was still visible in the voting patterns, and it survived to emerge again in future elections.

A critical realigning era is by no means the only occasion when changes in partisan affiliation are accommodated. In truth, every election produces realignment to some degree, since some individuals are undoubtedly pushed to change parties by events and by their reactions to the candidates. Recent research suggests that partisanship is much more responsive to current issues and personalities than had been believed earlier, and that major realignments are just extreme cases of the kind of changes in party loyalty registered every year.[8]

Secular Realignment.   Although the term *realignment* is usually applied only if momentous events such as war or depression produce enduring and substantial alterations in the party coalitions, political scientists have long recognized that a more gradual rearrangement of party coalitions could occur. Called **secular realignment,** this piecemeal process depends not on convulsive shocks to the political system, but on slow, almost barely discernable demographic shifts—the shrinking of one party's base of support and the enlargement of the other's, for example—or simple generational replacement (that is, the dying off of the older generation and the maturing of the younger generation).[9] A recent version of this theory, termed "rolling realignment,"[10] argues that in an era of weaker party attachments (such as we currently are experiencing), a dramatic, full-scale realignment may not be possible. Still, a critical mass of voters may be attracted for years to one party's banner in waves or streams, if that party's leadership and performance are consistently exemplary.

Some scholars and political observers also contend that the decline of party affiliation has left the electorate dealigned and incapable of being realigned as long as party ties remain tenuous for so many voters.[11] Voters shift with greater ease between the parties during dealignment, but little permanence or intensity exists in identifications made and held so lightly. If nothing else, the obsolescence of realignment theory may be indicated by the calendar; if major realignments occur roughly every thirty-six years, then we are long overdue. The last major realignment took place between 1928 and 1936, and so the next one might have been expected in the late 1960s and early 1970s.

There is little question that we have been moving through an unstable and somewhat "dealigned" period at least since the 1970s. The foremost political question today is whether dealignment will continue (and in what form) or whether a major realignment is in the offing. Each previous dealignment has been a precursor of realignment,[12] but realignment need not succeed dealignment, especially under modern conditions.

secular realignment
The gradual rearrangement of party coalitions, based more on demographic shifts than on shocks to the political system.

TIMELINE
Patterns of Presidential Election Realignment and Dealignment

WEB EXPLORATION
What voters say before going to the polls, and who they actually vote for are sometimes different. To look at poll questions and answers that were asked before and after national elections, go to www.ablongman.com/oconnor

CONGRESSIONAL ELECTIONS

Many similar elements are present in different kinds of elections: Candidates, voters, issues, and television advertisements are constants. But there are distinctive aspects of each kind of election as well. Compared with presidential elections, congressional elections are a different animal.

First, most candidates for Congress labor in relative obscurity. While there are some celebrity nominees for Congress— television stars, sports heroes, and, in 2000, even the first lady—the vast majority of party nominees are little-known state legislators and local office holders. For them, just getting known, establishing name identification, is the biggest battle. No major-party presidential nominee need worry about this elementary stage because so much media attention is focused on the race for the White House. While U.S. Senate races increasingly rely on the media and involve well-known men and women, this is not so for most congressional contests. Elections for the House of Representatives receive remarkably little coverage in many states and communities.

WEB EXPLORATION To learn more about candidates you have supported in the past, or to familiarize yourself with future political candidates, go to www.ablongman.com/oconnor

The Incumbency Advantage

Under these circumstances the advantages of incumbency (that is, already being in office) are enhanced, and a kind of electoral inertia takes hold: Those people in office tend to remain in office. Reelection rates for sitting House members range well above 95 percent in most election years.

Frequently, the reelection rate for senators is as high, but not always. In a "bad" year for House incumbents, "only" 88 percent will win (as in the Watergate year of 1974), but the senatorial reelection rate can drop much lower on occasion (to 60 percent in the 1980 Reagan landslide, for example). There is a good reason for this lower senatorial reelection rate. A Senate election is often a high-visibility contest; it receives much more publicity than a House race. So while House incumbents remain protected and insulated in part because few voters pay attention to their little-known challengers, a Senate-seat challenger can become well known more easily and thus be in a better position to defeat an incumbent.

The 2000 congressional elections are yet another example of the power of incumbency. The majority of sitting representatives and senators who sought reelection won another term. Not a single woman who sought reelection lost. For the relatively few incumbent members of Congress who lose their reelection bids, three explanations are paramount: redistricting, scandals, and coattails.

Redistricting. The U.S. Constitution requires that a census, which entails the counting of all Americans, be conducted every ten years.

POLITICS NOW

SENATE RACE STEALS SPOTLIGHT

Every now and then, a race for a governorship or U.S. Senate seat becomes the headline race of an election season, defining the political year or providing an exceptionally memorable match-up. It was clear from the moment that First Lady Hillary Rodham Clinton expressed interest in an open New York Senate seat that 2000 would be such a year and the contest in the Empire State would be the race. It was not simply that a first lady had never in American history run for any public office, nor that her likely Republican opponent, New York City Mayor Rudolph Giuliani, was almost as well known as Clinton and an exceptionally feisty campaigner. Rather, the Senate contest would top the charts because it would inevitably encapsulate all of the important current issues and personalities in American politics today, from President Clinton and his scandals to splits within the Republican Party and the voracity of the press.

The situation was further complicated by Giuliani's unexpected withdrawal following his diagnosis of cancer in the summer before the election. Representative Rick Lazio, whose name had briefly been mentioned in the Republican nominating process, reappeared to carry the Republican torch. As a relatively young and unknown congressman, Lazio had a hard time filling Giuliani's shoes, although his campaign did profit from the direct inheritance of the anti-Clinton vote.

Lazio raised $38 million; Clinton raised $29 million. In the end, Clinton easily took the election by a 12-point margin in spite of having far less to spend. As a junior senator with a high profile and some political baggage, it remains to be seen what role she will play in the Senate and on the national political scene.

Every ten years, after the census, all congressional district lines are redrawn (in states with more than one congressperson) so that every legislator represents about the same number of citizens.

This process of redrawing congressional districts to reflect increases or decreases in seats allotted to the states, as well as population shifts within a state, is called redistricting. When shifts occur in the national population, states gain or lose congressional seats. For example, in the 2000 Census (as in most censuses since 1960), many Northeastern states showed a population decline and lost congressional seats, whereas states in the South, Southwest, and West showed great population growth and gained seats.

Through redistricting, the political party in each statehouse with the greatest number of members tries to assure that the maximum number of its party members can be elected to Congress. This redistricting process, which has gone on since the first census in 1790, often involves a creative redrawing of district lines called **gerrymandering.**

gerrymandering
A creative redrawing of district lines.

TABLE 12.4   Congressional Election Results and Coattail Effects, 1948–2000

GAIN (+) OR LOSS (–) FOR PRESIDENT'S PARTY

Presidential Election Years			Midterm Elections		
President/Year	House	Senate	Year	House	Senate
Truman (D): 1948	+76	+9	1950	-29	-6
Eisenhower (R): 1952	+24	+2	1954	-18	-1
Eisenhower (R): 1956	-2	0	1958	-48	-13
Kennedy (D): 1960	-20	-2	1962	-4	+3
Johnson (D): 1964	+38	+2	1966	-47	-4
Nixon (R): 1968	+7	+5	1970	-12	+2
Nixon (R): 1972	+13	-2	Ford: 1974	-48	-5
Carter (D): 1976	+2	0	1978	-15	-3
Reagan (R): 1980	+33	+12	1982	-26	+1
Reagan (R): 1984	+15	-2	1986	-5	-8
Bush (R): 1988	-3	-1	1990	-9	-1
Clinton (D): 1992	-10	0	1994	-52	-9*
Clinton (D): 1996	+10	-2	1998	+5	0
Bush (R): 2000	-2	-4			

*Includes the switch from Democrat to Republican of Alabama U.S. Senator Richard Shelby.

Creative redistricting and the actions of state legislators often create problems that end up in litigation. Over the years, the Supreme Court has ruled that:

- Congressional as well as state legislative districts must be apportioned on the basis of population.[13]
- Purposeful gerrymandering of a congressional district to dilute minority strength is illegal under the Voting Rights Act of 1965.[14]
- Redrawing of districts for obvious racial purposes to enhance minority representation is unconstitutional because it denies the constitutional rights of white citizens.[15]

Scandals.   Scandals come in many varieties. The old standby of financial impropriety (bribery and payoffs, for example) has been supplemented by other forms of career-ending incidents, such as personal improprieties (sexual escapades, for instance). The power of incumbency is so strong, however, that many legislators survive even serious scandal to win reelection.

Coattails.   Historically, the defeat of a congressional incumbent has also occurred as a result of the presidential coattail effect. Successful presidential candidates usually carry congressional candidates of the same party into office in the year of their election (see Table 12.4). Notice the overall decline in the strength of the coattail effect in modern times, however, as party identification has weakened and the powers and perks of congressional incumbency have grown.

A major mobilizer of the youth vote, Rock the Vote registers new voters and lobbies for legislation of interest to young people and the record industry. The band Angry Salad performs here at a 2000 event in Philadelphia. (Photo courtesy: Rock the Vote. www.rockthevote.org.)

Midterm Elections.   Elections in the middle of presidential terms, midterm elections, generally present a different threat to incumbents. This time it is the incumbents of the president's party who are most in jeopardy. Just as the presidential party usually gains seats in presidential election years, it usually loses seats in off years. The problems and tribulations of governing normally cost a president some popularity, alienate key groups, or cause the public to want to send the president a message of one sort or another. An economic downturn or a scandal can underline and expand this circumstance, as the Watergate scandal of 1974 and the recession of 1982 demonstrated. Thus, many political pundits were shocked when Democrats actually picked up seats in the House in 1998.

Senate elections are less inclined to follow these rules than are House elections. The idiosyncratic nature of Senate contests is due to both their intermittent scheduling (only one-third of the seats come up for election every two years) and the existence of well-funded, well-known candidates who can sometimes swim against whatever political tide is rising. Also worth remembering is that midterm elections in recent history have a much lower voter turnout than presidential elections. As Analyzing the Data shows, midterm elections generally draw only 35 percent to 40 percent of adult Americans to the polls (1998's 34 percent was a modern record low). A presidential contest attracts between 50 percent and 55 percent (1996 was obviously an exception, producing the lowest voter turnout in a presidential general election since 1924).

VOTING BEHAVIOR

Whether they are casting ballots in congressional or presidential elections, voters behave in certain distinct ways and exhibit unmistakable patterns to political scientists who study them.

Voter Participation

turnout

The proportion of the voting-age public that votes.

Turnout is the proportion of the voting-age public that votes. The first clear division is between citizens who turn out and those who do not. About 40 percent of the eligible adult population in the United States vote regularly, whereas 25 percent are occasional voters. Thirty-five percent rarely or never vote. Several factors are associated with voter participation rates.

ANALYZING THE DATA

VOTER TURNOUT IN PRESIDENTIAL AND MIDTERM CONGRESSIONAL ELECTIONS

The twentieth century has seen a gradual and erratic but generally consistent decline in voter turnout. Various factors influence turnout. The high percentages of 1876 and 1960 both occurred in open races (i.e., when no incumbent was running), and in the latter, the new TV debates energized and engaged the electorate. The low midterm election turnout of 1998 is unfortunately all too typical of off-year (i.e., nonpresidential) elections. Following the historic 2000 election, many anticipate high voter turnout in the 2004 presidential election.

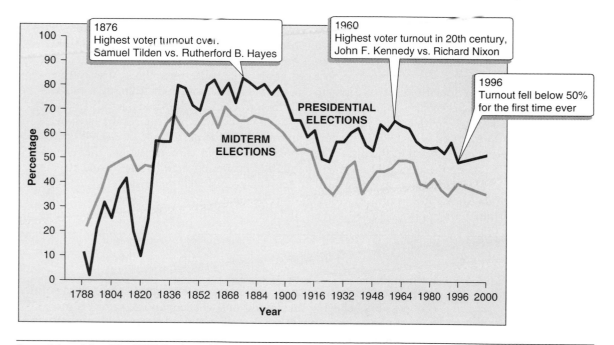

Source: Adopted from Harold W. Stanley and Richard G. Niemi, *Vital Statistics on American Politics*, 1997–1998, 5th ed. (Washington, D.C.: CQ Press, 1998), Figure 3-1, p. 85. Updated by authors.

Income.   A clear relationship between income and voting turnout rates exists. A considerably higher percentage of citizens with annual incomes over $40,000 vote than do citizens with incomes under $10,000. Income level is, to some degree, connected to education level, as wealthier people tend to have more opportunities for higher education and more education also may lead to higher income. Wealthy citizens are also more likely than poor ones to think that the "system" works for them and that their votes make a difference.

H I G H L I G H T

VOTING RIGHTS ACT OF 1965 AND ITS EFFECTS

Both the Civil Rights Act of 1964 and the Voting Rights Act of 1965 were intended to guarantee voting rights to African Americans nearly a century after passage of the Fifteenth Amendment. Often now heralded as the most successful piece of civil rights legislation ever passed, the VRA targeted states that had used literacy or morality tests or poll taxes to exclude blacks from the polls. The act has two key provisions: (1) Section 2, which makes it illegal to use any voting device or procedure that denies or hinders a minority citizen's right to vote, and (2) Section 5, which requires certain states throughout the South and in other areas where minority registration was not in proportion to the racial composition of the district to obtain approval from the Justice Department concerning any proposed changes in voting qualifications or procedures. It also authorized the federal government to monitor all elections in areas where discrimination was found to be practiced or where less than 50 percent of the voting-age public was registered to vote in the 1964 election.

The impact of the act was immediate. Black voter registration skyrocketed and the number of African Americans elected to office skyrocketed. For example, in 1965 there were 280 black elected officials at any level in the United States. By 1997 there were 8,656 black elected officials nationwide. Since 1965, African American voters have used their strength at the ballot box to elect black officials at all levels of government. But while the results have been encouraging, the percentage of elected offices held by African Americans in the eleven Southern states covered by the Voting Rights Act remains relatively small.

While many believed that the days of voter intimidation that the law was designed to address

By contrast, lower-income citizens often feel alienated from politics, possibly believing that conditions will remain the same no matter for whom they vote. A factor that contributes to this feeling of alienation is that American political parties, unlike parties in many other countries which tend to associate themselves with specific social classes, do not attempt to link themselves intimately to one major class (such as the "working class"). Therefore, the feelings of alienation and apathy about politics prevalent among many lower-income Americans should not be unexpected.

Age.   There is also a correlation between age and voter participation rates. The Twenty-Sixth Amendment, ratified in 1971, lowered the voting age to eighteen. While this amendment obviously increased the number of *eligible* voters, it did so by enfranchising the group that is least likely to vote. A much higher percentage of citizens age thirty and older vote

were long gone, the 2000 election put the Voting Rights Act back in the spotlight when charges of major irregularities were made by civil rights groups when it appeared that a disproportionate number of minority votes were not counted in Florida. In January 2001, just as the U.S. Civil Rights Commission was wrapping up hearings investigating possible violations of the act, several civil rights groups filed suit against Katherine Harris, the Florida secretary of state, alleging gross violations of the Voting Rights Act and the equal protection clause of the Fourteenth Amendment to the U.S. Constitution. Groups including the NAACP, the ACLU, the NAACP Legal Defense Fund, and People for the American Way allege that Florida officials knew that there would be an unprecedented minority voter turnout in Florida and took actions to deter those voters. They charged that officials took actions that forced African Americans to wait in unusually long lines to vote, purged thousands of minority voters from the polls, and used anti-

quated machines in minority districts, which were far less likely to record votes. Other allegations included "a pattern of targeted racial profiling," according to Reverend Jesse Jackson,[*] that included the razing of one majority African American polling place with no notice as to where the new polling place was, and random police roadblocks on the roads leading to minority polling places. The lawsuit also asks the federal court to order remedies, including the adoption of standard measures for poll workers and restoring purged voters to the polls. Whatever the outcome of this lawsuit, it is likely that the election and the mandates of the Voting Rights Act will require substantial changes in the kinds of ballot procedures used around the nation, as well as heightened awareness of the act and its mandates.

---

[*]Scott Martelle, "Decision 2000: America Waits: Rights Leaders Add to Charges of Vote Fraud in Florida," *Los Angeles Times* (November 30, 2000): A35.

than do citizens younger than thirty, although voter turnout decreases over the age of seventy, primarily because of physical infirmity, which makes it difficult to get to the polling location. Regrettably, less than half of eligible eighteen- to twenty-four-year-olds are even registered to vote.

PARTICIPATION
The Prepared
Voter Kit

Race. Another voter difference is related to race: Whites vote more regularly than do blacks, though recently the proportions have been more nearly equal. In 2000, black voter turnout reached record highs in many sections of the nation.

Much of the difference in turnout is due in part to the relative income and educational levels of the two racial groups. African Americans tend to be poorer and have less formal education than whites; and, as mentioned earlier, both of these factors affect voter turnout. Significantly, though, highly educated and wealthier African Americans are at least equally likely to vote, and sometimes more so, than whites of similar background.

Anti-Bush protesters lined the inauguration route to show their dissatisfaction with the 2000 election outcome. (Photo courtesy: Christy Bowe/Corbis Sygma)

Gender.   There have been elections throughout the twentieth century where gender was a factor, although precise data are not always available to prove the conventional wisdom. For example, journalists in 1920 claimed that women—in their first presidential election after the passage of the Nineteenth Amendment granted woman suffrage—were especially likely to vote for Republican presidential candidate Warren G. Harding. In the sexist view of the day, women were supposedly taken in by the handsome Harding's charm. Recent evidence is more clear that women act and react disproportionately to some candidacies, including those of other women. For instance, Democratic women were more likely than Democratic men to support Walter Mondale's presidential ticket in 1984 because of former Vice President Mondale's selection of New York Representative Geraldine Ferraro for the second slot on his presidential ticket. However, Republican women at the time were more likely than GOP men to support Ronald Reagan's candidacy because of Ferraro's presence on the Democratic ticket; Republican women were opposed to Ferraro's liberal voting record and views. Since 1980, the so-called gender gap (the difference between the voting choices of men and women) has become a staple of American politics.

Interest in Politics.   Although socioeconomic factors undoubtedly weigh heavily in voter participation rates, an interest in politics must also be included as an important factor. Many citizens who vote have grown up in families interested and active in politics, and they in turn stimulate their children to take an interest. Conversely, many nonvoters simply do not care about politics or the outcome of elections, never having been taught their importance at a younger age.

People who are highly interested in politics constitute only a small minority of the U.S. populace. For example, the most politically active Americans—party and issue-group activists—make up less than 5 percent of the country's 250 million people. Those who contribute time or money to a party or a candidate during a campaign make up only about 10 percent of the total population. On the other hand, although these percentages appear low, they translate into millions of Americans who contribute more than just votes to the system.

WEB EXPLORATION
To access the most up-to-date data on voting, public opinion, and public participation, go to www.ablongman.com/oconnor

Why Is Voter Turnout So Low?

There is no getting around the fact that the United States has one of the lowest voter participation rates of any nation in the industrialized

FIGURE 12.2　Why People Don't Vote

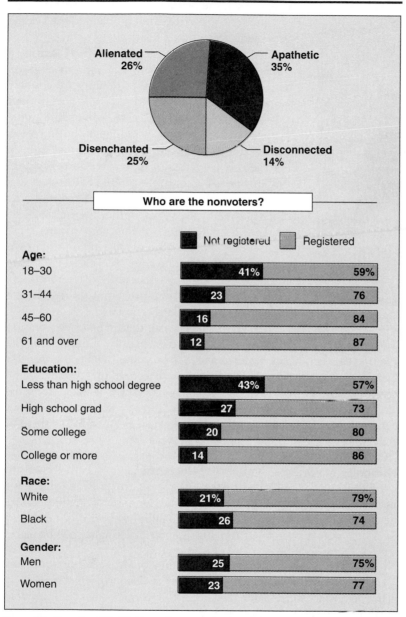

Who are the nonvoters?

■ Not registered　　▨ Registered

Age:
	Not registered	Registered
18–30	41%	59%
31–44	23	76
45–60	16	84
61 and over	12	87

Education:
	Not registered	Registered
Less than high school degree	43%	57%
High school grad	27	73
Some college	20	80
College or more	14	86

Race:
	Not registered	Registered
White	21%	79%
Black	26	74

Gender:
	Not registered	Registered
Men	25	75%
Women	23	77

Pie chart: Alienated 26%, Apathetic 35%, Disenchanted 25%, Disconnected 14%

Source: "The Non voters," *The Washington Post,* November 4, 2000. Copyright ©2000, The Washington Post. Reprinted with permission.

world, and it continues to decline. Only 50.7 percent of the eligible electorate (that is, those age eighteen and over) voted in the 2000 general presidential election, compared with 62 percent in 1960. Several explanations have been offered as to why Americans often opt not to vote. (See Figure 12.2.)

In an effort to improve voter turnout, Oregon allowed voters either to mail in their ballots or to deliver them to one of several dropoff locations. In 1996 this led to some delays in voting when over 20 percent of voters opted to mail their ballots. (Photo courtesy: Shane Young/AP/Wide World Photos)

Difficulty of Registration.   Interestingly, of those who are registered, the overwhelming majority vote. The real source of the participation problem in the United States seems to be that a relatively low percentage of the adult population is registered to vote. There are a number of reasons for the low U.S. registration rates. First, while nearly every other democratic country places the burden of registration on the government rather than on the individual, in the United States the registration process requires individual initiative—a daunting impediment in this age of political apathy. Thus the cost (in terms of time and effort) of registering to vote is higher in the United States than it is in other industrialized democracies. Second, many nations automatically register all of their citizens to vote. In the United States, however, citizens must jump the extra hurdle of remembering on their own to register. Indeed, it is no coincidence that voter participation rates dropped markedly after reformers pushed through strict voter registration laws in the early part of the twentieth century.

In 1993, a major advance toward easier registration was achieved with the passage by Congress of the motor-voter bill, which required states to permit individuals to register by mail, not just in person. The law, strongly backed by President Clinton, also allows citizens to register to vote when they visit any motor vehicles office, public assistance agency, or military recruitment division. Studies reveal that millions of new voters have been added to the poll since the enactment of the Motor Voter Act.

WEB EXPLORATION
For more on absentee ballots and their importance in the 2000 election, see www.ablongman.com/oconnor

Difficulty of Absentee Voting.   Stringent absentee ballot laws are another factor in the United States' low voter turnout. Many states, for instance, require citizens to apply in person for absentee ballots, a burdensome requirement given that one's inability to be present in his or her home state is often the reason for absentee balloting in the first place.

Number of Elections.   Another explanation for low voter turnout in this country is the sheer number and frequency of elections, which few if any other democracies can match. Yet an election cornucopia is the inevitable result of federalism and the separation of powers, which result in layers of often separate elections on the local, state, and national levels.

Voter Attitudes.   Although some of the reasons for low voter participation are due to the institutional factors we have just reviewed, voter attitudes play an equally important part. Some nations try to get around the effects of voter attitudes with compulsory voting laws, as in Australia and Belgium, or by taxing citizens who do not vote. Not surprisingly, voter turnout rates in Australia and Belgium are often greater than 95 percent.

GLOBAL POLITICS

THE AMERICANIZATION OF PARLIAMENTARY CAMPAIGNS

Election campaigns in the United States, for example, have the distinction of being the longest and most expensive of any in the industrial democracies. Institutions like political action committees (PACs), the "horse race" media coverage of presidential campaigns, and the concentration on "momentum" in presidential primaries are unknown in the other six democracies.

Observers in the European countries have worried in recent years about the "Americanization" of parliamentary campaigns, by which they mean in particular the growing use of television as a campaign tool. In the most recent rounds of parliamentary elections in Great Britain and Germany, the winning parties' campaign teams closely studied how the Clinton campaign had used media techniques to deliver effective messages. In 1998, Gerhard Schroeder's winning team used focus groups and speeches deliberately geared to television during the campaign for the German Bundestag. It is not clear, however, how far American-style campaigning can go; in France and Japan, the government carefully regulates media coverage of campaigns, and candidates are prohibited from buying television and radio time. Polling, a key tool in any national campaign in the United States, is less widely used in other democracies. In France, Italy, and Canada, the government prohibits public dissemination of poll results in the days prior to an election.

In almost all the G-7 parliamentary systems (Japan until recently was an exception) the parties are the candidates' major source of funding.

Sympathetic interest groups channel their campaign contributions through the parties. Not only do PACs not exist, but pronouncements such as U.S. Senator Russ Feingold's that one way to lessen the expense of campaigns is to refuse "soft money" from the national parties and their committees* would baffle a candidate in any of the other six countries.

In addition, no other major democratic political system has primaries (Mexico's PRI experimented with presidential primaries in the mid-1990s). Candidates are selected by the political party organizations, not the rank-and-file voters in all other countries surveyed in this book. The public does not have to go to the polls twice in a year to elect a government.

Parliamentary general election campaigns in other countries are short. The campaign season typically lasts less than a month. Japan's 1996 and 2000 parliamentary election campaigns each lasted less than two weeks, and prompted some observers to ask whether the campaigns were too short to allow the public to make informed candidate choices. Election dates are not fixed in the parliamentary systems. Except for Germany and France, elections occur whenever the prime minister calls for them (the French president has that power). Moreover, the Parliament elects the prime minister, so direct election of the executive (except for the presidents of France and Russia) is not possible.

*Russ Feingold, "Running and Winning a 'Restrained' Campaign," *Extensions* (Spring 1999): 4.

As noted previously, alienation afflicts some voters, and others are just plain apathetic, possibly because of a lack of pressing issues in a particular year, satisfaction with the status quo, or uncompetitive (even uncontested) elections. Furthermore, many citizens may be turned off

VISUAL LITERACY
Voter Turnout: Who Votes? Do Americans Vote as Much as Other Citizens?

TABLE 12.5   How America Votes

The U.S. voting system relies on a patchwork of machines to tally voters' choices. More than a third use punch-card systems similar to the ones involved in the 2000 ballot dispute in Florida. Florida outlawed their use in 2001.

	How they work	Percentage of precincts that use them
Punch cards	Punch holes in a card next to candidate's name.	37%
Optical scan	Shade in area next to candidate's name.	25%
Lever machine	Inside booth, voters pull levers to choose candidate.	22%
Electronic	Use keyboard or touch-screen to record votes.	7%
Mixed	Voters mark ballots with pen or pencil.	6%
Paper ballots	More than one system.	3%

Source: "How America Votes," *The Washington Post*, December 14, 2000. Copyright ©2000, *The Washington Post*. Reprinted with permission.

by the quality of campaigns in a time when petty issues and personal mudslinging are more prevalent than ever. Finally, perhaps turnout has declined due to rising levels of distrust of government. More and more people are telling pollsters that they lack confidence in political leaders. In the past some scholars argued that there is no correlation between distrust of political leaders and nonvoting. But as the levels of distrust rise, these preliminary conclusions might need to be revisited.

Those who do vote use a variety of different mechanisms, as the 2000 election made abundantly clear. See Table 12.5 for a list of voting systems.

Weak Political Parties.   Political parties today are no longer as effective as they once were in mobilizing voters, ensuring that they are registered, and getting them to the polls. Today candidate-centered campaigns have resulted in a somewhat more distant party with which most people do not identify very strongly. All of the factors represent major challenges to candidates as they structure their campaigns to entice voters.

MODERN CAMPAIGN CHALLENGES

The modern candidate faces two major challenges: communicating through the media and raising the money needed to stay in the race.

The goal of all limits is the same: to prevent any single group or individual from gaining too much influence over elected officials, who naturally feel indebted to campaign contributors.

Given the cash flow required by a campaign and the legal restrictions on political money, raising the funds necessary to run a modern campaign is a monumental task. See Figure 12.3 detailing a typical budget for a Senate candidate. Presidential and congressional campaigns have squads of fund raisers on staff. These professionals rely on several standard sources of campaign money.

Individual Contributions.   Individual contributions are donations from private citizens. The maximum allowable contribution under federal law for congressional and presidential elections is $1,000 per election to each candidate, with primary and general elections considered separately. Individuals are also limited to a total of $25,000 in gifts to all candidates combined in each calendar year. Most candidates receive a majority of all funds directly from individuals, and most individual gifts are well below the maximum level.

Political Action Committee (PAC) Contributions.   As explained in chapter 11, donations from political action committees (PACs) are those from interest groups (labor unions, corporations, trade associations, and ideological and issue groups). Under federal law, these organizations are required to establish officially recognized fundraising committees, called PACs, to participate in federal elections. (Some but

FIGURE 12.3   Campaign for Senate, 2000: A "Typical" Candidate's Budget of $7 Million
The breakdown of a sample budget for a typical Senate campaign. Note how most of the revenue comes from individual contributions, and how the greatest expense is media advertising.

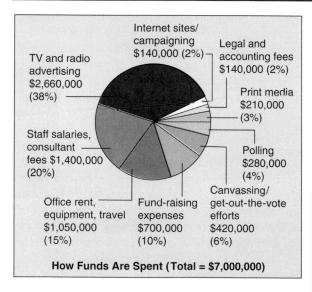

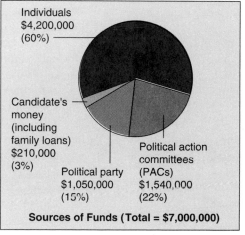

not all states have similar requirements for state elections.) Because a small number of PACs make up such a large proportion of campaign war chests, they have influence disproportionate to that of individuals. Recent studies, in fact, show that PACs effectively use contributions to punish legislators and affect policy, at least in the short run.[16] Legislators who vote contrary to the wishes of a PAC see their donations withheld, but those who are successful in legislating in the PAC's wishes are rewarded with even greater donations.[17]

Political Party Contributions.   Candidates also receive donations from the national and state committees of the Democratic and Republican Parties. Political parties can give substantial contributions to both presidential and congressional nominees. According to the FEC, in 2000, national, state, and local political parties raised over $1.2 billion, a 37 percent increase in fundraising over the 1995–1996 presidential cycle. Republican committees contributed $33.7 million directly to candidates and $29 million in coordinated expenditures. Democrats contributed $253.4 million directly and spent nearly that much in coordinated expenses. In addition to helping elect party members, campaign contributions from political parties have another, less obvious benefit: Helping to ensure party discipline in voting. One study of congressional voting behavior in the 1980s, for instance, found that those members who received a large percentage of their total campaign funds from their party voted with their party more often than they were expected to.[18]

Member to Candidate Contributions.   In Congress and in state legislatures, well-funded, electorally secure incumbents often contribute campaign money to their party's needy legislative candidates.[19] This activity has long occurred in some state legislatures (notably California), but it has recently become increasingly important at the congressional level.[20] Generally, members contribute to other candidates in one of two ways. First, some members have established their own PACs—informally dubbed "leadership" PACs—through which they distribute campaign support to candidates. Second, members also make contributions to other candidates directly from their own reelection accounts. Either way, members are limited in what they may contribute to other candidates: $1,000 per candidate per election to federal candidates from their reelection committees and $5,000 per candidate per election to candidates through a leadership PAC.

Candidates' Personal Contributions.   Candidates and their families may donate to the campaign. In 1976, the Supreme Court ruled in *Buckley* v. *Valeo* that no limit could be placed on the amount of money candidates can spend from their own families' resources, since such spending is considered a First Amendment right of free speech.[21] For wealthy politicians such as U.S. Senator Jon Corzine (D–N.J.), this

 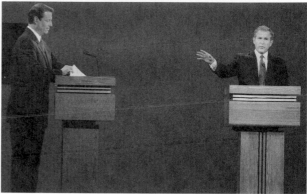

Presidential debates have come a long way—at least in terms of studio trappings—since the ill-at-ease Richard M. Nixon was visually bested by John F. Kennedy in the first televised debate. In the first of three 2000 debates, Al Gore's aggressive debating style contrasted sharply with that of George W. Bush. (Photos courtesy: left, Bettmann/Corbis; right, Al Behrman/AP/Wide World Photos)

allowance meant personal spending on his campaign of over $60 million of his own fortune. Most candidates, however, commit much less than $100,000 in family resources to their election bids.

Public Funds.   **Public funds** are donations from general tax revenues. Only presidential candidates (and a handful of state and local contenders) receive public funds. Under the terms of the Federal Election Campaign Act of 1971 (which first established public funding of presidential campaigns), a candidate for president can become eligible to receive public funds during the nominating contest by raising at least $5,000 in individual contributions of $250 or less in each of twenty states. Once the receipt of this money is certified, the candidate can apply for federal **matching funds,** whereby every dollar raised from individuals in amounts less than $251 is matched by the federal treasury on a dollar-for-dollar basis. This assumes there is enough money in the Presidential Election Campaign Fund to do so. The fund is accumulated by taxpayers who designate $3 of their taxes for this purpose each year when they send in their federal tax returns. (Only about 20 percent of taxpayers check off the appropriate box, even though participation does not increase their tax burden.)

For the general election, the two major-party presidential nominees are given a lump-sum payment in the summer before the election, from which all their general election campaign expenditures must come. A third-party candidate receives a smaller amount proportionate to his or her November vote total if that candidate gains a minimum of 5 percent of the vote. Note that in such a case the money goes to third-party campaigns only *after* the election is over; no money is given in advance of the general election. The only third-party candidate to qualify for general election funds before Ross Perot did so was John Anderson, the Independent candidate for president in 1980, who garnered 7 percent of the national vote. While Ross Perot chose not to take public funds for his campaign in 1992, a campaign which was

public funds

Donations from the general tax revenues to the campaigns of qualifying presidential candidates.

matching funds

Donations to presidential campaigns from the federal government that are determined by the amount of private funds a qualifying candidate raises.

largely self-financed, in 1996 Perot accepted public funding. He qualified for this funding by securing 19 percent of the popular vote in the 1992 presidential election. Pat Buchanan, the Reform Party candidate in 2000, failed to win 5 percent of the vote, calling the continued viability of the Reform Party into question. The Green Party also failed to meet the national 5 percent threshold.

SIMULATION
You Are a Professional Campaign Consultant

Independent Expenditures and Soft Money.   In the landmark case of *Buckley* v. *Valeo* (1976), the Supreme Court ruled that it is unconstitutional for Congress to limit the amount of money that an individual or a political committee may spend supporting or opposing a candidate *if the expenditures are made independently of the candidate's campaign.*[22] In a 1996 case, *Colorado Republican Federal Campaign Committee* v. *Federal Election Commission,* the Supreme Court extended this ruling to political parties.[23] Hence, individuals, PACs—and now political parties as well—may spend unlimited amounts of money directly advocating the election or defeat of a candidate as long as these expenditures are not made in coordination with the candidate's campaign. Often, when a group spends independently of a candidate, it will do so for television advertisements urging voters to support or defeat a particular candidate. However, because **independent expenditure** advertisements expressly advocate the election or defeat of a specific federal candidate, they must be paid for with *hard* money—that is, with money raised under the guidelines of the Federal Election Campaign Act. This stands in direct contrast to *soft-money ads.*

independent expenditure
The amount of money an individual or political committee may spend supporting or opposing a candidate as long as those funds are not made in coordination with a candidate's campaign.

As we saw in chapter 11, *soft money* is campaign money raised and spent by political parties and interest groups that is not subject to the regulations of the Federal Election Campaign Act. In a 1978 advisory opinion, the Federal Election Commission ruled that political parties could raise these unregulated funds in order to pay for expenses—such as overhead and administrative costs—and grassroots activities that did not directly influence campaigns for federal elections. In 1979, Congress passed an amendment to the Federal Elections Campaign Act allowing parties to *spend* unlimited sums on these same activities.[24] In the years immediately following the rule changes, the national parties began raising five- and six-figure sums from individuals and interest groups to pay for expenses such as rent, employee salaries, and building maintenance. The national parties also began transferring large sums of soft money to state parties in order to help pay for grassroots activities (such as get-out-the-vote drives) and campaign paraphernalia (such as yard signs and bumper stickers).

However, the line separating expenditures that influence federal elections from those that do not has proven to be quite blurry, and this blurriness has resulted in a significant campaign finance loophole. The largest controversy has come in the area of campaign advertisements. The federal courts have ruled that only campaign advertisements that use explicit words—for example, "vote for," "vote against," "elect," or "support"—qualify as *express advocacy* advertisements. Political advertisements that do not use these words are considered *issue-advocacy* advertisements.[25] The distinction here is crucial. Because express advocacy advertisements are openly intended to influence federal elections, they must be paid for with strictly regulated hard money. Issue-advocacy advertisements, on the other hand, can be paid for with unregulated soft money. The parties' response to these rules has been to create issue-advocacy advertisements that very much resemble express advocacy ads. Typically, for example, such advertisements call attention to the voting record of the candidate supported or opposed and are replete with images of the candidate. However, the parties ensure that the magic words "vote for" or "vote against" are never uttered in the advertisements, allowing them to be paid for with soft rather than hard money.

The national parties have not been the only groups to exploit the soft money loophole: Interest groups also have increasingly joined the fray by running their own "issue" advocacy ads and conducting other soft money–financed campaign activities. The introduction of huge sums of soft money in federal campaigns has the potential to transform campaigns from candidate-centered to interest group– and party-centered affairs.[26] It has also focused increased attention on the need for campaign finance reform. Government watchdog groups such as Common Cause and Public Campaign believe that the soft money/issue advocacy loophole has created a complete meltdown of federal campaign laws and argue that political parties should be banned from raising soft money.

The 2000 elections witnessed record campaign contributions, much to the dismay of campaign finance reformers. Every session of Congress of late has tried to address the question of campaign finance reform. Voters are afraid that some politicians are bought and paid for by special interests who, at times, appear to be running Washington.

Prior to the 1994 congressional elections, Democrats supported setting a limit on the amount of money congressional candidates could spend in an effort to win office. Republicans, long the congressional minority, were adamantly against these spending caps. They argued that the limits mainly hurt challengers who are not as well known as incumbents and who need to spend more money to increase their name identification. The Democrats responded that without limits on total campaign spending, personally wealthy candidates, like Steve Forbes, have an advantage over less affluent candidates. This advantage results from the present federal contribution limits and the Supreme Court decision in *Buckley* v. *Valeo,* which ruled that limits on a candidate's spending of personal funds violates his constitutional right to free speech.

Democratic President Bill Clinton and Republican lawmakers championed campaign finance reform only to later renege on their pledges. Prior to the 1992 presidential election, then candidate Bill

Clinton pledged to support and sign strong campaign finance reform legislation. Once in office, this promise fell by the wayside. In 1994, Democratic legislators were swept out of office and replaced with Republicans, who had also campaigned on the promise of change. Yet campaign finance reform was conspicuously absent from the Republican Contract with America. In 1995, after months of stalling by the House Republican leadership, the House passed the Shays-Meehan campaign finance reform bill in the 105th Congress (1995–96), which, among other provisions, banned the national parties from raising soft money. Unfortunately for reform proponents, however, senators could not muster enough votes to stop a filibuster on the Senate version of the Shays-Meehan bill (authored by Senators John McCain and Russ Feingold), and campaign finance reform died still another death.

The Internet and Campaign Finance

The Internet has the potential to alter radically the way candidates raise funds for their campaigns. After all, making an online appeal for campaign contributions costs significantly less than raising funds through expensive direct-mail campaigns or pricey fund-raising events—the standard means of raising campaign resources. Still, it's not necessarily clear that online fund-raising appeals would be all that successful. The Internet, veteran political consultant Hal Malchow reminds us, is a self-directed medium, and "it is not human nature to seek out places to give money."[27] Nevertheless, the potential weaknesses of Internet fundraising are unlikely to stop candidates from experimenting with it. Indeed, Republican presidential candidate John McCain was able to raise tens of thousands of dollars on his Web site during the primaries.

The Internet also promises to create headaches for the Federal Election Commission. Already, the FEC has been forced to rule on issues such as whether a business site link to a campaign site constitutes an in-kind contribution from the business to the campaign and whether funds raised online by presidential candidates are eligible to be matched with public funds from the Presidential Election Campaign Fund. (In the first case, the FEC ruled yes; in the second case it ruled no.) Clearly, these issues are only the beginning of a seemingly limitless plethora of issues regarding the Internet and campaign finance that the FEC will be asked to address. "Every day," noted former FEC Chair Trevor Potter, "I'm running into people in my practice who are saying, 'This is what I want to do on the Internet—are there any Federal Election law implications?'" Indeed, campaign finance experts have wondered aloud whether the agency has the resources to regulate and monitor the newly unfolding campaign activity on the Internet.[28]

PARTICIPATION

The Net Election: Campaigning on the Internet

The Effects of Technology on Campaigns and Candidates

The age of modern technology has brought many changes to the traditional campaign. Labor-intensive community activities have been replaced by carefully targeted messages disseminated through the mass media, and candidates today are able to reach voters more quickly than at any time in our nation's history. Consequently, the well-organized party machine is no longer essential to winning an election. The results of this technological transformation are candidate-centered campaigns in which candidates build well-financed, finely tuned organizations centered around their personal aspirations.

At the heart of the move toward today's candidate-centered campaigns is an entire generation of technological improvements. Contemporary campaigns have an impressive new array of weapons at their disposal: faster paper printing technologies, instantaneous Internet publishing and mass e-mail, fax machines and video technology, and enhanced telecommunications and teleconferencing. As a result, candidates can gather and disseminate information better than ever.

One outcome of these changes is the ability of candidates to employ "rapid-response" techniques: the formulation of prompt and informed responses to changing events on the campaign battlefield. In response to breaking news of a scandal or issue, for example, candidates (as well as journalists) can conduct background research, implement an opinion poll and tabulate the results, devise a containment strategy and appropriate "spin," and deliver a reply. This makes a strong contrast with the campaigns of the 1970s and early 1980s, which were dominated primarily by radio and TV advertisements, which took much longer to prepare and had little of the flexibility enjoyed by contemporary campaigners.

The first widespread use of the Internet in national campaigning came in 1996. According to one source, 26 percent of the public regularly logged on to the Internet to get campaign and election information.[29] Similarly, CNN's AllPolitics site reported an estimated 50 million hits on election night 1996—a number that paled in comparison to that of 2000. All the candidates for the 2000 presidential campaign set up Web sites even before their formal declarations. These sites presented platforms, offered easily accessible information on how to get involved in the campaign, and, for the very enthusiastic Web surfer, information on how to contribute money.

As bandwidth on the Internet continues to improve, real-time video clips enable Web users to view speeches, press conferences, state-of-the-nation addresses, and other typically "live" events at their own convenience, independent of the schedule of the original television coverage or rebroadcast. Campaign sites often offer the text of the speech as well as multiple video and audio versions of the real public event. Whatever the real benefit of such an embarrassment of riches, the goal is to suggest a candidate's technological mastery, sophistication, and depth of resources. The new media appear to be serving the current paradigm of

TIMELINE
Presidential Candidates and Their
Television Ads

FIGURE 12.4   Landmarks in the 2000 Presidential Campaign

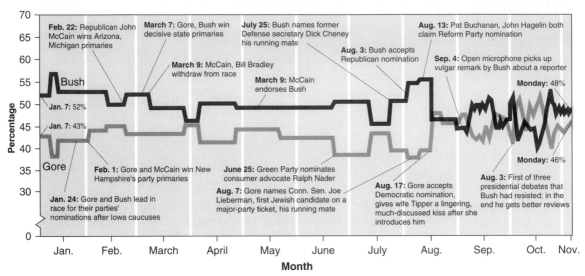

Source: "Tracking the Campaign that Was Too Close to Call.," *USA Today,* November 8, 2000, p. 15A. Copyright 2000, USA TODAY. Reprinted with permission.

mass-media, candidate-centered campaigns, but it is possible that with time they may reshape the campaign landscape.

Election Results

On November 7, just over half of all eligible Americans cast their votes for their next president and went home to watch the election returns on TV. (Figure 12.4 shows the landmark events of the 2000 campaign.) Exit polls showed the two candidates running neck and neck, and as results trickled in after polls closed across the nation, audiences were on the edge of their seat as precinct after precinct, state after state, fell alternately to Bush and to Gore. Around mid-evening, the major networks placed the all-important state of Florida in Gore's "win" column and, coupled with a victory in Pennsylvania, Gore seemed to be pulling ahead, even as continually arriving results started to show Bush retaking the lead in Florida. The nation was stunned when the networks retracted their verdict on Florida and the entire election was suddenly wide open again. Late that night, Gore conceded to Bush, only to learn of the closeness of the race and call Bush to retract his concession! When America went to bed on Tuesday night, the outcome of the election was utterly unclear.

If Americans expected definite information about their president's identity when they read their morning paper, however, they awoke to a rude surprise: the voting in Florida was so close that a final verdict was still unavailable. Indeed, only as the day progressed did the number of issues involved, and their true complexity, begin to come clear: absentee votes yet to be counted in Florida; possible irregularities in the ballot presentation in key Florida counties; critical absentee votes still

FIGURE 12.5   Exit Poll Results for 2000 Election

Demographic data based on surveys of voters leaving polling sites from across the United States (as of 9:56 P.M. ET Tuesday, November 7, 2000.)

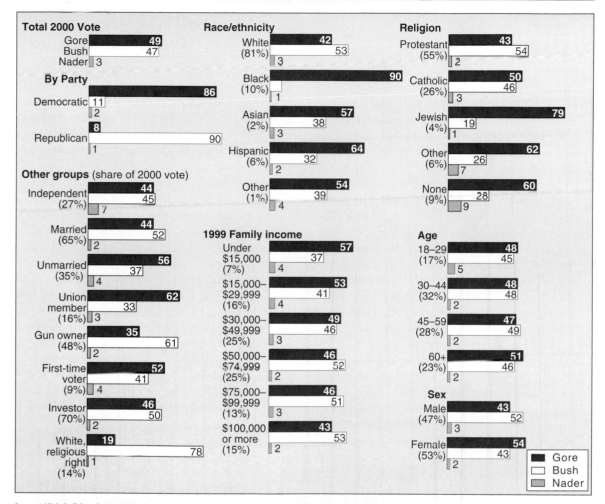

Source: "Exit Poll Results," *USA Today*, November 8, 2000, p. 8A. Copyright 2000, USA TODAY. Reprinted with permission.

pending in the close contest in Oregon; uncertainty in vote counts in other key states such as New Mexico; a possible discrepancy between one candidate's majority in the popular vote and the other's majority in the electoral college; a possible tie in the electoral college and an unclear outcome should Congress have to break the tie; and a host of other minor electoral and constitutional issues not confronted in decades when the Supreme Court ruled weeks later against a new Florida recount and Bush won Florida and the presidency.

As Figure 12.5 reveals, however, *how* people voted yielded few surprises. The gender gap continued, African Americans voted overwhelmingly for Gore, and white males cast their votes for Bush.

Continuity & Change

Election Technology—Past, Present, and Future

In the nineteenth century, political parties ran the elections, supplying not only paper ballots but also many of the poll-watchers and election judges. This was a formula for fraud, of course—there was not even a truly secret ballot, as people voted on different colors of ballot depending on their choice of party! The twentieth century saw widespread improvements in election practices and technology. The states now oversee the election process through official state boards of election, and the use of voting machines, nearly universal in America by the 1970s, permit truly secret mechanical voting. These measures helped effect enormous reductions in fraud and electoral ambiguity—though as the irregularities of the election of 2000 proved, there is still a long way to go.

As more and more Americans become computer savvy and as computer technology continues to evolve, Internet voting has become the likely way to cast votes in the coming years. Rightly or wrongly, Internet voting equates in the minds of many Americans with the ideals of instant democracy and greater citizen input in major decisions. Many states are formally studying the feasibility and impact of Internet voting. In 2000, Arizona pioneered online balloting by allowing citizens to vote via the Internet in the state's Democratic presidential primary. Opponents and proponents alike recognize potential problems, but technical solutions draw ever nearer.

The use of mail-in ballots, whereby registered voters are mailed ballots and given several weeks to mail them back in with their votes, increases participation but delays final tabulation of the ballots for several weeks. Oregon, the only state that votes entirely by mail-in ballots, did not have its 2000 presidential results finalized until several weeks after Election Day. Washington, which has extremely liberal laws regarding mail-in votes, was also much later than the rest of the country in announcing its presidential and senatorial winners.

The nation also lacks a standardized method by which votes should be recounted in close elections. Many reformers favor a national uniform ballot system for the entire country—a single ballot that would list the appropriate candidates for each voting locale. A national ballot is highly unlikely, however. If the federal government mandates a ballot form, it would almost certainly have to pay for it at a price tag of up to several billion dollars. In addition, there are over 41,000 voting localities in states and jurisdictions across the United States electing hundreds of thousands of officials, making it extremely difficult to create a uniform ballot.

Another change likely to result from the chaos of the 2000 election addresses the technology of the ballot itself. Americans can look forward to the elimination of the "butterfly ballot," which featured prominently in the heavily contested county of Palm Beach, Florida. Although the ballot was approved for use, it gained national attention because of its confusing layout. After the debacle of ambiguously punched ballots, Americans can also expect to see fewer stylus punch-card ballots, a technologically obsolete method of voting whereby voters use increasingly antiquated and faulty voting machines to stamp out a circle of paper, or chad, to indicate their vote.

Many Americans believe that the federal government should assist states in updating outdated and faulty voting equipment. Some localities across the country use computerized touch-screen machines, which are expensive but

(continued)

much more secure and accurate than the older mechanical devices still in widespread use. An analysis of Florida's voting machines found that older, punch-card machines failed to indicate a vote for president on 1.5 percent of the ballots, while newer, optical-scanning machines failed on only 0.3 percent of the ballots. Additionally, older, error-ridden machines are commonly assigned to low-income and African American precincts, which reintroduces a troublesome discriminatory dimension into the voting process. Although updating equipment across the country would cost billions of dollars, it seems a small price to pay to modernize our democracy. As Charles M. Vest, the president of the Massachusetts Institute of Technology, said, "A nation that can send a man to the moon, that can put a reliable ATM machine on every corner, has no excuse not to deploy a reliable, affordable, easy-to-use voting system."

1. What kind of voting machine does your precinct use? What about the precincts of your friends and family? Did you or someone you know vote by mail? Ask around, and then determine how the perceived experience of voting, especially after the year 2000, differs depending on the technology one uses.

2. We tend to take fair elections and private voting for granted in the United States, but in many countries such conditions are still not widespread. What do the lessons of election reform in America teach us about ways of improving the integrity of elections in other nations? What can a country without a long stable democratic tradition do to ensure fraud-free elections and private voting?

Cast Your Vote. How can America improve voter turnout? To cast your vote, go to **www.ablongman.com/oconnor**

SUMMARY

The explosion of elections we have experienced in over 200 years of voting has generated much good and some harm. But all of it has been done, as Hamilton insisted, "on the solid basis of the consent of the people." In our efforts to explain the complex and multilayered U.S. electoral system, we covered these points in this chapter:

When it comes to elections, the United States has an embarrassment of riches. There are various types of primary elections in the country, as well as general elections, initiatives, referenda, and recall elections. In presidential elections, primaries are sometimes replaced by caucuses, in which party members choose a candidate in a closed meeting, but recent years have seen fewer caucuses and more primaries.

A campaign for office is structured into the general election campaign, personal campaign, organizational campaign, and media campaign. To stay in the race, the modern candidate relies on individual, PAC, party, and personal contributions. Candidates can also apply for federal matching funds.

No U.S. election can compare to the presidential contest. This spectacle, held every four years, brings together all the elements of politics and attracts the most ambitious and energetic politicians to the national stage. No longer closed affairs dominated by deals cut in "smoke-filled rooms," today's conventions are more open made-for-television events in which the party platform is drafted and adopted, and the presidential ticket is formally nominated.

Many similar elements are present in different kinds of elections: Candidates, voters, issues, and television advertisements are constants. But there are distinctive aspects of each kind of election as well. Compared with presidential elections, which are played out on the national stage, congressional elections are a different animal. Most candidates for Congress labor in relative obscurity.

Whether they are casting ballots in congressional or presidential elections, voters behave in certain distinct ways and exhibit unmistakable patterns to political scientists who study them.

KEY TERMS

blanket primary, p. 385
campaign manager, p. 391
closed primary, p. 384
contrast ad, p. 393
critical election, p. 403
crossover voting p. 384
direct mailer, p. 391
elector, p. 396
electoral college, p. 396
free media, p. 393
front-loading, p. 386
general election, p. 385
gerrymandering, p. 406

get-out-the-vote (GOTV), p. 391
independent expenditure, p. 420
initiative, p. 385
inoculation advertising, p. 393
matching funds, p. 419
media consultant, p. 391
negative ad, p. 393
nonpartisan primary, p. 385
open primary, p. 384
paid media, p. 393
party realignment, p. 403

political consultant, p. 391
pollster, p. 391
positive ad, p. 393
primary election, p. 384
public funds, p. 419
raiding, p. 385
recall, p. 385
referendum, p. 385
runoff primary, p. 385
secular realignment, p. 404
spot ad, p. 393
turnout, p. 408
voter canvass, p. 391

SELECTED READINGS

Ansolabehere, Stephen, and Shanto Iyengar. *Going Negative: How Attack Ads Shrink and Polarize the Electorate.* New York: Free Press, 1996.

Berelson, Bernard R., Paul F. Lazarsfeld, and William N. McPhee. *Voting: A Study of Opinion Formation in a Presidential Campaign.* Chicago: University of Chicago Press, 1954.

Burnham, Walter Dean. *Critical Elections and the Mainsprings of American Politics.* New York: Norton, 1970.

Campbell, Angus, et al. *The American Voter.* New York: Wiley, 1960 (reprinted ed., Chicago: University of Chicago Press, 1980).

Carrol, Susan J. *Women as Candidates in American Politics,* 2nd ed. Bloomington: Indiana University Press, 1994.

Fiorina, Morris P. *Retrospective Voting in American National Elections.* New Haven, Conn.: Yale University Press, 1981.

Herrnson, Paul S. *Congressional Elections: Campaigning at Home and in Washington,* 2nd ed. Washington, D.C.: CQ Press, 1998.

Jacobson, Gary C. *The Politics of Congressional Elections,* 5th ed. New York: Addison Wesley, 2000.

Kahn, Kim Fridkin. *The Political Consequences of Being a Woman: How Stereotypes Influence the Conduct and Consequences of Political Campaigns.* New York: Columbia University Press, 1996.

Nie, Norman H., Sidney Verba, and John R. Petrocik. *The Changing American Voter (enlarged edition).* Cambridge, Mass.: Harvard University, 1980.

Pika, Joseph A., and Richard A. Watson. *The Presidential Contest,* 5th ed. Washington, D.C.: CQ Press, 1995.

Polsby, Nelson W., and Aaron Wildavsky. *Presidential Elections: Strategies and Structures of American Politics,* 10th ed. Chatham, N.J.: Chatham House, 2000.

Sabato, Larry J., ed. *Toward the Millennium: The Elections of 1996.* Boston: Allyn & Bacon: 1997.

Sorauf, Frank J. *Inside Campaign Finance.* New Haven, Conn.: Yale University Press, 1992.

Troy, Gil. *See How They Ran: The Changing Role of the Presidential Candidate.* Cambridge, Mass.: Harvard University Press, 1996.

Verba, Sidney, Kay Lehman Schlozman, and Henry E. Brady. *Voice and Equality: Civic Voluntarism in American Politics.* Cambridge, Mass.: Harvard University Press, 1995.

Wayne, Stephen J. *The Road to the White House,* 6th ed. New York: Palgrave, 2000.

(Photo courtesy: Alex Wong/Liaison Agency/Getty Source)

Public Policy 13

One of the signature actions of the Clinton administration was fulfillment of his promise to "end welfare as we know it." With passage of the Personal Responsibility and Work Opportunity Reconciliation Act (PRWORA) of 1996, rules changed significantly. The Aid to Families with Dependent Children (AFDC) program was abolished and replaced with the new program Temporary Assistance for Needy Families (TANF). The aim of TANF was to foster the philosophy of work rather than welfare dependence. The new program stipulated that the majority of families could not receive benefits for more than five years. Furthermore, the head of each family on welfare was required to work within two years after assistance payments began. If these requirements were not followed, states could lose a significant amount of federal money.

In addition to changing the requirements to qualify for welfare payments, the PRWORA fundamentally altered responsibilities of the national and state governments. The PRWORA gave states more flexibility in reforming their welfare programs toward work-oriented goals. The most fundamental alteration in family cash assistance programs came about when the PRWORA switched funding to states from an open-ended matching grant program to a block grant program. The block grant was based on past federal contributions to other programs such as AFDC, the Job Opportunities and Basic Skills (JOBS) program, and Emergency Assistance. States had considerable flexibility under the block grant, although spending was earmarked to assist low-income families with children. Supporters of welfare reform noted that large numbers of people who were on welfare prior to 1996 found gainful employment. Such jobs not only represented additional tax revenue but were believed to represent an initial step on an individual's road toward self-sufficiency. Critics of reform claimed that low-wage jobs did not pay enough to remove families from poverty, or guarantee future access to better pay. These critics also expressed the view that reductions in welfare rolls were largely attributed to a remarkably strong economy, and that when the economy weakened, citizens would suffer from a fraying of the social safety net. Social welfare policy, as illustrated by ANF, is just one kind of public policy.

public policy
A purposive course of action followed by government in dealing with some problem or matter of concern.

Public policy is a purposive course of action followed by government in dealing with some problem or matter of concern.[1] Public policies are governmental policies based on law; they are authoritative and binding on people. Individuals, groups, and even government agencies that do not comply with policies can be penalized through fines, loss of benefits, or even jail terms. As the phrase "course of action" implies, policies develop or unfold over time. They involve more than a legislative decision to enact a law or a presidential decision to issue an executive order. Also important is how the law or executive order is carried out. Whether a policy is vigorously enforced, enforced only in some instances, or not enforced at all helps determine its meaning and impact.

In this chapter we discuss social and economic policy. Policies in both areas follow similar patterns, what is called the policy process. First, we examine the stages of the policy process. We then discuss a few important social welfare policies in the context of the policy process. Finally, we review key economic policies.

THE POLICY PROCESS

Political scientists and other social scientists have developed many theories and models to explain the public policy process. Here, we present a widely used model (see Figure 13.1) of the policy-making process that views it as a sequence of stages or functional activities. Public policies do not just happen; rather, they are typically the products of a predictable pattern of events. Models for analyzing the policy-making process do not always explain *why* public policies take the specific forms that they do, however. That depends on the political struggles over particular policies. Nor do models necessarily tell us *who* dominates or controls the formation of public policy. The model in Figure 13.1 can be applied and used to analyze any of the issues discussed throughout this book.

Despite the limitations of models, however, policy making frequently does follow the sequence of stages. Sometimes some of the

FIGURE 13.1   The Policy Cycle

A look at how policy is made, put in place, carried out, and finally evaluated. A continuous process that flows in a natural order.

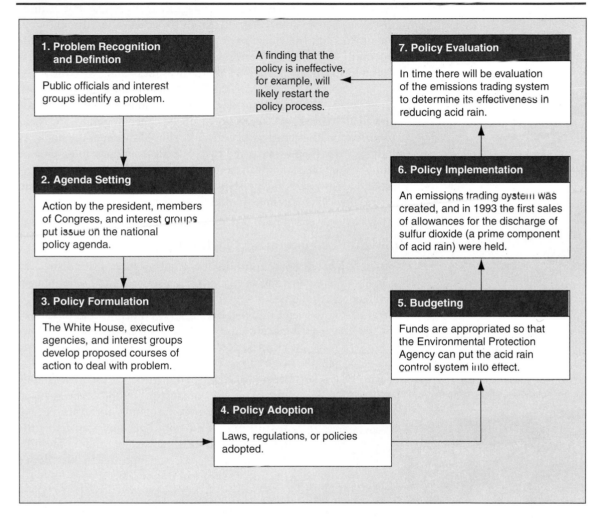

1. Problem Recognition and Defintion

Public officials and interest groups identify a problem.

2. Agenda Setting

Action by the president, members of Congress, and interest groups put issue on the national policy agenda.

3. Policy Formulation

The White House, executive agencies, and interest groups develop proposed courses of action to deal with problem.

4. Policy Adoption

Laws, regulations, or policies adopted.

5. Budgeting

Funds are appropriated so that the Environmental Protection Agency can put the acid rain control system into effect.

6. Policy Implementation

An emissions trading system was created, and in 1993 the first sales of allowances for the discharge of sulfur dioxide (a prime component of acid rain) were held.

7. Policy Evaluation

In time there will be evaluation of the emissions trading system to determine its effectiveness in reducing acid rain.

A finding that the policy is ineffective, for example, will likely restart the policy process.

stages may merge, such as the policy formulation and adoption stages. Another instance of stages merging occurs when administrative agencies like the Occupational Safety and Health Administration (OSHA) are making policy through rule-making at the same time that they are implementing it. Finally, we need to recognize that what happens at one stage of the policy-making process affects action at later stages, and sometimes such action is done deliberately in anticipation of these effects. Thus, particular provisions may be included in a law either to help or hinder its implementation, depending on the interests of the provisions' proponents.

STAGES OF THE POLICY PROCESS

Basically, the policy process has seven stages. (1) A *problem* that disturbs or distresses people gives rise to demands for relief, often through governmental action. Individual or group efforts are then made to get the problem (2) placed on a governmental *agenda*. If successful, this step is followed by (3) the *formulation* of alternatives for dealing with the problem. (4) *Policy adoption* involves the formal enactment or approval of an alternative. (5) *Budgeting* provides financial resources to carry out the approved alternative, which can now truly be called a "policy." (6) *Policy implementation*, the actual administration or application of the policy to its targets, may then be followed by (7) *policy evaluation* to determine the policy's actual accomplishments, consequences, or shortcomings. Evaluation may restart the policy process by identifying a new problem and touching off an attempt to modify or terminate the policy.

Problem Recognition and Definition

A problem involves some condition or situation that causes distress or dissatisfaction or generates needs for which some kind of relief or corrective action is sought—often from the government (national, state, or local). At any given time, there are many conditions that disturb or distress people—polluted air, unsafe workplaces, earthquakes and hurricanes, too much or too little rain, the rising cost of medical care, the poor academic performance of high school students, too many handguns, too few "dedicated" public officials, or no prayers in the public schools, for example. All disturbing conditions do not automatically become problems; some of them may be accepted as trivial, appropriate, inevitable, or beyond the control of government.

For a condition to become a problem, there must be some criterion—a standard or value—that leads people to believe that the condition does not have to be accepted or acquiesced to and, further, that it is something with which government can deal effectively and appropriately. Hurricanes, for example, are unlikely to become a policy problem because there is nothing that government can do about them directly. The consequences of hurricanes, the human distress and property destruction that they bring, are another matter. Their relief can be a focus of government action, as it was in the instance of Hurricane Floyd in 1999, for which Congress

"Rescue of Children from a Drunken Mother"—an artist's depiction of an early crusader for the Society for the Prevention of Cruelty to Children. (Photo courtesy: Bettmann/Corbis)

appropriated several million dollars for recovery activities. Conditions that at one time are accepted as appropriate and beyond government responsibility may at a later time be perceived as problems because of changes in public attitudes.

Usually there is not a single agreed-on definition of a problem. Indeed, political struggle often occurs over defining the problem because how the problem is defined helps determine what sort of action is appropriate. Problems differ not only in terms of how they are defined, but also in terms of how easy they are to ameliorate or resolve. For instance, problems that affect large numbers of people or require widespread behavioral changes are more difficult to resolve.

One additional point needs to be made. Public policies themselves are frequently viewed as problems or the causes of problems. Thus, for some people, gun control legislation is a solution to the handgun problem. To the National Rifle Association (NRA), however, any law that restricts gun ownership is a problem because of the NRA's view that such laws inappropriately restrict an individual's right to keep and bear arms. To conservatives, overly generous welfare programs are a problem; for many liberals, laws restricting the right to abortion falls into the problem category.

Agenda Setting

Once a problem is recognized and defined, it must be brought to the attention of public officials and it must secure a place on an **agenda,** a set of problems to which policy makers believe they should be attentive. Political scientists Roger W. Cobb and Charles D. Elder have identified two basic agenda types: the systemic agenda and the governmental or institutional agenda.[2] The **systemic agenda** is essentially a discussion agenda; it is made up of "all issues that are commonly perceived by the members of the political community as meriting public attention and as involving matters within the legitimate jurisdiction" of governments.[3] Every political community—national, state, and local—has a systemic agenda.

A **governmental** or **institutional agenda** includes only problems to which legislators or other public officials feel obliged to devote active and serious attention. Not all the problems that attract the attention of officials are likely to have been widely discussed by the general public, or even the "attentive" public—those who follow certain issues closely.

Problems or issues (an issue emerges when disagreement exists over what should be done about a problem) may move onto an institutional agenda, whether from the systemic agenda or elsewhere, in several ways.

Policy Formulation

Policy formulation involves the crafting of appropriate and acceptable proposed courses of action to ameliorate or resolve public problems. It

In 2000, actor Michael J.Fox, who suffers from Parkinson disease, testified before a Senate Appropriations subcommittee hearing on stem cell resarch. Celebrities often use their clout to bring legislative attention to issues they feel strongly about.
(Photo courtesy: Kamenko Pajic/AP/Wide World Photos)

agenda
A set of problems to which policy makers believe they should be attentive.

systemic agenda
All public issues that are viewed as requiring governmental attention; a discussion agenda.

governmental (institutional) agenda
The changing list of issues to which governments believe they should address themselves.

policy formulation
The crafting of appropriate and acceptable proposed courses of action to ameliorate or resolve public problems.

has both political and technical components. The political aspect of policy formulation encompasses determining generally what should be done to reduce acid rain, for example—whether standard setting and enforcement or emissions testing should be used. The technical facet involves correctly stating in specific language what one wants to authorize or accomplish, so as to adequately guide those who must implement policy and to prevent distortion of legislative intent. Political scientist Charles O. Jones suggests that formulation may take different forms:[4]

1. *Routine formulation* is "a repetitive and essentially changeless process of reformulating similar proposals within an issue area that is well established on the government agenda." For instance, the formulation of policy on veterans' benefits represents a standard process of drafting proposals similar to those established in the past.
2. In *analogous formulation,* a new problem is handled by drawing on the experience of developing proposals for similar problems in the past. What has been done in the past to cope with the activities of terrorists? What has been done in other states to deal with child abuse or divorce law reform?
3. *Creative formulation* involves attempts to develop new or unprecedented proposals that represent a departure from existing practices and that will better resolve a problem. For example, plans to develop an anti-missile defense system to shoot down incoming missiles represents a departure from previous defense strategies.

Policy formulation may be undertaken by various players in the policy process—the president and his aides, agency officials, specially appointed task forces and commissions, interest groups, private research organizations (or "think tanks"), and legislators and their staffs. The people engaged in formulation are usually looking down the road toward policy adoption.

Policy Adoption

policy adoption
The approval of a policy proposal by the people with the requisite authority, such as a legislature.

Policy adoption involves the approval of a policy proposal by the people with requisite authority, such as a legislature or chief executive. This approval gives the policy legal force. Because most public policies in the United States are based on legislation, policy adoption frequently requires the building of majority coalitions necessary to secure the enactment of legislation.

In chapter 5 we discussed how power is diffused in Congress and how the legislative process includes a number of roadblocks or obstacles, including House subcommittees, House committees, the House Rules Committee, and so on. A bill must successfully navigate each potential roadblock before it becomes law. A majority is needed to clear a bill through each of these obstacles. Hence, not one majority but a series of majorities are needed for congressional policy adoption. To secure the needed votes, a bill may be watered down or modified at each of these decision points. Or the bill may fail to win a majority at one of them and die, at least for the time being.

Much negotiation, bargaining, and compromise are entailed in the adoption of major legislation. In some instances years or even decades may be needed to secure the enactment of legislation on a controversial matter. Federal aid to public education was considered by Congress off and on over several decades before finally winning approval in 1965. At other times, the approval process may move quickly. The Flag Protection Act, for example, was passed quickly by Congress after the Supreme Court ruled that a Texas statute banning flag burning was unconstitutional.[5] The Supreme Court, however, quickly found that the new federal law was also an unconstitutional violation of the First Amendment.[6]

Not all policy adoption necessitates formation of majority coalitions. Presidential decision making on foreign affairs, military actions, and other matters is often unilateral. Although the president has many aides and advisers and is bombarded with information and advice, the final decision rests with him. Ultimately, too, it is the president who decides whether to veto a bill passed by Congress. President Clinton's 1996 decision to veto a bill that would have outlawed the practice of late-term abortion and his 1999 veto of Republican plans to cut taxes and spending represent two examples of presidential veto power. In 2000, Clinton vetoed two Republican tax-cut measures: a repeal of the federal estate tax and eliminating the so-called marriage penalty tax.

Budgeting

Most policies require money to be carried out; some policies, such as those involving income security, essentially involve the transfer of money from taxpayers to the government and back to individual beneficiaries. Funding for most policies and agencies is provided through the budgetary process. Whether a policy is well funded or poorly funded has a significant effect on its scope, impact, and effectiveness.

A policy can be nullified by an absence of funding or refusal to fund. Other policies or programs often suffer from inadequate funding. For example, in 1999 the Federal Aviation Administration admitted that long recommended security measures were yet to be implemented at national airports due to underfunding.

The budgetary process also gives the president and the Congress an opportunity to review the government's many policies and programs, to inquire into their administration, to appraise their value and effectiveness, and to exercise some influence on their conduct. Not all of the government's hundreds of programs are fully examined every year. But, over a period of several years, most programs come under scrutiny.

Policy Implementation

Policy implementation refers to how public policies are carried out. Most public policies are implemented primarily by administrative

policy implementation
The process of carrying out public policy through governmental agencies and the courts.

agencies. Some, however, are enforced in other ways. Product liability and product dating are two examples. Product liability laws such as the Food and Drug Act of 1906, the National Traffic and Motor Vehicle Safety Act of 1966, and the Consumer Product Safety Act of 1972 are typically enforced by lawsuits initiated in the courts by injured consumers or their survivors. In contrast, state product-dating laws are implemented more by voluntary compliance when grocers take out-of-date products off their shelves or by consumers when they choose not to buy food products after the use dates stamped on them. The courts also get involved in implementation when they are called on to interpret the meaning of legislation, review the legality of agency rules and actions, and determine whether the administration of institutions such as prisons and mental hospitals conforms to legal and constitutional standards.

Administrative agencies may be authorized to use a number of techniques to implement the public policies within their jurisdictions. These techniques can be categorized as authority, incentive, capacity, and hortatory techniques, depending on the behavioral assumptions on which they are based.[7]

Authoritative techniques for policy implementation rest on the notion that people's actions must be directed or restrained by government in order to prevent or eliminate activities or products that are unsafe, unfair, evil, or immoral. Thus people who drive while intoxicated can, by law, have their driver's licenses revoked. On the federal level, consumer products must meet certain safety regulations and radio stations can have their broadcasting licenses revoked if they broadcast obscenities.

Many governmental agencies have authority to issue rules and set standards to regulate such matters as meat and food processing, the discharge of pollutants into the environment, the healthfulness and safety of workplaces, and the safe operation of commercial airplanes. Compliance with these standards is determined by inspection and monitoring, and penalties may be imposed on people or companies that violate the rules and standards set forth in a particular policy. For example, under Title IX, the federal government can terminate funds to colleges or universities that discriminate against female students. This pattern of action is sometimes stigmatized as "command and control regulation" by its detractors, although in practice it often involves much education, bargaining, and persuasion in addition to the exercise of authority. In the case of Title IX, for instance, the Department of Education will try to negotiate with a school to bring it into compliance before funding is terminated.

Incentive techniques for policy implementation are based on the assumption that people are utility maximizers who act in their own best interest and must be provided with payoffs or financial inducements to get them to comply with public policies. Tax deductions may be given to encourage charitable giving, or grants awarded to companies for the installation of pollution control equipment. Subsidies are given to farmers to make their production (or nonproduction) of wheat, cotton, and other commodities more profitable. Conversely, sanctions such as high taxes may be adopted to discourage the purchase and use of such products as tobacco or liquor, and pollution fees may be levied to reduce the discharge of pollutants by making this action more costly to businesses.

Capacity techniques provide people with information, education, training, or resources that will enable them to undertake desired activities. The assumption underlying the provision of these techniques is that people have the incentive or desire to do what is right but lack the capacity to act accordingly. Job training may enable able-bodied people to find employment, and accurate information on interest rates will enable people to protect themselves against interest-rate gouging. Financial assistance can help the needy acquire better housing and warmer winter coats and perhaps lead more comfortable lives.

Hortatory techniques encourage people to comply with policy by appealing to people's "better instincts" in an effort to get them to act in desired ways. In this instance, the policy implementers assume that people decide how to act on the basis of their personal values and beliefs on matters such as right and wrong, equality, and justice. During the Reagan administration, Nancy Reagan implored young people to "Just Say No" to drugs. Hortatory techniques also include the use of highway signs that tell us "Don't Be a Litterbug" and "Don't Mess with Texas" to discourage littering. Slogans such as "Only You Can Prevent Forest Fires" are meant to encourage compliance with fire and safety regulations in national parks and forests.

The capacity of agencies to administer public policies effectively depends partly on whether the agencies are authorized to use appropriate implementation techniques. Many other factors also come into play, including the clarity and consistency of the policies' statutory mandates, adequacy of funding, political support, and the will and skill of agency personnel. There is no easy formula that will guarantee successful policy implementation; in practice, many policies only partially achieve their goals.

Policy Evaluation

Practitioners of **policy evaluation** are concerned with determining what a policy is actually accomplishing. They may also try to determine whether a policy is being fairly or efficiently administered. In the case of welfare programs, for instance, uncovering evidence of "waste, fraud, or abuse" in their administration has often been of more interest to official evaluators than whether the programs are meeting the needs of the poor.

Policy makers frequently make judgments on the effectiveness and necessity of particular policies and programs. Carefully designed studies or inquiries by social scientists and qualified investigators are undertaken to measure the societal impact of programs and to determine whether

policy evaluation
The process of determining whether a course of action is achieving its intended goals.

POLICY IN ACTION

ENVIRONMENTAL POLICY AS FOREIGN POLICY

When President George W. Bush retracted a campaign promise and opted not to regulate carbon dioxide emissions to save consumers money in the face of escalating energy costs, shock waves were sent throughout the nation's environmentalist community. While they agreed that Bush's decision will save money—they argued that the real costs will be down the road in global warming. It is the president's decision on greenhouse gas emissions and its effect on global warming that also has European leaders questioning the new administration's commitment to curbing global climate change. "This is not just an environmental question," said Kjell Larsson, the Swedish environmental minister who is also the president of the European Union (EU). "The EU puts a very high priority on this subject and it is very important for foreign policy relations between the EU and the United States," says Larsson.[a] The EU is also concerned by Bush's reassertion of his opposition to the Kyoto Protocol, an international treaty largely fashioned by the Clinton administration, designed to trim carbon dioxide and other greenhouse gases by 5.2 percent worldwide by 2012. The U.S. signed the treaty in 1997 but has yet to agree on rules to regulate the treaty and to give it teeth. In a letter to Senator Chuck Hagel (R–Nebr.), President Bush not only rescinded his commitment to lower greenhouse gases, he also stated that the Kyoto Protocol "would cause serious harm to the U.S. economy," referring to "the incomplete state of scientific knowledge on the causes of global warming," sentiments that shocked European officials.[b]

President Bush believes the Kyoto Protocol is unfair because developing countries, including India and China, are not covered, thus putting U.S. companies at a costly disadvantage in a global economy. The caps on emissions would also force a shift from coal as a source of energy to natural gas, already in short supply in the western section of the United States.

---

[a]Peter Ford, "US Climate Policy Alarms Europe," *Christian Science Monitor* (March 19, 2001): 6.
[b]Ford, "US Climate Policy."

---

these programs are achieving their specified goals or objectives. The national executive departments and agencies often contain officials and units with responsibility for policy evaluation; so do state governments.

Policy evaluation may be conducted by a variety of players: congressional committees, presidential commissions, administrative agencies; university researchers, private research organizations, such as the Brookings Institution and the American Enterprise Institute, and the federal General Accounting Office (GAO).

Evaluation research and studies can stimulate attempts to modify or terminate policies and thus restart the policy process. Legislators and administrators may formulate and advocate amendments designed to correct problems or shortcomings in a policy. In 1988, for example, legislation was adopted to correct weaknesses in the enforcement of the Fair Housing Act of 1968 that banned discrimination in the sale or rental of most housing. Or, some people may decide that the best alternative is simply to eliminate the policy. On occasion, policies are terminated; for example, by the Airline Deregulation Act of 1978, Congress eliminated the Civil Aeronautics Board and its program of economic regulation of commercial airlines. The demise of programs is rare, however; more often, a troubled program is modified or allowed to limp along because it is doing something that some people strongly want done, even if the program is not doing it well.

SOCIAL WELFARE POLICY

Social welfare policy is a term that designates a broad and varied range of government programs designed to provide people with protection against want and deprivation, improve their health and physical well-being, provide educational and employment training opportunities, and otherwise enable them to lead more satisfactory, meaningful, and productive lives. The issue of who is deserving and what they deserve is at the heart of the debate over social welfare programs. Over time, the focus of social welfare programs has expanded from providing minimal assistance to the destitute to helping the working poor attain a degree of security and provide for their health, nutrition, income security, employment, and education needs.

social welfare policy
Government programs to protect people from deprivation and improve their physical well-being.

WEB EXPLORATION
To understand how public policies are prioritized and analyzed, go to www.ablongman.com/oconnor

The Roots of Social Welfare Policy

Most social welfare programs in the United States are largely a product of the twentieth century, although their origins can be traced far into the nation's past. As U.S. society became more urban and industrial, self-sufficiency declined and people became more interdependent and reliant on a vast system of production, distribution, and exchange. The Great Depression of the 1930s revealed that hard work alone would not provide economic security for everyone and that the state governments and private charities lacked adequate resources to alleviate economic want and distress. Beginning with the Social Security Act of 1935, a variety of national programs aimed at providing economic security have emerged.

Income Security.   The economic turmoil known as the Great Depression produced massive shock waves throughout American society. As a consequence of the Great Depression, social and economic thinking began to change. Prior to 1929, the works of Adam Smith, Herbert Spencer, and Charles Darwin were highly influential. These theorists focused on the value of limited government and a "hands off" economic

The Great Depression, beginning in late 1929 and continuing throughout the 1930s, dramatically pointed out to average Americans the need for a broad safety net and gave rise to a host of income, health, and finance legislation. (Photo courtesy: Bettmann/Corbis)

Social Security Act
A 1935 law that established old-age insurance (Social Security); assistance for the needy, children, and others; and unemployment insurance.

policy for government to follow. After 1929 and the collapse of confidence in the private sector, the idea that government could and should be used as a positive influence in society gained widespread approval.

With the election of Franklin D. Roosevelt in 1932, the federal government began to play a more active role in addressing hardships and turmoil growing out of the Great Depression. Roosevelt proposed, and the Congress eventually adopted, numerous pieces of legislation to restore confidence in banks, put Americans back to work, and provide income security for the elderly and those unable to work. A major legacy of Roosevelt's New Deal was the creation of permanent social welfare programs such as Social Security. The intent of Social Security was to go beyond the various emergency programs to provide at least a minimum of economic security for all Americans. Due to the nature of this commitment, passage of the **Social Security Act** in 1935 represented the beginning of a permanent welfare state in America and a dedication to the ideal of greater equity. The act consisted of three major components: (1) old-age insurance (what we now call Social Security); (2) public assistance for the needy, aged, blind, and families with dependent children (later, people with disabilities were added); and, (3) unemployment insurance and compensation.

The core of the Social Security Act was the creation of a compulsory old-age insurance program funded equally by employer and employee contributions. The act imposed a payroll tax, collected from the employer, equal to 1 percent from both employee and employer starting in 1937. The Social Security Act also addressed the issue of unemployment, requiring employers to pay 3 percent of a worker's salary into an insurance fund. If workers became unemployed, they could draw from this fund for a given period of time. During the time laid-off workers are drawing from the insurance fund, they are required to seek other jobs. This component of the Social Security Act served two basic purposes: On the individual level, it provided income to laid-off workers, expanding the social safety net; second, on the broader economic level, it acted as an automatic stabilizer, increasing payments to the system when the economy slowed.

Social Security is credited with replacing a piecemeal collection of local programs with a national system. This national system was widely praised but also was perceived to contain two basic flaws: The payroll tax was regressive (it fell disproportionately on lower-income contributors) and some workers were excluded from the program.

National health insurance was considered at the time Social Security legislation was passed. Because of the strong opposition from the American Medical Association (AMA), which was the dominant force in American medicine at the time, health insurance was omitted from Social Security legislation. It was feared that mention of this concept would jeopardize adoption of other important elements of the program. Health insurance remained on the back burner for many years

Health Care.   Governments in the United States have long been active in the health field. Local governments began to establish public health departments in the first half of the nineteenth century, and state health departments followed in the second half. Knowledge of the bacteriological causes of diseases and human ailments discovered in the late nineteenth and early twentieth centuries led to significant advances in improving public health. Public sanitation and clean-water programs, pasteurization of milk, immunization programs, and other activities reduced greatly the incidence of infectious and communicable diseases. The increase in life expectancy at birth in the United States from forty-seven years in 1900 to seventy-eight years in 2000 is mostly due to public health programs.

Beginning in 1798 with the establishment of the National Marine Service (NMS) for "the relief of sick and disabled seamen," which was the forerunner of the Public Health Service, the national government has provided health care for some segments of the population. Efforts have been made over the years to expand coverage of health care to more and more Americans. The current Medicare and Medicaid programs that provide hospital benefits for all aged people covered by Social Security (Medicare) and medical costs for the poor (Medicaid) were first passed by Congress in 1965. With the enactment of the Medicare and Medicaid programs, the share of health care expenditures financed by public spending rose from under 25 percent in 1960 to almost 40 percent in 1970. During this time, public expenditures on health care as a percent of total grass domestic product (GDP) rose by more than 100 percent.

Social Welfare Policy Today

Income security and health care encompass many complex policies and programs. While all levels of government (national, state, and local) are involved with the development and implementation of social welfare policies, we emphasize the national government's role although new programs give states greater control over public welfare and health care programs.

Income Security: Non-Means-Based and Means-Tested Programs. Income security programs protect people against loss of income due to

GLOBAL POLITICS

COMPARING HEALTH POLICIES

The American social welfare system is an anomaly in the developed world. Social welfare institutions in the United States are less extensive than in Europe and Canada in particular. Health care exemplifies the difference. Not only does the United States spend more on health care than other developed countries, but private expenditures on health care here are almost as high, measured in terms of gross domestic product, as public health expenditures elsewhere. The European countries have had national health care systems for decades. Germany maintains a private health insurance system in which the government provides insurance for those citizens who cannot afford regular coverage by a private company. Unlike the United States, however, all German citizens are covered by one or the other. Even Japan, with the lowest level of social welfare spending in the industrial democracies, has a national health insurance system that includes free access to physicians and medical facilities. Specialist referrals, a staple of the HMO system in place throughout the United States, are not necessary.

One belief in the United States is that private health care is more efficient than public. In terms of hospital stays, it may be. According to the World Bank, Americans spend less time in the hospital than citizens in other countries: eight days per year on average during the 1990s as opposed to sixteen days in the high-income countries as a whole. In terms of basic health indicators, the evidence is not so clear; infant mortality in the United States is slightly higher than in other industrial countries, and average life expectancy is shorter (see Global Politics, chapter 1). Despite the prevailing image that nationalized medicine leads to shortages of doctors, the United States has about as many physicians per capita as the high-income countries. Canada, Germany, and Japan report that their citizens have adequate access to essential drugs; the United States does not provide such data.

---

retirement, disability, unemployment, or death or absence of the family breadwinner. Although cases of total deprivation are now rare, many people are unable to provide a minimally decent standard of living for themselves and their families. They are poor in a relative if not an absolute sense. In 1999, the poverty threshold for a family of four with two children under the age of eighteen was $16,895.

non-means-based programs
Program such as Social Security where benefits are provided irrespective of the income or means of recipients.

Income security programs fall into two general categories. *Social insurance* programs are **non-means-based programs** that provide cash assistance to qualified beneficiaries. **Means-tested programs** require that people must have incomes below specified levels to be eligible for benefits. Benefits of means-tested programs may come either as cash or in-kind benefits, such as food stamps.

means-tested programs
Income security program intended to assist those whose incomes fall below a designated level.

Social Insurance: Non-Means-Based Programs.   Social insurance programs operate in a manner somewhat similar to private automobile or

Across Europe, North America, and Japan, the increasing age of national populations will challenge national health policies. If anything, the point at which 18.5 percent of the national population is age sixty-five years or older (Florida's current situation) will come earlier in the other industrial countries than it will here because their populations are aging more rapidly. (The developing countries of China, Russia, Indonesia, and Mexico have relatively younger populations, but they also spend less than 5 percent of GDP on health care.) In Italy, Japan, and Germany, the latter with the second-highest health expenditures in the industrial countries, nearly one-fifth of the total population will be retirement age almost immediately after the turn of the twenty-first century.

Despite the strains on public budgets that public welfare programs impose, polls continue to show that most Europeans support them. Reflecting the differences in political culture and public opinion noted in chapter 11, there is far less support in Europe and Canada than in the United States for significant privatization of key welfare programs, including health care.

Health Expenditures in the Industrial Democracies, 1990–98

Country	Total (% of GDP)	Private (% of GDP)	Year in Which Senior Population (%) Will Exceed Florida
Canada	9.2	2.8	2021
France	9.6	2.5	2016
Germany	10.7	2.5	2006
Italy	7.6	2.3	2003
Japan	7.1	1.4	2005
UK	6.8	1.0	2016
USA	**6.8**	**7.5**	**2023**
High Income Countries avg.	9.8	3.7	—

Sources: World Bank, *World Development Indicators, 2000.* Washington, D.C.: World Bank, 2000, 90–92: and Peter Peterson, "Grey Dawn: The Global Aging Crisis," *Foreign Affairs* 18 (January/February, 1999): 43–45.

life insurance. Contributions are made by or on behalf of the prospective beneficiaries, their employers, or both. When a person becomes eligible for benefits, the monies are paid as a matter of right, regardless of how much wealth or unearned income (for example, from dividends and interest payments) the recipient has. (For Social Security, a limit is imposed on earned income. There is no means test.)

Old Age, Survivors, and Disability Insurance.   This program began as old-age insurance, providing benefits only to retired workers. Its coverage was extended to survivors of covered workers in 1939 and to the permanently disabled in 1956. Customarily called Social Security, it is not, as many people believe, a pension program that collects contributions from workers, invests them, and then returns them with interest to beneficiaries. Instead the current workers pay taxes that directly go toward providing benefits for retirees. A payroll tax of 7.65 percent on

WEB EXPLORATION
To learn more about the most current Social Security benefits and statistics, go to www.ablongman.com/oconnor

HIGHLIGHT

CHILD POVERTY

In the year 2000, a study released by the National Center for Poverty Research at Columbia University indicated that while child poverty fell in many states during the economic good times, in all but a handful of states child poverty was still higher than it was in 1980. U.S. Census data indicated that nationally the child poverty rate rose to 18.7 percent in 1998 from a rate of 16.2 percent in 1979. In 2000, more than 13 million American children (3 million more than in 1979) lived with incomes that were under the official poverty line. When poverty was defined relative to median incomes (below 50 percent of median income), the United States had the second highest proportion of children in poverty among twenty-three industrialized nations. Between 1980 and 2000, countries such as Sweden, Norway, Finland, Belgium, Luxembourg, and Denmark were characterized by low child poverty levels of about 5 percent.

Many scholars cite continuing high rates of unwed childbearing and divorce as the primary reason for the persistence of child poverty. In the year 2000, about 60 percent of all poor children lived in one-parent homes. Children in mother-headed homes were five times more likely to be poor than children in married-couple homes. The explosion of one-parent homes in the 1970s and 1980s accounted for almost all of the rise in child poverty during that period.

Data also support that view that low wages also contributed to increases in child poverty. Between 1973 and 1997, real wages rose by 6.4 percent at the 90th percentile of wage earners but declined by 8 percent at the 20th percentile and

by 15 percent at the 10th percentile. The percent of those making one-fourth or less below the poverty line rose from 24 percent to 29 percent during this period. The Bureau of Labor Statistics projected that the greatest occupational job growth between 1996 and 2005 would be in low-wage job categories such as cashiers, janitors, and retail sales clerks. Only three of the top ten growth occupations (nurses, general managers, and systems analysts) were in higher-wage job classifications. Retail jobs were increasingly part-time, whether or not employees preferred such arrangements. In the early 1990s, the average fast food restaurant worker worked thirty hours a week, received no benefits, and got a pay raise only when the legal minimum wage rose.

Negative outcomes are linked to the growth and persistence of child poverty. Studies showed that prolonged poverty impairs infants' and young children's physical and mental growth, impairs their academic ability, and impedes social as well as emotional well-being. Sustained poverty is thought to inhibit effective parenting, to increase the chances that children will attend inferior schools, and to raise the odds of living in high-risk environments.

Sources: Don Terry, "U.S. Child Poverty Rate Fell as Economy Grew, but Is Above 1979 Level," *The New York Times* (August 11, 2000): A10; Jason O'Neale Roach, "One in Six Children Live in Relative Poverty," *British Medical Journal* 320(7250) (July 17, 2000): 1621; Charles Craypo and David Cormier, "Job Restructuring as a Determinant of Wage Inequality and Working-Poor Households," *Journal of Economic Issues* (March 2000): 21–42.

the first $62,700 of wages or salaries is paid by the employee and another 7.65 percent is paid by the employer into the Social Security trust fund. Nearly all employees and most of the self-employed (who pay a 15.3 percent tax) are now covered by Social Security. People earn-

TABLE 13.1   The Rising Cost of Entitlement Programs: Government Spending
on Automatic Pilot

The Biggest Entitlements in 1997 (in Billions)		*Projections for 2003 (in Billions)*	
1. Social Security	$366	1. Social Security	$472
2. Medicare	190	2. Medicare	256
3. Medicaid	101	3. Medicaid	143
4. Federal civilian retirement	42	4. Federal civilian retirement	54
5. Veterans' benefits and services	40	5. Veterans' benefits and services	47
6. Military retirement	30	6. Military retirement	36
7. Food stamps	28	7. Supplemental Security Income	32
8. Supplemental Security Income	27	8. Unemployment compensation	30
9. Earned Income Tax Credit	27	9. Food stamps	29
10. Unemployment compensation	21	10. Earned Income Tax Credit	27

Source: *Budget of the United States Government for Fiscal Year 1999* (Washington, D.C.: U.S. Government Printing Office, 1998), 261–91.

ing less money pay a greater share of their income into the Social Security program than do workers earning more. In 2000, earnings in excess of $76,200 were not subject to the payroll tax. The Social Security tax therefore is considered to be a regressive tax since it captures larger proportions of income of lower- and middle-income individuals than from high-wage earners.

In 2000, the average monthly Social Security benefit for all retired workers was $804, while the maximum monthly benefit was $1,443. Social Security is the primary source of income for many retirees and keeps them from living in poverty. However, eligible people are entitled to Social Security benefits regardless of how much *unearned* income (for example, dividends and interest payments) they also receive. As of January 2000, there was no limit on the amount of income recipients older than sixty-five could earn without penalty. Individuals under the age of sixty-five could earn up to $10,800 a year before they began to lose some benefits.

Expenditures for Social Security have greatly increased during the last couple of decades because the number of beneficiaries is growing, they are living longer, and benefit levels are rising. More than 40 million people, including some 3 million workers with disabilities, currently receive benefits. Social Security is by far the national government's largest entitlement program (see Table 13.1).

Social Security, however, is expected to be insolvent by 2032 because the ratio of workers to retirees will decline as Baby Boomers hit retirement age. The number of Americans reaching retirement age is projected to double from 35 million in 2000 to more than 70 million in 2035. In anticipation of this problem, several members of Congress have called for a round of new reforms, including the removal of the Social Security Administration from the Department of Health and Human Services to make it an independent agency.

President George W. Bush proposed to allow some portion of Social Security taxes to be invested in private stocks or bonds, arguing that the returns on such investments would exceed typical government investments. In addition, Bush proposed a separate program that would encourage individuals to set up personal savings accounts. Tax credits would be given to individuals who invested in such accounts.

Unemployment Insurance. As mentioned earlier, unemployment insurance is financed by a payroll tax paid by employers. The program pays benefits to covered workers who are covered by the government plan and are unemployed through no fault of their own. The Social Security Act provided that if a state set up a comparable program and levied a payroll tax for its support, most of the federal tax would be forgiven (not collected). The states were thus accorded a choice: Either they could set up and administer an acceptable unemployment program, or they could let the national government handle the matter. Within a short time, all states had their own programs.

Unemployment insurance covers employers of four or more people, but not part-time or occasional workers. Benefits are paid to unemployed workers who have neither been fired nor quit their jobs and who are willing and able to accept suitable employment. State unemployment programs differ considerably in levels of benefits, length of benefit payment, and eligibility for benefits. In 1997, average weekly benefit payments, for example, ranged from $269 in Hawaii and $263 in Massachusetts, to $142 in Mississippi and $133 in Louisiana. The most generous programs exist in the northern industrial states, where labor unions are more powerful and influence the nature of these programs. Nationwide, only about half of the people counted as unemployed at any given time will be receiving benefits.

Social Insurance: Means-Tested Programs. Means-tested income security programs are intended to help the needy, that is, individuals or families whose incomes fall below specified levels, such as a percentage of the official poverty line. Included in the means-tested categories are the Supplementary Security Income (SSI), Temporary Assistance for Needy Families (TANF), and Food Stamp programs.

Supplementary Security Income. This program began under the Social Security Act as a categorical grant-in-aid program to help the needy, aged, or blind. Financed jointly by the national and state governments from general revenues, the states played a major role in determining standards of eligibility and benefit levels. In 1950, Congress extended coverage to needy people who were permanently and totally disabled.

With the supportzΩZ of the Nixon administration, Congress reconfigured these programs into the Supplementary Security Income (SSI) programs in 1974. Primary funding for SSI is provided by the national government, which prescribes uniform benefit levels throughout the nation. To be eligible, beneficiaries can own only a limited amount of possessions. In 1997 monthly payments were about $360. The states may choose to supplement the federal benefits, and forty-eight states do. For years this program generated little controversy, as the modest benefits go to people who obviously cannot provide for themselves.

Temporary Assistance for Needy Families (TANF).   In 1950, Aid to Families with Dependent Children (AFDC), the predecessor to the Temporary Assistance for Needy Families (TANF program), was broadened to include not only dependent children without fathers but also mothers themselves or other adults with whom dependent children were living. The AFDC rolls expanded greatly since 1960 because of the increasing numbers of children born to unwed mothers, the growing divorce rate, and the migration of poor people to cities, where they are more likely to apply for and be provided benefits. Now, AFDC has been replaced by the Temporary Assistance for Needy Families (TANF) program, part of the Personal Responsibility and Work Opportunity Reconciliation Act (PRWORA) of 1996. Most families covered by TANF are headed by single mothers.

Personal Responsibility and Work Opportunity Reconciliation Act (PRWORA) of 1996.   Because of its clientele, the AFDC program was the focus of much controversy and was frequently stigmatized as "welfare." Critics who pointed to the rising number of recipients claimed that it encouraged promiscuity and out-of-wedlock births and promoted dependency, which results in a permanent class of welfare families. Much effort has been expended by public officials to restrict the availability of aid, to ferret out fraud and abuse, and hold down AFDC cost. In what was hailed as the biggest shift in social policy since the Great Depression, the new welfare bill, the Personal Responsibility and

WEB EXPLORATION
For a progress report on welfare reform, go to www.ablongman.com/oconnor

Workfare is a welfare strategy that gives adults the opportunity to learn skills that can lead to employment. Here, one workfare recipient tends to children at his new daycare center job.
(Photo courtesy: James Nubile/The Image Works)

Work Opportunity Reconciliation Act (PRWORA) of 1996, created the Temporary Assistance for Needy Families (TANF) program to replace AFDC. The shift from AFDC to TANF was meant to foster a new philosophy of work rather than welfare dependency. The most fundamental change enacted in the new law was the switch in funding for welfare from an open-ended matching program to a block grant to the states. PRWORA also gave states more flexibility in reforming their welfare programs toward work-oriented goals.

Significant features of the welfare plan included: (1) a requirement for single mothers with a child over five years of age to work within two years of receiving benefits; (2) a provision that unmarried mothers under the age of eighteen were required to live with an adult and attend school in order to receive welfare benefits; (3) a five-year lifetime limit for aid from block grants; (4) a requirement that mothers must provide information about a child's father in order to receive full welfare payments; (5) cutting off food stamps and Supplemental Security Income for legal immigrants; (6) cutting off cash welfare benefits and food stamps for convicted drug felons; and (7) limiting food stamps to three months in a three-year period for persons eighteen to fifty years old who are not raising children and not working.

The Food Stamp Program.   The initial food stamp program (1939–43) was primarily an effort to expand domestic markets for farm commodities. Attempts to reestablish the program during the Eisenhower administration failed, but in 1961 a $381,000 pilot program began under the Kennedy administration. It was made permanent in 1964 and extended nationwide in 1974. Although strongly opposed by the Republicans in Congress, Democrats put together a majority coalition when urban members agreed to support a wheat and cotton price support program wanted by rural and Southern Democrats in return for their support of food stamps.

In the beginning, food stamp recipients had to pay cash for them, but this practice ceased in 1977. Benefiting poor and low-income families, the program has helped to combat hunger and reduce malnutrition. Food stamps went to more than 25.5 million beneficiaries in 1996 at a cost of $22.4 billion. The average participant received $73 worth of stamps per month. In 1995, families of four earning less than $1,642 per month qualified for food stamps.

Growth in the size of the food stamp program (in 1974 the cost of 12.9 million beneficiaries ran $2.8 billion) made this a target for Republican budget cutters. While 1995 House and Senate efforts differed on specifics, both sought to save more than $30 billion in projected food stamp costs over the seven years leading up to an anticipated balanced budget in 2002.

The national government operates several other food programs for the needy. These programs include a special nutritional program for women, infants, and children (WIC); a school breakfast and lunch program; and an emergency food assistance program.

The Effectiveness of Income Security Programs.   Many of the income security programs, including Social Security, Supplementary Security Income, and food stamps, are **entitlement programs**. That is, Congress sets eligibility criteria—such as age, income level, or unemployment—and those who meet the criteria are legally "entitled" to receive benefits. Moreover, unlike such programs as public housing, military construction, and space exploration, spending for entitlement programs is mandatory. Year after year, funds must be provided for them unless the laws creating the programs are changed. This feature of entitlement programs has made it quite difficult to control spending for them.

Poverty and economic dependency have not been eliminated by income security programs. Income security programs, however, have improved the lives of large numbers of people. Millions of elderly people in the United States would be living below the poverty line were it not for Social Security. Income security programs are basically alleviative rather than curative or remedial in their consequences. Poverty and economic dependency will not be eradicated so long as the conditions that give rise to them persist. There will probably always be people who are unable to provide adequately for themselves, whether because of old age, mental or physical disability, adverse economic conditions, or youth. A panoply of income security programs is a characteristic of all democratic industrial societies.

entitlement program
Income security program to which all those meeting eligibility criteria are entitled.

Health Care.   Currently, many millions of people receive medical care through the medical branches of the armed forces, the hospitals and medical programs of the Department of Veterans' Affairs, and the Indian Health Service. Billions of dollars are expended for the construction and operation of facilities and for the salaries of the doctors and other medical personnel, making the government's medical business truly a big business.

Most medical research currently is financed by the national government, primarily through the National Institutes of Health (NIH). The National Cancer Institute, the National Heart, Lung, and Blood Institute, the National Institute of Allergy and Infectious Diseases, and the other NIH institutes and centers expend more than $10 billion annually on biomedical research. The research is conducted by NIH scientists and by scientists at universities, medical schools, and other research centers receiving NIH research grants.

In recent years, debate has surrounded the issue of whether Washington is doing enough to combat AIDS. Most Americans accept and support extensive government spending on medical research. Congress, in fact, often appropriates more money for medical research than the president recommends. The United States spends significant sums of money on public health, a larger proportion of its gross domestic product than most industrialized democracies. In 2000, the United States spent $3,724 per person on health, more per person on health care than any other country. While these sums were being spent, the United

WEB EXPLORATION
To learn more about the National Institutes of Health Funding and Scientific resources, go to www.ablongman.com/oconnor

States only ranked thirty-seventh in quality of health care, according to a World Health Organization analysis. Countries such as Japan and France far surpassed the United States in terms of how long their citizens live in good health.

Much of the increase in funding for health care as gone to the Medicare and Medicaid programs. Reasons for growth in medical spending include increased expectations of the public, increased demand for services, advances in health care technology, the perception of health care as a right, and the third-party payment system.[8]

Medicare.   Medicare, which covers persons receiving Social Security benefits, is administered by the Health Care Financing Administration in the Department of Health and Human Services. Medicare coverage has two components, Parts A and B. Benefits under Part A come to all Americans automatically at age sixty-five, when they qualify for Social Security. It covers hospitalization, some skilled nursing care, and home health services. Individuals have to pay about $700 in medical bills before they are eligible for Part A benefits. Medicare is financed by a payroll tax of 1.45 percent paid by both employees and employers on the total amount of one's wages or salary.

Part B, which is optional, covers payment for physicians' services, outpatient and diagnostic services, X-rays, and some other items not covered by Part A. Excluded from coverage are prescription drugs, eyeglasses, hearing aids, and dentures. This portion of the Medicare program is financed partly by monthly payments from beneficiaries and partly by general tax revenues.

Medicare has become a costly program because people live longer, the elderly need more hospital and physicians' services, and medical care costs are rising rapidly. Attempts to limit or cap expenditures for the program have had only marginal effects. Spending has grown exponentially in the Medicare program, partially fueled by larger numbers of enrollees. Spending increased from $37.5 billion in 1980 to $214.3 billion in 1997.

Medicare does not cover long-term or catastrophic health care costs. Congress sought to remedy this situation in 1988 when, with the support of the Reagan administration, it passed the Catastrophic Health Care Act. This act provided elderly people with expanded hospital and physicians' benefits and limited nursing home and prescription drug coverage. These expenses were to be financed by a small monthly fee levied on all Medicare recipients and also by a tax paid by the more well-to-do among Medicare recipients. President Reagan had insisted that the elderly themselves had to pay for the program.

Many better-off elderly people quickly mobilized to protest the new law. Outraged elderly constituents bombarded members of Congress with letters, petitions, and telephone calls and accosted legislators at town meetings. Overwhelmed by this stampede of opposition from the wealthier elderly, Congress rushed to repeal the Catastrophic Health Care Act in 1989. Although many of the wealthier elderly had private health insurance providing protection for themselves similar to that in the act, the poorer elderly were left with no protection.[9] Many people did not view this action as one of Congress's finer moments, but it demonstrated the power of well-funded, organized interest groups.

Medicaid.   Enacted into law at the same time as Medicare, the Medicaid program provides comprehensive health care, including hospitalization, physicians' services, prescription drugs, and long-term nursing home care (unlike Medicare) to all who qualify as needy under TANF and SSI.

In 1986, Congress extended Medicaid coverage for pregnant women and children under age six in families with incomes of less than 133 percent of the official poverty level. The states were also accorded the option of extending coverage to all pregnant women and to all children under one year of age in families with incomes below 185 percent of the poverty level. By 1993, twenty-nine states had chosen to provide this coverage. In 1996, Medicaid served 36.1 million people at a cost of $121.7 billion. Most of the benefits paid out under the program went to the elderly. Nursing facility services, in-patient general hospital services, home health services, and prescription drugs represented major categories of spending within the Medicaid program.

Medicaid is jointly financed by the national and state governments. The national government pays 50 to 79 percent of Medicaid costs on the basis of a formula based on average per capita income, which awards more financial support to poor than to wealthy states. Each state is responsible for the administration of its own program and sets specific standards of eligibility and benefit levels for Medicaid recipients within the boundaries set by national guidelines. Nearly all needy people are covered by Medicaid in some states; in others, only one-third or so of the needy are protected. Some states also award coverage to the "medically indigent," that is, to people who do not qualify for welfare but for whom large medical expenses would constitute a severe financial burden.

While the average amount paid for by the states varies, the portion of state budgets going to Medicaid is ever upward. If Medicaid expenditures continue to grow at their present rate, the proportion of funding that is available for other programs will be reduced.

New Health Initiatives.   The 1997 Balanced Budget Act (BBA) significantly influenced the nation's health care system. The BBA extended the life of the Medicare Trust Fund, strengthened preventive care, created more choice of plans, and permitted states to have greater flexibility in designing health programs. A major feature of the BBA provided funding for up to 5 million children in working families. Prior to the Balanced Budget Act, in 1996, President Clinton and Congress enacted a bill, the Health Insurance Portability and Accountability Act (HIPAA), which helped people keep their health insurance when they changed jobs and limited the ability of insurers to deny coverage due to preexisting conditions.

WEB EXPLORATION
For other health care policy initiatives and consumer health information, go to www.ablongman.com/oconnor

The Cost of Health Care.   The costs of Medicare and Medicaid, which vastly exceed early estimates, have been major contributors to the ballooning costs of health care and the budget deficit. In 1997, national expenditures for Medicare were $190 billion and for Medicaid $101 billion. In 1997, the states collectively spent another $72 billion on Medicaid. The Balanced Budget Act of 1997 represented a significant attempt to control some of these costs. The government's health spending for Medicare, Medicaid, medical research, and other purposes amounted to 40 percent of total health spending.

A number of factors have contributed to the high and rising costs of health care. First, more people are living longer and are requiring costly and extensive care in their declining years. Second, the range and sophistication of diagnostic practices and therapeutic treatments, which are often quite expensive, have increased. Third, the expansion of private health insurance, along with Medicare and Medicaid, has reduced the direct costs of health care to most people and increased the demand for services. More people, in short, can afford needed care. They may also be less aware of the costs of care. Fourth, the costs of health care have also increased because of its higher quality and because labor costs have outpaced productivity in the provision of hospital care. Fifth, U.S. medicine focuses less on preventing illnesses and more on curing them, which is more costly.

Public opinion polls indicate that the major cause of Americans' dissatisfaction with the health care system relates to its cost and extent of coverage. While most people indicate that they are satisfied with the quality of health care services provided by physicians and hospitals, a substantial majority express dissatisfaction over the costs and accessibility of health care. There is, as a consequence, a strong belief in the need to improve the nation's health care system.

ECONOMIC POLICY

WEB EXPLORATION
To learn about the government bureau for economic analysis, go to www.ablongman.com/oconnor

During our nation's first century, most economic regulation was undertaken by states. The national government defined its role narrowly, although it did collect tariffs, fund public improvements, and regulate interstate commerce. Only with the perception that problems had outpaced the ability of states to provide adequate controls did Congress become active in setting national standards.

Economic Policy in the Nineteenth Century

Although the U.S. economic system is a mixed free-enterprise system characterized by the private ownership of property, private enterprise, and marketplace competition, governments in the United States have always been deeply involved in the economy. The national government has long played an important role in fostering economic development through its tax, tariff, public lands disposal, and public works policies, and also through the creation of a national bank (see chapter 3). For much of the nineteenth century, however, national regulatory programs were few and were restricted to such topics as steamboat inspection and the regulation of trade with the Native American tribes.

The state governments, in comparison, were quite active in promoting and regulating private economic activity. They constructed such public works as the Erie Canal, built roads, and subsidized railroads to encourage trade within and among the states; they also carried on many licensing, inspection, and regulatory programs.

Following the Civil War, the United States entered a period of rapid economic growth. The rise of industrial capitalism brought about extensive industrialization and the creation of large-scale manufacturing enterprises. Many people began working in factories for wages and crowded into large cities. New problems resulted from industrialization—industrial accidents and disease, labor-management conflict, unemployment, and the emergence of huge businesses that could exploit workers and consumers. Another problem was the loss of income by people because of business cycles, which became more severe in the new industrial society. **Business cycles** involve fluctuations between growth and recession, or periods of "boom and bust," and seem an inherent part of modern capitalist economies. During recessions many people lose their jobs, and a low or even negative growth rate afflicts the economy.

business cycles
Fluctuation between expansion and recession that is a part of modern capitalist economies.

Many people, disturbed by the problems resulting from industrialization, turned to government for help. Because the states, with their limited jurisdictions, appeared inadequate to cope with industrial problems, the national government was called on to control these new forces. Businesses and conservatives, who had welcomed national action to aid economic development in the early decades of the nineteenth century, now proclaimed their faith in *laissez-faire*. Based on Adam Smith's *The Wealth of Nations* (published in 1776), the doctrine of **laissez-faire** holds that governmental regulation of the economy is wrong and that the role of government should be limited to the maintenance of order and justice, the conduct of foreign affairs, and the provision of necessary public works such as roads or lighthouses, which are not profitable for private persons to provide. Beyond that, individuals should be left free to pursue their self-interest. In so doing, Smith held, people would be guided by an "unseen hand" to promote the public welfare; that is, to provide consumers with a sufficient quantity of goods at reasonable prices. Competition and the laws of supply and demand would control their behavior and ensure that self-interest did not get out of hand.

laissez-faire
A French term literally meaning "to allow to do, to leave alone." It is a hands-off governmental policy that is based on the belief that governmental regulation of the economy is wrong.

Although opposed to regulation of their activities, businesses did not shun other forms of governmental intervention in the economy. They strongly supported tariffs that provided protection from foreign competitors. Other favored policies included the giveaway of public lands,

THE BOSSES OF THE SENATE

Here, a political cartoonist depicts how the U.S. government is perceived by some as being dominated by trusts such as Standard Oil and Steel. (Photo courtesy: Bettmann/Corbis)

WEB EXPLORATION
To compare various business cycle indicators, go to www.ablongman.com/oconnor

subsidies for railroad construction, and the use of armed force to put down strikes. Essentially, what businesses and their supporters wanted, and what they thought of as *laissez-faire,* was an economic system and a set of governmental policies that would be congenial to the amassing of business profits.

In time, because of pressures from small businesses, reformers in the cities, and the Grangers and other powerful agrarian protest groups in the Midwest, the national government was impelled to action. In 1887, following nearly two decades of agitation, Congress adopted the Interstate Commerce Act to regulate the railroads. The act, to be enforced by the new Interstate Commerce Commission (ICC), required that railroad rates should be "just and reasonable." The act also prohibited such practices as pooling (rate agreements), rate discrimination, and charging more for a short haul than for a long haul of goods.

Three years later Congress dealt with the problem of "trusts," the name given to large-scale, monopolistic businesses that dominated many areas of production, including oil, sugar, whiskey, salt, cordage, and meatpacking. The Sherman Antitrust Act of 1890 prohibits all restraints of trade and all monopolization or attempts to monopolize. The act was to be enforced by the Antitrust Division of the Department of Justice, which was empowered to sue violators in the federal courts. The Interstate Commerce Act and the Sherman Antitrust Act constitute the nineteenth- and early twentieth-century response of the national government to the new industrialization. A modern manifestation of the Antitrust Act is found in the Department of Justice's lawsuit against the computer software company Microsoft, which began in October 1998.

The Progressive Era (1901–1917)

The Progressive movement drew much of its support from the middle class and sought to reform the political, economic, and social systems of U.S. society. Economically, there was a desire to bring corporate power fully under the control of government and make it more responsive to democratic ends. Progressive administrations under Presidents Theodore Roosevelt and Woodrow Wilson strengthened regulatory programs to control railroads, business, and banking and to protect consumers. Several laws intended to make railroad regulation more effective were passed. Notable among these laws was the Hepburn Act (1906), which gave the Interstate Commerce Commission (ICC) authority to set maximum reasonable rates for railroads. Strongly opposed by most of the railroads, the Hepburn Act helped make the ICC a more effective regulator.

Consumer protection legislation came in the form of the Pure Food and Drug Act and the Meat Inspection Act, both enacted in 1906. These statutes mark the beginning of consumer protection as a major task of the national government. The Meat Inspection Act was passed partly in response to publication of Upton Sinclair's novel *The Jungle,* which graphically portrayed the unsavory and unsanitary conditions in Chicago meatpacking plants. The food and drug law prohibited the adulteration and mislabeling of foods and drugs, which were common practices at this time.

Passage of the Federal Trade Commission (FTC) Act and Clayton Act of 1914 strengthened antitrust policy. The FTC Act created the Federal Trade Commission and authorized it to prevent "unfair methods of competition." The commission also shared jurisdiction with the Department of Justice to enforce the Clayton Act, which prohibited a number of unfair business practices, such as price discrimination, exclusive dealing contracts, and corporate mergers that lessened competition. These statutes sought to prevent business from forming monopolies or trusts.

As the national government's functions expanded in the early twentieth century, the government began to experience shortages of revenue. New sources of revenue became necessary, and the attention of public officials focused on the income tax as a way to raise money. The passage of the Sixteenth Amendment in 1913 authorized the national government "to lay and collect taxes on incomes, from whatever source derived" without being apportioned among the states. Personal and corporate income taxes have since become the national government's major source of general revenues. They have also been a source of political controversy.

The Great Depression and the New Deal

The Depression and the New Deal marked a major turning point in U.S. history in general and in U.S. economic history in particular. During the 1930s, the *laissez-faire* state was replaced with the **interventionist state,** in which the government plays an active and extensive role in guiding and regulating the private economy. Until the 1930s, the national government's role in the economy was consistent with a broad interpretation of *laissez-faire* doctrine in that the government mostly provided a framework of rules within which the economy was left alone to operate. After the 1930s, however, that was no longer true. The New Deal established the national government as a *major* regulator of private businesses, as a provider of Social Security, and as ultimately responsible for maintaining a stable economy.

interventionist state
Replaced the *laissez-faire* state as the government took an active role in guiding and regulating the private economy.

Although the New Deal was not (and is not) without critics, most people today accept the notion that these areas of responsibility are properly within the scope of national governmental power. Specifically, *how* matters of Social Security and economic stability should be handled rather than *whether* they should be the province of the national government has been the basis for political conflict. Recently, however, Republicans have led a growing chorus of critics who argue that federal intervention is part of the problem and not the solution. These critics would replace Social Security with private retirement plans and allow the market a freer hand.

The New Deal brought about a number of reforms in almost every area, including finance, agriculture, labor, industry, and consumer protection.

Financial Reforms.   The first actions of the New Deal were directed at reviving and reforming the nation's financial system. The major New Deal banking laws were the Glass-Steagall Act (1933) and the Banking Act (1935). The Glass-Steagall Act required the separation of commercial and investment banking and set up the Federal Deposit Insurance Corporation (FDIC) to insure bank deposits, originally for $5,000 per account. Although it had long been opposed by conservatives, bank deposit insurance now has become an accepted feature of the U.S. banking system. The Banking Act reorganized the Federal Reserve System, removed the secretary of the treasury as an ex-officio member, and formally established the Open Market Committee (discussed later in this chapter).

Legislation was also passed to control other abuses in the stock markets. The Securities Act (1933) required that prospective investors be given full and accurate information about the stocks or securities being offered to them. The Securities Exchange Act (1934) created the Securities and Exchange Commission (SEC), an independent regulatory commission. The SEC was authorized to regulate the stock exchanges, to enforce the Securities Act, and to reduce the number of stocks bought on margin (that is, with borrowed money).

Agriculture.   The economic condition of U.S. agriculture, which had been weak even during the prosperous 1920s, became much worse with the Depression. The Agriculture Adjustment Act (AAA) of 1933 sought to boost farm income by restricting agriculture production in order to bring it into better balance with demand. Farmers who reduced their crop production in line with the program were eligible to receive cash payments and other benefits. In 1936, however, the Supreme Court held the AAA unconstitutional on the grounds that the national government lacked authority to regulate farming through any of its enumerated powers.[10] Congress quickly replaced the AAA with the Soil Conservation and Domestic Allotment Act, which paid farmers for taking land out of crop production and devoting it to soil conservation purposes. The crops taken out of production generally were those whose prices the AAA had been designed to increase. This ploy did not work very well to increase farm income.

In 1938 Congress adopted the second Agricultural Adjustment Act. The second AAA provided for subsidies to farmers raising crops such as corn, cotton, and wheat who grew no more than their allotted acreage. If two-thirds of the growers of a commodity voting in a referendum approved, then the allotments became mandatory, and farmers exceeding them were penalized. Direct payments and commodity loans were also available to participating farmers. In 1941 the Supreme Court upheld the constitutionality of the second AAA as an appropriate exercise of Congress's power to regulate interstate commerce.[11] The act, the foundation of the agricultural price support programs, has come under increasing attack today from conservatives who claim that the program promotes inefficiency.

Labor.   Organized labor had long been handicapped in its relationships with management by unfriendly public officials and hostile public policies. The fortunes of labor unions, which were strong supporters of the New Deal, improved significantly in 1935 when Congress passed the National Labor Relations Act. Better known as the Wagner Act after its sponsor, Senator Robert Wagner (D–N.Y.), this statute guaranteed workers' right to organize and bargain collectively through unions of their own choosing. A series of "unfair labor practices," such as discriminating against employees because of their union activities, was prohibited. The National Labor Relations Board (NLRB) was created to carry out the act and to conduct elections to determine which union, if any, employees wanted to represent them. Unions prospered under the protection provided by the Wagner Act.

The last major piece of New Deal economic legislation was the Fair Labor Standards Act (FLSA) of 1938. Intended to protect the interests of low-paid workers, the law set twenty-five cents an hour and forty-four hours per week as initial minimum standards. Within a few years, wages were to rise to forty cents per hour and hours to decline to forty per week. Not all employees were covered by the FLSA, however; farm workers, domestic workers, and fishermen, for example, were exempted. The act also banned child labor.

Industry Regulations.   Several industries were the subjects of new or expanded regulatory programs. The Federal Communications Commission (FCC), created in 1934 to replace the old Federal Radio Commission, was given extensive jurisdiction over the radio, telephone, and telegraph industries. The Civil Aeronautics Board (CAB) was put in place in 1938 to regulate the commercial aviation industry. The Motor Carrier Act of 1935 put the trucking industry under the jurisdiction of the Interstate Commerce Commission (ICC). Regulation of industries such as trucking and commercial aviation, like railroad regulation, extended to such matters as entry into the business, routes of service,

WEB EXPLORATION
To access the most current labor and wages data for your state or region, go to www.ablongman.com/oconnor

and rates. To a substantial extent, government regulation, as a protector of the public interest, replaced competition in these industries. Supporters of these programs frequently spoke of a need to prevent destructive or excessive competition, as could occur among large numbers of trucking companies. Critics warned that limiting competition resulted in users having to pay more for the services.

Consumer Protection.   Even though consumers as a group were poorly organized in the 1930s, a few laws were passed to help protect their interests. The Wheeler-Lea Act (1938) expanded the jurisdiction of the Federal Trade Commission (FTC) to include deceptive practices and false and misleading advertising. The act gave the FTC a clear mandate to engage in consumer protection.

The Pure Food, Drug, and Cosmetic Act (1938) represented an effort to plug some of the loopholes and remedy the shortcomings of the Pure Food and Drug Act of 1906. Cosmetic and therapeutic devices were added to foods and drugs as matters subject to government regulation. All traffic in foods that were injurious to health was banned. Also, factories producing foods, drugs, and cosmetics were brought under inspection by the Food and Drug Administration (FDA). Drugs and cosmetics had to bear informative labels relating to their use. Moreover, the marketing of any drug was prohibited until it had been tested and found safe when properly used. Most responsibility for enforcing the 1938 law was given to the Food and Drug Administration, which today is part of the Department of Health and Human Services.

Just as World War I brought down the curtain on the Progressive Era, the war clouds gathering in Western Europe in the late 1930s diverted Americans' attention from domestic reform to international affairs and brought an end to the New Deal era. Many of the New Deal programs, however, became permanent parts of our public policy landscape. Moreover, the New Deal established the legitimacy and viability of national governmental intervention in the economy. Passive government was replaced with activist government, and the government in Washington became the people's primary source of solutions for economic problems.

The Social Regulation Era

economic regulation
Governmental regulation of business practices, industry rates, routes, or areas serviced by particular industries.

social regulation
Governmental regulation of the quality and safety of products as well as the conditions under which goods and services are produced.

Economists and political scientists frequently distinguish between economic regulation and social regulation. **Economic regulation** focuses on such matters as control of entry into a business, prices or rates of charge, and service routes or areas. Regulation is usually tailored to the conditions of particular industries, such as railroads or stock exchanges. "Simply put, economic regulation places government in the driver's seat with respect to the economic direction and performance of the regulated industry." In contrast, **social regulation** is concerned with such areas as the quality and safety of products and the conditions under which goods are produced and services rendered. Put another way, social regulation strives to protect and enhance the quality of life. Regulation of product safety by the Consumer Product Safety Commission is an example of social regulation. Professor Michael Reagan, noted authority in the study of regulation, makes a helpful distinction: "Social regulation can generally be differentiated from economic regulation by the former's concern with harm to our physical (and sometimes moral and aesthetic) well-being, rather than harm to our wallets."[12]

Most of the regulatory programs established through the 1950s fell into the category of economic regulation. From the mid-1960s to the mid-1970s, however, a huge wave of social regulatory legislation emanated from the national government on such topics as consumer protection, health and safety, and environmental protection. Congress enacted this legislation under its commerce clause authority.

As a consequence of this flood of social regulation, many industries that previously had had limited dealings with government now found government regulation to be of major importance in the conduct of their operations. A good example is the automobile industry, which previously had been lightly touched by antitrust, labor relations, and other general statutes. By the early 1970s, however, the quality of its products was heavily regulated by EPA motor vehicle emissions standards and federally mandated safety standards. The automobile companies found this experience both galling and expensive. The chemical industry found itself in much the same situation.

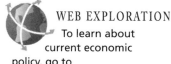

WEB EXPLORATION
To learn about current economic policy, go to www.ablongman.com/oconnor

Deregulation

Deregulation, which involves the reduction in market controls (such as controls on allowable rates or controls on who can enter the field) emerged as an attractive political issue even before the wave of social regulation began to wane. Deregulation, in theory, would increase market competition and lead to lower prices for consumers. The focus of the deregulation movement was on the economic regulatory programs for such industries as railroads, motor carriers, and commercial air transportation; most social regulatory programs continued to enjoy strong public support and were left largely alone by the deregulation movement.

Beginning in the 1950s and 1960s, economists, political scientists, and journalists began to point out defects in some of the economic regulatory programs. They contended that regulation sometimes produced monopoly profits, discrimination in services, and inefficiency in the operation of regulated industries. Moreover, regulation often made it difficult for industries to compete on the basis of prices and also for new competitors to enter the market. For instance, no new major commercial airline was permitted to enter the industry after the Civil Aeronautics Board (CAB) began to regulate the industry in 1938. Consequently, consumers paid higher prices for airfares and had fewer choices than they would in a more competitive market. Regulated firms like the commercial airlines, on the other hand, were comfortable with the higher profits and less competitive rigors of their regulated markets. Critics contended that regulatory commissions like the CAB and the Interstate Commerce Commission were more responsive to the interests of the regulated firms than to the public interest.

For some time, nothing changed in the regulatory arena despite these criticisms. In the mid-1970s, however, President Gerald R. Ford decided to make deregulation a focal point of his administration. He saw regulation as one cause of the inflation that was then besetting the economy. Also, as a conservative Republican, he found deregulation consistent with his beliefs in less government and a free market. About this time, Senator Edward M. Kennedy (D–Mass.) became chair of a subcommittee of the Senate Judiciary Committee. Wanting to use his new position and acting on the advice of his staff, he decided to hold hearings on airline deregulation. The combined actions of Ford and Kennedy put deregulation on the national policy agenda and got the deregulatory movement underway. Democrats and Republicans, liberals and conservatives, all found deregulation to be an appealing political issue.

Only one deregulation act was passed during the Ford administration. However, deregulation picked up momentum after Jimmy Carter became president in 1977. He made deregulation a high priority for his administration. Legislation that deregulated aspects of commercial airlines, railroads, motor carriers, and financial institutions was enacted during his term. Two additional deregulation laws were adopted in the early years of the first Reagan administration.

An exception to the usual rules and regulations guiding deregulation was the Airline Deregulation Act, which completely eliminated economic regulation of commercial airlines over several years. Although many new passenger carriers flocked into the industry when barriers to entry were first removed, they were unable to compete successfully with the existing major airlines. All of these new entrants have now disappeared. Indeed, so have some of the major airlines that were operating at the time of deregulation. Consequently there are now fewer major carriers than under the regulatory regime, although new airlines such as AirTran and JetBlue try to compete by offering low fares.

The deregulation of the savings and loan business, coupled with the failure of the Reagan administration to enforce the remaining controls on savings and loans adequately, led in time to a costly instance of deregulatory failure. Previously restricted to financing individual homes, deregulation took the lid off of what savings and loans could invest in. As a consequence of poor management, bad commercial investments, and corruption, hundreds of savings and loans, especially in southwestern states, went bankrupt, sometimes to the tune of hundreds of millions of dollars or more.[13] The Financial Institutions Reform, Recovery, and Enforcement Act (1989) revamped the regulatory system for savings and loans, provided for the liquidation of insolvent associations, and bailed out their depositors. Expectations are that the total direct cost to

A N A L Y Z I N G   T H E   D A T A

LONG–TERM ECONOMIC GROWTH IN THE UNITED STATES

Over the long term, economic growth in the United States has been strong. This growth, however, was not continuous and was marked by cycles of growth and decline. For example, the post-1929 period of the Great Depression represented an unusual period of sharp economic turmoil. In contrast, the 1992–2000 period represented a time of economic achievement. Reasons for growth during this period were attributed to increased productivity, deregulation, incentives for investors, and free trade.

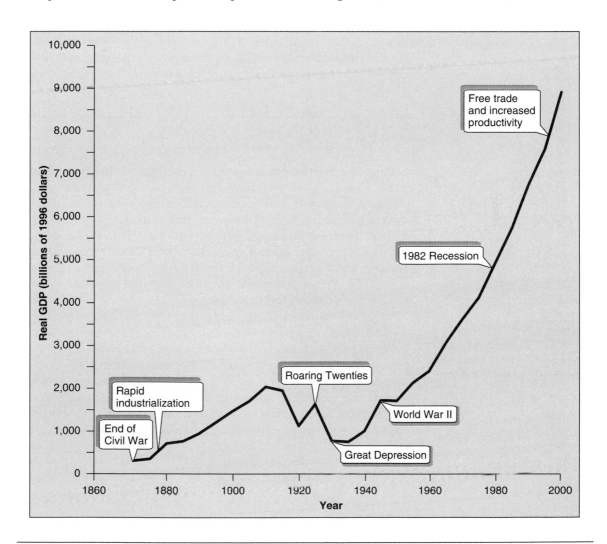

taxpayers of the bailout will be $150 billion to $200 billion. With interest, it was estimated that the cost may approximate $500 billion.[14] Much of the cost of the bailout could have been avoided by more timely and effective action. What is surprising is that the public has accepted this financial debacle with minimal complaint or criticism.

In some policy areas, the pendulum has now completed its deregulatory swing. The broad consensus that made possible "pro-competitive" or economic deregulation does not exist for the field of social regulation. Strong support continues for regulation to protect consumers, workers, and the environment. In some areas in which deregulation occurred, there have been calls to "reregulate." This has occurred in the airline industry because of concern about its safety and domination by a small number of companies.

In the following sections of this chapter, we take a detailed look at the government's role in stabilizing the economy, through policies that influence the overall performance of the economy.

STABILIZING THE ECONOMY

economic stability
A situation in which there is economic growth, rising national income, high employment, and steadiness in the general level of prices.

Economic stability is often defined as a situation in which there is economic growth, a rising national income, high employment, and a steadiness in the general level of prices. Conversely, economic instability may involve inflation or recession. **Inflation** occurs when there is too much demand for the available supply of goods and services, with the consequence that general price levels rise as buyers compete for the available supply. Prices may also rise if large corporations and unions have sufficient economic power to push prices and wages above competitive levels. A **recession** involves a decline in the economy. Investment sags, production falls off, and unemployment increases.

inflation
A rise in the general price levels of an economy.

recession
A short-term decline in the economy that occurs as investment sags, production falls off, and unemployment increases.

Typical tools by which government influences the economy include monetary policy (control of the money supply) and fiscal policy (spending and taxing decisions). Fiscal policy commitments as well as decisions related to the size of the deficit or surplus are observable in budget outputs. These outputs reflect the clash of various interest groups as they compete for advantage. The ultimate budget reflects the power of these groups as well as a mandate to stabilize the economy. Since the economy is not closed off from outside forces, national and global changes must be taken into account.

Monetary Policy: Regulating Money Supply

monetary policy
A form of government regulation in which the nation's money supply and interest rates are controlled.

Monetary policy, which is a form of influencing the total economy, involves regulating a nation's money supply and interest rates. A modern industrial economy operates on the basis of money, which is the medium through which nearly all income and all buying and selling transactions take place. When money is mentioned, most of us think of currency and coins, items we can feel, count, and carry in our pockets. But currency and coins are only a small portion of the nation's money supply. The term *money* also includes bank deposits and other financial assets. The Federal Reserve Board has three definitions of **money** based on this broader conception. *M1* (the first definition) includes currency, checking accounts, travelers checks, NOW accounts, and other checkable deposits. *M2* includes all of M1 plus savings and small-time deposits and money market account balances. *M3* includes M2 plus large-time deposits and institutional money market fund balances. The M2 definition is of the most concern to the Federal Reserve Board.

The **Federal Reserve Board** has responsibility for the formation and implementation of monetary policy because of its ability to control the credit-creating and lending activities of the nation's banks. When individuals and corporations deposit their money in financial institutions such as commercial banks (which accept deposits and make loans) and savings and loan associations (S&Ls), these deposits serve as the basis for loans to borrowers. In effect, the loaning of money creates new deposits or financial liabilities—new money that did not previously exist. But we are getting ahead of our story. First, we'll look at the Federal Reserve System and its authority.

The Federal Reserve System.   Created in 1913 to adjust the money supply to the needs of agriculture, commerce, and industry, the Federal Reserve System is comprised of the Federal Reserve Board (FRB) (formally, the Board of Governors of the Federal Reserve System; informally, "the Fed"), the Federal Open Market Committee, and the twelve Federal Reserve Banks in regions throughout the country. The Fed represents a mixture of private interests and governmental authority.

The primary monetary policy tools are the setting of reserve requirements for member banks, control of the discount, and open market operations. Formally, authority to use these tools is allocated to the FRB, the Federal Reserve Bank boards of directors, and the FOMC, respectively. In actuality, however, all three are dominated by the FRB, which in recent decades has been under the sway of its chair. Arthur Burns and Paul Volcker (past chairs) and Alan Greenspan, the current chair, have been influential and respected policymakers. Much attention is given by public officials and the financial community to the utterances of the Fed's chair for clues to the future course of monetary policy.

money
A system of exchange for goods and services that includes currency, coins, and bank deposits.

Federal Reserve Board
A seven-member board that sets member banks' reserve requirements, controls the discount rate, and makes other economic decisions.

WEB EXPLORATION
To learn more about regulation of financial markets via the Federal Reserve Board, go to www.ablongman.com/oconnor

Federal Reserve Board Chair Alan Greenspan helped shepherd the economy through one of its longest stretches of economic expansion. (Photo courtesy: Doug Mills/AP/Wide World Photos)

POLITICS NOW

A VOLATILE STOCK MARKET

The stock market is believed to be a predictor of future economic vitality. A positive stock market can also enhance an individual's wealth. Higher stock prices can lead to greater spending as individuals may sell some of their stock or simply have the confidence to spend more of their disposable income. This "wealth effect" can have a beneficial effect on growth in the overall economy.

In the late 1990s, stock prices soared, especially those related to the Internet or technology. Regardless of lackluster or even nonexistent profits, investors poured money into companies that promised to dominate the economy of the future. Confidence in these stocks, however, eroded over time. The seemingly unrelenting rise in stock prices and faith in future profitability gave way to several steep downturns and a severe slashing of some stock prices. Many stocks remain strong, but investors have discovered that no good thing lasts forever, and many have replaced confidence with caution.

In May 2000, a scenario that had become all too familiar to investors in previous months played itself out again. The Nasdaq, heavily rooted in technology names, dropped 172.63 points, or 4.36 percent. Associated more with industry and consumer-product stocks, the Dow Jones Industrial Average fell a less drastic 80.66 points or 0.75 percent. The drop in the market was attributed primarily to AT&T's decline of 14 percent after the company cut its earnings forecasts. AT&T's drop impacted people's feelings about the market because of its position as a market leader. Contributing to the impression of volatility and lack of a clear direction, the early May 4.36 percent drop in the Nasdaq was preceded by a 13.7 percent gain during the five previous trading days. In June 2000, the Nasdaq declined by about 10 percent in just eight days. As Nasdaq was falling, the Dow Jones Industrial Average was rising 0.66 percent, or by approximately 70 points, led by gains in older companies that were thought to be better positioned to withstand a slowdown in the economy.

The stock market decline of late June was attributed to negative sales and earnings reports from large communications companies such as Nokia and WorldCom. Nokia's stock fell 25 per-

---

reserve requirements
Governmental requirements that a portion of member banks' deposits must be retained to back loans made.

discount rate
The interest rate at which member banks can borrow money from their regional Federal Reserve Bank.

The FRB has several policy tools. **Reserve requirements** designate the portion of the banks' deposits that must be retained as backing for their loans and are directly related to a bank's capacity to offer new loans. The rate of interest at which member banks can borrow money from their regional Federal Reserve Bank is the **discount rate**. In open market operations, government securities are bought and sold by the FRB in the market. The FRB can use moral suasion to influence the actions of banks and other members of the financial community by suggestion, exhortation, and informal agreement. Because of its commanding position as a monetary policy maker, much attention and respect are given by the media, economists, and market observers to verbal signals about economic trends and conditions emitted by the FRB and its chair.

cent in one day followings its report of sluggish sales, a loss of almost $66 billion in market value. The price of WorldCom, another communications company, slid 12 percent as some investors rotated toward safer-looking drug, oil, bank, and consumer-products stocks in the Dow Jones index.

Individual stocks, particularly e-retailers, have felt the impact of the market's instability. After an influential Lehman Brothers Inc. bond analyst issued a warning in June 2000 about the finances of the Internet retailer Amazon.com Inc., its stock price fell precipitously—below $33 from a high of $113. The stock price rebounded 20 percent in one day in July, after a Wall Street analyst issued a bright forecast. Other e-retailers, however, did not recover. Online stores like Boo.com and Toysmart.com shut down their Internet operation. The Nasdaq suffered from another decline in early October 2000, dipping below 3,500. Volatility in the Nasdaq was most evident. Since its creation in 1971, the Nasdaq has moved up or down as much as 5 percent on only twenty-one days. More than one-third of those days were experienced in the first four months of 2000, and two-thirds have come since the summer of 1997.

Despite the great volatility in the market and the demise of individual stocks, the performance of the overall market did not seem disastrous. In the first four months of 2000, the broad Standard & Poor's 500 stock index was down only 1.6 percent. Over that period the Dow industrials declined 6.7 percent and the Nasdaq was down 7 percent.

By the end of 2000, however, the Standard & Poor index was down more than 10 percent, its worst performance since 1977. The Dow was down more than six percent for the year while the Nasdaq declined by more than 39 percent, its worst performance since its founding in 1971. Internet stocks were particularly hard hit. From its March 2000 high to the end of the year, the street.com's index of Internet stocks plunged more than 77 percent leading many to question the continued economic health of the U.S.

Sources: E. S. Browning, "Rate Fears Send Nasdaq Down 4.36%—Blue Chips Fall 0.75% and Bond Prices Slip," *Wall Street Journal* (May 3, 2000): C1; John Schwarz, "Amazon.com Shares Up 20% on Forecast," *The Washington Post* (July 15, 2000): E2; E. S. Browning, "Nasdaq Composite Tumbles 3.65%—Profit Warnings Hit Tech Stocks," *Wall Street Journal.* (July 28, 2000): C1

How the FRB uses these tools depends in part on how it perceives the state of the economy. If inflation appears to be the problem, then the Fed would likely restrict or tighten the money supply. If a recession with rising unemployment appears to threaten the economy, then the FRB would probably act to loosen or expand the money supply in order to stimulate the economy.

Fiscal Policy: Taxing and Spending

Fiscal policy involves the deliberate use of the national government's taxing and spending policies to influence the overall operation of the economy and maintain economic stability. Fiscal policy is formulated by the president and Congress and is conducted through the federal

fiscal policy
Federal government policies on taxes, spending and debt management, intended to promote the nation's macroeconomic goals, particularly with respect to employment, price stability and growth.

WEB EXPLORATION
To learn about cur-
rent fiscal policy, go to
www.ablongman.com/oconnor

budget process. The powerful instruments of fiscal policy are budget surpluses and deficits. These are achieved by manipulating the overall or "aggregate" levels of revenue and expenditures.

According to standard fiscal policy theory, at some level of total or aggregate spending, the economy will operate at a full employment level. Total spending is the sum of consumer spending, private investment spending, and government spending. If consumer and business spending does not create demand sufficient to cause the economy to operate at full employment, then the government should make up the shortfall by increasing spending in excess of revenues. This was essentially what Keynes recommended the national government do during the Great Depression. If inflation is the problem confronting policy makers, then government can reduce demand for goods and services by reducing its expenditures and running a budget surplus.[15]

Discretionary fiscal policy involves deliberate decisions by the president and Congress to run budget surpluses or deficits. This can be done by increasing or decreasing spending while holding taxes constant; by increasing or cutting taxes while holding spending stable; or by some combination of changes in taxing and expenditure.

The first significant application of fiscal policy theory occurred in 1964. When John F. Kennedy, an activist president committed to getting the country "moving again," took office in 1961, he brought Keynesian economists to Washington as his economic advisers. These advisers believed that government action was needed to stimulate the economy in order to achieve full employment, and they were able to convince President Kennedy of this. The need, as they saw it, was for a budget deficit to add to aggregate demand. The problem was, however, that budget deficits were strongly opposed by many conservatives as bad public policy and perhaps even as immoral. Thinking strategically, President Kennedy's advisers decided that many conservatives and members of the business community would find deficits more palatable, or less objectionable, if they were achieved by cutting taxes rather than by increasing government spending. (Businesses had been complaining about high taxes.) Furthermore, a tax cut would increase private sector spending on goods and services. Higher government spending, on the other hand, would mean more spending on public goods and services and bigger government.

The result was the adoption of the Revenue Act of 1964, which reduced personal and corporate income tax rates. This variant of fiscal policy, which was more acceptable to the business community, has been labeled "commercial Keynesianism." The tax-cut stimulus contributed to the expansion of the economy through the remainder of the 1960s and reduced the unemployment rate to less than 4 percent, its lowest peacetime rate and what many people then considered to be full employment.

In 1968, Congress enacted a tax increase at the urging of the Johnson administration in order to restrain inflation, which was stimulated

POINT / COUNTERPOINT

WHO SHOULD BENEFIT THE MOST FROM TAX CUTS?

A recurring controversy in economic policy relates to the issues of how much to tax and who should pay the taxes. Preferences for one position or another can be easily traced to fundamental differences in assumptions and philosophies. These differing assumptions determine perspectives of fairness.

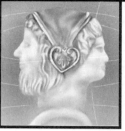

In general, conservatives on economic issues question the overall wisdom of expanding the government sector. Many of this persuasion advocate the position that the government that governs best is the one that governs least. They tend to fear the impact "big government" may have on personal liberties. Furthermore, economic conservatives are more skeptical of the value of anything connected with the public sector, contending that the private sector is more efficient and that expanding the size or scope of the public sector will result in lower levels of economic growth.

Due to skepticism over the value of government, economic conservatives prefer lower taxes and contend that tax cuts should be targeted to those at the upper end of the economic spectrum. They believe that these higher-income individuals pay the most taxes so they should get the most relief. In addition, they assume that targeting tax cuts to higher-income individuals will provide the proper incentives for risk taking, innovation, hard work, and productivity.

Economic liberals, on the other hand, take a contradictory view of the role of government and the position of taxes. Since they hold a much more positive view of government, they are less likely to advocate tax cuts and are more likely to subscribe to assumptions that underlie the progressive federal income tax. Progressive taxes are based on the perspective that those with higher abilities to pay (higher incomes) should pay more both in terms of absolute amounts paid and in terms of percentages of income. Advocates of progressive taxes argue that the marginal utility or marginal value of earnings for lower-income individuals is greater than the marginal utility of earnings for higher-income individuals. It is therefore efficient to take more money from those who earn more and need it less.

What do you think? Who should benefit from tax cuts?
Go to www.ablongman.com/oconnor

---

by increased spending for Great Society programs and the Vietnam War. The tax increase contributed to a balanced budget in fiscal year 1969, the last time the budget was balanced until 1998. Tax changes were also used during the 1970s to stabilize the economy. Beginning in the early 1980s and peaking in 1992, however, the government incurred large annual budget deficits. These deficits can be viewed as either "neutralizing" fiscal policy, because they politically foreclosed most major alterations in taxing and spending rates, or as a source of continuing stimulation to the economy.[16] Consequently, much of the burden of economic stabilization has been placed on FRB and monetary policy.

Continuity &Change

Exorcising the Deficit and Dealing with Surplus

In previous decades, America's economic policy was dominated by the scepter of deficits and debt. Beginning in the 1980s, as deficits seemed to explode, numerous economists warned of the dire consequences of this phenomenon. Economists asserted that deficits would increase the likelihood for:

- Increasing the supply of money, which would in turn lead to runaway inflation
- Crowding out or displacing private borrowers, which should increase interest rates and could reduce productivity as the scope of public sector activities expanded relative to those of the private sector
- Increasing the value of the dollar, which would contribute to the trade deficit
- Transferring money from middle-class taxpayers to upper-income bondholders
- Burdening future generations with debt obligations
- Transferring income from American citizens to citizens of other nations

In an effort to reduce the deficit, Congress passed various pieces of legislation in the 1980s and 1990s. Each plan relied on various mixtures of revenue enhancers (higher taxes) as well as spending cuts. Legislation of the 1980s and 1990s combined with a vibrant economy ultimately exorcised the deficit demon.

Unforeseen by many analysts, federal revenues began to surpass expenditures in 1999. This surplus environment shifted debate away from the question of what mix of tax increases and budget cuts were necessary to the newer question of how to spend the surplus. Should the funds be used to shore up Social Security or cut taxes? Should they be invested in an array of domestic programs? Some advocated investing government surplus funds in the stock market to yield a higher return on investments. Others were more skeptical about the wisdom of such actions, claiming that government bureaucrats should not wield so much influence on the private sector.

The new budget environment may be preoccupied with the best ways to spend the budget surplus, but some officials worry about earmarking the funds prematurely. Surpluses may disappear in the future as a result of generous tax breaks or economic downturn, both of which will result in lower levels of revenue. Unexpected expenditures such as military actions may further deplete government funds. If the experience of the "peace dividend" is an indication of future events, the impact of budget surpluses may be of brief duration.

1. In retrospect, what should Congress have done to eliminate deficits earlier?
2. How will budget surpluses change the nature of the debate over taxing and spending? What interests are likely to gain or lose in the new budget environment?

Cast Your Vote. How do you think the budget surplus should be spent? To cast your vote, go to **www.ablongman.com/oconnor**

SUMMARY

This chapter examined the policy-making process, social welfare policies, and economic policies. The policy-making process can be viewed as a sequence of functional activities beginning with the identification and definition of public problems. Once identified, problems must get on the governmental agenda. Other stages of the process include policy formulation, policy adoption, budgeting for policies, policy implementation, and the evaluation of policy.

The origins of social welfare policy can be traced back to early initiatives in the nation's history. Only after the Great Depression, however, was a public-sector role in the delivery of social services broadly accepted. Programs initiated in the Great Depression became a model for greater public-sector responsibilities in the area of social welfare.

Income security programs to relieve economic dependency and poverty were mostly handled by state and local governments, albeit in minimal fashion, through the nineteenth century. Most income security programs generally take two forms: non-means-based programs and means-tested programs, which indicate that all people who meet eligibility criteria are automatically entitled to receive benefits. Governments in the United States have a long history of involvement in the health of Americans. Most state and local governments have health departments, and the

U.S. government has several public health and medical research divisions. Medicare and Medicaid are the two most prominent national programs. As the cost of health care has risen, however, new demands have been made to restrain the rate of growth in costs.

Efforts by the national government to regulate the economy began with antimonopoly legislation. Under President Franklin D. Roosevelt, the interventionist state replaced the *laissez-faire* state. After World War II, many areas of economic policy were settled. Full employment, employee-employer relations, and social regulation became new concerns of government. Even before social regulation began to ebb, economic deregulation, which involves the reduction in the entry, rate, and other controls, emerged as an attractive political issue.

The national government continues to shape monetary policy by regulating the nation's money supply and interest rates. Monetary policy is controlled by the Federal Reserve Board. Fiscal policy, which involves the deliberate use of the national government's taxing and spending policies, is another tool of the national government and involves the president and Congress setting the national budget. Although the budget is initially suggested by the president, Congress has constitutional authority over the process.

KEY TERMS

agenda, p. 433
business cycles, p. 453
discount rate, p. 464
economic regulation, p. 458
economic stability, p. 462
entitlement program, p. 449
fiscal policy, p. 465
Federal Reserve Board, p. 463
governmental (institutional)
    agenda, p. 433

inflation, p. 462
interventionist state, p. 455
laissez-faire, p. 453
means-tested program, p. 442
monetary policy, p. 462
money, p. 463
non-means-based program,
    p. 442
policy adoption, p. 434
policy evaluation, p. 437

policy formulation, p. 433
policy implementation, p. 435
public policy, p. 430
recession, p. 462
reserve requirements, p. 464
social regulation, p. 458
Social Security Act, p. 440
social welfare policy, p. 439
systematic agenda, p. 433

SELECTED READINGS

Derthick, Martha, and Paul J. Quirk. *The Politics of Dereg-ulation.* Washington, D.C.: Brookings Institution, 1985.

Eisner, Marc Allen. *Regulatory Politics in Transition.* Baltimore, Md.: Johns Hopkins University Press, 1993.

Gold, Steven D., ed. *The Fiscal Crisis of the States.* Washington, D.C.: Georgetown University Press, 1995.

Harr, Johnathan. *A Civil Action.* New York: Random House, 1995.

Hart, Paul't. et. al., eds. *Beyond Groupthink: Political Group Dynamics and Foreign Policy Making.* Ann Arbor: University of Michigan Press, 1997.

Keech, William. *Economic Politics: The Costs of Democracy.* Cambridge: Cambridge University Press, 1995.

Kettl, Donald F. *Deficit Politics: Public Budgeting in Its Institutional and Historical Context.* New York: Macmillan, 1992.

Krugman, Paul. *The Age of Diminished Expectations.* Cambridge, Mass.: MIT Press, 1994.

LeLoup, Lance T., and Steven A. Shull. *Congress and the President: The Policy Connection.* Belmont, Calif.: Wadsworth, 1993.

Lindbloom, Charles E., and Edward J. Woodhouse. *The Policy-Making Process,* 3rd ed. Englewood Cliffs, N.J.: Prentice Hall, 1993.

Ripley, Randall B., and Grace A. Franklin. *Congress, the Bureacracy, and Public Policy,* 5th ed. Pacific Grove, Calif.: Brooks/Cole, 1991.

Sabatier, Paul A. *Theories of the Policy Process.* Boulder, Colo.: Westview Press, 1999

Stone, Deborah A. *Policy Paradox: The Art of Political Decision Making.* New York: W. W. Norton, 1997

Switzer, Jacqueline Vaughn. *Environmental Politics: Domestic and Global Dimension.* New York: St. Martin's, 1994.

Van Horn, Carl E., Donald C. Baumer, and William T. Gormley Jr. *Politics and Public Policy,* 2nd ed. Washington, D.C.: CQ Press, 1992.

Wilson, James Q., ed. *The Politics of Regulation.* New York: Basic Books, 1980.

Woolley, John T. *Monetary Politics: The Federal Reserve and the Politics of Monetary Policy.* London, England: Cambridge University Press, 1984.

THE DECLARATION OF INDEPENDENCE

In Congress, July 4, 1776

The Unanimous Declaration of the Thirteen United States of America

When in the Course of human events it becomes necessary for one people to dissolve the political bands which have connected them with another, and to assume, among the powers of the earth, the separate and equal station to which the Laws of Nature and of Nature's God entitle them, a decent respect to the opinions of mankind requires that they should declare the causes which impel them to the separation.

We hold these truths to be self-evident, that all men are created equal, that they are endowed by their Creator with certain unalienable Rights, that among these are Life, Liberty and the pursuit of Happiness. That to secure these rights, Governments are instituted among Men, deriving their just powers from the consent of the governed. That whenever any Form of Government becomes destructive of these ends, it is the Right of the People to alter or to abolish it, and to institute new Government, laying its foundation on such principles and organizing its powers in such form, as to them shall seem most likely to effect their Safety and Happiness. Prudence, indeed, will dictate that Governments long established should not be changed for light and transient causes; and accordingly all experience hath shewn that mankind are more disposed to suffer, while evils are sufferable, than to right themselves by abolishing the forms to which they are accustomed. But when a long train of abuses and usurpations, pursuing invariably the same Object evinces a design to reduce them under absolute Despotism, it is their right, it is their duty, to throw off such Government, and to provide new Guards for their future security.—Such has been the patient sufferance of these Colonies; and such is now the necessity which constrains them to alter their former Systems of Government. The history of the present King of Great Britain is a history of repeated injuries and usurpations, all having in direct object the establishment of an absolute Tyranny over these States. To prove this, let Facts be submitted to a candid world.

He has refused his Assent to Laws, the most wholesome and necessary for the public good.

He has forbidden his Governors to pass Laws of immediate and pressing importance, unless suspended in their operation till his Assent should be obtained; and when so suspended, he has utterly neglected to attend to them.

He has refused to pass other Laws for the accommodation of large districts of people, unless those people would relinquish the right of Representation in the Legislature, a right inestimable to them and formidable to tyrants only.

He has called together legislative bodies at places unusual, uncomfortable, and distant from the depository of their Public Records, for the sole purpose of fatiguing them into compliance with his measures.

He has dissolved Representative Houses repeatedly, for opposing with manly firmness his invasions on the rights of the people.

He has refused for a long time, after such dissolutions, to cause others to be elected; whereby the Legislative Powers, incapable of Annihilation, have returned to the People at large for their exercise, the State remaining in the mean time exposed to all the dangers of invasion from without, and convulsions within.

He has endeavored to prevent the population of these States; for that purpose obstructing the Laws of Naturalization of Foreigners; refusing to pass others to encourage their migration hither, and raising the conditions of new Appropriations of Lands.

He has obstructed the Administration of Justice, by refusing his Assent to Laws for establishing Judiciary powers.

He has made Judges dependent on his Will alone, for the tenure of their offices, and the amount and payment of their salaries.

He has erected a multitude of New Offices, and sent hither swarms of Officers to harass our people, and eat out their substance.

He has kept among us, in times of peace, Standing Armies without the Consent of our legislatures.

He has affected to render the Military independent of and superior to the Civil power.

He has combined with others to subject us to a jurisdiction foreign to our constitution, and unacknowledged by our laws, giving his Assent to their Acts of pretended Legislation:

For quartering large bodies of armed troops among us:

For protecting them, by a mock Trial, from punishment for any Murders which they should commit on the Inhabitants of these States:

For cutting off our Trade with all parts of the world:

For imposing Taxes on us without our Consent:

For depriving us in many cases, of the benefits of Trial by Jury:

For transporting us beyond Seas to be tried for pretended offences:

For abolishing the free System of English Laws in a neighboring Province, establishing therein an Arbitrary government, and enlarging its Boundaries so as to render it at once an example and fit instrument for introducing the same absolute rule into these Colonies:

For taking away our Charters, abolishing our most valuable Laws, and altering fundamentally the Forms of our Governments:

For suspending our own Legislatures, and declaring themselves invested with power to legislate for us in all cases whatsoever.

He has abdicated Government here, by declaring us out of his Protection and waging War against us.

He has plundered our seas, ravaged our Coasts, burnt out towns, and destroyed the lives of our people.

He is at this time transporting large Armies of foreign Mercenaries to compleat the works of death, desolation and tyranny, already begun with circumstances of Cruelty and perfidy scarcely paralleled in the most barbarous ages, and totally unworthy the Head of a civilized nation.

He has constrained our fellow Citizens taken Captive on the high Seas to bear Arms against their Country, to become the executioners of their friends and Brethren, or to fall themselves by their Hands.

He has excited domestic insurrections amongst us, and has endeavored to bring on the inhabitants of our frontiers, the merciless Indian Savages, whose known rule of warfare, is an undistinguished destruction of all ages, sexes and conditions.

In every stage of these Oppressions We have Petitioned for Redress in the most humble terms: Our repeated Petitions have been answered only by repeated injury: A Prince, whose character is thus marked by every act which may define a Tyrant, is unfit to be the ruler of a free people.

Nor have We been wanting in attention to our

British brethren. We have warned them from time to time of attempts by their legislature to extend an unwarrantable jurisdiction over us. We have reminded them of the circumstances of our emigration and settlement here. We have appealed to their native justice and magnanimity; and we have conjured them by the ties of our common kindred to disavow these usurpations, which would inevitably interrupt our connections and correspondence. They too have been deaf to the voice of justice and consanguinity. We must, therefore, acquiesce in the necessity, which denounces our Separation, and hold them, as we hold the rest of mankind, Enemies in War, in Peace Friends.

We, therefore, the Representatives of the United States of America, in General Congress, Assembled, appealing to the Supreme Judge of the world for the rectitude of our intentions, do, in the Name, and by Authority of the good People of these Colonies, solemnly publish and declare, That these United Colonies are, and of Right ought to be Free and Independent States; that they are Absolved from all Allegiance to the British Crown, and that all political connection between them and the State of Great Britain, is and ought to be totally dissolved: and that as Free and Independent States, they have full power to levy War, conclude Peace, contract Alliances, establish Commerce, and to do all other Acts and Things which Independent States may of right do. And for the support of this Declaration, with a firm reliance on the protection of divine Providence, we mutually pledge to each other our Lives, our Fortunes and our sacred Honor.

JOHN HANCOCK,

Attest
CHARLES THOMSON,
Secretary

NEW HAMPSHIRE
Josiah Bartlett,
Wm. Whipple,
Matthew Thornton.

MASSACHUSETTS BAY
Saml. Adams,
John Adams,
Robt. Treat Paine,
Elbridge Gerry.

RHODE ISLAND
Step. Hopkins,
William Ellery.

CONNECTICUT
Roger Sherman,
Samuel Huntington,
Wm. Williams,
Oliver Wolcott.

NEW YORK
Wm. Floyd,
Phil. Livingston,
Frans. Lewis,
Lewis Morris

NEW JERSEY
Richd. Stockton,
J. Witherspoon,
Fras. Hopkinson,
John Hart,
Abra. Clark.

PENNSYLVANIA
Robt. Morris,
Benjamin Rush,
Benjamin Franklin,
John Morton,
Geo. Clymer,
Jas. Smith,
Geo. Taylor,
James Wilson,
Geo. Ross.

DELAWARE
Caesar Rodney,
Geo. Read,
Tho. McKean.

MARYLAND
Samuel Chase,
Wm. Paca,
Thos. Stone,
Charles Caroll
    of Carollton.

VIRGINIA
George Wythe,
Richard Henry Lee,
Th. Jefferson,
Benjamin Harrison,
Thos. Nelson, jr.,
Francis Lightfoot Lee,
Carter Braxton.

NORTH CAROLINA
Wm. Hooper,
Joseph Hewes,
John Penn.

SOUTH CAROLINA
Edward Rutledge,
Thos. Heyward, Junr.,
Thomas Lynch, jnr.,
Arthur Middleton.

GEORGIA
Button Gwinnett,
Lyman Hall,
Geo. Walton.

THE CONSTITUTION OF THE UNITED STATES OF AMERICA

W e the People of the United States, in Order to form a more perfect Union, establish Justice, insure domestic Tranquility, provide for the common defence, promote the general Welfare, and secure the Blessings of Liberty to ourselves and our Posterity, do ordain and establish this Constitution for the United States of America.

ARTICLE I

SECTION 1. All legislative Powers herein granted shall be vested in a Congress of the United States, which shall consist of a Senate and House of Representatives.

SECTION 2. The House of Representatives shall be composed of Members chosen every second Year by the People of the several States, and the Electors in each State shall have the Qualifications requisite for Electors of the most numerous Branch of the State Legislature.

No person shall be a Representative who shall not have attained to the Age of twenty five Years, and been seven Years a Citizen of the United States, and who shall not, when elected, be an Inhabitant of that State in which he shall be chosen.

Representatives and direct Taxes shall be apportioned among the several States which may be included within this Union, according to their respective Numbers which shall be determined by adding to the whole Number of free Persons, including those bound to Service for a Term of Years, and excluding Indians not taxed, three fifths of all other Persons. The actual Enumeration shall be made within three Years after the first Meeting of the Congress of the United States, and within every subsequent Term ten Years, in such Manner as they shall by Law direct. The Number of Representatives shall not exceed one for every thirty Thousand, but each State shall have at Least one Representative; and until such enumeration shall be made, the State of New Hampshire shall be entitled to chuse three, Massachusetts eight, Rhode-Island and Providence Plantations one, Connecticut five, New-York six, New Jersey four, Pennsylvania eight, Delaware one, Maryland six, Virginia ten, North Carolina five, South Carolina five, and Georgia three.

When vacancies happen in the Representation from any State, the Executive Authority thereof shall issue Writs of Election to fill such Vacancies.

The House of Representatives shall chuse their speaker and other Officers; and shall have the sole Power of Impeachment.

SECTION 3. The Senate of the United States shall be composed of two Senators from each State chosen by the Legislature thereof, for six Years; and each Senator shall have one Vote.

Immediately after they shall be assembled in Consequence of the first Election, they shall be divided as equally as may be into three Classes. The Seats of the Senators of the first Class shall be vacated at the Expiration of the second year, of the second Class at the Expiration of the fourth Year, and of the third

Class at the Expiration of the sixth Year, so that one third may be chosen every second Year and if Vacancies happen by Resignation, or otherwise, during the Recess of the Legislature of any State, the Executive thereof may make temporary Appointments until the next Meeting of the Legislature, which shall then fill such Vacancies.

No Person shall be a Senator who shall not have attained to the Age of thirty Years, and been nine Years a Citizen of the United States, and who shall not, when elected, be an Inhabitant of that State for which he shall be chosen.

The Vice President of the United States shall be President of the Senate, but shall have no Vote, unless they be equally divided.

The Senate shall chuse their other Officers, and also a President pro tempore, in the Absence of the Vice President, or when he shall exercise the Office of President of the United States.

The Senate shall have the sole Power to try all Impeachments. When sitting for that Purpose, they shall be on Oath or Affirmation. When the President of the United States is tried, the Chief Justice shall preside: And no Person shall be convicted without the Concurrence of two thirds of the Members present.

Judgment in Cases of Impeachment shall not extend further than to removal from Office, and disqualification to hold and enjoy any Office of honor, Trust or Profit under the United States; but the Party convicted shall nevertheless be liable and subject to Indictment, Trial, Judgment and Punishment, according to Law.

SECTION 4. The Times, Places and Manner of holding Elections for Senators and Representatives, shall be prescribed in each State by the Legislature thereof; but the Congress may at any time by law make or alter such Regulations, except as to the Places of chusing Senators.

The Congress shall assemble at least once in every Year, and such Meeting shall be on the first Monday in December, unless they shall by Law appoint a different Day.

SECTION 5. Each House shall be the Judge of the Elections, Returns and Qualifications of its own Members, and a Majority of each shall constitute a Quorum to do Business; but a smaller Number may adjourn from day to day, and may be authorized to compel the Attendance of absent Members, in such Manner, and under such Penalties as each House may provide.

Each House may determine the Rules of its Proceedings, punish its Members for disorderly Behaviour, and with the Concurrence of two thirds, expel a Member.

Each House shall keep a journal of its Proceedings, and from time to time publish the same, excepting such Parts as may in their judgment require Secrecy; and the Yeas and Nays of the Members of either House on any question shall, at the Desire of one fifth of those present, be entered on the Journal.

Neither House, during the Session of Congress, shall, without the Consent of the other, adjourn for more than three days, nor to any other Place than that in which the two Houses shall be sitting.

SECTION 6. The Senators and Representatives shall receive a Compensation for their Services, to be ascertained by Law, and paid out of the Treasury of the United States. They shall in all Cases, except Treason, Felony and Breach of the Peace, be privileged from Arrest during their Attendance at the Session of their respective Houses, and in going to and returning from the same; and for any Speech or Debate in either House, they shall not be questioned in any other Place.

No Senator or Representative shall, during the Time for which he was elected, be appointed to any civil Office under the Authority of the United States, which shall have been created, or the Emoluments whereof shall have been encreased during such time; and no Person holding any Office under the United States, shall be a Member of either House during his Continuance in Office.

SECTION 7. All Bills for raising Revenue shall originate in the House of Representatives; but the Senate may propose or concur with Amendments as on other Bills.

Every Bill which shall have passed the House of Representatives and the Senate, shall, before it become a Law, be presented to the President of the United States; If he approves he shall sign it, but if not he shall return it, with his Objections to that

House in which it shall have originated, who shall enter the Objections at large on their journal, and proceed to reconsider it. If after such Reconsideration two thirds of that House shall agree to pass the Bill, it shall be sent, together with the Objections, to the other House, by which it shall likewise be reconsidered, and if approved by two thirds of that House, it shall become a Law. But in all such Cases the Votes of both Houses shall be determined by Yeas and Nays, and the Names of the Persons voting for and against the Bill shall be entered on the Journal of each House respectively. If any Bill shall not be returned by the President within ten Days (Sundays excepted) after it shall have been presented to him, the Same shall be a Law, in like Manner as if he had signed it, unless the Congress by their Adjournment prevent its Return, in which Case it shall not be a Law.

Every Order, Resolution, or Vote to which the Concurrence of the Senate and House of Representatives may be necessary (except on a question of Adjournment) shall be presented to the President of the United States; and before the Same shall take Effect, shall be approved by him, or being disapproved by him, shall be repassed by two thirds of the Senate and House of Representatives, according to the Rules and Limitations prescribed in the Case of a Bill.

SECTION 8. The Congress shall have Power To lay and collect Taxes, Duties, Imposts and Excises, to pay the Debts and provide for the common Defence and general Welfare of the United States; but all Duties, Imposts and Excises shall be uniform throughout the United States;

To borrow Money on the credit of the United States;

To regulate Commerce with foreign Nations, and among the several States, and with the Indian Tribes;

To establish a uniform Rule of Naturalization, and uniform Laws on the subject of Bankruptcies throughout the United States;

To coin Money, regulate the Value thereof, and of foreign Coin, and fix the Standard of Weights and Measures;

To provide for the Punishment of counterfeiting the Securities and current Coin of the United States;

To establish Post Offices and post Roads;

To promote the Progress of Science and useful Arts, by securing for limited Times to Authors and Inventors the exclusive Right to their respective Writings and Discoveries;

To constitute Tribunals inferior to the supreme Court;

To define and punish Piracies and Felonies committed on the high Seas, and Offences against the Law of Nations;

To declare War, grant Letters of Marque and Reprisal, and make Rules concerning Captures on Land and Water;

To raise and support Armies, but no Appropriation of Money to that Use shall be for a longer Term than two Years;

To provide and maintain a Navy;

To make Rules for the Government and Regulation of the land and naval Forces;

To provide for calling forth the Militia to execute the Laws of the Union, suppress Insurrections and repel Invasions;

To provide for organizing, arming, and disciplining, the Militia, and for governing such Part of them as may be employed in the Service of the United States, reserving to the States respectively, the Appointment of the Officers, and the Authority of training the Militia according to the discipline prescribed by Congress;

To exercise exclusive Legislation in all Cases whatsoever, over such District (not exceeding ten Miles square) as may, by Cession of particular States, and the Acceptance of Congress, become the Seat of the Government of the United States, and to exercise like Authority over all Places purchased by the Consent of the Legislature of the State in which the Same shall be for the Erection of Forts, Magazines, Arsenals, dock-Yards, and other needful Buildings;—And

To make all Laws which shall be necessary and proper for carrying into Execution the foregoing Powers, and all other Powers vested by this Constitution in the Government of the United States, or in any Department or Officer thereof.

SECTION 9. The Migration or Importation of such Persons as any of the States now existing shall think proper to admit, shall not be prohibited by the Congress prior to the Year one thousand eight hundred and eight, but a Tax or duty may be imposed on such Importation, not exceeding ten dollars for each Person.

The Privilege of the Writ of Habeas Corpus shall not be suspended, unless when in Cases of Rebellion or Invasion the public Safety may require it.

No Bill of Attainder or ex post facto Law shall be passed.

No Capitation, or other direct, Tax shall be laid, unless in Proportion to the Census or Enumeration herein before directed to be taken.

No Tax or Duty shall be laid on Articles exported from any State.

No Preference shall be given by any Regulation of Commerce or Revenue to the Ports of one State over those of another; nor shall Vessels bound to, or from, one State, be obliged to enter, clear, or pay Duties in another.

No Money shall be drawn from the Treasury, but in Consequence of Appropriations made by Law; and a regular Statement and Account of the Receipts and Expenditures of all public Money shall be published from time to time.

No Title of Nobility shall be granted by the United States: And no Person holding any Office of Profit or Trust under them, shall, without the Consent of the Congress, accept of any present, Emolument, Office, or Title, of any kind whatever, from any King, Prince, or foreign State.

SECTION 10. No state shall enter into any Treaty, Alliance, or Confederation; grant Letters of Marque and Reprisal; coin Money; emit Bills of Credit; make any Thing but gold and silver Coin a Tender in Payment of Debts; pass any Bill of Attainder, ex post facto Law, or Law impairing the Obligation of Contracts, or grant any Title of Nobility.

No State shall, without the Consent of the Congress, lay any Imposts or Duties on Imports or Exports, except what may be absolutely necessary for executing its inspection Laws: and the net Produce of all Duties and Imposts, laid by any State on Imports or Exports, shall be for the Use of the Treasury of the United States, and all such Laws shall be subject to the Revision and Controul of the Congress.

No State shall, without the Consent of Congress, lay any Duty of Tonnage, keep Troops, or Ships of War in time of Peace, enter into any Agreement or Compact with another State, or with a foreign Power, or engage in War, unless actually invaded, or in such imminent Danger as will not admit of delay.

ARTICLE II

SECTION 1. The executive Power shall be vested in a President of the United States of America. He shall hold his Office during the Term of four Years, and, together with the Vice President, chosen for the same Term, be elected as follows.

Each State shall appoint, in such Manner as the Legislature thereof may direct, a Number of Electors, equal to the whole Number of Senators and Representatives to which the State may be entitled in the Congress; but no Senator or Representative, or Person holding an Office of Trust of Profit under the United States, shall be appointed an Elector.

The Electors shall meet in their respective States, and vote by Ballot for two Persons, of whom one at least shall not be an Inhabitant of the same State with themselves. And they shall make a List of all the Persons voted for, and, of the Number of Votes for each; which List they shall sign and certify, and transmit sealed to the Seat of the Government of the United States, directed to the President of the Senate. The President of the Senate shall, in the Presence of the Senate and House of Representatives, open all the Certificates, and the Votes shall then be counted. The Person having the greatest Number of Votes shall be the President, if such Number be a Majority of the whole Number of Electors appointed; and if there be more than one who have such Majority, and have an equal Number of Votes, then the House of Representatives shall immediately chuse by Ballot one of them for President; and if no Person have a Majority, then from the five highest on the List the said House shall in like Manner chuse the President. But in chusing the President, the Votes shall be taken by States, the Representation from each State having one Vote; A quorum for this Purpose shall consist of a Member or Members from two thirds of the States, and a Majority of all the States shall be necessary to a Choice. In every Case, after the Choice of the President, the Person having the greatest Number of Votes of the Electors shall be the Vice President. But if there should remain two or more who have equal Votes, the Senate shall chuse from them by Ballot the Vice President.

The Congress may determine the Time of chusing the Electors, and the Day on which they shall give their Votes; which Day shall be the same throughout the United States.

No Person except a natural born Citizen, or a Citizen of the United States, at the time of the Adoption of this Constitution, shall be eligible to the Office of President; neither shall any Person be eligible to that Office who shall not have attained to the Age of thirty five Years, and been fourteen Years a Resident within the United States.

In Case of the Removal of the President from Office, or of his Death, Resignation, or Inability to discharge the Powers and Duties of the said Office, the Same shall devolve on the Vice President, and the Congress may by Law provide for the Case of Removal, Death, Resignation or Inability, both of the President and Vice President, declaring what Officer shall then act as President, and such Officer shall act accordingly, until the Disability be removed, or a President shall be elected.

The President shall, at stated Times, receive for his Services, a Compensation, which shall neither be encreased nor diminished during the Period for which he shall have been elected, and he shall not receive within that Period any other Emolument from the United States, or any of them.

Before he enter on the Execution of his Office, he shall take the following Oath or Affirmation— "I do solemnly swear (or affirm) that I will faithfully execute the Office of President of the United States, and will to the best of my Ability, preserve, protect and defend the Constitution of the United States."

SECTION 2. The President shall be Commander in Chief of the Army, and Navy of the United States, and of the Militia of the several States, when called into the actual Service of the United States; he may require the Opinion, in writing, of the principal Officer in each of the executive Departments, upon any Subject relating to the Duties of their respective Offices, and he shall have Power to grant Reprieves and Pardons for Offences against the United States, except in Cases of Impeachment.

He shall have Power, by and with the Advice and Consent of the Senate, to make Treaties, provided two thirds of the Senators present concur; and he shall nominate, and by and with the Advice and Consent of the Senate, shall appoint Ambassadors, other public Ministers and Consuls, Judges of the supreme Court, and all other Officers of the United States, whose Appointments are not herein otherwise provided for, and which shall be established by Law: but the Congress may by Law vest the Appointment of such inferior Officers, as they think proper, in the President alone, in the Courts of Law, or in the Heads of Departments.

The President shall have Power to fill up all Vacancies that may happen during the Recess of the Senate, by granting Commissions which shall expire at the end of their next Session.

SECTION 3. He shall from time to time give to the Congress Information of the State of the Union, and recommend to their Consideration such Measures as he shall judge necessary and expedient; he may, on extraordinary Occasions, convene both Houses, or either of them, and in Case of Disagreement between them, with Respect to the Time of Adjournment, he may adjourn them to such Time as he shall think proper; he shall receive Ambassadors and other public Ministers; he shall take Care that the Laws be faithfully executed, and shall Commission all the Officers of the United States.

SECTION 4. The President, Vice President and all civil Officers of the United States, shall be removed from Office on Impeachment for, and Conviction of, Treason, Bribery, or other high Crimes and Misdemeanors.

ARTICLE III

SECTION 1. The judicial Power of the United States, shall be vested in one supreme Court, and in such inferior Courts as the Congress may from time to time ordain and establish. The Judges, both of the supreme and inferior Courts, shall hold their Offices during good Behaviour, and shall, at stated Times, receive for their Services, a Compensation, which shall not be diminished during their Continuance in Office.

SECTION 2. The judicial Power shall extend to all Cases, in Law and Equity, arising under this Constitution, the Laws of the United States, and Treaties made, or which shall be made, under their Authority;—to all Cases affecting Ambassadors, other public Ministers and Consuls;—to all Cases of admiralty and maritime Jurisdiction;—to Controversies to which the United States shall be a Party;—to Controversies between two or more States;—between a State and Citizens of another State;—between Citizens of different States,—between Citizens of the same State claiming Lands under Grants of different States,—and between a State, or the Citizens thereof, and foreign States, Citizens of Subjects.

In all Cases affecting Ambassadors, other public Ministers and Consuls, and those in which a State shall be Party, the supreme Court shall have original Jurisdiction. In all the other Cases before mentioned, the supreme Court shall have appellate Jurisdiction, both as to Law and Fact, with such Exceptions, and under such Regulations as the Congress shall make.

The Trial of all Crimes, except in Cases of Impeachment, shall be by Jury; and such Trial shall be held in the State where the said Crimes shall have been committed; but when not committed within any State, the Trial shall be at such Place or Places as the Congress may by Law have directed.

SECTION 3. Treason against the United States, shall consist only in levying War against them, or in adhering to their Enemies, giving them Aid and Comfort. No Person shall be convicted of Treason unless on the Testimony of two Witnesses to the same overt Act, or on Confession in open Court.

The Congress shall have Power to declare the Punishment of Treason, but no Attainder of Treason shall work Corruption of Blood, or Forfeiture except during the Life of the Person attainted.

ARTICLE IV

SECTION 1. Full Faith and Credit shall be given in each State to the public Acts, Records, and judicial Proceedings of every other State. And the Congress may by general Laws prescribe the Manner in which such Acts, Records and Proceedings shall be proved, and the Effect thereof.

SECTION 2. The Citizens of each State shall be entitled to all Privileges and Immunities of Citizens in the several States.

A Person charged in any State with Treason, Felony, or other Crime, who shall flee from Justice, and be found in another State, shall on Demand of the executive Authority of the State from which he fled, be delivered up, to be removed to the State having Jurisdiction of the Crime.

No Person held to Service or Labour in one State under the Laws thereof, escaping into another, shall, in Consequence of any Law or Regulation therein, be discharged from such Service or Labour, but shall be delivered up on Claim of the Party to whom such Service or Labour may be due.

SECTION 3. New States may be admitted by the Congress into this Union; but no new State shall be formed or erected within the Jurisdiction of any other State; nor any State be formed by the Junction of two or more States, or Parts of States, without the Consent of the Legislatures of the States concerned as well as of the Congress.

The Congress shall have Power to dispose of and make all needful Rules and Regulations respecting the Territory or other Property belonging to the United States; and nothing in this Constitution shall be so construed as to Prejudice any Claims of the United States, or of any particular State.

SECTION 4. The United States shall guarantee to every State in this Union a Republican Form of Government, and shall protect each of them against Invasion, and on Application of the Legislature, or of the Executive (when the Legislature cannot be convened) against domestic Violence.

ARTICLE V

The Congress, whenever two thirds of both Houses shall deem it necessary, shall propose Amendments to this Constitution, or, on the Application of the Legislatures of two thirds of the several States, shall call a Convention for proposing Amendments, which, in either Case, shall be valid to all Intents and Purposes, as Part of this Constitution, when ratified by the Legislatures of three fourths of the several States, or by Conventions in three fourths thereof, as the one or the other Mode of Ratification may be proposed by the Congress; Provided that no Amendment which may be made prior to the Year One thousand eight hundred and eight shall in any Manner affect the first and fourth Clauses in the Ninth Section of the first Article; and that no State, without its Consent, shall be deprived of its equal Suffrage in the Senate.

ARTICLE VI

All Debts contracted and Engagements entered into, before the Adoption of this Constitution, shall be as valid against the United States under this Constitution, as under the Confederation.

This Constitution, and the laws of the United States which shall be made in Pursuance thereof; and all Treaties made, or which shall be made, under the Authority of the United States, shall be the supreme Law of the Land; and the Judges in every State shall be bound thereby, any Thing in the Constitution or Laws of any State to the Contrary notwithstanding.

The Senators and Representatives before mentioned, and the Members of the several State Legislatures, and all executive and judicial Officers, both of the United States and of the several States, shall be bound by Oath or Affirmation, to support this Constitution; but no religious Test shall ever be required as a Qualification to any Office or public Trust under the United States.

ARTICLE VII

The Ratification of the Conventions of nine States, shall be sufficient for the Establishment of this Constitution between the States so ratifying the Same.

Done in Convention by the Unanimous Consent of the States present the Seventeenth Day of September in the Year of our Lord one thousand seven hundred and Eighty seven and of the Independence of the United States of America the Twelfth. IN WITNESS whereof we have hereunto subscribed our Names,

Go. WASHINGTON,
Presid't. and deputy from Virginia

Attest
WILLIAM JACKSON,
Secretary

DELAWARE
Geo. Read,
Gunning Bedford jun,
John Dickinson,
Richard basset,
Jaco. Broom.

MASSACHUSETTS BAY
Nathaniel Gorham,
Rufus King.

CONNECTICUT
Wm. Saml. Johnson,
Roger Sherman.

NEW YORK
Alexander Hamilton.

NEW JERSEY
Wi. Livingston,
David Brearley,
Wm. Paterson,
Jona. Dayton.

PENNSYLVANIA
B. Franklin,
Thomas Mifflin,
Robt. Morris,
Geo. Clymer,
Thos. FitzSimons,
Jared Ingersoll,
James Wilson,
Gouv. Morris

NEW HAMPSHIRE
John Langdon,
Nicholas Gilman.

MARYLAND
James McHenry,
Dan of St. Thos.
  Jenifer,
Danl. Carroll.

VIRGINIA
John Blair,
James Madison, Jr..

NORTH CAROLINA
Wm. Blount,
Richd. Dobbs Spaight,
Hu. Williamson.

SOUTH CAROLINA
J. Rutledge,
Charles Cotesworth
  Pinckney,
Charles Pinckney.
Pierce Butler

GEORGIA
William Few,
Abr. Baldwin

Articles in addition to, and amendment of the Constitution of the United States of America, proposed by Congress and ratified by the Legislatures of the several states, pursuant to the Fifth Article of the original Constitution.

(The first ten amendments were passed by Congress on September 25, 1789, and were ratified on December 15, 1791.)

AMENDMENT I

Congress shall make no law respecting an establishment of religion, or prohibiting the free exercise thereof; or abridging the freedom of speech, or of the press; or the right of the people peaceably to assemble, and to petition the Government for a redress of grievances.

AMENDMENT II

A well regulated Militia, being necessary to the security of a free State, the right of the people to keep and bear Arms, shall not be infringed.

AMENDMENT III

No Soldier shall, in time of peace be quartered in any house, without the consent of the Owner, nor in time of war, but in a manner to be prescribed by law.

AMENDMENT IV

The right of the people to be secure in their persons, houses, papers, and effects, against unreasonable searches and seizures, shall not be violated, and no warrants shall issue, but upon probable cause, supported by Oath or affirmation, and particularly describing the place to be searched, and the persons or things to be seized.

AMENDMENT V

No person shall be held to answer for a capital, or otherwise infamous crime, unless on a presentment or indictment of a Grand Jury, except in cases arising in the land or naval forces, or in the Militia, when in actual service in time of War or public danger; nor shall any person be subject for the same offence to be twice put in jeopardy of life or limb; nor shall be compelled in any criminal case to be a witness against himself, nor be deprived of life, liberty, or property, without due process of law; nor shall private property be taken for public use, without just compensation.

AMENDMENT VI

In all criminal prosecutions, the accused shall enjoy the right to a speedy and public trial, by an impartial jury of the State and district wherein the crime shall have been committed, which district shall have been previously ascertained by law, and to be informed of the nature and cause of the accusation; to be confronted with the witnesses against him; to have compulsory process for obtaining witnesses in his favor, and to have the assistance of counsel for his defence.

AMENDMENT VII

In Suits at common law, where the value in controversy shall exceed twenty dollars, the right of trial by jury shall be preserved, and no fact tried by a jury, shall be otherwise re-examined in any Court of the United States, than according to the rules of the common law.

AMENDMENT VIII

Excessive bail shall not be required, nor excessive fines imposed, nor cruel and unusual punishments inflicted.

AMENDMENT IX

The enumeration in the Constitution, of certain rights, shall not be construed to deny or disparage others retained by the people.

AMENDMENT X

The powers not delegated to the United States by the Constitution, nor prohibited by it to the States, are reserved to the States respectively, or to the people.

AMENDMENT XI *(Ratified on February 7, 1795)*

The Judicial power of the United States shall not be construed to extend to any suit in law or equity, commenced or prosecuted against one of the United States by Citizens of another State, or by Citizens or Subjects of any Foreign State.

AMENDMENT XII *(Ratified on June 15, 1804)*

The Electors shall meet in their respective states, and vote by ballot for President and Vice-President, one of whom, at least, shall not be an inhabitant of the same state with themselves; they shall name in their ballots the person voted for as President, and in distinct ballots the person voted for as Vice-President, and they shall make distinct lists of all persons voted for as President, and of all persons voted for as Vice-President, and of the number of votes for each, which lists they shall sign and certify, and transmit sealed to the seat of the government of the United States, directed to the President of the Senate;—The President of the Senate shall, in the presence of the Senate and House of Representatives, open all the certificates and the votes shall then be counted;—The person having the greatest number of votes for President, shall be the President, if such number be a majority of the whole number of Electors appointed; and if no person have such majority; then from the persons having the highest numbers not exceeding three on the list of those voted for as President, the House of Representatives shall choose immediately, by ballot, the President. But in choosing the President, the votes shall be taken by states, the representation from each state having one vote; a quorum for this purpose shall consist of a member or members from two-thirds of the states, and a majority of all the states shall be necessary to a choice. And if the House of Representatives shall not choose a President whenever the right of choice shall devolve upon them, before the fourth day of March next following, then the Vice-President shall act as President, as in the case of the death or other constitutional disability of the President.—The person having the greatest number of votes as Vice-President, shall be the Vice-President, if such number be a majority of the whole number of Electors appointed, and if no person have a majority, then from the two highest numbers on the list, the Senate shall choose the Vice-President; a quorum for the purpose shall consist of two-thirds of the whole number of Senators, and a majority of the whole number shall be necessary to a choice. But no person constitutionally ineligible to the office of President shall be eligible to that of Vice-President of the United States.

AMENDMENT XIII *(Ratified on December 6, 1865)*

SECTION 1. Neither slavery nor involuntary servitude, except as a punishment for crime whereof the party shall have been duly convicted, shall exist within the United States, or any place subject to their jurisdiction.

SECTION 2. Congress shall have power to enforce this article by appropriate legislation.

AMENDMENT XIV *(Ratified on July 9, 1868)*

SECTION 1. All persons born or naturalized in the United States, and subject to the jurisdiction thereof, are citizens of the United States and of the State wherein they reside. No State shall make or enforce any law which shall abridge the privileges or immunities of citizens of the United States; nor shall any State deprive any person of life, liberty, or property, without due process of law; nor deny to any person within its jurisdiction the equal protection of the laws.

SECTION 2. Representatives shall be apportioned among the several States according to their respective numbers, counting the whole number of persons in each State, excluding Indians not taxed. But when the right to vote at any election for the choice of electors for President and Vice President of the United States, Representatives in Congress, the Executive and Judicial officers of a State, or the members of the Legislature thereof, is denied to any of the male inhabitants of such State, being twenty-one years of age, and citizens of the United States, or in any way abridged, except for participation in rebellion, or other crime, the basis of representation therein shall be reduced in the proportion which the number of such male citizens shall bear to the whole number of male citizens twenty-one years of age in such State.

SECTION 3. No person shall be a Senator or Representative in Congress, or elector of President and Vice President, or hold any office, civil or military, under the United States, or under any State, who, having previously taken an oath, as a member of Congress, or as an officer of the United States, or as a member of any State legislature, or as an executive or judicial officer of any State, to support the

Constitution of the United States, shall have engaged in insurrection or rebellion against the same, or given aid or comfort to the enemies thereof. But Congress may by a vote of two-thirds of each House, remove such diability.

SECTION 4. The validity of the public debt of the United States, authorized by law, including debts incurred for payment of pensions and bounties for services in suppressing insurrection or rebellion, shall not be questioned. But neither the United States nor any State shall assume or pay any debt or obligation incurred in aid of insurrection or rebellion against the United States, or any claim for the loss or emancipation of any slave, but all such debts, obligations and claims shall be held illegal and void.

SECTION 5. The Congress shall have power to enforce, by appropriate legislation, the provisions of this article.

AMENDMENT XV *(Ratified on February 3, 1870)*

SECTION 1. The right of citizens of the United States to vote shall not be denied or abridged by the United States or by any State on account of race, color, or previous condition of servitude.

SECTION 2. The Congress shall have power to enforce this article by appropriate legislation.

AMENDMENT XVI *(Ratified on February 3, 1913)*

The Congress shall have power to lay and collect taxes on incomes, from whatever source derived, without apportionment among the several States, and without regard to any census or enumeration.

AMENDMENT XVII *(Ratified on April 8, 1913)*

The Senate of the United States shall be composed of two Senators from each State, elected by the people thereof, for six years; and each Senator shall have one vote. The electors in each State shall have the qualifications requisite for electors of the most numerous branch of the State legislatures.

When vacancies happen in the representation of any State in the Senate, the executive authority of such State shall issue writs of election to fill such vacancies: Provided, That the legislature of any State may empower the executive thereof to make tempo-rary appointments until the people fill the vacancies by election as the legislature may direct.

This amendment shall not be so construed as to affect the election or term of any Senator chosen before it becomes valid as part of the Constitution.

AMENDMENT XVIII *(Ratified on January 16, 1919)*

SECTION 1. After one year from the ratification of this article the manufacture, sale, or transportation of intoxicating liquors within, the importation thereof into, or the exportation thereof from the United States and all territory subject to the jurisdiction thereof for beverage purposes is hereby prohibited.

SECTION 2. The Congress and the several States shall have concurrent power to enforce this article by appropriate legislation.

SECTION 3. This article shall be inoperative unless it shall have been ratified as an amendment to the Constitution by the legislatures of the several States, as provided in the Constitution, within seven years from the date of the submission hereof to the States by the Congress.

AMENDMENT XIX *(Ratified on August 18, 1920)*

The right of citizens of the United States to vote shall not be denied or abridged by the United States or by any State on account of sex.

Congress shall have power to enforce this article by appropriate legislation.

AMENDMENT XX *(Ratified on February 6, 1933)*

SECTION 1. The terms of the President and Vice President shall end at noon on the 20th day of January, and the terms of Senators and Representatives at noon on the 3d day of January, of the years in which such terms would have ended if this article had not been ratified; and the terms of their successors shall then begin.

SECTION 2. The Congress shall assemble at least once in every year, and such meeting shall begin at noon on the 3d day of January, unless they shall by law appoint a different day.

SECTION 3. If, at the time fixed for the beginning of the term of the President, the President elect shall have died, the Vice President elect shall become President. If a President shall not have been chosen before the time fixed for the beginning of his term, or if the President elect shall have failed to qualify, then the Vice President elect shall act as President until a President shall have qualified; and the Congress may by law provide for the case wherein neither a President elect nor a Vice President elect shall have qualified, declaring who shall then act as President, or the manner in which one who is to act shall be selected, and such person shall act accordingly until a President or Vice President shall have qualified.

SECTION 4. The Congress may by law provide for the case of the death of any of the persons from whom the House of Representatives may choose a President whenever the rights of choice shall have devolved upon them, and for the case of the death of any of the persons from whom the Senate may choose a Vice President whenever the right of choice shall have devolved upon them.

SECTION 5. Sections 1 and 2 shall take effect on the 15th day of October following the ratification of this article.

SECTION 6. This article shall be inoperative unless it shall have been ratified as an amendment to the Constitution by the legislatures of three-fourths of the several States within seven years from the date of its submission.

AMENDMENT XXI *(Ratified on December 5, 1933)*

SECTION 1. The eighteenth article of amendment to the Constitution of the United States is hereby repealed.

SECTION 2. The transportation or importation into any State, Territory, or possession of the United States for delivery or use therein of intoxicating liquors, in violation of the laws thereof, is hereby prohibited.

SECTION 3. This article shall be inoperative unless it shall have been ratified as an amendment to the Constitution by conventions in the several States, as provided in the Constitution, within seven years from the date of the submission hereof to the States by the Congress.

AMENDMENT XXII *(Ratified on February 27, 1951)*

No person shall be elected to the office of the President more than twice, and no person who has held the office of President, or acted as President, for more than two years of a term to which some other person was elected President shall be elected to the office of the President more than once. But this Article shall not apply to any person holding the office of President when this Article was proposed by the Congress, and shall not prevent any person who may be holding the office of President, or acting as President, during the term within which this Article becomes operative from holding the office of President or acting as President during the remainder of such term.

AMENDMENT XXIII *(Ratified on March 29, 1961)*

SECTION 1. The District constituting the seat of Government of the United States shall appoint in such manner as the Congress may direct:

A number of electors of President and Vice President equal to the whole number of Senators and Representatives in Congress to which the District would be entitled if it were a State, but in no event more than the least populous State; they shall be in addition to those appointed by the States, but they shall be considered, for the purposes of the election of President and Vice President, to be electors appointed by a State; and they shall meet in the District and perform such duties as provided by the twelfth article of amendment.

SECTION 2. The Congress shall have power to enforce this article by appropriate legislation.

AMENDMENT XXIV *(Ratified on January 23, 1964)*

SECTION 1. The right of citizens of the United States to vote in any primary or other election for President or Vice President, for electors for President or Vice President, or for Senator or Representative in Congress, shall not be denied or abridged by the United States or any State by reason of failure to pay any poll tax or other tax.

SECTION 2. The Congress shall have power to enforce this article by appropriate legislation.

AMENDMENT XXV *(Ratified on February 10, 1967)*

SECTION 1. In case of the removal of the President from office or of his death or resignation, the Vice President shall become President.

SECTION 2. Whenever there is a vacancy in the office of the Vice President, the President shall nominate a Vice President who shall take office upon confirmation by a majority vote of both Houses of Congress.

SECTION 3. Whenever the President transmits to the President pro tempore of the Senate and the Speaker of the House of Representatives his written declaration that he is unable to discharge the powers and duties of his office, and until he transmits to them a written declaration to the contrary, such powers and duties shall be discharged by the Vice President as Acting President.

SECTION 4. Whenever the Vice President and a majority of either the principal officers of the executive departments or of such other body as Congress may by law provide, transmit to the President pro tempore of the Senate and the Speaker of the House of Representatives their written declaration that the President is unable to discharge the powers and duties of his office, the Vice President shall immediately assume the powers and duties of the office as Acting President.

Thereafter, when the President transmits to the President pro tempore of the Senate and the Speaker of the House of Representatives his writ-ten declaration that no inability exists, he shall resume the powers and duties of his office unless the Vice President and a majority of either the principal officers of the executive department or of such other body as Congress may by law provide, transmit within four days to the President pro tempore of the Senate and the Speaker of the House of Representatives their written declaration that the President is unable to discharge the powers and duties of his office. Thereupon Congress shall decide the issue, assembling within forty-eight hours for that purpose if not in session. If the Congress, within twenty-one days after receipt of the latter written declaration, or, if Congress is not in session, within twenty-one days after Congress is required to assemble, determines by two-thirds vote of both Houses that the President is unable to discharge the powers and duties of his office, the Vice President shall continue to discharge the same as Acting President; otherwise, the President shall resume the powers and duties of his office.

AMENDMENT XXVI *(Ratified on July 1, 1971)*

SECTION 1. The right of citizens of the United States, who are eighteen years of age or older, to vote shall not be denied or abridged by the United States or by any State on account of age.

SECTION 2. The Congress shall have power to enforce this article by appropriate legislation.

AMENDMENT XXVII *(Ratified on May 7, 1992)*

No law varying the compensation for the services of Senators and Representatives shall take effect until an election of Representatives shall have intervened.

FEDERALIST NO. 10

November 22, 1787

James Madison

TO THE PEOPLE OF THE STATE OF NEW YORK.

Among the numerous advantages promised by a well constructed Union, none deserves to be more accurately developed than its tendency to break and control the violence of faction. The friend of popular governments, never finds himself so much alarmed for their character and fate, as when he contemplates their propensity to this dangerous vice. He will not fail therefore to set a due value on any plan which, without violating the principles to which he is attached, provides a proper cure for it. The instability, injustice and confusion introduced into the public councils, have in truth been the mortal diseases under which popular governments have every where perished; as they continue to be the favorite and fruitful topics from which the adversaries to liberty derive their most specious declamations. The valuable improvements made by the American Constitutions on the popular models, both ancient and modern, cannot certainly be too much admired; but it would be an unwarrantable partiality, to contend that they have as effectually obviated the danger on this side as was wished and expected. Complaints are every where heard from our most considerate and virtuous citizens, equally the friends of public and private faith, and of public and personal liberty; that our governments are too unstable; that the public good is disregarded in the conflicts of rival parties; and that

measures are too often decided, not according to the rules of justice, and the rights of the minor party; but by the superior force of an interested and over-bearing majority. However anxiously we may wish that these complaints had no foundation, the evidence of known facts will not permit us to deny that they are in some degree true. It will be found indeed, on a candid review of our situation, that some of the distresses under which we labor, have been erroneously charged on the operation of our governments; but it will be found, at the same time, that other causes will not alone account for many of our heaviest misfortunes; and particularly, for that prevailing and increasing distrust of public engagements, and alarm for private rights, which are echoed from one end of the continent to the other. These must be chiefly, if not wholly, effects of the unsteadiness and injustice, with which a factious spirit has tainted our public administrations.

By a faction I understand a number of citizens, whether amounting to a majority or minority of the whole, who are united and actuated by some common impulse of passion, or of interest, adverse to the rights of other citizens, or to the permanent and aggregate interests of the community.

There are two methods of curing the mischiefs of faction: the one, by removing its causes; the other, by controlling its effects.

There are again two methods of removing the causes of faction: the one by destroying the liberty which is essential to its existence; the other, by giving to every citizen the same opinions, the same passions, and the same interests.

It could never be more truly said than of the first remedy, that it is worse than the disease. Liberty is to faction, what air is to fire, an aliment without which it instantly expires. But it could not be a less folly to abolish liberty, which is essential to political life, because it nourishes faction, than it would be to wish the annihilation of air, which is essential to animal life, because it imparts to fire its destructive agency.

The second expedient is as impracticable, as the first would be unwise. As long as the reason of man continues fallible, and he is at liberty to exercise it, different opinions will be formed. As long as the connection subsists between his reason and his self-love, his opinions and his passions will have a reciprocal influence on each other; and the former will be objects to which the latter will attach themselves. The diversity in the faculties of men from which the rights of property originate, is not less an insuperable obstacle to a uniformity of interests. The protection of these faculties is the first object of Government. From the protection of different and unequal faculties of acquiring property, the possession of different degrees and kinds of property immediately results: and from the influence of these on the sentiments and views of the respective proprietors, ensues a division of the society into different interests and parties.

The latent causes of faction are thus sown in the nature of man; and we see them every where brought into different degrees of activity, according to the different circumstances of civil society. A zeal for different opinions concerning religion, concerning Government and many other points, as well of speculation as of practice; an attachment to different leaders ambitiously contending for pre-eminence and power; or to persons of other descriptions whose fortunes have been interesting to the human passions, have in turn divided mankind into parties, inflamed them with mutual animosity, and rendered them much more disposed to vex and oppress each other, than to cooperate for their common good. So strong is this propensity of mankind to fall into mutual animosities, that where no substantial occasion presents itself, the most frivolous and fanciful distinctions have been sufficient to kindle their unfriendly passions, and excite their most violent conflicts. But the most common and durable source of factions, has been the various and unequal distribution of property. Those who hold, and those who are without property, have ever formed distinct interests in society. Those who are creditors, and those who are debtors, fall under a like discrimination. A landed interest, a manufacturing interest, a mercantile interest, a monied interest, with many lesser interests, grow up of necessity in civilized nations, and divide them into different classes, actuated by different sentiments and views. The regulation of these various and interfering interests forms the principal task of modern Legislation, and involves the spirit of party and faction in the necessary and ordinary operations of Government.

No man is allowed to be a judge in his own cause; because his interest would certainly bias his judgment, and, not improbably, corrupt his integrity. With equal, nay with greater reason, a body of men, are unfit to be both judges and parties, at the same time; yet, what are many of the most important acts of legislation, but so many judicial determinations, not indeed concerning the rights of single persons, but concerning the rights of large bodies of citizens, and what are the different classes of legislators, but advocates and parties to the causes which they determine? Is a law proposed concerning private debts? It is a question to which the creditors are parties on one side, and the debtors on the other. Justice ought to hold the balance between them. Yet the parties are and must be themselves the judges; and the most numerous party, or, in other words, the most powerful faction must be expected to prevail. Shall domestic manufactures be encouraged, and in what degree, by restrictions on foreign manufactures? are questions which would be differently decided by the landed and the manufacturing classes; and probably by neither, with a sole regard to justice and the public good. The apportionment of taxes on the various descriptions of property, is an act which seems to require the most exact impartiality; yet, there is perhaps no legislative act in which greater opportunity and temptation are given to a predominant party, to trample on the rules of justice. Every shilling with which they over-burden the inferior number, is a shilling saved to their own pockets.

It is in vain to say, that enlightened statesmen will be able to adjust these clashing interests, and render them all subservient to the public good. Enlightened statesmen will not always be at the helm: Nor, in many cases, can such an adjustment be made at all, without taking into view indirect and remote considerations, which will rarely prevail over the immediate interest which one party may find in disregarding the rights of another, or the good of the whole.

The inference to which we are brought, is, that the *causes* of faction cannot be removed; and that relief is only to be sought in the means of controlling its *effects*.

If a faction consists of less than a majority, relief is supplied by the republican principle, which enables the majority to defeat its sinister views by regular vote: It may clog the administration, it may convulse the society; but it will be unable to execute and mask its violence under the forms of the Constitution. When a majority is included in a faction, the form of popular government on the other hand enables it to sacrifice to its ruling passion or interest, both the public good and the rights of other citizens. To secure the public good, and private rights, against the danger of such a faction, and at the same time to preserve the spirit and the form of popular government, is then the great object to which our enquiries are directed: Let me add that it is the great desideratum, by which alone this form of government can be rescued from the opprobrium under which it has so long labored, and be recommended to the esteem and adoption of mankind.

By what means is this object attainable? Evidently by one of two only. Either the existence of the same passion or interest in a majority at the same time, must be prevented; or the majority, having such co-existent passion or interest, must be rendered, by their number and local situation, unable to concert and carry into effect schemes of oppression. If the impulse and the opportunity be suffered to coincide, we well know that neither moral nor religious motives can be relied on as an adequate control. They are not found to be such on the injustice and violence of individuals, and lose their efficacy in proportion to the number combined together; that is, in proportion as their efficacy becomes needful.

From this view of the subject, it may be concluded, that a pure Democracy, by which I mean, a Society, consisting of a small number of citizens, who assemble and administer the Government in person, can admit of no cure for the mischiefs of faction. A common passion or interest will, in almost every case, be felt by a majority of the whole; a communication and concert results from the form of Government itself; and there is nothing to check the inducements to sacrifice the weaker party, or an obnoxious individual. Hence it is, that such Democracies have ever been spectacles of turbulence and contention; have ever been found incompatible with personal security, or the rights of property; and have in general been as short in their lives, as they have been violent in their deaths. Theoretic politicians, who have patronized this species of Government, have erroneously supposed, that by reducing mankind to a perfect equality in their political rights, they would, at the same time, be perfectly equalized and assimilated in their possessions, their opinions, and their passions.

A republic, by which I mean a government in which the scheme of representation takes place, opens a different prospect, and promises the cure for which we are seeking. Let us examine the points in which it varies from pure democracy, and we shall comprehend both the nature of the cure and the efficacy which it must derive from the union.

The two great points of difference, between a democracy and a republic, are, first, the delegation of the government, in the latter, to a small number of citizens, elected by the rest; secondly, the greater number of citizens, and greater sphere of country, over which the latter may be extended.

The effect of the first difference is, on the one hand, to refine and enlarge the public views, by passing them through the medium of a chosen body of citizens, whose wisdom may best discern the true interest of their country, and whose patriotism and love of justice, will be least likely to sacrifice it to temporary or partial considerations. Under such a regulation, it may well happen, that the public voice, pronounced by the representatives of the people, will be more consonant to the public good, than if pronounced by the people themselves, convened for the purpose. On the other hand the effect may be inverted. Men of factious tempers, of local prejudices, or of sinister designs, may by intrigue, by corruption, or by other means, first obtain the suffrages, and then betray the interest of the people. The question resulting is, whether small or extensive republics are most favorable to the election of proper guardians of the public weal, and it is clearly decided in favor of the latter by two obvious considerations.

In the first place, it is to be remarked that, however small the republic may be, the representatives must be raised to a certain number, in order to guard against the cabals of a few; and that however large it may be, they must be limited to a certain number, in order to guard against the confusion of a multitude. Hence, the number of representatives in the two cases not being in proportion to that of the constituents, and being proportionally greatest in the small republic, it follows, that if the proportion of fit characters be not less in the large than in the small republic, the former will present a greater option, and consequently a greater probability of a fit choice.

In the next place, as each Representative will be chosen by a greater number of citizens in the large than in the small Republic, it will be more difficult for unworthy candidates to practise with success the vicious arts, by which elections are too often carried; and the suffrages of the people being more free, will be more likely to center on men who possess the most attractive merit, and the most diffusive and established characters.

It must be confessed, that in this, as in most other cases, there is a mean, on both sides of which inconveniences will be found to lie. By enlarging too much the number of electors, you render the representatives too little acquainted with all their local circumstances and lesser interests; as by reducing it too much, you render him unduly attached to these, and too little fit to comprehend and pursue great and national objects. The Federal Constitution forms a happy combination in this respect; the great and aggregate interests being referred to the national, the local and particular, to the state legislatures.

The other point of difference is, the greater number of citizens and extent of territory which may be brought within the compass of Republican, than of Democratic Government; and it is this circumstance principally which renders factious combinations less to be dreaded in the former, than in the latter. The smaller the society, the fewer probably will be the distinct parties and interests composing it; the fewer the distinct parties and interests, the more frequently will a majority be found of the same party; and the smaller the number of individuals composing a majority, and the smaller the compass within which they are placed, the more easily will they concert and execute their plans of oppression. Extend the sphere, and you take in a greater variety of parties and interests; you make it less probable that a majority of the whole will have a common motive to invade the rights of other citizens; or if such a common motive exists, it will be more difficult for all who feel it to discover their own strength, and to act in unison with each other. Besides other impediments, it may be remarked, that where there is a consciousness of unjust or dishonorable purposes, communication is always checked by distrust, in proportion to the number whose concurrence is necessary.

Hence it clearly appears, that the same advantage, which a Republic has over a Democracy, in controlling the effects of faction, is enjoyed by a large over a small Republic—is enjoyed by the Union over the States composing it. Does this advantage consist in the substitution of Representatives, whose enlightened views and virtuous sentiments render them superior to local prejudices, and to schemes of injustice? It will not be denied, that the Representation of the Union will be most likely to possess these requisite endowments. Does it consist in the greater security afforded by a greater variety of parties, against the event of any one party being able to outnumber and oppress the rest? In an equal degree does the increased variety of parties, comprised within the Union, increase this security? Does it, in fine, consist in the greater obstacles opposed to the concert and accomplishment of the secret wishes of an unjust and interested majority? Here, again, the extent of the Union gives it the most palpable advantage.

The influence of factious leaders may kindle a flame within their particular States, but will be unable to spread a general conflagration through the other States: a religious sect, may degenerate into a political faction in a part of the Confederacy but the variety of sects dispersed over the entire face of it, must secure the national Councils against any danger from that source: a rage for paper money, for an abolition of debts, for an equal division of property, or for any other improper or wicked project, will be less apt to pervade the whole body of the Union, than a particular member of it; in the same proportion as such a malady is more likely to taint a particular county or district, than an entire State.

In the extent and proper structure of the Union, therefore, we behold a Republican remedy for the diseases most incident to Republican Government. And according to the degree of pleasure and pride, we feel in being Republicans, ought to be our zeal in cherishing the spirit, and supporting the character of Federalists.

PUBLIUS

FEDERALIST NO. 51

February 22, 1787

James Madison

TO THE PEOPLE OF THE STATE OF NEW YORK.

To what expedient then shall we finally resort for maintaining in practice the necessary partition of power among the several departments, as laid down in the constitution? The only answer that can be given is, that as all these exterior provisions are found to be inadequate, the defect must be supplied, by so contriving the interior structure of the government, as that its several constituent parts may, by their mutual relations, be the means of keeping each other in their proper places. Without presuming to undertake a full development of this important idea, I will hazard a few general observations, which may perhaps place it in a clearer light, and enable us to form a more correct judgment of the principles and structure of the government planned by the convention.

In order to lay a due foundation for that separate and distinct exercise of the different powers of government, which to a certain extent, is admitted on all hands to be essential to the preservation of liberty, it is evident that each department should have a will of its own; and consequently should be so constituted, that the members of each should have as little agency as possible in the appointment of the members of the others. Were this principle rigorously adhered to, it would require that all the appointments for the supreme executive, legislative, and judiciary magistracies, should be drawn from the same fountain of authority, the people, through

channels, having no communication whatever with one another. Perhaps such a plan of constructing the several departments would be less difficult in practice than it may in contemplation appear. Some difficulties however, and some additional expense, would attend the execution of it. Some deviations therefore from the principle must be admitted. In the constitution of the judiciary department in particular, it might be inexpedient to insist rigorously on the principle; first, because peculiar qualifications being essential in the members, the primary consideration ought to be to select that mode of choice, which best secures these qualifications; secondly, because the permanent tenure by which the appointments are held in that department, must soon destroy all sense of dependence on the authority conferring them.

It is equally evident that the members of each department should be as little dependent as possible on those of the others, for the emoluments annexed to their offices. Were the executive magistrate, or the judges, not independent of the legislature in this particular, their independence in every other would be merely nominal.

But the great security against a gradual concentration of the several powers in the same department, consists in giving to those who administer each department, the necessary constitutional means, and personal motives, to resist encroachments of the others. The provision for defense must in this, as in all other cases, be made commensurate to the danger of attack. Ambition must be made to counteract ambition. The interest of the man must be connected with the constitutional right of the place. It may be a reflection on human nature, that such devices should be necessary to control the abuses of government. But what is government itself but the greatest of all reflections on human nature? If men were angels, no government would be necessary. If angels were to govern men, neither external nor internal controls on government would be necessary. In framing a government which is to be administered by men over men, the great difficulty lies in this: You must first enable the government to control the governed; and in the next place, oblige it to control itself. A dependence on the people is no doubt the primary control on the government; but experience has taught mankind the necessity of auxiliary precautions.

This policy of supplying by opposite and rival interests, the defect of better motives, might be traced through the whole system of human affairs, private as well as public. We see it particularly displayed in all the subordinate distributions of power; where the constant aim is to divide and arrange the several offices in such a manner as that each may be a check on the other; that the private interest of every individual, may be a sentinel over the public rights. These inventions of prudence cannot be less requisite in the distribution of the supreme powers of the state.

But it is not possible to give to each department an equal power of self defense. In republican government the legislative authority, necessarily, predominates. The remedy for this inconveniency is, to divide the legislature into different branches; and to render them by different modes of election, and different principles of action, as little connected with each other, as the nature of their common functions, and their common dependence on the society, will admit. It may even be necessary to guard against dangerous encroachments by still further precautions. As the weight of the legislative authority requires that it should be thus divided, the weakness of the executive may require, on the other hand, that it should be fortified. An absolute negative, on the

legislature, appears at first view to be the natural defense with which the executive magistrate should be armed. But perhaps it would be neither altogether safe, nor alone sufficient. On ordinary occasions, it might not be exerted with the requisite firmness; and on extraordinary occasions, it might be prefidiously abused. May not this defect of an absolute negative be supplied, by some qualified connection between this weaker department, and the weaker branch of the stronger department, by which the latter may be led to support the constitutional rights of the former, without being too much detached from the rights of its own department?

If the principles on which these observations are founded be just, as I persuade myself they are, and they be applied as a criterion, to the several state constitutions, and to the federal constitution, it will be found, that if the latter does not perfectly correspond with them, the former are infinitely less able to bear such a test.

There are moreover two considerations particularly applicable to the federal system of America, which place that system in a very interesting point of view.

First. In a single republic, all the power surrendered by the people, is submitted to the administration of a single government; and usurpations are guarded against by a division of the government into distinct and separate departments. In the compound republic of America, the power surrendered by the people, is first divided between two distinct governments, and then the portion allotted to each, subdivided among distinct and separate departments. Hence a double security arises to the rights of the people. The different governments will control each other; at the same time that each will be controlled by itself.

Second. It is of great importance in a republic, not only to guard the society against the oppression of its rulers; but to guard one part of the society against the injustice of the other part. Different interests necessarily exist in different classes of citizens. If a majority be united by a common interest, the rights of the minority will be insecure. There are but two methods of providing against this evil: The one by creating a will in the community independent of the majority, that is, of the society itself, the other by comprehending in the society so many separate descriptions of citizens, as will render an unjust combination of a majority of the whole, very improbable, if not impracticable. The first method prevails in all governments possessing an hereditary or self appointed authority. This at best is but a precarious security; because a power independent of the society may as well espouse the unjust views of the major, as the rightful interests, of the minor party, and may possibly be turned against both parties. The second method will be exemplified in the federal republic of the United States. While all authority in it will be derived from and dependent on the society, the society itself will be broken into so many parts, interests and classes of citizens, that the rights of individuals or of the minority, will be in little danger from interested combinations of the majority. In a free government, the security for civil rights must be the same as for religious rights. It consists in the one case in the multiplicity of interests, and in the other, in the multiplicity of sects. The degree of security in both cases will depend on the number of interests and sects; and this may be presumed to depend on the extent of country and number of people comprehended under the same government. This view of the subject must particularly recommend a proper federal system to all the sincere and considerate friends of republican government: Since it shows that in exact proportion as the territory of the union may be formed into more circumscribed confederacies or states, oppressive combinations of a majority will be facilitated, the best security under the republican form, for the rights of every class of citizens, will be diminished; and consequently, the stability and independence of some member of the government, the only other security, must be proportionally increased. Justice is the end of government. It is the end of civil society. It ever has been, and ever will be pursued, until it be obtained, or until liberty be lost in the pursuit. In a society under the forms of which the stronger faction can readily unite and oppress the weaker, anarchy may as truly be said to reign, as in a state of nature where the weaker individual is not secured against the violence of the stronger: And as in the latter state even the stronger individuals are prompted by the uncertainty of their condition, to submit to a government which may protect the weak as well as themselves: So in the former state, will the more powerful factions or parties be gradually induced by a like motive, to wish for a government which will protect all parties, the weaker as well as the more powerful. It can be little doubted, that if the state of Rhode Island was separated from the confederacy, and left to itself, the insecurity of rights under the popular form of government within such narrow limits, would be displayed by such reiterated oppressions of factious majorities, that some power altogether independent of the people would soon be called for by the voice of the very factions whose misrule had proved the necessity of it. In the extended republic of the United States, and among the great variety of interests, parties and sects which it embraces, a coalition of a majority of the whole society could seldom take place on any other principles than those of justice and the general good; and there being thus less danger to a minor from the will of the major party, there must be less pretext also, to provide for the security of the former, by introducing into the government a will not dependent on the latter; or in other words, a will independent of the society itself. It is no less certain than it is important, notwithstanding the contrary opinions which have been entertained, that the larger the society, provided it lie within a practicable sphere, the more duly capable it will be of self government. And happily for the *republican cause*, the practicable sphere may be carried to a very great extent, by a judicious modification and mixture of the *federal principle*.

PUBLIUS

APPENDIX V

PRESIDENTS, CONGRESSES, AND CHIEF JUSTICES: 1789–2001

Term	President and Vice President	Party of President	Congress	Majority Party		Chief Justice of the United States
				House	Senate	
1789–1797	**George Washington** John Adams	None	1st 2d 3d 4th	(N/A) (N/A) (N/A) (N/A)	(N/A) (N/A) (N/A) (N/A)	John Jay (1789 1795) John Rutledge (1795) Oliver Ellsworth (1796–1800)
1797–1801	**John Adams** Thomas Jefferson	Federalist	5th 6th	(N/A) Fed	(N/A) Fed	Oliver Ellsworth (1796–1800) John Marshall (1801–1835)
1801–1809	**Thomas Jefferson** Aaron Burr (1801–1805) George Clinton (1805–1809)	Democratic-Republican	7th 8th 9th 10th	Dem-Rep Dem-Rep Dem-Rep Dem-Rep	Dem-Rep Dem-Rep Dem-Rep Dem-Rep	John Marshall (1801–1835)
1809–1817	**James Madison** George Clinton (1809–1812)[a] Elbridge Gerry (1813–1814)[a]	Democratic-Republican	11th 12th 13th 14th	Dem-Rep Dem-Rep Dem-Rep Dem-Rep	Dem-Rep Dem-Rep Dem-Rep Dem-Rep	John Marshall (1801–1835)
1817–1825	**James Monroe** Daniel D. Tompkins	Democratic-Republican	15th 16th 17th 18th	Dem-Rep Dem-Rep Dem-Rep Dem-Rep	Dem-Rep Dem-Rep Dem-Rep Dem-Rep	John Marshall (1801–1835)
1825–1829	**John Quincy Adams** John C. Calhoun	National-Republican	19th 20th	Nat'l Rep Dem	Nat'l Rep Dem	John Marshall (1801–1835)
1829–1837	**Andrew Jackson** John C. Calhoun (1829–1832)[b] Martin Van Buren (1833–1837)	Democrat	21st 22d 23d 24th	Dem Dem Dem Dem	Dem Dem Dem Dem	John Marshall (1801–1835) Roger B. Taney (1836–1864)
1837–1841	**Martin Van Buren** Richard M. Johnson	Democrat	25th 26th	Dem Dem	Dem Dem	Roger B. Taney (1836–1864)
1841	**William H. Harrison**[a] John Tyler (1841)	Whig				Roger B. Taney (1836–1864)

Term	President and Vice President	Party of President	Congress	House	Senate	Chief Justice of the United States
1841–1845	**John Tyler** (VP vacant)	Whig	27th 28th	Whig Dem	Whig Whig	Roger B. Taney (1836–1864)
1845–1849	**James K. Polk** George M. Dallas	Democrat	29th 30th	Dem Whig	Dem Dem	Roger B. Taney (1836–1864)
1849–1850	**Zachary Taylor**[a] Millard Fillmore	Whig	31st	Dem	Dem	Roger B. Taney (1836–1864)
1850–1853	**Millard Fillmore** (VP vacant)	Whig	32d	Dem	Dem	Roger B. Taney (1836–1864)
1853–1857	**Franklin Pierce** William R.D. King (1853)[a]	Democrat	33d 34th	Dem Rep	Dem Dem	Roger B. Taney (1836–1864)
1857–1861	**James Buchanan** John C. Breckinridge	Democrat	35th 36th	Dem Rep	Dem Dem	Roger B. Taney (1836–1864)
1861–1865	**Abraham Lincoln**[a] Hannibal Hamlin (1861–1865) Andrew Johnson (1865)	Republican	37th 38th 38th	Rep Rep Rep	Rep Rep Rep	Roger B. Taney (1836–1864) Salmon P. Chase (1864–1873)
1865–1869	**Andrew Johnson** (VP vacant)	Republican	39th 40th	Union Rep	Union Rep	Salmon P. Chase (1864–1873)
1869–1877	**Ulysses S. Grant** Schuyler Colfax (1869–1873) Henry Wilson (1873–1875)[a]	Republican	41st 42d 43d 44th	Rep Rep Rep Dem	Rep Rep Rep Rep	Salmon P. Chase (1864–1873) Morrison R. Waite (1874–1888)
1877–1881	**Rutherford B. Hayes** William A. Wheeler	Republican	45th 46th	Dem Dem	Rep Dem	Morrison R. Waite (1874–1888)
1881	**James A. Garfield**[a] Chester A. Arthur	Republican	47th	Rep	Rep	Morrison R. Waite (1874–1888)
1881–1885	**Chester A. Arthur** (VP vacant)	Republican	48th	Dem	Rep	Morrison R. Waite (1874–1888)
1885–1889	**Grover Cleveland** Thomas A. Hendricks (1885)[a]	Democrat	49th 50th	Dem Dem	Rep Rep	Morrison R. Waite (1874–1888) Melville W. Fuller (1888–1910)
1889–1893	**Benjamin Harrison** Levi P. Morton	Republican	51st 52d	Rep Dem	Rep Rep	Melville W. Fuller (1888–1910)
1893–1897	**Grover Cleveland** Adlai E. Stevenson	Democrat	53d 54th	Dem Rep	Dem Rep	Melville W. Fuller (1888–1910)
1897–1901	**William McKinley**[a] Garret A. Hobart (1897–1899)[a] Theodore Roosevelt (1901)	Republican	55th 56th	Rep Rep	Rep Rep	Melville W. Fuller (1888–1910)
1901–1909	**Theodore Roosevelt** (VP vacant, 1901–1905) Charles W. Fairbanks (1905–1909)	Republican	57th 58th 59th 60th	Rep Rep Rep Rep	Rep Rep Rep Rep	Melville W. Fuller (1888–1910)

Term	President and Vice President	Party of President	Congress	House	Senate	Chief Justice of the United States
1909–1913	**William Howard Taft** James S. Sherman (1909–1912)[a]	Republican	61st 62d	Rep Dem	Rep Rep	Melville W. Fuller (1888–1910) Edward D. White (1910–1921)
1913–1921	**Woodrow Wilson** Thomas R. Marshall	Democrat	63d 64th 65th 66th	Dem Dem Dem Rep	Dem Dem Dem Rep	Edward D. White (1910–1921)
1921–1923	**Warren G. Harding**[a] Calvin Coolidge	Republican	67th	Rep	Rep	William Howard Taft (1921–1930)
1923–1929	**Calvin Coolidge** (VP vacant, 1923–1925) Charles G. Dawes (1925–1929)	Republican	68th 69th 70th	Rep Rep Rep	Rep Rep Rep	William Howard Taft (1921–1930)
1929–1933	**Herbert Hoover** Charles Curtis	Republican	71st 72d	Rep Dem	Rep Rep	William Howard Taft (1921–1930) Charles Evans Hughes (1930–1941)
1933–1945	**Franklin D. Roosevelt**[a] John N. Garner (1933–1941) Henry A. Wallace (1941–1945) Harry S Truman (1945)	Democrat	73d 74th 75th 76th 77th 78th	Dem Dem Dem Dem Dem Dem	Dem Dem Dem Dem Dem Dem	Charles Evans Hughes (1930–1941) Harlan F. Stone (1941–1946)
1945–1953	**Harry S Truman** (VP vacant, 1945–1949) Alben W. Barkley (1949–1953)	Democrat	79th 80th 81st 82d	Dem Rep Dem Dem	Dem Rep Dem Dem	Harlan F. Stone (1941–1946) Frederick M. Vinson (1946–1953)
1953–1961	**Dwight D. Eisenhower** Richard M. Nixon	Republican	83d 84th 85th 86th	Rep Dem Dem Dem	Rep Dem Dem Dem	Frederick M. Vinson (1946–1953) Earl Warren (1953–1969)
1961–1963	**John F. Kennedy**[a] Lyndon B. Johnson (1961–1963)	Democrat	87th	Dem	Dem	Earl Warren (1953–1969)
1963–1969	**Lyndon B. Johnson** (VP vacant, 1963–1965) Hubert H. Humphrey (1965–1969)	Democrat	88th 89th 90th	Dem Dem Dem	Dem Dem Dem	Earl Warren (1953–1969)
1969–1974	**Richard M. Nixon**[c] Spiro T. Agnew (1969–1973)[b] Gerald R. Ford (1973–1974)[d]	Republican	91st 92d	Dem Dem	Dem Dem	Earl Warren (1953–1969) Warren E. Burger (1969–1986)
1974–1977	**Gerald R. Ford** Nelson A. Rockefeller	Republican	93d 94th	Dem Dem	Dem Dem	Warren E. Burger (1969–1986)
1977–1981	**Jimmy Carter** Walter Mondale	Democrat	95th 96th	Dem Dem	Dem Dem	Warren E. Burger (1969–1986)
1981–1989	**Ronald Reagan** George Bush	Republican	97th 98th 99th 100th	Dem Dem Dem Dem	Rep Rep Rep Dem	Warren E. Burger (1969–1986) William H. Rehnquist (1986–)

Term	President and Vice President	Party of President	Congress	House	Senate	Chief Justice of the United States
1989–1993	**George Bush** J. Danforth Quayle	Republican	101st 102d	Dem Dem	Dem Dem	William H. Rehnquist (1986–)
1993–2001	**William J. Clinton** Albert Gore Jr.	Democrat	103d 104th 105th 106th	Dem Rep Rep Rep	Dem Rep Rep Rep	William H. Rehnquist (1986–)
2001–	**George W. Bush** Richard Cheney	Republican	107th	Rep	Dem	William H. Rehnquist (1986–)

[a]Died in office.
[b]Resigned from the vice presidency.
[c]Resigned from the presidency.
[d]Appointed vice president.

MAJOR SUPREME COURT CASES

- **Brown v. Board of Education (1954):** U.S. Supreme Court decision holding that school segregation is inherently unconstitutional because it violates the Fourteenth Amendment's guarantee of equal protection; marked the end of legal segregation in the United States.

- **Civil Rights Cases (1875):** Name attached to five cases brought under the Civil Rights Act of 1875. In 1883 the Supreme Court decided that discrimination in a variety of public accommodations, including theaters, hotels, and railroads, could not be prohibited by the act because it was private and not state discrimination.

- **Gibbons v. Ogden (1824):** The Court upheld broad congressional power over interstate commerce.

- **Immigration and Naturalization Service v. Chadha (1983):** Legislative veto ruled unconstitutional by the Supreme Court.

- **Marbury v. Madison (1803):** Supreme Court case in which the Court first asserted the power of judicial review in finding that a congressional statute extending the Court's original jurisdiction was unconstitutional.

- **McCulloch v. Maryland (1819):** Supreme Court upheld the power of the national government and denied the right of a state to tax the bank. The Court's broad interpretation of the necessary and proper clause paved the way for later rulings upholding expansive federal powers.

- **Miranda v. Arizona (1966):** The Fifth Amendment requires that individuals arrested for a crime must be advised of their right to remain silent and to have counsel present.

- **New York Times Co. v. Sullivan (1964):** Supreme Court decision ruling that simply publishing a defamatory falsehood is not enough to justify a libel judgment. "Actual malice" must be proved to support a finding of libel against a public figure.

- **Plessy v. Ferguson (1896):** *Plessy* challenged a Louisiana statute requiring that railroads provide separate accommodations for blacks and whites. The Court found that separate but equal accommodations did not violate the equal protection clause of the Fourteenth Amendment.

- **Roe v. Wade (1973):** The Supreme Court found that a woman's right to an abortion was protected by the right to privacy that could be implied from specific guarantees found in the Bill of Rights and the Fourteenth Amendment.

- **United States v. Nixon (1974):** There is no constitutional absolute executive privilege that would allow a president to refuse to comply with a court order to produce information needed in a criminal trial.

GLOSSARY

administrative adjudication:
A quasi-judicial process in which a bureaucratic agency settles disputes between two parties in a manner similar to the way courts resolve disputes.

administrative discretion: The ability of bureaucrats to make choices concerning the best way to implement congressional intentions.

agenda: A set of problems to which policy makers believe they should be attentive.

amicus curiae: "Friend of the court"; a third party to a lawsuit who files a legal brief for the purpose of raising additional points of view in an attempt to influence a court's decision.

Anti-Federalists: Those who favored strong state governments and a weak national government; opposed the ratification of the U.S. Constitution.

appellate court: Court that generally reviews only findings of law made by lower courts.

appellate jurisdiction: The power vested in an appellate court to review and revise the decision of a lower court.

Articles of Confederation: The compact among the thirteen original states that was the basis of their government. Written in 1776, the Articles were not ratified by all the states until 1781.

bicameral legislature: A legislature divided into two houses; the U.S. Congress and almost every U.S. state legislature are bicameral (Nebraska is unicameral).

bill of attainder: A law declaring an act illegal without a judicial trial.

Bill of Rights: The first ten amendments to the U.S. Constitution.

blanket primary: A primary in which voters may cast ballots in either party's primary (but not both) on an office-by-office basis.

block grant: Broad grant with few strings attached given to states by the federal government for specified activities, such as secondary education or health services.

brief: A document containing the collected legal written arguments in a case filed with a court by a party prior to a hearing or trial.

Brown **v.** *Board of Education* **(1954):** U.S. Supreme Court decision holding that school segregation is inherently unconstitutional because it violates the Fourteenth Amendment's guarantee of equal protection; marked the end of legal segregation in the United States.

bureaucracy: A set of complex hierarchical departments, agencies, commissions, and their staffs that exist to help carry out the president's constitutionally mandated charge to enforce the laws of the nation.

business cycles: Fluctuation between expansion and recession that is a part of modern capitalist economies.

Cabinet: The formal body of presidential advisers who head the fourteen departments. Presidents often appoint others to this body of formal advisers.

campaign manager: A professional who directs the various aspects of a campaign.

capitalism: The economic system that favors private control of business and minimal governmental regulation of private industry.

checks and balances: A governmental structure that gives each of the three branches of government some degree of oversight and control over the actions of the others.

civil law: The body of law that regulates the conditions and relationships between private individuals or companies.

civil liberties: The personal rights and freedoms that the federal government cannot abridge by law, constitution, or judicial interpretation.

civil rights: Refers to the positive acts governments take to protect individuals against arbitrary or discriminatory treatment by governments or individuals based on categories such as race, sex, national origin, age, or sexual orientation.

Civil Rights Act of 1964: Legislation passed by Congress to outlaw segregation in public facilities and racial discrimination in employment, education, and voting; created the Equal Employment Opportunity Commission.

civil service laws: These acts removed the staffing of the bureaucracy from political parties and created a professional bureaucracy filled through competition.

civil service system: The system created by civil service laws by which many appointments to the federal bureaucracy are made.

clear and present danger test: Test used by the Supreme Court to draw the line between protected and unprotected speech; the Court looks to see if there is an imminent danger that illegal action would occur in response to the contested speech.

closed primary: A primary election in which only a party's registered voters are eligible to vote.

cloture: Motion requiring 60 Senators to cut off debate.

collective good: Something of value that cannot be withheld from a nonmember of the group, for example, a tax write-off, a good feeling.

Committees of Correspondence: Groups formed in the colonies to exchange ideas and information about resisting British rule.

concurrent powers: Powers shared by the national and state governments.

confederation: Type of government in which the national government derives its powers from the states; a league of independent states.

conference committee: Joint committee created to iron out differences between Senate and House versions of a specific piece of legislation.

congressional review: The process by which Congress can nullify an executive branch regulation by a resolution passed in both houses within sixty days of announcement of the regulation.

congressionalist: A view of the president's role in the lawmaking process that holds Article II's provision that the president should ensure "faithful execution of the laws" should be read as an injunction against substituting presidential authority for legislative intent.

conservative: One thought to believe that a government is best that governs least and that big government can only infringe on individual, personal, and economic rights.

constitutional courts: Federal courts specifically created by the U.S. constitution or by Congress pursuant to its authority in Article III.

content regulation: Governmental attempts to regulate the electronic media.

Contract with America: Campaign pledge signed by most Republican candidates in 1994 to guide their legislative agenda.

contrast ad: Ad that compares the records and proposals of the candidates, with a bias toward the sponsor.

cooperative federalism: A term used to characterize the relationship between the national, state, and local governments that began with the New Deal.

criminal law: The body of law that regulates individual conduct, is enforced by the state, and provides punishment for violations.

critical election: An election that signals a party realignment through voter polarization around new issues.

crossover voting: Participation in the primary of the party with which the voter is not affiliated.

Declaration of Independence: Document drafted by Thomas Jefferson in 1776 that proclaimed the right of the American colonies to separate from Great Britain.

delegate: Role played by elected representatives who vote the way their constituents would want them to, regardless of their own opinions.

department: A major administrative unit with responsibility for a broad area of government operations. Departmental status usually indicates a permanent national interest in that particular governmental function, such as defense, health, or agriculture.

direct democracy: A system of government in which members of the polity meet to discuss all policy decisions and then agree to abide by majority rule.

direct incitement test: The advocacy of illegal action is protected by the First Amendment unless imminent action is intended and likely to occur.

direct mailer: A professional who supervises a political campaign's direct-mail fundraising strategies.

direct primary: The selection of party candidates through the ballots of qualified voters rather than at party nomination conventions.

discharge petition: Petition that gives a majority of the House of Representatives the authority to bring an issue to the floor in the event of committee inaction.

discount rate: The interest rate at which member banks can borrow money from their regional Federal Reserve Bank.

disturbance theory: The theory offered by political scientist David B. Truman that posits that interest groups form in part to counteract the efforts of other groups.

divided government: The situation that arises when the congressional majority and the president are from different political parties.

dual federalism: The belief that the national government should not exceed its enumerated powers expressly set out in the constitution.

due process clause: Clause contained in the Fifth and Fourteenth Amendments. Over the years, it has been construed to guarantee to individuals a variety of rights ranging from economic liberty to criminal procedural rights to protection from arbitrary governmental action.

due process rights: Procedural guarantees provided by the Fourth, Fifth,

Sixth, and Eighth Amendments for those accused of crimes.

economic regulation: Governmental regulation of business practices, industry rates, routes, or areas serviced by particular industries.

economic stability: A situation in which there is economic growth, rising national income, high employment, and steadiness in the general level of prices.

elastic clause: A name given to the "necessary and proper clause" found in the final paragraph of Article I, section 8, of the U.S. Constitution. It gives Congress the authority to pass all laws "necessary and proper" to carry out the enumerated powers specified in the Constitution.

elector: Member of the electoral college chosen by methods determined in each state.

electoral college: Representatives of each state who cast the final ballots that actually elect a president.

electronic media: The newest form of broadcast media, including television, radio, cable, and the Internet.

entitlement program: Income security program to which all those meeting eligibility criteria are entitled.

enumerated powers: Seventeen specific powers granted to Congress under Article I, section 8, of the U.S. Constitution; these powers include taxation, coinage of money, regulation of commerce, and the authority to provide for a national defense.

enumerated powers: A name given to the clause found in the final paragraph of Article I, section 8, of the U.S. Constitution giving Congress the authority to pass all laws "necessary and proper" to carry out the enumerated powers specified in the Constitution; the "elastic" clause.

equal protection clause: Section of the Fourteenth Amendment that guarantees that all citizens receive "equal protection of the laws"; has been used to bar discrimination against blacks and women.

equal time rule: The rule that requires broadcast stations to sell campaign air time equally to all candidates if they choose to sell it to any.

establishment clause: The first clause in the First Amendment. It prohibits the national government from establishing a national religion.

***ex post facto* law:** Law passed after the fact, thereby making previously legal activity illegal and subject to current penalty; prohibited by the U.S. Constitution.

exclusionary rule: Judicially created rule that prohibits police from using illegally seized evidence at trial.

Executive Office of the President (EOP): Establishment created in 1939 to help the president oversee the bureaucracy.

executive order: A rule or regulation issued by the president that has the effect of law. All executive orders must be published in the *Federal Register*.

executive privilege: An assertion of presidential power that reasons that the president can withhold information requested by the courts in matters relating to his office.

exit poll: Poll conducted at selected polling places on Election Day.

Federal Employees Political Activities Act: 1993 liberalization of Hatch Act. Federal employees are now allowed to run for office in nonpartisan elections and to contribute money to campaigns in partisan elections.

Federal Reserve Board: A seven-member board, that sets member banks' reserve requirements, controls the discount rate, and makes other economic decisions.

federal system: Plan of government created in the U.S. Constitution in which power is divided between the national government and the state governments and in which independent states are bound together under one national government.

federalism: The philosophy that describes the governmental system created by the Framers; see also federal system.

The Federalist Papers: A series of eighty-five political papers written by John Jay, Alexander Hamilton, and James Madison in support of ratification of the U.S. Constitution.

Federalists: Those who favored a stronger national government and supported the proposed U.S. Constitution; later became the first U.S. political party.

Fifteenth Amendment: One of the three Civil War amendments; specifically enfranchised black males.

filibuster: A formal way of halting action on a bill by means of long speeches or unlimited debate in the Senate.

First Continental Congress: Meetings held in Philadelphia from September 5 to October 26, 1774, in which fifty-six delegates (from every colony except Georgia) adopted a resolution that opposed the Coercive Acts.

fiscal policy: Federal government policies on taxes, spending and debt management, intended to promote the nation's macro-economic goals, particularly with respect to employment, price stability and growth.

Fourteenth Amendment: One of the three Civil War amendments; guarantees equal protection and due process of the law to all U.S. citizens.

free exercise clause: The second clause of the First Amendment. It prohibits the U.S. government from interfering with a citizen's right to practice his or her religion.

free market economy: The economic system in which the "invisible hand" of the market regulates prices, wages, product mix, and so on.

free media: Coverage of a candidate's campaign by the news media.

free rider: A problem that occurs when those who don't join or work for the benefit of the group still reap the rewards of the group's activity.

front-loading: The tendency of states to choose an early date on the primary calendar.

gender gap: The difference between the voting choices of men and women.

general election: Election in which voters decide which candidates will actually fill elective public offices.

gerrymandering: The legislative process through which the majority party in each statehouse tries to assure that the maximum number of representatives from its political party can be elected to Congress and the statehouse through the redrawing of legislative districts.

get-out-the-vote (GOTV): A push at the end of a political campaign to encourage supporters to go to the polls.

***Gibbons v. Ogden* (1824):** The Court upheld broad congressional power over interstate commerce.

government corporation: Business set up and created by Congress that performs functions that could be provided by private businesses (such as the U.S. Postal Service).

governmental (institutional) agenda: The changing list of issues to which governments believe they should address themselves.

grandfather clause: Statute that allowed only those whose grandfathers had voted before Reconstruction to vote unless they passed a wealth or literacy test.

Great Compromise: A decision made during the Constitutional Convention to give each state the same number of representatives in the Senate regardless of size; representation in the House was determined by population.

hard money: Federal campaign contributions strictly regulated by federal law.

Hatch Act: Law enacted in 1939 to prohibit civil servants from taking activist roles in partisan campaigns. This act prohibited federal employees from making political contributions, working for a particular party, or campaigning for a particular candidate.

hold: A tactic by which a Senator asks to be informed before a particular bill is brought to the floor.

impeachment: The power delegated to the House of Representatives in the Constitution to charge the president, vice president, or other "civil officers," including federal judges, with "Treason, Bribery, or other high Crimes and Misdemeanors." This is the first step in the constitutional process of removing such officials from office.

implementation: The process by which a law or policy is put into operation by the bureaucracy.

implied power: A power derived from an enumerated power and the necessary and proper clause. These powers are not stated specifically but are considered to be reasonably implied through the exercise of delegated powers.

implied powers: Power given to the national government through inference from the enumerated powers.

in forma pauperis: Literally, "in the form of a pauper"; a way for an indigent or poor person to appeal a case to the U.S. Supreme Court.

incorporation doctrine: Principle in which the Supreme Court has held that most, but not all, of the specific guarantees in the Bill of Rights limit state and local governments by making those guarantees applicable to the states through the due process clause of the Fourteenth Amendment.

incumbency: The status derived by one who holds an office or elected position. This usually provides a substantial advantage in seeking selection.

independent executive agency: Governmental unit that closely resembles a Cabinet department but has a narrower area of responsibility (such as the Central Intelligence Agency) and is not part of any Cabinet department.

independent expenditure: The amount of money an individual or political committee may spend supporting or opposing a candidate as long as those funds are not made in coordination with a candidate's campaign.

independent regulatory commission: An agency created by Congress that is generally concerned with a specific aspect of the economy.

indirect (representative) democracy: A system of government that gives citizens the opportunity to vote for representatives who will work on their behalf.

inflation: A rise in the general price levels of an economy.

inherent powers: Powers of the president that can be derived or inferred from specific powers in the Constitution.

initiative: A process that allows citizens to propose legislation and submit it to the state electorate for popular vote.

inoculation advertising: Advertising that attempts to counteract an anticipated attack from the opposition before the attack is even launched.

interest group: An organized group that tries to influence public policy.

intergovernmental lobby: The pressure group or groups that are created when state and local governments hire lobbyists to lobby the national government.

interventionist state: Replaced the *laissez-faire* state as the government took an active role in guiding and regulating the private economy.

iron triangle: The relatively stable relationship and pattern of interaction that occur among an agency, interest groups, and congressional committees or subcommittees.

J

judicial activism: A philosophy of judicial decision-making that argues judges should use their power broadly to further justice, especially in the areas of equality and personal liberty.

judicial implementation: Refers to how and whether judicial decisions are translated into actual public policies affecting more than the immediate parties to a lawsuit.

judicial restraint: A philosophy of judicial decision-making that argues courts should allow the decisions of other branches of government to stand, even when they offend a judge's own sense of principles.

judicial review: Power of the courts to review acts of other branches of government and the states.

Judiciary Act of 1789: Established the basic three-tiered structure of the federal court system.

jurisdiction: Authority vested in a particular court to hear and decide the issues in any particular case.

L

laissez-faire: A French term literally meaning "to allow to do, to leave alone." It is a hands-off governmental policy that is based on the belief that governmental regulation of the economy is wrong.

legislative courts: Courts established by Congress for specialized purposes, such as the Court of Military Appeals.

legislative veto: A procedure by which one or both houses of Congress can disallow an act of the president or executive agency by a simple majority

vote; ruled unconstitutional by the Supreme Court.

libel: False statements or statements tending to call someone's reputation into disrepute.

liberal: One considered to favor extensive governmental involvement in the economy and the provision of social services and to take an activist role in protecting the rights of women, the elderly, minorities, and the environment.

libertarian: One who favors a free market economy and no governmental interference in personal liberties.

line-item veto: The power to veto specific provisions of a bill without vetoing the bill in its entirety.

lobbying: The activities of groups and organizations that seek to influence legislation and persuade political leaders to support a group's position.

M

majority leader: The elected leader of the party controlling the most seats in the U.S. House of Representatives or the Senate; second in authority to the Speaker of the House, and in the Senate is regarded as its most powerful member.

majority party: The political party in each house of Congress with the most members.

mandates: National laws that direct states or local governments to comply with federal rules or regulations (such as clean air or water standards) under threat of civil or criminal penalties or as a condition of receipt of any federal grants.

Marbury v. Madison **(1803):** Supreme Court case in which the Court first asserted the power of judicial review in finding that a congressional statute extending the Court's original jurisdiction was unconstitutional.

matching funds: Donations to presidential campaigns from the federal government that are determined by the amount of private funds a qualifying candidate raises.

McCulloch v. Maryland **(1819):** The Supreme Court upheld the power of the national government and denied the right of a state to tax the bank. The Court's broad interpretation of the necessary and proper clause paved the way for later rulings upholding expansive federal powers.

means-tested programs: Income security program intended to assist those whose incomes fall below a designated level.

media consultant: A professional who produces political candidates' television, radio, and print advertisements.

media effects: The influence of news sources on public opinion.

merit system: The system by which federal civil service jobs are classified into grades or levels to which appointments are made on the basis of performance on competitive examinations.

minority leader: The elected leader of the party with the second highest number of elected representatives in either the House or the Senate.

minority party. Party with the second most members in either house of Congress.

***Miranda* v. *Arizona* (1966):** The Fifth Amendment requires that individuals arrested for a crime must be advised of their right to remain silent and to have counsel present.

monetary policy: A form of government regulation in which the nation's money supply and interest rates are controlled.

money: A system of exchange for goods and services that includes currency, coins, and bank deposits.

muckraking: A form of newspaper publishing concerned with reforming government and business conduct.

national convention: A party conclave (meeting) held in the presidential election year to nominate a presidential and vice-presidential ticket and adopt a platform.

national party platform: A statement of the general and specific philosophy and policy goals of a political party, usually promulgated at the national convention.

natural law: A doctrine that society should be governed by certain ethical principles that are part of nature and, as such, can be understood by reason.

necessary and proper clause: A name given to the clause found in the final paragraph of Article I, section 8, of the U.S. Constitution giving Congress the authority to pass all laws "necessary and proper" to carry out the enumerated powers specified in the Constitution; the "elastic" clause.

negative ad: Advertising on behalf of a candidate that attacks the opponent's platform or character.

New Deal: The name given to the program of "Relief, Recovery, Reform" begun by President Franklin D. Roosevelt in 1933 designed to bring the United States out of the Great Depression.

New Jersey Plan: A framework for the Constitution proposed by a group of small states; its key points were a one-house legislature with one vote for each state, a multiperson "executive," the establishment of the acts of Congress as the "supreme law" of the land, and a supreme judiciary with limited power.

***New York Times Co.* v. *Sullivan* (1964):** The Supreme Court ruled that "actual malice" must be proved to support a finding of libel against a public figure.

non-means-based programs: Program such as Social Security where benefits are provided irrespective of the income or means of recipients.

nonpartisan primary: A primary used to select candidates without regard to party affiliation.

obscenity: Those things considered disgusting or morally unhealthy.

open primary: A primary in which party members, independents, and sometimes members of the other party are allowed to vote.

original jurisdiction: The jurisdiction of courts that hear a case first, usually in a trial. Courts determine the facts of a case under their original jurisdiction.

paid media: Political advertisements purchased for a candidate's campaign.

pardon: An executive grant providing restoration of all rights and privileges of citizenship to a specific individual charged or convicted of a crime.

party identification: A citizen's personal affinity for a political party, usually expressed by his or her tendency to vote for the candidates of that party.

party realignment: A shifting of party coalition groupings in the electorate that remains in place for several elections.

patronage: Jobs, grants, or other special favors that are given as rewards to friends and political allies for their support.

Pendleton Act: Reform measure that created the Civil Service Commission to administer a partial merit system. It classified the federal service by grades to which appointments were made based on the results of a competitive examination. It made it illegal for federal political appointees to be required to contribute to a particular political party.

***Plessy* v. *Ferguson* (1896):** *Plessy* challenged a Louisiana statute requiring that railroads provide separate accommodations for blacks and whites. The Court found that separate but equal accommodations did not violate the equal protection clause of the Fourteenth Amendment.

pocket veto: If Congress adjourns during the ten days the president has to consider a bill passed by both houses of Congress, without the president's signature, the bill is considered vetoed.

policy adoption: The approval of a policy proposal by the people with the requisite authority, such as a legislature.

policy evaluation: The process of determining whether a course of action is achieving its intended goals.

policy formulation: The crafting of appropriate and acceptable proposed courses of action to ameliorate or resolve public problems.

policy implementation: The process of carrying out public policy through governmental agencies and the courts.

political action committee: A federally registered fund-raising committee that represents an interest group in the political process through campaign donations.

political consultant: Professional who manages campaigns and political advertisements for political candidates.

political culture: Attitudes toward the political system and its various parts, and attitudes toward the role of the self in the system.

political ideology: An individual's coherent set of values and beliefs about the purpose and scope of government.

political machine: A party organization that recruits its members with tangible incentives and is characterized by a high degree of control over member activity.

political party: A group of office holders, candidates, activists, and voters who identify with a group label and seek to elect to public office individuals who run under that label.

political socialization: The process through which an individual acquires particular political orientations; the learning process by which people acquire their political beliefs and values.

politico: Role played by elected representatives who act as trustees or as delegates, depending on the issue.

pollster: A professional who takes public opinion surveys that guide political campaigns.

pork barrel: Legislation that allows representatives to "bring home the bacon" to their districts in the form of public works programs, military bases, or other programs designed to benefit their districts directly.

pornography: Depictions of sexual lewdness or erotic behavior.

positive ad: Advertising on behalf of a candidate that stresses the candidate's qualifications, family, and issue positions, without reference to the opponent.

precedent: Prior judicial decision that serves as a rule for settling subsequent cases of a similar nature.

preemption: A concept derived from the Constitution's supremacy clause that allows the national government to override or preempt state or local actions in certain areas.

presidentialist: One who believes that Article II's grant of executive power is a broad grant of authority and power allowing a president wide discretionary powers.

press briefing: A restricted engagement with the press usually conducted by aides to a public figure.

press conference: An unrestricted appearance by public figure to talk with the press.

press release: An official statement on an issue or news event.

primary election: Election in which voters decide which of the candidates within a party will represent the party in the general election.

print press: The traditional form of mass media, comprising newspapers, magazines, and journals.

prior restraint: Judicial doctrine stating that the government cannot prohibit speech or publication before the fact.

privacy: The right to be left alone; a judicially created doctrine encompassing an individual's decision to use birth control or secure an abortion.

public funds: Donations from the general tax revenues to the campaigns of qualifying presidential candidates.

public interest group: An organization that seeks a collective good that will not selectively and materially benefit the members of the group.

public opinion: What the public thinks about a particular issue or set of issues at any point in time.

public opinion poll: Interviews or surveys with a sample of citizens that are used to estimate public opinion of the entire population.

public policy: A purposive course of action followed by government in dealing with some problem or matter of concern.

raiding: An organized attempt by voters of one party to influence primary results of another party.

random sampling: A method of selection that gives each potential voter or adult the same chance of being selected for a poll.

recall: Removal of an incumbent from office by popular vote.

recession: A short-term decline in the economy that occurs as investment sags, production falls off, and unemployment increases.

redistricting: The redrawing of congressional districts to reflect increases or decreases in seats allotted to the states, as well as population shifts within a state.

referendum: A procedure whereby the state legislature submits proposed legislation to the state's voters for approval.

regulation: Rule that governs the operation of a particular government program and has the force of law.

republic: A government rooted in the consent of the governed; a representative or indirect democracy.

reserve (or police) powers: Powers reserved to the states by the Tenth Amendment that lie at the foundation of a state's right to legislate for the public health and welfare of its citizens.

reserve requirements: Governmental requirements that a portion of member banks' deposits must be retained to back loans made.

revenue sharing: Method of redistributing federal monies back to the states with "no strings attached"; favored by President Richard M. Nixon.

Roe v. *Wade* **(1970):** The Supreme Court found that a woman's right to an abortion was protected by the right to privacy that could be implied from specific guarantees found in the Bill of Rights and the Fourteenth Amendment.

rule making: A quasi-legislative administrative process that has the characteristics of a legislative act.

Rule of Four: At least four justices of the Supreme Court must vote to consider a case before it can be heard.

runoff primary: A second primary election between the two candidates receiving the greatest number of votes in the first primary.

sampling error or margin of error: A measure of the accuracy of a public opinion poll.

Second Continental Congress: Meeting convened in Philadelphia on May 10, 1775, at which it was decided an army should be raised and George Washington of Virginia was named commander-in-chief.

secular realignment: The gradual rearrangement of party coalitions, based more on demographic shifts than on shocks to the political system.

senatorial courtesy: A process by which presidents, when selecting district court judges, defer to the senator in whose state the vacancy occurs.

separation of powers: A way of dividing power among three branches of government in which members of the House of Representatives, members of the Senate, the president, and the federal courts are selected by and responsible to different constituencies.

slander: Untrue spoken statements that defame the character of a person.

social contract theory: The belief that people are free and equal by God-given right and that this in turn requires that all people give their consent to be governed; espoused by John Locke and influential in the writing of the Declaration of Independence.

social regulation: Governmental regulation of the quality and safety of products as well as the conditions under which goods and services are produced.

Social Security Act: A 1935 law that established old-age insurance (Social Security), assistance for the needy, children, and others; and unemployment insurance.

social welfare policy: Government programs to protect people from deprivation and improve their physical well-being.

soft money: Under a loophole in federal campaign law, money donated to a political party for noncandidate specific purposes; not covered by federal campaign spending laws.

solicitor general: The fourth-ranking member of the Justice Department; responsible for handling all appeals on behalf of the U.S. government to the Supreme Court.

Speaker of the House: The only officer of the House of Representatives specifically mentioned in the Constitution; elected at the beginning of each new congress by the entire House; traditionally a member of the majority party.

spoils system: The firing of public-office holders of a defeated political party and their replacement with loyalists of the newly elected party.

spot ad: Television advertising on behalf of a candidate that is broadcast in sixty-, thirty-, or ten-second duration.

Stamp Act Congress: First official meeting of the colonies; first step toward unified nation.

standing committee: Committee to which proposed bills are referred.

stare decisis: In court rulings, a reliance on past decisions or precedents to formulate decisions in new cases.

stratified sampling: A variation of random sampling; census data are used to divide a country into four sampling regions. Sets of counties and standard metropolitan statistical areas are then randomly selected in proportion to the total national population.

straw poll: Unscientific survey used to gauge public opinion on a variety of issues and policies.

strict constructionist: An approach to constitutional interpretation that emphasizes the Framers' initial intentions.

strict scrutiny: A heightened standard of review used by the Supreme Court to determine the constitutional validity of a challenged practice.

suffrage movement: The drive for women's right to vote that took place in the United States from 1890 to 1920.

supremacy clause: Portion of Article IV of the U.S. Constitution that mandates that national law is supreme to (that is, supersedes) all other laws passed by the states or by any other subdivision of government.

suspect classification: Category or class, such as race, which triggers the highest standard of scrutiny from the Supreme Court.

symbolic speech: Symbols, signs, and other methods of expression generally also considered to be protected by the First Amendment.

systemic agenda: All public issues that are viewed as requiring governmental attention; a discussion agenda.

term limits: Legislation designating that state or federal elected legislators can serve only a specified number of years.

third-partyism: The tendency of third parties to arise with some regularity in a nominally two-party system.

Thirteenth Amendment: One of the three Civil War amendments; specifically bans slavery in the United States.

Three-Fifths Compromise: Agreement reached at the Constitutional Convention stipulating that each slave was to be counted as three-fifths of a person for purposes of determining population for representation in the U.S. House of Representatives.

ticket-split: To vote for candidates of different parties for various offices in the same election.

tracking poll: Continuous surveys that enable a campaign to chart its daily rise or fall.

trial court: Court of original jurisdiction where cases begin.

trustee: Role played by elected representatives who listen to constituents' opinions and then use their best judgment to make final decisions.

turnout: The proportion of the voting-age public that votes.

two-party system: The political system in which two major parties dominate the electoral process; rules and customs operate to make it very difficult for third parties to become dominant.

United States v. Nixon (1974): The Supreme Court ruled that there is no constitutional absolute executive privilege that would allow a president to refuse to comply with a court order to produce information needed in a criminal trial.

veto power: The formal, constitutional authority of the president to reject bills passed by both houses of Congress, thus preventing their becoming law without further congressional action.

Virginia Plan: The first general plan for the Constitution, proposed by James Madison. Its key points were a bicameral legislature, an executive chosen by the legislature, and a judiciary also named by the legislature.

voter canvass: The process by which a campaign gets in touch with individual voters: either by door-to-door solicitation or by telephone.

War Powers Act: Law requiring presidents to obtain congressional approval before introducing U.S. troops into a combat situation; passed in 1973 over President Nixon's veto.

Watergate: Term used to describe the events and scandal resulting from a break-in at the Democratic National Committee headquarters in 1972 and the subsequent coverup of White House involvement.

whip: One of several representatives who keep close contact with all members and take "nose counts" on key votes, prepare summaries of bills, and in general act as communications links within the party.

writ of *certiorari*: A formal document issued from the Supreme Court to a lower federal or state court that calls up a case.

Y

yellow journalism: A form of newspaper publishing that featured pictures, comics, color, and sensationalized, oversimplified news coverage.

CHAPTER 1

1. The English and Scots often signed covenants with their churches in a pledge to defend and further their religion. In the Bible, covenants were solemn promises made to humanity by God. In the colonial context, then, covenants were formal agreements sworn to a new government to abide by its terms.
2. The term *men* is used here because only males were considered fit to vote.
3. Frank Michelman, "The Republican Civic Tradition," *Yale Law Journal* 97 (1988): 1503.
4. Gabriel A. Almond and Sidney Verba, *The Civic Culture: Political Attitudes and Democracy in Five Nations* (Princeton, N.J.: Princeton University Press, 1963), 4.
5. Susan A. MacManus, *Young v. Old: Generational Combat in the 21st Century* (Boulder, Colo.: Westview Press, 1995), 3.
6. MacManus, *Young v. Old*, 4.
7. Jack C. Plano and Milton Greenberg, *The American Political Dictionary*, 6th ed. (New York: Holt, Rinehart and Winston, 1982).
8. William Safire, *Safire's New Political Dictionary* (New York: Random House, 1993), 144–45.
9. Safire, *Safire's New Political Dictionary*.
10. Philip E. Converse, "The Nature of Belief Systems in Mass Publics," in David E. Apter, ed., *Ideology and Discontent* (New York: Free Press, 1964), 206–21.
11. Colin Powell with Joseph E. Persico, *My American Journey* (New York: Random House, 1995).
12. David Broder and Richard Morin, "Americans See 2 Distinct Bill Clintons," *Washington Post* (August 23, 1998): A10.
13. Howard Wilkinson and Patrick Crowly, "Campaign '98: Races Offer Definite Choices."
14. "Apathetic Voters? No, Disgusted," *Ledger* (July 12, 1998): A14.
15. Scott Shepard, "Non-Voters. Too Busy or Apathetic?" *Palm Beach Post* (August 1998): 6A.
16. Shepard, "Non-Voters." (August 1998): 6A.
17. 1999 Poll Questions on the Federal Government, National Journal's *Cloak Room Poll Track*. Questions from the Center of Policy Attitudes, conducted January 26–31, 1999.

CHAPTER 2

1. See Richard B. Bernstein with Jerome Agel, *Amending America* (New York: Times Books, 1993), 138–40.
2. *Oregon v. Mitchell*, 400 U.S. 112 (1970).
3. Bernstein with Agel, *Amending America*, 139.
4. For an account of the early development of the colonies, see D. W. Meining, *The Shaping of America*, Vol. 1: *Atlantic America, 1492–1800* (New Haven, Conn.: Yale University Press, 1986).

5. For an excellent chronology of the events leading up to the writing of the Declaration of Independence and the colonists' break with Great Britain, see Calvin D. Lonton, ed., *The Bicentennial Almanac* (Nashville, Tenn.: Thomas Nelson, 1975).

6. See Gary Wills, *Inventing America: Jefferson's Declaration of Independence* (New York: Random House, 1978). Wills argues that the Declaration was signed solely to secure foreign aid for the ongoing war effort.

7. For more about the Articles of Confederation, see Merrill Jensen, *The Articles of Confederation* (Madison: University of Wisconsin Press, 1940).

8. Charles A. Beard, *An Economic Interpretation of the Constitution of the United States,* reissue edition (New York: Free Press 1996).

9. Quoted in Richard N. Current, et al., *American History: A Survey,* 6th ed. (New York: Knopf, 1983), 170.

10. John Patrick Diggins, "Power and Authority in American History: The Case of Charles Beard and His Critics," *The American Historical Review* 86 (October 1981): 701–30.

11. Robert Brown, *Charles Beard and the Constitution: A Critical Analysis of "An Economic Interpretation of the Constitution"* (Princeton, N.J.: Princeton University Press, 1956).

12. Jackson Turner Main, *The Anti-Federalists* (Chapel Hill: University of North Carolina, 1961).

13. Gordon S. Wood, *The Creation of the American Republic, 1776–1787,* reissue edition (New York: Norton, 1969).

14. For more on the political nature of compromise at the convention, see Calvin C. Jillson, *Constitution Making: Conflict and Consensus in the Federal Constitution of 1787* (New York: Agathon, 1988).

15. Slavery is nowhere specifically mentioned in the Constitution. Although many of the Framers were morally opposed to slavery, they recognized that if the convention attempted to abolish or seriously restrict it in the short term, the Southern states would walk away from the new union (as they eventually did, resulting in the Civil War).

16. See E. P. Panagopoulos, *Essays on the History and Meaning of Checks and Balances* (Lanham, MD: University Press of America, 1985).

17. Federal Republicans favored a republican or representative form of government (do not confuse this term with the modern Republican Party, which came into being in 1854; see chapter 12). Ultimately, the word *federal* came to mean the form of government embodied in the new Constitution, just as *confederation* meant the "league of states" under the Articles, and later came to mean the "Confederacy" of 1861–65.

18. Numerous editions of *The Federalist Papers* exist. They are now available in their entirety on the World Wide Web at: www.intergo.com/library/history/federalist/contents.html.

19. See Ralph Ketcham, ed., *The Anti-Federalist Papers and the Constitutional Debates* (New York: New American Library, 1986).

20. See Alan P. Grimes, *Democracy and the Amendments to the Constitution* (Lexington, MA: Lexington Books, 1978).

21. David E. Kyvig, *Repealing National Prohibition* (Chicago: University of Chicago Press, 1978).

22. See Jane J. Mansbridge, *Why We Lost the ERA* (Chicago: University of Chicago Press, 1986).

23. Speech by Attorney General Edwin Meese III before the American Bar Association, July 9, 1985, Washington, D.C. See also Antonin Scalia and

Amy Gutman, eds, *A Matter of Interpretation: Federal Courts and the Law* (Princeton, N.J.: Princeton University Press, 1998).

24. Speech by William J. Brennan, Jr., at Georgetown University, Text and Teaching Symposium, October 10, 1985, Washington, D.C.

25. Mark V. Tushnet, *Taking the Constitution Away from the Courts* (Princeton, N.J.: Princeton University Press, 1999).

26. Bruce Scherman, *We the People: Foundations* (Cambridge, Mass.: Belknap Press, 1991).

CHAPTER 3

1. *New Jersey* v. *New York,* 523 U.S. 767 (1998).

2. Linda Greenhouse, "Skeptical High Court Hears Case Over Pride and Acreage on Ellis I," *New York Times* (January 13, 1998): B1. See also Lisa Anderson, "Land of the Free, Home of the Silly Dispute," *Chicago Tribune* (June 5, 1998): 8.

3. *New Jersey* v. *New York,* 523 U.S. 767 (1998).

4. Nancy Plevin, "Ohio Frees Indian-Rights Activist 'Little Rock' Reed," *Santa Fe New Mexican* (March 12, 1999): B1.

5. *New Mexico ex rel. Ortiz* v. *Reed,* 524 U.S. 151 (1998).

6. *Gibbons* v. *Ogden,* 22 U.S. 1 (1824).

7. *Lane County* v. *Oregon,* 74 U.S. 71 (1869).

8. 163 U.S. 537 (1896).

9. *Panhandle Oil Co.* v. *Knox,* 277 U.S. 71 (1928).

10. *Indian Motorcycle Co.* v. *United States,* 238 U.S. 570 (1931).

11. *Pensacola Telegraph* v. *Western Union,* 96 U.S. 1 (1877).

12. *United States* v. *E. C. Knight,* 156 U.S. 1 (1895).

13. *NCRB* v. *Jones and Laughlin Steel Co.* 301 U.S. 1 (1937).

14. *United States* v. *Darby,* 312 U.S. 1 (1937).

15. *Wickard* v. *Filburn,* 317 U.S. 111 (1942).

16. Morton Grodzins, "Centralization and Decentralization in the American Federal System," in Robert A. Goldwin, ed., *A Nation of States* (Chicago: Rand McNally, 1963), 3–4.

17. Alice M. Rivlin, *Reviving the American Dream* (Washington, D.C.: Brookings Institution, 1992), 92.

18. Rivlin, *Reviving the American Dream,* 98.

19. Aaron Wildavsky, "Birthday Cake Federalism," in Robert E. Hawkins, ed., *American Federalism: A New Partnership for the Republic* (New Brunswick, N.J.: Transaction Press, 1982), 182.

20. Richard P. Nathan, et al., *Reagan and the States* (Princeton, NJ: Princeton University Press, 1987), 4.

21. Quoted in David E. Anderson, "Conservative Think Tanks Go Local," *UPI* (June 10, 1991).

22. Stephen G. Bragaw, "Federalism's Defense Fund: The Intergovernment Lobby and the Supreme Court, 1982–1997," paper delivered at the 1999 annual meeting as the Midwest Political Science Association.

23. John Kincaid, "From Cooperation to Coercion in American Federalism: Housing, Fragmentation, and Preemption, 1789–1992," *Journal of Law and Politics* 9 (Winter 1993): 333–430.

24. This discussion of preemption relies heavily on Joseph F. Zimmerman, *Contemporary American Federalism: The Growth of National Power* (New York: Praeger, 1992), 55–81.

25. The Close Up Foundation, "Federalism," http://www.closeup.org/federal.html.
26. Timothy J. Conlan and David R. Beam, "Federal Mandates: The Record of Reform and Future Prospects," *Intergovernmental Perspectives* (Fall 1992): 9.
27. Paul West, "Era of Big Government May Not Be Over After All," *Times-Picayune* (January 13, 1998): A5.
28. *Harper* v. *Virginia Board of Elections*, 383 U.S. (1966).
29. 469 U.S. 528 (1985).
30. 492 U.S. 490 (1989).
31. 112 S.Ct. 931 (1992).

CHAPTER 4

1. This vignette draws heavily on Jamie Raskin, "In Defense of Students' Rights," *Washington Post* (August 27, 2000): B8.
2. *Barron* v. *Baltimore*, 7 Pet. 243 (1833).
3. *Allgeyer* v. *Louisiana*, 165 U.S. 578 (1897).
4. 268 U.S. 652 (1925).
5. Philip Kurland and Ralph Lerner, eds., *The Founders' Constitution*, vol. 5 (Chicago: University of Chicago Press, 1987), 61.
6. *Cantwell* v. *Connecticut*, 310 U.S. 296 (1940).
7. *Zobrest* v. *Catalina Foothills School District*, 506 U.S. 813 (1992).
8. *Engel* v. *Vitale*, 370 U.S. 421 (1962).
9. *Lee* v. *Weisman*, 505 U.S. 577 (1992).
10. *Santa Fe Indep. Sch. District* v. *Doe*, 530 U.S. 290 (2000).
11. *Widmar* v. *Vincent*, 454 U.S. 263 (1981).
12. *Lamb's Chapel* v. *Center Moriches Union Free School District*, 508 U.S. 384 (1993).
13. *Rosenberger* v. *University of Virginia*, 115 S. Ct. 2510 (1995).
14. *Mitchell* v. *Helms*, 530 U.S. 793 (2000).
15. *Sherbert* v. *Verner*, 374 U.S. 398 (1963).
16. *Employment Division, Dept. of Human Resources of Oregon* v. *Smith*, 494 U.S. 872 (1990).
17. *Chaplinsky* v. *New Hampshire*, 315 U.S. 568 (1942).
18. *Schenck* v. *United States*, 249 U.S. 47 (1919).
19. *Brandenburg* v. *Ohio*, 395 U.S. 444 (1969).
20. See Donald Downs, "Obscenity and Pornography," in Kermit Hall, ed., *The Oxford Companion to the Supreme Court of the United States* (New York: Oxford University Press, 1992), 602.
21. 413 U.S. 15 (1973).
22. *Jenkins* v. *Georgia*, 418 U.S. 153 (1974).
23. *Jacobellis* v. *Ohio*, 378 U.S. 184 (1964).
24. *Barnes* v. *Glen Theater*, 501 U.S. 560 (1991).
25. Joan Biskupic, "Decency Can Be Weighed in Arts Funding," *The Washington Post* (June 26, 1998): A1, A18.
26. *National Endowment for the Arts* v. *Finley*, 118 S.Ct. 1550 (1998).
27. *Reno* v. *ACLU*, 117 S.Ct. 2329 (1997).
28. 376 U.S. 254 (1964).
29. 403 U.S. 713 (1971).
30. *Nebraska Press Association* v. *Stuart*, 427 U.S. 539 (1976).

31. *Stromberg* v. *California*, 283 U.S. 359 (1931).
32. *Tinker* v. *Des Moines Independent Community School District*, 393 U.S. 503 (1969).
33. 491 U.S. 397 (1989).
34. *U.S.* v. *Eichman*, 496 U.S. 310 (1990).
35. 7 Peters 243 (1833).
36. 19 How. 393 (1857).
37. 307 U.S. 174 (1939).
38. 464 U.S. 863 (1983).
39. *Printz* v. *United States*, 117 S.C. 2365 (1997).
40. *Wilson* v. *Arkansas*, 115 S.Ct. 1914 (1995).
41. *U.S.* v. *Sokolov*, 490 U.S. 1 (1989).
42. *U.S.* v. *Matlock*, 415 U.S. 164 (1974).
43. *Johnson* v. *U.S.*, 333 U.S. 10 (1948).
44. *Winston* v. *Lee*, 470 U.S. 753 (1985).
45. *South Dakota* v. *Neville*, 459 U.S. 553 (1983).
46. *Michigan* v. *Tyler*, 436 U.S. 499 (1978).
47. *Hester* v. *U.S.*, 265 U.S. 57 (1924).
48. *Carroll* v. *U.S.*, 267 U.S. 132 (1925).
49. *Chandler* v. *Miller*, 520 U.S. 305 (1997).
50. *Skinner* v. *Railway Labor Executives' Association*, 489 U.S. 602 (1989).
51. *Vernonia School District* v. *Acton*, 115 S.Ct. 2386 (1995).
52. Richard Willing, "Reno: Study Broad DNA Testing," *USA Today* (March 1, 1999): A1.
53. *Counselman* v. *Hitchcock*, 142 U.S. 547 (1892).
54. *Brown* v. *Mississippi*, 297 U.S. 278 (1936).
55. *Miranda* v. *Arizona*, U.S. (1966).
56. *Arizona* v. *Fulminante*, 500 U.S. 938 (1991).
57. No. 99–5525 (June 26, 2000).
58. *Weeks* v. *United States*, 232 U.S. 383 (1914).
59. *Johnson* v. *Zerbst*, 304 U.S. 458 (1932).
60. 372 U.S. 335 (1963).
61. *Strander* v. *West Virginia*, U.S. 303 (1880).
62. *Taylor* v. *Louisiana*, U.S. 522 (1975).
63. *Batson* v. *Kentucky*, U.S. 79 (1986).
64. 497 U.S. 836 (1990).
65. 65 497 U.S. 836 (1990).
66. 408 U.S. 238 (1972).
67. *Gregg* v. *Georgia*, 428 U.S. 153 (1976).
68. *McCleskey* v. *Kemp*, 481 U.S. 279 (1987).
69. *Olmstead* v. *United States*, 277 U.S. 438 (1928).
70. 381 U.S. 481 (1965).
71. *Eisenstadt* v. *Baird*, 410 U.S. 113 (1972).
72. 410 U.S. 113 (1973).
73. 492 U.S. 490 (1989).
74. 502 U.S. 1056 (1992)
75. The National Abortion and Reproductive Rights Action League, "Congressional Votes on Reproductive Choice, 1977–1995," February 1996.
76. "House Sends Partial Birth Abortion Bill To Clinton," *Politics USA* (March 28, 1996): 1.
77. *Stenberg* v. *Carhart*. 530 U.S. 914 (2000).

78. *Hill* v. *Colorado*. 530 U.S. 703 (2000).
79. *Board of Education of City of Oklahoma City* v. *National Gay Task Force*, 470 U.S. 903 (1985).
80. 478 U.S. 186 (1986).
81. Reported in David M. O'Brien, *Constitutional Law and Politics*, vol. 2. (New York: Norton and Co., 1991), 1223.
82. *Romer* v. *Evans*, 517 U.S. 620 (1996).
83. 530 U.S. 640 (2000).
84. *Cruzan by Cruzan* v. *Director, Missouri Dept. of Health*, 497 U.S. 261 (1990).
85. *In re Quinlan*, 70 N.J. 10 (1976).
86. *Vacco* v. *Quill*, 521 U.S. 793 (1997), and *Washington* v. *Glucksberg*, 95–1858, 521 U.S. 793 (1997).

CHAPTER 5

1. Michael Cooper, "Officers in Bronx Fire 41 Shots, and an Unarmed Man Is Killed," *The New York Times* (February 5, 1999): A1.
2. Amy Wilentz, "New York: The Price of Safety in a Police State," *Los Angeles Times* (April 11, 1999): M1.
3. N. R. Kleinfield, "Veterans of 60's Protests Meet the Newly Outraged in a March," *The New York Times* (April 16, 1999): B8.
4. Jessica Lee, "Women Speak to House about Unwarranted Customs Strip-Searches," *USA Today* (May 21 1999): 10A.
5. Edward Walsh, "The Racial Issue Looming in the Rear-View Mirror," *The Washington Post* (May 19, 1999): A3; Ralph Siegel, "Turnpike Arrest Cases Explore Use of Racial Profiling Defenses," *The Record* (May 12, 1999): A3.
6. Judith Evans, "Suit Claims Race Bias at Fla. Hotel," *The Washington Post* (May 21, 1997):
7. *The Slaughterhouse Cases*, 83 U.S. (16 Wall.) 36 (1873) and *Bradwell* v. *Illinois*, 83 U.S. (16 Wall.) 130 (1873).
8. *Minor* v. *Happersett*, 88 U.S. (21 Wall.) 162 (1875). See also Karen O'Connor, *Women's Organizations' Use of the Courts* (Lexington, Mass.: Lexington Books, 1980).
9. 109 U.S. 3 (1883).
10. 163 U.S. 537 (1896).
11. *Missouri* ex rel. *Gaines* v. *Canada*, 305 U.S. 337 (1938).
12. *Sweatt* v. *Painter*, 339 U.S. 629 and *McLaurin* v. *Oklahoma*, 339 U.S. 637 (1950).
13. 347 U.S. 483 (1954).
14. But see Gerald Rosenberg, *Hollow Hope: Can Courts Bring About Social Change* (Chicago: University of Chicago Press, 1991).
15. Quoted in Juan Williams, *Eyes on the Prize: America's Civil Rights Years, 1954–1965* (New York: Penguin, 1987), 10.
16. 349 U.S. 294 (1955).
17. 358 U.S. 1 (1958).
18. Jo Freeman, *The Politics of Women's Liberation* (New York: Longman, 1975), 57.
19. *Hoyt* v. *Florida* 368 U.S. 57 (1961).
20. Betty Friedan, *The Feminine Mystique* (New York: Dell, 1963).
21. *Reed* v. *Reed* 404 U.S. 71 (1971).
22. *Rostker* v. *Goldberg*, 453 U.S. 57 (1981).

23. Joyce Gelb and Marian Lief Palley, *Women and Public Policies* (Charlottesville: University of Virginia Press, 1982).

24. Rennard Strickland, "Native Americans," in Kermit Hall, ed., *The Oxford Companion to the Supreme Court of the United States* (New York: Oxford University Press, 1992), 557.

25. *White* v. *Register,* 412 U.S. 755 (1973).

26. *San Antonio Independent School District* v. *Rodriguez,* 411 U.S. 1 (1973).

27. 478 U.S. 186 (1986).

28. *Romer* v. *Evans,* 517 U.S. 620 (1996).

CHAPTER 6

1. Valerie Richardson, "A Massacre in Colorado; Students Killed, Injured in Blood Bath," *The Washington Times* (April 21, 1999): A1.

2. Ceci Connolly, "Littleton Alters the Landscape of Debate on Guns," *The Washington Post* (May 5, 1999): A3.

3. Helen Dewar, "Senate Turns Down Rules to Tighten Gun Show Sales," *The Washington Post* (May 13, 1999): A1.

4. Helen Dewar and Juliet Eilperin, "Senate Backs New Gun Control, 51–50," *The Washington Post* (May 21, 1999).

5. Juliet Eilperin, "House Democrats Seek a New Edge, Members Look for Ways to Get Votes of White Men,"*The Washington Post* (December 8, 2000): A28.

6. David C. Kimball and Samuel C. Patterson, "Living Up to Expectations: Public Attitudes Toward Congress," *Journal of Politics* (August 1997): 701–28.

7. John R. Hibbing and Elizabeth Theiss-Morse, "The Media's Role in Fomenting Public Disgust with Congress," *Extensions* (Fall 1996): 15–18.

8. *Wesberry* v. *Sanders,* 376 U.S. 1 (1964).

9. *Thornburg* v. *Gingles,* 478 U.S. 30 (1986). The act was amended in 1982.

10. *Shaw* v. *Reno,* 113 S.Ct. 2816 (1993).

11. Norman Ornstein, ed., *Vital Statistics on Congress* (Washington, D.C.: CQ Press, 1998), 135.

12. *U.S. Term Limits, Inc.* v. *Thornton,* 115 U.S. 1842 (1995).

13. Katharine Seelye, "Congressional Memo; New Speaker, New Style, Old Problem," *The New York Times* (March 12, 1999): A18.

14. Kenneth A. Shepsle, *The Giant Jigsaw Puzzle: Democatic Committee Assignments in the Modern House* (Chicago: University of Chicago Press, 1978).

15. Jack Anderson, "Subcontractor Oversight Absent," *Press Journal* (May 17, 1999): A8.

16. Barbara Sinclair, "The Struggle Over Representation and Lawmaking in Congress: Leadership Reforms in the 1990s," in James A. Thurber and Roger H. Davidson, eds., *Remaking Congress: Change and Stability in the 1990s* (Washington, D.C.: CQ Press, 1995), 105.

17. Steven S. Smith and Eric D. Lawrence, "Party Control of Congress in the Republican Congress," in Lawrence C. Dodd and Bruce I. Oppenheimer, *Congress Reconsidered,* 6th ed (Washington, D.C.: Congressional Quarterly Press, 1997), 163–64. For more on the role of parties in the organization of Congress, see Forrest Maltzman, *Competing Principals: Committees, Parties, and the Organization of Congress* (Ann Arbor: University of Michigan, 1997).

18. "A Short History of the Democratic Caucus," 1. Homepage; HillSource, House Republican Conference, "Our Mission," 1.

19. Woodrow Wilson, *Congressional Government: A Study in American Government* (New York: Meridian Books, 1956, originally published in 1885), 79.

20. Roger H. Davidson, "Congressional Committees in the New Reform Era: From Combat to the Contract," in Thurber and Davidson, *Remaking Congress*, 28.

21. Kenneth A. Shepsle, *The Giant Jigsaw Puzzle: Democratic Committee Assignments in the Modern House* (Chicago: University of Chicago Press, 1978).

22. Guy Gugliotta, "Term Limits on Chairman Shake Up House," *Washington Post* (March 22, 1999): A4.

23. Miles Benson, "New Faces Inevitable Among House Leadership," *Times-Picayune* (June 15, 2000): A7.

24. James A. Thurber, "If the Game Is Too Hard, Change the Rules: Congressional Budget Reform in the 1990s," in Thurber and Davidson, *Remaking Congress*, 140.

25. *Clinton* v. *City of New York,* 118 S.Ct. 2091 (1998).

26. John Kingdon, *Congressmen's Voting Decisions*, 3rd ed. (Ann Arbor: University of Michigan, 1989).

27. Jonathan D. Salant, "LSOs Are No Longer Separate, the Work's Almost Equal," *Congressional Quarterly* 53 (May 27, 1995): 1483.

28. Steven J. Balla, "Legislative Organization and Congressional Review of Agency Regulations," paper delivered at the 1999 annual meeting of the Midwest Political Science Association.

29. This discussion draws heavily on Balla, "Legislative Organization and Congressional Review."

30. 462 U.S. 919 (1983).

31. Quoted in Stewart M. Powell, "Lee Fights Signals Tougher Battles Ahead on Nomination," *Commercial Appeal* (December 21, 1997): A15.

CHAPTER 7

1. Richard E. Neustadt, *Presidential Power: The Politics of Power from FDR to Carter* (New York: Wiley, 1980).

2. Michael Waldman, "Bush's Presidential Power," *The Washington Post* (December 26, 2000): A29.

3. Winston Solberg, *The Federal Convention and the Formation of the Union of the American States* (Indianapolis: Bobbs-Merrill, 1958), 235.

4. "Is the Vice Presidency Necessary?" *Atlantic* 233 (May 1974): 37.

5. Benjamin I. Page and Mark P. Petracca, *The American Presidency* (New York: McGraw-Hill, 1983), 262.

6. *Clinton* v. *City of New York,* 118 S.Ct. 2091 (1998).

7. Richard J. Newman, et al, "Making War from 15,000 ft." *U.S. News & World Report* (May 10, 1999): 32.

8. Quoted in Richard E. Neustadt, *Presidential Power,* 9.

9. Quoted in Paul F. Boller Jr., *Presidential Anecdotes* (New York: Penguin Books, 1981), 78.

10. Quoted in Page and Petracca, *The American Presidency,* 57.

11. Franklin D. Roosevelt, Press Conference, July 23, 1937.

12. See, generally, Richard Pious, *The American Presidency* (Boston: Allyn and Bacon, 1996), 213, 254, 255.

13. Lyndon B. Johnson, *The Vantage Point* (New York: Holt, Rinehart and Winston, 1971), 448.

14. Morris Fiorina, *Divided Government* (New York: Macmillan, 1992).

15. See Cary Covington, J. Mark Wrighton, and Rhonda Kinney, "A 'Presidency-Augmented' Model of Presidential Success on House Roll Call Votes," *American Journal of Political Science* 39 (November 1995): 1001–24; and Wayne P. Steger, "Presidential Policy Initiation and the Politics of Agenda Control," *Congress and the Presidency* 24 (Spring 1997): 42–59.

16. Quoted in Thomas E. Cronin, *The State of the Presidency*, 2nd ed. (Boston: Little, Brown, 1980), 169.

17. Waldman, "Bush's Presidential Power."

18. *Congressional Quarterly Weekly Report* (December 1, 1990): 4034.

19. Richard W. Stevenson, "Political Memo: Clinton Ending Term on a Busy Note," *The New York Times* (December 25, 2000): A27.

20. Thomas Cronin, *The State of the Presidency* (Boston: Little, Brown, 1975).

21. Paul C. Light, *The President's Agenda: Domestic Policy Choice from Kennedy to Carter* (Baltimore: Johns Hopkins University Press, 1983).

22. George Reedy, *The Twilight of the Presidency* (New York: New American Library), 38–9.

23. Samuel Kernell, *New Strategies of Presidential Leadership*, 2nd ed. (Washington, D.C.: CQ Press, 1993), 3.

24. Jeffrey Cohen, "Presidential Rhetoric and the Public Agenda," *American Journal of Political Science* 39 (February 1995): 87–107.

25. Reedy, *Twilight of the Presidency*, 33.

26. Neustadt, *Presidential Power*, 1–10.

27. Waldman, "Bush's Presidential Power."

29. William E. Gibson, "Job Approval Ratings Steady; Personal Credibility Takes a Hit," *News and Observer* (August 19, 1998): A16.

30. See Kenneth Collier and Terry Sullivan, "New Evidence Undercutting the Linkage of Approval with Presidential Support and Influence," *Journal of Politics* 57 (February 1995): 197–209; and George C. Edwards III, "Aligning Tests with Theory: Presidential Approval as a Source of Influence in Congress," *Congress and the Presidency* 24 (Autumn 1997): 121–35.

CHAPTER 8

1. Jack Kelley, "Poll: Most Support Elian Raid," *USA Today* (April 25, 2000): A1.

2. Stephen Barr, "Users Mostly Rate Agencies Favorably," *Washington Post* (April 13, 2000): A29.

3. Harold D. Lasswell, *Politics: Who Gets What, When and How* (New York: McGraw-Hill, 1938).

4. H. H. Gerth and C. Wright Mills, *From Max Weber* (New York: Oxford University Press, 1958).

5. *NLRB v. Jones & Laughlin Steel Corp.*, 301 U.S. 1 (1937).

6. David Osborne and Ted Gaebler, *Reinventing Government* (Reading, MA: Addison-Wesley, 1992), 20–1.

7. Osborne and Gaebler, *Reinventing Government*.

8. On the difficulty of counting the exact number of government agencies, see David Nachmias and David H. Rosenbloom, *Bureaucratic Government: U.S.A.* (New York: St. Martin's Press, 1980).

9. *Humphrey's Executor* v. *U.S.*, 295 U.S. 602 (1935).

10. "Federal News: Hatch Act," *Inc.: Government Employee Relations Report* (October 11, 1993): 1317.

11. Michael Lipsky, *Street-Level Bureaucracy: Dilemmas of the Individual in Public Services* (New York: Russell Sage Foundation, 1980).

12. Lipsky, *Street-Level Bureaucracy.*

13. For more on iron triangles, see Randall Ripley and Grace Franklin, *Congress, Bureaucracy and Public Policy*, 4th ed. (Homewood, Ill.: Dorsey Press, 1984).

14. Cornelius M. Kerwin, *Rulemaking: How Government Agencies Write Law and Make Policy*, 2d ed. (Washington, DC: CQ Press, 1999), xv.

15. Jack C. Plano and Milton Greenberg, *The American Political Dictionary*, 6th ed. (New York: Holt, Rinehart and Winston, 1982), 236.

16. Irene Murphy, *Public Policy on the Status of Women* (Lexington, Mass.: Lexington Books, 1974).

17. Rosemary O'Leary, *Environmental Change: Federal Courts and the EPA* (Philadelphia: Temple University Press, 1993).

18. James F. Spriggs III, "The Supreme Court and Federal Administrative Agencies: A Resource-Based Theory and Analysis of Judicial Impact," *American Journal of Political Science* 40 (November 1996): 1122.

19. Spriggs, "The Supreme Court."

20. Wendy Hansen, Renee Johnson, and Isaac Unah, "Specialized Courts, Bureaucratic Agencies, and the Politics of U.S. Trade Policy," *American Journal of Political Science* 39 (August 1995): 529–57.

CHAPTER 9

1. 5 U.S. 137 (1803).

2. This discussion draws heavily on Jack C. Plano and Milton Greenberg, *The American Political Dictionary*, 10th ed. (Fort Worth, Tex.: Harcourt Brace, 1996), 247.

3. Cases involving citizens from different states can be filed in state or federal court.

4. John R. Vile and Mario Perez-Reilly, "The U.S. Constitution and Judicial Qualifications: A Curious Omission," *Judicature* (December/ January 1991): 198–202.

5. Quoted in Lawrence Baum, *The Supreme Court*, 3rd ed. (Washington, D.C.: CQ Press, 1989), 108.

6. See Barbara A. Perry, *A Representative Supreme Court? The Impact of Race, Religion and Gender on Appointments* (New York: Greenwood Press, 1991).

7. Clarence Thomas was raised a Catholic but attended an Episcopalian church at the time of his appointment, having been barred from Catholic sacraments because of his remarriage. He again, however, is attending Roman Catholic services.

8. Robert H. Bork, *Tempting of America: The Political Seduction of Law* (New York: Free Press, 1989).

9. Marcia Coyle, "How Americans View High Court," *National Law Journal* (February 26, 1990): 1.

10. John Brigham, *The Cult of the Court* (Philadelphia: Temple University Press, 1987).

11. Stephen L. Wasby, *The Supreme Court in the Federal Judicial System*, 4th ed. (Chicago: Nelson-Hall, 1988), 194.

12. David W. Neubauer, *Judicial Process: Law, Courts and Politics* (Pacific Grove, Calif.: Brooks/Cole, 1991), 370.

13. William P. McLauchan, "The Business of the United States Supreme Court, 1971–1983: An Analysis of Supply and Demand," paper presented at the 1986 annual meeting of the Midwest Political Science Association.

14. Paul Wahlbeck, James F. Spriggs II, and Lee Sigelman, "The Influence of Law Clerks on Supreme Court Opinions," paper delivered at the 1999 annual meeting of the Midwest Political Science Association.

15. Richard A. Posner, *The Federal Courts: Crisis and Reform* (Cambridge, MA: Harvard University Press, 1985), 114.

16. Edward Lazarus, *Closed Chambers: The First Eyewitness Account of the Epic Struggles Inside the Supreme Court* (New York: Random House, 1998).

17. "Retired Chief Justice Warren Attacks . . . Freund Study Group's Composition and Proposal," *American Bar Association Journal* 59 (July 1973): 728.

18. Kathleen Werdegar, "The Solicitor General and Administrative Due Process," *George Washington Law Review* (1967–68): 482.

19. Rebecca Mae Salokar, *The Solicitor General: The Politics of Law* (Philadelphia: Temple University Press, 1992), 3.

20. Richard C. Cortner, *The Supreme Court and Civil Liberties* (Palo Alto, Calif.: Mayfield, 1975), vi.

21 Gregory A. Caldeira and John R. Wright, "*Amicus Curiae* before the Supreme Court: Who Participates, When and How Much?" *Journal of Politics* 52 (August 1990): 803.

22. See also John R. Hermann, "American Indians in Court: The Burger and Rehnquist Years," Ph.D. dissertation, Emory University, 1996.

23. Stanley C. Brubaker, "Reconsidering Dworkin's Case for Judicial Activism," *Journal of Politics* 46 (1984): 504.

24. Donald L. Horowitz, *The Courts and Social Policy* (Washington, D.C.: Brookings Institution, 1977), 538.

25. *Webster* v. *Reproductive Health Services*, 492 U.S. 518 (1989).

26. 112 S.Ct. 2791 (1992).

27. See, for example, Tracy E. George and Lee Epstein, "On the Nature of Supreme Court Decision Making," *American Political Science Review* 86 (1992): 323–37.

28. Jeffrey A. Segal and Harold Spaeth, *The Supreme Court and the Attitudinal Model* (Cambridge: Cambridge University Press, 1993).

29. Gerard Gryski, Eleanor C. Main, and William Dixon, "Models of State High Court Decision Making in Sex Discrimination Cases," *Journal of Politics* 48 (1986): 143–55; and C. Neal Tate and Roger Handberg, "Time Binding and Theory Building in Personal Attribute Models of Supreme Court Voting Behavior, 1916–1988," *American Political Science Review* 35 (1991): 460–80.

30. Donald R. Songer and Sue Davis, "The Impact of Party and Region on Voting Decisions in the U.S. Courts of Appeals, 1955–86," *Western Political Quarterly* 43: 830–44.

31. See, generally, Lee Epstein and Jack Knight, "Field Essay: Toward a Strategic Revolution in Judicial Politics: A Look Back, A Look Ahead," *Political Research Quarterly* 53 (September 2000): 663–76.

32. Thomas R. Marshall, "Public Opinions, Representation and the Modern Supreme Court," *American Politics Quarterly* 16 (1988): 296–316.

33. William H. Rehnquist, "Constitutional Law and Public Opinion," paper presented at Suffolk University School of Law, Boston, April 10, 1986, 40–1.

34. Thomas R. Marshall, *Public Opinion and the Supreme Court* (Boston: Unwin and Hyman, 1989).

35. Timothy R. Johnson and Andrew D. Martin, "The Public's Conditional Response to Supreme Court Decisions," *American Political Science Review* 92 (June 1998): 299–309.

36. 377 U.S. 533 (1964).

37. Charles Johnson and Bradley C. Canon, *Judicial Policies' Implementation and Impact* (Washington, D.C.: CQ Press, 1984), ch. 1.

CHAPTER 10

1. Gallup Organization, Poll Release, "The Florida Recount Controversy from the Public's Perspective: 25 Insights," http:www.gallup. com/poll/resleases. All data discussed here are drawn from this compendium of polls concerning the 2000 Florida recount.

2. Allan M. Winkler, "Public Opinion," in Jack Greene, ed., *The Encyclopedia of American Political History* (New York: Charles Scribner's Sons, 1988), 1035.

3. *Literary Digest* 122 (August 22, 1936): 3.

4. *Literary Digest* 125 (November 14, 1936): 1.

5. Robert S. Erikson, Norman Luttbeg, and Kent Tedin, *American Public Opinion: Its Origin, Content, and Impact* (New York: Wiley, 1980), 28.

6. Richard Dawson et al., *Political Socialization*, 2nd ed. (Boston: Little, Brown, 1977), 33.

7. Statistical Abstract of the United States, 1996, 929.

8. Lyman A. Kellstedt et al., "Has Godot Finally Arrived? Religion and Realignment," *Public Perspective* (June/July 1995): 19.

9. Pamela Johnson Conover and Virginia Sapiro, "Gender, Feminist Consciousness and War," *American Journal of Political Science* 37 (November 1993): 1079–99.

10. "*Newsweek*: No Gender Gap on Impeachment Question," *Hotline* (December 14, 1998).

11. "*Newsweek*."

12. Edward S. Greenberg, "The Political Socialization of Black Children," in Edward S. Greenberg, ed., *Political Socialization* (New York: Atherton Press, 1970), 181.

13. Wes Allsion and David Adams, "Family to Dad: Elian Stays with Us," *St. Petersburg Times* (April 1, 2000): 1A.

14. Gallup Organization, Poll Releases, "Americans Approve of U.S. Government Decision to Return Boy to Cuba," http://www.gallup.com/poll/releases/pr000112.asp.

15. Susan A. MacManus., *Young* v. *Old: Generational Combat in the 21st Century* (Boulder, CO: Westview Press, 1995).

16. Richard Morin, "Southern Exposure," *The Washington Post* (July 14, 1996): A18.

17. F. Christopher Arterton, "The Impact of Watergate on Children's Attitudes Toward Political Authority," *Political Science Quarterly* 89 (June 1974): 273.

18. Diana Owen and Jack Dennis, "Kids and the Presidency: Assessing Clinton's Legacy," *Public Perspective* (April 1999), NEXIS.

19. Statistical Abstract of the United States, 1011.

20. Sandor M. Polster, "Bad News for Much TV News," *Bangor Daily News* (May 18, 1996): NEXIS.

21. Peggy Fikas, "A Funny Thing Happened on the Way to the White House," *San Antonio Express* (October 31, 2000): 1F.

22. Anne Miller, "Students Fighting National Apathy Trend," *San Antonio Express* (November 1, 2000): 3H.

23. Julie Mason, "Avalanche of Politico-tainment Seems to Benefit Presidential Candidates," *Houston Chronicle* (October 1, 2000): A38; and Lois Romano, "For the Candidates, It's Showtime," *Washington Post* (October 20, 2000): A11.

24. Andrew Glass, "News About the Net," *Atlanta Journal and Constitution* (November 17, 2000): 2D.

25. David Bauder, "Young Voters Turning Out in Droves, MTV Says," *Dayton Daily News* (October 20, 2000): 6A.

26. Everett Carl Ladd, "Fiskin's 'Deliberative Poll' Is Flawed Science and Dubious Democracy," *Public Perspective* (December/January 1996): 41.

27. Gerald M. Pomper, *The Performance of American Government* (New York: Free Press, 1972); Benjamin I. Page, *Choices and Echoes in Presidential Elections* (Chicago: University of Chicago Press, 1978).

28. Norman H. Nie, Sidney Verba, and John R. Petrocik, *The Changing American Voter* (Cambridge, Mass.: Harvard University Press, 1976).

29. Ladd, "Fiskin's 'Deliberative Poll,' " 42.

30. John E. Mueller, *War, Presidents and Public Opinion* (New York: Wiley, 1973), 69.

31. Michael W. Traugott, "The Polls in 1992: Views of Two Critics: A Good General Showing, But Much Work Needs to Be Done," *Public Perspective* 4 (November/December 1992): 14–16.

32. Traugott, "The Polls in 1992," 14.

33. Traugott, "The Polls in 1992."

34. For a delightful rendition of this episode, see Shelley Ross, *Fall from Grace* (New York: Ballantine, 1988), ch. 12.

35. The name strictly derived from printing the comic strip "Yellow Kid" in color.

36. Doris A. Graber, *Mass Media and American Politics*, 3d ed. (Washington, D.C.: CQ Press, 1989), 12.

37. See Thomas C. Leonard, *The Power of the Press: The Birth of American Political Reporting* (New York: Oxford University Press, 1986), ch. 7.

38. Richard L. Rubin, *Press, Party, and Presidency* (New York: Norton, 1981), 38–39.

39. Stephen Bates, *If No News, Send Rumors* (New York: St. Martin's Press, 1989), 185.

40. "TV Tops for News," *Atlanta Constitution* (May 29, 1997): G6.

41. This was the fundamental conclusion of Shanto Iyengar and Donald R. Kinder, *News That Matters* (Chicago: University of Chicago Press, 1987).

42. Shanto Iyengar and Donald R. Kinder, *News That Matters* (Chicago: University of Chicago Press, 1987).

43. L. Peer and B. Chestnut, "Deciphering Media Independence: The Gulf War Debate in Television and Newspaper News," *Political Communication* 12 (January 1995): 81–95.

44. M. Just, T. Buhr, and A. Crigler, "Voice, Substance, and Cynicism in Presidential Campaign Media," *Political Communication* 16: 1 (January 1999): 25–44.

45. "Internet Takes Off," PEW Research Center for the People and the Press, http://www.people-press.org/med98rpt.html.

46. Thomas Patterson, *Out of Order* (New York: Vintage, 1994).

47. Harold W. Stanley and Richard G. Niemi, *Vital Statistics on American Politics*, 4th ed. (Washington, D.C.: CQ Press, 1994), 28.

48. Bob Woodward, *The Shadow: Five Presidents and the Legacy of Watergate* (New York: Simon and Schuster, 1999).

49. See Tom Wolfe, *The New Journalism* (New York: Harper & Row, 1973), especially 9–32.

50. The first and best in White's series was *The Making of the President 1960* (New York: Atheneum, 1961). See also Joe McGinniss, *The Selling of the President 1968* (New York: Trident, 1969).

51. See James David Barber, *The Presidential Character*, 4th ed. (Englewood Cliffs, N.J.: Prentice Hall, 1992).

52. 376 U.S. 254 (1964). See also Steven Pressman, "Libel Law: Finding the Right Balance," *Editorial Research Reports* 2 (August 18, 1989): 462–71.

53. *Curtis Publishing Co.* v. *Butts,* 388 U.S. 130 (1967); *Associated Press* v. *Walker,* 388 U.S. 130 (1967).

54. William Schneider and I. A. Lewis, "Views on the News," *Public Opinion* 8 (August/September 1985): 6–11, 58–59; and Shanto Iyengar and Richard Reeves, eds., *Do the Media Govern?: Politicians, Voters, and Reporters in America* (Beverly Hills, Calif.: Sage, 1997).

55. See Dom Bonafede, "Crossing Over," *National Journal* 21 (January 14, 1989): 102; Richard Harwood, "Tainted Journalists," *Washington Post* (December 4, 1988): L6; Jim Naureckas and Janine Jackson, eds., *The Fair Reader: An Extra! Review of Press and Politics in the '90s* (Boulder, Colo.: Westview Press, 1996).

56. "*Roe* v. *Webster,*" *Media Monitor* 3 (October 1989): 1–6. See also David Shaw, "Abortion and the Media" (four-part series), *Los Angeles Times* (July 1, 1990): A1, 50–51; (July 2, 1990): A1, 20; (July 3, 1990): A1, 22–23; (July 4, 1990): A1, 28–29.

57. David C. Barker, "Rushed Decisions: Political Talk Radio and Vote Choice, 1994–1996," *Journal of Politics* 61:2 (May, 1999): 527–39.

58. Benjamin I. Page, Robert Y. Shapiro, and Glenn R. Dempsey, "What Moves Public Opinion?" *American Political Science Review* 81:1 (March 1987): 23–44.

59. Iyengar and Kinder, *News That Matters.*

60. Martin P. Wattenberg, *The Decline of American Political Parties, 1952–1994* (Cambridge, MA: Harvard University Press, 1996).

61. 403 U.S. 713 (1971).

CHAPTER 11

1. John Mintz, "Some in GOP Upset by Lobbyist's Appearance at Caucus," *Washington Post* (June 27, 1999): A10.

2. Graham Wilson, *Interest Groups in the United States* (New York: Oxford University Press, 1981), 4.

3. V. O. Key Jr., *Politics, Parties, and Pressure Groups* (New York: T. J. Crowell, 1942), 23.

4. John H. Aldrich, *Why Parties? The Origin and Transformation of Party Politics in America* (Chicago: University of Chicago Press, 1995).

5. The National Republican (one forerunner of the Whig Party) and the Anti-Masonic parties each had held more limited conventions in 1831.

6. By contrast, Great Britain did not develop truly national, broad-based parties until the 1870s.

7. Voter turnout in presidential elections from 1876 to 1900 ranged from 75 percent to 82 percent of the potential (male) electorate, compared with 50 percent to 55 percent in contemporary elections. See *Historical Statistics of the United States: Colonial Times to 1970,* Part 2. Series Y-27–28 (Washington, DC: Government Printing Office, 1975), based on unpublished data prepared by Walter Dean Burnham.

8. Frank J. Sorauf, *Party Politics in America,* 5th ed. (Boston: Little, Brown, 1984), 22.

9. Christian Collet and Martin P. Wattenberg, "Strategically Unambitious: Minor Party and Independent Candidates in the 1996 Congressional Elections," in John C. Green and Daniel M. Shea, eds., *The State of the Parties: The Changing Role of Contemporary American Parties*, 3rd ed. (Lanham, MD: Rowman and Littlefield, 1999).

10. See Steven E. Finkel and Howard A. Scarrow, "Party Identification and Party Enrollment: The Difference and the Consequence," *Journal of Politics* 47 (May 1985): 620–42.

11. Robert D. Putnam, "Bowling Alone: America's Declining Social Capital," *Journal of Democracy* 6 (1) 1995: 65–66.

12. Richard Movin, "Who Says We're Not Joiners," quoting Everett Carll Ladd, *Washington Post* (May 2, 1999): B5.

13. Kay Lehman Schlozman and John T. Tierney, *Organized Interests and American Democracy* (New York: Harper & Row, 1986).

14. David B. Truman, *The Governmental Process: Political Interests and Public Opinion* (New York: Knopf, 1951), ch.16.

15. Robert H. Salisbury, "An Exchange Theory of Interest Groups," *Midwest Journal of Political Science* 13 (1969): 1–32.

16. Jack L. Walker, "The Origins and Maintenance of Interest Groups in America," *American Political Science Review* 77 (June 1983): 390–406.

17. Allan J. Cigler and Anthony J. Nownes, "Public Interest Entrepreneurs and Group Patrons," in Allan J. Cigler and Burdett A. Loomis, eds., *Interest Group Politics,* 4th ed. (Washington, DC: CQ Press, 1995), 77–100.

18. Alexis de Tocqueville, *Democracy in America,* Vol. 1, trans. Phillips Bradley (New York: Knopf, Vintage Books, 1945; orig. published in 1835), 191.

19. Mancur Olson Jr. *The Logic of Collective Action: Public Goods and the Theory of Groups* (Cambridge, MA: Harvard University Press, 1965).

20. Jeffrey Berry, *Lobbying for the People: The Political Behavior of Public Interest Groups* (Princeton, NJ: Princeton University Press, 1977), 7.

21. Peter Steinfels, "Moral Majority to Dissolve; Says Mission Accomplished," *The New York Times* (June 12, 1989): A14.

22. Steve Goldstein, "The Christian Right Grows in Power," *Atlanta Journal* (November 11, 1994): A8.

23. Matthew Vita and Susan Schmidt, "The Interest Groups: Religious Right Mutes Voice, Not Efforts," *The Washington Post* (November 2, 2000): A20.

24. Robert Scheer, "The NRA-Friendly Candidate: Bush's Stance on Guns Proves That He Is No Compassionate Conservative," *Pittsburgh Post-Gazette* (May 11, 2000): A29.

25. Juliet Eilperin, "A Pivotal Election Finds NRA's Wallet Open," *The Washington Post* (November 1, 2000): A16.

26. David Mahood, *Interest Groups Participation in America: A New Intensity* (Englewood Cliffs, N.J.: Prentice-Hall, 1990), 23.

27. Tom Walker, "Business Press: Microsoft Tops Political Donations," *Atlanta Journal and Constitution* (November 7, 2000): 6D.

28. Nancy Cleeland, "Decision 2000: Unions Mobilize to Get out Vote," *Los Angeles Times* (November 8, 2000): A3.

29. Sam Lowenberg, "Now, The Tricky Part: Dividing Profits," *Legal Times* (May 31, 1999): 4.

30. Influence, Inc., at http://www.opensecrets.org/pubs/lobby98/index.htm.

31. Thomas Cronin, *The State of the Presidency* (Boston: Little, Brown, 1975), 123.

32. Some political scientists speak of iron rectangles, reflecting the growing importance of a fourth party, the courts, in the lobbying process.

33. Jane Fritsch, "Sometimes, Lobbyists Strive to Keep Public in the Dark," *The New York Times* (March 19, 1996): A1.

34. Joel Brinkley, "Cultivating the Grass Roots to Reap Legislative Benefits," *The New York Times* (November 1, 1993): A1.

35. Marilyn J. Cohodas, "Digital Activism," *Governing Magazine* (August 2000): 70.

CHAPTER 12

1. Paul Allen Beck, *Party Politics in America*, 8th ed. (New York: Longman, 1998). David Adamany, "Cross-over Voting and the Democratic Party's Reform Rules," *American Political Science Review* 70 (1976): 536–41. Ronald Hedlund and Meredith W. Watts, "The Wisconsin Open Primary: 1968 to 1984," *American Politics Quarterly* 14 (1986): 55–74. Gary D. Wekkin, "The Conceptualization and Measurement of Crossover Voting," *Western Political Quarterly* 41 (1988): 105–14.

2. Beck, *Party Politics in America*. Alan Abromowitz, John McGlennon, and Ronald Rapoport, "A Note on Strategic Voting in a Primary Election," *Journal of Politics* 43 (1981): 899–904. Gary D. Wekken, "Why Crossover Voters are not 'Mischievous' Voters," *American Politics Quarterly* 19 (1991): 229–47.

3. Larry J. Sabato, "Presidential Nominations: The Front-Loaded Frenzy of 1996," in Larry J. Sabato, ed., *Toward the Millenium: The Elections of 1996* (New York: Allyn and Bacon, 1997).

4. Paul S. Herrnson, "Campaign Professionalism and Fundraising in Congressional Elections," *Journal of Politics* 54 (1992): 859–70.

5. Stephen K. Medvic and Silvo Lenart, "The Influence of Political Consultants in the 1992 Congressional Elections," *Legislative Studies Quarterly* 22 (February 1997): 61–77.

6. Barbara Farah and Helmut Norpoth, "Trends in Partisan Realignment, 1976–1986: A Decade of Waiting," paper prepared for delivery at the annual meeting of the American Political Science Association, Washington, D.C., August 27–31, 1986.

7. Earl Black and Merle Black, *Politics and Society in the South* (Cambridge, Mass.: Harvard University Press, 1989).

8. Morris P. Fiorina, *Retrospective Voting in American National Elections* (New Haven, Conn.: Yale University Press, 1981); and Charles H. Franklin and John E. Jackson, "The Dynamics of Party Identification," *American Political Science Review* 77 (1983): 957–73.

9. V. O. Key Jr., "A Theory of Critical Elections," *Journal of Politics* 17 (February 1955): 3–18.

10. The less dynamic term *creeping realignment* is also sometimes used by scholars and journalists.

11. Byron E. Shafer, ed., *The End of Realignment? Interpreting American Electoral Eras* (Madison: University of Wisconsin Press, 1991); and Robert W. Fogel, *The Fourth Great Awakening: The Political Realignment of the 1990s and the Fate of Egalitarianism* (Chicago: University of Chicago Press, 1997).

12. See Paul Allen Beck, "The Dealignment Era in America," in Russell J. Dalton et al., *Electoral Change in Advanced Industrial Democracies: Realignment or Dealignment?* (Princeton, NJ: Princeton University Press, 1984), 264. See also Philip M. Williams, "Party Realignment in the United States and Britain," *British Journal of Political Science* 15 (January 1985): 97–115.

13. *Wesberry* v. *Sanders*, 376 U.S. 1 (1964).

14. *Thornberg* v. *Gingles*, 478 U.S. 30 (1986).

15. *Shaw* v. *Reno*, 113 S.Ct. 2816 (1993).

16. Steven T. Engel and David J. Jackson, "Wielding the Stick Instead of Its Carrot: Labor PAC Punishment of Pro-NAFTA Democrats," *Political Research Quarterly* 51 (September 1998): 813–28.

17. Janet M. Box-Steffendsmeier and J. Tobin Grant, "All in a Day's Work: The Financial Rewards of Legislative Effectiveness," *Legislative Studies Quarterly* 24 (November 1999): 511–23.

18. Kevin M. Leyden and Stephen A. Borrelli, "An Investment in Goodwill: Party Contributions and Party Unity Among U.S. House Members in the 1980s," *American Politics Quarterly* 22 (October 1994): 421–52.

19. Amy Keller, "Helping Each Other Out: Members Dip into Campaign Funds for Fellow Candidates," *Roll Call* (June 15, 1998): 1.

20. For member contribution activity at the state level, see Jay K. Dow, "Campaign Contributions and Intercandidate Transfers in the California Assembly," *Social Science Quarterly* 75 (1994): 867–80. For member contribution activity at the congressional level, see Bruce A. Larson, "Ambition and Money in the U.S. House of Representatives: Analyzing Campaign Contributions from Incumbents' Leadership PACs and Reelection Committees" (Ph.D. dissertation, University of Virginia, 1998). For a briefer account, see Paul S. Herrnson, "Money and Motives: Spending in House Elections," in Lawrence C. Dodd and Bruce I. Oppenheimer, eds., *Congress Reconsidered*, 6th ed. (Washington, D.C.: Congressional Quarterly Press, 1997).

21. 424 U.S. 1 (1976).

22. 424 U.S. 1 (1976).

23. 116 S.Ct. 2309 (1996).

24. Anthony Corrado, "Party Soft Money," in Anthony Corrado, et al., eds., *Campaign Finance Reform: A Sourcebook* (Washington, D.C.: Brookings, 1997).

25. Trevor Potter, "Issue Advocacy and Express Advocacy," in Anthony Corrado et al., eds., *Campaign Finance Reform: A Sourcebook* (Washington, D.C.: Brookings, 1997).

26. David Magleby and Marianne Holt, "The Long Shadow of Soft Money and Issue Advocacy Ads," *Campaigns and Elections* (May 1999): 22.

27. Michael Cornfield, "The On-Line Campaigner: Interacting for Campaign Dollars," *Campaigns and Elections* (June 1999): 31.

28. Amy Keller, "Experts Wonder About FEC's Internet Savvy: Regulating Web Is a Challenge for Watchdog Agency," *Roll Call* (May 6, 1999): 1, 21.

29. *Public Perspective* (December/January, 1997): 4.

CHAPTER 13

1. James E Anderson, *Public Polymaking: An Introduction*, 2nd ed. (Boston: Houghton Mifflin, 1994), 5. This discussion draws on Anderson's study.

2. Roger W. Cobb and Charles D. Elder, *Participation in American Politics: The Dynamics of Agenda Building*, 2d ed. (Baltimore: Johns Hopkins University Press, 1983), ch.5.

3. Cobb and Elder, *Participation in American Politics*, 85.

4. Charles O. Jones, *An Introduction to the Study of Public Policy*, 3rd ed. (Monterey, Calif.: Brooks/Cole, 1984), 87–89.

5. *Texas* v. *Johnson*, 492 U.S. 397 (1989).

6. *U.S.* v. *Eichman*, 496 U.S. 310 (1990).

7. This discussion draws on Anne Schneider and Helen Ingram, "Behavioral Assumptions of Policy Tools," *Journal of Politics* 52 (May 1990): 510–29.

8. Henry J. Aaron, *Serious and Unstable Conditions: Financing America's Health Care* (Washington D.C.: Brookings Institution, 1991), ch. 2.

9. Marilyn Werber Serafina, "Medicrunch," *National Journal* 27 (July 29, 1995): 1937.

10. *U.S.* v. *Butler*, 297 U.S. 1 (1936).

11. *Wickard* v. *Filburn*, 317 U.S. 111 (1942).

12. Quoted in Larry N. Gerston, Cynthia Fraleigh, and Robert Schwab, *The Deregulated Society* (Pacific Grove, Calif.: Brooks/Cole, 1988), 27.

13. Martin Mayer, *The Greatest-Ever Bank Robbery: The Collapse of the Savings and Loan Industry* (New York: Scribner's, 1990).

14. L. William Seidman, *Full Faith and Credit: The Great S&L Debacle and Other Washington Sagas* (New York: Times Books, 1993). Seidman was in charge of the Resolution Trust Corporation during the early years of the S&L bailout.

15. James D. Savage, *Balanced Budgets and American Politics* (Ithaca, N.Y.: Cornell University Press, 1988), 176–79.

16. Herbert Stein, *Presidential Economics: The Making of Economic Policy from Roosevelt to Reagan and Beyond* (New York: Simon & Schuster, 1984), 290-91.

INDEX